AFTER IMPERIALISM

MICHAEL BARRATT BROWN

AFTER
IMPERIALISM

William Heinemann Ltd
LONDON   MELBOURNE   TORONTO
JOHANNESBURG   AUCKLAND

Printed by Redwood Press Limited of
Trowbridge & London.

Preface

This book is an attempt to understand the world economy of today and the inter-relationships especially of the rich and poor peoples within it. It is primarily concerned with Britain and the Commonwealth; but the picture here presented is painted on a wide canvas. The past is examined as much as the present in order to try to get bearings for the future.

The urgency of such a study is dictated by the historic choice that faces Britain today. With the colonial empire behind us, we stand at a divide in the road. Along one way lies an immediate future within the confines of a United States of Europe; the other way the prospect is more distant, for it involves the establishment of nothing less than an all-embracing world-wide economic and political association. It is in the belief that there is here a real divide, that the first road does not lead on to the second, but is a cul-de-sac, and that only the second road can provide the possibility of assuring the livelihood of the British people and at the same time of establishing peace and prosperity among all peoples, that this book is written.

The book is directed primarily to that growing body of readers who, though not themselves specialists, have more than the smattering of economic concepts of the ordinary man in the street. Its writing has arisen directly from lectures given in adult-education classes over more than ten years under the auspices of Technical Colleges, the Workers

Educational Association and University Extramural departments. Herein lies the explanation for what may seem a rather surprising variation throughout the book on the level of sophistication of treatment.

The general argument of the book, where it draws on widely accepted findings of the specialists, is pitched at a fairly unsophisticated level. It is hoped that the reader will be able to follow along easily enough, aided by the introduction and conclusion to each chapter, to keep him on the main line of argument. At the same time, certain specific arguments which challenge accepted findings, as in the case of Lenin's imperialism, the terms of trade or the causes of post-war inflation, are deliberately pitched at a rather higher level, so that the reader may have the chance to evaluate for himself the material that is presented. The rather exhaustive references and the comprehensive nature of some of the statistical tables are designed to provide the reader with the tools for further study in addition to underpinning the argument of the book.

When all this has been said, specialists may still find the often crude and cursory historical, economic and political judgements irritating and even inadequately based. My defence is that an attempt has sometimes to be made to connect the pieces of individual research together and to see the picture whole. This is such an attempt. If it provokes discussion and disagreement, not only on detail, but on the general thesis that is put forward, then it will have done its job.

I have had much help in writing the book from Charles Feinstein of Cambridge, especially in the early stages of its preparation, and from John Hughes of Oxford and John Saville of Hull, especially in the later stages. I am greatly indebted to all three of them for their suggestions and also to Norman Birnbaum of Oxford, who read the manuscript, when it was originally prepared for a series of *New Left* books, and gave me the benefit of his views. I am happy also to record here my debt to the late Gunther Stein whose papers I was fortunate to inherit and whose researches, especially on comparisons between communist and capitalist economies, I have made full use of. They must all be absolved completely from responsibility for any inadequacy of the final text that has resulted.

I am most grateful to Mrs J. M. Clarke and Mr R. Fisher for typing a presentable copy from my confused typescripts, and to Mr W. Hampton for assisting me with proof-reading and with the preparation of an index. Without the unfailing forbearance and encouragement of my wife and my children, particularly throughout a long and wet English summer holiday, the book could never have been written.

Sheffield
May 1962

Preface to the Second Edition

A second edition of a book provides the author with the opportunity to answer his critics. The very fact of a second edition is one answer; but in my case the criticisms were in general so friendly and so helpful that what follows is more in the nature of the continuation of a dialogue than of the latest round in a contest. I want to take up in this new Preface, first, some general criticisms of the book and in doing this I shall have briefly to restate the theme of the book; second some examination of the conclusions I drew for socialist strategy in Britain; third, some new developments in the crisis of imperialist relations since the book first appeared six years ago; fourth, some further thoughts on the Marxist theory of economic growth.

1. *Criticisms of the Book and its Theme*

A few violent attacks on the book came from those who can have read the title and gone no further, assuming that it implied the belief that imperialism was over[1]. A brief look inside at the chapter headings would have dispelled such an assumption. The book is divided into three parts, the first "Imperialism as it was"; the second "Imperialism

---

[1] R. Bellamy, *The Spark*, Accra, Ghana 24. xii. 1965.

Today" and the third headed "Towards an International Economy".
The title thus looks to the future as the last sentence of the book makes
clear.

Some friends have wished me to add a question mark after the title.
I have not done so because this would suggest precisely what the more
violent critics accuse me of: viz, that I must believe that even if
imperialism is not definitely finished there is some question about this.
On the contrary my belief is that imperialism is still without question a
most powerful force in the sense that I have used the word, to describe
a complex of economic, political and military relations by which the
less economically developed lands are subjected to the more economically developed. We may still look forward to its ending.

Other friends have asked me why I did not use the French term
which has since entered the English language as "Neo-colonialism"[2].
Writing today it would be sheer eccentricity not to use the word.
Seven years ago I was held back not only by a personal distaste for new
words, and especially words and phrases with 'new' and 'neo' in them
(as in the advertisers' captions all products today are 'new'), but also by
the conviction that imperialism remains the best word for the general
system of unequal world economic relations. The political form of
colonial status was never universal but only one kind of imperialism.
Different phases of imperialism were distinguished in my book and it
was my aim in Chapter 8 on "The New Empires—of the Great
Corporations" to characterise the most recent phase as centering around
the international company. But this is not a new phenomenon, as I
tried to show in the book. Lenin's association of imperialism with
monopoly capital, although inapplicable to Nineteenth Century
Britain, had always been true of the newer industrial powers and
became increasingly true of Britain. But it was not limited to direct
political colonisation. The title of Lenin's book is not "Colonialism".
"Neo-colonialism" still seems to me an inadequate term and perhaps
even dangerous, like other definitory terms, the defining of which
becomes for some social scientists a substitute for the analysis of
content[3]. There do not seem to me to have been sufficient changes in
the content of imperialist relations to demand a new name; but I
intend to develop the point in a later section of this Preface.

[2] E. Mandel, After Imperialism? in New Left Review No. 25, May–June 1964.

[3] This remark is not of course aimed at Ernest Mandel whose contribution to
analysing the true content of Monopoly Capitalist relations in his Treatise of
Marxist Economic Theory and elsewhere I regard as of the utmost value.

The most sustained attack on the book came from the dogmatic Marxists who wrote in outraged tones of my "breath-taking impudence" in criticising some part of Lenin's analysis of Imperialism. I will concede at once that the passage on page 97 of the book concerning Lenin's 'composite picture' of imperialism not only failed to attribute this phrase to Lenin himself, but is badly expressed. I had wished only to emphasise that, while Lenin's analysis mainly of German imperialism led him to see the connexion between monopoly capital and the outward drive to imperialism and thus correctly to predict the future, this was not to be taken to mean either that British capital was very far concentrated by 1913 or that British overseas investment was at that time mainly direct investment by monopolistic companies. British imperialism had to be understood in the light of a much longer history of the advantages of free trade for Britain as the most advanced industrial power. I would not suggest that Lenin did not realise this but only that those who quote Lenin as gospel tend to overlook this.

My purpose in this argument was to emphasise several related points about free trade and imperialism that I still believe to be of the greatest importance and which I shall recapitulate here in order to take up some of the more important criticisms which have been made. The several points are:—

(1) that free trade or the opening of markets is of the greatest benefit to the technically most advanced country once its industrial superiority is established, as Britain's was in the Nineteenth Century and that of the United States is today;

(2) that as a corollary free trade is a disaster for the technically more backward countries. Protection was the device behind which industrial capital developed in a monopolistic manner in Germany and the U.S.A. Any other country wishing to industrialise would have to protect its infant industries and its whole economic development from the influence of the most advanced industrial powers;

(3) that the economic advance of Britain and other developed imperialist powers was less the result of colonial tribute than of the "mopping up" of overseas markets by destruction of native handicrafts and by the increased productivity in the metropolitan industries resulting from free trade;

(4) that correspondingly the disadvantage for the less developed lands was not so much the tribute (heavy though this was) than the holding back and distortion of economic development into mainly primary production which resulted from their inability to develop

their own industries in a world of free trade; the lands which became dependent in the imperialist system suffered not simply from negative lack of development but from the positive distortions of *under*development which include of course political distortions.

I should add here that the current practice of speaking of 'developing' lands, while it is a commendable concession to the *amour propre* of their peoples is really incorrect. It conceals the fact that the economies of many of them are *not* developing and that they do not start from the same point from which European countries began their economic development but from a special condition which is the result of the long period of dependence. I tried to make this clear in the book, but I can see now that my use of the concept of "enclaves" of development (of raw materials for export), which has since been amplified by others[4] into the concept of "dual" economies—one part technically advanced and the backward—may have served to conceal the *total* distortion of these economies by imperialism[5].

(5) that it was rather the development of the white dominions than the exploitation of the colonies that expanded British industry's markets and productivity in the Nineteenth Century. There was an obvious contradiction in the idea that capital would flow to impoverished colonies, except to enclaves of direct raw material extraction. Capital has in fact increasingly flowed to the rich lands and rich markets, today in the form mainly of what can be called "cross-investment" between the most advanced industrial lands;

(6) that, although those persons in Britain who derive income from property benefitted and still benefit from investment in the Colonies (whether before 1913 by rentiers in overseas governments' stock or after 1913 and especially after 1945 by monoply companies in their subsidiaries), the majority of the British people shared with the colonial people in the disadvantages of imperialist relations. They paid the taxes and manned the armies without sharing the dividends; and more still suffered in the end from the growing backwardness of the British economy as home industry was starved of capital and export markets were increasingly impoverished by adverse terms of trade and rising debts;

(7) finally, that the corruption of the metropolitan working class by empire has been much more a moral than an economic corruption.

[4] See H. Myint *The Economics of Developing Countries*, pp. 69–85

[5] See A. G. Frank "The Development of Underdevelopment" in *Monthly Review* (New York) September 1966.

The crumbs from the rich man's table have been less important than the overlaying of working class consciousness first by national consciousness after universal suffrage was conceded and then by what was largely a myth of some universal imperial interest.

I regard this last point as of immense importance in the failure of socialist nerve which we have seen so often in British history, and not least in the Labour Governments of 1964 and 1966. The references in my book to Vespucci, to Kipling, to the collapse of the internationalism of the Labour Movement in 1914 and to Bevinite imperialism all point this way. But I think now that I failed to make this sufficiently explicit in my summary at the beginning of Chapter 12 (especially p.452). I am happy to accept Victor Kiernan's comments on this point [6].

The theses here outlined have been criticised from the right and from the left. The critics on the right may best be exemplified in D. K. Fieldhouse's extremely fair and friendly review in the *Economic History Review*[7]. The essence of this criticism is that "the economic preponderance of Europe should have been enough to prevent industrialisation everywhere else, irrespective of imperial political control" and Fieldhouse goes on: "If freedom to impose tariffs . . . was the factor that differentiated Australia from India . . . why could Brazil not have used her still greater political freedom to protest nascent industries? Conversely, why could Japan. . . ?" I hope that I nowhere suggest that the freedom to impose tariffs was the *only* factor differentiating developed and under developed lands. It was, I believe, a very important factor, but I associate with it, throughout my historical analysis, the freedom for an indigenous industrial capitalist class to emerge.

The central problem of the underdeveloped lands has always been the dependence of the ruling landowning, merchant or comprador class on the imperial trade connections and the determination of the imperial powers to see that it stayed that way—from Omichund the millionaire Hindu merchant in Clive's day to the Sheikh of Kuwait in our own time. Free trade did not only prevent the developement of nascent industries, it also provided better opportunities for money making through handling the imperial trade than through the establishment of local industries. A great part of the first chapter of the book is concerned to suggest that great landlords and merchants rarely become industrialists. What is said here is as true of the economic colonies like

[6] V. Kiernan, Farewell to Empire, *The Socialist Register*, 1964 p. 275.

[7] *Economic History Review*, April 1964, pp. 579–81.

Brazil as of the political colonies like India. European investment
in the Brazilian trade was on a large scale. Japan avoided economic
colonisation by largely cutting herself off from European trade and
investment, until her industries were firmly established. There are
complex historical reasons for the Japanese isolationism, but the sheer
distance from Europe and the absence of important raw material
resources in her islands undoubtedly contributed.

The lands of white settlement including the U.S.A. were able to
develop their own industries, because they had no indigenous ruling
landlord or merchant class to be corrupted, (or if they had it was small
enough to be wiped out along with the rest of the indigenous peoples)
and were settled by European proto-industrial capitalists. These came
mainly from Britain which was already on the way to industrialisation,
and with strong protestant and rebellious origins. It is precisely because
of this that I give so much space to the causes of the settlement of New
England. It was natural for such men as Bradford and Brewster and
those that followed them to attempt to develop indigenous industry
rather than to become mere agents for the products of metropolitan
industry. It was equally natural for their grandchildren when they won
political independence to demand economic freedom. (Incidentally,
and contrary to what Fieldhouse suggests I never said that Britain
granted this voluntarily, but only that kith and kin succeeded in winning it, where alien peoples failed).

The main criticisms from the Left of the line of argument presented
above have been of two kinds: the first concerns the advantage or
disadvantage of the terms of trade between industrial and primary
producers and is most clearly made by Ernest Mandel[8]; the second
concerns the real importance to Britain of the imperial investment and
is most clearly made by Hamsa Alavi[9]. The argument about the terms
of trade is highly complex and is developed at length at the end of
Chapter 2 and in the annexes both to Chapter 2 and to Chapter 4 of the
book. I do not intend to recapitulate here but only to emphasise that
I made it perfectly clear (page 69ff) that the trading relationship was an
unequal one between the industrial countries selling manufactured
goods and the non-industrialised countries confined by colonial rule or
by free trade to primary production alone. What I insisted was *first*
that exports of manufactures from the developed countries preempted
or "mopped up" the markets of the non-industrialised countries,

[8] *Opcit* (2) above.

[9] H. Alavi "Imperialism Old and New" *Socialist Register* 1964, p. 104 ff.

thereby strengthening the manufacturers in the developed countries and destroying the base for industrial revolution elsewhere; *second*, that the terms of trade thus established on the basis of an initial inequality did not continuously move against the primary products and in favour of manufactured goods. There was, of course, a movement against the primary producers in the 1920s and 1930s but the 1940s saw a great recovery back to the 1913 position, and the adverse movement since 1951, serious as it has been, has not brought the terms of trade any where near back to the adverse position of 1937–8 (See Table XXV and supplementary Table XXV below). Competition between manufacturers helped to ensure that this did not happen but the main reason was that *thirdly*, when the terms of trade did move against primary products and in favour of manufactures in certain periods, this led to the impoverishment of the underdeveloped primary producers and worked back through reduced purchasing power upon the export industries of the manufacturing countries themselves. The unemployed in Britain's export industries in the 1930s were obvious sufferers form this process.

Thus when I spoke of "the wealth of rich lands such as Britain not being a function of the poverty of poor lands, but (having) followed rather from the steadily growing productivity of industry over nearly two centuries" (p. 448) I had already excepted the initial period when British industrialisation grew by "mopping up", and in the process impoverishing, the markets of Asia and South America. Had this process of impoverishment been all that there was to Britain's foreign trade it would soon have died of inanition. In fact in Europe and then in North America and in the Dominions economic independence *was* established which made industrialisation there possible with steadily rising purchasing power. It was British exports to these developing industrial economies and not to the impoverished colonies and semi-colonies that provided the dynamic for British industrial advance, until competition and beggar-my-neighbour policies between the advanced industrial countries in the 1930s halted this process too.

It needs to be emphasised here also that cheap labour no longer provides the cheapest form of production. Accumulation of capital still emerges from the surplus value which human labour produces, but costs are more easily reduced today with fewer men working with more machinery at high wages than more men with less machinery at low wages. Oil for example is being produced in the North Sea and Alaska with some of the most highly paid labour in the world. The

importance for capital accumulation of the existence of a much lower
paid layer of labour in the underdeveloped lands, and among negro
and immigrant groups in the developed lands also, is that this layer
acts to keep down the general level of wages which would otherwise
cut sharply into profits. But this is a general problem of capitalist
economic relations and not of some sort of colonial super-profits. I
point out in the book that the return to British capital is no higher on
investment in oil and only a little higher on investment in other
primary products than it is on investment in manufacturing industry at
home. More recent figures confirm this fact (See Supplementary Table
XIII). Of course competition among mining and other raw material
producing campanies could be keeping down sales prices and passing
some of the surplus on to the consumers. The fact remains, as I argue
in the book, that the cost of raw materials and even of fuel is becoming
a smaller and smaller part of total production costs as synthetic replace
natural materials and more and more working up and less and less
material is involved in modern manufactures. To give one illustration,
the value of imports into Britain of basic materials and fuels in 1968 was
equivalent to about 5.5% of the Gross Domestic Product; in 1956–8 it
had been about 8.5% and in the early 1950s about 10%. While the
proportion of total British capital invested in oil has been maintained
that in other overseas raw materials producing companies has steadily
declined (See Supplementary Table XIII).

The question of the role of imperial investment raised by Hamsa
Alavi must be answered in a similar manner. I do not, and did not,
deny the importance of the development of mining and plantations by
British capital both in preempting supplies of raw materials for monopolistic British companies and in providing high rates of return for
British investors. But this very process of extracting high rates of return
on capital exported overseas left the countries from which the extraction took place undeveloped and thus poor markets not only for
British goods but for further British capital investment. The bulk of
the outflow of British capital overseas between 1880 and 1913, the
period of maximum expansion of the Colonial Empire, was to the
Dominions, Europe and the U.S.A. (over 55%). Only 18% of the
total in the 1880s and 16% in 1911–13 went to the colonial empire and
another 22% to South America. Alavi confuses the importance of
British overseas investment, which I do not deny, with its colonial
direction, which I dispute.

Alavi speaks again of neo-colonial investment in the most recent period of the post-1945 flow of British overseas investment. I myself wrote (p. 420) of the preemption by the subsidiaries of British and American firms of the newly growing markets in his own country, Pakistan. But, I cannot accept his claim that such markets provide "a rich new field for exploitation . . . by monopoly capitalism". I wish they were so rich. I was concerned to emphasise once again that British (and now *a fortiore* American) capital was flowing not into the poor lands but into the already advanced industrialised lands. Between 1938 and 1959, as I showed, the share of private British investment in the developed lands was raised from 40% to 60%, that in the more developed lands of the Sterling Area alone from 38% to 45% (Table XVII, p. 282). Similarly I showed U.S. private investment in Canada and Europe as rising from 44% in 1922–29 to 49% in 1955–59. The process has gone much further since 1959 as the Supplementray Tables XIX and XXX indicate.

Alavi and others[10] also question my view that the return on the overseas investment has since 1913 made fairly insignificant additions to the U.K. national income. Before 1913 the gross inflow of investment income was around 8% of the national income and there was very little outflow of income on foreign investments in Britain. Since 1945 the inflow has been around 3½% and the outflow about 2% giving a net inflow of 1½% of national income. This is, I maintain a major change. But Alavi and others suggest that I am neglecting the importance of this income from abroad in relation to the total income received by property owners in Britain. Far from neglecting this, I spent a large part of Chapter 8 insisting on this very fact, especially (on p. 267) that for every £3,000 million of net Company income earned in a year at home, another £1,000 million was earned abroad taking the years 1958–60 together. The share of property income derived from overseas in 1913, however, was not a quarter of the total as today, but over a half; and while about 45% of this came from underdeveloped lands then, only about 30% does so today. Perhaps a twelfth of all property income therefore, can be ascribed now to investment in underdeveloped lands. Investment in the already developed lands is far more important (See Supplementary Table XIX).

My purpose in the latter part of the book was to examine critically the importance of the new wave of British overseas investment, continued since the book was written at an even faster rate (See

[10] H. Rathbone "Problems of Imperialism" *Marxism Today*, April and May 1964.

Supplementary Table XVIII), first as a dynamic element in capital formation, secondly, as a contribution to the growth of the national income at home and finally, as a further check to the economic growth of the underdeveloped economies. The outward flow of capital is the result of intensified competition among giant international companies. What I emphasised seven years ago may seem almost common-place today in the year of the mergers of A.E.I., G.E.C. and English Electric, Allied Breweries and Unilever, Citroen and Fiat, Agfa and Gevaert. The flow has been resumed on a massive scale despite the maintenance of demand with full employment at home. This is what made nonsense of John Strachey's argument in *End of Empire* and led me to question the Hobson thesis upon which Strachey's book was based (pp. 92–6 and 330–1). If overseas investment followed from under-consumption at home, as Hobson suggested, then the maintenance of demand at home was supposed to explain the abandonment of empire and of overseas investment, according to Strachey. If the foreign investment had been largely unrelated to Empire, however, and the result rather of real development through economic independence of the dominions overseas and of growing competition between the advanced industrial powers in each others' markets, then Empire did not provide "the life blood of British capitalism" nor did the ending of colonial empire imply the collapse of British capitalism. I criticised these two suppositions of communist writers like Mr. R. P. Dutt (See pages 13 and 295) but I equally criticised the Strachey view that the welfare state had solved the problems of capitalism (pp. 452–3). Capitalist contradictions deepen with the increasing concentration of wealth in the rich lands and of poverty in the poor lands, despite the fact that an understanding of Keynesian techniques of market management have combined with the emerging challenge of the Communist world to force upon capitalist governments the provision of some aid for the economic development of the poor.

One reviewer, R. H. S. Crossman[11], succeeded in confusing my argument with Strachey's and indeed in attributing my ideas to his book, despite all the evidence to the contrary. Crossman was so anxious to discredit the *New Left* ("declining almost as speedily as it rose") that he failed to see that the implications of my argument were the very opposite of Strachey's. Crossman accepted my conclusions for reviving world trade and claimed that a Labour Government would

[11] R. H. S. Crossman "After John Strachey" *The Guardian* p. 9. 63.

not be "seduced by the lure of the Common Market". But he regarded
my view that these conclusions required a total reorientation of
British foreign economic policy towards positive neutralism as
"spatchcocked awkwardly into the argument (since) without it there
would be nothing New Leftish about either the analysis or the conclusions". This is partly because he refers to my proposals as being
concerned with "reviving world *free* trade", whereas in fact they were
for *planning* at least our part of world trade. It is largely, however,
because Crossman evidently cannot bring himself to see Socialists as
really beginning, or perhaps ever needing, to challenge the power and
pressures of the giant capitalist companies that he assumes that arguing
for unity between industrial workers and colonial peasants implies
believing in "harmonious relations between capitalism and the colonial
peoples". It is of course this failure that leaves Crossman looking rather
foolish in a government that has both rejected proposals for world
trade expansion and in fact been seduced by the lure of the Common
Market. This failure to challenge the power of the giant companies is
of course also the cause of the general failure of the Labour Government·

2. *Unity of Struggle between Rich and Poor Countries*

My purpose in going over some of this ground again in a new
Preface is to reaffirm the main conclusions for socialist strategy: *first*
for the advanced countries that imperialist relations today involve
primarily the control over sources of supply and markets by the giant
international companies. The actual direct tribute in "super profits" is
not so important; so its drying up will not lead to some collapse of
capitalism (a la Palme Dutt). On the other hand the welfare state has
not solved the problems of capitalism without henceforth, therefore,
requiring imperialist relations, because in fact these problems never
were simple problems of underconsumption; *second*, for the underdeveloped countries the ending of the tribute will not suddenly free
them from their poverty, burdensome though this tribute is. Underdevelopment is a condition of total economic and political distortion,
which will require a long struggle by the peoples of these countries to
correct; *third*, for the relations between the working people of the
advanced and the underdeveloped countries of the capitalist world we
need not accept that there is an inevitable opposition of interests because of the imperialist relationship; we have to find a framework for
common action between them and also with those who are bound by
Russian domination in the communist world.

But some of my friends on the Left, while accepting the truth of the first two propositions cannot accept the truth of the last which involves a total rejection of the current concept of rich capitalist nations and poor proletarian nations as to the main line of class struggle in the world today[12]. This concept has of course become the central theme of Maoist criticism of the Soviet Union and its acceptance of the partition of the world between the Russian and American Empires. I concede at once that the kind of Third World that emerged from the Bandoeng meetings is no more. In a sense only China is left as a Third World uncommitted to either of the Power Blocs. At the time that I wrote the book a real possibility seemed to exist of associating Britain with the countries of the "Third World" in the schemes for world economic development. These were predicated upon the development of a framework of positive neutralism (p. 465) which, far from being "spatch-cocked awkwardly into the argument" as Crossman averred, was essential to it. The fact has to be faced six years later that the "Third World" in the sense I was speaking of it then has largely dissolved. At that time Pandit Nehru in India, Goulart in Brazil, Sukarno in Indonesia, Ben Bella in Algeria, Kassim in Iraq, Nkrumah in Ghana combined with Castro, Tito and Nasser to make a reality of the Bandoeng powers. Nationalist and populist regimes deriving a large part of their power from the Left but uncommitted to either Bloc gave to the Third World a perspective of planned development in the direction of Socialism[13]. A Labour Britain moving in the same direction would have found ready allies in embarking on a new foreign economic policy to sustain a new economic policy at home. It is easy enough to look back today and laugh, but the fact is that at least a part of the explanation for the collapse of such hopes of the Third World lies in the total abrogation by the Labour Government itself of nearly all the advances to the Left for which socialists voted in Britain in 1964. A Britain moving towards Socialism with such allies could have challenged the power of the United States bloc.

The collapse of these populist and nationalist regimes indicates that my hope for a Third Force in the world was unfounded. The pressures

---

[12] See J. P. Sartre's Introduction to Frantz Fanon's *The Wretched of the Earth*, Paris 1961 and London 1965 and see K. Buchanan's "The Third World" in *New Left Review* No. 18, January, February 1963; my reply "Third World or Third Force" in *New Left Review*, No. 20 and Buchanan's further comments in "UNO or Bingo" *New Left Review*, No. 21.

[13] P. Worsley *The Third World*, London 1963.

of the two blocs proved too strong and the power of populism too weak. One must draw the conclusion that the analysis of the agency of change in non-industrialised lands was faulty and to this question I shall return in a later section. This is no reason, however, for supposing that it will be necessary to accept the concept of "proletarian nations" opposed to "affluent capitalist nations". No revised analysis is likely to reveal the sudden disappearance of class struggle and gross inequalities of income inside both the rich and the poor countries in the capitalist system. To mix up peasants, landlords and comprador merchants in one mish-mash in the underdeveloped countries makes no more sense than mixing up property owners, managers and workers in the developed countries. The interests of each group are not only different but antagonistic[14]. The interests, moreover, of the industrial worker and the peasant producer are more nearly the same. They each have products to exchange. They have a common enemy in the giant international company which exploits them both.

The problem is to find a framework for common action. All workers will desire an improvement in contacts through the International Trade Union movements, but these are still very much movements of the cold war. Mr. Hugh Scanlon, President of the Engineers' Union in Britain has recently emphasised that international companies need to be offset by international unions, but unions provide only a countervailing force in such a conception. The nationalisation of international companies is part of socialist doctrine but this becomes increasingly not only a difficult legal operation but a complex political operation. Moreover, the bureaucratic and indeed exploitative role of giant state corporations in capitalist (and indeed in communist) countries warns us that nationalisation does not necessarily mean democratic control. A framework is required within which principled fraternal cooperation can be developed between groups of workers who are struggling for control over their working lives and within which the power of the international company can be challenged.

The argument about relations between rich and poor countries generally revolves around the giving by the rich of larger and more effectively distributed grants of aid. While private capital is now increasingly concentrated in other rich countries, government aid goes mainly to the underdeveloped countries. It is still derisorily small

---

[14] See K. Buchanan *opcit.*

in quantity and mainly directed by military and political considerations, as the information collected in Supplementary Table XXXIII quite clearly indicates. It is not just that the flow of funds from rich to poor is wholly inadequate to encourage economic development. The private flows are counted by the rich countries in assessing the proportion of their national income that they provide in "aid for underdeveloped lands". At the U.N.C.T.A.D. Conference in 1968 they promised to raise this to 1% but they refused the claim of the poor countries that 0.8% should be official aid and only 0.2% private investment and that there should be a time table for this target. The poor countries at this U.N.C.T.A.D. meeting complained bitterly that the effect of private investment is often to hold back economic development. First, the rate of return is high; a third of the gross flow of funds flowing from rich to poor is now mortgaged for debt interest and repayments, and the proportion is rising. Secondly, the profits are remitted to banks in London and New York and these include, at least in the case of oil investment, the profits due to the host government as well as those due to the operating company; thirdly the investment tends to be directed into the luxury market and not into basic industry. This is partly because the tariff walls are highest on luxuries but also because of the process of mopping up developing markets by the giant companies which I have referred to above.

Official aid has also important limitations from the point of view of the underdeveloped lands. Even official aid that is not directly military tends to go to governments in underdeveloped countries which do not propose to make fundamental changes; and that is of course disastrous for the economic development of these poor countries just because such development precisely demands fundamental changes. The changes are needed to develop markets that are now restricted by feudal land ownership and to release the forces that will carry through industrialisation even against the interests of landowners and comprador merchants whose whole economic base depends upon their connexion with foreign trade and foreign capital. No industrial revolution was ever carried out without a prior political revolution.

At a time when grants for overseas aid have become remarkably unpopular in Britain, it may be well once more to rehearse the argument about the purposes of economic aid. Mr. Enoch Powell in leading the attack on such aid is reported as saying that "the two grounds given for development aid—charity and self-interest—are first of all contradictory and secondly untenable since the charity does not help and the self-interest is fictitious". The question is whose charity and whose self-interest. For property owners in the rich countries, and especially for those with investments made in the poor countries, aid may be regarded by them as charity which they pay taxes to provide, but Mr. Powell is undoubtedly right in speaking also of self-interest. Much of the aid is associated with private investment and with orders for equipment supplied by private firms in the rich countries. Now it is perfectly possible to argue on Keynesian grounds that aid that expands the world market and brings into use unutilised resources is well worth the taxes paid to provide it. The argument was in fact used by the Federation of British Industries in its 1963 pamphlet on *Overseas Trade Policy*. It is just as true overseas as at home that a smaller share (after taxes) of a larger cake may give a bigger slice to rich tax-payers than a larger share of a smaller cake. The attitudes revealed by the rich countries' governments at the U.N.C.T.A.D. Conferences show, however, that it is much harder to persuade the rich to think in Keynesian welfare terms abroad than at home. National governments can ensure that all pay their taxes; international conferences cannot. Welfare payments at home can be used to hold back demands for fundamental changes in the economic system. Similar payments abroad may only encourage such things. There is a real contradiction here for the managers of capital in the advanced industrial countries. Deliberate development of the underdeveloped world still seems too hazardous to become a major point of policy.

There remains the possibility of expanding trade rather than aid between rich and poor countries. This is what many leaders in the underdeveloped countries demand. If more trade means freer trade, then the problem arises that free trade increases the exchanges amongst the rich countries but holds back the growth of the infant industries and thus of the economic development of the poor countries. On the other hand, protection imposed by the poor countries impairs the advantages they can derive from foreign trade unless thay can establish common markets amongst themselves. Some Latin American countries have attempted to do this but the influence of the U.S.A. has been enough to prevent a common external tariff wall from being raised. If, however, such customs unions were to be established in a number of regions, S.E. Asia and Africa as well as Latin America, there would be a danger for the capitalist world that its trade exchanges would be seriously reduced.

The most promising suggestion which I recommended six years ago,

and which would unite the demands of socialists in the rich countries
and of those elsewhere who wished to see an extension of planning in
their economies, was the introduction of increased planning in international trade exchanges. Many critics of the book referred disparag-
ingly to the absence of original solutions. I accept the rebuke and reaffirm my conclusion that the scheme suggested by Professor Ragnar
Frisch of Norway provides by far the most practical and most effective
way forward[15]. Orginally put forward in an academic journal, it was
repeated at Conferences on "Britain, E.F.T.A. and the Commonwealth"
in 1962 and 1963. It has received extraordinary little discussion,
although a vague and modified form of the scheme was incorporated in
the Labour Party Manifestos of 1964 and 1966, in which the importance
of Britain developing long-term trade agreements was emphasised.
Nevertheless it must be said that in recent weeks the T.U.C. has set up
a committee to investigate the possibilities of developing planned
trade exchanges with some of Britain's trading partners. This was
designed to support the T.U.C.'s proposals for a major extension of
economic planning contained in its 1969 *Economic Review*.

The essence of Professor Frisch's scheme is simple enough. It is a
scheme for planning international trade not by a *supra*-national agency
but by national governments establishing a multilateral trade clearing
agency to act as a secretriat for those countries who wished to co-operate in the scheme. These would be countries which have economic
plans even of an indicative type. Their governments would draw up
estimates of the volumes of growth (or of decline in some cases) in the
main lines of goods they were likely to import over the next several
years and in those goods they were likely to have available for export.
These growth figures would be examined for mutual consistency
at the multilateral clearing agency with the use of computers, and adjustments would be made by negotiation until a consistent mix of trade
plans was agreed. Governments would then contract to fulfil their
plans, subject to annual reviews of progress when revised contracts
could be negotiated. Payments would be made through the agency
and balances would need only to be settled over an agreed period of
years, poorer countries being provided with aid from the richer and
with longer terms of settlement than the richer. The scheme would thus
avoid the limitations of bilateral trade agreements and provide for
multilateral compensations at an optimum rate of growth. If only a

[15] R. Frisch "The Problem of Multicompensatory Trade" *Review of Economics and
Statistics* XXX, November 1948.

beginning were made between a few countries and in a few lines of goods, these countries could plan with confidence for the growth (or the rundown) of particular sectors of their economies within a widening world division of labour.

The disastrous results of the failure of any new international economic planning to emerge from this last decade can best be illustrated from the case of Yugoslavia. Her economic position in the early 1960s depended upon the development of modern industries which needed wider markets than her own 15 million people could justify. With a large part of her foreign trade firmly based in the "Third World" she could safely distribute the rest equally between the U.S.A. and E.E.C. on the one hand and the communist bloc on the other. When one by one the regimes in the "Third World" were overthrown by coups from the right or were gravely weakened, as in the case of India, by internal dissensions, she was faced with having to trade more and more with the 'Eastern' or 'Western' bloc. To expand in either created difficulties in the other, since expansion beyond a certain point involved politico-economic strings which the Yugoslav regime had wished at all costs to avoid—the Russian controlled COMECON on the one hand, the private capital of the Common Market on the other. Critics of the most recent policies of the Yugoslav Government should not forget the responsibility of British socialists for helping to create the dilemma of a small country caught between such fires.

The problem illustrated by the Yugoslav dilemma arises not only from the collapse of populist regimes in the "Third World"; it follows also from the failure of the communist ecomonies to expand as fast as had been expected. It must be added here that I fell into the extrapolation trap in assuming in the book that the fast economic growth rates of the communist countries in the 1950s and the slow growth rate of the U.S.A. would continue in the 1960s. In fact the annual growth rate which was 11.5% in the Soviet Union and East Europe has dropped to 8.5% and that of the U.S.A. and Canada, which was 3.3% has risen to nearly 6%. The result is that instead of the communist states catching up with the capitalist world in industrial output by the early 1970s, as I suggested in Table XXXI and Supplementary Table XXXI, they may still only be producing about a half of the capitalist output by then*. Such is the effect of quite small changes in compound interest. The importance of this changed perpective for our purpose is that I had

---

* I say nothing of the growth of Chinese output which may well surprise us all.

assumed that with near equality in the industrial strengths of the 'East' and the 'West' the opportunities for developing lands to "shop around" for aid and trade would be greatly increased and the area of planned trade in the 'East' enormously increased. In fact one of the aggravating elements in the world liquidity crisis which we shall be considering is that Soviet aid to underdeveloped countries reached a peak in 1963, which has not been nearly equalled since. Soviet resources of foreign currency have been preempted for their own needs of imported grains.

The continued failures in Soviet agriculture are of course one reason for the slowing down in the growth rate. The other reason must surely be the desperately slow pace of liberalisation in the Soviet Union and throughout the Russian Empire despite the Liebermann economic reforms. The failure of social or individual incentive to increase production, to which Ota Sik was directing attention in the Czechoslovak reforms, must provide the main explanation for reduced growth rates. Judged by recent events in Czechoslovakia it would seem unlikely that the malaise will be quickly cured. At the same time the more rapid American growth rate, depending as it does on enormously swollen government military spending, has, as we have seen, provided increased spending power to a few favoured lands, but this has been combined with an actual cut-back in aid programmes as the balance of payments deficit has persisted. The rosy prospect of the early 1960s for peaceful if competitive coexistence between the two great power blocs, with each striving by grants in aid to win the allegiance of the underdeveloped world, has perceptibly darkened.

The question remains how far the advanced capitalist countries will be forced to step up what are best described as international Keynesian measures of economic aid in order to sustain and expand the world market, and then how far they can be forced by the demands of workers at home and the resistance of the peoples overseas to make this aid serve real economic development. There can be no doubt that Keynesian measures for maintaining aggregate demand at home have not only helped private capitalism as an economic system to survive but have also created through full employment a unity and bargaining strength among industrial workers, and at the same time a confidence that did not exist before that economic forces can be mastered, that the capitalist is no longer indispensable, that social control of social production is a possibility. The question is now who controls the controllers.

An international extension of Keynesian measures to sustain and expand the world market can hardly have a lesser effect in the rest of the world than Keynesian measures have had in the advanced countries[16]. The opportunity thus opened up to end the divisions between workers in the rich countries and the peoples of the poor and the possibility created of easing the bitter process of capital accumulation for industrial revolution in underdeveloped countries can only be realised by powerful pressures from below. Keynesian type welfare measures were not handed down on a plate. Their introduction had to be fought for and their extension is still being fought for. Welfare provision is always the first item to be cut in an economic crisis and its replacement by authoritarian measures is always possible, as the Labour Governments recent proposals for Trade Union legislation have shown. Although the Labour Movement in Britain has fought for welfare provision, such struggles do not of course establish socialism in the sense of social control of the productive process. What they do is to create a basis of unity and self confidence from which to advance to socialism. Anyone who regards the welfare state as no more than a reformist device to buy off radical change must prove that workers divided and opposed by unemployment and poverty will be more prepared for radical change than those who begin to feel the unity and confidence of full employment but are still denied control over their working lives and the product of them.

The book as it stands is based upon the assumption that measures of reform have to be pushed to the limits of what any economic system is capable of. In Marx's words "No social order ever disappears before all the productive forces for which there is room in it have been developed; and new higher relations of production never appear before the material conditions of their existence have matured in the womb of the old society"[17]. But it is out of growing human consciousness "of the contradictions of material life, from the existing conflict between the social forces of production and the relations of production" that radical change will occur. I shall return at the end of this Preface to the question of human consciousness and economic change. I want to consider first the point to which the contradiction between technological forces of production and the economic structure of property

[16] See N. Kaldor "The Case for an International Commodity Reserve Currency" in *Essays on Economic Policy* Vol. II, 1964.

[17] K. Marx Preface to *Introduction to a Critique of Political Economy*.

relations have developed. For there can be no doubt that these contradictions have been developing rapidly in the last few years.

3. The Present Crisis of Imperialist Relations, and the Possibility of Keynesian Solutions

The warning that I gave in my book of the imminent breakdown
of the very core of imperialist relations—the international monetary
system—has been proved only too correct. Under the multilateral
world trading system that now exists outside the Communist bloc each
country's exporters and importers freely push their goods so long as
their efforts are profitable. Tariffs may not be raised and subsidies are
frowned on as a result of international agreement under the General
Agreement on Tariffs and Trade (GATT). International accounts are
cleared multilaterally and most of the trade is in fact invoiced in pounds
sterling and dollars and now in euro-dollars too (the euro-dollar being
a claim on a dollar that can be more profitably used outside the U.S.A.).
When any country's payments for goods and services fail to be balanced
by receipts, then its government can run down the reserves of currency that it holds and can borrow from other governments or from
the International Monetary Fund. This may provide time for the im-
balance to be rectified, but in the end if deficits persist, it must act, as
the British people have learnt in the last few years, either to devalue its
currency, i.e. to lower its exchange rate in relation to others, or to
take other measures internally to reduce the country's imports and/or
increase exports. The British government has had recently both to
devalue and to deflate overall home demand in the hope of reducing
imports and encouraging exports.

Until the post-war monetary agreements were reached in 1946,
exchange rates were adjusted automatically as demand for and supply
of a country's currency rose and fell. While it is certainly in the interests
of stability that these rates are now fixed within narrow limits and only
altered infrequently, the result is to encourage enormous speculative
movements of funds as soon as a currency like the £ sterling becomes
suspect. There is unfortunately a built-in contradiction in the use of
national currencies for international reserves and this has become
increasingly obvious in the 1960s. A currency is kept as an official
reserve currency because it is available and because it is stable, i.e.
unlikely to be devalued. But the more available the currency is, as a
result of over spending by the nationals whose currency it is, the more
suspect its stability becomes. The deficits run by the U.S.A. and

Britain since 1960 have been reaching a combined annual average of about $2000 millions a year (See Supplementary Table XXX). That is to say that about 2% of world imports were being financed out of these deficits or nearly 15% of the annual average increase in world trade. Nobody believes that these deficits can continue and the Governments of both the U.S.A. and the U.K. have been taking desperate measures to change their deficits into surpluses by deflating internal demand and controlling the outflow of funds. For both countries to attempt to do this simultaneously, however, is bound to lead to a check to the rate of growth of world trade unless alternative sources of demand take their place.

It needs perhaps to be emphasised here that the problem of liquidity in the world monetary system is no longer a problem of credit for the traders concerned. Enormously improved communications, the network of modern banking and government credit guarantees have all combined to solve that problem. There remains a problem of long term credit for underdeveloped countries to buy equipment for industrialisation, but this is really a matter of aid and, as these countries so frequently insist, of developing trade. The fundamental problem facing not only the governments of such countries, which are genuinely attempting to speed up their economic development, but facing all governments with an important stake in world trade, is the problem of balancing their trade at the maximum and not the minimum level. This is the problem to the solution of which the last chapter of the book is directed. When the government of one country, finding itself in balance of payments deficit, adopts measures of internal deflation or import control, in order to reduce its imports, these imports, of course, are some other country's exports; and such other countries will in the end themselves have to cut back *their* imports. As a result world trade is balanced at a level well below the optimum that is possible and a vicious spiral of declining trade such as occurred after 1930 is always a danger. The problem is not too serious for the richest countries with the largest reserves of foreign currencies nor for the giant companies with their own reserves and international trading networks. They simply swallow up the smaller fish. The ultimate battle of the giant pikes in the fish pond is horrible to contemplate. In the mean time there are plenty of smaller fry to be absorbed. The problem is serious for a country like Britain with heavy overseas debts, though these could easily be paid off by liquidating the portfolios of foreign investments held by rich British citizens. It is desperately serious for poor countries with little or no official reserves and no private foreign holdings to liquidate.

Since the book was published the problem of reserves—of international liquidity—has become infinitely more serious. In 1963 the capitalist world's official reserves consisted of $43 billions of gold and $27 billions of dollars and pounds sterling; in 1968 there were $40 billions of gold and $30 billions of the two key currencies. The total was unchanged; but during these five years world trade had grown by 65%. Reserves became equal to 33% instead of 55% of the value of annual trade exchanges. Moreover, the distribution of the reserves had changed so that the underdeveloped countries held 17% of the total instead of the 23% that they had held five years earlier. And if we exclude just six small favoured countries—viz. Israel, Venezuela, Kuwait, Saudi Arabia, Malaysia and Thailand—the remaining underdeveloped countries, including India, Pakistan and Brazil, held only 10% of the total. This meant that, whereas in 1963 their reserves equalled over a third of the value of their imports, by 1968 they equalled less than a fifth[18].

It will be noted that official gold reserves declined over this period and this was despite the annual output of $1.5 billions of gold in the capatalist world, plus another $500m. contributed by Russia and China in most of these years to pay for their grain and other imports. The reason for this apparently strange disappearance of some $10 billions of gold in five years is that private hoarding has been taking place on a fabulous scale in anticipation of a rise in the official price of gold, which has remained for 30 years at its pre-war level. The rise was expected because the value of gold, which remains the basis of the world's money, was so obviously out of line with the world's trade. Gold sales became so serious at the beginning of 1968 that the central bankers agreed to try to hold their official gold reserves off the market and allow a free market in private gold. It was a temporary expedient dictated by the refusal of the U.S. Government to agree to the price of gold being raised. To raise it would be in effect to devalue the dollar and this was unthinkable for the American bankers.

The crisis of the world's money is at the heart of the crisis of capitalist and imperialist economic relations which are the central subject of the book. The currencies of the two great imperialist powers are the key currencies and they are based on gold. These currencies and

[18] For details see M. Barratt Brown "Marxism and the Capitalist World Economy" in *World Economy and Revolution* Bari 1969.

particularly the £ sterling are under challenge from the newly established economic power of the Common Market and especially of
Western Germany. The exports of the six countries of the E.E.C. in
1960 were equal to 23% of the world total; by 1968 this was 27%, and
their reserves had risen from 28% to 37% over the period. Meanwhile
the exports of the U.S.A. and U.K. together had fallen from 24% of the
total to 21% and their reserves from 40% to 24%. By far the greater
part of the fall in these reserves was in the sales of gold by the U.S.A.
and the reasons for these sales was the huge outflow of the giant
American company's funds in buying subsidiaries and extending their
operations in other countries plus the drain on official reserves of
financing the Vietnam war. The $1500 million annual deficit in the
U.S. balance of payments which we noted earlier provided finance for
favoured countries in Europe and the Far East who provided sites for
American business or services for American forces. The trade of the
world grew, albeit lopsidedly and heavily concentrated in military
goods and services, but even the giant United States became over-
extended.

To re-establish the capitalist world's trade on an expanding civilian
base, involving the encouragement of real economic growth in the
underdeveloped lands must seem to be an impossible task. All the
attempts to develop an alternative world money to gold and the two
key currencies built upon it have got no further than they had five years
ago despite the increasing urgency of the situation. The International
Monetary Fund and the International Bank, which Keynes had hoped
would provide the new world money, have never been given adequate
funds or freedom from the strings of the bankers in their administration. Even today the reserves of the I.M.F. total only $13 billions
out of the $70 billions total of gold and other reserves and the latest
proposal to add Special Drawing Rights would make no more than a
marginal increase; while the loans of the International Bank for longer
term development have never exceeded $700 millions a year. All the
other proposals for a new world currency which I discuss in the last
chapter have come to nothing and the reason is not far to seek. One
and all they involve a major diminution of the power of the capitalist
nation's central bankers. There need be no surprise that the main line
of thought that has developed among bankers for meeting the problem
of world liquidity has been an extension of the currency swapping and
standby credit arrangements that have already been made available to
Britain and more recently to France. For these are swaps between the

bankers and controlled by the bankers with interest paid to the bankers. They are of course of little or no help to the poorer countries which have nothing to swap and enjoy poor "credit—worthiness" in a banker's eyes.

So much has been written in recent years about the role of the international bankers, the gnomes of Zurich and the currency manipulators particularly, in laying blame for Britain's economic difficulties, that it is necessary to describe rather precisely the relationship of private and state banks and of banking and industry as a whole. Lenin spoke of the merging of industrial and finance capital under the domination of the latter[19]. For many years the outstanding feature of United States capitalism was undoubtedly the "empires of high finance"[20]—the Mellon, du Pont, Rockefeller, Cleveland, Chicago and Morgan Groups of holding companies. In these empires, the bankers undoubtedly played a dominant and organising role. The increase in the scale of state finance for military and space programmes and in the subsequent scale of the internal generation of company capital has undoubtedly raised the importance of the international industrial company at the expense of the finance groups. The banks and insurance companies still have an important role in mobilising funds for the giant companies and especially in managing overseas finance.

The important new role of the "euro-dollar" in financing international trade and investment can be seen from the fact that, whereas the London deposits of the English Clearing Banks rose between December 1965 and December 1968 from £10,600 m. to £11,700m., the London deposits of American banks in the same three years rose from £1,400m. to £5,300m. and the London deposits of other foreign banks from £1,450m. to £3,700m. In addition to these deposits of American and foreign banks the London deposits of British Commonwealth Banks and London Merchant Banks—much of whose capital derives from overseas—rose from £2,700m. to £4,500m.[21].

The emergence of this secondary banking system[22] with deposits exceeding in size the deposits of the Clearing Banks raises problems for the British government, not only in controlling the money supply at

[19] V. I. Lenin *Imperialism*, Chapter III.

[20] V. Perlo *The Empires of High Finance*.

[21] Figures from Bank of England *Quarterly Bulletin*, March 1969.

[22] J. Revell *Changes in British Banking*, Hill Samuel & Co., May 1968.

home but also in controlling capital movements between sterling and other currencies. For only about a third of the deposits in this secondary system consists of sterling. The so-called "waves of speculation" that have attacked the £ and the Franc in recent months are not caused primarily by private persons speculating against a revision of exchange rates or of gold prices; nor are they now only the result of the "leads and lags" of international trade payments as they were in the late 1950s[23]. They are today a combination of leads and lags with the shifting of great blocks of funds from one financial centre to the other by the giant international companies. Thus the London *Times* reported on November 20th, 1968 that Unilever, B.P., British American Tobacco and I.C.I. had moved balances from Paris and London to Bonn during a week of pressure on the Franc and the £ sterling. Financial journalists have been regaling us for some time now with stories of the tax avoidance devices and tax havens which the international companies have developed in Switzerland, Luxemburg, Lichtenstein (more companies registered than inhabitants!), the Bahamas and so forth[24].

The new role of the bankers is not so much, however, the concealing of funds; it is much more the maintaining of some law and order in this jungle of battling giants. The banker's role is now more a partnership with the finance directors of the giant companies and the bankers themselves have become most important as intermediaries between the companies and the state. What the finance groups did before to co-ordinate movements of private capital in an otherwise anarchic market, the bankers do now to co-ordinate the otherwise unplanned allocation of state funds and unplanned international trade and investment. The contradiction between increasingly planned production on a gigantic scale and the continuing anarchy of private appropriation through the market has to be brought under some sort of control. In Britain as well as the United States this control is the key role of the bankers who straddle the boards of the largest industrial and financial companies and sit on the main Government Committees from the Court of the Bank of England downwards[25].

---

[23] J. Spraos "Speculation, Arbitrage and Sterling" *Economic Journal*, March 1959.

[24] for example P. Ferris *Men and Money*, 1968.

[25] for details see M. Barratt Brown "Who Controls British Industry" in K. Coates (ed) *Can The Workers Run Industry*, Sphere Books, 1968.

The capitalist-imperialist system can only be understood as a whole and operated as a whole and in this Lenin was entirely right. Governments—and this is of course what happened to the Labour Government —have to be brought to understood that the investment plans of the giant companies, the movements of private capital and the provision of state funds have today to be combined. Duplication and mistiming of investment can be exceedingly costly; so can the loss of a major market. While it is true, however, that inside any advanced capitalist country the market can be managed, increasingly the giant companies operate internationally and it is the international market that has to be managed.

The most difficult problem the bankers face is that the new flood of overseas investment from both Britain and the U.S.A. places an excessive strain upon the international balance of payments of these two countries. The outflow of direct company investment from the U.K. now averages nearly £400m. a year; that from the U.S.A. over $4,000m. a year. It has proved quite impossible to cover these huge sums from current foreign earnings, so that both countries have been running the balance of payments deficits throughout the 1960s which we noted earlier, Moreover the establishment and expansion of foreign subsidiaries by international companies have tended to reduce the direct exports of these companies which are of course an essential part of the foreign earnings in the balance of payments. In the case of Britain's exports the top 50 companies provide less than a quarter of the exports but own probably nearer a third of the assets of plants in the U.K. and account for more than a third of the turnover in the home market[26].

Many people have been astonished at the size of the loans made available to a Labour Government to cover its payments deficits since 1964—amounting in all to some £2,500 millions. The fact is that, although the central bankers of the advanced capitalist countries are incapable of agreeing on a new world money, they are bound to try to hold the existing system together. The world role of sterling as a key currency is in this way being steadily replaced by the dollar and mark but Britain could not be permitted to opt out of the system by reducing its overseas military and investment commitments or to reduce too heavily its imports from other capitalist countries, for fear of the repercussions that would follow. There is no sign that the bankers are prepared as yet to apply the Keynesian measures on a

[26] See M. Barratt Brown, "Labour and Sterling" in *International Socialist Journal*, No. 25, February, 1968.

world scale that they have swallowed at home. This is not to say that they will not do this, provided that they can maintain their control over the system.

What is happening at the moment is a gigantic mopping up operation by the largest companies of the markets of the smaller companies, above all by United States companies but also to some extent by U.K. and West German companies, of the markets of the less technologically advanced countries and companies. This is the explanation for the great wave of mergers and take-overs in Britain which was valued at over £3,000m. in 1968 alone, compared with £1,000m. the year before, £500m. in 1966 and £125m. in 1965. The same process is going on in the European Common Market. It is not simply, as we are usually told, that European companies are rationalising in order to be more competitive with the giant American Companies [27]. It is much more a question of preempting markets before the Americans capture them. The fact is that even the rich markets of the advanced capitalist countries cannot absorb the huge productive capacity of modern technology, given the capitalist system of economic relations and the distribution of incomes that it generates. The proportion of new income generated that goes into savings tends to rise, particularly in periods of boom and particularly in the United States[28]. The result is a permanent threat of over production countered only by massive state expenditure on preparations for war, on war itself and on the space race.

A part of this state spending spills over into the underdeveloped countries, as we saw earlier, through direct military aid and offshore purchases and economic aid to to favoured regimes. We deferred final consideration of the prospects of a switch from such military aid to more specific development aid with the deliberate aim among the advanced capitalist countries of extending Keynesian measures of demand management on a world scale. Having now examined some of the features of the current crisis of the capitalist world financial system what conclusion are we to draw? Despite the huge sums in military aid and offshore spending over the last decade the fact is that the

[27] See J. S. Schreiber *The American Challenge*, London 1968.

[28] I have given detailed evidence for this in an essay on "Marxism and the Capitalist World Economy" in *World Economy and Revolution* de Donato Bari 1969. Further evidence may be found in M. Kidron *Western Capitalism since the War*, London 1968, and in P. M. Sweezey and P. Baran *Monopoly Capital*, New York 1966.

underdeveloped lands' share of the world's trade has declined at an accelerated rate. The revisions to Table XXVII show how both the share of primary products in world trade and the share of the under-developed countries of the trade in primary products have declined. While the exports of the underdeveloped lands (excluding the Communist bloc) amounted before the war to over a third of the world's trade (even at low pre-war prices), today they amount to not much more than a sixth. This collapse of such a major part of the capitalist world market has had disastrous consequences for Britain, most of whose trade was traditionally oriented towards lands of primary production, but it has also involved a shrinking of the area of trade for all capitalist countries. Besides this the organisation of the trade of the Communist bloc on a largely autarchic basis of planned mutual trade exchanges has withdrawn another tenth of the world's trade from capitalist control. The overall result of these developments is to concentrate the capitalist pikes in a rich but narrow fishpond. How far, then, to continue the metaphor, are they prepared deliberately to extend the size of the fish pond? For movements of capital in Myrdal's phrase, wealth attracts and poverty repels[29].

What private investment does flow from advanced capitalist countries into underdeveloped countries still today flows almost entirely into primary production. This pattern has changed hardly at all; only the scale is greatly reduced. I criticised earlier the concept of "neo-colonialism" if by this is meant something different from the older imperialism. For the most part, as I have said, the old imperialist relations depended less on political (colonial rule) than on the economic ties of trade and investment and on the artificial division of labour in the world between manufacturing and primary production. These remain and these still provide the essence of imperialist relations. There is none the less the beginnings of a development that might be called "neo-colonialism" although it also has a long history. This is the subordinating of in-dustrialisation where it does occur in underdeveloped countries to the interests of metropolitan capital. United States, Canadian, Australian and other ex-colonials can all recall the early subordination of their industrial development to British capital. Only certain lines of pro-duction were encouraged, or only the assembly of finished products leaving essential processes to be carried out in Britain. The banking system, insurance and shipping services were operated from London.

---

[29] G. Myrdal, *Economic Theory and Underdeveloped Regions*, London 1957.

The Sterling Area was a London based system, in which the gold and foreign earnings of the whole area were banked in London. The independent Sterling Area members have today achieved a large measure of economic freedom and have in fact benefitted in recent years from the Sterling system, as I show in the book (pp. 220ff). But a subordinate capitalist development was what originally took place.

It is such a development, which might be described as being of a neo-colonialist type, and which can be expected to result in those under-developed countries which have attracted large amounts of investment either because of their natural resources, for example oil producing countries like Venezuela or Algeria, or because they are regarded as important bulwarks against the spread of revolutionary changes nearby, like Taiwan or South Korea. The concentration of private investment in the former group and of official aid in the latter combined with local political pressure for some real economic development could lead in such special cases to the beginnings of industrialisation. Industries might be developed by subsidiaries of the international companies for example in motor car assembly. Already, in 1968 assembly lines in Venezuela were producing 5,000 cars and 1,500 commercial vehicles a month or seven times the 1962 figure and in Spain and Portugal the 1968 total was 30,000 cars and 10,000 commercial vehicles a month compared with a fifth of that number in 1962. Plants are now established also in Korea, Taiwan and Algeria and output has been doubled over the same period in Brazil and Argentina to a figure of some 12,000 cars a month in each of these two countries[30]. For the establishment of such plants to lead to a wider and deeper process of industrialisation the profits and incomes generated will have to be retained in the countries themselves and not repatriated.

It seems at least possible that some development of this sort might occur in what may be called the "back gardens" of the major industrial powers but it is likely to be limited to industries that do not compete with home-based plants and to countries that are thought to be politically safe. How far such development might extend elsewhere will depend on the political response of the major powers to world-wide economic changes and on political changes in the underdeveloped lands themselves.

The question remains how far the workers in advanced capitalist countries can push their governments to apply Keynesian measures on

[30] Figures from United National *Statistical Yearbook*, 1967.

a world scale and how far these pressures can be linked with the
demands of the people of the underdeveloped lands for fundamental
changes. Socialists in Britain and in other rich countries cannot rely
only on a long term revolutionary strategy for the overthrow of
capitalism. Nor can they wait for the revolution to be carried out for
them by the peoples of the underdeveloped countries. Short and
medium term programmes are needed which begin to cut into the
power of the giant company both at home and in its international
operations. Controls at home by Trade Unions and workers representatives through the opening of the companies' books and through
more and more open public control of company policy will be limited
in their effect if they are not complemented by the opening of the
accounts of international company transactions and by international
control of international company policy.

This is not to suggest any kind of supra-national government
authority being acceptable to a wide range of rich and poor nations—
this is not even acceptable to the six nations of the Common Market.
But international agreements for some planning of trade exchanges
along the lines of the Frisch proposals considered earlier would seem
to be possible, if they could be supported not only by governments but
by control through workers' representatives in the various plants and
companies concerned. Just as national economic planning means only
an extension of the management of the market in the interests either of
private capital or of a state bureaucracy unless there is built into the
plan a major element of workers' control over costs and prices and
direction of production, so any kind of international economic planning must be complemented by the extension of control from below.
Not only this, but any advance towards a major challenge to the power
of the giant international companies is hard to envisage unless it
includes a steady process of encroachment upon the arbitrary and
hierarchical authority of the company by the workers in it. This brings
us to the last section of this Preface in which I try to re-evaluate the
Marxist theory of economic change.

4. *Marxist Theory and Economic Development*

The approach in the book to the problems of the world economy
is a Marxian one; it is neither reformist in the sense of concentrating
on reforms today which only serve to patch up a dying economic
system nor revolutionary in the sense of concentrating on a revolution
one day in the future which will come automatically as the old system

dies. It seems to me to be worthwhile to set down the basis of this
approach in a quite simple manner in order to clear the way for making
explicit what I believe is involved in economic development. The
fundamental Marxian proposition is accepted that changing technology
both creates and requires for its fulfilment changes in the economic
system of human relations in production. But what is here insisted on
is that *men* make the changes as they become conscious of the need for
them. Just as it is men who develop new techniques in the struggle
with nature so they must develop new relations to make full use of the
new techniques. Only a class of men with a common consciousness of
what is needed can generate the confidence and the will for such
changes. This common consciousness derives from the relationship of
such a class of men to the new techniques of production. It can be held
back by classes of men who own and control older techniques of
production and by the common consciousness which they brought
to the development of the old. Men are engaged not only in struggles
with nature and in class struggle but in a struggle for a new consciousness of what technological change requires.

Economic change and growth then are matters essentially of
accumulating resources for assisting men in their struggle with nature
to make tools and machines to strengthen and extend human hands and
arms and backs and brains. But they involve also the discovery of the
relations between men that will make possible the full use of the new
machines. In the past small groups of men saw what could be done with
new tools and machines by following a quite narrow self-interest and
hardly aware of the implications for whole societies and peoples of
what they were doing. The invention of the market as a place which
brought together the different products of different men served enormously to increase the division of labour upon which technical advances rested. It served also to conceal that what occurred day by day in
the market was a relationship of men and not simply an exchange of
products. Men were barely conscious of the enormous difference that
it made in the market that a few owned land or capital and most owned
only their hands and brains. Those who were conscious of this unequal distribution accepted it as their fate. Few knew anything of what
happened beyond the confines of their fields and villages, their workshops and towns.

Today the market still brings together the different producers and
still serves to conceal the true relationship of the owners of land
and of capital and of labour power. But human consciousness has

nevertheless made a quite critical advance. The market can be managed by the owners of great concentrations of capital; it can be managed also by governments. Increasing numbers of people know this. They know also how vast is the gulf between the condition of those in the few rich countries and those in the many which are still poor; and the poor know that they need not forever accept this as their fate. What men have done in one land to control their environment other men can do elsewhere. The revolution of rising expectations, as it is called, is a change in human consciousness. But the accumulation of resources for making new tools and machines is a terrible process; it means giving up some part of the little a poor man has today in order to build for tomorrow. Throughout history the few who accumulated did so at the expense of the many who contributed. Voluntary self denial for those on the margins of subsistence is an almost impossible request to make of any man.

In all countries where the accumulation has occurred and the process of carrying through an industrial revolution has been undertaken, a small class of men has forced the process through, and very largely at the expense of the many whose consumption has been held down so that investment could take place. I think I am over-optimistic in the book (p. 433) that "a high rate of investment need not mean a cut in consumption". It is hard to see how it could be otherwise. This is particularly true today when the capital required to establish modern industry is so enormous. No peoples are prepared to go through the long slow growth from small beginnings of Britain's industrial revolution, not even the Chinese with their kitchen iron furnaces. All will wish to jump straight to the most modern equipment and would be quite out-classed in world markets if they were to do anything else. Only China is big enough and so self-sufficient in food and raw materials to cut herself off completely from world trade. The rest, as we saw in the case of Yugoslavia, are bound to move towards large-scale industrial production through the international division of labour.

John Knapp, in a private communication, has criticised the book on the ground that, while it accepts from Marxism the role of technology and class agency in economic change, it describes again and again the importance of the market without acknowledging this in the theoretical framework. Certainly I ascribe the successful early advance of the industrial revolution in Britain to the "mopping up" by the products of a superior technology of long established markets overseas, first, in Europe and in the Americas, then in Asia. And I ascribe to the impoverishment of many of these markets the later stagnation of British industry. I also regard the real economic development in Western Europe and in North America and Oceania, and the consequent real growth of markets in these areas, as the sustaining force in the hey-day of Britain's industrial expansion. My conclusion, moreover, is that the present "mopping up" of markets by the most advanced giant international companies is once more fatal to the economic development of industry in the less advanced countries; and only a new framework of expanded world trade exchanges can save them. And I can see that this conception may seem to fit uneasily in a Marxist analysis that puts its main emphasis on technology and class agency.

I concede at once that the importance which Marxists have attributed to accumulation in economic growth provides an inadequate analysis. Hoarding manifestly fails to provide the stimulus for growth; it is the process of dishoarding, whether it be in pyramid or cathedral building or on manufacturing industry, that provides for growth. But Marx's simple formula $M-C-M^1$ made this point perfectly clear. It is money laid out on commodities to make more money that is the essence of capitalism; and money laid out on buying labour power (itself a commodity) to manufacture commodities that may be sold to make more money that is the essence of industrial capitalism. $M-C-M^1$ is a model of the very engine of capitalist growth and it is worthwhile examining the socio-economic assumptions that surround it [31]. These are that production is for the market, incomes are unequal, large sums of capital are accumulated, the means of production are in relatively few hands, labour power is itself a commodity (free from feudal ties etc.) and a class of capitalists exists who are motivated to make money in a particular way. A further crucial assumption is that there is competition between capitalists so that each wishing to sell his products at a profit must reduce his costs by improving his machinery and widening the market for his product. Technological advances not only require the accumulation of capital *and* the widening market; they are further generated by these processes.

Marx's whole critique of capitalism however, rested on the innate contradiction of accumulation and a widening market, since extra profit for capitalist accumulation must always mean less spending power for the masses. In the anarchy of the market it will only be by chance that what is set aisde by all the capitalists for investment

---

[31] I have done this at greater length in a contribution to a volume of essays in honour of Lelio Basso *World Economy and Revolution* p.67, De Donato, Bari, 1969.

exactly equals in any period their actual investments and what is left
for consumption by the masses in the same period exactly equals the
value of goods which it is profitable for capitalists to produce for
consumption. Indeed there is every reason to suppose that these
elements in the equation will not balance as booms lead to excessive
investment which has to be cut back in subsequent slumps. Marx was
perfectly aware of the importance of the market in capitalist growth;
what he did not expect was that governments would be able to "manage" demand in the market by Keynesian measures, which would be
acceptable to capitalists in fear of something worse.

The proposals in the last Chapter of the book, for sustaining demand
in the poor lands, are put forward not so much as an extension of
Keynesian measures to the solution of the problems of the world
capitalist economy, but as a framework for united action by the
peoples of the rich and poor countries alike. Of course Keynesian
measures by governments to maintain full employment at home provide
some solution for capitalist stagnation and slump. They also unite
workers and strengthen their unions, which would otherwise be
divided and weakened by unemployment. It is also clear that Keynesian
full employment policies do not permanently solve the contradictions
of capitalism. Inflation takes the place of unemployment in depriving
the workers of their gains, and accumulation by the giant companies
at the expense of the smaller fry constantly renews the ranks of the
unemployed and requires ever more intervention by governments to
maintain demand. In the international field as within capitalist nations
the mopping up of markets by the giant companies creates ever new
areas of underdevelopment. The prospect of the day when there are
only pikes in the fish pond is always there before us as a dreadful
warning of what must come.

While Marx's prediction of the increasing concentration and
centralisation of capital every day sees new fulfilment and while
governments are forced increasingly to intervene to manage the market
for the giant companies, one lesson is again and again spelt out to the
people. Economic events are not the uncontrollable forces of nature
that they once seemed. If giant companies and their governments can
essay to control them, so can the people. The feed-back in consciousness
from the conflict of new technology and an old economic system of
production relations is not limited to the owners and managers of
capital. This too is what Marx foresaw and why he believed in the
property-less workers as the agents of future economic change. They

had no property to lose; the very nature of their work in great in dustrial plants united them; and their growing consciousness of the unused or distorted potentialities of the processes in which they were engaged would make them socialists. With all the corruption of higher living standards today, the growing demand for workers' control in an advanced but increasingly second-rate capitalist country like Britain reveals this growing socialist consciousness at work.

What has happened in the underdeveloped countries has turned out far differently, however, from what Marx expected. From his preface to the first (German) edition of *Capital* and from his essay on "The Future Results of the British Rule in India" he evidently believed that "The country that is more developed industrially only shows, to the less developed, the image of its own future"[32]. "The free press" . . . "a fresh native class" . . . "a net work of railways" . . . "will become in India truly the forerunner of modern industry" . . . "when you have once introduced machinery into the locomotion of a country, which possesses iron and coal, you are unable to withold it from its fabrication"[33]. This was, however, almost exactly just what the imperialism of free trade succeeded in doing. And if no modern industry can develop, then it follows that there will be no indigenous capitalist class to generate further capitalist economic growth and no working class to make the advance to Socialism. Of course India was not left at the end of colonial rule without any modern industry, but many parts of Asia, Africa and South America remain to this day almost in that condition of underdevelopment. Whence then will come the agency, the class, that can carry through the process of industrialisation in such countries?

I have said in this Preface that I reject the concept of neo-colonialism as implying that imperialism had changed in some important way, since there had always been many parts of the world contained within the relations of imperialism which were never actual colonies. I reject it also for another more important reason, that the basis of this *neo*-colonialism is supposed to be the suborning of a new indigenous capitalist class in the one-time colonies to the needs and interests of the imperialist powers and the giant international company in particular·

[32] K. Marx *Capital* Volume 1. Authors Preface to the first edition, Allen and Unwin, p. XVII.

[33] K. Marx "Future Results of British Rule in India" in K. Marx and F. Engels *On Colonialism*, FLPH Moscow, p. 57 ff.

This is to assume that there is some indigenous modern industry in the underdeveloped lands, but in fact there is generally very little. There were in most colonies before decolonisation enclaves of mines and estates under European ownership and some of these have since been nationalised. There was for long a comprador merchant class in the colonies engaged in the export and import trade with the metropolitan countries and some of this trade which was in European hands has now been transferred to native merchants. These elements always provided an important base for imperialist relations and they provide a more important base today; but it would seem to be exaggerating the role of indigenous *industrial* capitalists to suppose that there is already a new element in the situation. This is not to say that, where indigenous modern industry does emerge in underdeveloped countries, it will not be suborned to the wider operations of the international companies. The most important fact in the situation remains that modern industrial development, apart from mining and oil production, is still being largely prevented in the underdeveloped lands by imperialist trading relations of the old type. This was the significance of the overthrow of the Ben Bellas and Goularts and Sukarnos.

I have already indicated earlier in this Preface that the assumption of the last chapter of the book, that populist and nationalist regimes would successfully engage in industrial development has been falsified by the overthrow of these regimes. What then are the prospects for the under-developed lands and where should we look for the agency of change? Paul Baran assumed in the 1950s that, however, serious the distortions of imperialism, "the general direction of the historial movement seems to have been the same for the backward echelons as for the forward contingents"[34]. He spoke of the "revolution from above that con-solidated the social order in Russia[35], but Russia in 1917 had the beginnings of an industrial base and a sufficient industrial proletariat to supply the leaders of the Communist Party in carrying out that "revolution from above." Baran accepted that "the revolutionary break could not have been achieved with the consent of the irrational, illiterate and ignorant peasantry", although he also accepted Oscar Lange's judgement that their "assent was obtained *ex post facto* through the propaganda and educational activities of the state and of the

[34] P. Baran *The Political Economy of Growth*, New York 1957, p. 140.

[35] *Ibid* p. 281

Communist Party"[36]. Without any industrial base and with no industrial proletariat from which to build even a Communist Party as proxy for the working class, what would have been achieved? What can be achieved in those underdeveloped countries that are now in that condition?

The answer which I am going to suggest here seems to me to be in line with the fundamental element of Marx's thinking if not with the detail of its working out. Marx singled out the industrial working class in contemporary Europe as the agency of future economic change, in struggles with the capitalist class which had accomplished the previous great changes. The industrial workers had nothing to lose, they were united by their activity into a class, solidarity was developed by their evident exploitation in the process of work and they had the occasion to develop a socialist consciousness from their awareness of the conflict between the changing productive forces and the existing relations of production. A new consciousness is the essence of the process. If this is so, then other groups of men can be imagined today, besides industrial workers, both other groups of workers in the advanced capitalist countries and many different groups in the underdeveloped lands, as sharing these essential attributes.

There are indeed millions in the underdeveloped lands with nothing to lose; the new systems of communication by press and transistor radio and T.V. have made them all conscious as never before of the vast contradiction between their miserable condition and the fantastic advances of man's control over his environment, reaching out from the earth itself to the moon and the stars. In this growing consciousness it is likely that students, intellectuals, clerks, artisans, small shopkeepers and peasants too, all those under pressure from the products and sales network of the giant international companies of the advanced capitalist lands, may readily be espected to play the role ascribed by Marx to the industrial working class. Nkrumah's attempt in Ghana, under western communist advice, to build his regime upon the few proletarians instead of the many cocoa farmers, who were just as much threatened by the international cartels, was an evident failure and should have taught a lesson to others. Certainly, Mondiane in Mozambique with his guerilla army drawn from the villages seems more likely to succeed in creating a base for real economic advance; and in such guerilla units we may perhaps identify in one form the missing attribute

[36] *Ibid* p. 279

in this picture of a new agency of change—that organisational unity which the factory supplied to the industrial workers in Marx's model. This form of organisation is the military unit of liberation armies. Where peasants join guerilla armies to defend their land they take a first step from individual to social consciousness, but it is a long way still from socialist consciousness.

This is not perhaps to say anything very new. The economic successes of Mao Tse Tung and the Chinese communists cannot be separated from their foundation in the military resistance of an almost entirely peasant army to the Japanese invaders. The economic successes of the Vietnamese have been born in the fire of battle against French and American invaders. Perhaps it was after all more the solidarity deriving from the resistance of the Red Army to armed invasion by the Allies than anything learned in the factories before 1917 that sustained the Soviet Communist Party's advance to industrialisation. Certainly it is true that many of the cadres of industrial workers in the early Soviets were killed in the Civil War. Does this mean that the key to organising united action for economic change lies in the presence of an external enemy? The failure of Che Guevara's little band in Bolivia may have been partly due to the fact that they were not directly fighting against United States forces, as the Vietnamese are, or as the Chinese fought the Japanese and Mondiane's guerillas are fighting the Portugese. The appeals of nationalism and of zenophobia are powerful human emotions.

To accept such arguments, however, would lead us back to belief in the viability of the nationalist, populist regimes of the "Third World' which have so signally collapsed. They were built upon anti-European, anti-colonial, zeno-phobic emotions. These were not enough. They were not, of course, expressed in the organisational form of the guerilla unit but only in the mob riot, the street demonstration, the mass meeting. The need for the "discipline of the mountains" is the clear message of Regis Debray[37]. It is even more clearly the message of the Chinese, the Vietnamese and the Africans of Mozambique and Guinea.[38] The guerilla unit appears to provide not only the discipline, but the confidence, the unity, the mutual trust and the group consciousness in face of a common external enemy that Marx saw in the capitalist factory. But just as the unity, confidence and

[37] R. Debray *Revolution in the Revolution?* New York 1967.
[38] B. Davidson *The Liberation of Guiné* 1969

socialist consciousness of factory workers had to be built in common actions to win small improvements in conditions year by year, and developed by socialist theory, so the same is true of the guerilla units. Careful attention to the people's needs before any engagements are fought are the hall-mark of the successes of the Chinese, the Vietnamese and the African guerillas, just as their lack was the mark of Guevara's failure.

Today it must seem a long road from the agricultural work of the guerilla units of Mozambique (especially after the tragic murder of Mondiane himself) to the foundations of modern industry in Africa, where the bullock and plough have often still to take the place of the digging stick. Isaac Deutscher in one of his last essays wrote of the Russian Revolution as "a combination of bourgeois and proletarian revolutions, though both were accomplished under bolshevik leadership"[39], but if the categories are just meaningful, though doubtfully applicable, to the Russian case, they are quite meaningless in Africa. They conceal the fact that it is an industrial revolution in all its stages, first, second and third, that has to be carried through in underdeveloped lands, with all the changes in economic relations that this demands. For, underdevelopment is a specific condition, different from non-development, a condition in which consciousness has lept ahead while the technical base has been held back from developing. In such a condition utopian hopes abound, but when the elan of fighting on the mountains dies away, the "iron heel of primitive accumulation" must descend, as Preobrezhensky described it in the Russia of the 1920s.[40] This is the more true the lower the level of economic development in the country concerned. For accumulation to industrialise means giving up today, even the little that separates subsistence from near starvation, in order to build for tomorrow.

The very deformities, however, of the Russian Revolution under Stalin are today paralleled by the idolising of Tito, Castro and Mao Tse Tung while their critics are outlawed without any open discussion of the issues involved.[41] Together these experiences should warn socialists of the dangers inherent in movements for economic change which are

[39] I. Deutscher "The Unfinished Revolution 1917–67", *New Left Review*, No. 43, 1967

[40] E. Preobrezhensky *The New Economics* (tr. B. Pearce) Oxford 1965.

[41] After reading Joan Robinson's *The Cultural Revolution in China*, 1969. I am bound in part to revise this judgement. The argument of the paragraph, I believe, still stands.

based upon the experiences of guerilla warfare. With all its comrade-ship, common discipline and co-operation, unity in any kind of fighting involves a strict line of command and unquestioning obedience. It is a bad seed bed for democracy. Of course democratic decisions may be rendered impossible in the period of accumulation of an industrial revolution in just the same way as they are rendered impossible in war time. The greater the amount of truly principled fraternal aid that can be given from the rich developed countries to the peoples of the underdeveloped countries attempting to industrialise, the more pos-sible it will be for them to avoid the deformities of central autocratic or bureaucratic authority.

Apart from the guerilla units which we have just considered as one possible agency of social and economic change, the only hope for the underdeveloped countries lie in the industrial workers. The beginnings of motor car assembly which we noted earlier and the spread of the international company into the underdeveloped lands mopping up markets wherever they appear are still on a very small scale. As this process extends, however, we are bound to see a more rapid development even though it may be suborned to the interests of the giant company. Although an indigenous industrial capitalist will not be permitted to develop, an indigenous proletariat may. The links between this proletariat and the workers in the advanced capitalist countries will become increasingly important. Groups of workers in the same giant companies in different lands will be forced to come together to concert action. These links will be greatly encouraged by the fact that the whole trend of the growth of the giant international company implies that not only the poorest underdeveloped countries but many of the half developed and even some of the smaller advanced countries will be driven into subordinate roles. The polarisation of wealth and poverty which Marx so well understood as the essential feature of capitalism[42] tends always to eliminate the middle groups—first the small land owner and small capitalist, then the self employed now the medium sized business and small national economy. Resistance against this process will tend to unite increasing sections of the workers in the more advanced countries with those in the underdeveloped countries.

Already, the problem of building new relations between workers in the rich countries and the Vietnamese people is no longer to be

---

[42] K. Marx *Capital* Vol. I, Chapter XXV, Section 2.

solved solely on the level of demonstrations of solidarity and protest. A programme of common action needs to be worked out; and this cannot stop at criticism of the role of the international companies and the governments associated with them or even at boycott of their plans. It is no longer fanciful to think of 'workers' control' in Britain extending to the point where workers demand that the products of their plants go to supply the industrial needs of the peoples of South-East Asia or of Africa, and not to meet the military needs of their common enemies. And such a demand will require the further demand for a new framework of planned trade exchanges between rich and poor countries that would truly begin to build the relationships that must follow after imperialism.

At the end of this long preface I should like to take the opportunity of paying tribute to all those who have written to me personally and often at great length in discussion of the book. These include Basil Davidson, Ioan Davies, Isaac Deutscher, Royden Harrison, Geoff Kay and John Knapp. Without their criticisms the conclusions reached here would not have emerged. They are not of course to be held responsible for the conclusions. This second edition also gives me the opportunity to repair an inexplicable omission from the acknowledgements in the original Preface to the book and to thank my old friend David Leacock, lately of the United Nations Economic Commission for Europe, who gave me so much help and encouragement in the early stages of preparing the book.

Sheffield, March 1969.

'But a people may be too rich; because it is the tendency of the commercial, and more especially of the manufacturing system, to collect wealth rather than to diffuse it. Where wealth is successfully employed in any of the speculations of trade, its increase is in proportion to its amount; great capitalists become like pikes in a fish pond, who devour the weaker fish; and it is but too certain that the poverty of the one part of the people seems to increase in the same ratio as the riches of another.'

Robert Southey, *Sir Thomas More or Colloquies on the Progress and Prospects of Society*

Contents

PREFACE   v

PREFACE TO SECOND EDITION   vii

LIST OF TABLES   lv

INTRODUCTION – ONE WORLD   1

   10,000 Million People   2

   The Great Divide – between Rich and Poor   3

   How did it Happen? Was Imperialism the Cause?   7

   Lenin's 'Imperialism'   11

   The Questions to be Answered – The Meaning of
     Imperialism   14

   After Empire   16

PART ONE: IMPERIALISM AS IT WAS

CHAPTER 1. THE RISE OF EMPIRE – WHY
     DIDN'T THEY COLONISE US?   25

   Slave and Peasant Empires   25

   East and West – the Basic Difference in Agri-
     cultural Production   28

   Merchant Adventurers and a Manufacturing
     Interest   31

   The First English Manufacturers and the Old
     Colonial System   35

   Plunder and Industrialisation   38

   The Conquest of India   41

   The Destruction of Competition from the East   44

l CONTENTS

CHAPTER 2. CAPITALISM AND EMPIRE –
(1) THE SUCCESS OF FREE TRADE: 1824–
1870   51
The Establishment of Free Trade   52
Lands of White Settlement   54
The Origins of Underdeveloped Lands   56
Enclaves of Development   58
Advantages of Free Trade for Britain   61
Overseas Investment and the Empire   63
The World Division of Labour   66
Britain's Gain from the Terms of Trade   69
Annexe on the Terms of Trade   72

CHAPTER 3. CAPITALISM AND EMPIRE –
(2) THE DEFEAT OF PROTECTION: 1870–
1913   80
The Great Depression and British Industrial
  Decline   81
Overseas Investment and the Economy at Home   84
Overseas Investment and the Expansion of Empire   86
Hobson's View of Investment as the Drive to
  Empire   91
Lenin's 'Imperialism' Examined   95
The Role of Joseph Chamberlain   101
The Campaign against Free Trade   104

CHAPTER 4. WAR, STAGNATION AND EMPIRE:
1914–1945   117
War and Empire   117
German Expansionism   119
British Overseas Investment in the 1920s   122
Monopoly and World Cartels   125
Foreign Investment, Crisis and Stagnation at
  Home   131
Imperial Trade and Preference   135

Were the Terms of Trade Favourable for Britain
    in the 1930s? 140
Who Gained in Britain from 'Imperial Tribute'? 142
Capitalism and the Second World War 147
Annexe on the Terms of Trade in the 1930s 150

CHAPTER 5. RESULTS OF EMPIRE – IN THE
    COLONIES 158
What Economic Dependence meant for a Colony 160
Lands of European Settlement 163
Cheap Labour in the Colonies 166
Mining and Plantation Wealth 169
The Wealth and Poverty of India 174
The Results of Indirect Rule 177
The Native Middle Class and Industrialisation 180

PART TWO: IMPERIALISM TODAY

CHAPTER 6. END OF COLONIAL EMPIRE:
    1945–1962 189
The Colonial Liberation Movements 190
Japanese Occupation and Communist Rebellion 192
The Successor States 195
The Remaining Colonies 198
The Basis of African Nationalism 200
The Cold-War Context of Liberation and the
    Supremacy of United States Capitalism 204
Internal and External Limitations to Economic
    Independence 208

CHAPTER 7. WHAT REMAINS OF EMPIRE? 216
The Sterling Area – a New Form of Imperialism? 217
Should Ex-Colonies leave the Sterling Area? 220
What is the Importance of Imperial Preference
    Today? 222
The Challenge to British Privilege 227

'Economic Imperialism' in the Plantation and
    Mining Companies   230
The Oil Protectorates   236
The Empires of Oil Today   238
Oil Investment and the British Economy   242

CHAPTER 8. THE NEW EMPIRES – OF THE
    GIANT CORPORATIONS   253
The New Wave of British Overseas Investment   254
Can it Continue?   258
The Nature of British Overseas Investment Today   263
Who are the Investors?   268
Why so much Overseas Investment?   273

CHAPTER 9. CAPITALISM WITHOUT EMPIRE   291
The Causes of the Post-war Boom   293
    (a) More Tribute   293
    (b) More Exports   296
    (c) More Equal Incomes   301
    (d) More Government Spending and Techno-
        logical Change   304
The Check to Growth in Britain after 1955   307
Should We Blame the City?   311
The Comparison with West Germany and France   314
Has Capitalism Changed?   320
The Role of the Giant Corporations   324
Home versus Foreign Investment   327

PART THREE: TOWARDS AN INTERNATIONAL
ECONOMY

CHAPTER 10. THE WORLD TRADE BLOCS   345
The Trade of the Industrialised and Non-Indus-
    trialised Lands   348
The Rise of Trade Blocs   355
The Sterling Area   358

The Dollar Area   364
Foreign Investment of United States Capital   369
The Common Market   372
The Rouble Area   380

CHAPTER 11. INDUSTRIALISATION OF THE
    WORLD   404
The Necessary Conditions for Industrial Develop-
    ment   405
The Checks to Development   408
The Need for Land Reform   412
Industrial Evolution or Revolution   415
Can Capitalism do the Job?   418
Planned Economic Development   422
Communist Agricultural Policy   425
The Indian and Chinese Plans Compared   430
The Role of Foreign Aid   436

CHAPTER 12. BRITAIN IN A WORLD OF
    EQUALS   447
The Questions Answered: A Summary of Con-
    clusions   447
The Way Forward for Britain   454
International Aid and Investment   458
    (a) Bilateral Contributions   458
    (b) Multilateral Contributions   461
The Framework of Positive Neutralism   465
Higher and More Stable Earnings for Primary
    Producers   468
Growing Points of an International Economy   472
Towards a True Division of Labour in the World   475

Select Bibliography   489
Index   502

Tables

Chapter	Table	Title	Page
Intro.	I–A	Rich and Poor, 1938 and 1958	19
	I–B	Rich and Poor Countries by groups in *Per Capita* Income Order, 1958	20
2	II	Balance of Britain's Foreign Payments in the Nineteenth Century	75
	III	Boom and Slump in Britain's Industrial Output and Foreign Trade, 1822–1960	76
3	IV	Growth of National Income in Britain and Relationship of Trade and Investment, 1865–1961	108–9
	V	Geographical Distribution of British Overseas Trade and Investment, 1860s–1930s	110
	VI	Volume of Britain's Trade and Empire Share in it, 1850s–1960s	111
	VII	Shares and Directions of Different Commodity Exports in U.K. and Eight Countries' Trade, 1830–1960	112
4	VIII	Character of British Overseas Investment, 1913, 1930, 1934	153

Chapter	Table	Title	Page
	IX	Movement in Real National Income, Real Earnings and Unemployment, U.K. and Germany, 1913–40	154
5	X	Distribution of Revenue from African Mining, 1937–56	183
6	XI	Distribution of U.S. Foreign Aid, 1945–59	212–13
7	XII	Shares in Overseas Sterling Area Markets, 1938–61	247
	XIII	Return on Investment in British Home and Overseas Companies, 1955–61	248
8	XIV	U.K. Imports and Means of Payment, 1913–61	278
	XV–A	U.K. and Sterling Area Aggregate Balance of Payments, 1946–60	279
	XV–B	U.K. Balance of Payments Current Account, 1958–61	280
	XVI	U.K. Net Foreign Investment Balance, 1959	281
	XVII	Estimated Distribution of British Overseas Investment, 1938 and 1959	282
	XVIII	Nature of British Overseas Investment in the 1950s	283
	XIX	U.K. Company Direct Overseas Investments and Earnings, 1958–59, 1960	284
	XX	Overseas Interests of British Commercial and Industrial Companies, 1959–60	285–7

Chapter	Table	Title	Page
9	XXI	Industrial and Export Performance of U.K. in Relation to other Manufacturing Countries, 1913–61	334
	XXII	Changes in Distribution of Incomes in the U.K., 1938–57	335
	XXIII	Annual Movements in Real Product, Consumption, Wages, Prices and Profits, 1948–61	336
	XXIV	Distribution of West German National Product, 1950–59	337
10	XXV	Capitalist World Production, Trade and Prices of Manufactures and Primary Products, 1876–1961	388
	XXVI	Output and Prices of Selected Primary Commodities: 1948–54, 1954–60	390–1
	XXVII–A	Trade of Industrial and Non-Industrial Lands, 1928 60	392
	XXVII–B	Trade of Industrial and Non-Industrial Lands, 1953, 1956, 1960	393
	XXVIII	World Trade Blocs, 1959	394
	XXIX	Rate of Growth and Shares of World Trade, 1938–59	395
	XXX	United States Balance of Payments and Long-Term Foreign Investment, 1919–59	396–7
	XXXI	Growth Rates and Shares of World Manufacturing Industry, 1937–59, with an Estimate for 1970	398
11	XXXII	The Indian and Chinese Plans Compared	440–1
12	XXXIII	World Aid and Investment for Underdeveloped Lands, 1955–59	485

lviii

LIST OF SUPPLEMENTARY TABLES

Table I   —Rich and Poor 1958 and 1968

XIII   —Return on Investment in British Home and Overseas Campanies 1952–68

XVIII   —Nature of British Overseas Investment in the 1960s.

XIX   —U.K. Company Direct Overseas Investment 1960–67

XXV   —Capitalist World Production Trade and Prices of Manufactures and Primary Products 1958–67

XXVII   —Trade of Industrial and Non Industrial Lands 1953–67
A—by Area
B—by Commodity

XXIX   —Rate of Growth and Shares in World Trade 1959–70

XXX   —United States Balance of Payments and Long Term Foreign Investment 1960–68

XXXI   —Growth Rates and Shares of World Industrial Activity 1950–70

XXXIII —World Aid and Investment for Underdeveloped Lands 1955–66
A—Aid and Investment—Capitalist and Communist Countries
B—Official Aid (excl. Military) by Source and Destination
C—Major Donors and Beneficiaries of Official International Aid.

Introduction – One World

The human race is rapidly becoming a major biological success. Having slowly and painfully, and with many setbacks in 170,000 years, increased its population to a thousand millions, it has trebled this figure in little more than a hundred years. At the present rate of growth, it will be twice as large again in less than forty years. Unless we destroy ourselves in nuclear warfare, by the turn of the century there will be at least six thousand million men, women and children on the face of the earth.[1] It is a prospect to terrify the misanthropist, encourage the humanist and challenge us all. Such a change in quantity cannot but demand a change in the quality of the lives we live.

We shall not only have to find enough food and clothing and living-space and shelter, and all the other things that make life worth living; we shall have to find how to live together at much closer quarters. Even without the huge advance in the ease and speed of modern transport, the very increase in our numbers would bring us closer together and end the isolation in which many thousands of communities have lived in the past.

Little more than a quarter of the surface of the earth consists of land, and of this man can only at present inhabit about a third. The rest is ice and tundra, tropical forest and desert. But there is still room for expansion. Two-thirds of mankind are at present crowded together on little more than 7 per cent of the land-surface; and we cultivate a bare tenth of the land itself.[2]

10,000 *Million People*

Over the next hundred years man's survival will depend not only upon avoiding a new world war, but upon our ability to apply the knowledge we have gained in controlling the forces of nature to the opening up of new lands for cultivation and human habitation in the virgin forests and deserts of the earth. There is no reason to suppose that the growth of population will not ease off by conscious control everywhere, as it has already done in the richer communities whenever higher standards of education and life are achieved. With a stabilised world population of, say, 10,000 million, there should be no need to fear over-population. Such a figure, between three and four times the present number, would mean about two hundred people to the square mile of land-surface. In England we have more than a thousand to the square mile, in the United Kingdom as a whole about five hundred.[3]

The opening up of new lands, however, demands as its precondition the raising of the whole level of life of those peoples whose population is so rapidly increasing. For it is among the very peoples who have shared least in man's recent advances towards controlling his environment that the numbers are rising. Looked at from one point of view, the peoples of Asia and Africa are beginning to re-establish the share of the world's population which they held before the eighteenth century. Between 1800 and 1950 their populations barely doubled, while Europeans in Europe and overseas multiplied fourfold. In 1750 Asians and Africans made up 80 per cent of the world's people; they are today a little more than 60 per cent.[4] But every year they are increasing their share; for now it is their turn and that of the South Americans to grow while the Europeans stabilise.

The expansion of the European peoples over the last two hundred years has been a part of the revolutionary changes pioneered by Europeans in man's control over nature. As a result, their lives have been changed out of all recognition. Their health and expectation of life, their material possessions, their forms of work, their hours of leisure, their opportunities for education and recreation have risen at an unprecedented pace. But these changes have not yet become very widely diffused among non-Europeans. The main spread to date has been in the field of health and expectation of life, which has led to the new high rate of growth of world population which we have been considering. For the rest, the great majority of the people of the earth live lives that are little different from those of their ancestors going back two, three and even four thousand years.

Thus, not much more than a quarter of the world's people live in communities which have gone through their industrial revolution. These are the peoples of northern Europe, including Russia, of North America and Japan. Another small group of peoples in eastern Europe, in the lands of white settlement in southern Africa and Oceania, and here and there in Latin America may be said to have established an industrial base for their economies. This leaves two-thirds of the world's people in lands where industrialisation has barely begun (see Table I): in China, in the successor states of the European empires in Africa, India and Indonesia, and in South America. Of these countries only China may be said to be firmly set upon the road to industrialisation, but with a population of 680 millions her task is the greatest.

The Great Divide – between Rich and Poor

The different stages of industrial development of the peoples of the world are reflected in very great differences in national wealth. At one extreme, as Table I shows, North Americans enjoy an annual income of about £700 for every

man, woman and child. At the other extreme, the figure for
the two-thirds of the world's people in the underdeveloped
lands is less than £30. And the gap is widening: before the
war the two figures would have been £120 and £10. The
difference has doubled – from a ratio of just over 10 to 1 to
one of well over 20 to 1.*

Thus, while less than one-fifth of the world's people in
industrialised lands (including Japan) enjoy three-fifths of
the world's wealth, three-fifths of the world's people in China
and the poorest lands share little more than a tenth of the
wealth. The North Americans alone, with 7 per cent of the
world's population, have nearly 40 per cent of the total
income. Only a very few peoples, notably those in the communist lands, in lands of white settlement and in oil-bearing
lands, have kept up with or surpassed the pace of growth set
by the Americans. Even the people of other industrialised
lands have fallen back in relation to the North Americans.

The most remarkable feature of Table I is the apparent
rate of growth of wealth in the communist lands between
1938 and 1958, despite the much greater extent of destruction
which they suffered during the Second World War than any
of the other belligerents. Even the most conservative estimates of industrial output in the communist third of the
world (those of Mr Allen Dulles[5]) give them 25 per cent of
world output. (The figures are shown in Table XXX, below.)
In our calculation we have given them 28 per cent of world
income. What is more important is that at present growth-
rates, even on the Dulles basis, the Communists will have a
half of the world's industrial output by 1970. This will probably not mean half of the world's income, but it will not be

* Comparisons of national wealth over space and time are fraught
with difficulties, especially those of allocating correct weight to food,
clothing and housing in non-money sectors of a largely subsistence
economy. The comparisons in physical terms that follow may give the
reader a fairer picture than money income estimates.

far off. The Communists are showing the other poor lands how to catch up.

Can the system of economic ownership and organisation that we call 'Capitalism', which industrialised Europe and the lands of European settlement, do the same for Asia, Africa and South America? Or do the communist techniques of the Soviet Union and China provide the only way forward in the world today? Or is there a third alternative distinct from each? This last is the crucial question of our time and it is to answering it that this book is devoted. Our task will be to discover how capitalism carried through the industrialisation of the lands where Europeans live and how it came about that it has failed to do the job elsewhere (with the single exception of Japan, which we shall have to take into account). But first we need to make the leap in the imagination from the wealth of our rich lands to the poverty of the poor lands. For unless we can understand what holds back their development, we shall not know how we may help them.

Statistics mean little unless translated into real terms. We know what life is like in an advanced industrialised land, for we live in one ourselves. Britain is not one of the richest lands; we only come seventh in the roll-call of lands according to the level of national income per head – after the North Americans, the Australians, the Swiss and the Swedes.[6] But we are more industrialised than any others; only four out of every hundred employed persons in Britain work on the land.[7] The vast majority of our people live in cities and towns of over 100,000 population.[8] We spend less than a third of our personal incomes on food, only a tenth on clothing and little more than another tenth on housing, fuel and light. That leaves half of our money to spend on things that are not basic necessities.[9] Moreover, in addition to our personal expenditure, half as much again is spent on our behalf by the State in public services and by industry in capital formation.[10] If we reckon our wealth in material possessions, we may note that, in 1960, two-thirds of our households here in Britain had television, one in three had a motor-car and a washing machine, and one in five had a refrigerator.[11]

It is not difficult to think of doubling our income to North American standards, but it is hard for us to imagine how the two-thirds of the world lives whose annual income per head is less than a tenth of our own. We must first distinguish between the great areas of land in Africa and South America, where populations are small, and desert and jungle make development technically difficult, and the heavily populated lands of South-East Asia, with their complex social structures and long cultural histories. As more than half the world's people live in Asia south and east of the Soviet Union, and only the 90 million of them in Japan have gone through the main stages of industrialisation, much of our attention must be given to them.

To begin with, three-quarters of the people live and work on the land. Less than a tenth live in cities or towns of over 100,000 population.[12] Houses are grouped together in villages with large areas of land between them. Land is farmed by peasant families, but is generally owned by a local landlord or mortgaged to a money-lender. The landlord's and money-lender's share in the crop may be as much as 60 per cent, while the peasant is little more than a sharecropper or serf tied by feudal relations to the lord.[13] The typical land-holding in South-East Asia is one of three to five acres, suited to working by a family with hand tools and producing about 30 per cent of the crop for sale.[14] In addition, some part of the land is reserved for the production of crops for export – a quarter in Indonesia and as much as two-thirds in Malaya and Ceylon.[15] The greater part of this area is owned by foreign companies, for whom the local population work as labourers on large estates and plantations.[16] Here some modern equipment may be found, but elsewhere the most primitive tools are used.

In South-East Asia, more than half of the peasant's income is spent on food, but his average daily consumption is only just over 2,000 calories, compared with our 3,500, and 5 to 10 grams of animal protein compared with our 40 to 50.[17] Though the climate is not always warm, his annual purchases of clothing weigh less than 5 pounds compared with our 30 pounds.[18] His house is a mere hovel of mud and reeds. His annual fuel consumption is 200 to 300 pounds, often including precious dung that is burned to cook with, when it should be used to fertilise the crops. Our demands for heating and lighting every year are the equivalent of 10,000 pounds of fuel per head of the population.[19] In South-East Asia, after the landlord or money-lender is paid, and food, clothing and shelter are found, little or nothing remains for the other needs, and when the crop fails from drought or flood, millions die of starvation. Children born in India can expect, on average, to live for thirty years; in Britain we may expect to live until we are seventy. Fifteen out of every hundred Indian babies die within the first year of their lives; only two die in Britain.[20]

How did it Happen? Was Imperialism the Cause?

It is a long and terrible catalogue; and it is the purpose of this book to discover how such a disparity has come about and what may now be done to rectify it. We shall have to consider the geological, climatic and other natural conditions, as well as the whole historical development from which this great division of the world into rich and poor has emerged. For we must know how the division came about if we are to understand how it may be ended. The simple answer of Socialists has been to say that this situation is the work of imperialism, that we are rich and they are poor because we have exploited them and, to some extent, still do exploit them. The cheap labour of colonial workers has brought us cheap food and raw materials. Such simple answers conceal a complicated web of political and economic relations, and a detailed balance sheet of gains and losses which we shall have to disentangle.

Let us first imagine an argument between a Socialist and a moderate defender of empire. The riposte to this simple, Socialist critique of imperialism will be that most of our food and raw materials never came from colonies, and that colonial food and raw materials are not particularly cheap; output of the same products in advanced industrial countries is often cheaper. The Socialist may persist in maintaining that, nevertheless, huge profits were made out of the operation. He will then probably be told that we are not rich because of this fact – colonial tribute has never provided more than a small proportion of our national income – but we are better off than others because of our high industrial productivity. And the Socialist will answer that it was colonial tribute anyway that helped us to industrialise, and that we have steadily enhanced our position since then by holding back industrial development in the colonies.

The defender of empire will claim that in fact we *have* industrialised our colonies one by one – the United States, Canada, Australia, New Zealand, South Africa, and now Rhodesia and India – and that, without us, the other colonial lands, including those in South-East Asia and Africa, would not have even what development they have today. At this the Socialist's hackles will rise, and he will say that we only industrialised the lands of European settlement and will ask sharply what we did for India in three hundred years. He will be told that we gave the Indians peace and better health, and as a result their population is now pressing against their resources – and that this is the cause of their poverty. But, the Socialist will retort, it is the Europeans' population that has been growing fastest in the last three hundred years and the peoples of Asia and Africa are no more than catching up again, which is all the more serious now since we have held back their economic development in the past.

Again, the defender of empire will reply that European populations were able to develop economic resources but that these Asian and African countries simply do not have the economic resources to be developed or could not mobilise them for the world market; we did what we could for them. At this point, the Socialist must deliver his *coup de grâce*. On the contrary, he will say, it was the East that once had the riches of which every European trader from the Greeks to the English went in search; but we destroyed the competition of Indian and Chinese cottons and silks, and other products of Eastern handicraft industries, when we opened up these countries to the factory-made goods of Manchester and Birmingham. And we have done all we could to hold back this competition ever since.

Where is the truth in this argument? This is what this book is about; but one point must be cleared up at once. In what has just been said we have spoken of empire and imperialism and of imperialist relations of exploitation. What precise meaning can we give to these phrases? First, in popular usage empire is generally thought of in terms of political sovereignty only, but the argument we have considered was as much concerned with economic as with political dependence. Indeed, it is the economic, rather than the political, relationship of dependence that is referred to when imperialism is blamed for the world division between the rich and the poor lands. Second, the terms 'imperialism' and 'imperialist' are surrounded with emotional associations, involving an assertion of racial superiority that we can reject at once as an explanation of the differences whose causes we are seeking, although we may have to recognise that the assertion is widely believed. Third, 'imperialism' was used by Lenin in a very special sense, which we must examine but which implies a particular view of the relationship of imperialism to capitalism,* that is of being capitalism's

* 'Capitalism' is used throughout this book to describe that economic and social system which is based on predominantly private ownership

'highest stage', which we may or may not wish to accept.[21]

We may grant that there is a clear meaning to be attached to these words as describing the whole complex of political and economic relations between the rich industrialised lands and the poor underdeveloped lands which are in various ways dependent upon them. Yet we may still hesitate to use the words because of the danger of confusion with the vulgar, and with Lenin's rather special, usage. A word here, therefore, may be in order on both these uses of 'imperialism'. First, vulgar usage tends to equate imperialism with the conquest and domination of one whole society or people over another. Yet the domination over the lives of other peoples in empires throughout history has always been exercised by a dominant group or class for its own ends – that is to extend the numbers who will work for them in various forms of servile labour. The fact that this group has shared with their own people some part of the advantages accruing to them – the free bread and circuses of imperial Rome, for example – need not lead us to consider imperialist relations in terms of the domination of one whole society over another.

When we look for the causes of the mastery of the world achieved by Britain and other European powers, we shall not, therefore, expect to find them in the emergence of a national 'will to rule' from some mystical folk source, embodied in the persons of heroic empire-builders.* We shall be concerned with examining rather the social and economic relations inside the societies themselves which were caught up in ties of domination and subjection. It will be different

of capital, where capital ownership (rather than land-owning, slave-owning or tribal custom) and the reward to capital are the main determinants of what goods are produced and how they are distributed. Within this general definition certain stages of capitalism will be distinguished – merchant, industrial and finance.

* It is an extraordinary feature of John Strachey's *The End of Empire*,[22] that he retains the concept of empire as 'the domination of one people by another people' and introduces the theory of a 'daemonic will to empire', 'which is now leaving us', in an otherwise largely economic Marxist explanation of empire, without any attempted reconciliation.

techniques of production that Marxists would expect to underlie these different social relations; but Marxists should not forget that the point of Marx's analysis was precisely that social relations, and the whole structure of ideas that grows out of them, gain a life of their own, which may carry them on long after the base in productive techniques is changed.

Lenin's 'Imperialism'

The expansion of empires in the last three hundred years has always been associated in socialist thinking with the development of capitalism; and this association will be examined in this book, particularly in relation to the British empire and British capitalism. But Lenin used the term 'imperialism' precisely to define the last stage in the development of capitalism. He called it the 'highest stage', indicating thereby that there would be no later stage, or only a moribund, dying capitalism thereafter. He did so because he regarded imperial expansion as essential to capitalism; its ending would be an indication of imminent decay in capitalism at home; indeed, the decay began at home partly as a result of expansion overseas. Stagnation was to be associated with imperialism, he believed.[23]

This process would not affect capitalism in every country at the same time, such was Lenin's law of unequal development. Capitalism in some new countries would be advancing while it decayed in the older and more mature countries. This unequal development Lenin considered to be the main cause of wars, bringing to a head the struggle for the redivision of the world between the unequally developed capitalist groups. For the basis of Lenin's analysis was that capitalism would have reached a stage 'in which the dominance of monopolies and [the dominance of] finance capital has established itself; in which the export of capital has acquired pronounced importance; in which the division of the world among the inter-national trusts has begun; in which the division of all territories of the globe among the great capitalist powers has been completed'.[24] These were Lenin's five points which provide his special definition of imperialism.

We may imagine how Lenin would have contributed to the argument between the Socialist and the Imperialist which we presented earlier. The cause of the expansion of empire, he would have said, was the outward pressure of capitalism towards monopoly and especially of finance capital towards overseas investment. Political rule was necessary to protect overseas investment not only from the colonial peoples but from other monopoly capitalist groups. The countries which had been brought under capitalist rule as colonies would have no chance of becoming industrialised so long as the imperialist relationship continued. The outward pressure of investment would, however, reach its limit in the poverty of the exploited peoples overseas; and thus, at the same time, it would be increasingly associated with stagnation at home. Each would react upon the other in a vicious circle of decay.

The result, Lenin would have concluded, was bound to be the collapse of capitalism and its replacement by social control in the hands of the workers at home and in the colonies. To this general picture Lenin, however, added another contradictory feature. In spite of stagnation, the 'imperial tribute' did provide the wherewithal for the capitalists to bribe the workers, or at least an upper section of them, and so, for a time, to hold back the grave-diggers from digging capitalism's grave. When colonial rule was challenged and the tribute dried up, then indeed the moment of truth for capitalism would come.[25]

Thus, we shall have to consider whether the present dissolution of imperial political ties does not presage the collapse of capitalism. In the early 1920s, Lenin could be forgiven for thinking that capitalism looked moribund; yet the gravediggers failed to bury it. Today the system looks much more viable, however inefficient and unjust it may seem to its many critics. We shall have to decide by the end of the book what has really been happening. Leninism could still be maintained on three different lines of argument. One could attempt to establish that it is only an illusion of strength that capitalism shows. The collapse is really at hand.* Another that the ending of political rule has been accompanied by little or no economic change, so that the form only of imperialism is altered.† A third that capitalism itself has changed since Lenin's day. Other ways of expanding have been found in the welfare state.‡

If Lenin's analysis was right, then one of these alternatives must be found to fit the facts. But it may be that Lenin was in part wrong, that monopoly and finance capital were not the chief cause of the outward pressure into empire, at least for Britain, that stagnation had other causes than those associated with imperial ties and overseas investment, that the imperial tribute never played so important a role in British life, and especially in corrupting the working class, as Lenin imagined.

If this rather sceptical view is preferred, then we shall not expect capitalism to be indissolubly tied to colonial exploitation for its survival. We shall still have to discover whether capitalism is capable of developing the one-time colonial lands, now that they have won their political freedom, so that they too will become new industrial rivals in the unequal

---

* This is the view of Mr Palme Dutt in his book *The Crisis of Britain and the British Empire*[26]:

'This is the essence of the truth about Britain's crisis, that it is the crisis of *the parasitic metropolis of a world empire* [his italics]; that the whole economic and social structure of Britain has been built on this assumption of empire; that this basis of empire is now beginning to crack, and therefore the whole traditional economic and social basis in Britain is plunged into increasing difficulties; that the desperate efforts to maintain the basis of empire domination and exploitation are only worsening Britain's home economic situation.'

† This has much in common with the view expressed by Mr Paul Baran in *The Political Economy of Growth*.[27]

‡ This is the view of Mr John Strachey in his book *The End of Empire*.[28]

development of capitalism. Lenin evidently thought that this was unlikely, because the world-wide power of the existing capitalist combines would prevent it.[29] We shall have to study this power and its effects very closely.

The Questions to be Answered – The Meaning of Imperialism

We may now summarise the questions with which this book will be concerned. In doing so, we shall use the words 'empire', 'imperialism' and 'imperialist' only for shorthand purposes, and we shall continue the same usage throughout the book, in chapter titles and headings. In the text we shall speak of relationships of political or of economic dependence, of dependencies, and of sovereign or metropolitan powers, so that the confusion of meanings can be avoided. When Lenin's special definition of 'imperialism' is being referred to, it will be made clear that this is so.

The questions we are asking may be grouped into five major inquiries, each having two aspects, one that faces inwards to Britain and the other advanced industrial lands, and another that faces outwards to the colonies and other underdeveloped lands:

1. How far has the gap between the rich and the poor lands in the world been due to the political and economic dependence of the poor upon the rich? What have been the gains and losses for the two parties from this dependent relationship at different periods?

   This is the central *question of* what are called '*imperialist relations*'.

2. What enabled Britain to industrialise first and to establish these relations of dependence throughout the world? Why did industrialisation not then spread to every land? Was there a natural division of labour between industrial and primary producers?

This may be called the *question of capitalism and industrialisation*.

3. Why, having carried through its own process of industrialisation, did British capitalism continue to push out to colonise half the world? What were the pressures at different stages and in the very different development of the lands of white settlement and of those colonies where Asians, Africans or American Indians were already established?

This may be called the *question of capitalism and 'imperialist expansion'*.

4. What changes in our society and in that of the colonies are reflected in the recent ending of political rule over colonies by Britain and other European powers? Does this ending of political dependence involve also the ending of economic dependence? What is the role now of the great imperial companies?

This may be called the *question of the end of 'imperialism'*.

5. What will be the effect of the dissolution of the dependent relationship, both on the development of our wealth and advancement and on the development of the ex-colonies? Can capitalism survive in the advanced lands without their colonies and can capitalism carry through the industrialisation of the underdeveloped lands? If not, what will? Is communism the only alternative? or can a genuine third way be found?

This may be called the *question of what happens after 'imperialism'*.

All these questions and their answers are naturally closely interwoven, because we are considering one complex of relations of political and economic dependence. We have to examine how and why these relations were established, were maintained and are now being dissolved. We have also to study the results of dependence at each stage. And all along we have to look at the relationship from both sides.

Thus in this book we shall examine, first, the original establishment of the relationship of dependence and the immediate effects, on both sides, of its establishment (Chapter 1); second, the maintenance and extension of the relationship in the period of expanding trade (Chapter 2) and of expanding investment overseas (Chapter 3); third, the effects of this dependent relationship between the wars on the imperial powers (Chapter 4) and on the dependencies (Chapter 5); fourth, the dissolution of the political relationship (Chapter 6) and the results for the ex-dependencies (Chapter 7), for the great imperial companies (Chapter 8) and for the economies of the old imperial powers as a whole (Chapter 9); finally we shall consider the future of the economic relationship that remains today (Chapter 10) and the implications for the ex-dependencies (Chapter 11), and for Britain and the other capitalist states (Chapter 12). In fact, throughout we shall give most attention to Britain and her dependencies, because this is our responsibility and because we had the greatest empire.

After Empire

All the old unequal relationships are being challenged, as colonial rule ends. The great problem of our time is to establish a new relationship between the peoples of the advanced and of the underdeveloped lands, whose economies have both been distorted by the previous system of relations. Can capitalism do this and, if not, what can? This is the main question we must answer. We are at the end of an epoch, which will surely be seen by future historians as the epoch of the opening-up of the world's empty lands by European settlers. We are entering the epoch of the renewed advance of the earlier-settled lands whose development has been held back; and this no doubt will be followed by the opening-up of the deserts and tropical jungles.

There can be no return to a world of accepted inequality.

The three-quarters of the world's peoples who have so far been largely excluded from the industrial revolution of mankind are demanding economic equality; and the one-third who have pulled out of the capitalist system are rapidly achieving it. It matters very much for the underdeveloped lands how quickly they can begin to achieve economic equality. While they are doing so, their position is inevitably weak. In the modern world no small state has much freedom to follow its political and economic interests; those that have most are those whose all-round economic development is most advanced or which are large enough or sufficiently united with others to stand up for themselves.

The economic advance of the underdeveloped lands matters very much also to us in Britain. Our people must live by processing raw materials into machines and instruments for other peoples as well as for ourselves to use. We can only gain from a world that is growing richer. The advantages derived from maintaining inequality are disappearing. It is a smaller and smaller number of people – it was never large – who benefit from the remaining unequal relationships. The British people certainly have nothing to lose from the complete replacement of these relationships by ties of co-operation on equal terms.

For many years now, infinitely greater benefits have accrued to ordinary people from the application of man's growing knowledge of how his natural environment may be controlled than ever came from plunder and exploitation. But this control involves men in ever-widening interdependence. The advance of one is conditional upon the advance of all. What men can do by co-operating together exceeds by far anything that was won in the past by war and conquest. The possibilities of man's fullest personal development, free from cold and hunger and ill-health, insecurity and heavy toil, unite us together as never before, in one world. Should we forget, there is the bomb hanging over all our heads to remind us.

The whole complex that we call 'imperialism' has always involved an attitude of mind as well as a political and economic relationship. The effects of three hundred years of imperial rule will not disappear overnight, either for the rulers or the ruled, because the economic *raison d'être* of imperial rule has gone. It cannot be too often repeated that attitudes of mind, individual and public responses, the institutions of political and social action, survive long after the economic and technological developments to which they owe their origin.

It is 450 years since the writer who used Amerigo di Vespucci's name to give a title to a new-found continent, and to provide Europe's bankers with their information about its peoples, first put forward the grotesque and vicious myth of white superiority.[30] The picture that he drew then, of the supposedly lazy, feckless, over-sexed, idolatrous, cannibalistic 'Indian', has been used ever since to justify European rule – the paternalistic white man's burden as well as massacre, exploitation and slavery. It will require a positive act of will for Europeans to bring themselves to think of African, Asian and American-Indian people as not only deserving of our aid, to repair past sins, but as comrades with whom to build the one world of the human race. It is to this act of human emancipation that this book is dedicated.

Table 1A

RICH AND POOR, 1938 and 1958

Group	Countries (For details of groupings see over)	National Income 1938 $b.(%) Current	National Income 1958 $b.(%) Current	Population 1938 Millions (%)	Population 1958 Millions (%)	Average Per Capita Income 1938 $	Average Per Capita Income 1958 $	Real Growth of Per Capita Income 1938-1958 1938=100 at 1953 U.S. Export Prices
1.	U.S. and Canada	71 (31)	390 (37)	141 (7)	192 (7)	500	2040	178
2.	Other Advanced Industrialised Countries	76 (33)	210 (20)	230 (12)	270 (10)	330	780	105
3.	Middle Group (Communist)	35 (15)	240 (23)	280 (15)	325 (12)	125	740	250
4.	Middle Group (Non-Communist)	19 (8)	100 (10)	236 (12)	365 (14)	80	275	150
5.	China	8 (3)	50 (5)	460 (24)	680 (25)	17	75	190
6.	Other Poor Lands	20 (9)	60 (6)	580 (30)	820 (31)	35	70	90
	TOTALS*	230 (100)	1050 (100)	1930 (100)	2650 (100)	137	405	130

* Note: This Table excludes countries with an aggregate population of about 100 million in 1938 and 200 million in 1958, for which National Income details are not available.

Sources: For 1938: W. S. and E. S. Woytinsky, *World Population* (New York: 20th Century Fund, 1953), pp. 36–40.

For 1958: Capitalist Countries – United Nations, *Yearbook of National Account Statistics – 1958* (New York, 1959).

Communist Countries – United Nations, *World Economic Survey – 1958* (New York, 1959), and United Nations, *Economic Survey of Europe – 1959* (Geneva, 1959), and Chinese State Statistical Bureau, *The Ten Great Years* (Pekin, 1960).

TABLE IB

RICH AND POOR COUNTRIES BY GROUPS IN
PER *CAPITA* INCOME ORDER, 1958 IN $ U.S.

Advanced Industrialised		Middle (Communist)		Middle (Non-Communist)		Poor Lands (Excl. China)	
Sweden	1310	U.S.S.R.	850	(Venezuela	840)*	Ecuador	150
Switzerland	1300	Poland	810	South Africa	350	Algeria	150
New Zealand	1130	East Germany	800	Argentina	340	Rhodesias	135
Australia	1120	Czechoslovakia	740	Spain	340	Iraq	133
U.K.	970	Hungary	700	Jamaica	315	Korea	130
Norway	915	Yugoslavia	550	Cuba	300	Morocco	125
Denmark	910	Bulgaria	520	Chile	300	Egypt	125
Belgium	870	Rumania	360	Greece	290	Ceylon	115
France	815			Malaya	275	Peru	100
Israel	800			Turkey	265	Thailand	100
West Germany	735			Japan	250	Paraguay	95
Netherlands	715			Mexico	250	Kenya	90
Austria	570			Colombia	215	Formosa	85
Eire	480			Brazil	205	Nigeria	70
Italy	435			Ghana	200	Belgian Congo	65
				Portugal	200	India	60
				Philippines	190	Uganda	55
						Indonesia	55
						Tanganyika	50
						Pakistan	50
						Burma	45

* Note: Venezuela's income is grossly inflated by the value of oil exports; most of the income leaves the country.

N.B. In both Tables the income figures given for the Communist Group are not strictly comparable with the others, for the Communist Group figures are based on reported percentage increases in real income on a dollar valuation for 1938. In both Tables these have then been inflated for the dollar price increase between 1938 and 1958. The figures for all the other countries are the result of converting estimates of income in national currencies into dollars at the current rate of exchange. The last column of Table A is found in the case of these countries by deflating for the dollar price increase between 1938 and 1958, the figure of 230% being used for this purpose.

References

1. United Nations, *Future Growth of World Population*, New York, 1958.
2. Food and Agricultural Organisation, *Yearbook of Food and Agricultural Studies, 1956*, Part I, Rome, 1957.
3. W. S. and E. S. Woytinsky, *World Population and Production*, New York, 1953, p. 41.
4. ibid., p. 36.
5. *New York Times*, 2.8. 59.
6. United Nations, *Yearbook of National Account Statistics – 1960*, New York, 1960.
7. United Kingdom Central Statistical Office, *Annual Abstract of Statistics*, H.M.S.O., 1961.
8. *Whitaker's Almanack, 1960*, 'Municipal Directory'.
9. United Kingdom Ministry of Labour, *Family Expenditure Survey, 1957–59*, H.M.S.O., 1961.
10. Central Statistical Office, *National Income and Expenditure, 1961* (Bluebook), H.M.S.O., 1961.
11. L. Needleman, 'The Demand for Domestic Appliances' and L. A. Dicks-Mireaux, 'Prospects for the British Car Industry', *Economic Review* of the National Institute for Economic and Social Research, respectively for November 1960 and September 1961.
12. Woytinsky and Woytinsky, op. cit., p. 117.
13. J. de Castro, *Geography of Hunger*, Gollancz, 1952, pp. 155–6.
14. United Nations, Economic Commission for Asia and the Far East, *Economic Survey of Asia and the Far East, 1950*, Bangkok, 1950, pp. 3–4.
15. ibid., pp. 173–7.
16. K. M. Stahl, *Metropolitan Organisation of the British Colonial Trade*, Faber and Faber, 1951, pp. 84 and 103.
17. Food and Agricultural Organisation, *State of Food and Agriculture – 1960*, Rome, 1960, Annex Table 14.b.
18. United Nations, *Statistical Yearbook – 1960*, New York, 1960, Tables 128 and 129.
19. ibid., Table 120.
20. United Nations, *Demographic Yearbook – 1960*, New York, 1960.
21. V. I. Lenin, *Imperialism*, Petrograd, 1917; Little Lenin Library Edition, Lawrence and Wishart, 1944, p. 77.
22. J. Strachey, *The End of Empire*, Gollancz, 1959, especially pp. 7 and 217.
23. ibid., especially Preface to the French and German editions, 1920, published in E. Varga and L. Mendelsohn, *New Data for Lenin's Imperialism*, New York, 1940.

24. V. I. Lenin, *Imperialism*, Little Lenin Library 1944 ed., p. 77.
25. ibid., p. 112.
26. R. P. Dutt, *The Crisis of Britain and the British Empire*, Lawrence and Wishart, 1953, p. 381.
27. P. Baran, *The Political Economy of Growth*, New York, 1957.
28. J. Strachey, *The End of Empire*, Chapter VI.
29. V. I. Lenin, op. cit., p. 53.
30. C. R. Markham, *Letters of Amerigo Vespucci*, Hakluyt Society, 1894.

PART ONE

Imperialism As It Was

CHAPTER 1

The Rise of Empire –
Why Didn't They Colonise Us?

This chapter is concerned with the establishment of the domination of the European powers over the peoples of Asia, Africa and America. We have to discover not only what pushed groups of Europeans into establishing their ruling position, but also how they were able to maintain their rule over numerically vastly superior peoples. Why did we colonise them and not they us? There had been slave and serf empires in the past, but the European empires created after the sixteenth century did not have their basis primarily either in slaves or serfs. It will be suggested in this chapter that these empires were established in the process of capital accumulation and of industrialisation, and that it was their advanced social organisation which enabled Britain and other European powers to industrialise, and thus gave them the edge on the rest of the peoples of the world. There was no natural division of labour between the advanced industrial manufacturers and backward primary producers; the division was an artificial creation of European industrial expansion.

Slave and Peasant Empires

There were empires long before the Portuguese and Spaniards, English and Dutch and French established their dominion over the rest of the world from the sixteenth century onward. There were slave empires from Sumeria to Rome, merchant empires from Greece to Venice, and peasant empires from China to the Ottomans. Yet few survived the rise of the new empires built by Britain and Holland and France. One is bound to ask why. Slave empires, designed to keep up the supply of slaves for a dominant exploiting class, collapsed from internal decay before they yielded to external attack. When labour, the actual exercise of man's control over his environment, became a slave's affair, the rot set in.[1] For slaves there existed no incentive to improve productive techniques; for their masters there remained neither the need nor the practical knowledge to do so. Peasant empires, based upon the wider extraction of surplus through rent and taxation or through feudal dues, suffered from a similar weakness, but it was not so debilitating. The peasant empires lasted longer, the Chinese for more than 2,000 years.

The peasant empires outside Europe established and spread some of man's most triumphant successes in the long process of controlling his environment. Yet their civilisation was easily disrupted and destroyed by European adventurers in the sixteenth and seventeenth centuries, and many of their people were subjected to European rule thereafter. How did it happen?

Civilisations were built and flourished in Asia for thousands of years, while Europe lingered in the stone age. South American Indian civilisation preceded the settlement of North America. Africans had an Iron Age that, by the fourteenth century, reached a level almost comparable with that of their contemporaries in Britain.[2] Europe by the sixteenth century had scarcely pioneered a single human invention of real importance. The three discoveries which Francis Bacon singled out in 1620 as those 'which have changed the whole face and state of things throughout the world'[3] were printing, gunpowder and the magnet – all of them invented by the Chinese at least a thousand years earlier and brought to Europe by the Arabs.[4] Our letters had their origin in western Asia and our numerals in India, and were, also, brought to Europe by the Arabs.[5]

Perhaps the very fact of these civilisations' early successes led to their institutions' becoming fossilised over the years and incapable of responding to a new challenge? Perhaps the very wealth of their resources reduced the stimulus to overseas trade? Perhaps the very poverty of Europe's resources drove her merchants to bring back the wealth of the East?[6] Whatever the case, we shall have to examine why Europe was the first to break through the ossification of feudalism, or its equivalent in ancient society, and thus lead the world into capitalism and industrialisation. For this was the key to Europe's development – the emergence of a merchant and then of a manufacturing class as the dominant element in society. Why did no Chinese or Indian merchant-adventurers emerge from China or India to conquer Europe, as the Golden Horde had once threatened to do? How did a merchant class emerge as the dominant element in European society and not in Asia?

Merchants and the towns they developed grew within the peasant society of China and India as they did in Europe. Akbar, the great sixteenth-century Mogul emperor of India, was interested in commerce and encouraged trade, as Queen Elizabeth of England was doing at the same time, and what he did was on a much grander scale than anything Elizabeth attempted;[7] but the merchants never became a dominant class in India. In China the merchants even rose for a brief period (221–217 B.C.) to supreme power in establishing the Ch'in Empire, but they were soon incorporated into the governing class and became landowners.[8] Why then did a mercantile class separate from the landowning rulers never emerge?

The first answer is that, in both China and India, manufacture and trade in most scarce goods were a state monopoly.

So they were in England, but the monopoly was granted to a merchant or company for a payment. We only have to say it to realise the difference: what could any mere merchant pay to Akbar? Can we for a moment imagine Akbar, like James I of England, selling monopolies to keep up the payments for his court expenses? The very idea is ridiculous. The wealth of Akbar, as the English merchant-adventurer of the Levant Company, Ralph Fitch, bore witness, far surpassed anything that might then have been found in Europe.[9] Marco Polo, the thirteenth-century Venetian merchant, had reported similarly on the wealth of the great emperor of China, Kublai Khan.[10] There were two reasons for this wealth: not only were the natural resources of India and China far richer than those of Europe, and the population cultivating them far more numerous, but a much greater proportion of the wealth was channelled directly to the central power.

East and West – the Basic Difference in Agricultural Production

What was the reason, then, for the concentration of wealth upon a central power which held back the emergence of an independent merchant class in India or China? Its basis must lie in the fundamentally different system of land-ownership in European feudalism and in Asiatic society. 'The absence of property in land is indeed the key to the whole of the East,' Engels wrote in a letter to Marx.[11] It is true at least of India though not of China. Although, in theory, medieval European kings might claim title to all the lands of their kingdom, in practice they had to dispute their claim with their barons, who disputed title with the knights, who further carried the dispute down to the free peasants. Ancient society in the East saw battles enough for the produce of the land but not primarily for its ownership. In India, the ownership and the working of the land remained with the communities.

The surplus was collected by tax-gatherers, a bureaucracy whose power stemmed from the emperor and who took no part in the working or administration of production.

The Indian nobility existed by direct favour of the king and not by virtue of past settlement of their families on certain lands. As François Bernier, the sixteenth-century traveller, put it: 'The nobles of Hindustan cannot be proprietors of land or enjoy an independent revenue, like the nobility of France and the other states of Christendom. Their incomes consist exclusively of pensions which the King grants or takes away according to his own will or pleasure.'[12]

In China the position was somewhat different after the fourth century B.C. There were landowners, both large and small, but they were themselves the bureaucrats. At the beginning of a dynasty they owned little land; the free peasants paid their taxes in kind through the bureaucracy to the state. As a dynasty progressed, a peasant's debts accumulated until he became a tenant. The bureaucracy took over the land. Rent grew and the government's revenue declined. Neither public works nor the army could be maintained. In a period of chaos the peasants revolted, a new dynasty from the nomadic north established itself; and after famine and decimation of the population, the irrigation works were re-established.[13]

Here, surely, lies part of the essential difference between Europe and the East. The basis of food-production in the East was irrigated agriculture, which in India involved communal working, in China a free peasantry, in both cases within a framework of large-scale water-control. Irrigated agriculture demanded a centralised state and put immense power into its hands.[14] But this was only a partial explanation, which has its critics.[15] In both India and China, moreover, a strong central power was essential to preserve peace from invasion.[16]

By contrast, in Europe the year-round rain falling gently and in adequate supplies in all areas put a premium upon individual initiative, not communal activity, encouraged decentralisation, and greatly weakened the power of the central state. The English Channel, moreover, gave Britain a special immunity from invasion once the Normans established a minimal, central control over defence. A merchant class emerging in the medieval towns throughout Europe could attain an independent position that their Indian and Chinese counterparts could not.

It was on the basis of the overwhelming power they drew from the land that the state in China and India could establish a monopoly over trade as well. The Chinese state was peculiarly strengthened further by its monopoly of iron as well as of bronze from the time of the Ch'ins,[17] which may have been partly due to the fact that iron-ore occurs much more rarely in easily accessible sources in China than in other lands. It should not be concluded that there was no merchant class and no mercantile capital in China or India. There were both; the merchant class never became independent of the central state, however, but was always absorbed into the bureaucracy which was based on land-revenue.

One of the results of the concentration of power in a centralised state, based on rich land-revenue, was a lack of interest in navigation and foreign commerce. The point is emphasised by the fact that it was precisely during the period of eunuch-rule in China during the first half of the Ming dynasty, when the landed bureaucracy was temporarily superseded, that Chinese overseas navigation reached its highest peak. The reassertion of the authority of the bureaucracy at the end of the fifteenth century led to the closing-down of the shipyards and, by the Edict of 1525, to the destruction of all sea-going junks and the arrest of all mariners who continued to sail them, for the ocean trade had been the chief source of the eunuchs' wealth and power. The Edict of 1525 was a catastrophic decision.[18]

Since the end of the thirteenth century the Chinese had been carrying on trade right across the Indian Ocean to East

Africa and Arabia. They were launching vessels of 700 tons two hundred years before the Armada sailed, whose unwieldy barges did not exceed 500 tons, while the average English man-of-war averaged less than 200 tons. It is one of the most incredible ironies of history, to which Basil Davidson has recently drawn our attention, that the Chinese withdrew from the Indian Ocean just as the Europeans entered it.[19] When at length a Chinese and Indian merchant class did establish some independence of their central state, it was as agents of the Europeans' trade. This fact has had profound effects to this very day.

Merchant Adventurers and a Manufacturing Interest

The overseas empires founded by the European powers in the sixteenth century were not primarily the result either of the extension of slave-rule or of feudal domains. It is true that slavery of Indians and of Africans was an essential part of the colonisation of the American continent. It is true also that the empires of Spain and Portugal and France stemmed from an essentially feudal society at home. Nevertheless, it was a rising merchant class that was the driving force, especially in Britain and Holland, though not in Spain, behind the extension of European rule overseas. The merchant city-states of Italy and of Germany, and especially of Venice, had shown the way. At the very centre of the story of the founding of the first English colonies was the struggle of the rising merchant and manufacturing class for independence from a feudal monarchy and social system. The two processes were intimately associated. But what was involved was more than the rise of a merchant class.

The growing strength of the merchant class in Europe, and the great wealth which the European merchants plundered from the rest of the world, would not of itself have challenged European feudalism. Merchants in Europe, as in China, tended to be absorbed into the landowning class, mercantile capital to be invested in land. The merchant adventurers of Europe also held royal monopolies. The revolutionary significance of the so-called 'voyages of discovery' in the sixteenth century did not lie only in the wealth that they brought back to build the first foundations for the growth of industry at home. Even more important was the emergence of an independent merchant class, the so-called 'outsiders', who were encouraged in the sea-girt lands, and especially in England, to chance their hand against the monopolists.

It was from the ranks of the 'outsiders', and from the tiny but growing manufacturing interest, that the challenge to feudalism in England came.[20] Their emergence had been made possible by the solvent effect upon feudalism of the money-economy in the towns. The import of gold and silver from the Indies greatly increased the working of this effect. Money was also used in China and India, but it remained secondary to payments in kind, with a share of the harvest from the land. In England, land was being replaced by money as the prevailing form of property from the beginning of the fifteenth century, but it was a long process; feudalism was not finally defeated until the middle of the seventeenth century.

That the plunder was not enough to ensure capital accumulation may be seen from the experience of the Spanish and Portuguese empires and, to some extent, of the Dutch too. Drake brought back booty including more than a ton of gold and silver from the voyage of the *Golden Hind*, but the Spanish-government fleet alone brought back from the Americas between 1521 and 1660 as much as 200 tons of gold and 18,000 tons of silver.[21] The Spanish empire, however, was not even a merchant empire; it was feudal. The wealth, which the *conquistadores* spilt their own blood and that of the Indians and of African slaves to win, ended up mainly in the merchant coffers of Protestant Europe. Every attempt was made by the Spanish court to preserve its monopoly of the colonial trade: no foreign ships were permitted to visit Spain's colonial ports, and trade with foreign countries was forbidden; but Spain did not benefit. The fact was that she did not have the manufactures which her growing colonies required for their survival, nor did she have the slaves. As a result, smuggling on a grand scale was combined with piracy by the Protestant sea-rovers, and particularly by the English, who found the slaves and had the manufactures.[22]

The moral of Spain's failure to utilise the tribute from the New World was not lost upon the young English merchant 'outsiders' with a manufacturing interest; but they first had to break the power of the great merchants with a royal monopoly. The great merchant-adventurers had opened up the prospect of rich foreign trade, but the nature of their operation limited its scale. They plundered or bought cheap to sell dear in the English and European markets – silks, spices, precious stones. Such trade was of no value to the 'outsiders' and was a positive menace to the manufacturing interest, whose cloth had to compete with foreign textiles. The basis of the whole operation was monopoly profit.[23]

Each chartered company deriving from the old Merchant Adventurers' Company had its own province – Russia, the Eastlands (Scandinavia), the Levant, Hudson Bay, Africa, the East Indies. Their main enemies were the Dutch and Portuguese monopolies. The East India Company had been founded at a meeting of London merchants 'in my Lord Mayor's parlour, to consider the unchristian price of pepper';[24] but it was less the price than the fact that it was controlled by the Dutch United East India Company that was worrying them. The forts that the companies built along the coast line of Africa and India and North America were designed less to overawe the native inhabitants, though this was useful, than to protect company interests against foreigners and interlopers.

The essence of trade was monopoly. 'The governors of

these companies by their monopolising orders have so handled the matter as that the mass of the whole trade of the realm is in the hands of some 200 persons at most, the rest serving for a show and reaping small benefit'[25] – so spoke Sir Edwin Sandys; and we may best take the story of Sandys's struggle for control over the Virginia Company to illustrate the battle of the manufacturing interest and of the merchant 'outsiders', who were both largely independent of the landed interest, against the monopolists, who had made their peace with feudalism.

First, how had an influential manufacturing interest emerged already from the womb of feudalism? There were cloth manufacturers in India and China – handicraftsmen, but with an international market which the Arabs and then the Europeans developed. But a cloth-making 'interest' represented in Parliament by a man like Sandys, indeed a Parliament at all with a House of Commons, was inconceivable in the centralised empires of the East. In part, the answer is to be found in the fact that the same conditions of crop-production and land-ownership, which encouraged decentralisation in Europe and permitted the rise of a powerful merchant class, also permitted the rise of a manufacturing interest.

The large number of streams and small rivers in Europe, as well as the absence of any centralised water-control, prompted free peasants and landlords alike to build water-mills, first for grain and then for fulling and sawing; and from these they developed crushing hammers, forge-hammers, bellows, pumps and other machines, which though invented a thousand years earlier had never been worth any-one's while to apply.[26] Here we reveal an absolutely crucial difference between Europe and the East – the fact that a landlord or knight might actually engage in the processes of production in Europe, as the bureaucrat, tax-collector or scholar gentry could never do in India or China. Once again we must associate this situation with the centripetal forces of irrigated agriculture, hardened by tradition and institution through thousands of years.

The First English Manufacturers and the Old Colonial System

We should not, however, entirely deny the contribution of the overseas adventurers to the growth of a manufacturing interest in Britain. Merchant-adventuring itself encouraged boat-building, rope-yards, sail-cloth making and other similar crafts in the ports and along the rivers of England. Moreover, the stimulus of wars to the production of cannon and other military-equipment and scientific-instrument making was of the greatest importance in encouraging the development of manufacturing experience in many local communities. In England, particularly, the advantages accruing from preparations for war were not offset by the disadvantages of being fought over. It is an important difference, but the reasons for Britain's advance towards manufacture ahead of the rest of Europe are not so easily explained.

By the middle of the fifteenth century, England had definitely passed from being a wool-producer to being a manufacturer and exporter of cloth.[27] The same forces which we see to have been operating throughout Europe worked perhaps a little more strongly in England than elsewhere. Neither the king nor the barons were ever quite so powerful or rich in England as in France, for instance; the towns never grew to such a size or strength.[28] The cloth manufacture which began in the villages of East Anglia and Hampshire and the South-west was the more easily developed in a capitalist manner, by the early clothiers.[29] To these considerations we must add the very important factor of Britain's long sea-coast, which permitted the development of a national market through cheap coastwise transport, in addition to placing British sailors and traders in the very forefront of the great 'discoveries' across the Atlantic. With the opening of the Atlantic routes and the decline of the continental trade-routes, the German and Italian trading cities, until then certainly the most advanced in Europe in commerce and manufacture, declined. The results in the delayed growth of German and Italian industry are with us still today, and will be met later in this book.

The crucial changes in British life that nurtured Britain's industrial revolution were social and political changes. We have seen the background to the political demands which began to be made at the beginning of the seventeenth century by Sir Edwin Sandys and his associates among the smaller merchants and the manufacturers. Knowing this background, we shall not be surprised that they seized on the possibility of developing North America with their capital and enterprise, and in challenge to the Catholic Spaniards who claimed the whole New World as their own. Sandys, who had spent some years in Venice, had become convinced, on the one hand, of man's ability to master his environment, through the discoveries of the scientists like Galileo whom he had met, and, on the other, of the absolutely reactionary force of the Catholic Church in holding back man's progress.[30]

To succeed, however, Sandys and his friends had first to win control over the new colonies from the king and the old aristocratic clique of merchant monopolists. The colonisation of Virginia had been a slow and precarious business. Raleigh's first settlements, established in 1585 and 1587 at Roanoke, were wiped out by the Indians. The settlement established under a Royal Council in 1607 at Jamestown barely survived its first few years, after the settlers discovered that there was no gold in the neighbourhood, but only marshes and Indians, whose hostility had been assured by raids on their corn.[31]

Sandys determined to act. Representing the progressive seafaring and cloth-making county of Hampshire in the House of Commons, he threw himself into the attack on the royal monopolies, introduced a bill for freeing trade and, in 1606, helped in drawing up the Bill of Grievances against the crown. It was in that year that James I set up a Royal Council for Virginia, consisting of the inner merchant clique of the City of London, whom Sandys had been attacking. The leading member was Sir Thomas Smythe who, like a modern merchant-banker, sat on the boards of half a dozen companies, including the East India, and became Treasurer of the Virginia Company in 1609.[32]

In 1609 and in 1612, Sandys won successively more 'democratic' constitutions for the Virginia Company – that is, control over the company was obtained for the small stockholders, any holder of a twelve-guinea share having equal voting rights with the holder of a large number of shares. By 1619, Sandys had unseated Smythe and taken his place as treasurer. Despite the splendid reports of Captain Smith on the progress of the colony in tobacco-cultivation, and the visit to England of John Rolfe and his Indian wife, Pocahontas, there was no escaping the fact that, after ten years of settlement, the stockholders were not getting any return on their money. The company was riddled with the same kind of inefficiency, extravagance, peculation and corruption that was destroying the Spanish empire.[33] Sandys, as treasurer, cleaned all this up, and sent out forward-looking gentlemen farmers as settlers in place of the adventurers and criminals who had founded the colony. With the farmers he sent London paupers, often boys and girls, as indentured labourers; to these were added, in 1619, the first boat-load of negroes.[34]

Thus the result of Sandys's efforts was to establish the slave-owning plantation-culture of the south, but at the same time to ensure supplies of Virginian tobacco and cotton for the British manufacturers. These were to become far more important than all the spices and silks of the East. The American colonies later became, in fact, the main markets outside Britain for the products of England's new manu-

factories, although this was the result not only of the founding of the southern colonies, but also of the establishment of
the northern colonies on a capitalist basis from the very
beginning.*[35]

Plunder and Industrialisation

Sandys and his friends had founded a new colonial system,
in which trade could develop, out of the old system of
monopoly plunder. But lest we should think of Sandys as a
nineteenth-century free-trader, it is well to remember that his
last acts were to obtain a heavy duty on imports of Spanish
tobacco, which competed with Virginian, and to begin the
attempts by annual proclamations, supported by militia
action, to prohibit the growing of tobacco in England. It
was another 150 years before the benefits of free trade could
be recognised in a by then industrialised Britain.

The victory of Parliament over the king in the Civil War
completed what Sandys and his friends had begun; and,
although the monarchy was restored, the power of the royal
monopolies was broken and feudal society finally ended. By
1688, the new and now dominant merchant class had their
own merchant prince on the throne. It was still a privileged
class, but its privileges no longer stemmed from the monarch.
The implications for the future were immense. In the long
run, independence of the monarch meant dependence on the
electorate. And, as Schumpeter has pointed out, it was inevitable from 1688 that English foreign policy should have an
economic rather than a political motivation.[37]

What were the immediate results of the Parliamentary
victory? It was a great victory but the effort had been great

* They became capitalist because their leaders were capitalists and
despite the ironic fact that it was King James and the merchant clique
around him who evidently diverted the *Mayflower* from Virginia to Cape
Cod in the hope of pulling the new settlers out of the sphere of Sandys's
Virginia Company and putting them under the Royal Council of New
England.[36]

too. The general crisis of the seventeenth century, as Dr Hobsbawm has called it, involved not only the wars and revolutions through which European society passed in emerging from the restraints of feudalism, but the decline and exhaustion that accompanied the social and political changes.[38] In fact, only England and the Low Countries did break through. This fact itself, while leading to a concentration of capital in the maritime lands, meant also some impoverishment of the rest of Europe. The European market certainly declined and with it the profit to be made from overseas trade. The English Africa Company and the Dutch West India Company were wound up in the 1670s and even the great East India Company failed to pay a dividend sixteen times between 1627 and 1687.[39]

By the end of the seventeenth century, all the conditions necessary for the industrial revolution in Britain might have seemed to have been established. The enclosures had already done much to concentrate capital in land.[40] Industrial techniques had been developing rapidly in coal-mining, the iron industry and in textiles. The Darbys of Coalbrookdale were smelting iron with coal soon after 1700. Capital had been accumulating for a century or more from the profits of overseas operations; a new form of colonial system was being established in North America which was beginning to provide the sources of raw material and the markets for expanded manufacture in Britain.[41] Why then was the final revolutionary leap so long delayed?

In part, the answer must be that the processes we have just noted took a long time to mature, particularly the social changes in the countryside, involving the expropriation of the peasants.

The agricultural revolution, which we may think of in terms of Jethro Tull's and Lord Townshend's introduction of turnips for winter fodder in the rotation of crops and of Robert Bakewell's improvements in stock-breeding, could not be carried out until the size of the holdings had been increased and the old open-field system replaced. Increased food-production was a necessary condition for an increase of industrial workers in the towns.[42]

In part, however, the delay in the maturing of the industrial revolution may be attributed to the fact that trade revived, the old plundering trade of the merchants, who bought cheap to sell dear. Far from at this stage aiding Britain's industrial revolution, the East India Company's revival may actually have held it back.

In 1700 the East India Company had been reconstituted on a wider basis and thereafter its fortunes recovered. The famous three-cornered trade was begun – manufactures from England to Africa, slaves from Africa to the Americas, silver from Mexico to India and China, silks and spices from the East for Europe.[43] How then did the very recovery of trade after the Anglo-French wars at the beginning of the eighteenth century contribute to holding back the growth of British industry? The fact is that trade, and particularly the slave-trade, was too profitable for capital to be attracted into manufacturing. The profit on each slave was between £20 and £30 and it is estimated that some three millions were transported in British ships in the eighteenth century.[44] As a result, capital which might otherwise have been attracted to industry went back into financing more trade. The Dutch, who at the beginning of the eighteenth century were the greatest traders in the world, never developed their own manufactures, so profitable were their trading enterprises; and they never, therefore, changed from the old colonial system until their rivals had leapt far ahead of them.[45]

Even a particularly well-informed Englishman like Daniel Defoe, standing at the threshold of the eighteenth century and considering the decay of the Spanish empire, the loosening of the control of Portugal over her colonies, the struggling settlements on the Atlantic coast of North America, the string of tiny forts around the African coast and in India, could not have anticipated the world dominion that England was to establish within a hundred years. Nevertheless, there is in Defoe's hero, Robinson Crusoe, a picture of the technical ability, the attention to financial detail, the inventive resourcefulness, the self-confidence, the assurance of command over native peoples that gives us a surer clue to what was to be than all the wealth of the Whig merchants.

Yet, while the young manufacturing interest was developing a new kind of trade with North America, albeit held back by old mercantilist ideas of monopoly restraint, the old system received a new and fabulous lease of life in the conquest of India. After Clive's defeat of the Nawab of Bengal at Plassey in 1757, gold and jewels and other forms of tribute began to flow back to Britain on a scale that makes the plunder of the early adventurers look paltry indeed. Under the treaties that followed Plassey, treasure valued at £4 million sterling (perhaps £40 million of our currency) was received by the Company and its servants. Clive took nearly a quarter of a million and an estate which brought him in £27,000 a year. For fifty years after Plassey, the tribute drained from Bengal may have amounted to £15 million a year and certainly exceeded £5 million, most of it going not to the company but to establish the private fortunes of its servants.[46]

The Conquest of India

To understand how the quite small number of English soldiers defeated the very much more numerous Indian forces, we have to remember the whole of the different development of Britain and India since the two peoples first met in the sixteenth century. We have sketched in some of the changes in Britain, but we should be wrong to see Clive as an agent of the rising British *bourgeoisie*. It was in the West Indies and North America that the young manufacturers were developing in peaceful trade their new interests, and especially their interest in the growing of cotton, which was to be the catalyst of the industrial revolution. The East India

Company, like so many imperial agencies that were to follow, was the happy hunting-ground for the rascals, the misfits, the spivs and speculators, who found the home country either too dull or too 'hot' for them. And the British armed forces were the preserve of the old aristocratic families.[47]

It was a combination of these two – Company and Army – that conquered India. A similar combination reappeared in Africa at the end of the nineteenth century. But on both occasions there stood behind them at home the growing industrial power, technical knowledge and self-confidence of a people that were changing their lives at a rapid rate. The bourgeoisie of England regarded the army with fear and hatred; but the army drew from the manufacturers not only its arms but its confidence in British superiority. Behind the armed forces which Clive had at his command lay the long record of successes of British arms against France, first in Europe and then in Canada.

The object of the British military operation in Bengal in the first instance had been to secure the forts of the East India Company against the growing influence of the French. But the point for us to notice is the discipline and experience and self-confidence that the troops had learnt in almost continuous and overwhelmingly successful fighting.* What had happened meanwhile in India? The great Mogul Empire had begun to disintegrate. An alien court drawing heavier and heavier tribute from the land had been opposed by peasant revolt, internal separatism and external attack.

Indian metallurgy anticipated European developments by several centuries, not only in copper and brass but in high-grade steels.[49] Indian textiles had been selling in Europe at an immense profit to the traders ever since the eastern trade

---

* Mr Strachey, in his recent book on *The End of Empire*, regards the military discipline of Clive's soldiers as absolutely crucial in the defeat of the Indian army at Plassey and at Buxar. Both sides were equally well-armed; it was only at a later stage of empire that we could say that 'We had got the Gatlin' gun, and they had not'.[48]

had begun. When the English manufacturers wished to protect their textiles from Indian competition, nothing less than 75 per cent duties were needed to do the job.[50] There was, however, no strong and independent merchant or manufacturing class capable of replacing the decaying imperial rule in India, for reasons which we have already noted. Part of India's tragedy was that the merchants in Bengal and elsewhere had already become oriented towards the trade with Europe.

The contrast with the British merchant capitalists was complete. The officers of the East India Company in Madras, who decided to fight back after they had been evicted from their fort in Calcutta, had not only the self-confidence of a hundred years of colonial operations, a trained and disciplined army, and a huge personal financial stake in the outcome; they knew also that they had a trojan horse in the enemy camp. We have only to read Orme's account of Clive's dealings with Omichund, the millionaire Hindu merchant of Calcutta, to realise this.[51] The conquest of Bengal may have added only a little to the acceleration of the industrial revolution in Britain; in India it meant the absolute impoverishment and devastation of a once flourishing Indian state. The first Bengal famine followed in 1770; a third of the population perished. By 1789 Lord Cornwallis had to minute 'that one-third of the Company's territory in Hindustan is now a jungle inhabited only by wild beasts'.[52]

The loss to India from the plunder was certain; what was the gain to England? 'Such a prize in solid money', as Clive called it, must have done something to nourish Britain's industrial revolution. It arrived at a crucial moment in technical developments. Arkwright's and Wyatt's inventions in textile manufacture, and Tull's and Turnbull's discoveries in agriculture were just beginning to be put to use. A host of new inventions followed in the years immediately after Plassey – Hargreaves's spinning-jenny, Watt's steam-engine, Crompton's mule and Cartwright's loom all were introduced within fifteen years of Plassey – and coal soon replaced wood for smelting. Yet there is little evidence that much of the Indian plunder was invested in industry directly; most of it was reinvested in trade or went into building great houses, but some went into agriculture. Here it played its most crucial role in developing the agricultural revolution that was the necessary prelude to the industrial revolution. The country banks, moreover, built up funds which were of perhaps more importance for industrial development than readers of George Rae's *Country Banker* might suppose.[53]

It is not only plunder from India that is claimed, for example by R. P. Dutt,[54] as the main source of finance for industrialisation in Britain; more recently Basil Davidson has emphasised the claims of the slave-trade for this honour.[55] Yet, while there can be little doubt that the West African and East Indian trade helped to provide the infra-structure of industrialisation in Britain, in ports, shipping, communications, banking and above all in investment in agriculture, it is essential to remember that the traders did not invest directly in industry. Indeed, profits from trade may even, as was suggested earlier, have tended to hold back industrial investment. Certainly a richer home market was established for the products of the manufacturing industry, and rising naval and military orders encouraged metal manufacture; but the crucial developments for British industry were taking place elsewhere.

The Destruction of Competition from the East

It is an arguable question whether the critical breakthrough to full industrialisation came from the technological developments in iron-manufacture in the 1780s – particularly in the invention of the puddling process – or whether, as we have already suggested, cotton provided the catalyst for the really revolutionary pace of Britain's industrial change at the end of the eighteenth century. For cotton could be grown easily, quickly and cheaply (compared with sheep), and was much more susceptible than wool to mechanical processing.[56] Plantations in the West Indies had been developed to supply the greater part (about 70 per cent) of the growing demand of the English mills for cotton. Imports into Britain doubled between 1796 and 1800. Whichever view is accepted, the crucial problem after the initial breakthrough was the expansion of the market. It seems reasonable to conclude that the importance of the conquest of India lay less in the plunder derived than in the markets opened up. One thing still remained to be done before the English manufactures could establish their dominant position, before the industrial revolution could be completed: competition from eastern and particularly from Indian textiles and other handicrafts had to be ended. The East India Company had to be destroyed. At the same time, new overseas markets had to be added to the American market for the large scale of investment in manufacture to be realised.

English industry had been built up behind high protective walls. The colonies, according to mercantilist ideas, were expected to provide raw materials for export to Britain but to import their manufactured goods from Britain. 'It was the intention in settling our plantations in America,' wrote the Commissioner for Trade and Plantations in 1699, 'that the people there should be only employed in such things as are not the produce of England to which they belong.'[57] Thus iron was produced in New England, but was exported to Old England for working up into manufactures. By 1765, a Boston newspaper was complaining that: 'A colonist cannot make a button, a horse-shoe or a hobnail, but some ironmonger or respectable button-maker of Britain may bawl and squawl that his Honour's worship is most egregiously maltreated, injured and robbed by the rascally American republicans.'[58]

This was in part what provoked the rupture between the

American colonies and the mother country. Their secession ended Britain's monopoly of their market. It seemed a heavy blow, at the time, although the upshot was in fact a steady growth of the North American market as New England industrialised, and of the southern states as the main source of raw cotton for the English mills. But this could not then be foreseen; at the end of the eighteenth century the Indian market seemed more than ever important, competition from Indian textiles more than ever insufferable.

From 1720 the East India Company had been prohibited by British Government act from importing Indian silks and calicoes, and increasingly heavy duties were imposed upon Indian cotton manufactures as a result of the pressure of the Lancashire manufacturers. The Company's trade with India thereafter consisted mainly of re-exports to the rest of Europe, always one of the most profitable sides of its business and the justification for its export of bullion. After Plassey no more bullion was exported; in fact practically nothing was taken *to* India, while exports *from* India were valued at well over £6 million a year.[59] Dacca exported three million rupees' worth of muslin in 1787.[60]

After Bengal had been devastated, the English manufacturers turned once more to attack the East India Company. The reasons advanced by their spokesmen, such as Fox in the House of Commons, were the corruption, maladministration and peculation of the Company's servants. This led to the impeachment of Warren Hastings, but the real objective was the end of the Company's monopoly of the Indian trade, the elimination of Indian competition and the opening-up of this vast new market to English manufactures. It may be a point of some importance that the very diversion of the East India Company from trade with India to military conquest and direct pillage probably aided substantially the final victory of the manufacturing interest.* In 1813, at the end of the Napoleonic wars, the East India Company's monopoly

* I am indebted to John Hughes for the suggestion.

of the India trade was at last ended; its monopoly of the
China trade continued until 1840.

Between 1814 and 1835, British manufacturers increased
their exports of cotton goods to India from a million yards
valued at £26,000 to 51 million yards at £400,000; that was
a quarter of all their cotton exports. Exports of silk and
woollen goods, iron, pottery, glass and paper increased like-
wise. India provided a captive market for British manufactures. Meanwhile, Indian spinners, weavers and metal-
workers were steadily driven out of business. Dacca exported
nothing in 1817. Total Indian exports of cotton goods,
amounting to a million and a quarter pieces in 1814 and
valued at £1.3 million, had fallen to 300,000 pieces valued at
£100,000 by 1832, and to 63,000 pieces by 1844.[61] The
population of Dacca, Surat, Murshidabad and other centres
for manufacture in India was decimated in a generation and
India's balefully increasing dependence on agriculture had
begun.

The same process was completed in China in 1842. China,
whose empire 'had possessed all things' and had no need for
manufactures of 'barbarians', gave the East India Company
its last fling. The Company had always paid silver for the tea it
exported through the Hong merchants in Canton, until it
discovered that opium could be sold to the Chinese populace.
When the import of opium was forbidden by the emperor,
the company grew poppies on great estates in Bengal and
smuggled the seeds in to the China coast by private traders
in their own fast-running vessels. The great merchant house
of Jardine Matheson was founded on the opium-trade. But
the English private traders were anxious to open up the
Chinese market for other goods than smuggled opium. The
campaign of the Manchester Chamber of Commerce was
largely responsible for the ending, in 1834, of the East India
Company's China trade monopoly. The sale of cottons still
went badly in China. The two Opium Wars against China
were concerned far more with opening the Chinese market

to British manufactures than with imposing opium on an unwilling people. The Treaty of Nanking of 1842, which ended the wars, opened the main ports of China to foreign trade and conceded Hong Kong as an imperial base for the British trade.[62]

The great Indian and Chinese markets were now wide open to the English manufacturers. The village handicraft industries were destroyed – the same which had supplied the eastern trade of more than a thousand years and had provided Greek and Roman, Arab and Venetian, English and Portuguese traders with their wealth. 'The bones of the weavers,' – and an English Governor-General said it – 'were bleaching the plains of India.'[63] Manchester and Birmingham ruled supreme, distorting even the great centralised states of the irrigated plains of Asia to their ends. Capitalism, which had grown from the tiny villages and valleys of England, had achieved world dominion and divided the nations into rich and poor – advancing industrial manufacturers and declining primary producers. It was the freeing of the trade, not the building of the empire, that was the essence of the process; but that is the subject of the next chapter.

References

1. S. Lilley, *Men, Machines and History*, Cobbett Press, 1948, Chapter III.
2. B. Davidson, *Old Africa Rediscovered*, Gollancz, 1959.
3. Francis Bacon, *The Great Instauration*, Part II, *Novum Organum*, Aphorism 129, London 1620; Everyman Library, 1954.
4. J. Needham, *Science and Civilisation in China*, Vol. I, Cambridge, 1954.
5. A. C. Moorhouse, *Writing and the Alphabet*, Cobbett Press, 1946.
6. Paul Baran, *The Political Economy of Growth*, p. 138.
7. R. Mukherjee, *The Rise and Fall of the East India Company*, Berlin, 1955, Chapter 4.
8. Wu Ta K'un, 'An Interpretation of Chinese Economic History', *Past and Present*, No. 1, 1953.
9. R. Mukherjee, op. cit., p. 106.
10. E. Power, *Mediaeval People*, Penguin 1937, Chapter II.
11. Marx-Engels, *Selected Correspondence*, Lawrence & Wishart, 1934, Letter of 6 June 1853.
12. quoted in R. Mukherjee, op. cit., p. 129.
13. Wu Ta K'un, op. cit.
14. K. Wittwogel, *Oriental Despotism*, New Haven, 1957.
15. E. R. Leach, 'Hydraulic Society in Ceylon', *Past and Present*, No. 15, 1959.
16. O. Lattimore, *Inner Asian Frontiers of China*, Oxford, 1940.
17. Wu Ta K'un, op. cit.
18. J. Needham, op. cit., p. 144.
19. B. Davidson, *Old Africa Rediscovered*, p. 163.
20. M. H. Dobb, *Studies in the Development of Capitalism*, Routledge, 1946, p. 193 ff.
21. H. Hamilton, *History of the Homeland*, Allen and Unwin, 1947, p. 158.
22. E. J. Hobsbawm, 'The Crisis of the Seventeenth Century', *Past and Present*, Nos. 5 and 6, 1954.
23. M. H. Dobb, op. cit., pp. 218–19.
24. quoted by G. W. Southgate, *The British Empire and Commonwealth*, Dent, 1953, p. 174.
25. quoted by M. H. Dobb, op. cit., p. 168.
26. S. Lilley, op. cit., Chapter V.
27. E. Lipson, *Economic History of England*, Black, 1931, Vol II, p. 10 ff.
28. H. Pirenne, *History of Europe*, Allen and Unwin, 1936, p. 213.
29. E. M. Carus Wilson, 'Industrial Growth in some Fifteenth Century Manors', *Economic History Review*, December 1959.
30. Sir Edwin Sandys, *Europae Speculum*, London, 1638; The Hague, 1629.

31. J. H. Lawson, *The Hidden Heritage*, New York, 1950, p. 292 ff.
32. ibid., p. 287.
33. ibid., p. 408 ff.
34. ibid., p. 471 ff.
35. ibid., p. 506.
36. ibid., p. 487 ff.
37. J. Schumpeter, *Imperialism*, Meridian Books ed., New, York, 1955, p. 15.
38. E. J. Hobsbawm, op. cit., *passim*.
39. ibid., Part I, p. 36.
40. M. H. Dobb, op. cit., p. 172 ff.
41. E. J. Hobsbawm, op. cit., Part II, p. 60 ff.
42. M. H. Dobb, op. cit., p. 226 ff.
43. H. Hamilton, op. cit., p. 448.
44. B. Davidson, *Black Mother*, Gollancz, 1961, pp. 77 and 87.
45. E. J. Hobsbawm, op. cit., Part II, p. 54.
46. J. Strachey, *The End of Empire*, pp. 33 and 39 ff.
47. B. Williams, *The Whig Supremacy, 1715-60*, Oxford, 1939, p. 205 ff.
48. J. Strachey, op. cit., p. 38, note.
49. D. H. Buchanan, *Development of Capitalist Enterprise in India*, New York, 1934, p. 274.
50. James Mill, continued by H. H. Wilson, *History of British India*, London, 1840, Vol. I, p. 385.
51. R. Orme, *History of the Military Transactions of the British Nation in Indostan*, London, 1768, Vol. II.
52. Minute of September 18, 1789, quoted by J. Strachey, op. cit., p. 44.
53. G. Rae, *A Country Banker*, London, 1885, and L. S. Pressnell, *Country Banking in the Industrial Revolution*, Oxford, 1956.
54. R. P. Dutt, *India Today*, Bombay, 1947, p. 93 ff.
55. B. Davidson, *Black Mother*, pp. 74-5.
56. L. S. Pressnell, *Studies in the Industrial Revolution*, Athlone Press.
57. E. Lipson, op. cit., Vol. III, p. 173.
58. quoted in W. Z. Foster, *Outline Political History of the Americas*, New York, 1951, p. 125.
59. E. Thompson and G. T. Garrett, *Rise and Fulfilment of British Rule in India*, Macmillan, 1934, p. 99.
60. Sir Henry Cotton, quoted in R. P. Dutt, *India Today*, p. 102.
61. R. P. Dutt, op. cit., p. 101.
62. for this whole paragraph see M. Greenberg, *British Trade and the Opening of China*, Cambridge, 1951.
63. Quoted by Karl Marx in *Capital*, Vol. I, Chapter XV, section 5, Allen and Unwin, 1938, p. 432.

CHAPTER 2

Capitalism and Empire –
1 The Success of Free Trade: 1824–1870

In this chapter we have to note first the varied development of the different types of colony established in the nineteenth century:

(a) those largely empty lands, lands colonised by Europeans, i.e. colonised in the proper sense of the word;

(b) those already populous territories which were dependencies of the metropolitan powers, including some that avoided political rule but were nonetheless economically dependent, and

(c) those enclaves of mining and plantation where there was no large-scale settlement either of Europeans or of indigenous peoples.

We shall then want to discover how far the relationship with Britain and the other metropolitan European powers advanced or retarded the economic development of each of these three groups. This will lead us to ask what were the relative advantages of industrial and agricultural specialisation, which was established and maintained by free trade. All our questions will be related to the central issue of free trade. How far was Britain's industrial advance dependent upon possession of colonies? Was it free trade, or a protected imperial market for goods and capital, that gave Britain her ascendancy? Was it the terms of trade established with primary producing lands, or the expansion of the scale of trade, that benefited Britain most?

The Establishment of Free Trade

Britain's industries were reared behind protective walls, nourished on imperial tribute and encouraged by the destruction of all competition from the East. But, once established, they needed protection, plunder and protected markets no more. Protection became a drag on development; the factory product could undersell the work of handicraftsmen in any country in the world. All the industrialists asked was freedom to trade – to obtain food and raw materials wherever they were most cheaply produced and to open up the whole world as markets for their wares. To the great markets of India and China, and of North America and Europe, which we have already considered, Central and South America were added.

We may take these as an example of the process. In 1823, the Manchester Chamber of Commerce declared that the Central and South American markets were 'of the first magnitude'.[1] Britain's Foreign Secretary, Canning, was forced, under pressure from the merchants of London and against the monarchist principles of the king and of his own party, to recognise the new republics of Latin America in 1824, and to sign trade agreements, incorporating the principles of free trade. On this basis, trade expanded until, by 1829, South America was taking a quarter of the total British exports. Thereafter, the share declined, but British merchants had become so well established that the Barings, in the 1850s, were able to negotiate a virtually state-guaranteed market for British merchandise and British capital. Britain's 'informal empire in the Argentine'[2] had been established.

The 'Manchester School' free-traders have been held

responsible for promoting the growth of empire, at least of informal empire.[3] The judgement is not hard to maintain. The repeal of the Corn Laws was the beginning of the end of all imperial preferences. The repeal of the Navigation Laws opened the colonial trade to the whole world.

By the middle of the nineteenth century, free trade had made Britain the workshop of the world. The fact was that the British naval and military victories of the early nineteenth century, consolidated by Britain's industrial advance far ahead of any other nation, made the whole world, in a sense, Britain's colony. The actual colonial territories were retained, however, not so much to exploit but as military bases of world power.

Thus the bases won during the Napoleonic Wars – the Cape of Good Hope, Guiana, Trinidad, Tobago, Mauritius, Malta – were retained. In 1819, Sir Stanford Raffles staked his claim to Singapore, and on the islands throughout the Pacific and Indian Oceans the Union Jack was soon fluttering in the wind. Moreover, the conquest of India had to be extended if the original provinces brought under British rule were to be retained. Throughout the first half of the nineteenth century, the Indian Empire was expanded to include Ceylon, most of central India, the Sind, the Punjab, Kashmir, Nepal, Assam and Burma. Nor was this done without bitter fighting in the Maratha, Sikh and Afghan Wars.

Nonetheless, to saddle the free-traders with this catalogue of expansion is unfair. They were genuinely anti-colonial, in at least two senses: they were opposed to the cost in money and lives of all overseas adventures, which Palmerston was quite prepared to risk; and they wished to see the colonies separated off from the home country as soon as possible, partly because they were a charge on the budget, but from libertarian principles also.[4] There were, in fact, two absolutely opposed views in Britain about colonies throughout the nineteenth century, and the protagonists fought continuously for public support.

In broad terms, we may think of the aristocracy, and later the Tories, as expansionist, and the manufacturers, and later the Liberals, as contractionists. But there are two sources of confusion here. First, there is the changing role of the parties in mid-Victorian politics. Palmerston was as much a Whig 'imperialist' as Disraeli was a Tory 'imperialist'. Second, there were two distinct types of colony. Disraeli was expressing a widely-held view when he made his famous remark in 1852 about the Colonies being 'millstones around our necks'.[5] But the strategic bases and the Indian possessions were always specifically excluded, even by Liberals, in the 'millstones around our necks' critique of colonies. The radical Dilke, for example, clearly distinguished between the dependencies such as India, and the colonies proper. It was the latter which should be separated.[6] These colonies were the settlements of new lands by English emigrants. Canada had not been exchanged for Guadeloupe as had been suggested to Pitt in the negotiation with France in 1763. The reason had been strategic, but, as the frontier was pushed west right across North America, Canada attracted a share of the great flood of emigrants from Britain. Settlements grew rapidly in the first half of the nineteenth century in South Africa, in Tasmania and on the Australian mainland, and then in New Zealand.

Lands of White Settlement

The pressure behind this settlement of largely empty lands, where the indigenous populations were non-existent or almost wiped out, was the extremely rapid growth of Britain's population. This was combined with the special circumstances of the ruin of Irish agriculture and handicrafts. Ireland was England's first colony; the extraction of high rents by English absentee landlords and the destruction of native industries finally created the catastrophe of the 1840s. In the next fifty years, while England's population doubled,

Ireland's was halved. Not only in Ireland, but throughout Britain, people were leaving the rural areas – three millions between 1850 and 1890. Of these, for every three who went into the towns, two went overseas. As small farmers continued to be slowly[7] squeezed out by large, and as rural handicrafts collapsed in the face of factory competition, still more were forced or attracted off the land at home to join the emigrants, or start work in the towns. For many years in the middle of the nineteenth century three thousand emigrants left British ports every week.[8] Most of them, however, were bound for the United States and not for the colonies. Indeed, some part of the interest in colonies in the mid-1850s arose from awareness of this very fact.

Soon there were enough emigrants in Canada, Australia and New Zealand to be demanding representative institutions and to achieve what came to be called 'dominion' status. Once they had achieved independence, they rapidly developed their own industry behind protective tariffs as the United States had done before them. Although the free-traders protested when Canada, in 1859, established a protective tariff on certain goods mainly imported from Britain, the British Government did not venture to override the colony on the matter.[9] British industry could afford to be generous and was soon to benefit from the growing market for its products. The railway boom was still on and, as the lines were completed at home, rails and locomotives were being shipped across the Atlantic to supply the great transcontinental railroads of America.

Exporting capital equipment such as rails and locos, however, was a different business from exporting consumer goods such as textiles. A merchant or trader, even in a quite undeveloped country, can fairly quickly dispose of cotton piece-goods where there is a large population of consumers, and raw materials to be bought in exchange. But railway equipment is an investment. From the very start, the railway-export business involved heavy exports of capital, and often of men, too, for the duration of the job. Thomas Brassey and Morton Peto, and their backers, had large shares in the continental lines they built between 1840 and 1870, and it was believed in 1857 that £80 million of American railway stock was then held in England.[10] By 1870, the total British foreign investment was about £700 million, of which more than a quarter was in the United States and only about a third inside the empire.[11]

The results of this period of British capitalist expansion were of central importance for Britain's future development and we shall return to this point below; they were also decisive for the rest of the world. Foreign investment established capitalism throughout Europe and in the lands of white settlement. Industrialisation was most rapid in the United States and Germany, but, by 1870, it was proceeding apace also in France, in the rest of western Europe and even in eastern Europe. At the same time, the construction of ports, railways, roads and bridges, and internal communications in Canada, South America and Australasia laid the foundations for their economic development.

The Origins of Underdeveloped Lands

The progress of Britain's overseas possessions steadily diverged during the nineteenth century. It was not only that the lands of white settlement attained political independence, while India, Burma, Ceylon and other Asian and African lands remained in colonial status, but Europe and the lands settled by Europeans went ahead rapidly in economic development while the rest of the world marked time. The division of the world into industrially developed and underdeveloped lands deepened. It is essential that we should understand the reasons for this difference.

The division was not simply the result of colonial status. China, which remained independent, failed equally with India to advance towards industrialisation. Nor was it any lack of resources to be developed, as is often assumed.[12] The resources of China and India were far greater than those of Canada and Australia.[13] Nor was it that no steps were taken to open up these lands. Railways were, in fact, built in India and China, and ports and harbours were constructed. Why then did these works not generate economic development as Marx had expected that they would?[14]

The central fact which we must seize upon is that these lands with huge settled populations failed to raise agricultural productivity and to produce a food surplus, such as would have enabled them to begin the process of accumulation which, in Britain, was essential to industrialisation. The reasons for this circumstance were several: first, there was the stultifying effect of traditional techniques and an irrigation system that denied individual initiative. Far more important, in India there was the British land-settlement, which created a class of landowner/money-lenders, divorced from the productive process and yet drawing a huge surplus from the land for their own consumption.[15] This in its turn held back the emergence of an entrepreneurial class. British rule after the mutiny came increasingly to rely on Indian princes and landlords, as we shall see later.

In China, the land-owning bureaucracy had the same effect. The great rebellion of the Taipings, which might have brought China into the modern world a hundred years before 1949, was put down by the Manchus with the aid of Anglo-French forces under the command of General Gordon.[16] Only Japan of the great eastern states succeeded, by a lucky combination of circumstances, in carrying through her industrial revolution.

Japan's industrialisation precisely confirms the analysis we have made of the failure of oriental society in India, China and elsewhere to develop economically as European society did. The factors we have emphasised were the power of the central state, based primarily on the particular forms of agricultural technique appropriate to the great irrigated river-valleys, the consequent failure of an independent merchant and manufacturing class to emerge, and, finally, the destruction of local craftmanship that followed the opening of markets to European manufactures. Japan, divided into four separate islands and a hundred small valleys, had a centralised state only as a borrowing from China, without any real basis. Her island position, and the luck of European rivalry in China, insulated her from European colonisation so that a combination of southern landowners and merchants, who had understood the power of European arms and technical achievement, were able themselves to impose an industrial revolution upon Japan from above, turning state power to their own ends, much as the Junkers were doing in Prussia.[17]

Enclaves of Development

It was the actual destruction of native industries by the competition of British manufacture that resulted in the steady increase in both China and India of the proportion of the population dependent wholly on agriculture for a livelihood. The division of labour thus created between European manufacturers and Asian primary producers was then perpetuated by free trade. To this was added, in the middle of the nineteenth century, a new factor, namely European investment in the growing of crops for export. The increased need for raw materials in Britain and other industrialised lands, and the growing demand for food imports, provided the means for economic development by European settlers of North and South America and Australia. A part of these same needs was also met by plantations in the West Indies and in India and Ceylon. Exports of raw cotton, jute, hides, oil and wool from India grew at a very rapid rate in the second half of the nineteenth century.[18] Tea and, in Ceylon, coffee and rubber were added to the list of export crops towards the end of the century.

The sale of these crops would have helped forward the process of economic development much more than it did, had it not been for four crucial limitations we shall consider in detail below (Chapter 5). These were, first, the difficulty of raising agricultural productivity, which we have already noted; second, the dependence on fluctuating earnings from one or two crops; third, the fact that most of the value from their sale went to the British and other European investors and merchants who initiated, and often managed, their production; and finally, that the whole purpose of the operation, i.e. to provide raw materials for British and European industry, worked against the development of industries in the primary producing countries. In India, for example, the first textile mill was established in the 1850s, but it was not until the end of the century that production developed on any scale.[19]

The result of the whole process was disaster. The expanding acreage of land devoted to export crops, at the expense of food crops, combined with a rise in population to cause a rapidly mounting death-roll from famine in India – half a million in the second quarter of the nineteenth century, rising to fifteen millions in the last quarter.[20] Most of the export crops were grown on British-owned plantations, some of the planters having originally had experience as slave-drivers in the West Indies before the abolition of slavery.[21] Most of the earnings were remitted to the home country either to investing companies or with the planters when they retired.

India had been opened up at the beginning of the nineteenth century as a market for British manufactures. In the process, as we have seen, Indian exports of manufactures were annihilated; but exports of food and raw materials were rapidly expanded. Until the last quarter of the century, Indian exports thus continued to exceed imports, and in fact by a rising margin. What was begun in India was later continued in Egypt, in South-East Asia, and especially in Malaya and the East Indies, in Africa and in South America. The result was especially disastrous in Egypt. The area of irrigated land was increased – by a fifth – but only to be devoted largely to growing cotton for export. Food production hardly kept up with the growth in population. The cotton provided the means for paying the foreign bond-holders, whose tribute equalled a half of the value of exports and more than half of the annual government budget. More serious was the distortion and arrest of economic development that we have already noted in India and China; indigenous handicrafts were undermined by imperial manufactures; the whole population was concentrated upon agriculture; a few thousand great landlords were maintained in power; the peasant burdened by rent and debt had no strength, initiative, or capital to improve on age-old techniques of production.[22]

As industrialisation in Europe and North America advanced in the decade before 1914, development of mining was added to the spread of plantations. Enclaves of development occurred in many parts of the world, in Malaya, in Africa and especially in South America. Much of this development was in colonies, and the Latin American states became virtually United States colonies.[23] They may best be thought of as enclaves of metropolitan development because they remained within a largely unchanged subsistence economy. In this first decade of the twentieth century, the Malayan states were added to the British Empire by the partition of South-East Asia with the French; and rubber plantations were rapidly developed with Indian and Chinese labour, the Malayan population being almost unaffected. The sharp rise in rubber prices after Henry Ford introduced his motor-car brought rubber estates into being in Ceylon and Java also. But this takes us beyond the period of our present chapter. The distortion of the economies of the countries thus opened up we shall have to examine in more detail in a later chapter (Chapter 5).

Advantages of Free Trade for Britain

Now that we have distinguished the main types of colonial development, we have to look at this whole process from the point of view of the metropolitan power, and particularly from the British point of view. What were the gains for Britain from the empire in the mid-nineteenth century? If the disadvantages of the opening-up of markets, the tightening of imperial rule, and the exploitation of mineral and raw material sources were great indeed for the non-European-settled colonies, what advantages were there for the imperial powers? Here there has been much confused explanation, especially in attempts at explaining the grab for Africa at the end of the nineteenth century and the relation between overseas investment and empire during the whole period prior to 1913. To these we shall return later.

We need first to be clear about the effects of Britain's foreign economic relations upon her growth at home in the middle decades of the century. The situation here is clear. The opening of Britain's own markets to free trade and the opening up of the world's markets to the new factory products of Britain brought great wealth. The year 1848 had been one of revolution in Europe; but the British landed aristocracy were able to count on the full support of the capitalist middle class in meeting the Chartists with a show of force, and to make no concession to their demand for working-class participation in the parliamentary life of the country. The workers turned to self-protection through thrift and craft unions. The Anti-Corn Law League had been more successful. After the early 1840s customs rates began to be cut step by step from about 36 per cent of import values in 1840 to less than 8 per cent in 1870.[24] Free trade began to bring its reward.

Within three years of 1848, the whole nation was celebrating British industrial pre-eminence at the Great Exhibition in the Crystal Palace built in Hyde Park. Increased productivity in British industry – far ahead of the rest of the world – was the secret. Industrial output doubled between 1850 and 1870, although the number of industrial workers probably rose only by about a half.[25] The number of miners rose by less than a half, though their output was doubled. Numbers in iron and steel and in machine-making and ship-building doubled but output nearly trebled. Cotton textile output doubled in the ten years 1850–1860 with a labour force no larger.[26] Exports of all goods were also doubled within the decade of the 'fifties alone and nearly doubled again in the 'sixties and first years of the 'seventies as the markets in one country after another were prised open (see Table III below).[27] For long, nearly two-thirds of Britain's exports were textiles, and a half of all those engaged in manufacture were in the textile industries.[28]

Textiles had been the pace-setters of the industrial re-volution in Britain and they were long to continue to dominate the manufacturing sector of the economy. From its earliest days, the overseas market had been crucial for the textile industry's development. We have already noted the influence of the Manchester Chamber of Commerce on government policy in India, China and the Argentine. We should not be surprised. Some four-fifths of Lancashire's output went to foreign markets throughout the nineteenth century, although the share of textiles in Britain's total exports fell steadily from two-thirds in 1850 to one-third in 1913 – of cotton goods alone from a half to a quarter.[29]

Britain's exports as a whole came to equal in value about a fifth of the national income.[30] This was the point to which industrial specialisation had brought Britain. But the great advantage of free trade was that the whole level of world trade was raised. This was considerably aided by the doubling of the world's gold output between 1850 and 1885.[31] The total result was remarkable. World trade increased fivefold between 1840 and 1874, and in that year Britain probably accounted for two-fifths of it, nearly as much as the total of France, Germany and the United States together.[32]

It cannot be too strongly emphasised that free trade worked both ways. After the repeal of the Corn Laws, English ports were opened to the products of the whole world. Apparently, not far short of one-third of the exports of the rest of the world found their way into the United Kingdom in the 1850s and 1860s.[33] A quarter of the country's food, including a million tons of wheat, came from overseas in these years.[34] Little of this came from the empire, less than a quarter in fact. Our largest single trading-partner was the United States, accounting for nearly a quarter of all imports and of all exports. Another quarter was accounted for by the countries of Europe, which were beginning, like the U.S.A., to industrialise themselves with British equipment and ideas. The share that the empire took of Britain's exports fluctuated, falling in the 'forties, rising in the 'fifties, and then falling again in the 'sixties, but it never rose above a third of our total exports. The rise in the 'fifties certainly coincided with the most rapid rise in British exports, the main advance taking place in the new dominions (see Table V at end of Chapter 3).[35] How important was this?

Overseas Investment and the Empire

It was during these years between the late 1840s and the late 1850s that exports of capital goods expanded so rapidly − from 11 per cent to 22 per cent of the total.[36] Exports of engineering goods, rails and other capital equipment required, as we noted earlier, a considerable flow of overseas investment. Did this mean that the imperial connection became more important than world-wide free trade? We can certainly say that British investments in the new dominions aided the growth in exports, but can we say that it was because the dominions were within the British Empire that investment and exports grew? Both were growing also in the

U.S.A. and in Europe, in which two regions, in fact, more than half of British overseas capital was established by 1870 (see Table V at end of Chapter 3).[37] Certainly, investment in India grew rapidly after the Mutiny of 1857 in Dalhousie's railway schemes, to make up by 1870 another fifth of Britain's overseas capital. Military and strategic necessity demanded the lines and a 5 per cent minimum of interest on the investment was given government guarantee. In India there was indeed an advantage derived from imperial possessions for British investors and exporters.

It is clear that the whole episode of Indian railway investment, upon which Marx placed his hopes of India's ultimate regeneration,[38] was due to a succession of rather exceptional events. The first pressure to establish a market for British manufactures may be said to have culminated in the grant of the 5 per cent guarantee in 1849. Thereafter, the mutiny in 1857 and then the growing fear in Lancashire of excessive dependence on cotton from the southern United States, soon to be engulfed in civil war, contributed to maintain the pressure. But it is noteworthy that, even after the concession of the 5 per cent guarantee, pressure from manufacturers continued to be brought to bear on the Government to extend the railway system with a view to expanding markets. Thus, for example, the cutlers of Sheffield were petitioning the House of Lords to this effect in 1853.[39]

Dalhousie himself minuted that aid for the railways will encourage 'a more extensive employment of similar capital and similar efforts hereafter in connexion with the production and trade of India'.[40] He had in mind the movement of salt and coal as well as of cotton; but in fact the railways created very little local development since they opened up a market mainly for British and not for Indian manufactures. The only big British investment in India in the nineteenth century was in the railways. Even Dalhousie's irrigation schemes, designed to increase cotton cultivation, accounted for no more than £18 million compared with the £95 million invested in railways in 1860. And the railways never made a profit, at least up to 1866. The Government of India found the 5 per cent guaranteed interest mainly out of taxation of the Indians.[41]

Outside India there is little evidence that the empire gave much direct advantage to British capital. In the pressure to sell rails to foreign governments, loans were often made that brought little or no return to the rentiers. Failures were as frequent inside the Empire (with the exception of India) as they were outside.[42] The fact was that Britain's pre-eminent position had supplied her with the capital to invest. But free trade rather than imperial protection was the basis of the pre-eminence. The advantage of the strategic lines of the empire was the preservation of a world of free trade. What we must emphasise here was that free trade for any country that was not strong enough to challenge Britain involved the opening of its markets to British manufactures, and, as a consequence, the holding back of its own industrial development. Britain's monopoly as the workshop of the world was soon to be challenged from many quarters; but that is the subject of the next chapter.

How were the funds found for this overseas investment, and what was the balance of advantage for Britain in this outward movement of capital? First of all, there has been a long misunderstanding of the source of British capital for overseas investment. This capital was always supposed to be the result of an export surplus in the middle decades of the nineteenth century. But, as Imlah has shown, there never was a surplus on merchandise account in the whole nineteenth century, and there was only very rarely, in the 1860s and early 1870s, a surplus on all goods and services.[43] Indeed, between 1890 and 1905 there was a heavy deficit.* The surplus in Britain's annual balance of payments with foreign countries was found from the return of interest and dividends

* Services include ship-building, shipping, insurance, commodity brokerage, migrant's remittances, etc.

on previous investments. This meant that, year by year, a part, often a large part, of the income from investment overseas was re-invested abroad. In this way capital overseas accumulated, at first slowly but later in great leaps (see Table II, below).

This error about the source of funds for overseas investment has led to a crucial misunderstanding of the relation between exports and overseas investment, which persists today. It is still supposed that overseas lending must be made possible by creating a surplus on goods and services; in the absence of competitive exports, imports must be cut down. In fact, as we shall see, reducing imports only pulls down our exports, since it deprives trading partners of the wherewithal to buy our goods. Britain's exports expanded in the nineteenth century precisely because Britain's imports rose steadily, and because import prices kept in line with export prices, so that Britain's customers could afford to pay for our products.[44] This raises the central question of the terms of Britain's trade with overseas primary producers, and the advantages and disadvantages of Britain's specialisation on industrial production, involving as it did such a large flow of overseas investment to sustain the rising tide of exports.

The World Division of Labour

The great advantage for the British people from the overseas investment in the middle of the nineteenth century was undoubtedly cheap food. The reduction of transport costs, the building of railways and harbours for Baltic grain and then for North American grain, as the prairies were opened up, and finally the advent of the new iron ships plying the Atlantic all combined to bring food prices tumbling. The nation's rising demand for grain was met from overseas. After 1870, a third of the nation's food was imported including nearly a half of its bread grains.[45] The price of a quarter of wheat, which had been 60s. before 1840 and over 50s. for two decades after 1850, fell below 20s. at the end of the century, although rising again to 30s. by 1913.[46] Refrigeration enabled frozen beef to come from the United States, and mutton from Australia and New Zealand.

Overseas investment also brought cheaper supplies of raw materials. Britain had become pre-eminently a processor of imported materials. Raw material imports rose sharply in the mid-1860s. Within a decade, the total value of Britain's imports was equivalent to nearly a third of the national income.[47] Free trade had opened up the world's markets and was bringing in supplies of food and raw materials from the cheapest sources. Were there any disadvantages from this process? Apart from the effect on tin- and lead-mining, where Britain's reserves of ores were in any case small, the main result was the decline of agriculture at home. The ending of the Corn Laws was followed by a generation of rising demand and limited world supplies of foodstuffs. British agriculture was never so prosperous as in the 1850s and 1860s, but free trade in the end had its effect. Collapse followed the poor harvests of the 1870s and the subsequent flood of prairie grains.[48] The wheat acreage in Britain was halved between 1874 and the end of the century; total land under cultivation fell from 17 million acres to 13 million in 1913. Pasturage took up some of the gap, as dairying and market-gardening developed at the turn of the century.[49]

We shall have to consider in the next chapter whether there were important disadvantages for the development of industry at home in the flow of investment overseas, whether industry at home in fact was starved of capital. What we have first to be clear about is the precise nature of the advantage to Britain of the growing concentration on industrial production, involving such a huge expansion of exports. It used to be assumed that Britain gained from the Ricardian principle of comparative costs. In so far as the difference between the productivity in British industry and productivity in British agriculture was greater than the similar differences in other countries, Ricardo supposed that it paid us to trade textiles for food and also paid our trading partners to trade food for textiles. E. A. G. Robinson has pointed out that it is very doubtful if this was ever true in relation to our main trading-partners in the U.S.A., Canada or Europe, although it probably was true in relation to Australia and South America.[50]

Ricardian theory was based on the explicit assumption that capital and labour did not in fact move across national boundaries, as equilibrium theory would expect them to do.[51] In fact they did move, but only to lands of European settlement. Britain's advantage lay in her higher overall productivity, but her monopoly of industrial specialisation was short-lived. Others soon caught up, but some were left behind. The result was that any country able to move resources out of agriculture and into industry could be expected to gain just because some countries were not free to do so. Robinson's argument, which so many others have overlooked, is that what Britain gained from – and the U.S.A. and other European countries soon joined us – was the terms of trade subsisting everywhere between manufactured and primary products.[52]

It is precisely these terms of trade, that is the nation's net barter terms of trade, or the prices received for its exports compared with the prices paid for imports, from which we should therefore expect to discover the relative advantages of industrial and primary producers in mutual trading. There are two main considerations here: first, if, as we have already suggested, it has proved more difficult to raise productivity in agriculture in most areas than in industry, then the restriction of any country to agricultural production will tend to harm its terms of trade[53]; second, it is clear that, if the numbers of industrial producers could be limited, as they were, and if the number of primary producers was almost without limit, then we should expect the terms of trade to primary producers to suffer. It is not a simple matter, however, to measure the terms of trade. We can measure the *changes* in import and export prices, but we do not know what meaning to give to the original relationship of prices from which we start, nor can we be sure that changes in an apparently favourable direction necessarily bring advantage and vice versa. We are left in this position for two reasons.

In the first place, falling prices of exports may reflect falling costs, as the long fall in Britain's export prices after 1815 obviously did; there might in this case be no disadvantage in an adverse movement of the terms of trade, so long as trade expanded and the widening market permitted the realisation of falling costs from the introduction of machinery. This brings us to the second point: the maintenance of a high and rising quantity of exports (usually referred to as the volume of exports, that is the value adjusted for price changes) may, therefore, be just as important as raising the terms on which exports are exchanged for imports. It was, indeed, likely to become more important with the growing dependence of employment in Britain on the level of her exports after the mid-nineteenth century, when a fifth of the national income began to be derived from sales abroad.

Britain's Gain from the Terms of Trade

To raise the volume of exports obviously implies the ability of trading-partners to earn enough from their sales to purchase this extra volume. As Britain's main trading-partners were and are producers of food and of other primary products, an expansion of exports may only be possible when the terms of trade are moving in favour of the primary producers or when capital movements are taking place in their direction. By contrast, rising export prices in relation to import prices for a manufacturing country like Britain may lead to a decline in the volume of exports, because the earnings and balance of payments of our trading-partners suffer. Thus rising import prices in relation to export prices may be needed, in the absence of investment moving overseas, to ensure a growth in export volume. Which is very largely the situation we find in examining the movements of prices in the nineteenth century.

The evidence is examined in an annexe to this chapter, but here we may draw one seemingly firm conclusion. This is that the behaviour of the advanced industrial economy – in this case Britain – was the dynamic factor.[54] The variation in prices that we have been considering between exports and imports, and the variations in trade volumes, took place within a general rise and fall that keeps in beat with the rise and fall of manufacturing output in Britain. This is generally true for the whole period, although there is some evidence of 'crisis exports' being what we would now call 'dumped' in the late 1870s, when exports continued to rise while manufacturing output in general was stagnant. Although exports were somewhat better maintained in periods of slump than sales at home, the big advances of exports (there were few actual falls) coincide with the periods of general prosperity (*see* Table III below). The export proportion in the economy was sufficiently large to influence general prosperity; but, no less important, prosperity at home also meant increased demand for imports, which thus raised the earnings of primary producers and stimulated British exports.

The dynamic factor was the growth of industrial demand aided by reduced costs of production and transport. Demand of primary producers for industrial products was a function of the demand of industrial producers for primary products, and not vice versa. An upward thrust in industrial producers' demand with terms of trade moving favourably for primary producers led to a spiral of growth; a downward movement with unfavourable terms for the primary producers resulted in a downward spiral of contracting trade. The agricultural producers thus became largely dependent economically, if not politically, upon their industrial markets.

From this study of the development of trade in the first two-thirds of the nineteenth century we may draw three general conclusions about the world division of labour: first, there were great advantages to be derived from specialisation on industrial production for any nation that was free to transfer resources from agriculture to industry, and particularly for Britain, which had a head start from her technical, historical and geographic position. Further, there were advantages only in a very few areas (Australia and parts of South America) from specialisation in agricultural production; in most cases this was an enforced specialisation which held back economic development and imposed economic dependence of primary producers on their industrial trading-partners. Finally, the gain to Britain as an industrial power from expanding the total volume of her trade was largely made possible by the opening of her home markets to overseas products, thus allowing the terms of trade to move adversely for her own manufactured products, or at least not too unfavourably for the primary products of her overseas trading-partners.

To these conclusions we may add our earlier conclusion about the nature of British overseas investment and the expansion of the British empire in the first half of the nineteenth century. With the outstanding exception of India, neither process was concerned primarily with drawing a higher rate of profit or some other form of tribute directly from overseas lands. Both were concerned with expanding trade. Free trade was the instrument of Britain's industrial supremacy holding back development elsewhere; this condition would, in the end, have checked British growth too, as foreign markets were impoverished. But British capital investment in Europe and North America, and in other lands of European settlement created the necessary expanding markets for manufactured exports. In the not so long run, it created also new competitors for British industry.

Annexe on the Terms of Trade

We may divide the nineteenth century after 1815 into five periods: 1815–57; 1858–73; 1874–81; 1882–1900; 1901–13. Between 1815 and 1857, the terms of trade moved steadily in favour of the primary producers, as the prices of the products of Britain's new factories were cut much more sharply than the prices of food and raw materials. The volume of Britain's exports doubled three times in the forty-two years. They almost doubled again in the next fourteen years after 1857, when in fact British export prices rose ahead of import prices; but these were years of capital investment overseas and of heavy reductions in freight costs, so that the funds available to primary producers probably did not fall. In the 1870s, the volume of British exports was almost stagnant, despite the fall in export prices well ahead of import prices during the Great Depression. This third period, then, does not exhibit the correlation of high volumes of exports from Britain with more favourable terms of trade for primary producers and vice versa. The advantage from the improved terms of trade for primary producers must have been offset by the lower level of sales of primary products in Britain and the other industrial lands during the depression years.

After 1880, for more than twenty years, both export and import prices fell, but in this period Britain's import prices fell most; and these unfavourable terms for primary producers were accompanied by a very slow rate of growth in Britain's export volumes. After 1900, however, the terms of trade again turned in favour of the primary producers and Britain's exports once more leapt ahead as demand for primary products grew in Britain and in other industrial lands. This view – that, in general, the terms of trade for Britain (and for other industrial producers) moved in their favour in a depression and unfavourably in boom periods – has been challenged by Martin and Thackeray taking only the period after 1870.[55] Before 1870, the major booms in Britain (except 1843–6), as Table III shows, coincided with unfavourable movements in the terms of trade and the terms of trade only improved very slightly in the smaller booms. Half of the slumps coincided with favourable movements and half with unfavourable movements. But the fifty years before 1870 witnessed a steadily unfavourable trend in the terms of trade for Britain; and this in itself is significant, for it was the period of the most rapid rise in Britain's foreign trade and industrial output. Rapid rates of growth did not take place again until the 1900s, when once more the terms of trade moved unfavourably for Britain.

Should we conclude then that the greater gain accrued to Britain from the increased volume of trade than from more favourable terms of trade? Two opposite arguments need to be considered. On the one hand, it is often said that what was happening was simply that, as imports cost relatively more than exports, more goods had, consequently, to be exported to pay for them.[56] What then was the gain from the growth in the whole level of trade? How can we estimate it? We can link the index of the terms of trade to that for the volume of trade (or, in a more refined way, Imlah links in also the index of the gross barter terms of trade, that is the relationship of the volume of imports compared with the volume of exports). In this case, a more than thirty-fold rise in gain occurred between 1815 and 1913, with a steady growth apart from minor set-backs in the mid-1820s, late 1840s, mid-1850s, early 1860s, 1870s and early 1890s.[57] On this calculation the gain in volume would seem easily to have outweighed any loss in terms of trade.

On the other hand, it is said that what was happening, when the terms of trade moved in favour of primary producers, was that the pressure to export more goods because of falling home demand involved cutting manufacturers' export prices, not that the better earnings of primary producers allowed the volume of British exports to rise. That there were such crisis exports we may readily concede, but the question is: On what scale? An inverse movement of the terms of trade and the export proportion does not of itself provide proof of large crisis exports, as Schloete suggests.[58] It would equally well justify our argument to say that better prices for primary producers expanded Britain's exports.

To discover which is the better explanation of what was happening, we could find, first, whether there was a better correlation between the movement of export volumes and the movement of export prices or of import prices, and then whether movements in export prices or movements in import prices generally led to changes in the terms of trade. What we find from a careful study of Imlah's figures is that what happened before 1860 was different from what happened after.

Before 1860, the correlation is undoubtedly between export volumes and export prices. Britain's export prices were falling faster than import prices as the rising efficiency of manufacturing production and expanding markets led to reduced costs. The pressure to export from expanding capacity might be said to have brought down export prices, but increased productivity was the ultimate cause.[59] Movements in import prices, moreover, were more often the immediate cause of changes in the terms of trade than movements in export prices.

After 1860, there seems to be little to choose between the prices of imports and of exports as the determining factor in swinging the terms of trade; but movements in volume of exports more often accompany movements in import prices than in export prices, the volume of Britain's exports rising with a rise in import prices and falling with a fall.

TABLE II
BALANCE OF BRITAIN'S FOREIGN PAYMENTS IN THE NINETEENTH CENTURY
(Annual Averages for Five-year periods)

	Balance on Goods, i.e. Merchandise trade (£m.)	Balance on Services (£m.)	Balance on Goods and Services (£m.)	Net Interest and Dividends (£m.)	Overall Balance of Current Account (£m.)	Accumulated Balance of Credit abroad by end of 5-year periods (£m.)
1815–20	−9	+14		+2	+7	46
1821–25	−8	+14		+4	+10	98
1826–30	−13	+14		+5	+3	111
1831–35	−13	+11		+5	+6	143
1836–40	−24	+19		+8	+3	156
1841–45	−17	+15		+7	+6	185
1846–50	−27	+22		+9	+5	209
1851–55	−27	+23		+12	+8	249
1856–60	−34	+43	+9	+16	+26	380
1861–65	−57	+57	0	+22	+22	490
1866–70	−58	+68	+10	+31	+40	692
1871–75	−62	+87	+25	+50	+75	1,065
1876–80	−125	+94	−31	+56	+25	1,189
1881–85	−104	+101	−3	+65	+62	1,497
1886–90	−91	+94	+3	+84	+88	1,935
1891–95	−130	+88	−42	+94	+52	2,195
1896–1900	−161	+101	−50	+100	+40	2,397
1901–05	−175	+111	−64	+113	+49	2,642
1906–10	−142	+136	−6	+151	+146	3,371
1911–13	−134	+152	+18	+188	+206	3,990

Note: Services include Ship sales and Bullion.
Source: A. H. Imlah, *Economic Elements in the Pax Britannica* (Cambridge, Mass.: Harvard Univ. Press, 1958), Table 4.

TABLE III

BOOM AND SLUMP IN BRITAIN'S INDUSTRIAL OUTPUT AND FOREIGN TRADE, 1822–1960

Boom or Slump	Years	Industrial Index	Trade Volume	Terms of Trade	i.e. (Export Price Index / Import Price Index)
Boom	1822–24	16–18	8–10	155–149	Down
Slump	1825–26	20–18	11–9	147–157	Up
Boom	1827–30	20–23	12–13	148–150	Up, slight
Slump	1831–32	24–23	13–12	138–128	Down
Boom	1833–36	25–27	13–16	123–124	Up, slight
Slump	1837	28	14	130	Up
Boom	1838–41	31–33	17–19	120–110	Down
Slump	1842	32	18	105	Down
Boom	1843–46	34–40	19–22	113–120	Up
Slump	1847	39	25	112	Down
Boom	1848–53	39–52	25–37	122–101	Up-down
Slump	1854–55	52–51	36–34	95–89	Down
Boom	1856–60	51–63	41–49	92–95	Up, slight
Slump	1861–62	60–58	48	98–106	Up
Boom	1863–70	61–80	49–69	107–102	Down
Boom	1871–74	85–92	77–81	109–117	Up
Slump	1875–79	91–85	84–91	112–102	Down
Boom	1880–83	100–110	100–111	100–99	Down, slight
Slump	1884–86	104–101	108–109	100–106	Up
Boom	1887–91	106–122	114–130	106–107	Up, slight
Slump	1892–93	116–113	128–125	107–109	Up, slight
Boom	1894–99	120–142	134–160	111–112	Up, slight
Slump	1900–04	142–141	160–175	120–113	Down
Boom	1905–07	151–160	182–198	113–115	Up, slight
Slump	1908–09	152–154	187–193	115–109	Down
Boom	1910–13	159–184	203–232	108–116	Up
War	1914–18	173–149	200–127	—	Up
Boom	1919–20	163–168	169–187	134–146	Up
Slump	1921	105	153	165	Up
Boom	1922–29	143–195	186–260	153–138	Down
Slump	1930–32	183–168	226–195	150–171	Up
Boom	1933–37	179–240	196–286	173–153	Down
Slump	1938	216	222	166	Up
War	1939–45	—	—	—	Down
Boom	1946–51	227–312	184–298	153–120	Down
Slump	1952	304	281	129	Up
Boom	1953–57	321–367	292–350	135–144	Up, slight
Slump	1958	362	340	156	Up
Boom	1959–60	383–420	356–390	155–162	Up, slight

Notes: (a) In each column the first figure relates to the first year in the period, the second to the last year.
 (b) Boom or Slump italicised implies a major boom or slump in industry and trade.
 (c) Cross lines indicate periods during which output and trade were roughly doubled.

Sources: W. G. Hoffman, *British Industry, 1750–1950* (Oxford: Blackwell, 1955), Table 54-b recalculated for 1880 = 100.
 A. H. Imlah, op. cit., Table 8.
 London and Cambridge Economic Service, *Bulletin*, Tables on 'External Trade'.

References

1. quoted in E. L. Woodward, *The Age of Reform, 1815–70*, Oxford, 1938, p. 199.
2. for this whole paragraph see H. S. Ferns, 'Britain's Informal Empire in Argentina, 1806–1914', *Past and Present*, No. 4, November 1953.
3. J. Gallagher and R. Robinson, 'The Imperialism of Free Trade', *Economic History Review*, Second Series, Vol. VI, 1953.
4. O. Macdonagh, 'The Anti-Imperialism of Free Trade', *Economic History Review*, April 1962.
5. In a letter to Lord Malmesbury, 13 August 1852.
6. C. A. Bodelsen, *Studies in Mid-Victorian Imperialism* (1923), Heinemann, 1960, p. 32, p. 13 ff. and pp. 63–7.
7. G. E. Mingay, 'The Size of Farms in the Eighteenth Century', *Economic History Review*, April 1962.
8. for whole paragraph see Brinley Thomas, *Migration and Economic Growth*, National Institute for Economic and Social Research, 1954.
9. E. L. Wooward, op. cit., p. 367, and see A. B. Keith, *Responsible Government in the Dominions*, Oxford, 1928, pp. 1159–64.
10. Sir J. Clapham, *An Economic History of Modern Britain*, Cambridge, 1937, Vol. II, p. 234 ff.
11. C. H. Feinstein, *Home and Foreign Investment, 1870–1913*, Department of Applied Economics, Cambridge, 1960.
12. W. W. Rostow, *The Stages of Economic Growth*, Cambridge, 1960, p. 109 ff., or Ritchie Calder, *The Inheritors*, Heinemann, 1961, pp. 265–6.
13. L. Dudley Stamp, *Our Developing World*, Faber, 1960, Tables XXV and XXVI.
14. Karl Marx, 'Future Results of British Rule in India', *New York Daily Tribune*, 8 August 1853; Lawrence and Wishart, 1959.
15. J. de Castro, *Geography of Hunger*, p. 89 and p. 155 ff.
16. I. Epstein, *Unfinished Revolution in China*, Bombay, 1947, pp. 24–7.
17. E. H. Norman, *Japan's Emergence as a Modern State*, New York, Institute of Pacific Relations, 1940.
18. V. Anstey, *Economic Development of India*, fourth ed., Longmans, 1952, p. 331.
19. ibid., p. 260 ff.
20. A. Loveday, *History and Economics of Indian Famines*, G. Bell, 1914.
21. D. H. Buchanan, *Development of Capitalist Enterprise in India*, pp. 36–7.
22. C. Issawi, *Egypt at Mid-Century*, Royal Institute of International Affairs, Oxford, 1954, Chapter III.
23. H. Herring, *History of Latin America*, Cape, 1954, Part XI.

24. A. H. Imlah, *Economic Elements in the Pax Britannica*, Harvard, 1958, p. 160.

25. W. G. Hoffmann, *British Industry, 1850–1950*, Blackwell, 1955, p. 38.

26. ibid., Table 54B, and see E. L. Woodward, op. cit., p. 581.

27. W. Schloete, *British Overseas Trade from 1700 to the 1930s*, Blackwell, 1952, Appendix, Table 9.

28. E. A. G. Robinson, 'The Changing Structure of the British Economy', *Economic Journal*, September 1954, pp. 459–60.

29. Sir J. Clapham, *An Economic History of Modern Britain*, Vol. II, p. 228.

30. W. Schloete, op. cit., p. 49, Table 10.

31. Sir T. Layton and G. Crowther, *An Introduction to the Study of Prices*, Macmillan, 1935, pp. 239–40.

32. E. A. G. Robinson, *United Kingdom Policy–Foreign, Economic, Political*, Royal Institute of International Affairs, 1950, p. 97.

33. E. A. G. Robinson, 'The Changing Structure of the British Economy'.

34. ibid.

35. W. Schloete, op. cit., for whole of preceding paragraph.

36. ibid., p. 74, Table 27.

37. C. H. Feinstein, op. cit., Table 2.13.

38. Karl Marx, 'Future Results of British Rule in India'.

39. W. J. Macpherson, 'Investment in Indian Railways, 1845–75', *Economic History Review*, December 1955.

40. ibid.

41. ibid.

42. C. H. Feinstein, op. cit., and see R. Wilson, *Capital Imports and the Terms of Trade*, Melbourne, 1931.

43. A. H. Imlah, op. cit., Chapter III.

44. ibid., Chapter VI.

45. E. A. G. Robinson, 'The Changing Structure of the British Economy', p. 449.

46. Sir J. Clapham, *An Economic History of Modern Britain*, Vol. II, p. 279.

47. E. A. G. Robinson, 'The Changing Structure of the British Economy', p. 448.

48. Sir J. Clapham, *An Economic History of Modern Britain*, Vol. II, p. 283.

49. R. C. K. Ensor, *England 1870–1914*, Oxford, 1936, pp. 116, 512.

50. E. A. G. Robinson, 'The Changing Structure of the British Economy', p. 451.

51. D. Ricardo, *Principles of Political Economy and Taxation*, Everyman Library, Chapter VII, p. 77 ff.

52. E. A. G. Robinson, 'The Changing Structure of the British Economy', p. 452; for opposite view see C. P. Kindleberger, *Economic Development*, New York, 1958, p. 246 ff.

53. H. W. Singer, 'The Distribution of Gains between Investing and Borrowing Countries', *American Economic Review*, XL (1950), p. 477.

54. D. J. Coppock, 'The Causes of the Great Depression, 1873–96,' *The Manchester School of Economic and Social Studies*, September 1961.

55. K. Martin and F. G. Thackeray, 'The Terms of Trade of Selected Countries, 1870–1938', *Oxford University Bulletin of Statistics*, November 1948.

56. for example, see R. C. Marris, 'The Purchasing Power of British Exports', *Economica*, February 1955.

57. A. H. Imlah, op. cit., Table 8.

58. W. Schloete, op. cit., pp. 77–9.

59. K. Martin and F. G. Thackeray, op. cit.

CHAPTER 3

Capitalism and Empire—
2 The Defeat of Protection: 1870–1913

This chapter is concerned with the response of British capitalism to the new situation that arose in the years after 1870, when Britain's monopoly as the world's workshop was successively challenged by the United States, and by Germany, France and other European powers. It has been widely argued from Hobson and Lenin to Stalin and Dutt that the British response was to fall back on developing protected markets in the empire for her overseas trade and investment, and that this was the pressure behind the great expansion of the area of the British Empire at the end of the nineteenth century. At the same time, according to this argument, while the home economy stagnated in this process, enough tribute was wrung from the colonies with which to bribe at least the leadership of the working class.

We have to consider how far this explanation fits the facts of Britain's expanding overseas trade and investment between 1870 and 1914. If it does not, then we must discover what was the pressure behind the great expansion of the empire after 1880 and of Britain's foreign investment right up to 1913. We shall, finally, have to consider why Joseph Chamberlain in fact failed in his plans to develop the British Empire as a more organic whole, and, above all, why he failed in his campaign against free trade and for a system of protection and imperial preference.

The Great Depression and British Industrial Decline

We have first to consider the effect of Britain's expanding overseas connections on the economy at home. We have suggested so far that capital investment, first in Europe and then overseas, expanded the markets for British exports, which acted as an important stimulus for growth at home. The very process of industrialising other lands, however, called forth new industrial competitors for Britain. In the long run, such a process might be expected to expand the whole level of world trade exchanges through ever widening markets and more extended division of labour. In the short run, while new industrial lands were developing their young industries, they were bound to protect themselves if they could against British goods. Had British industry become excessively export-oriented?

The year 1872 marked a peak in Britain's exports which was not to be reached again for eighteen years, a peak in manufactured exports which was not surpassed for thirty years. It may be argued that the 1872 level of exports was due to the exceptional circumstances of the Franco-Prussian war; but the fact is that 1873 heralded the Great Depression in Britain. The rate of growth of industrial output and of exports had already fallen in the 1860s from the heights of the 1850s, but the early 1870s showed a marked recovery. It was not maintained. Financial crises on the continent associated with company speculation in the Austro-Hungarian Empire and with the adoption of the gold standard by Germany led to a collapse of European markets.[1]

The raising of tariff walls to protect their own growing industries against British goods in Germany in 1879 and in Russia, France and Austria-Hungary in the following years perpetuated this initial decline.[2] At the same time, the United States, unified and strengthened after the civil war, had doubled her industrial output in a decade.[3] United States imports from Britain were rapidly cut down, falling from a fifth to a tenth share of Britain's foreign markets between the peaks of the 1850s and 1860s and the trough of the 1870s. Thereafter the share declined steadily further to little more than 6 per cent by the end of the century.[4] Britain's major markets had been in the United States and in Europe and these were now challenged by the development of American and German industry. Between 1880 and 1890 United States steel production overtook Britain's; within another decade German output also had surpassed ours.[5]

The 1880s saw some recovery. British exports renewed their upward trend, a steadily increasing proportion of them consisting of metal and engineering goods.[6] Shipbuilding was greatly expanded in the 1880s compared with the 1870s; and, although a greater proportion was for foreign owners – a fifth after 1880 compared with a tenth before – British shipowners held on to something like a half of the world's carrying trade.[7] In 1890 came a further check to expansion. The McKinley tariff in the U.S.A. only crowned the process of United States mastery that had been growing since the mid-1860s. Britain's exports hardly increased in the decade after 1890, while American exports leapt ahead and German exports advanced almost as quickly. Was Britain's failure to compete the result of the neglect of investments at home in the interest of supporting trade overseas?

Since they were faced by the challenge of new competitors to their position in established markets, especially in Europe and the United States, it seemed natural for British exporters to turn to new markets. Looking back with wisdom after the event, we may consider that the right approach would have been to look for new products to sell. British capitalists should, in other words, have accepted that textiles, coal and iron were no longer growth sectors and, from the immensely strong industrial foundations already laid, gone on to develop new technical inventions. These were just then opening up in a way that could have revolutionised industrial processes – in electricity, in chemicals, and in the use of the internal combustion engine. But this was not done, for various and important reasons. Before we examine these reasons, we have to remember that the crisis was, in part, concealed by the rise in living standards owing to the fall in import prices which continued until the end of the century, and to the increased productivity[8] which followed from the long-sustained high level of home investment up to the mid-1870s (see Table IV below).

The first explanation of the failure of British industry to maintain its technological advance after the mid-1870s is the continuous availability of cheap labour, especially from Ireland.[9] This led through low rates of wages to high rates of profit, and thus created the possibility for the essential accumulation of capital in the early years of industrialisation. Thereafter, however, so the argument goes, cheap labour became a drag on further technological progress. The American shortage of labour in relation to the great wealth of land and natural resources is cited as the contrasting case. America's rich resources were clearly as important as her labour shortage; and surplus labour did not prevent profits from falling in Britain, though the second explanation is to be found precisely in this fact. Despite the fall in raw-material costs, there was a real fall in the rate of profit after 1873, to which Feinstein has drawn attention. This was caused partly by failing overseas markets, but also by the increasing strength of working-class bargaining power. Real wages were kept up throughout the Great Depression.[10] A third factor was the continuing small scale and inflexible structure of manufacturing enterprises.

The establishment of limited liability after 1856 had little effect on family businesses. A decade followed before the beginnings of mergers and trade associations. The Salt Union, United Alkali, Brunner Mond, J. & P. Coats, Lever Bros. and Vickers, and the tobacco and cement company amalgamations all date from the Great Depression.[11] The overwhelming majority of firms continued to be small and highly specialised. A large measure of competition remained and only few enterprises had the resources, when profits declined, to undertake major new developments. Allied to the small size of production unit was a growing conservatism and lack of aggressive enterprise, as founders of firms were followed by sons and grandsons who had not the founder's know-how and moved in a world of finance that was increasingly remote from the actual processes of production.[12] The dogmatic adherence of governments to the principles of *laissez-faire* prevented any measures being taken by the state for encouragement of economic development. The lack of technical education in the country at large, and the lack of interest of entrepreneurs in science, all added to a general rigidity and inflexibility in the face of the need for structural changes.[13]

Overseas Investment and the Economy at Home

How important, then, was the remaining factor in Britain's failure to keep up with her new competitors in the last quarter of the nineteenth century: the attraction of capital into foreign investment and the steady rise in income from this source? After the early 1870s a large balance of payments surplus was achieved by virtue of the growing income from past investments (see Table II at end of Chapter 2). This surplus could be re-invested overseas if suitable openings presented themselves.

To this surplus was added, especially after the turn of the century, a considerable gain in funds for investment from multilateral settlements through India. The surplus in India's trade with the rest of the world rose in the latter half of the century from £4 million to £50 million. This second surplus was earned not with Britain, but with the U.S.A., western Europe and Japan from sales of cotton and jute, and later of textile manufactures also. At the same time, Britain continued to export more to India than she imported from India. British exporters found a market in India for textiles, sheet steel and other products that were being challenged in other markets. In addition to the direct-trade balance, Britain's balance of payments with India was augmented by receipts from the 'Home Charges' – for the British administration – and from interest on the Indian Government debt (which rose from £70 million to £225 million in the last quarter of the century). The resulting surplus had risen by 1910 to over £60 million.[14]

Thus not only the funds for investment in India itself but a large part of the total investment-income from overseas, that gave Britain her balance of payments surplus in the last quarter of the nineteenth century, was provided by India. India was in truth the jewel in the imperial diadem. The Koh-i-noor diamond was added to the imperial crown in 1850 and Victoria became Empress of India in 1857. 'Imperialism' may have been a vote-catching word for Disraeli, as Schumpeter insists;[15] in India, it was very much a reality supporting Britain's balance of payments.

The whole capital market of the City of London was, in fact, oriented towards foreign investment.[16] Loans to foreign governments were very profitable to the City merchant houses and carried a good rate of interest and a large measure of security for investors. Home industrial developments simply did not seem to have the same security as home and overseas government bonds. Security was what the growing class of rentiers wanted. There were failures from time to time and investors were frightened away from the foreign field, but this did not necessarily make them invest at home; and, if they did, it was not in industry but in building, in railways or in local government.[17] For there were even more frequent failures at home, particularly at the end of the 1870s. According to Shannon, insolvencies within five years of formation grew from 6.6 per cent of the companies formed in the period from 1856 to 1859 to 21.5 per cent of those

formed in 1878–80. The mortality rate of companies continued at the steady rate of over a third of those formed each
year.[18]

Not only was the financial mechanism of the City oriented
overseas, but state protection was increasingly given to
investors overseas rather than to home investment. It was the
other way round in Germany. An example of early measures
of state intervention to protect British holders of foreign
bonds had been the prompt action of the Governor of the
Bank of England, with the Chancellor of the Exchequer's
backing, when Barings, the merchant bankers who had been
adding heavily to the £150 million already invested in the
Argentine since the first trade agreements of the 1820s,
became over-committed in 1892 and nearly defaulted.[19]
State aid to guarantee foreign loans had for long before that
been built into the system in the loans to India.[20]

Overseas Investment and the Expansion of Empire

The advantage derived from foreign investment was
primarily the expansion of the market for Britain's traditional
exports, coal, iron and textiles especially. With rising competition in world markets and a growing stake in overseas
investment, it would not have been surprising if British
capitalists had once again begun to look to the empire.

But was this new interest in overseas investment in fact the
cause of the truly amazing expansion of the British Empire
after 1880, when some four million square miles, or twice the
whole area of the Indian empire, were added to its territory
in less than twenty years?[21] Those who have accepted this
view, from Hobson and Lenin onwards, have perpetuated
three major confusions: first, there has been a failure to
distinguish the original colonies (by 1870 the dominions)
from the dependencies such as India and the other territories
added after 1880. The main interest of imperialist thought in
the 1870s – the word imperialism was first commonly used

around 1840[22] – was in strengthening the ties of the dominions to the mother country. There was good reason for this, and this is the second confusion, for, while the growth of British overseas investment has been associated with the empire, in fact most of the investment took place outside the empire (see Table V below). There was a considerable growth of investment in the dominions, but little or none in the dependencies. The third confusion has arisen from supposing an inevitable connection between the expansion of empire and the protection of trade. Britain remained devoted to free trade until after the First World War.

What was at issue was precisely the defence of Britain's world-wide freedom to trade. When Britain's world monopoly was challenged, the actual control of territory became increasingly important, to anticipate the moves of rivals. Many quite separate reasons may be adduced for each step in the great expansion of the British Empire that took place after 1880: one may emphasise the protection of investments in Egypt, the opening-up of new sources of raw material in Malaya, the ambitions of speculators such as Rhodes, the concern of missionaries and travellers such as Livingstone, or the enthusiasm of local military commanders, as in Burma.

We may take as an example the annexation of Egypt in 1882, following a period of dual control with France. Disraeli had made the first moves in 1875 with the purchase of the Khedive's Suez Canal shares and the dispatch of Evelyn Baring, Lord Cromer, to Egypt as Consul-General. That the first decision was entirely Disraeli's is clear;[23] but what was his objective? It may be argued that it was to collect the debts of British bondholders in Egypt[24] or, on the contrary, that British investors were but the instrument of Disraeli's foreign and imperial policy.[25]

But by 1880 Gladstone had succeeded Disraeli. Faced by an Arab nationalist revolt, a Liberal Government bombarded Alexandria, occupied Egypt, estranged France and destroyed the Arabi Movement that might have brought Egypt into the modern world seventy-five years before Colonel Nasser. Payments on the British loans were maintained, but Gladstone refused to guarantee the 1885 Egyptian loan and the other European Powers moved in.[26] It is clear from Cromer's account[27] that, despite Gladstone's pacific warnings and hesitation, particularly in the Sudan, strategic considerations were paramount, particularly the maintenance against French or German penetration of overall control over the Nile valley and the life-line to India.

It may well be asked, as John Strachey does in his *The End of Empire*,[28] what the objective of the strategy was. Strachey's *simpliste* answer – that it was to retain the wealth of British investors – is surely inadequate. What was at issue was not only the route to India, but Britain's world-wide freedom to trade and invest wherever her traders and investors wished. Nevertheless, the direct investment interest in empire was well illustrated in the southern part of the continent of Africa. In 1870, diamonds were discovered at Kimberley and in 1886 gold at Witwatersrand. It was in part due to the personality of Cecil Rhodes, who made a fortune in diamonds which he applied to the mining of gold, that the British Empire expanded as it did in Africa.[29]

The 1870s had witnessed the Zulu wars and the purchase of the Gold Coast from the Dutch, followed by the Ashanti wars; the United Africa Company was established. The 1880s saw not only the discovery of gold at Witwatersrand but the foundation of the three great British companies in Africa: the Royal Niger in 1886, the British East Africa in 1888 and the British South Africa in 1889. To the first the empire owed what is now Nigeria, to the second Kenya and Uganda, and to the third, Rhodes's own company, Northern and Southern Rhodesia. Government support for the companies operating in Africa was assured by their charters, but to attribute great prescience to Gladstone or even to Disraeli in this matter would be to run far ahead of events. King Leopold II of the Belgians, who, with the help of H. M.

Stanley, the explorer, had founded what came to be the Belgian Congo in 1879, alone of Europe's statesmen would seem to have foreseen the importance of African development.[30]

Lord Salisbury, whose agreements in the 1890s with Germany, France and Portugal settled the map of Africa, saw the new continent largely as an element in the central picture of European diplomacy, and of importance for strategic reasons rather than for any direct local interest.[31] There is no reason to dissent from his judgement, so long as we clearly understand the purpose of the strategy, which was the overriding general interest that as much as possible of the world should be kept open to the British principle of free trade. This interest found its fullest expression in the national preoccupation with the strength of the navy and of strategic bases. The Union Jack was planted on an endless succession of islands in the 1880s, stretching right across the Pacific and Indian Oceans to the Persian Gulf and Cyprus in the Mediterranean. In every decade after 1880 a new class of battleship was launched which made all existing vessels obsolete. The 'Admirals' of the 'eighties were followed by the 'Magnificents' of the 'nineties, and they in turn by the 'Dreadnoughts' of the 1900s.[32]

The aims of a man like Rhodes, however, were quite clear. These were to obtain mining concessions for Britain against French and Portuguese prospectors, and for his company, the British South African, against all competitors. The strength of de Beers, the firm he founded in the diamond business, has always been in its monopoly of the market. The concessions which he obtained for the British South African Company throughout the Rhodesias gave him the monopoly of all mining in the territory, from which the company still draws royalties today. The protection which the British Government offered to tribal chiefs in Africa in the last decade of the century was in all cases in exchange for mineral rights.[33] As time went on and the new century dawned, the protection of interests and markets entered more and more into contemporary British thought, reaching a climax in Chamberlain's campaign against free trade. But the issue was, from an early date, confused by the arguments which Rhodes and others used to win state support for their private enterprises. The validity of these arguments has been far too easily accepted ever since by imperialists and anti-imperialists alike. Lenin gave especial fame to W. T. Stead's report of Rhodes's statement after a visit to a meeting of unemployed in the East End of London in 1882: 'In order to save the 40 million inhabitants of the United Kingdom from a bloody civil war, we colonial statesmen must acquire new lands to settle the surplus population, to provide new markets for the goods produced by them in the factories and mines.'[34] Lands for settlement of the unemployed, and markets for British goods – these were the explicit aims of the imperialists such as Rhodes. How far were they genuine? Markets were certainly a real problem in the 1890s, with the raising of tariff barriers and the competition of Germany and U.S.A.

The growth of population must at that time have seemed equally threatening. We know now that only another quarter were to be added to the population of Britain in the sixty-five years after 1895, but in the previous sixty-five years the number had doubled. The turning-point was 1870, when the birth rate was at its peak of over 35 per thousand; from this time it declined steadily and consistently until the early 1940s, when it was only just over 14 per thousand.[35] The prosecution of Bradlaugh and Mrs Besant in 1877 for publishing their Malthusian pamphlet advertised birth control for the first time; but in the 1890s it was too early for anyone to tell that it was having an effect.[36] In the 1880s, the flood of emigration to America reached a new peak. After 1895, the flow was reduced by the check to economic growth in the U.S. and the simultaneous recovery at home.[37]

No wonder statesmen looked round for new outlets, but

interest in the colonies as fields for emigration was of long standing. Rhodes was saying nothing new. Rhodes, moreover, knew very well that the greater part of the lands brought under British rule in Africa was desert, scrub or tropical jungle unsuitable for emigration, and that the markets offered by the tribal Africans were extremely limited. Yet Rhodes succeeded in winning the support not only of the City of London but of the Government also for his dreams of a British Africa from the Cape to Cairo. How did he do it? The answer lies partly in the interests of certain City investors, partly in the personality of Joseph Chamberlain and the interests he represented, partly in the British imperial tradition. Nevertheless, apart from Rhodes and Africa, Chamberlain was singularly unsuccessful in his campaigns for imperial unity and for protection. We shall take up this part of the story later, but we must bear this fact in mind in examining the drive to empire at the end of the nineteenth century.

Hobson's View of Investment as the Drive to Empire

We must consider first in more detail the varied drives to empire. As a starting-point, we may note that, in 1879 at the Trade Union Congress held in Edinburgh, James Bradshaw of Manchester moved and carried a resolution that the trade unions should invest in the proposed African Corporation.[38] Rhodes's arguments had proved telling enough to convince trade unionists that in Africa lay the remedy for depression in England. Imperialist sentiment had shown itself in the working-class press in the early 1870s.[39] By the 1880s, the British working man had won the vote and universal education. Parliamentary democracy involved the two great parties in the state in widening their appeal to the whole nation. Not all the workers followed the imperialists. Socialist agitation was growing among the working class, some of it Marxist-led, and the dock strike of 1889 started the organisation of unskilled workers into unions.[40] Disraeli had been the first to see clearly that the Liberal Party's appeal to trade unionists could best be countered by a mixture of social reform and imperialism.[41]

The responsibilities of empire were given new emphasis by Social-Darwinist ideas. It was only too easy for the popular press, founded at this time to cater for the new literate public, to popularise these ideas in the gospel of the 'white man's burden' and of Britain's divine mission to bring order and Christian faith to those 'lesser breeds without the law'.[42] The last decade of the nineteenth century witnessed that outburst of imperialist jingoism in which Kipling's voice was the most distinguished. There can be no doubting the popular pressure behind government support for the proconsuls, missionaries, traders, soldiers and speculators who were carving up the African continent and other lands besides. Was the long imperialist tradition, with its implications of unlimited opportunity for the adventurers and reflected glory for the stay-at-homes, the main pressure behind the expansion of empire? Or was direct economic pressure more important? If so, we must be sure about its sources.

In 1902, Hobson published his attack on Imperialism. By the end of the Boer War, a more critical note was once more being sounded in the public estimation of empire. The war had been costly in men and money, and rather shaming, not only in the successive defeats suffered by the British forces, but in the manner of final victory, with its herding of women and children into concentration camps. Hobson's aim was to expose the 'economic taproot of Imperialism' in the 'failure of consumption to keep up with the growing powers of production'.[43] Lack of investment opportunities at home drove capital abroad and imperial rule followed to protect the capital, he argued. Hobson's 'under-consumptionist' analysis we shall correct in a moment, but his association of the drive to empire with overseas investment also needs correction.

Hobson pointed to the facts: the new territories added to the empire in the previous fifteen years were unsuitable for emigration and poor markets for English manufactures. They could be of no interest to the British people; but, he averred, they were of great value to those with capital to invest in gold and other mining enterprises, and to those who officered and provisioned the whole imperial apparatus of colonial government and armed services. The cost of this apparatus was rising and was quite excessive in relation to the annual value of Britain's foreign trade. It was time to pull back to 'Little England', and to raise the standard of consumption at home.

The appeal fell mainly on deaf ears, although Campbell-Bannerman, the Liberal leader, was interested.[44] Events certainly seemed to confirm Hobson's analysis. After the brief home-investment boom in the last years of the century there followed a further decline at home and, at the same time, a spectacular rise in investment overseas which continued almost without break from 1902 to 1915 (see Table IV below). By 1913, the annual investment overseas exceeded investment at home and the total of British capital held abroad may have equalled a third, and was certainly more than a quarter, of all the holdings of British investors.[45] The reasons for this orientation towards overseas investment we have already examined. There can be no doubt that the openings for capital overseas kept up the rate of return on capital when the rate was declining at home. But the connection between the investment and the empire is far from clear.

The fact is that there was little or no increase in the proportion of foreign investment directed towards the empire after the great additions to its territory in the 1880s (see Table V below). The main increase in empire investment actually took place during the 1880s, in Australia and Canada. After 1890, apart from the investment boom in South Africa, the main flow of investment continued to be to the independent and developing lands of North America, Oceania and Europe. In the great boom of British investment between 1900 and 1913, the United States and Canada each took a fifth, Argentina took a tenth, the rest of Latin America another sixth; that is, the American hemisphere took two-thirds of the total. Europe took just under a tenth, Africa and Asia each an eighth (Table V). It might be argued that the Latin American lands were virtual colonies, but the important fact was that the new British colonial possessions in Asia and Africa, with the outstanding exception of South Africa, hardly received any capital for their development at all in this period, not 5 per cent of the total.

It is also clear that there was little or no increase in the empire share of British trade after the 1880s (see Table V). Hobson saw this point only too clearly. About a third of all exports of home products continued to go to the empire – a not dissimilar value of goods to that imported, owing to the large annual excess of imports over exports. The main increase in Britain's exports after 1904 was to agrarian countries in Europe, such as Russia, which were beginning to industrialise, to Japan which was doing the same, and to Latin America. Nevertheless, Table VII below shows that half of Britain's exports of iron and steel did go to empire countries and nearly half of the old staple export of textiles. Textile exports had fallen by 1913, however, to a mere third of all the goods exported. Metal and engineering exports had by then risen to over a quarter of the total, but Britain was already falling steadily behind Germany and the U.S.A. in this most dynamic sector of world trade, and in spite of the high level of British capital exports.[46]

The most interesting feature of Table V is the extreme sluggishness with which an expansion of exports followed the growth of investment in the Dominions and in South America. Only in Africa, where the proportion of the total was very small indeed (1 per cent to 2 per cent), was the rise in investment followed by a sharp rise in exports. At the same time, the Table shows the maintenance of British exports to Europe despite the decline of British investment there. Only in the U.S.A. did the declining share of British exports run fairly steadily in line with the declining share of investment. This is not, of course, to say that overseas investment did not aid British exports. The volume of exports doubled between 1880 and 1913, and it seems hardly likely that this would have happened without the corresponding doubling of overseas investment.

The main feature of this period is clearly shown, however, not to have been any considerable growth of investment and exports in the dependent empire, but the continued industrialisation of the lands of Europe and of European settlers overseas. Investment and empire were not so closely connected as Hobson thought. Hobson was, not surprisingly, blinded by the single glaring case of Rhodes and South Africa to make a general analysis that did not apply elsewhere. His error was perpetuated by Marxist writers like Hilferding and Bukharin and, above all, by Lenin.[47]

Lenin's 'Imperialism' Examined

Writing fourteen years after Hobson, Lenin had witnessed a great sharpening of imperialist rivalry ending in world war. He rejected Hobson's under-consumptionist theory, but replaced it with the theory of the natural expansionism of the great and growing monopolies,[48] a theory which equally supported Hobson's insistence on investment as the root of empire-building.* But he was certainly echoing Hobson when he declared that 'the necessity for exporting capital

* John Strachey in his *The End of Empire* accepts something near to the Hobson analysis and argues from it that the welfare state of today has ended the era of imperialism.[49]

arises from the fact that in a few countries capitalism has become "over-ripe" and owing to the backward state of agriculture and *the impoverished state of the masses*, capital cannot find "profitable" investment'.[50]*

Lenin defined imperialism precisely as 'capitalism in its highest stage'; and the grab for territory leading to inter-necine war between the capitalist powers in the years leading up to 1916, when he wrote his book, certainly seemed to justify the definition. The cause of this drive to empire of fully developed capitalism Lenin saw in the continuous development of capitalism towards monopoly, first at home and then in world markets, and the simultaneous increasing centralisation of capital in the hands of financiers with enormous power in both commerce and industry. Having won a near monopoly of the home market, finance capital had still to solve the problem of foreign competition.

Moreover, given the Marxist analysis of crisis in the cycle of reproduction, it seemed clear to Lenin that it was capita-lism's tendency for the capacity to produce to run ahead of the capacity to consume that was forcing capital to look over-seas for profitable investments. Investment in colonies, where capital was scarce and labour cheap, kept up the rate of profit by the addition of 'super-profit' from the exploita-tion of colonial workers.[51]

By rejecting Hobson's under-consumptionism and em-phasising what he called the 'over-ripeness' – that is the high organic composition of capital – of the lands rich in capital as the cause of falling profits, Lenin escaped from the con-tradiction that Hobson was involved in. Profits were sup-posed to be declining at home, according to Hobson, because of the impoverishment of the masses at home, while super-profits were to be earned overseas through the still greater impoverishment of the masses overseas. But Lenin still accepted Hobson's argument that falling profits were the economic force behind the drive to empire. At the same time,

* My emphasis. M.B.B.

he wanted to find a source in colonial exploitation for the corruption of the working class at home. He found the link, he thought, in overseas investment income.[52] We may consider the three elements in Lenin's argument separately: the falling rate of profit at home, the outward drive of monopoly, and colonial exploitation and the investment income.

Lenin's analysis of imperialism was based on what has been called a 'composite picture' of imperialism,* into which he drew separate elements from German, French, British and United States economic developments. It was not the result of the analysis of general tendencies to be found in all capitalist economies. The composite picture thus breaks down on examination, but from it Lenin was able brilliantly to foretell what was to come. The composite picture was to fit Britain in the 1920s, and the U.S.A. in the 1950s, far better than it fitted Britain or Germany or the U.S.A. before 1913.

Lenin's picture of the great monopolies, increasingly subordinated to finance capital pressing outwards to invest their surplus funds and using the flag to bring markets for capital and goods under their direct control, was based upon what he knew of German capitalism. The description undoubtedly fits German pressure after 1900 in Africa and down the Berlin-Baghdad railway line.[53] It does not fit the British situation.

In the first place, monopoly and finance capital were not as fully developed nor as interconnected in Britain before 1913 as they were in Germany and on the continent.[54]

Further, British overseas investment was, at that time, investment by rentiers mainly in rails and in government stocks, and not investment by imperial companies in overseas operations (Table VIII, Chapter 4).

Third, and most important, British industry still regarded the whole world as its market for goods and capital, and relied on free trade and the navy to hold what it already had.

Fourth, it was precisely to the developing industrial lands

* I am indebted to John Hughes for the phrase.

of North America and Europe, and not to the new colonies, that British investors were attracted (Table V).

Fifth, the export of capital did certainly help to maintain the rate of profit, which showed signs of sagging in the years after the mid-1870s;[55] but it was not colonial 'super-profit' that did the trick.

Nevertheless, British moves in Africa and elsewhere may rightly be seen as a reaction to the challenge of German and American capitalists to Britain's dominant position as *the* world power. To emphasise the overall interests of British capitalism is not to replace economic by political explanations for the expansion of empire, as some writers have done,[56] but rather to show the political as arising out of the total economic interest. Power, prestige and security were aims which reflected Britain's basic economic interest in world free trade.

Lenin saw the crisis of capitalist reproduction as forcing capital overseas, but he saw the stagnation of the metropolitan power as the result of the subsequent dependence on super-profit. We suggested earlier, however, that the low level of home investment was largely due to the constant supply of cheap labour, the small scale of industrial enterprises, the inflexibility of entrepreneurs, dogmatic *laissez-faire*, neglect of technical education, etc. The diversion of capital into foreign investment was then as much a result as the cause of stagnation at home. Moreover, there was a rise and fall in the total rate of investment between 1870 and 1913, as well as an inverse movement in the home and overseas shares of the total (see Table IV).[57]

What is at issue is Marx's critique of British capitalism in the 1860s and 1870s, which Lenin applied to the developments of the next forty years. To explain the rise and fall of investment at home and overseas would involve a full-scale study of the trade cycle in the last hundred years; no such attempt will be made here, although more will be said on the subject later. What may be said here is that, whatever the evidence may be for the long-term falling rate of profit, which Marx postulated,[58] because of the growing plethora of fixed capital, we do not need to doubt that rates of profit at home were falling in the last quarter of the nineteenth century.

The falling rate of profit was a fact in the late 1870s,[59] and in pointing to other institutional factors that held back investment at home, we have not excluded the possibility that the main factor was a structural fault in capitalism itself. What we do have to deny is that investors turned primarily to the colonies for higher rates of profit or that the investors were primarily monopolists seeking guaranteed overseas markets. The very special historic role of the British merchant bankers and their control over the London capital market certainly did encourage the export of capital, and Britain's long imperial history certainly did lead to a growing interest in the empire. But colonial exploitation must be said to have supplied a very small part of Britain's growing wealth. It is true that, by 1913, nearly a tenth of the national income was accounted for by payments received from overseas investments (see Table IV) and this formed perhaps a quarter of all property incomes.[60] Only about a sixth of this could, however, be said to come from India and the other dependent colonies; the very much greater part came, as we have seen (Table V), from the other developing industrial lands, the United States, European countries and the independent British dominions.

How far, nevertheless, did this overseas investment advance or retard Britain's economic development? The best explanation seems to be the one we accepted in the period before 1870, that the overseas investment did aid the economy at home in so far as it aided real development overseas.[61] Far from exploiting the newly developed lands of Canada and Australia, as well as the U.S.A. and Europe, British capital enabled them to lay the foundations of their industrialisation, and thus created markets for British goods, and cheaper sources of food and raw materials. The empire then did help the British economy, not through exploitation of the colonies, but through economic development of the dominions. Rising exports, especially after 1890, provided a strong growth factor for the home economy.[62]

At the same time, there can be little doubt that the success of British sales in these markets of traditional exports – especially iron and textiles – did much to hold back the development of new industries in Britain.[63] Again, it must be emphasised that it was not only, or even mainly, empire markets that were involved. In the case of textiles, empire trade, and especially Indian trade, certainly helped to keep up the share of cotton piece-goods in total British exports, but iron and steel exports to the empire never rose much above 4 per cent of total exports (see Table VII). What is true is that the re-export of mainly empire products played an important part in assuring Britain's trade surplus (see Table VII).

This leads us to the final aspect of Lenin's analysis which we must consider. Lenin saw the 'imperial tribute' as in its turn enabling the capitalists to bribe a section of the workers and thus put off the day of revolution.[64] When the colonial workers refused their 'tribute', the moment of truth for a, by then, moribund and parasitic capitalism would be at hand. (Granted that investment income was not primarily colonial in origin, the correlation between tribute and working-class corruption is far from clear.)

Marx had always insisted that it was foreign trade and Britain's predominant share of it that provided super-profits.[65] His view, however, was a gloomy one of increasing misery for the workers from the system, despite the fact that he saw quite clearly that there was no reason why the capitalists should retain the whole of the extra profit, if the trade unions fought for some part of it.[66] It was Engels who seized on the idea that an aristocracy of labour gained.[67] That there did arise a growing differential among workers' incomes is clear from Hobsbawm's work on the labour aristocracy in the nineteenth century.[68] On the other hand, there is evidence of a similar process of growing differentials especially for white-collar and skilled workers in other industrial countries, in Scandinavia, for example, where empire and overseas investment were absent.[69]

Furthermore, it was just in the years before 1914, when the 'tribute' reached its peak, that working-class militancy was at its highest. The years between 1911 and 1914 were marked by an unprecedented wave of strike-action and by increasing unity in the Socialist movement with the growth of trade-union membership from 2.5 to 4 million.[70] The workers were more concerned about stagnation in industry at home than about the source of the rentiers' income abroad.

It was true, however, that the long history of empire had assured to British nationalism a strength which class-consciousness could not divide. Given the latent jingoism and arrogance of the British people, which the new popular press was able to evoke, and the gains already won from rising productivity at home and from investment overseas, it was hardly necessary to offer bribes. Chauvinism easily asserted itself over international working-class solidarity in 1914. The interests of the nation appeared to all but a tiny minority to be one, for rich and poor, for worker and investor. The British situation can be most clearly studied in relation to Joseph Chamberlain's imperial campaign.

The Role of Joseph Chamberlain

It was, as we have seen, in the critical decline of trade after 1890 that the thoughts of British statesmen had begun to turn more and more towards the empire. The first Conference of Empire Prime Ministers had been held during the Jubilee in 1887 at the suggestion of the Imperial Federation League. The League had been created by J. R. Seeley and J. A. Froude with W. E. Forster as its chairman and included among its supporters Lord Rosebery and James Bryce from

the Liberals and W. H. Smith from the Tories. But neither
the League nor the conference was able to agree on any
positive policy for uniting the empire.[71] There was a real
clash here between the Liberal imperialists, who looked back
to the world-wide empire of free-trade and banking, and the
Conservatives, reinforced after 1886 by the Duke of Devonshire and the Whig landlords as well as by Chamberlain's
Liberal Unionists, who were beginning to look forward to a
narrower, but more privileged and protected, empire of the
dominions and colonies which flew the British flag.

The first imperial conference, however, set a precedent for
other meetings, which were to provide a forum for the
tremendous efforts which Joseph Chamberlain made, as
Colonial Secretary from 1895 to 1903, to strengthen the
imperial connection. Chamberlain's aims were to unite the
empire closer together in a consultative Council of Empire,
to bring under common command the naval and military
strength of the empire and to expand empire trade by a
system of imperial preferences. He failed in all three, but his
attempt reflected a part of the pressures behind the empire-
building of the late nineteenth century.

In 1868, Bismarck wrote to von Roon that: 'All the
advantages claimed for the Mother Country are for the most
part illusions. England is abandoning her colonial policy;
she finds it too costly.' [72] Within fifteen years Chamberlain
was sounding a new note. 'Is there any man in his senses,' he
said in 1884, 'who believes that the crowded population of
these islands could exist for a single day if it were to cut adrift
from us the great dependencies, which now look to us for
protection and assistance and which are the natural outlets
for our trade?'[73] What had supervened was the crisis of the
1870s. Less was heard of 'the great dependencies' during the
recovery of the 1880s, but after 1890 interest revived. A
wave of imperialism swept through the country with the
news of the Matabele wars (1893–95) and the British advance
across the continent of Africa.[74] This played some part in the

return of a Conservative Government in the election of 1895 and in Chamberlain's unexpected choice of the Colonial Office.[75]

For a decade after 1895, Joseph Chamberlain dominated the political scene, Salisbury and then Balfour allowing him 'usually the power of a co-Premier and on some rare occasions more'.[76] Chamberlain was nearly sixty when he entered the Colonial Office, with a fortune solidly built in the manufacture of screws, with a 'terrific socialist'[77] reputation in municipal enterprise and a parliamentary career as a radical and liberal until he, and so many others like him, broke with Gladstone over Home Rule for Ireland. His interest in the empire was direct. In 1882 he was one of the initial subscribers for shares in the Royal Niger Company. For him, commerce was 'that greatest of all political interests'.[78] As the new Colonial Secretary, he said in the House of Commons in the summer of 1895, 'I regard many of our colonies as being in the condition of undeveloped estates, and estates which can never be developed without imperial assistance.'[79] Two days later he added, to a deputation on West African railways, '. . . and it is only in such a policy of development that I can see any solution to those great social problems by which we are surrounded.'[80]

The test came at the turn of the century. In 1898, South Africa yielded £15 million worth of gold. Mining for gold in the deep rock of the Rand was not 'easy money', like diamond prospecting. It had required heavy British investment of capital and needed large supplies of cheap labour.[81] The threat of the Boer farmers to the security of tenure of those they called the 'Uitlanders' in Johannesburg had to be resisted, if the capital already invested in the mines was to be protected. Rhodes, who had close contact with Chamberlain, had no difficulty in involving the British Army in that most humiliating and despicable of all colonial wars, the Boer War. Whatever Rhodes might say in line with Chamberlain about the empire as a bread-and-butter question, it was the defence of private investment that was involved here, as Hobson so clearly saw.[82]

The Campaign against Free Trade

As the twentieth century opened, a powerful movement arose among certain British industrialists for imperial protection and tariff reform. Again it was Joseph Chamberlain who took the lead. The 1902 Imperial Conference was his great opportunity. The colonies had been united in action with the mother country over the Boer War. Chamberlain appealed to the colonial premiers for assistance with the cost of imperial defence: 'The weary Titan staggers under the too vast orb of its fate,' were his words.[83] They turned him down, but he got a resolution in favour of imperial trade preference. Within a year, he had left the cabinet to campaign for tariff reform as the way forward to imperial unity, but not before he had given the Johannesburg Chamber of Mines, now desperate to lower their wage costs, the go-ahead to import indentured labourers from Hong Kong, if the Transvaal legislative council voted for it. They did, thanks to wholesale bribery; and the storm of protest that this raised in England fell upon the shoulders of Chamberlain's successor.[84]

Chamberlain easily gathered strong supporters for his Tariff Reform League, to end Britain's sixty-year-old adherence to the principles of free trade. It is important to note who they were: the great landlords, ever faithful to protection for Britain's agriculture increasingly squeezed by imports from America; the leaders of heavy industry – mainly in steel – including the Chairmen of Armstrong-Whitworth, Vickers, Bessemer and Guest Keen, who were faced by German 'dumping' and severe American competition; finally Hewins the Director of the London School of Economics, and Charles Booth. Against Chamberlain were ranged the Liberals in all their fury, the cotton industry, the coal miners, the shipbuilding and engineering employers, who enjoyed the advantage of cheap German steel, the economists, including Marshall, Pigou and Clapham, and the Trade Union Congress.[85] In the end, the leaders of the Tory Party, too, turned solidly against Chamberlain, but they were nonetheless overwhelmed in the 1906 General Election. Why did Chamberlain fail? Why did he never impress the City of London? Why did the great industrialists not get what they wanted?

The fact is that industrialists were divided. Monopoly exporting from behind protective walls by its very nature aids only the monopolists. And these were not yet predominant in the Britain of the early twentieth century. The remaining industrialists believed in, and really gained from, free trade and the kind of overseas investment that was then in fact expanding markets in the lands of European settlement. They even gained from the exports of German and American monopolists, whose 'dumping' of cheap steel – forgings as well as plates and girders – actually reduced their costs.[86]

Marx, we saw earlier, had insisted from the 1840s onwards that free trade, and not protection, was of the essence of capitalism;[87] and Schumpeter, taking up the point, argued against Lenin that this was as true of the later stages of capitalism as of the earlier.[88] We shall have to consider this further when examining the inter-war period; but we may agree here that it was certainly true for the most advanced capitalist power; which Britain remained until 1913. Schumpeter's argument may well, however, be relevant to Germany before the First World War. All young industries absolutely need protection, as we saw when Britain was industrialising at the end of the eighteenth century. Without protection, infant industries cannot grow at all, as English manufacturers in the seventeenth century had already recognised before J. S. Mill gave the principle his authority;[89] but, once established, capitalism needs free trade for its fullest development.

The demand for protection continues to be made, however, by the monopolists who have established themselves behind protective walls, although the result may do actual harm to the economy as a whole and even to the protected industry, by protecting inefficiency and high costs. Chamberlain could see only the success and the challenge of Germany, and associated it with her protective-monopoly structure; but the success derived rather from the excellence of Germany's educational system than from the system of protection.[90]

What defeated Chamberlain in the last analysis was the City of London, which still dominated the British economy,[91] and whose wealth did not derive any longer from manufacturing industry by the time of the first decade of the twentieth century. It derived from the issue and promotion and management of foreign loans, from brokerage and insurance, from the issue of bills to finance trade throughout the whole world. Re-exports to Europe of colonial products through the London markets were growing once more, to equal more than a fifth of the value of home-produced exports by 1910–13. Shipping earned another fifth (Table XIV, Chapter 8). Coal made up a tenth of all exports (Table VII, below). Investment income from past overseas investments was rising year by year from £100 million in 1900 to £170 million in 1910 (Table IV, below). It was all these items, far greater than steel or engineering exports, that the City relied on for financing the further capital exports that actually exceeded £220 million in 1913 (Table II, Chapter 2).

The City merchant bankers who were engaged in overseas finance not only dominated the economy; even more surely they dominated Government circles. Sir Ernest Cassel was Edward VII's confidant.[92] Evelyn Baring was Consul-General in Egypt and might, had he wished, have been Foreign Secretary in 1905.[93] Two Chancellors of the Exchequer – Goschen and McKenna – were merchant bankers. Lord Rosebery married a Rothschild, and Hobson in his book on imperialism asks rhetorically whether 'a great war could

be undertaken by any European state, or a great loan sub-
scribed, if the house of Rothschild and its connections set
their face against it.'[94] Chamberlain and his friends from the
Midlands were still comparatively small beer. Another
twenty years were to pass before they would provide the
country's Prime Minister, who should introduce the tariff
reform and imperial preference for which they campaigned.

Keynes, in his essay on *The Economic Consequences of the
Peace,* emphasised the now almost unrecognisable 'inter-
nationalisation of the economy' prior to the First World
War.[95] British finance had then no need to cultivate the
restricted field of the empire, when the whole world was still
open to it, when the London capital market was prepon-
derant and when sterling was the equivalent of gold. The
value of the empire was not so much the privileged position
it gave to British manufacturers or investors – India was the
main example of this – but the strategic position it conferred
in world power-politics over against Britain's German and
American rivals. They too were pushing outwards in the
first decade of our century, America realising her 'manifest
destiny' under President Theodore Roosevelt in the remains
of the Spanish Empire, Germany pressing eastwards along
the Berlin-Baghdad line. What drove them was the need not
merely for markets and sources of raw materials, and profitable investment opportunities, but the need to challenge
Britain's domination of governments and their economic
activities, not in the empire only but in the world as a whole.

TABLE IV

GROWTH OF NATIONAL INCOME IN BRITAIN AND RELATIONSHIP OF TRADE AND INVESTMENT, 1865–1961

Year	Real National Income Index 1890–99 prices	Real National Income Index 1913 = 100	Actual Net National Income (Current Prices) (£m.)	Relationship to National Income in each year (%)				Gross (net) Investment Income from Overseas
				Investment Home (net)	Investment Foreign (net)	Trade Imports (c.i.f.)	Trade Exports (f.o.b.)	
1865–69	47	35	840	6·2	4·5	35	21	3·3
1870–74	52		1,060	6·4	6·8	33	22	4·5
1875–79	55	47	1,075	7·7	2·3	35	19	4·4
1880–84	61		1,120	5·7	4·8	37	21	4·75
1885–89	70	60	1,210	3·8	7·2	31	19	6·35
1890–94	75		1,350	4·2	4·7	31	17	5·7
1895–99	86	77	1,560	5·9	2·7	29	15	6·2
1900–04	87		1,720	8·2	2·2	31	17	6·3
1905–09	93	87	1,880	5·2	6·7	32	20	7·5
1910–13	100	92	2,120	4·1	9·3	33	22	8·6
1920–24		100	4,430	5	2·3	29	18	4·3
1925–29		109	4,160	7	1·6	30	17	5·5
1930–34		116	3,850	5	−0·7	21	11	4·3
1935–39		136	4,710	6[1]	−1·3	19	10	3·9

TABLE IV (contd.)

Year	Real National Income Index 1890–99 prices 1913 = 100	Actual Net National Income (Current Prices) (£m.)	Relationship to National Income in each year (%)				Gross (net) Investment Income from Overseas
			Investment		Trade		
			Home (net)	Foreign (net)	Imports (c.i.f.)	Exports (f.o.b.)	
1946–49	144	9,310	6[2]	1·2[2][3]	23[2]	18[2]	3·7 (1·7 net)
1950–54	162	13,100	6·8	0·8	25	19	4·0 (1·6 net)
1955–59	183	18,000	8·5	1·0[4]	21	18	3·8 (1·3 net)
1960–61	195	21,000	10·0	−1·0	21	17	3·3 (1·2 net)

Notes: 1 = 1938 only

2 = 1948–49 only

3 = Foreign Investment almost entirely offset by capital grants from Overseas Governments

4 = Outward flow of £400m. less inward flow of £200m.

Sources: Figures prior to 1939 from:
J. B. Jeffreys and D. Walters, 'National Income and Expenditure of U.K., 1870–1952', *Income and Wealth Series V* (1955) (London: Bowes and Bowes, 1955), p. 38.
W. Schloete, *British Overseas Trade from 1700 to the 1930s* (Oxford: Blackwell, 1952), Table 10.

C. Feinstein, *British Home and Foreign Investment, 1870–1913* (Cambridge: Cambridge Univ. Press, 1960).

Figures after 1946 from:

H.M. Treasury, *Balance of Payments, 1945–57* (London: H.M.S.O., 1958).
H.M. Treasury, *Balance of Payments, 1958–60* (London: H.M.S.O., 1961).
London and Cambridge Economic Service, *Bulletin*, Tables on 'External Trade'.
H.M. Statistical Office, *Annual Abstract of Statistics* for 1952 and 1961 (London: H.M.S.O., 1953 and 1962).

TABLE V

GEOGRAPHICAL DISTRIBUTION OF BRITISH OVERSEAS TRADE AND INVESTMENT, 1860s–1930s

Years	1860–70		1881–90		1901–10		1911–13		1927–29		1933–35
Area	Exports (%)	Invest-ment (%)	Exports (%)	Invest-ment (%)	Exports (%)	Invest-ment (%)	Exports (%)	Invest-ment (%)	Exports (%)	Invest-ment (%)	Exports (%)
Total Empire	32	36	34	47	34	47	36	46	42	59	43
Of which Dominions	12	12	16	29	17	30	18	30	20	37·5	22
India	11	21	11	15	12	12	11·5	10·5	11	14	9
Africa (ex. S. Africa)	1	—	1	0·5	2	2·5	2	2·5	3	2	3·5
Europe	39	25	36	8	36	5	36	6	34	8	38
S. America	12	10·5	11	20	10·5	21	12	22	11	22	9
U.S.A.	13	27	14	22	9	21	9	19	7	5·5	6
Other	4	3·5	5	3	10·5	6	7	7	6	5·5	4
Total	100	100	100	100	100	100	100	100	100	100	100
in £m.	144	770	230	2,040	333	3,770	474	4,415	720	4,000	407

Notes: Export figures are averages over the decade or period.
Investment figures are totals at the last year of decade or period, except for 1927–29 where figures given are for 1930.

Sources: W. Schloete, op. cit, for export shares.
C. Feinstein, op. cit, for investment 1860s–193.
R.I.I.A., *The Problem of International Investment* (London: Oxford Univ. Press, 1937), pp. 186–7, for investment in 1930.

TABLE VI
VOLUME OF BRITAIN'S TRADE AND EMPIRE SHARE IN IT, 1850s–1960s

Year	IMPORTS Volume (1913 = 100)	IMPORTS Shares (%) Old Dominions	IMPORTS Shares (%) Other Empire	EXPORTS Volume (1913 = 100)	EXPORTS Shares (%) Old Dominions	EXPORTS Shares (%) Other Empire	CAPITAL EXPORTS Volume[4] (1913 = 100)	CAPITAL EXPORTS Share to[5] Empire (%)
1850–59	17·5	8	16	21	14	18	—	—
1860–69	26	7·5	18·5	27·5	12	19	14	37
1870–79	40	9	13	40	13	16	20	42
1880–89	57·5	10·5	12·5	55	15·5	18·5	38	47
1890–99	70	12	10	59·5	15·5	17·5	31	50
1900–09	85	13	10	73	16	18	42	47
1910–13	95	13	12	94	18	18	91	46
1914–19	83	16	13	62	15·5	17	—	—
1920–24	93	17	10	70	16·5	20·5	18	—
1925–29	103	16	12	75	20	22	17	57
1930–34	105	19	12	53	20	22	—	—
1935–39[2]	111	22(9)[1]	17·5	60	24(5)[1]	25	—	50
1940–45[2]	80	20·5(16)[1]	17·5	45	33(10)[1]	22·5	—	—
1946–49[2]	87	26(10·5)[1]	22	72	26(5)[1]	31·5	—	65
1950–54[2]	104	23(8)[1]	26	59	23(5)[1]	31	—	—
1955–59[2]	125	22(8)[1]	25	115	24(6)[1]	27	—	—
1960–61	149	21(8)[1]	20	126	23(6)[1]	22	—	60[3]

Notes: Old Dominions = territories which were Dominions in 1938.
1 Canada is included in all the figures for the old Dominions but her share of Dominion imports and exports after 1955 is shown in brackets as she was not part of the Sterling Area.
2 Figures after 1935 include U.K. trade with Eire which equalled in 1935–39 2·5% of imports, 4·5% of exports.
3 Figure is for 1958–60.
4 Foreign investment index divided by export price index.
5 Figures include investment in Canada up to 1931, 3% of total in 1870; 13% in 1913; 14% in 1930.

Sources: W. Schloete, op. cit., for Imports and Exports prior to 1935. London and Cambridge Economic Bulletin, for volumes after 1935.
Annual Abstract of Statistics, for shares after 1935.
Charles Feinstein, op. cit, for shares in capital exports before 1913.
Mark Abrams, ed. *Britain and her Export Trade* (London: Pilot Press, 1948).
Tables II and III, Chapter 2, shares in capital exports, 1932–34. Tables XVIII and XIX, Chapter 8 for shares in capital exports in 1950–60.

TABLE VII

SHARES AND DIRECTIONS OF DIFFERENT COMMODITY EXPORTS IN U.K. AND EIGHT COUNTRIES' TRADE, 1830–1960
(% of Total exports of Home Products)

YEAR	TEXTILES U.K.	of which to Empire	Eight Countries	METAL AND ENGINEERING U.K.	of which Iron & Steel alone to Empire	Eight Countries	COAL U.K. only	RE-EXPORTS U.K. only
1830	67	15	—	11	2	—	1	24
1850	63	17	—	18	4	—	2	19
1870	56	15	—	21	3·5	—	3·	22
1890	43	16·5	20	25	3·5	22	7	27
1913	34	14	19	27	5	26	10	21
1925	34	11	12	18	4	36	9	27
1937	24	10·5	12	35	4·5	38	7	13
1950	18	6		49	3	60	2	5
1960	7	2	8·5	58	1·5		1	4·5

Notes: 1. Empire Market = Canada, Newfoundland, India, Australia, New Zealand, South Africa, British West Indies.
2. 8 Countries = U.K., Germany, France, Italy, Belgium, Switzerland, Sweden and U.S.A.
3. Empire figures are for 1827, 1854, 1876, 1900, 1913, 1929, 1934, 1950 and 1960.
4. 8 Countries' figures are for 1913, 1928, 1938, 1950 and 1959.
5. Iron and Steel up to 1957 includes bicycles and cutlery.

Sources: E. A. G. Robinson, 'The Changing Structure of the British Economy', *Economic Journal*, September 1954, p. 540.
W. Schloete, op. cit., Table 25.
I. Svennilson, *Growth and Stagnation in the European Economy* (Geneva: 1959), Table A-59.
Board of Trade, *Journal*, 30 March 1957 and 22 July 1960.

References

1. Sir J. Clapham, *An Economic History of Modern Britain*, Vol. II, Chapter IX.
2. ibid., p. 247.
3. U.S. Department of Commerce, *Historical Statistics of the U.S.A. 1789–1945*, Washington, 1952, p. 179.
4. W. Schloete, op. cit., Table 31.
5. I. Svennilson, *Growth and Stagnation in the European Economy*, Geneva, 1954, Table A29, p. 260.
6. W. Schloete, op. cit., Table 27, p. 74.
7. R. C. K. Ensor, op. cit., pp. 278–9.
8. Colin Clark, *Conditions of Progress*, second edition, Macmillan, 1951, p. 63.
9. H. J. Habbakuk, *American and British Technology in the 19th Century*, Cambridge, 1962.
10. C. H. Feinstein, op. cit., p. 227; and A. L. Bowley, *Wages and Income in the United Kingdom since 1860*, Cambridge, 1937.
11. Sir J. Clapham, op. cit., Vol. III, Chapter IV.
12. ibid., Vol. III, Chapter III, especially p. 203; and see M. H. Dobb, *Studies in the Development of Capitalism*, pp. 264–5.
13. D. Burn, *Economic History of Steel-making*, Cambridge, 1940, Chapter XI; and see J. D. Bernal, *Science and Industry in the Nineteenth Century*, Routledge, 1953, p. 107.
14. R. B. Saul, *Studies in British Overseas Trade*, Liverpool, 1960, pp. 58 and 62.
15. J. Schumpeter, *Imperialism*, p. 13.
16. C. H. Feinstein, op. cit., Chapter IV.
17. ibid., Chapters VI and VII.
18. H. Shannon, article in *Economic History Review*, 1933.
19. H. S. Ferns, op. cit.
20. W. J. Macpherson, article in *Economic History Review*, December 1955.
21. Woytinsky and Woytinsky, op. cit., Table 19, pp. 48–9.
22. C. A. Bodelsen, op. cit., p. 127 and *passim*.
23. R. C. K. Ensor, op. cit., pp. 37–8.
24. J. Strachey, *The End of Empire*, pp. 89–90.
25. L. H. Jenks, *The Migration of British Capital to 1875*, Cape, 1938, p. 325.
26. R. C. K. Ensor, op. cit., pp. 77–86.
27. Lord Cromer, *Modern Egypt*, Macmillan, 1908.
28. J. Strachey, op. cit., pp. 89–90.
29. R. C. K. Ensor, op. cit., p. 189.
30. ibid., p. 187 ff.

31. ibid., p. 191 ff.

32. ibid., p. 364.

33. A. J. Hannah, *The Beginnings of Nyasaland and Northern Rhodesia, 1859–95*, Oxford, 1956, e.g. pp. 64, 141, 160, 174.

34. quoted from M. Beer's *Modern British Imperialism*, Berlin, 1898, in Lenin's *Imperialism*, Little Lenin Library, 1944 edition, p. 68.

35. Woytinsky and Woytinsky, op. cit., Table 63, p. 142; and U.K. Government, *Annual Abstract of Statistics*, H.M.S.O., 1961.

36. R. C. K. Ensor, op. cit., p. 104.

37. Brinley Thomas, *Emigration and Economic Growth*.

38. In a speech entitled 'Africa, the Remedy for the Trade Depression of England', quoted by R. Harrison in an unpublished thesis on *The English Positivists and Labour Movements*, Oxford, 1949.

39. *The Beehive* of 19 February 1870, is quoted by C. A. Bodelsen, op. cit., p. 87 to this effect.

40. S. and B. Webb, *History of Trade Unionism*, Longmans, 1920, p. 380 ff; and see A. E.P. Duffy, 'New Unionism in Britain, 1889–90, A Reappraisal', *Economic History Review*, December, 1961.

41. D. C. Somervell, *English Thought in the 19th Century*, Methuen, 1929, p. 173 ff.

42. B. Semmell, *Imperialism and Social Reform*, Allen and Unwin, 1960, Chapter II.

43. J. A. Hobson, *Imperialism*, London, 1902; Third Edition, Allen & Unwin, 1938, p. 81.

44. W. Scovell Adams, *Edwardian Heritage*, Muller, 1949, p. 65.

45. C. H. Feinstein, op. cit.

46. I. Svennilson, op. cit., pp. 260–1.

47. R. Hilferding, *Das Finanz Kapital*, Vienna, 1912, and N. I. Bukharin, *Imperialism and World Economy*, Martin Lawrence, 1930.

48. V. I. Lenin, *Imperialism*, Little Lenin Library, 1944 edition, p. 57 ff.

49. J. Strachey, *The End of Empire*, Chapter VII.

50. V. I. Lenin, op. cit., p. 54.

51. ibid., p. 53.

52. ibid., pp. 93–4.

53. W. K. Hancock, *The Wealth of Colonies*, Cambridge, 1950, pp. 11–12, points out that the age of German cartels came after the first years of German expansionism in Africa in the 1880s.

54. Sir J. Clapham, *Economic History of Modern Britain*, Vol. III, Chapter IV, and especially p. 203.

55. C. H. Feinstein, op. cit., p. 227.

56. W. W. Rostow, *The Stages of Economic Growth*, p. 108 ff, and D. K. Feldhouse, ' "Imperialism": an Historiographical Revision', *Economic History Review*, December 1961.

57. C. H. Feinstein, op. cit., Figs. 5.1 and 5.4, which correct A. K. Cairncross, *Home and Foreign Investment 1870–1940*, Cambridge, 1953.

58. Karl Marx, *Capital*, Vol. III, Chapter XIII, C. H. Kerr ed., 1909, p. 247 ff.; and see J. M. Gillman, *The Falling Rate of Profit*, New York, 1957.

59. J. M. Keynes, *Treatise on Money*, Vol. II, Macmillan, 1930, p. 199.

60. C. H. Feinstein, op. cit.

61. A. K. Cairncross, op. cit., p. 187 ff.

62. C. P. Kindleberger, 'Foreign Trade and Economic Growth, Lessons from Britain and France, 1850–1914', *Economic History Review*, December 1961.

63. ibid., and J. Saville, 'Some Retarding Factors in the British Economy before 1914', *Yorkshire Bulletin of Economic and Social Research*, May 1961.

64. V. I. Lenin, *Imperialism*, Introduction to the French and German Editions.

65. Karl Marx, op. cit., pp. 278–80.

66. Karl Marx, *Value, Price and Profit*, 1865; Allen and Unwin, 1899, Chapter XIV especially.

67. F. Engels, Preface to the 1892 edition of *The Condition of the Working Class in England, 1844*.

68. E. J. Hobsbawm, 'Labour Aristocracy in Nineteenth Century Britain', *Democracy and the Labour Movement*, ed. J. Saville, Lawrence and Wishart, 1954, p. 228–9, surprisingly ignored in a study of this question by H. B. Davis, 'Imperialism and Labour: an analysis of Marxist views', *Science and Society*, Winter 1961–62.

69. J. J. Kuczynski, *Short History of Labour Conditions under Industrial Capitalism*, Muller, 1942, Vol. III, Part I, *passim*; and I. Svennilson, op. cit., p. 38.

70. S. and B. Webb, *History of Trade Unionism*, 1920 ed., p. 473.

71. R. C. K. Ensor, op. cit., p. 178; and Bodelsen, op. cit., p. 205 ff.

72. quoted in R. P. Dutt, *The Crisis of Britain and the British Empire*; and see A. J. P. Taylor, *The Course of German History*, Hamish Hamilton, 1945, pp. 134–6.

73. quoted in W. Scovell Adams, op. cit., p. 66.

74. R. C. K. Ensor, op. cit., p. 212.

75. ibid., p. 225.

76. J. L. Garvin, *Life of Chamberlain*, Vol. III, Cape, 1934, p. 7.

77. F. Whyte, *Life of W. T. Stead*, Cape, 1925, Vol. II, p. 109.

78. W. Scovell Adams, op. cit., p. 84.

79. Joseph Chamberlain speaking in the House of Commons, 22 August 1895.

80. *The Times*, 24 August 1895, quoted in R. P. Dutt, op. cit., p. 79.

81. S. H. Frankel, *Capital Investment in Africa*, Oxford, 1935.
82. J. A. Hobson, op. cit., especially pp. 94 ff.
83. W. Scovell Adams, op. cit., p. 186.
84. ibid., pp. 101–2.
85. ibid., pp. 190–1, taken from W. S. Hewins, *Apologia of an Imperialist*, Constable, 1929.
86. R. C. K. Ensor, op. cit., p. 504.
87. K. Marx, 'Address on the Question of Free Trade', Brussels, 9 January 1848, Martin Lawrence edition, 1935, printed as an appendix to *The Poverty of Philosophy*, pp. 192–208.
88. J. Schumpeter, *Imperialism*, p. 76, Meridian Books edition.
89. J. Viner, 'English Theories of Foreign Trade before Adam Smith', *Studies in the Theory of International Trade*, Allen and Unwin, 1955.
90. D. L. Burn, *Economic History of Steel-making*, p. 66, and *passim*; and Sir J. Clapham, *The Economic Development of France and Germany, 1815–1914*, Cambridge, 1923.
91. W. Scovell Adams, op. cit., p. 198.
92. ibid., p. 15.
93. ibid., p. 172.
94. J. A. Hobson, *Imperialism*, p. 57.
95. J. M. Keynes, *The Economic Consequences of the Peace*, Macmillan, 1920, pp. 9–10.

CHAPTER 4

War, Stagnation and Empire – 1914–1945

In this chapter we must consider the results in the metropolitan economies, and particularly in the British economy, of the unequal economic relations established with the underdeveloped lands and colonies in the nineteenth century. In the period between the two wars the outward movement of investment dried up after a further spurt in the 1920s, but the return of income on earlier investments continued. Was this a period of enjoyment of the fruits of conquest by the so called 'Have' powers (while the 'Have-nots' in Europe and the Far East prepared to pounce)? We shall consider the results in the colonies in the next chapter. What were the results at home? What was the balance of advantage to be gained from unequal economic relations in this period? In particular, we must examine again, in this new period, Lenin's theses: that, on the one hand, capitalism in its 'imperialist stage' led to stagnation in the old mature capitalist powers and brought the threat of war from the new rising capitalist states, but on the other hand, that imperial tribute, even in the stagnating mature states, could be used by the capitalists to buy off the top levels of the working class and prevent, for a time, the replacement of capitalism by socialism.

War and Empire

At times when no major war is being waged, it seems to

most rational beings inconceivable that any issue could
warrant such an outbreak of organised genocide. Yet when
war is actually in progress, its occurrence appears inevitable
and its aims adequately justified to the great majority on both
sides. The instincts of self-preservation and of group con-
formism, sedulously evoked by the arts of propaganda, make
sure of this. Today, more than ever before, we are bound to
ask what kind of difference could bring men to the point of
mass mutual suicide. It is impossible to consider here the
whole complex of causes, psychological, political and
economic, which are involved in the resort to war. But
something must be said of the connection between imperialism and war in a period marked at each end by the
holocausts of the two World Wars.

We have already noted the temptation to make others
work for their profit that opened up before the empire-
builders from the earliest period of civilisation, through the
long line of slave masters, *conquistadores*, merchant companies and concession-hunters. In each case, the armed
forces of the state became involved in support of adventurers'
activities. Those who attempt to avoid economic explanations for the causes of war generally accept the crucial
importance of the self-determination of nations, without
examining the cause also of this phenomenon.[1] Indeed, the
rise of nation-states, which has distinguished European
development, can be properly understood only in relation to
the emergence of a *bourgeoisie*. For unity of language and
communication, unification of the market, a common
system of law and government and a single national armed
force were all essential to capitalist development.

How has this led to war? There were wars enough between
the European conquerors and the American, Asian and
Africa peoples over whom they established their dominion;
but we are as much concerned here with the causes of war
between the Europeans themselves. The steady outward
pressure of German capitalism to win new markets and

sources of raw materials, and new opportunities for investment was noted in the last chapter. As Germany and other
advanced capitalist states emerged in Europe and North
America to challenge Britain's world dominion, so their
outward pressure led to war. Indeed, some would see the
struggle for colonies from the earliest times merely as a
reflection of the struggle for power inside Europe. The truth
of this lies in the all-sided rivalry of competing capitalist
states, which goes beyond the mere scramble for colonies,
trade and investment, but need not for that reason be
regarded as non-economic.[2]

What was the basis of the rivalry, however? Should we see
it in the competition of the major economic groupings in
each state for control over world markets for goods and
capital? German manufactured goods rapidly caught up with
British goods in the world market at the end of the nineteenth
century and almost overtook them by 1913; they did over-
take in 1938 (Chapter 9, Table XXI below). The dates are
significant. Did the Germans, at a certain stage, reach some
blockage from the political power of the British Empire
which they thought could only be shifted by war?*

German Expansionism

Let us first consider German foreign economic policy
before 1914. The basis of German expansionism was the
extremely rapid rate of advance in industrial production.
Coal production was increased fourfold between 1880 and
1913, while Britain's output doubled. German steel production was two-fifths of Britain's in 1880, and two and a half
times Britain's in 1913.[3] To compete with Britain, the young

---

* German exports overtook Britain's again in 1958. What conclusion should we draw? We shall consider later whether expansion
inside the Common Market may not be an alternative to preparation for
war.

German industrialists had invoked state aid to give tariff
protection, to encourage research institutes and to establish a
national educational system far ahead of any other in the
world.[4] Tariffs stimulated the formation of trade associations
and then of cartels; the economies of scale developing in the
1880s led to the establishment of large production units;
while the absence of a capital market brought into existence
the many consortia of bankers and industrialists that were to
dominate the German economy.[5]

The outstanding characteristic of German industrial
organisation came to be the large-scale trust, combining
financial, commercial and industrial interests and engaging
in a whole range of manufacturing processes. At the centre of
these trusts were the great coal, iron and steel, and engineering combines, like Krupp's, which dominated the trade
associations and cartels.[6] The combination of landowning
Prussian Junkers; and of banking and commercial consortia,
created the specifically German concentration of interest
upon armament. The Junkers provided the unifying
national force in control of the army and the civil administration; the bankers provided the industrialising force
in control of a manufacturing economy oriented towards
heavy industry.

Even without the Junkers and the history of German
unification, German capitalism, emerging when it did in
competition with Britain, would have been bound to push
outwards for markets and, given the connection between
markets for capital goods and capital investment, this was
bound to mean a search for protected investment opportunities. But Prussia had established its dominion over the
states of Germany through the Zollverein; the concept of
Mittel-Europa (as of the European Economic Community
today) was based on the development of a common
market into political unification.[7] The special feature of
German capitalism – large-scale, cartelised and finance-
capital-dominated enterprises growing behind protective

tariffs – only exaggerated the tendencies towards expansion, economically by permitting the maintenance of monopoly prices at the expense of the home consumer, politically by excluding the growth of a liberal and free-trade party.

British capitalism did not, as we pointed out earlier, share before 1914 the special characteristics of the German industrial structure, which Lenin saw as the essence of what he called the 'imperialist stage' of capitalist evolution.

After 1919, however, Britain also began to exhibit more and more of these characteristics of monopoly concentration and finance-capital domination that Lenin had analysed in Germany. Not only the growth of oligopoly, but conversion to protection from free trade and concentration on empire markets, all marked the British economy in the inter-war years. And it was increasingly in relation to the closed doors of empire trade that Germany, Italy and Japan were challenging the 'Have' powers. Britain and the other Allied powers presented a barrier to the natural development of the German economy.

While German industry was busily engaged in home investment, that is up to the 1880s, Bismarck took little interest in colonies but his interest in European expansion was very evident. By the time that German capital began to look outwards for profitable investment opportunities, most of the best openings had been entered by the British and French. The Germans were a few years too late in Africa and in the Far East, but the most obvious field for expanding markets must always have appeared to be in eastern Europe. Investment opportunities, we have emphasised before, were much greater in the developing lands of Europe than in undeveloped Asia and Africa. Germany's eastward pressure through Europe, which had begun with large-scale colonisation in Poland and continued down the railway line through Turkey to Baghdad, however, met British and Russian resistance at every step. For it challenged the balance of power in Europe.[8]

The First World War has generally been regarded by
Socialists as an imperialist war, in the sense that it involved a
real clash of economic interests of rival capitalists. There
were many other factors – the clumsy arrogance of the
Kaiser; the uncertainty, right up to the last minute, about the
British Government's intentions; the rising German and
declining French populations – but at bottom it is hard to
avoid Lenin's characterisation of the war as a reflection of the
unequal development of capitalist states. It was *the* cause of
war that Lenin was most anxious to discover in the capitalist
system.[9]

To accept Lenin's view does not entail supposing that
there was a grand conspiracy of a few all-powerful financiers
and industrialists to foment war, although arms manufacturers did undoubtedly do just this to sell their wares in
South America. What seems to have been involved was that
the forces of competition between the largest capitalist
groups created tensions and frictions, which were not easily
solved by diplomatic means and tended to an explosion,
such as that in 1914, which finally engulfed the world in a war
that no one wanted.

British Overseas Investment in the 1920s

While we may recognise that it was not simply a struggle
for empire that was the cause of the World Wars, what we
have to decide is whether the general rivalry of great monopolistic groupings was not the crucial factor. We have to
consider, in particular, what were the real advantages which
the metropolitan powers derived between the wars from
their colonial possessions.

Here we must distinguish between the benefits received
from overseas trade and investment in total, and those
received from specifically *empire* trade and investment. We
have suggested so far that, in Britain's case, the former were
infinitely greater than the latter, but that the whole far-flung

range of imperial connections may have been central to Britain's world-wide trade and investment. By 1913 income from overseas – nearly half of it from investment in the empire, but only 16 per cent from the colonies – amounted to nearly a tenth of the national income. It amounts to little more than a hundredth part of the national income today, but how important was it between the wars? (See Table I at end of Chapter 3.)

In considering a period, like that of the 1920s and 1930s, marked by such long stagnation and such deep crisis at home, one is bound to wonder how real were the advantages for the British economy as a whole from these overseas operations. The City of London certainly made every effort in the 1920s to re-establish its pre-eminence in overseas investment and the power of the Pound Sterling in world banking and commerce.[10] How far, then, had British capitalism begun to move closer towards Lenin's picture of great combines pressing outwards their imperial claims, and how was this related to stagnation at home? We need first to make certain comparisons between British overseas investment in the 1920s and in the years immediately before 1913.

Between 1910 and 1913 the level of overseas investment was more than double that of capital formation at home. By contrast, even in the peak years of 1928–9 overseas lending never rose to more than a quarter of home investment (see Table IV at end of Chapter 3). Before 1913 the annual export of capital exceeded the income from earlier overseas investments (see Table II at end of Chapter 3). After the war, capital exports never rose above half the level of investment income. Before 1913, this investment income had been equal to nearly a tenth of the whole national income and a quarter of the incomes from property. After the war, it was reduced to about 5 per cent of national income and perhaps a fifth of property incomes (see Table IV).

These big changes in investment income were caused partly by the sale of securities to pay for United States supplies during the war, and particularly by the almost complete disposal of British holdings in the U.S. railways (see Table VIII below). The nominal value of British overseas investments was re-established by 1926 at about the 1913 level of £4,000 million; but this meant a reduction in their real worth, since the value, at least of the government and municipal stocks, had not risen in line with the 100 per cent increase in other prices in the war and post-war years.

There were two important results of the sale of the U.S. and other American railway stocks, which amounted to nearly a fifth of the British portfolio. These were a marked change in the composition of British overseas investment and a change in the empire proportion of the investment. The gap arising from the sale of American stock was filled mainly by new issues to governments and especially to dominion governments. Table VIII shows that municipal and government stocks rose between 1913 and 1930, and that there was, at the same time, also some increase in investment in British companies engaged in overseas raw-material production and in industrial investments overseas. The main investors were still individual rentiers, but the direct investments of companies (which made up more than a half of United States overseas investment in the 1920s[11]) were increasing. Some incentive had been given to such investment by the raising of tariff walls around the dominion markets, which led British steel and engineering companies, such as Dorman Long and Stewart and Lloyds, to establish subsidiaries and joint companies in Australia and South Africa.[12]*

There can be no doubt that profits from overseas raw materials provided an exceedingly important part of the total profits of the great combines that were formed in Britain in the 1920s. Nearly a half of the Lever Group profits in 1928, for example, came from overseas operations, and the basis of

---

* In 1927, British companies had attempted to prevent the South African government from establishing a state-owned steel mill; see Chapter V.

the profits at home was, of course, the raw materials obtained from Africa and South-East Asia.[13]

The second result of this change in the composition of British investment was that a much larger proportion of British capital was directed to the Empire – about 59 per cent in 1930 compared with 47 per cent in 1913 (see Table V at end of Chapter 3). This tendency was increased by the sales in 1929 of some £40 million of British companies' shares mainly in South American operations to United States companies. These sales were in many cases a *quid pro quo* for continued British control of operations in empire countries.[14] The 1920s saw the first major struggle between British and American interests for control of Rhodesian copper.[15]

We may detect here the beginning of the outward pressure of monopoly within protected imperial fields, of which Lenin was speaking. The huge scale of the total British investment in companies operating overseas, some £2,000 million in 1930 (about £1,200 million of it in companies registered in the U.K. but operating abroad, and the rest in companies registered abroad) gave a heavy overseas emphasis to British capitalism.[16] This was, of course, a carry-over from Britain's world monopoly of the nineteenth century, but it was increasingly involving the kind of struggle for monopoly in cartels and market spheres of influence which Lenin regarded as the essence of imperialism.

Monopoly and World Cartels

Lenin, in 1916, foresaw the complete 'division of the world among the great international trusts'.[17] The 1920s saw this process most actively at work. In the much needed rationalisation and reconstruction of British industry after the First World War, concentration through merger, purchase and trusts proceeded at a more rapid pace. By 1930 single firms controlled over 80 per cent of capacity in salt, chemicals, dyes and fertilisers (Imperial Chemicals), in cement (the Associated Group), in cotton thread (J. & P. Coats), in tobacco (Imperial Tobacco), in spirit distilling (Distillers Co.), in soap and margarine (Unilever), in rubber tyres (Dunlop), in matches (Bryant & May).[18] Increasingly, the competition that remained was the competition of giants – five or six firms each in banking, coal and steel (vertically integrated), railways, shipping, cotton and so on. These were linked in cartels and trade associations which were especially strong in heavy industry, the mines and iron and steel owners receiving government aid to this end.[19] Moreover, the new industries – in chemicals, petroleum, aluminium, motors, artificial textiles – which were belatedly being developed in Britain, did so inside monopoly or quasi-monopoly structures.

This development in Britain was matched, had indeed been vigorously preceded, by similar formations in the U.S.A., Germany, France, Belgium, Holland, Italy and Japan. Now the giant monopolies met each other in the world market in the search for raw materials. The result was the extension of cartel agreements to cover the whole world. In 1916, Lenin could already refer to the agreements on electrical products between Allgemeine Elektrische Gesellschaft of Germany and General Electric Company of America in 1907, to the struggle for the control of oil between Rockefeller and Sir Henry Deterding, to the International Zinc Syndicate, to the International Rail Cartel of 1904, to the International Dynamite Trust.[20] During the 1920s all the international cartels mentioned by Lenin had been revived after the disruption of the war; many more were added, especially in the field of raw materials, not only for oil and zinc but for tin and copper and aluminium and rubber.[21]

The nature of a cartel should be clearly understood. It is a temporary and, by its nature, unstable agreement among competitors to limit the competition among themselves for a period of time and in certain respects. Prices may be fixed, or production regulated, to agreed output quotas, or markets may be shared out, or patents exchanged and frozen. Any or all of these forms of action may enter the agreement. The essential point is that competition does not cease; but it is not allowed to lead to suicidal price-cutting or to dividing the common front of employers to their employees or of buyers of raw materials to the producers. The struggle for markets goes on as fiercely as ever, changes in the balance of forces being recognised in each revision of the agreement.

It is a pre-condition of the effective working of a cartel, of course, that it should embrace all the producers, if not in the whole world, then at least in part of the world; and if it operates only in a part of the world, that part must be able to be separated off from outside competition by some form of protective barrier. Thus cartels are, in effect, the product of tariffs, and it is not, therefore, surprising that they had their origin in Germany, where industry, as we have seen, was built up behind protective walls. This association between cartels and tariffs helps us to understand the importance of the customs union in German industrial thinking – from the Zollverein to the Common Market.

Lenin saw cartels becoming the 'foundations of the whole economic life' after the boom and crisis of 1900–03 and from that time, he comments, 'Capitalism has become transformed into imperialism'.[22] Lenin believed this to be the result of the concentration of production, to which, as Marx had foreseen, free competition gave rise. But we noted in the last chapter that Britain, at least up to the First World War, held on to her free trade principles and showed only the beginnings of development towards monopoly. Between the wars, we have now seen, monopoly structures grew apace in Britain too behind protective walls. Must we conclude that the drive towards monopoly is an inevitable tendency of capitalism, representing Lenin's 'imperialist stage' of capitalism? Schumpeter has argued vigorously against this view.[23] Large-scale production is certainly an inevitable attribute of modern technological developments, but economies of scale cannot be realised beyond an optimum point. Giant companies are not the same as monopolies, Schumpeter argued, and there are powerful factors at work to prevent the 'drive to monopoly'. These arise from the large number of smaller concerns, who suffer from protective monopoly action and from the competitors outside the ring who are always striving to break in. He therefore regards cartels and monopolies as a far from stable and inevitable part of capitalism, taking into account in addition the interests of the increasingly vocal citizen-consumer.

Lenin would have been the last to doubt that there were contradictions in the development of capitalism; but what Schumpeter's argument would seem to miss, even if we accept his view of the technological limits to company size,* is the unity among all capitalists as a class that overrides the divisions between them. In face of the working class or of the colonial primary producers the most antagonistic groups of capitalists may find a common front. We need only to notice how the great oil companies may compete for markets but find a common bond in face of the Arab oil-workers or of Soviet oil-supplies. We may now also see how the whole period since Lenin *wrote* in 1917 has been dominated by the results of what Lenin *did* in 1917. Fear of the Soviet revolution has proved a stronger force than all the divisive forces of monopolistic practices.

Lenin saw the cartel primarily as a reflection of the antagonistic forces, which came into operation as a result of the uneven development of capitalism in different lands. But, as we look back from the standpoint of the 1960s, the importance of cartels may seem to have been even more that they were able to some extent to contain the divergence of interests of the great competing oligopolies. In the Twentieth

---

* With the growing use of computers we may today say that this leaves room for some very large companies as we shall see in Chapter VIII.

Century Fund study of international cartels between the wars, the authors, although highly critical of the workings of the cartels they examine, sum up their analysis of the chemical cartels in words that may be more widely applied: 'The cartels provide a relatively stable framework within which conflicting interests may be reconciled by manœuvre, bargain and compromise'.[24]

In the light of the whole range of international competition, it may be thought that the cartels failed to hold the conflicting interests in Germany and among the Allies in 1939; but this was the result of the Frankenstein monster which German nationalists and the German industrialists' fear of communism had conjured up. All the evidence shows that the cartels were working overtime in 1938 to prevent an explosion. As late as March of 1939, the Federation of British Industries was able to reach agreement at Duesseldorf with the Reichsgruppe Industrie 'to ensure that as a result of an agreement between their industries unhealthy competition shall be removed'.[25] And, in answer to a question in the House of Commons, the President of the Board of Trade, Mr Oliver Stanley, added that 'There is nothing in the agreement intended to be, or that would be, in conflict with the interests of American industry'.[26]

It was precisely Germany's exclusion from the raw-material cartels that had strengthened the German claim to colonies, which Hitler began to press in the 1930s. Although only about 3 per cent of the world's output of raw materials came from colonial territories, this included nearly all the natural rubber and palm oil, over half of the tin and a quarter of the copper;[27] and of course the colonial proportion of output of raw materials outside the United States of America was very high. How far was Germany cut off from these supplies?

There is no doubt that Hitler's arguments were strong ones. First, although German firms were not prevented from purchasing raw materials, primary product prices fluctuated outside their control and it was often difficult for them to obtain the appropriate currencies from sales of German goods in what were in effect restricted markets. Second, although primary producers were only too anxious to expand their sales after the excessive development of capacity in the First World War, nevertheless British firms, as we have seen, found it necessary and profitable to ensure their raw material supplies by vertical integration. German firms were excluded from such action and prices were sometimes raised against German buyers in this way. Thirdly, there was the fear that Germany's supplies might be cut off in time of war. In fact, to increase its self-sufficiency, German industry developed many synthetic substitute materials – of which naphtha and Buna for oil and rubber were the chief – and raised her own agricultural output – particularly of sugar – and in this way enjoyed a great stimulus to industrial advance. In addition to the argument about raw materials, there was the demand for *lebensraum*, lying behind the claim to colonies, although this was probably mainly a good propaganda point for home and foreign consumption.[28]

Finally, perhaps the most important point, which neither Hitler nor his appeasers, nor the stream of League of Nations, Chatham House and P.E.P. pamphlets on raw materials and colonies[29] ever mentioned, was that German capital was excluded from the opportunities enjoyed by the 'Haves' to profit from the exploitation of essential raw materials. Of course the 'Have-nots' could have put capital into raw-material exploitation inside other countries' colonies, but without flag protection and control over the labour-force through poll-taxes and other inducements, the prospects would have been unattractive.[30] In this sense of raw-material exploitation, investment and 'the flag' were certainly closely associated. Colonial possessions were an aspect, an extremely important aspect, of the whole struggle of the giant world monopolies. If this is the conclusion to the first part of the question of the relationships between colonial expansion and economic interests at home, we still have to answer how this outward pressure towards monopoly was related to the stagnation of the economy at home.

Foreign Investment, Crisis and Stagnation at Home

The shares of home and foreign investment in the total of British capital formation were reversed between the pre-war and post-war years. We have already noted that, in the four years before 1913, three-quarters of the average of £250 million of annual net British capital investment consisted of overseas lending; between 1920 and 1928, three-quarters of the average of £400 million of annual net British capital investment consisted by contrast of capital formation at home (see Table IV at end of Chapter 3). No longer could the flow of capital overseas be said to be starving development at home, although ship-building and steel were certainly starved of capital and the City was still oriented towards foreign rather than home investment, as the Macmillan Report complained.[31]

The export of capital was, moreover, much less securely based in the 1920s than it had been before 1913. Annual surpluses on the balance of payments averaging £100 million were achieved in all years of the post-war decade except for 1926, but the gap in the trade account, which had to be filled by other means, was wider than ever.[32] Although imports were kept down by deflation at home, less than two-thirds were paid for by exports compared with three-quarters before 1913 (see Table II at end of Chapter 2 and Table XIV at end of Chapter 8). Britain suffered especially because the quantum of world trade had not risen after 1920 in line with the increase in world manufacturing output.[33] Earnings from shipping still filled a large part of the gap, although the share of British ships in world carrying had fallen (from nearly a half of the total to under 40 per cent).[34] But the greater part of the gap was covered by income from past investments abroad, which amounted to about £250 million a year (Table XIV). To these sums was added a much increased figure (£60 million) of interest on short-term investments and commissions.[35] At the same time, a great increase in short-term borrowing, i.e. of 'hot money' deposited in London, also made available funds for long-term lending overseas. It was these funds that fled from London after the Austrian and German financial crisis of 1931 and forced the abandonment of the gold standard.[36]

The tying of the pound to the price of gold at the pre-1914 rate, which Winston Churchill had effected as Chancellor of the Exchequer in 1925, had been the culmination of a whole series of measures urged upon post-war governments by the City of London. These are of central importance to our inquiry; for their aim was to re-establish the international strength of sterling and to encourage once more the flow of funds overseas. To this end, the inflation of the war and immediate post-war years had to be checked; but the measures adopted led to the deflation of the whole economy. There was no doubt that, as the result of the abrupt de-controlling of prices at the end of the war when many goods were in very short supply, British prices had moved right out of line with those in America. This was partly the result also of the great reduction of costs in American industry following the war-time increases in productivity. Rather than devalue the pound to take account of this, the City led the Government to make a headlong assault on wages, salaries, Government expenditure and business credit at home in order to deflate prices.[37]

This policy created heavy unemployment, but it enabled the pound to be put back on gold and also created the conditions for the great wave of mergers and rationalisation schemes that we have noted. Putting the pound back on gold at the pre-war parity greatly aggravated the difficulties being experienced by Britain in her foreign trade. Foreigners were attracted to hold sterling and, as we have seen, long-term investment overseas was re-established, but on the other hand British exports were very nearly priced out of the world markets. The volume of British exports never recovered even in 1929 to more than four-fifths of the 1913 level (see Table VI at end of Chapter 3); and this was at least in part a question of price. The collapse of the export industies pulled down the whole level of industrial production. Output of manufactures even in 1929 was barely 5 per cent above the level in 1913.[38]

The other main reason for Britain's export failure was structural, resulting from declining world demand for coal and textiles. Despite the rationalisation schemes of the 1920s, British industry was desperately slow to adapt to the needs of the post-war world. This failure is best illustrated by a table in Arthur Lewis's *Economic Survey, 1919–1939*, which shows the continued concentration of British manufactured exports in those groups (over 40 per cent of Britain's total exports) such as textiles, which expanded least in the years between 1913 and 1929, and the very small part British industry was playing in those groups (only 4 per cent of British exports), such as machinery and transport equipment, which expanded most. The United States, by contrast, had nearly 30 per cent of her exports in the expanding groups and only 17 per cent in the contracting groups. Germany was almost as well placed.[39]

British industry certainly suffered from the traditional policies urged by the City of London. The apparently parasitic dependence of the balance of payments on the overseas investment income of £250 million seemed to give strength to Lenin's forecast of 'the increasing parasitism and decay of the countries which are richest in capital (such as England)'.[40] But the stagnation at home cannot be said to have been the result of a simple diversion of resources from home to foreign investment. With the home economy so heavily damped down, however, it was not surprising that rentiers turned to overseas government stocks. There were, moreover, other causes besides the Government's deflationary measures for the backwardness of British industry.

There is much evidence of conservatism, nepotism, inefficient management, lack of scientific awareness, low level of technical education – all the attributes, which we noted already at the end of the nineteenth century, of a once progressive society that has for too long rested content with earlier successes.[41] What may be said is that the overseas investment income, and the privileged position of British exports in many markets, delayed the adjustments that were being forced upon British industrialists, and that the City's concentration on strengthening sterling aggravated the situation.

The crisis, when it came in 1929, was the result of the crash of the uncontrolled American boom which engulfed the whole capitalist world. It was not a crisis of empire or even primarily a crisis of overseas lending. United States foreign investment between 1919 and 1929 was running at a high level, but it accounted for little more than 1 per cent of United States national income, or about a tenth of the annual rate of net capital formation.[42] It was a crisis involving the whole complex of capitalist relations, and especially the drive of the giant combines from oligopoly towards monopoly, and the consequent pressure to increase capacity to produce, as if, as Marx said, 'only the absolute power of consumption of the entire society would be their limit'.[43] When overproduction saturated the market, the collapse came. As Professor Galbraith has pointed out, productivity rose throughout the 1920s but wages and prices remained stable.[44] As profits boomed, savings grew and the propensity to spend declined. The great mass of wage-earners could not buy back what, as workers, they had produced. The great corporations drove each other into the Great Crash.

In this crisis the British combines played their part; but the British economy had enjoyed little of the boom. It suffered somewhat less from the slump, although the world-wide effects of the collapse of U.S. foreign lending and purchases of food and raw materials hit Britain especially hard on account of the openness of her economy. Why then did Britain survive better than some of the other capitalist states? Was this the result of her empire? First, we must be clear that even 1929 was not the final crisis which Lenin might have expected. Capitalism survived and capitalists learned two important lessons. The first, we have already noted, was to use cartels and output agreements to contain the divergent economic interests, while allowing brand competition to stimulate innovation. The second was to use the power of the state and particularly to adopt protective policies.

British capitalists were no more active than their German and French opposite numbers in applying these lessons – on the contrary they were less active – but British industry recovered sooner and more vigorously than German, French or U.S. industry.[45] This recovery cannot be dissociated from the slow process of adaptation to the modern world which British industry had been making in the 1920s; nor can it, however, be dissociated from the special relations which Britain enjoyed with her colonial possessions and the independent dominions overseas, and, indeed, with food and raw-material producers the world over. We need to consider, then, what state intervention in British foreign economic policy amounted to in the 1930s.

Imperial Trade and Preference

Many protective measures were taken after 1931 by a British Government that had by then begun, at last, to abandon *laissez-faire*. Their purpose was primarily to protect British capital and British industrialists operating overseas. They did little, however, to expand trade, as we shall see by examining some of the steps taken. Using the threat to impose tariffs and deploying the bargaining strength of the world's largest importer of foodstuffs and raw materials, the Government signed bilateral trade agreements in 1933 with the Argentine, the Baltic states, the U.S.S.R., Poland and indeed with Germany herself. The resultant expansion of trade with these countries was small in the extreme.

Trade expansion was, however, only a secondary object in the agreements to debt-collection – mainly of interest on past investments and to a less extent of trade debts. Argentina was promised that Britain would continue meat imports at the pre-Ottawa level, for example, and in her turn was obliged to allocate to debt repayment practically 100 per cent of the sterling earned from her exports to Britain.[46] The difference between imports at £150 million by Britain from these 'trade agreement' countries and exports at £50–70 million was largely covered by dividends and loan interest. Britain's export industries gained little.[47]

In the breakdown of world trade and payments after 1930, British capitalism turned, more specifically than before, to the empire. The first step was, as ever, to strengthen the position of the pound. The gold standard was abandoned and the pound devalued by 20 per cent in 1931. Thereafter, in theory, the pound was allowed to fluctuate according to market demand instead of being tied to the market value of gold. In fact, the fluctuations were managed by the Bank of England through the Exchange Equalisation Account, and gold was steadily accumulated in the Gold Reserve, until this had risen by 1938 to £840 million from £121 million in 1931, without the pound being permitted to appreciate in value.[48] The result of this was that sterling, which had always been regarded as the equivalent of gold, took the place of gold as a monetary standard and an international currency.

The currencies of the British colonies, including India, were pegged to the pound; the Dominions did the same and a group of other countries, which had for long looked to London for capital short-term finance of trade, and banked their reserves in London, followed suit. These countries included Egypt, Iraq, Portugal, Norway, Sweden, Denmark, Iran, Japan, Argentina, Uruguay, Yugoslavia. Thus the so-called 'Sterling Bloc' came into existence, without agreement or organisation, but preserving the tie with the City of London.[49] Fortunately, one lesson, at least, of the 1920s had been learnt; sterling was not overvalued. Indeed it was devalued again by 10 per cent in 1932 and the subsequent rise in the gold reserve was mildly reflationary in relation to Britain's economy as a whole. For a time the devaluation also gave British exports a much needed fillip until the rest of the world devalued too.[50]

The most important act of the National Government in the crisis of the 1930s was the final abandonment of free trade. Already, tariffs had been imposed to protect British industries; behind these the motor and electrical and other light-engineering industries at last made some real headway. This did something to meet one of Britain's major post-war problems, which we noted earlier, that Britain's exports were concentrated not on those products for which the world market was expanding, viz., transport equipment and machinery, but on those for which the market was declining, viz., textiles and miscellaneous manufactures.

Tariffs were used after 1930, however, primarily in negotiating international cartel agreements. By 1937, British industries and financial interests were involved in agreements covering iron and steel, aluminium, coke, nitrogen, railway rolling stock and rails, and heavy chemicals, as well as in empire commodity control agreements for the companies producing copper, rubber, lead, sugar, tea and tin.[51] The tariffs imposed on imported steel, which were operated by the semi-governmental Import Duties Advisory Committee, actually enabled the steel firms not only to rationalise and control the expansion of capacity, but to raise steel prices at home, while subsidising exports.[52] Lord Nuffield, Mr George Lucas and other industrialists frequently complained about the effect that this had on the competitiveness of their engineering products in international markets, but the steel industry strengthened itself.[53] Here was a good example of

Schumpeter's monopoly export-dumping that in fact harms the economy. It was nevertheless allowed to continue.

The main effect of the new imposition of tariffs on imports after 1931 was in the preference that it was then possible to give to empire produce. In exchange, Britain's goods received preference in empire markets. Agreements on these preferential duties were the result of the Imperial Economic Conference held at Ottawa in 1932. These gave definite advantages to the farmers of the dominions and to the mines and plantations of the colonies. Table VI at the end of chapter 3 shows that the share of the empire in Britain's imports rose from around 25 per cent in 1929, as in 1913, to nearly 40 per cent in the years after 1935. Some part of this was the result of the great expansion of oil imports from the Middle East, as the number of motor-cars on the roads rapidly increased. The main part followed from the switch from Russian, East European and United States supplies of food grains to empire sources mainly in Canada and Australia.[54] This rise in imports from the empire was hardly balanced by an equivalent rise in the empire share of Britain's exports (Table VI).

What gains there were in the protected empire markets were, in any case, largely balanced by losses in the unprotected;[55] the volume of exports rose after 1932, but only to two-thirds of the 1913 level, three-quarters of 1929 (Table VI). Exporters did rather better from the sixfold increase in the Government's underwriting of commercial credits through the Export Credit Guarantees Department between 1933 and 1937, some of the guarantees amounting to considerable loans to foreign governments.[56] None of these measures, however, could replace the broken system of international trade and finance. Indeed, imperial preference and bilateral trade after 1930 greatly reduced the old multilateral payments-system, and especially the three-cornered flow of materials from the empire to the European continent, of manufactures from Europe to Britain, and of goods and services from Britain to the empire.[57]

One of the many tragedies of the 1930s was the failure of the World Economic Conference in 1933, and the rejection of later proposals like that of the I.L.O. for International Public Works.[58] The United States refused to stabilise the dollar; she cut down her imports and stopped lending. Each country in turn attempted to reduce imports and expand exports. The vicious contracting spiral of world trade, illustrated on the frontispiece of the League of Nations *World Economic Survey, 1932–3*, leaves an unforgettable impression.[59]

The Sterling Bloc, the Dollar Area, the Franc Area and the rest were no substitute for an expansion of the whole world's trade. The volumes of food and raw materials entering international trade only seemed to grow because their values were so low. World trade in manufactures had not recovered to 1913 levels by 1937.[60] A new recession in the United States in 1938 reduced British and empire exports once more. Britain faced a major crisis in her balance of payments. Gold had to be shipped across the Atlantic to stop the gap, and, as war approached, capital fled once more from Europe to America. The critical situation which Britain faced at the end of the Second World War should not blind us to the crisis that existed already in 1938.

Compared with the advantages that an expansion of world trade between the wars would have brought, the privileges obtained by British traders inside the empire were poor compensation. Undoubted advantages were gained from privileged markets in which British industry could widen the sale of the new lines in engineering and chemicals that were being pioneered. But the low overall level of world trade meant that the necessary reorganisation of Britain's industrial structure came in the cruellest possible manner for the unemployed and for those who were driven to migrate from the depressed areas to the Thames valley. In the long run, privileged empire markets cushioned British exporters from the hard facts of international industrial competition in a way that we may still rue today. The links between the giants of the economy at home and the colonial empire had, however, been forged. Free trade in an international economy had been abandoned for the cultivation of privileged and protected markets.

Were the Terms of Trade Favourable for Britain in the 1930s.

It now remains to consider how far Britain, at least, benefited from the relative movement in prices of manufactured goods and of primary products during the 1930s. For it is often argued by Socialists that it was largely through the terms of Britain's trade with the colonies and with the other primary producing lands that most advantage was drawn from the unequal dependent relationship of metropolitan industrial power and primary producing colony.[61]

That there was over-expansion of investment in raw-materials production during, and immediately after, the war is clear.[62] Raw-material productive capacity proved to be far in excess of the demand from European and American industry in the 1920s. The terms of trade for primary producers worsened. By 1921, their terms were only 70 per cent of 1913 and, although they recovered between 1922 and 1929 to 84 per cent of 1913, they fell again after 1930 to a level below even that of 1921.[63] Britain got her food and raw materials cheaper but, with her large interests in overseas food and raw-material production, and her large export market among food and raw material producers, she was bound to be adversely affected at the same time. The slump was both worsened and deepened by the collapse of the earnings of the primary producers.

Such unfavourable movements in the terms of trade for primary producers might be regarded, and indeed often are regarded, as being *per contra* favourable for the industrial producers. What was in fact the balance of advantage for Britain? It is essential that we decide this question, not only because the terms of trade are often quoted as the main expression of the unequal relationship between advanced and underdeveloped lands,[64] but because they are also said to provide the essential illustration of Lenin's thesis. This included the concept of imperial tribute as the cause of parasitic decay, as the source of corruption for holding back the advance of the working class, and as the explanation for the failure of Marx's prophesy of increasing misery for the workers.

We noted in considering the extension of trade in the nineteenth century that Britain's free-trade policy, while destroying Asian competitors, did give overseas producers of food and materials, particularly in the lands of European settlement, the means of payment for British exports. However fair or unfair may have been the original terms of trade established in the first exchanges between primary and industrial producers, the prices of their separate products moved steadily more favourably for the primary producers for fifty years from 1805 to 1857, and the period was marked by the most rapid growth of British exports. Thereafter, the trend was less favourable to the primary producers and British exports rose much more slowly, until the trend changed again at the turn of the century. The movement in the terms of trade before the 1850s was, we saw, dominated by the falling prices of manufactured goods, which were flooding into every land and destroying the handicrafts industries the world over. After 1860, however, we have suggested, it was the movement of the prices of primary products that determined the level of trade and periods of stagnation in foreign trade followed a fall in primary-product prices just as periods of growth followed a rise. At the same time, these interacting factors were found themselves to depend upon growth or stagnation in the economy of the industrial country, i.e. Britain.

We may leave the detailed argument, once more, to an annexe.* The conclusion from the 1930s cannot be

* Annexe on the Terms of Trade in the 1930s will be found at the end of the chapter.

challenged. The failure of British industry to expand in the 1920s, and the world-wide industrial collapse after 1929, drove down the prices of food and raw materials. While industrial producers could keep up their prices by cartel- and price-agreements, primary producers were largely helpless. The industrialists' terms of trade improved, but at the expense of the volume of trade. Those in work got cheaper food at the expense of the unemployed at home, especially in the export industries, as well as at the expense of the primary producers overseas.

Who Gained in Britain from 'Imperial Tribute'?

That the primary producers suffered no one need doubt; but who gained in Britain? The British plantation and mining companies operating overseas might be expected to have been as badly hit as the colonial producers, but they sought to protect themselves by restriction and control schemes, especially in coffee-, sugar-, rubber- and tin-output.[65] It was just during this period that the largest concerns bought up many smaller firms that had been ruined and proceeded to build up vertically integrated combines, by which the final processing end of the business actually gained from the low raw-material prices.[66] Some of these great combines – Unilever, Imperial Tobacco, Tate and Lyle, Dunlop – established a near monopoly of the market which made them more than ever into the giants of the economy. They may certainly be said to have benefited from the low level of raw-material prices, because their semi-monopoly position and their cartel-agreements enabled them to keep up their final prices and thus to maintain a high level of profits.

The rest of British industry gained to the extent that it benefited from cheap imports but lost from the impoverishment of the markets for its manufactured exports. British export industries were particularly oriented towards the less developed lands. What was more important for British industry as a whole than cheaper imports was the deep dive of exports, even below the levels of the 1920s, to nearly half the 1913 volume in 1931–3. Exports recovered slowly but they did not regain the 1929 level and were still only two-thirds of the 1913 level by 1937. In 1938 they collapsed again (see Table V at end of Chapter 3). The results were to be seen in the depressed areas all over Britain – in the Lancashire cotton towns and the Yorkshire woollen industry, in the shipyards of the Tyne, the Clyde and the Lagan, in the coal-mines and steel-works everywhere. England's export industries stayed depressed. The smaller companies, which had not been absorbed by the great combines and could not benefit from vertical integration, were especially hard hit. There were never less than a tenth of the labour force, nearly two million people, unemployed between the wars, and for three years there were more than a fifth without work (Table IX below).

Of course this decline was, in part, a result of the structural shift in the commodities entering into world trade, as we noted earlier. Textiles, iron and steel faced a declining market as the newly industralised lands built up their own basic industries. But Britain's very capacity to adapt to this structural change was undoubtedly for long held back (and still is held back) both by the overseas orientation of British capital and by the protected markets of the empire, upon which exporters of textiles and iron and steel could continue to rely.

On the other hand, the empire did provide a protected market for Britain's infant motor and chemical industries to expand in, and did provide some part of the cheap food and raw materials that were so important in the 1930s. The protected earnings of the monopolies, added to this small rise in real income at home, was enough in the end to create a market for the new industries that British capital had been so long in establishing. It is not, therefore, surprising that the new industries were not only highly monopolistic, but also directed largely to the high-income groups. The state financed the electric grid, but private capital built up the electrical, chemical and motor industries. Much of the capital was, in fact, American.[67] The foundation for these new industries had been laid in the concentration of production-units by the process of mergers in the 1920s and by the take-over of bankrupt firms in the early 'thirties. In this process, the banks, for the first time in the history of British capitalism, took on a leading role at home and the interlocking of industrial and finance capital grew.[68]

Thus, slowly and in the most inefficient manner, with the maximum wastage of unemployed human potential and amidst the desolation of whole regions of the land, British capitalism made the adjustment to the modern world. That British capitalism finally made the adjustment suggests that Lenin was wrong in forecasting parasitic decay as the future for the 'over-ripe' capitalist empires.

How far was he right in his other thesis, which appears to contradict the first, that it was the tribute of empire that enabled the imperialists to buy off the leaders of the working class and that saved the workers from increasing impoverishment? 'The high monopoly profits for a handful of very rich countries,' Lenin said, 'created the economic possibility of corrupting the upper strata of the proletariat and thereby fostered, gave form to and strengthened opportunism.'[69] As early as 1892, Engels had said, and Lenin quoted him, that 'the workers merrily share the feast of England's monopoly of the colonies and the world market'. [70] There was some truth in Engels's picture at that time and reformism certainly sank deep roots in the British working class in the last years of the old century; but we saw earlier that the reason lay rather in the rise of British industrial productivity and the reduction of the transport costs of imports, resulting from investment in railways, docks, ships, etc., than in the direct tribute flowing into Britain.

What was the position between the wars? Of course, none need doubt that some in Britain gained very considerably from the unequal relationship between the metropolitan power and the colonial people and other primary producers. To begin with, there were those who had shares in overseas companies and other foreign stocks that gave a higher return than investment at home. There cannot, however, have been many such shares: the average return on nominal capital from all overseas investment had been 5.2 per cent in 1907–8. It rose to 6.2 per cent in 1929, but fell back to 4.3 per cent in 1934. It was nearer 10 per cent on shares in raw-material producing companies, but again this fell back sharply in the early 1930s. By comparison, yields at home were not much worse: Consols dropped in 1935 to 3.8. per cent, but yields on equity shares never fell below 4.5 per cent and were as high as 8 per cent in 1931.[71]

The flow of income from earlier overseas investment certainly provided an addition to Britain's national income of about 5 per cent to 6 per cent. It dropped from about £250 million to about £150 million after 1930 (Table IV at end of Chapter 3). How much did such a sum amount to? It would have provided each of the three million unemployed in 1932 with £1 a week – that is much the same as he was receiving in family benefit, but less than a third of what he would have received from a job. The £150 million was, moreover, less than a quarter of the drop in net national income between 1929 and 1932.

We should, however, take into account the transfer of income from the movement in the terms of trade. For, although, as we have shown, the whole economy suffered from this movement, those who continued to be employed may be said to have gained. We may estimate this transfer of income from the shift in prices between 1929 and 1932 at nearly £300 million in 1932. Thus, as rentier incomes from overseas dropped by £100 million, we may take the net addition to incomes to have been of the order of £200 million. The employed part of the population plus the rentiers were £200 million better off. The national income as a whole,

however, had dropped by over £500 million over the same
period ('Table IV) – a loss that fell mainly on the additional
1.5 millions unemployed in 1932 who had had jobs in
1929.

There were other forms of tribute, which advantaged some
and disadvantaged others. We have already considered the
advantages of a privileged and protected market for the great
integrated corporations, and the disadvantages of the
resulting narrowing of world trade for the smaller exporter
and for workers in export industries who lost their jobs.
Then we must remember the earnings of the City from
insurance, brokerage, commodity marketing and other
financial operations such as the floating of foreign stocks.
These were not inconsiderable; but we must set against them
the disadvantages flowing from the economic policies
dictated by the City, which we have also considered. There
were jobs in the empire for some 20,000 administrators and
posts in the Army, the Navy and the Air Force. These all
provided interesting employment for the second-class
graduates of Oxford and Cambridge – the firsts went into the
Home Civil Service – and no doubt they added to the
country's wealth and somewhat relieved the pressure of
graduates at the employment exchanges.[72]

If there was not a 'feast for the workers' in the 1930s, there
were certainly crumbs thrown to the growing number of
domestic servants around the tables of the rich; there were
two and a half million men and women engaged in personal
service in England and Wales in 1931.[73] Varga regarded this
fact as evidence of parasitism in the British economy,[74] but
should luxury services be regarded as any more parasitic than
luxury goods? Only in so far as they were at the expense of
the development of production for export to help balance
Britain's foreign payments, which were so dependent on
earnings from past investment overseas, could both be
regarded in this light. Employment and real earnings
provided a better test of economic strength. The figures in

Table IX below are important and the last figures in the columns are the crucial ones.

As we look at the rise in real earnings of those employed, the cheap food from overseas must seem to have saved the British worker from increasing misery. Looking at the high level of unemployment throughout these years – never less than 1.5 million – doubts rise in the mind. Looking further, at the check that came in the end to the rise in real wages and in national income in 1936 and at the new crisis of 1938, solved only by rearmament and war in 1939 (Table IX), one may see that the initial gains were at the expense of long-term losses. The impoverishment of the primary producers worked back in the end after 1936 to pull down the whole economy in the industrial metropolis.

Capitalism and the Second World War

How did capitalism survive? What we have to say of this period as of earlier periods is that the whole history of European, and especially of British, world-domination made capitalism, and especially British capitalism, seem to be immensely strong. Protest against stagnation was thus more easily diverted from challenge to the system as a whole into criticism of the stupidity or cupidity of particular capitalists – the mine-owners, the City bankers, the war profiteers. The years after 1917 in Britain also were years of unrest, but they ended in the débâcle of the General Strike. The working-class leaders failed then to seize the opportunity of the near collapse of British capitalism and to convince the British people as a whole of the necessity and possibility of an alternative. The same failure marked the working-class movements – Lenin's 'grave-diggers of capitalism' – throughout Europe. Everywhere, except in Russia, capitalism had a second chance.

Even the crisis of the 1930s did not lead to the collapse of capitalism. Indeed, in Britain, industry emerged from the early 1930s better organised and more soundly based than it had been for fifty years. But the new capitalism in Britain centring around the giant imperial companies looked much more like the picture which Lenin drew in 1917. Industry was much more concentrated, capital more centralised, the control of finance-capital over industry much greater and the influence of the representatives of the most powerful sections of banking and industry upon government policy much more profound. We have already examined the effects of these changes on government policy. The key to this period was to be found in the new links between the great vertically integrated combines and the colonial empire that we have seen being forged in the 1930s.

This was the crucial development of the 1930s; it was a development which, in one more respect, brought the facts of British economic life nearer to Lenin's picture of imperialism. Britain could not hope to retain the monopoly of world power that she had held in the nineteenth century, once her industrial monopoly had been challenged. The defeat of Germany, with the help of the United States, in the First World War could not re-establish it. American economic power was bound to emerge supreme. German industry was bound to recover and to demand a place in the sun. The tragedy was that the narrow and restrictive policies pursued by the 'Have' powers in the inter-war years, replacing the freer expansion of the nineteenth century, made it inevitable that German industry should turn to a Hitler for its advancement.

Demonic theories of history are singularly inadequate. It is no use blaming Hitler's maniacal policies for the outbreak of the Second World War, without seeing the real economic developments that underlay them. It was not just that the 'Have' powers refused to part with their colonial territories in face of Hitler's demands – 'No Christians for that poor lion!' as Leonard Barnes put it.[75] Colonial possessions may well not, perhaps, have been the advantage that the Germans felt them to be. They were but one example of the restrictive, 'spheres of influence' policies pursued by the great monopoly and semi-monopoly groups after 1919.

It was Lenin's clear grasp of this point that gave to his book its really prophetic character. The establishment by Britain, France and the United States of exclusive trading areas in the 1930s drove Japan, Germany and Italy to seek their own alternative spheres of influence. Japan followed the programme laid down by her militarists in the Tanaka memorial of 1927, first into Manchuria, then China and finally South-East Asia.[76] Italy moved into the Balkans, North Africa and Abyssinia; Germany through south-east Europe to the Middle East. The great monopolies, which dominated the governments of these countries, unable to find an outlet for their greatly expanded capacity, particularly in heavy industry, turned once more to war.[77]

For six terrible years two new empires appeared upon the stage of world history. The whole industry of continental Europe was brought under the ownership and control of the giant German trusts – Krupp's, Thyssen's, I.G., etc., and the banks that interlocked with them – who had put Hitler into power in 1934.[78]* On a lesser scale Japanese industry did the same in Northern China. Slave labour was brought into existence again. The peoples of south-east Europe and South America who had lost their markets in Britain fell easy prey to Dr Schacht's economic penetration. The wealth of whole peoples and of minority groups at home, even to the watches and jewellery of the seven million Jews consigned to the gas-chambers, was taken as tribute to the leaders of the master race.

No more terrible justification of Lenin's prophecy of the results of the uneven development of capitalist states could

---

* A subversive ditty current among German troops in 1940 ran:
'Who follows behind the leading tank?
It's Dr Rasche of the Dresdener Bank!'[79]
Dr Rasche was also a director of Metallgesellschaft and one of Göring's principal lieutenants.

have been imagined. Yet the gains for the German people, even before the bombing and destruction of their cities, were slight indeed. The advantage of colonies was a chimera compared with what might have been gained by peaceful co-operation in international trade. But the 'Have' powers blocked the way.

German and Japanese combines had a real complaint that they were excluded from markets and control over sources of raw materials. The militaristic gangsters, whom they employed to make good their claim to a place in the sun, however, succeeded in uniting the peoples of the 'Have' nations against them, as nothing else could, and in bringing into the balance also the growing might of the first non-capitalist world power. The Second World War thus became something more than a second war between rival imperialists, although the origin of Japanese and German fascism in the outward pressures of monopoly capitalism cannot be missed. It was not only the recruitment of slave labour but the taking over of rival companies that marked the German occupation of Europe.

Annexe on the Terms of Trade in the 1930s

There can be no question about the strong correlation in the 1930s between movements in the terms of trade and in the volume of British exports – the improving terms of trade for primary producers bringing a rise in exports from Britain in the 1920s, but the unfavourable changes for primary producers after 1929 bringing a sharp fall in the volume of Britain's exports (Table III, Chapter 2). Moreover, the changes in import prices during this period were much more violent than changes in export prices and were, therefore, mainly responsible for the swings in the terms of trade.[80] There was no longer much evidence of falling export prices being associated with a rise in export volumes. Export prices, in fact, fell continuously throughout the 1920s and early 1930s, and export volumes, though they rose briefly in the early and late 1920s, never regained the levels attained in the years before 1913. What had happened was that, during the First World War, export prices had risen far ahead of import prices and created a general setback in earnings of primary producers from which they did not recover. This situation both reflected and aggravated the stagnation of production in Britain in the post-war years. There was the same downward spiral of import prices and export volumes that we noted after the mid-1860s, and after 1929 this was of catastrophic proportions.

Throughout the nineteenth century, however, the general trend of exports and of manufacturing output was upwards. The cuts in prices, and particularly the reduced costs of railway- and sea-transport, brought real gains to Britain. Was there no similar advantage gained for Britain between the wars from the movement in the terms of trade that would generally be regarded as being in her favour? One would have expected the market at home to have been expanded by virtue of the cheaper prices of food and raw materials. Alan Day, for example, has argued that unfavourable terms of trade for industrial producers do, in fact, involve just as much a forgoing of resources as do unfavourable terms of trade for primary producers.[81]

There can be no doubt that there must be some advantage to industrial producers from obtaining cheaper rather than more expensive food and raw materials; but the idea of a forgoing of resources begs the question of whether such resources would have been evoked at all, that is, what level of output would have resulted in the industrial country without the demand for exports from the earnings of primary producers. This is the significance of the correlation of high import prices and a high export volume for a country like Britain that must live by processing imported materials into manufactures for export.

Moreover, in a situation of oligopoly with price-fixing

cartels, the crucial question is how far the lower prices of food and raw materials are in effect passed on to consumers and not used merely to maintain profits. Such profits may provide resources for investment which will in time lead to a general expansion of incomes, but the time-lag is important. A stagnation situation with a measure of unemployment may last long enough to start, or to accelerate, a recession both among primary producers and in the industrial country. It appears that this is just what happened in the early 1930s; for these years were marked by a vicious spiral of declining demand and at the same time by high profits among the largest near-monopoly producers. It was, indeed, precisely the high degree of monopoly and of cartelisation of the industrial producers which enabled them to maintain their prices so much better than the primary producers the world over.[82]

TABLE VIII

CHARACTER OF BRITISH OVERSEAS INVESTMENT, 1913, 1930, 1934

Type of Stock	1913 (%)	1930 (%)	1934 (%)
Government Stock	30	42	44
of which Empire	21	32	34
Foreign	9	10	10
Railways	41	24	24
of which Indian	4	3	3
Other Empire	8	7	7
U.S.A.	16	1	1
Other Foreign	12	13	13
Public Utilities and Shipping, etc.	5	6	6
Commerce and Industry	6	7	6
Mines	7	4	5
Other Raw Materials	3	9	8
Banks and Finance	8	7	7
Total	100	100	100
in £m.	3,763	3,425	3,414

Note: Total includes only quoted securities, leaving another £300 million un-
quoted.
Source: Royal Institute of International Affairs, *The Problem of International Investment* (London: Oxford Univ. Press, 1937), pp. 153–4.

TABLE IX

MOVEMENT IN REAL NATIONAL INCOME, REAL
EARNINGS AND UNEMPLOYMENT, U.K. AND
GERMANY, 1913–40

Year	Real National Income per head (1925–29 = 100) U.K.	Germany	Real Weekly Earnings U.K.	Germany	Unemployment as % of Labour Force U.K.	Germany
1913–14	99	103	100	100	—	—
1919	106	—	—	—	—	—
1920	98	—	—	—	—	—
1921	85	—	—	—	17	3
1922	89	—	—	—	14	1·5
1923	93	—	—	—	12	10
1924	94	—	111	—	10	14
1925	95	93	112	87	10	7
1926	95	95	113	90	12·5	18
1927	103	102	117	98	10	9
1928	103	105	117	108	11	8
1929	105	104	118	109	10	13
1930	103	100	122	105	16	22
1931	102	88	129	101	21	34
1932	101	78	129	94	22	44
1933	108	81	131	98	20	—
1934	111	89	132	102	17	—
1935	115	96	132	103	15·5	—
1936	119	105	134	106	13	—
1937	119	113	133	109	11	—
1938	119	124	128	114	13	—
1939	126	133	—	—	—	—
1940	124	136	—	—	—	—

Note: 10% of British labour force = roughly 1·5 million workers.
Source: I. Svennilson, op. cit., Tables 3, A-1, A-3.

References

1. W. W. Rostow, *The Stages of Economic Growth*, p. 106 ff.
2. E. Staley, *War and the Private Investor*, Chicago, 1935.
3. I. Svennilson, op. cit., Tables 22–33.
4. R. Pascal, *Growth of Modern Germany*, Cobbett Press, 1946, p. 64 ff.
5. Sir J. H. Clapham, *Economic Development of France and Germany*.
6. H. Levy, *Industrial Germany*, Cambridge, 1935, p. 52 ff.
7. E. Strauss, *Common Sense about the Common Market*, Allen and Unwin, 1958, p. 22 ff.
8. R. C. K. Ensor, op. cit., p. 258 ff.
9. V. I. Lenin, *Imperialism*, preface to French and German Editions, July 1920.
10. H. W. Arndt, *Economic Lessons of the 1930s*, Oxford, 1944, pp. 21 and 95 ff.
11. Royal Institute of International Affairs, *The Problem of International Investment*, Oxford, 1937, pp. 186–7.
12. D. L. Burn, *Economic History of Steel-making*, p. 374.
13. Labour Research Department, *Labour Research*, October, 1928, p. 223.
14. Royal Institute of International Affairs, *The Problem of International Investment*, pp. 145-6.
15. J. H. Frankel, op. cit.
16. Royal Institute of International Affairs, op. cit., pp. 152.
17. V. I. Lenin, *Imperialism*, Chapter V.
18. P. E. Hart and S. J. Prais, 'Analysis of Business Concentration', *Journal of the Royal Statistical Society*, Part II, 1956; and H. Leak and H. Maizels, 'The Structure of British Industries', *Journal of the Royal Statistical Society*, 1945, Parts I and II.
19. H. W. Arndt, op. cit., pp. 109 and 115.
20. V. I. Lenin, op. cit., Chapter V.
21. H. W. Arndt, op. cit., p. 115; and E. Varga and L. Mendelsohn, *New Data for Lenin's Imperialism*, New York, 1937, p. 153 ff.
22. V. I. Lenin, *Imperialism*, Little Lenin Library, 1944 edition, pp. 75–6.
23. J. Schumpeter, *Imperialism*, Meridian Books edition, p. 68.
24. G. W. Stocking and M. W. Watkins, *Cartels in Action*, New York, 1949, p. 516.
25. J. S. Martin, *All Honourable Men*, New York, 1950, p. 96.
26. ibid., p. 172.
27. League of Nations Committee on Raw Materials, *Report*, A27, Geneva, 1937.
28. L. Birch, *The Demand for Colonies*, League of Nations Union, London, 1936.

29. The above two may be cited and Royal Institute of International Affairs pamphlets 18 on *Raw Materials*, 1936, and 18 A., on *Raw Materials and Colonies*, 1939.

30. H. D. Henderson, Oxford Pamphlet on *Colonies and Raw Materials*, No. 7, Oxford, 1939, pp. 12–13.

31. Committee on Finance and Industry, *Report*, H.M.S.O., 1931, Chapter IV.

32. *London and Cambridge Economic Bulletin*, Statistical Series on External Trade.

33. League of Nations, *World Economic Survey, 1931–32*, Geneva, 1933, p. 151.

34. P. Jaffé, 'World Trade and British Shipping', *Britain and Her Export Trade*, ed. Mark Abrams, Pilot Press, 1946, pp. 218 and 229.

35. U.K. Government, *Statistical Abstract for the United Kingdom, 1923–36*, H.M.S.O., 1938, Table 295.

36. H. W. Arndt, op. cit., pp. 14 and 23.

37. W. A. Lewis, *Economic Survey, 1919–1939*, Allen and Unwin, 1949, p. 80.

38. W. Hoffmann, *British Industry, 1700–1950*, Table 54 B.

39. W. A Lewis, op. cit., p. 78.

40. V. I. Lenin, *Imperialism*, Little Lenin Library, 1944 ed., p. 109.

41. S. Lilley, *Men, Machines and History*, Cobbett Press, 1948, Chapter IX.

42. U.S. Dept. of Commerce, *Historical Statistics of the United States, 1789–1945*.

43. K. Marx, *Capital*, Vol. III, Clark Kerr edition, p. 568.

44. J. K. Galbraith, *The Great Crash, 1929*, Hamish Hamilton, 1955, p. 157.

45. I. Svennilson, op. cit., Table A. 68, p. 307.

46. H. W. Arndt, op. cit., pp. 111 and 116.

47. Political and Economic Planning, *Report on International Trade*, 1937, pp. 287–9.

48. H. W. Arndt, op. cit., p. 96 ff.

49. European Co-operation Administration, *The Sterling Area*, London, 1951, pp. 25–6.

50. H. W. Arndt, op. cit., p. 96 ff.

51. ibid., pp. 114–15.

52. D. L. Burn, op. cit., Chapter XVI.

53. H. Owen, *Steel – The Facts*, Lawrence and Wishart, 1946, pp. 60–1.

54. Political and Economic Planning, *Report on International Trade*, p. 268.

55. ibid., p. 248.

56. ibid., p. 185 ff.; and H. W. Arndt, op. cit., p. 114.

57. I. Svennilson, op. cit., Chapter IX.

58. H. W. Arndt, op. cit., p. 246 ff.

59. League of Nations, *World Economic Survey, 1932–33*, Geneva, 1933, p. 8.
60. League of Nations, *World Economic Survey, 1937–38*; and E. A. G. Robinson's article in *United Kingdom Foreign Policy*, Royal Institute of International Affairs, 1950, Table I, p. 97.
61. J. Strachey, *The End of Empire*, Chapter X.
62. League of Nations, *World Economic Survey, 1931–32*, Geneva, 1932, pp. 22 and 111.
63. Food and Agricultural Organisation, *The State of Food and Agriculture, 1956*, Rome, 1957, p. 65.
64. e.g. R. P. Dutt, review of J. Strachey's *The End of Empire*, in the *Daily Worker*, 7.1. 60.
65. J. W. F. Rowe, *Markets and Men*, Cambridge, 1936.
66. P. L. Cook and R. Cohen, *Effects of Mergers*, Cambridge, 1937.
67. H. W. Richardson, 'New Industries between the Wars', *Oxford Economic Papers*, October, 1961.
68. Sir J. Clapham, *An Economic History of Modern Britain*, Vol. III, Epilogue, p. 536 ff.; and T. Balogh, *Financial Organisation*, National Institute for Economic and Social Research, 1947, p. 274 ff.
69. V. I. Lenin, *Imperialism and the Split in Socialism*, Selected Works, Lawrence and Wishart, Vol. XI, p. 748 ff.
70. F. Engels, Preface to the second edition of *The Condition of the Working Class in England, in 1844.*
71. Royal Institute of International Affairs, *Problems of International Investment*, p. 160.
72. L. Birch, op. cit., p. 23.
73. A. M. Carr Saunders and D. Caradog Jones, *Social Structure of England and Wales*, 2nd edition, Oxford, 1937, Table XXIV, p. 48.
74. E. Varga and L. Mendelsohn, op. cit., p. 223 ff.
75. L. Barnes, *Empire or Democracy*, Gollancz, 1939.
76. Baron Tanaka, Memorandum on the 'Positive Policy in Manchuria', quoted in G. D. R. Philips, *Russia, Japan and Mongolia*, Muller, 1942, Chapter VIII.
77. R. Sasuly, *I. G. Farben*, New York, 1947, p. 180 ff.
78. ibid., p. 69 ff.; and J. S. Martin, *All Honourable Men, passim*; and J. E. Dubois, *Generals in Grey Suits*, Bodley Head, 1953.
79. J. E. Dubois, op. cit.
80. London and Cambridge Economic Service *Bulletin*, Series on External Trade. This explanation is accepted for the post-1919 period by Martin and Thackeray, op. cit.
81. A. C. L. Day, article in *Lloyd's Bank Review*, July 1958.
82. The League of Nations *World Economic Survey, 1931–32* gives some remarkable contrasts of the movements in cartelized and non-cartelized prices, p. 127 ff.

CHAPTER 5

Results of Empire –
in the Colonies

We now turn to the results in the colonial territories of the unequal economic relations established between them and the European metropolitan powers, distinguishing once again between the lands of European settlement, where industries were being developed, and the already settled lands, where primary production alone was encouraged. What was the balance of advantage and disadvantage from the relationship for each? While possession of colonies has been shown to have brought less advantage to the metropolitan country than its citizens had been led to suppose, it does not follow that the *disadvantages* for the colonial peoples have been any less. As John Strachey has rightly noted, 'The unrequited transfer of say £100 million a year may mean a minor addition to the wealth of the [highly developed country], but the imposition of a crushing burden upon the poverty of the [underdeveloped].'[1] If the movement of the terms of trade in the 1930s was only doubtfully 'favourable' to the British workers, even to those in employment, it was certainly unfavourable to the colonial and other primary producers.

In the years between the wars, no colony achieved its freedom except the Philippines. A third of the world's peoples, or 800 million, lived under colonial rule. In addition, another 500 million in China, 150 million in Central and South America, and 100 million in South-East Europe had very limited economic freedom of manœuvre against the economic strength of the great industrial powers. In most of the lands where these peoples lived, the main economic resources, and especially the minerals, were exploited by foreign companies from among the industrial powers. We have to judge the balance of advantage in such unequal economic relations during the inter-war period, not forgetting the politico-economic as well as the direct economic effects.

In the earliest period of colonial rule the crucial element in the relationship between Europe and the overseas dependencies was the flow of tribute from the Americas and India to Europe. This was followed by the no less important elimination of native industries, above all in the opening-up of India and China to British manufactures. It is this actual destruction of competitors that is missed in Professor Rostow's theory[2] of the incapacity of traditional societies, as he calls them, to organise a surplus for export without the help of Western European business, or to develop anything but raw materials for export. The main exports entering world markets for two thousand years before 1800 were precisely the textiles and spices of China and India. The same point is missed in the otherwise infinitely more valuable theory of Professor Nurkse[3] and Dr Gunnar Myrdal[4] that the widening gulf between rich and poor nations results from the vicious circle of free trade: that rich lands attract wealth and poor lands repel it.

Dr Myrdal, in his *Economic Theory and the Underdeveloped Regions*, quotes the biblical phrases, 'For unto everyone that hath shall be given, and he shall have abundance; but from him that hath not shall be taken away even that which he hath',[5] to illustrate Nurkse's concept of a process of circular and cumulative causation that is involved in the unregulated free play of economic forces. In the nineteenth century, free trade froze the world division of labour between primary producers and manufacturers; but the division had first to be made by the opening-up of the world's markets to European manufacturers. This artificial division of labour was the essence of the unequal relationship between advanced and underdeveloped lands. The division was finally confirmed in the exploitation by European capital of the minerals and of the plantation-crops produced for export from the lands of primary production. And, as Myrdal is the first to concede, the advanced industrial lands have not been above doing all they could to prevent the division of labour from being altered.[6]

What Economic Dependence meant for a Colony

What has been the disadvantage, then, in being confined to primary production? Canada, Australia, New Zealand and South Africa all seem to have done well out of it (Table I at end of Introduction). But none of them has in fact been a colony, in this century at least. All have used the wealth from their primary production to establish many of their own industries. It is an extremely important fact that, by 1938, none had a majority of its population engaged in agriculture.[7] Only countries for whose natural products there has been a steadily growing world demand have been in a position to begin industrialising. But more than this was needed. To industrialise requires economic independence, so that the wealth produced may be retained for internal development, and political independence, so that infant industries may be protected.

These courses have not been open to colonies, whose wealth was remitted to the investors of capital away in the metropolitan country, and who were often specifically prevented from introducing protective tariffs, and whose natural resources were developed by an artificially created proletariat at low wages from migrant, indentured and poll-tax labour. Colonial countries, along with other primary producers, have, in addition, suffered, as we have seen, in the terms of their trade with the manufacturers for two reasons. Their exports were generally limited to one or two crops or minerals upon which their whole livelihood increasingly depended, and in which productivity was difficult to raise; at the same time, the markets for their products were generally restricted to the metropolitan investing country. This 'enforced bilateralism' is, as Myrdal points out, what the imperialists call 'close cultural and economic ties with the mother country'.[8]

Moreover, the channelling of all sales through the London commodity markets, as far as British Empire products were concerned, and through New York, Amsterdam, Paris, etc., for other products, has had disadvantages as well as advantages for primary producers. The main claims made for these markets have been, first, that they are markets, bringing together buyers and sellers from all over the world and thus establishing a price; and, second, that they reduce the risks inherent in fluctuating prices by providing a system of re-insurance to the merchants, against price movements.[9] The disadvantages arise because these markets also greatly exaggerate the fluctuations: a very small excess of supply over demand and the price collapses; a very small excess of demand over supply and the price soars. The primary producer has no insurance, unless he or his government can stockpile supplies. But this is just the sort of thing that colonial producers (as opposed to U.K. firms operating in the colonies) have not been able to do.

The free operation of market forces has been the cause of the violent instability of primary-commodity prices. High prices in the First World War encouraged, as we saw earlier, an excessive extension of crop areas, particularly of rubber, and also of some mining capacity. The subsequent slump in prices left a trail of ruin among primary producers which in the end reacted back on the manufacturing countries too. What must also not be forgotten is that the control of the production of many colonial exports came in this period increasingly into the hands of great imperial companies, such as Unilever, Imperial Tobacco, Dunlop, or Tate and Lyle, whose business has been to obtain cheap raw materials for processing.

Was there no advantage at all to colonies, then, from European investment in them? The answer we saw earlier was that the position differed completely in the lands colonised by European settlers, and in the Asian and African lands brought under colonial rule. The greater part of overseas investment was in railways, ports and harbour installations, roads, telegraph and telephones, plantation and mining. To determine how far European investment actually advanced the condition of the peoples in the regions concerned, however, it is necessary to find what spread took place from the investment to the rest of the economy.

The object of the investment in such mining installations, plantations and transport was chiefly to facilitate the extraction of primary products for export. If the investment created enclaves of development within a largely-unchanged subsistence economy then it might well happen that the net result might be to leave the region as a whole poorer than it was before.[10] This is a conclusion so much at variance with the widely fostered view of the role of European capital that we shall have to examine rather closely what has happened in several different regions. But we may accept now that actual impoverishment might take place, if there was little or no spread into the rest of the economy from the developed enclaves, if the work in mines or on plantations gravely debilitated the workers, if the plantations and the concentration on crops for export seriously reduced the area available for food production, or if the irreplaceable natural wealth of the country was exhausted so that the future income of the inhabitants was mortgaged.

The extent of the spread from foreign investment into the development of the whole economy has depended on a wide range of factors: the amount of capital brought in from outside; the rate of return on the capital invested; the proportion of the new value created, which remained in the region as the result of taxation and native share-holding; the extent to which secondary employment was provided by the establishment of processing and refining industries in the region and by the placing of orders locally for food and other stores for the mines and plantations, the degree to which a native entrepreneurial class was encouraged, the range of health and educational services and local housing provided by the mining or plantation companies. These are the points which we must look for in studying the results of European colonisation.

Lands of European Settlement

The lands of white settlement are those, as we should expect, where economic development with European capital has been carried furthest. The United States was the first and is the foremost, then follow Canada, Australia, New Zealand and southern Africa. Native populations, where they existed, were largely wiped out. Slaves and indentured and convict labour were brought in. It is interesting to remember that half the population of the United States at the Revolution was of slave or indentured origin.[11] The immensely rich resources of these lands were first developed by the colonisers with their own capital.[12] Later, capital obtained from investors in Britain was a crucial factor in their development, but the return on this capital never became the major call on the earnings of their exports. Indeed, British investors in the great land speculation of the 1880s in Australia actually lost a good part of their capital.[13] Only Canada of these lands became heavily dependent on outside capital, because of the large British investment in railways before the First World War and the still larger United States investment in industry thereafter.[14]

The colonisers of these lands were all lucky in the products they had to offer on the world market, but the crucial factor was their freedom to develop their own agricultural and mineral output and build up their own industries. Control over their own trade and industry enabled them to import capital equipment from Britain and develop their own economies without running into debt. For they had all won the political freedom to protect their own infant industries against British competition and to spend their earnings of foreign currency much as they wished. Very soon a majority of their rapidly growing populations were engaged in trade and industry, and only a minority in agriculture. But it was the basis of capitalist agriculture that was crucial to their development. The schemes for colonisation promoted from Britain, and especially in Australia and New Zealand by Gibbon Wakefield,[15] quite explicitly re-created a capitalist system of agriculture. One may conclude that, in all these lands of white settlement, capitalism was successfully transplanted from the home country, and that the shortage of labour and the wealth of resources generated high wages and rapid economic development.

The settler lands of Africa provide a halfway house between the empty lands of white settlement, and the mining and plantation colonies. One can see the two elements side by side in Southern and Northern Rhodesia, or in the mining and settler communities in South Africa. The Dutch voortrekkers and the early British settlers in Southern Rhodesia employed native labour in a more or less servile state, but brought their own capital to develop the land for their own needs and to produce a surplus for export. Rhodes and his successors obtained capital in far larger amounts to mine the diamonds and gold of South Africa and the copper of Northern Rhodesia. But the capital came largely from investors in Britain and the return on this capital flowed back to Britain. Gold-mining dividends paid overseas between 1887 and 1932 were £190 million; investment including reinvestment £120 million.[16] Thus, although the wealth produced by these British companies was immensely greater than that which the settlers contributed, it was largely the settlers and not the mining companies in both South Africa and Rhodesia who stimulated the industrialisation of their economies.

The settlers, however, were able to make use of the mines to develop the economy in South Africa, not only by direct and indirect taxation but by meeting many of the demands of the mines for stores of clothing, food, explosives, and similar necessities from local production instead of from imports. They had to fight for this, but, as Europeans themselves, it was not an impossibly unequal struggle. In South Africa and the Rhodesias there has for long been strong antagonism between the mine-owners and the white settlers, particularly the European trade unionists, who have fought for higher wages, for the exclusion of Africans from skilled jobs and for the retention of a larger share of the profits inside the colony.[17] It was Sir Roy Welensky, the present Prime Minister of the Central African Federation, who, as a Northern Rhodesian railway-union leader, used to complain bitterly that more than 45 per cent of the colony's whole national income went to outside investors every year.

A major aim of the Rhodesian Federation today is precisely to capture by taxation and other means some part of the Northern Rhodesian copper companies' wealth for Southern Rhodesia's industrial development.[18] This development got under way during the Second World War; at that time imports had to be cut down while the demand for manufactures grew with the large number of Empire forces stationed in the colony. Employment and output in non-mining industry in Southern Rhodesia trebled between 1938 and 1948; production of electric energy increased more than fourfold.[19] The basis of the expansion was the rather special one of the Forces' expenditure; it had almost nothing to do with the wealth of the mines in the north.

Similarly, industrialisation in South Africa took its two

major forward leaps in the two World Wars, when imports were cut off and armed forces had to be supplied. Between the wars it was the Nationalist Government of General Hertzog who, in the 'twenties, introduced protective duties and invested public funds, for example in Iscor (the Iron and Steel Corporation of South Africa set up in 1928), in order to encourage industrial development. African labour in private manufacturing doubled between 1929 and 1938; it doubled again in the decade of the war.[20]

The mine-owners have regarded the process of industrialisation without enthusiasm, although they have rather slowly begun to take advantage from it by investing some of their own resources in processing plants and secondary industry. The point is that they did not initiate industrialisation. As the whole output of the gold-mine is exported, the owners have had no interest in expanding the local market, but would rather see it held back so that there should be no competitive pressure on their wages and prices. In the case of South African gold, not much less than £500 million was paid to investors over the sixty years from 1887 to 1947,[21] but even in 1945, 56 per cent was going direct to foreign investors.[22] Nevertheless, the share going overseas has been steadily reduced, especially since 1945, and it has been from the taxation of the gold-mines that the Government has drawn a large part of its revenue, and with gold exports that it has been able to pay for industry's imports of machinery.

Cheap Labour in the Colonies

The conclusion would seem to be that the wealth produced from mines, or from plantations, will not of itself generate economic development, no matter how great the wealth may be. It took two World Wars and a non-mining settler community to develop local industry in South Africa. This is not perhaps surprising when it is remembered that the average wage paid to African labour in the mines, in addition to his keep, remained at 2s. a day from 1890 to 1940.[23] The spending of such pay as this was not likely to create demand for goods on a scale which would stimulate local industry. Here is the dilemma: industrial and economic development must be slow, indeed, where the market is so poor, but the basis of mining and planting overseas has always been cheap labour.

The wages paid in mines and plantations were based on the assumption that the worker's family stayed in the subsistence economy. Mining in Africa, and elsewhere too, largely depends on migrant labour, and the mine-owners want to keep it that way. Hence their support in the past for *apartheid* policies, which imply the restriction of native Africans to special reserves of land. The point has indeed been put most clearly by the South African Chamber of Mines: 'The ability of the mines to maintain their native labour-force by means of tribal natives from the reserves at rates of pay which are adequate for this migratory class of native but inadequate in practice for the de-tribalised urban native is a fundamental factor in the economy of the gold-mining industry.'[24] The basis of *apartheid* in South Africa and of segregation policies elsewhere is to retain those features of an enclave economy which are of advantage to the mine- and plantation-owners. Thus Africans are confined, as far as possible, to native reserves except for the periods when they are required for contract labour in the mines and on the farms; but more and more escape into the towns as industry expands and as those in the reserves are confined to narrower and narrower areas of land.[25]

By 1941, the South African government had scheduled 10 per cent of the land for the three million Africans already in the reserves. For the full implementation of *apartheid*, another 2.5 per cent of the land was to be added to the reserves to provide for the six million who had established themselves in the towns and on 'European' farms. That would leave 87.5 per cent for the two and a half million whites.[26] In Southern Rhodesia, the native Africans, who comprise more than nine-tenths of the country's population, are permitted to occupy only a third of the land.[27]

Overcrowding on the reserves leads to impoverishment and erosion of the soil, and the desperate attempt to gate-crash the urban economy, despite the pass system, the arrests, the shanty towns, the humiliation for the 'native' of life in a white-dominated city. In the end, of course, urban indus-trialisation will destroy *apartheid* and the enclave mining and plantation system. For the present, the system continues, illustrating most horribly the limitations of colonial enclave development.

The debilitation of the African population, already deci-mated by two centuries of slavery, confirms the view that European capital has so far retarded rather than advanced the African peoples' development. Those who think of Africans as savages emerging from the primeval forest are referred to Basil Davidson's *Old Africa Re-discovered*[28] for a description of the civilisations which Africans established prior to the coming of the European. Those who are im-pressed with Europe's civilising mission should then read the companion volume *Black Mother*[29] for a clear picture of the effects of the slave trade.

African health figures are universally appalling.[30] 'For one brief period of his life, the African achieves parity with infants of other races,' wrote Dr H. C. Trowell of the British Colonial Service, 'during the brief months of breast-feed-ing.'[31] European mine-workings have added new diseases to those which were endemic. The chief of these is T.B. Deaths from T.B. among South African miners are con-cealed by the dispatch home of the suspect as soon as the disease appears; but in Natal, in 1947, such deaths amounted to 900 per hundred thousand of the population compared with 64 in London.[32] In 1935, 55 per cent of the 75,000 Southern Rhodesian mine-workers were reported by the government medical director as casualties of disease.[33] The carrying of T.B. by the mine-workers back to their families has for long combined with the low level of nutrition in the reserves to produce a gravely debilitated people.

The result of these conditions is that the problem of replacing the labour force in the mines has become increasingly acute. As early as 1901, the South African Chamber of Commerce tried importing indentured Chinese labourers, a practice that was successful in Malaya and other colonies. But the Chinese could not stand the conditions in the mines. Since then the net has been spread wider and wider throughout Africa, to find men tough enough for the work. The whole continent is crossed with the tracks that bare feet have made to the city of 'Goli', and today the mining companies fly the labourers in and out in their own fleet of Dakotas, so that they shall not be caught up in the urban economy *en route*. They draw upon all the neighbouring territories. Two-thirds of the mine-workers of South Africa come from Portuguese and British colonies.[34] The Northern Rhodesian copper belt has drawn on the comparatively dense population of Nyasaland (as many Nyasas worked outside the territory in 1958 as worked for money inside it),[35] just as the Katanga mines of the Belgian Congo have depended on Ruanda-Urundi.

Mining and Plantation Wealth

We have looked so far at the developed lands of European settlement and at the part-developed lands of southern Africa, where European capital investment has been high and where European settlers have encouraged the development of an industrial economy. We must now turn to look at other parts of Africa and at South-East Asia, where there have been less capital and fewer settlers. The result has been both better and worse – less debilitation and less industrialisation. The amount of capital invested was certainly an important factor. As we have noted earlier, the essence of the situation in underdeveloped lands was that they were starved of capital.

Only a quarter of all British investment in 1913 was in the colonies and, as 10 per cent was in India and 8 per cent in South Africa, that left 7 per cent for all the rest (see Table V, Chapter 3). But even size is not all; the rate of return on capital invested has often been so high as to leave absolutely nothing for 'spread' into local development. Table X below gives a remarkable picture, especially for the pre-war period, of the high proportion of dividends and royalties in the total value of African mineral output. This is the corollary of the cheap labour, which the Table also reveals.

It is only since the war that local taxation has begun to bite into the revenues of overseas-operating companies. Almost equally important is the rise, at least in South Africa and Southern Rhodesia, of the share of ownership in mines and plantations held inside the country. This has been kept in the hands of Europeans, of course, but nonetheless it has created funds available for local spending or reinvestment. In South Africa, well over a half of the profit in mining now accrues to local capital; in Rhodesia, the proportion is very much lower, but since the war there has been much reinvestment of profits by the copper companies and a new net inflow of private capital.[36] Where there were no European settlers, in West Africa for example, there was before the war virtually no development.

We may take Nigeria as a case in point. The wealth of Unilever was based to a considerable extent on Nigerian vegetable oils,[37] yet the Nigerians remained one of the poorest peoples of a poor continent.[38] Half the children in Niger province did not survive their fifth year. After three-quarters of a century of British rule in West Africa, where 80 per cent of the population suffer from malaria, the British authorities had built only one fever hospital for a population of 30 million Nigerians. Compared with Britain's ration of a doctor to every thousand inhabitants, Nigeria had one to 60,000.[39]

Nonetheless, for all that we have said, investment in

primary production brought some advantage to a colony. The infra-structure of ports and railways involved some extra employment. Mining and plantation wages added something to subsistence. Urban centres did establish themselves, despite segregation policies, and the growth of towns, which received a great impetus during the Second World War, became the basis of African nationalism. This part of the story we must take up in the next chapter. We have looked briefly at Africa; it will be well to examine the effects of colonial rule in South-East Asia also.

In the trade of each of the countries of South-East Asia (excluding that of China, the U.S.S.R. and Japan), only two primary commodities account for around 80 per cent of exports.[40] Although the total share of these lands in world trade is only 3 per cent, the share of their trade in some commodities is very high. All but a tiny fraction of the world's natural rubber, jute, tea and tin are produced and exported from South-East Asia.[41] The greater part of these crops was sold before the war through markets in London. Production was mainly on large estates owned by imperial companies. Two-thirds of Malayan rubber, nearly all Malayan palm oil and 70 per cent of Malayan tin production were controlled by foreign, mainly British, companies.[42] Dunlop alone owns 90,000 acres of rubber in Malaya, as their advertisements proclaim. In Ceylon, 80 to 90 per cent of the tea and rubber was grown on estates, and three-quarters of the tea and half the rubber estates were owned by British companies. In Ceylon, the copra processing for the market was entirely in British hands. There is a further point: in Ceylon and Malaya, agency houses, such as Harrisons and Crosfield, J. H. Vavaseur and Co. and others, carried on a large part of the merchanting, shipping, and import and export business, as well as owning large estates.[43] A similar picture could be drawn for the West Indian sugar islands, with Tate and Lyle owning estates and Booker, McConnell doing the merchanting and shipping.

It was not only through their weak bargaining position over the terms of trade that mining and plantation colonies suffered, but through the fact that the greater part of the profit from the sale of their products was taken right out of their hands. In his study of British investment in Latin America, Rippy gives some comparative figures of dividends on nominal capital in ordinary shares in different British colonies. Twenty tin-mines in Malaya, for example, show annual returns on investments over a 30-to-40-year period of between 15 per cent and 30 per cent with earnings in the best five years – in the late 1930s – of 40 to 50 per cent on a total capital of about £5 million. Twenty tea plantations in India and Ceylon show returns over 50 to 60 years averaging 15 to 25 per cent with dividends in the best years – mainly in the 1920s this time – 40 to 50 per cent on a total capital of about £3 million.[44] Earnings on the overall ordinary and loan stock of £90 million held, according to the Chatham House study of international investment, in rubber plantations were not much over 5 per cent in the 1930s, but they had been well over 10 per cent in the early 1920s. Earnings on overall stocks of about £120 million held in oil in 1930 were over 12 per cent.[45]

Rates of profit for investors were high partly because wages were desperately low, and wages were low because there was no alternative employment. Mines and plantations were enclaves in a subsistence economy. Sometimes they were quite large enclaves: in Malaya, half the arable land was under rubber; two-thirds of the crop-area in Ceylon was taken up with the three export crops – tea, rubber and copra; a quarter of the cultivated land in Indonesia was covered by rubber, tea, sugar, copra, tobacco, all crops for export.[46] The total value of Indonesian exports was equal to a quarter of the national income in 1938 and exceeded the value of imports by 50 per cent. Exports formed an even higher proportion of income in Burma (41 per cent), Ceylon (48 per cent) and Malaya (about 75 per cent); in the case of Burma, exports

were more than double the value of imports.[47] The result of
the concentration on export crops was that food had to be
imported. Before the war, Indonesia, Ceylon and Malaya
all relied on imports for a third of their consumption of
rice.[48]

The earnings from the sale of these export crops accrued
largely to Europeans. The wealth from the rubber and
tobacco plantations, and from the tin and petroleum workings in Indonesia, which flowed back to the Netherlands, was
estimated to be equal to a sixth of the Dutch national income
before the war.[49] Yet, so small was the spread from these
enclaves of development to the rest of the Indonesian
economy that every kind of iron goods, even to every nail
used for building and packing, had to be imported.[50] Britain,
as we have seen, was far less dependent on her colonies than
Holland. Less than 5 per cent was added each year to Britain's
national income from overseas investment during the 1930s,
and only a fifth of this was drawn from investment in
colonial territories including India (see Tables IV and V,
at end of Chapter 2). But this did not necessarily mean that
no really large sums were taken from the colonies. Out of a
value of £60 to £70 million of exports from Malaya in the
middle 1930s, the return on tin and rubber investments
valued at about £100 million probably amounted to £10
million a year, which would be somewhat over a tenth of
Malaya's national income.[51]

In South-East Asia, however, as elsewhere in underdeveloped lands, the process of urbanisation had been going
on, often encouraged by the agrarian slump between the
two World Wars. Thus Singapore had a population of
300,000 in 1913, over half a million in 1938 and very nearly
a million by 1948.[52] But this movement has been greatly
accelerated of recent years and must concern us later. Up
to the Second World War urbanisation in mining and
plantation colonies had only affected a very small proportion
of the population. The mines and plantations remained

developed islands in the wide ocean of a bare subsistence economy.

The Wealth and Poverty of India

The last countries to be considered are those which were brought under imperial rule for the wealth which they had already created, rather than for that which lay hidden and awaiting exploitation in the soil or the rocks of their land. Of these, India and Pakistan have been the most important for Britain, but the semi-colonial status of China after the beginning of the nineteenth century should not be overlooked.

The story of these two great sub-continents of Asia in their relations with Europe is a cruel one. We have already seen the exaction of a rich tribute, the destruction of competitive industry, and the opening of markets to European and particularly British manufactures. The result was to set off the terrible series of famines in Bengal and the Sind, which were to hold back the growth of Indian population for a century; to cause the ruin of Indian handicraft industry and the great towns based upon it; and to create that over-population of the land and that over-pressure on the agricultural sector of the economy which is India's tragedy today. What is little realised is that this whole disastrous process continued right up to the ending of Britain's colonial rule.

Between 1891 and 1931, the population of India dependent upon agriculture rose from 61 per cent to 75 per cent,[53] and this was after the main blows at the handicraft industry had already been absorbed. At the same time, yields per acre were falling, in rice, for instance, from nearly 1,000 pounds in the First World War to just over 700 pounds in the second, and similar steady falls were recorded for other crops.[54] Moreover, more and more land was being taken for export crops and, while before the First World War the area under food crops was also being increased by irrigation works and reclamation, after 1920 the food-crop acreage actually declined – by two million acres in the succeeding twenty years.[55] The area under export crops rose to almost a fifth of the total cultivated land.[56] Exports, mainly of cotton, jute and tea, rose steadily until, in the five years after 1931, they were on average, including bullion, £60 million a year in excess of imports.[57]

This difference between the value of exports and imports went each year to pay the 'Home Charges', loan interest and dividends. The so-called 'Home Charges', drawn from Indian revenues for British services, rose from £2·5 million in 1851 to £33 million in 1937, and with them the remittances of individual Britons rose steadily. This was the estimate of a semi-official American report in 1945, which added the loans made to the Indian Government for building the railways and telegraph system carrying annual payments of interest of nearly £50 million, and also incomes of another £50 million earned by British companies in trade and shipping, from which Indians were excluded.[58] Thus, by the Second World War, the annual flow of wealth from India to Britain amounted to over £130 million. The average flow of tribute for the first seventy-five years of British rule in India had been between £2 million and £3 million a year,[59] and the difference between that and the 1945 figure can only in some small part be accounted for by the depreciation in the value of the Pound.

The Indian tribute may have been a small addition to Britain's national wealth in the 1930s, perhaps of the order of 3 per cent (see Table IV, Chapter 3). It was a larger loss to India – about a tenth of her national income.[60] In the 1930s, India was forced to cover her losses with gold, which was paid into Britain's reserves to the astonishing amount of £240 million during the six years from 1931 to 1937.[61] The traditional savings of the Indian peasantry, the heirlooms of an ancient people, were melted down and shipped to

London and then to America to cover Britain's own deficit on her foreign trade.

There was, however, one important difference between what happened in India and in the smaller plantation and mining colonies. Some part of the crops for export were produced by Indian peasants rather than on British or other European-owned plantations. A rather larger proportion of the earnings from the sale of these crops, therefore, stayed in India. Some of the processing of the crops and the secondary industries associated with them were also established in India. Many of these were British-owned and thus their British owners tended to take the profits made in them out of the country. Some, however, were Indian-owned, and this development led to the emergence of a small Indian capitalist, manufacturing class.

The Indian textile industry had first been established in the 1850s, but made little progress until the late 1880s.[62] Expansion up to 1913 was rapid, when, as we have seen, exports of cotton yarn and jute manufactures became of major importance. During the First World War, Indian cotton- and jute-mills enjoyed high profits and attracted a new flow of investment immediately after 1918, partly owing to the government's over-valuation of the rupee, but mainly to war-time demand and high prices. Capital equipment was exported to India, and Indian-owned as well as British companies flourished. The boom crashed in 1921, the smaller Indian firms being the worst hit, and the proportion of the population engaged in industry actually declined during the next decade. It had been over 11 per cent in 1911; by 1931 it was under 10 per cent.[63] Exports of yarns collapsed but exports of piece-goods grew.[64]

The development of Indian industrialisation had been recommended in 1918 in the light of war-time experience by the Montagu-Chelmsford report;[65] and for strategic, economic and political reasons it was decided to give protection first to cotton manufacture and then to the infant iron and steel industry. When, after 1921, other industries applied for protection, only the British-owned match industry received it. In 1927, the whole policy was reversed: the iron and steel tariff was lowered and a system of imperial preference for imports of British manufactures was introduced. In 1930, this was extended to cotton textiles and, after the Ottawa Conference of 1932, a measure of protection for Indian textiles was combined with protection for British exporters in the Indian market, albeit over strong Congress protests.[66] Thus, not only was Indian economic development held back, until a second World War created conditions which encouraged it once more, but the share of imports from Britain in a much smaller total of trade after 1931 was steadily increased.[67]

Despite the obstacles we have considered, Indian industry did develop between the wars, but very slowly. By 1937, the Tata mills were producing nearly a million tons of steel, enough at least for India's own restricted needs; and Indian mills were meeting three-quarters of the country's textile requirements. Cement and paper output had doubled in a decade but there had been practically no development in heavy engineering, chemicals and machinery manufacture.[68] Thus, the initial impetus given to industrialisation by increased export earnings before and during the war was checked first by the collapse of export markets and then by imperial policies that worked against industrialisation.

The Results of Indirect Rule

What held back development in India and elsewhere, more even than direct economic limitations, were the political and politico-economic effects of imperialist rule on the colonial society itself. We may examine these in India here, but we shall meet them again when we look at the position in the oil-bearing and mineral-producing lands of the Middle East and South America, which avoided colonisation, but failed to emerge from a very low level of economic development. These politico-economic effects of colonial status are essential to our study.

Imperialists have nearly always preferred some form of indirect rule through local princes, chiefs, sheikhs and landlords to direct government by imperial satraps. We saw earlier how Clive's success in Bengal against the Mogul Empire was in part due to the already existing orientation of the Bengal merchants towards the European trade. The Permanent Land Settlement established by Lord Cornwallis in 1793, affecting Bengal, Bihar, Orissa and later Madras, not only formed the basis for taxation but established a permanent class of landowner. The zamindars, who had been originally just tax-collectors for the Mogul, collecting a certain share of each year's crop produced by the village commune which had owned the land since time immemorial, became landlords. The peasant was expropriated and the tax was fixed with little regard to crop fluctuations.[69]

'The Permanent Settlement, though a failure in many other respects and in most important essentials, has this great advantage at least,' said Lord William Bentinck, the Governor-General in 1829, 'of having created a vast body of rich landed proprietors deeply interested in the continuance of the British dominion and having complete command over the mass of the people.'[70] Fifty years later, when Queen Victoria was proclaimed Empress of India, the Viceroy, then Lord Lytton, claimed that this marked the beginning of a 'new policy by virtue of which the Crown of England should henceforth be identified with the hopes, the aspirations, the sympathies and the interests of a powerful native aristocracy'.[71] The princes and the landlords became the foundation of British rule.

Many landlords were also money-lenders, and money-lenders in the nature of things tended to become landlords. The share of the Indian peasant's crop taken by the landlord, money-lender and tax-collector, often all rolled into one person, might be as much as two-thirds – and good land would produce three crops a year.[72] A succession of bad years – which became more frequent with the over-pressure on the land, the use of dung for fuel, the subdivision of plots, the lack of capital for improvements – created a crushing burden of debt. Debts grew steadily. By 1919 only 17 per cent of peasants in the Punjab were free of debt.[73] But this situation also meant that the surplus, over and above immediate needs and available for possible economic development, was drawn into the hands of a class with no interest whatever in industrialisation. Why should the landlords be interested in industry when the return on investment in agriculture was so high? This is still the basic problem of Indian economic development. Feudal land-ownership holds back progress in many other ways, too, besides the dissipation of the surplus in luxurious living. We shall take up this question in a later chapter (Chapter 11).

Moreover, the opening-up of markets for British manufactures and the later expansion of export crops encouraged the growth of a merchant 'comprador'* class, depending on the colonial system and not interested in the growth of local industry. This phenomenon occurred not only in India, but more widely in other colonial territories, wherever marketing and crop-collection were not directly in the hands of imperial companies. Where these companies were operating, as in the plantation economies, even the native trader was squeezed out. In West Africa, for example, Unilever's subsidiary, the United Africa Company, not only bought the oils for soap and margarine direct from the peasant but ran a chain of stores at which he could make his purchases.[74]

* 'Comprador' was the name given to the Chinese merchants who operated European 'factories' in China's treaty ports, originally from the Portuguese *comprador* – a purveyor.

The Native Middle Class and Industrialisation

The imperial government not only needed princes and landlords and merchants but had also to train a native middle class for clerical and other administrative work, for teaching, for medicine and the law. In India, especially, the number of these was considerable, but civil servants are not entrepreneurs any more than landlords and merchants are. One of the major weaknesses of Indian industry in the 1920s and 1930s was the 'agency' management system, which reflected the divorce between ownership with its narrow interest in profit and management with its lowly status in Indian society.[75] Nevertheless, from all these groups a native bourgeoisie, and a class of industrial entrepreneurs even, did emerge in India; and this generated the pressure for native industries. But the process was desperately slow, not only because of the obstacles to industrialisation, which we considered earlier, but because the landlord and middle classes were built up around the colonial system itself.

The origins of the Indian National Congress are to be found just in the emergence of such a class, which was in the end to challenge imperialist rule. But the form that Congress took was the direct result of imperialist intervention: 'to provide a safety-valve for the escape of great and growing forces', as the Marquis of Dufferin's official adviser on the subject put it in 1884.[76] Extremists, as Lord Dufferin explained, could be sidetracked and repressed, loyalist and even reactionary elements encouraged. The aim was to direct the movement for self-government into channels that could be controlled by persons who would be fundamentally in sympathy with the British. And if this failed, the movement could be split on communal lines.

'*Divide et impera* was the old Roman motto and it should be ours,' wrote Mountstuart Elphinstone, Governor of Bombay, in 1859;[77] and thirty years later Mr Strachey's ancestor, Sir John, was writing, 'The truth plainly is that the existence side by side of these hostile creeds is one of the strong points in our political position.'[78] And yet for centuries communal strife in India had been almost non-existent. No wonder the founding of the Moslem League in 1906 was regarded by a British official writing to the Viceroy, then Lord Minto, as 'a work of statesmanship that will affect India and Indian history for many a long year'[79] – a revealing and prophetic utterance! The policy of divide and conquer was to appear again in British imperial history between Jews and Arabs in Palestine, between Chinese and Malays in Malaya, between Greeks and Turks in Cyprus, between Indians and Negroes in British Guiana.

Establish and maintain a native feudal aristocracy, hold back the emergence of a truly entrepreneurial class, divert the nationalist movement into safe channels, hold down the peasant in debilitating poverty, divide and rule – it is not too much to say that these have been the harsh realities, often openly pursued, behind the lofty phrases about the white man's burden and preparation for self government. The day of liberation has revealed that the preceding period, far from being a preparation for self-rule, was often one of deterioration and disintegration, which left almost insuperable problems for the successor governments.

The example of the partition of India and the establishment of independent governments in Pakistan, India, Burma and Ceylon is but one among several. The much-boasted services in health and education revealed a picture almost as backward as the industrial base, from which the future economy had to be built. After two hundred years of British rule in India, over 80 per cent of the people were still unable to read or write. Illiteracy was at the same high level throughout all the Asian and African colonies.[80] A small aristocracy of princes and great landlords sent their sons to Eton and Oxford or Cambridge; the middle class could educate their children through Indian schools and colleges; but the chance of schooling for the great mass of the peasants was rare, and the advance to higher education barred by obstacles which only the most outstanding child could surmount. Nevertheless, the movements for national liberation in Africa and Asia are led mainly by men from middle-class or even aristocratic origins, who in many cases boast an Oxford or Cambridge degree. Education is not a weapon whose effects can be limited.

TABLE X

DISTRIBUTION OF REVENUE FROM AFRICAN MINING, 1937–56

Year	Country	Value of output (£m.)	Govt. Revenue (£m.)	Dividends & Royalties (£m.)	Employment Ratio*	Wages paid Europeans (£m.)	Wages paid Africans (£m.)	Average per African Worker Wage (£ per year)	Average per African Worker Output
1937	N. Rhodesia	12	·7	5·5	1:110	·8	·25	14	700
1956	N. Rhodesia	115	21	34	1:6	13·6	7·7	165	2,450
1956	S. Rhodesia	23	—	—	1:20	3·4	2·6	47	415
1958	S. Africa (gold only)	140	19	43	1:7	52	23	68	680
1957	S. Africa (all minerals)	337	—	—	1:7	67	32	65	700
1937	Nigeria	2·5	—	1·3	1:150	—	·3	9	69
1956	Nigeria	12	—	4	1:150	—	3·3	57	205

Note: * Employment Ratio = of Europeans to Africans employed.
Sources: 1937 figures:
L. Barnes, *Empire and Democracy* (London: Gollancz, 1939), p. 153.
Margery Perham, *Mining, Commerce and Finance in Nigeria* (London: Oxford Univ. Press, 1939).
1956–58 figures:
United Nations, *Economic Survey of Africa since 1950* (New York, 1960), pp. 67–8.
A. Hazlewood and P. D. Henderson, articles on Nyasaland in Oxford University Institute of Statistics, *Bulletin*, February 1960.
Mining Year Book, 1960.
Union of South Africa Department of Mines publications quoted in unpublished article by Dr H. J. Simons in reference 17, Chapter 5.

References

1. J. Strachey, *The End of Empire*, p. 187.
2. W. W. Rostow, *The Stages of Economic Growth*, p. 109.
3. R. Nurkse, *Problems of Capital Formation in Underdeveloped Countries*, Blackwell, 1953, p. 4 and Chapter VI *passim*.
4. G. Myrdal, *Economic Theory and the Underdeveloped Regions*, Duckworth, 1957, Chapter II.
5. ibid., p. 34.
6. ibid., p. 71.
7. Woytinsky and Woytinsky, op. cit., Table 169, pp. 356–7.
8. G. Myrdal, op. cit., p. 62.
9. O. Hobson, *How the City Works*, *News Chronicle*, Book Department, Sixth Edition, 1959, p. 77.
10. G. Myrdal, op. cit., p. 53.
11. E. C. Kirkland, *A History of American Economic Life*, New York, 1933, p. 387.
12. T. A. Coghlan, *Labour and Industry in Australia*, Oxford, 1918.
13. C. H. Feinstein, op. cit., Chapter VIII.
14. E. C. Kirkland, op. cit., p. 693.
15. E. Gibbon Wakefield, *A View of the Art of Colonisation*, London, 1849; and see Karl Marx's comments in *Capital*, Vol. I, Chapter XXXIII, Allen and Unwin Ed., p. 801 ff.
16. S. H. Frankel, *Capital Investment in South Africa*, op. cit., p. 127.
17. for much of the material on South Africa in this section I am indebted to Dr H. J. Simons of the University of Cape Town.
18. A. Hazlewood and P. D. Henderson, 'Nyasaland, The Economics of Federation', Oxford University Institute of Statistics, *Bulletin*, February 1960, pp. 43 and 45–6.
19. B. Davidson, *Report on Southern Africa*, Cape, 1952, pp. 226–7.
20. ibid., pp. 109–10.
21. S. H. Frankel, op. cit., p. 127.
22. Dr Albert Hertzog, in an address to the Peoples' Congress of the Dutch Reformed Churches, 1947, quoted by Dr H. J. Simons, op. cit.
23. Mine Native Wages Commission, U.G. No. 21, 1944, quoted in B. Davidson, *Report on Southern Africa*, p. 93.
24. quoted by H. J. Simons, op. cit.
25. B. Davidson, *Report on Southern Africa*, p. 78 ff. and 117 ff.
26. ibid., p. 51.
27. ibid., p. 226.
28. B. Davidson, *Old Africa Rediscovered*, Gollancz, 1959.
29. B. Davidson, *Black Mother*, Gollancz, 1961.

30. J. Woddis, *Africa, the Roots of Revolt*, Lawrence and Wishart, 1961, p. 164 ff.
31. quoted in D. Kartun, *Africa, Africa!*, Lawrence and Wishart, 1954, pp. 29–30.
32. B. Davidson, *Report on Southern Africa*, p. 194.
33. D. Kartun, op. cit., p. 35.
34. B. Davidson, *Report on Southern Africa*, pp. 96–7.
35. A. Hazlewood and P. D. Henderson, op. cit., p. 81 ff.
36. ibid., p. 12.
37. C. Wilson, *History of Unilever*, Vol. I, p. 250 ff.
38. United Nations, *Economic Survey of Africa since 1950*, New York, 1959, Table I (iii), p. 15.
39. D. Kartun, op. cit., pp. 30–1.
40. United Nations, Economic Commission for Asia and the Far East, *Economic Survey of Asia and the Far East, 1955*, Bangkok, 1956, p. 32.
41. ibid., p. 33.
42. K. M. Stahl, *Metropolitan Organisation of British Colonial Trade*, pp. 84 and 103.
43. ibid., pp. 166 and 174.
44. J. F. Rippy, *British Investments in Latin America*, University of Minnesota, 1959, Tables on pp. 181 and 182.
45. Royal Institute of International Affairs, *The Problem of International Investment*, p. 160.
46. United Nations, Economic Commission for Asia and the Far East, *Economic Survey of Asia and the Far East, 1950*, Bangkok 1951, pp. 173–7.
47. United Nations Economic Commission for Asia and the Far East, *Economic Survey of Asia and the Far East, 1955*, Bangkok, 1956, p. 35.
48. United Nations, Economic Commission for Asia and the Far East, *Economic Survey of Asia and the Far East, 1954*, Bangkok, 1955, p. 1.
49. H. B. D. Derksen and J. Tinbergen, *Calculations about the Economic Significance of the Netherlands East Indies for the Netherlands*, Netherlands Information Bureau, New York, 1947, quoted in P. M. Kattenburg, chapter on 'Indonesia' in *The State of Asia*, ed. L. K. Rosinger, New York, 1951, p. 406.
50. Neill Stewart, *New Democracy in Asia*, Changing Epoch Series, Birch Books, 1947.
51. calculated from U.K. Government, Board of Trade, *Statistical Abstract of the British Empire, 1928–37*, H.M.S.O., 1938, Table 136-B; Royal Institute of International Affairs, *The Problem of International Investment*, pp. 143 and 160; and F. Benham, *The National Income of Malaya, 1947–49*, Singapore, 1951.
52. Woytinsky and Woytinsky, op. cit., p. 122.
53. V. Anstey, *Economic Development of India*, Longmans, 1929, p. 60.

64. W. Burns, *Technological Possibilities of Agricultural Development in India*, 1944, p. 55 ff.
55. ibid.
56. V. Anstey, op. cit., Table II, p. 607.
57. *Statistical Abstract of the British Empire, 1928–37*, Tables 117-A and -B, pp. 211–12.
58. L. K. Rosinger, *Independence for Colonial Asia, the Cost to the Western World*, Foreign Policy Association of America, 1945.
59. H. Furber, *John Company at Work*, Harvard, 1948.
60. calculated from United Nations, *Statistical Yearbook, 1949–50*, New York, 1951, Table 14, p. 148.
61. *Statistical Abstract of the British Empire*, Table 117-B, p. 211.
62. V. Anstey, op. cit., pp. 260 and 279.
63. ibid., p. 612, Occupational Census.
64. ibid., pp. 620–2, Table XIV.
65. H.M. Government, India Office, *Report on Indian Constitutional Reform*, H.M.S.O., 1918, p. 267.
66. V. Anstey, op. cit., pp. 505–8.
67. *Statistical Abstract of the British Empire, 1928–37*, Table 117.
68. V. Anstey, op. cit., p. 253 and p. 519 ff.
69. ibid., pp. 98–9.
70. quoted in A. B. Keith, *Speeches and Documents on Indian Policy, 1750–1921*, World Classics, 1922, Vol. I, p. 215.
71. quoted by R. P. Dutt, *India Today*, p. 359.
72. R. C. Dutt, *Economic History of India*, London, 1908; and J. de Castro, *Geography of Hunger*, Gollancz, 1952, p. 155–6.
73. M. L. Darling, *The Punjab Peasant in Prosperity and Debt*, Oxford, 1925.
74. C. Wilson, *The History of Unilever*, Vol. II, p. 323.
75. V. Anstey, op. cit., pp. 273–4, and 524–5.
76. Sir W. Wedderburn, *Alan Octavian Hume, Father of the Indian National Congress*, Fisher Unwin, 1913.
77. quoted in R. P. Dutt, *India Today*, p. 355.
78. Sir J. Strachey, *India*, Macmillan, 1888, p. 255.
79. Lady Minto, *India, Minto and Morley*, Macmillan, 1934, p. 47.
80. UNESCO, *World Illiteracy at Mid-Century*, Paris, 1957, p. 39.

PART TWO

Imperialism Today

CHAPTER 6

End of Colonial Empire:
1945—1962

In this chapter will be described the dissolution of imperial rule over the colonial peoples of Asia and Africa. We shall consider the cold-war context in which this has taken place. In the world-wide struggle between capitalism and communism the attempt is always being made from either side to determine the type of government succeeding imperial rule. But we shall see that many of the emerging countries have successfully contracted out of the framework built for them. We shall have to decide in this and the succeeding chapter how far political freedom has ended the economic inequality, which we have seen to be the essential element in the relationship of advanced industrial powers and their underdeveloped colonies. As a first step towards answering this question, we shall examine the nature of the aid offered in the cold war and the special role played by the United States in the post-war world. In what sense, if any, is the U.S.A. an imperialist power today?

In 1945, something like 780 million people, more than a third of the people in the world at that time, lived in the colonial possessions of the imperial powers. Most of them lived in Britain's Indian Empire; but Britain ruled nearly 200 million people in colonies outside the sub-continent of India, and there were the same number in aggregate in the French, Dutch, Belgian and Portuguese colonies. One might well have added to the colonial list the 500 million Chinese people, great parts of whose lands were in Japanese occupation. Another 150 million people in Central and South American states, and 100 million in south-east Europe had little power of economic or political decision, where their interests ran against those of the great powers. Even without these last 250 million, the total of some 1,300 million comprised three out of every five people living on two-fifths of the earth's surface marked on the map with the colours of the colonial powers.[1]

The wildest enthusiast for colonial liberation could scarcely have dared in 1945 to hope that, within fifteen years, all but a few million of these people would have freed themselves from subject status. Perhaps we should be more surprised that so many human beings should have remained under the yoke of inequality for so long. However that may be, it is true that, after 1962, there will be no more than at most 100 million people living under colonial rule. We have indeed been living through one of the great transformations of human history. How has it come about?

The Colonial Liberation Movements

This great change cannot be dissociated from the nature of the World War which ushered in this period of our history. During the grim years of the war, millions of men, women and even children fought for what they believed to be liberation from human oppression. The German, Italian and Japanese empires seemed to them to incarnate all that was worst in the empires of the past. There could be no going back to imperial rule after victory over the Axis Powers. The early defeats of the Allies, the destruction especially of the British, American and French navies, had shown that the old imperial powers were not, after all, invincible. The recruitment of millions of Asians and Africans into the Allied armies had given them not only the mastery of many skills of the modern world but a self-confidence and an awareness of their equality with those whose skins were white that they had not had before.

In the common struggle, aims were espoused which could not easily be limited in their application. The Atlantic Charter laid down the principle embraced by the United Nations, that: 'They respect the right of all people to choose the form of government under which they live.'[2] In vain did Mr Winston Churchill seek to exclude 'India, Burma and other parts of the British Empire'.[3] The American President was unmoved and the words stand in the Charter, without qualification.[4]

The war ended with the seizure of power by those popular forces which had led the movements of resistance to the Axis, even in Europe itself – in Yugoslavia and Greece – but above all in Asia – in China, in Indo-China, in Indonesia, in Burma.[5] Britain's Indian Empire itself was on the verge of revolt. It is customary for British statesmen today to claim great credit for the granting of independence to India. The claim is made equally by Labour leaders, who carried through the act, and by Conservatives, who opposed it. 'There was, in fact,' to quote Lord Ismay, who was Earl Mountbatten's Chief of Staff in India, 'no option before us but to do what we did.'[6] It is a commonplace today, moreover, to contrast British wisdom, in thus recognising the inevitable, with Dutch and, more especially, French obstinacy and recklessness in carrying on long and exhausting colonial wars before finally recognising defeat. For the British to make the contrast thus baldly is an unjust piece of chauvinism. Britain too fought a major colonial war in Malaya, and supported the Dutch in Indonesia and the French in Indo-China.

The distinction should rather be drawn between those colonies in which a non-communist-led group existed, to which power could be handed over, and those where the only obvious successors to colonial rule were the communists and their allies. India, Pakistan, Burma and Ceylon came into the former category and the transference of power was made as rapidly as possible. Malaya and Indo-China came into the latter category, and, before 1948, Indonesia also, and thus they became battle-grounds in the post-war struggle against communism.[7] (The future of the African and eastern Mediterranean colonies did not arise so immediately after the ending of the war; we shall consider them in a moment.)

Communist and socialist ideas had spread fairly widely among students and intellectuals in Asia in the 1920s and 1930s, and had put down roots into the proletariat where it existed, as in Indian industry and on Indonesian plantations.[8] These ideas were most effective where imperial corporations – Royal Dutch Shell, Unilever and the like – had retained in their hands a good part of the country's internal as well as external trade, and had, therefore, held back the growth of a native merchant and trading class. The existence of a non-communist leadership in any colony naturally depended also on its degree of political development based on the emergent native middle class which the colonial power had encouraged. Communists were naturally strongest where this had been least. In this matter, the British had shown some shrewdness, belatedly enough, in the 1930s, with the measures of self-government granted to Indians, which certainly, by giving power to Congress ministries, helped further to divide Hindu and Moslem.[9]

There was, however, one special circumstance, from which Malaya, Indonesia and Indo-China had suffered, which India, Pakistan and Ceylon had escaped. That was Japanese occupation. The case of Burma lay both geographically and politically between the two groups.

Japanese Occupation and Communist Rebellion

Japanese occupation had not only temporarily disrupted European rule and shown up its weakness; it had also provoked guerilla warfare and thus brought much kudos to the young men and women who led the resistance movements. But this kudos should not be exaggerated; the Japanese were in many places regarded as deliverers from white domination. They directed much of their propaganda against European rule to the youth. This proved a double-edged weapon. The youth were stirred with nationalist ideas and many came under the influence of communist students. When Japanese rule collapsed, communist-led governments were set up in Indo-China and Indonesia some months before the French and Dutch reappeared on the scene to claim their inheritance. When they came, moreover, they came with British forces, which only emphasised their own weakness and the alien nature of European rule.[10]

The Dutch attempt to re-establish what they could of political and economic control over Indonesia led to four years of open war followed by the almost incredible series of cloak-and-dagger plots, secessionary intrigues and military *coups d'état*, which ended finally in 1957 and 1958 with the expropriation of Dutch businesses and the repatriation of Dutch citizens. By 1961 the Dutch still held on to West Irian (the western half of New Guinea), which had been the base of their operations against the Indonesian Republic in the years after 1945; but it is hard to see what else they gained from their efforts. If the aim was to protect the £750-million investment in the East Indies, then it was hopelessly miscalculated. The Dutch people were wise to develop at the same time their own natural resources at home, of rich land, and of horticultural and engineering skills.[11]

The bitter and bloody campaign of the French to hold Indo-China was no less costly, but had a rather different end from that of the Dutch in Indonesia. When the French Army withdrew after the disaster at Dien-Bien-Phu in 1954, the cost to the French exchequer of the nine years of fighting was over £2,000 million, much of it found from American aid; 100,000 French lives were lost, including not only ex-Nazi and other Legionnaires, but also the flower of the French officer-corps.[12] The result was to pull out from the communist-led Viet Minh the southern half of Viet Nam, together with the small kingdoms of Laos and Cambodia. This was achieved in the end by the growing force of American intervention. The whole operation thereafter ceased to be primarily aimed at protecting French investment, which was mainly concentrated in southern Viet Nam, but had already been partly abandoned; it was increasingly aimed at holding back the advancing influence of China which had come under communist leadership after the defeat of Chiang Kai-shek on the Chinese mainland in 1949.

The inspiration of the Chinese communist victories, not only on the field of battle but in land reform and the beginnings of industrialisation as well, was especially profound among the peoples along China's south-eastern frontier and among the large Chinese community in Malaya. Every dollar of the $300 million supplied annually to the southern half of Indo-China as aid from the United States,[13] was needed by 1961 to counter the attraction of the communist programme in the north, which included literacy (85 per cent of the Indo-Chinese were still illiterate after 80 years of French rule),[14] land reform and industrial development. We shall return in a moment to the role of the U.S.A. in these events.

The communist rebellion against the re-establishment of British rule in Malaya involved Britain in her one major colonial war after 1945. It was not a small affair; the cost to Britain, at its peak, was over £50 million a year, plus another £25 million borne by the Malayan Government. More than 100,000 British soldiers were at one time involved, together with 300,000 local auxiliaries.[15] Before the war Malaya had been described as 'an ideal dependency to govern . . . a paradise of high profits and low taxation . . . devoid of all but advisory and appointive political bodies'.[16] Chinese and Indian labour had been brought into the country to work the tin-mines and rubber estates; the Malays were left alone to get on with their primitive rice growing and fishing.

It was the Chinese element, who had become equal in numbers to the Malays before the war, who led the resistance to the Japanese and led the rebellion against the British in 1948; but there was never any evidence that they received aid from China.[17] After eight years of jungle warfare, the rebellion petered out, not only as the result of military pressure, which included collective punishment and transportation of whole villages, but with the emergence of a Malayan leadership which was capable of reflecting popular aspirations sufficiently to deprive the communists of their unique appeal. Thus, it may be said that the Malayan war achieved its objective in that the communist leadership was eliminated and a government emerged to which power could be handed over without fear that British investments would be expropriated.

The Successor States

The general picture of colonial liberation in Asia was of imperial powers making political concessions to *force majeure* and turning all their attention to securing successor governments which would not challenge their economic interests. The framing of appropriate constitutions was the all-important exercise in this whole operation. Political power in India, Pakistan, Burma and Ceylon was not handed over to the colonial people for them to choose a constituent assembly and frame their own constitution in the first instance. Power was delegated 'into responsible Indian hands', as the Mountbatten Declaration had it, and under a constitution which had already been laid down.[18] The same procedure was adopted in the British African and West Indian colonies.

The manner of succession was obviously regarded as of great importance, if the length of time spent in constitutional conferences is anything to judge by. It was not that limitations were put on the voting registers or that some matters were withdrawn from the competence of the people's representatives. Those were the marks of constitutions granted before independence. What the final constitution did in each colony was to assure continuity of institutions, copied from British democracy, and of administration, based on Colonial Service methods and even politics. To aid continuity, many British servants stayed on at their posts, while 'natives' were trained and instructed in their ways.

It would not be right to decry the very real democratic safeguards won by the British people in the course of parliamentary struggle, or the genuine devotion of many colonial civil servants, or the importance of this continuity in preventing anarchy after liberation. The Congo has shown what the alternative might be. But the transplanting of Westminster and Whitehall to the soil of Ceylon or Ghana, complete with Mr Speaker's wig and mace, was bound to produce some rather strange growths and not a little obfuscation of reality in the defence of tradition. Continuity in the Police and Armed Forces has been of particular importance in ensuring that the object of security precautions shall continue to be on the extreme left of the political spectrum. The tragedy has been that, with the outstanding exception of India, all the elaborate constitution-making has been of no avail in preventing the establishment of military dictatorship in Pakistan and the Sudan, or of other forms of personal dictatorship elsewhere.

More important even than constitution-mongering, in determining the way forward for the ex-colonial peoples after liberation, has been the nature of the regions over which sovereignty has been transferred. The partition of India and of Palestine, the Federation of Central Africa, the separation of Malaya and Singapore are obvious examples; no less ridiculous has been the retention of trading-fort hinterland boundaries in the establishment of separate 'nations' on the Gold Coast, the Ivory Coast, Sierra Leone, French Guinea. The nationalism which colonial peoples, feeling their way to independence and self-confidence, have espoused has greatly encouraged this development. The result has been an added element of continuity from colonial rule into independence. At the same time, divisions which had been exploited in the past by the imperial power are unhappily perpetuated. The one example mentioned above where it was hoped that colonies would be united on attaining independence, the incorporation of Northern Rhodesia and Nyasaland into the Central African Federation, forms a special case to which we shall return.

Since the British Parliament enacted the Statute of Westminster in 1931,[19] all the Parliaments of the British Commonwealth, as it thereafter was termed, attained equality both among themselves and with the Parliament at Westminster. Colonies granted independence since then have attained equal rights. Most have chosen to stay inside the Commonwealth, although Burma and Eire withdrew. Some accept the Queen as Chief of State; others, like India and Ghana, have become republics. Independence has brought the right to conduct their own foreign as well as home affairs. In military matters, a remnant of imperial power remains in the Chief of the Imperial General Staff and his co-ordinating authority over Commonwealth defence; but even here Commonwealth members are free to dissociate themselves, a great deal freer than they would be as members of most international alliances.

The sole tenuous links of the Commonwealth lie in history and tradition, common language and adopted institutions, the playing of cricket and some exchange of state papers. This last culminates in the now annual Conference of Commonwealth Prime Ministers, at which broad questions of common interest are discussed but without decisions of any binding character being reached. There remain also the system of Imperial Preferences left over from the Ottawa Conference of 1931 and the mechanism of the Sterling Area, of which we shall say more later (Chapter 7).

A somewhat similar, but rather more organic, association of ex-colonial states has been adopted by the Government of General de Gaulle, in the granting of independence within the French Community to the French African colonies. Both the Commonwealth and the Community may be compared with the Organisation of American States under the leadership of the U.S.A. It is to be noted that, although none of the Latin American states has ever been a direct colony of the United States, the U.S. has used the Organisation to reach decisions binding on all members.[20] The smaller states have, moreover, acted, for example in the United Nations, with much less independence than the new Commonwealth members have shown. This fact suggests that the cold war alliances, which we have already considered, and the economic ties of great imperial companies, which we have yet to examine, may be far more important than the purely political links of empire.

It is the hangovers of empire, some of which we have already seen, that we must now examine more closely. It is clear that the British Commonwealth can no longer be thought of as an empire, no matter what the League of Empire Loyalists (or Mr Palme Dutt[21]) may say. Yet something remains.

The Remaining Colonies

There are a large number of fairly small territories over which the writ of Whitehall still runs. Most of them, and particularly the islands in the Pacific and Indian Oceans, are too small to become viable economies. The islands range from important sugar-producing islands like Fiji and Mauritius, which each have a population of between a third and half a million – mainly Indians (And perhaps, therefore, more appropriately transferred to Indian sovereignty?) – to Tristan da Cunha and Pitcairn, the latter with a few hundred inhabitants, still all of them descendants of the *Bounty* mutineers. Many of Britain's smaller colonies scattered across the oceans of the world have always derived their importance from strategic considerations – Hong Kong, Singapore, Cyprus, Malta, Gibraltar, Aden, Bermuda (now a U.S. naval base), the Maldives.[22]

Their future must hang upon the future of the cold war. They form part – a small part – of the ring of NATO, CENTO, and SEATO bases that surrounds China and the Soviet Union. The problem of retaining bases on Cyprus has at length been solved, but difficulties may still arise in retaining Singapore and Hong Kong. The former wishes to join Malaya, to which it geographically belongs. The latter can hardly avoid being claimed ultimately by China. Their problems will be in part the same as those of Malta: finding employment for a grossly inflated naval and military garrison community. In addition to this, they also have the task of retaining the entrepôt trade that they have attracted by their special economic position in imperialist trade relations in the past. There can be no doubt that the opportunity should be given to every dependent territory to choose its own future;* but the retention of these smaller territories cannot in itself be regarded as evidence of active imperialism at this time.

Some of the smaller mainland colonies, especially in Africa, will naturally become part of neighbouring lands, from which they were only divided by the rivalry of imperial powers. British Somaliland has already been joined to ex-Italian Somalia, and it is possible and natural that French Somaliland should follow suit. Gambia, which runs along the river for two hundred miles, has only a width of some fifteen miles and is entirely surrounded by the new states formed from French Senegal and French Sudan.[24]

Gambia is a good example of the distorting role of imperialism. The French have had to export their large ground-nut production from Senegal by rail to Dakar instead of by

* The Labour Party is committed to this view by the third of its small pamphlets on 'Labour's Colonial Policy'.[23]

the much cheaper river-route to Bathurst. The union of
Gambia with its neighbours would seem the most logical
solution, but Senegal and Sudan failed to make their own
federation of Mali. Africans have always tended to move
across the frontiers drawn by Europeans with singular
impunity,[25] and European intrigue cannot be exempted from
responsibility for the tiny states that are emerging as successors to European colonies throughout Africa. The
dangers of Balkanisation are clearly recognised by African
leaders like Dr Nkrumah.[26] The small states are surely bound
to form unions, once the first bloom of national identifica-
tion has worn off. The prompt assistance of Ghana to the
Congo in the summer of 1960 revealed their sense of
solidarity.

On the other hand, the effects of this fragmentation of
Africa should not be underestimated. Whatever may have
been the intentions of the imperial powers in retaining old
ties with the metropolitan land, the actual result of this fragmentation has undoubtedly been to strengthen the role of
the imperial companies. This question will be examined
closely in the next chapter, but it may be said now that the
small and divided successor states can be no match in
economic power for the closely integrated and united imperial companies like Unilever. Pan-Africanism becomes an
urgent economic necessity to ensure both stronger bargaining power in relations with foreign capital and an integrated
local market, as well as a political necessity to offset the
centrifugal and reactionary forces of traditional leaders –
tribal, professional or comprador.

The Basis of African Nationalism

The emergence of an African nationalism is one of the most
potent political forces of our time. Its history is important.[27]
Africa had no Japanese invasion to discredit the European
powers and stimulate anti-European movements. Except in

the northern, Arab states, Africa had enjoyed practically no economic development to create a native middle class. There was only a class of small traders and shopkeepers – in the north mainly Arabs and in the south mainly Indians. Because of the migrant labour-system in the mines, and the predominantly peasant rather than plantation culture of export crops[28] and the almost complete absence of local industry, Africans had had little or no experience of trade union organisation.[29]

As was the case in India, the contact of African students with the British and French Labour Movements, and especially with the Communist Parties, had begun to spread European ideas of liberty, socialism or communism; but the small numbers of students involved had meant that the process had not gone far in Africa before the Second World War. There was an equivalent force in the revolutionary influence of the Protestant missionaries' emphasis on the freedom of the individual to interpret the Bible for himself.[30] Yet within twenty years of its birth African nationalism has grown to the point of taking over power from the imperial masters throughout almost the whole of the continent.

How has this happened? One half of the answer arises from the Second World War, in the world-wide influence of the Asiatic liberation movements, the Russian and Chinese revolutions, the promises of freedom and equality spoken in the war, and in the training and service of Africans in the war-time armies.[31] The other half of the answer follows from the growth during and after the war of the world's demand for certain African products.

First, there are the minerals – gold, copper, uranium, tin, cobalt – which have attracted investment to Africa. Port installations, railways and electric power have been further developed, and some part of the wealth has filtered through from the developed enclaves to Africans, despite the continued low level of African wages and the huge profits taken out of the country. Where migrant labour is not typical, trade unionism has been stimulated, on the railways for example. The Labour Government in Britain may take some credit for encouraging this, while doing its best to steer trade unions away from political activity.[32]

Secondly, there are the agricultural products – cocoa and vegetable oils – grown very largely by individual peasant farmers in West Africa. Peasant farmers do not make revolutionaries, and there are few European plantations in West Africa to encourage proletarian organisation. But the collection and merchanting of these crops has been the cause of the growth of the towns, which are the crucial element in the emergence of African nationalism.[33] Much of this commerce has been retained in the hands of the great European houses, such as the United Africa Company, but some has gone to native traders and merchants.

Thus, the growth of the towns in Africa has begun to create a demand for clothing, household equipment, cafés, drink and other luxuries, and thus to stimulate some local industry. Moreover, in West Africa, which has been the pace-setter of the nationalist movements, considerable contributions have been made since the war to local revenues by the agricultural marketing companies, and particularly by the Cocoa Marketing Board. These have made possible a rapid growth in schools, hospitals and other government services. Advance in West Africa has been easier, not only because of the demand for its export products but because of the absence of European settlers. The difficulties facing the multi-racial communities of East and Central Africa are far greater. The key to the future lies in the towns.

The urbanisation of Africans encouraged the forming of associations to fill the void left by the break with tribalism and these have been the basis of the nationalist parties. Nationalism has been greatly strengthened in Africa by the fact that it has been possible to maintain a certain unity among conflicting elements. There has been no native-owned industry and so no major division between the trade unions and the middle class. The chiefs, although they were always used by the British for indirect rule, never became landlords and, therefore, never gained an economic as well as tribal hold upon the people.

Africa has thus largely avoided involvement in the cold war, because there was no native propertied class anxious to defend its possessions against expropriation and because there is no Communist Party except in the Arab north and (illegally) in South Africa.* The only influences of the cold war on Africa have been in the establishment of bases in Libya and Kenya, and the very large sums (nearly 25 per cent of the total of British Government loans and grants made to the Sterling Area in the period 1954-59 – see Table XVIII, Chapter 8, below) provided for the colonial armed and police forces. India was always made to pay for 'its' armed services! Africa has been given them free. The services of British advisers have generally been continued after liberation, although without much enthusiasm on either side,[34] and the Colonial Office and the Commonwealth Office have been careful to warn successor governments about the 'political' background of left-wing advisers and even of university lecturers and teachers applying for posts.

In welcoming the successes of Ghana and contrasting them with the catastrophe of the Congo, it is important to remember that the absence of communists is no guarantee either, on the one hand, that imperial companies will escape being expropriated or, on the other, that progressive economic policies will be pursued. Even where the imperial companies do lose out, it is not impossible for them to be replaced by small-scale local capitalism which holds back economic development; but this must be the subject of a later chapter (11). When a colony did elect an apparently communist-led government, moreover, in British Guiana,

* Cold-war attitudes may account for the rather greater sympathy that has been accorded to South Africa than one might have expected on the basis of her racial policies.

constitutional advance was suspended. Such actions only serve to emphasise the element in the cold war of direct defence of the economic positions of some of the great imperial corporations. The fact is that in Africa power is being transferred, as we saw it was in Asia, to governments who do not, on the face of it, seem likely to expropriate Unilever or Shell, although Ghana and Guinea, and even Nigeria, have made a beginning with the nationalisation of some smaller imperial companies.[35]

The Cold-War Context of Liberation and the Supremacy of United States Capitalism

It is not possible to consider the process of colonial liberation without taking into account the wider context of the cold war since 1945 in which it has taken place. Here it is important to recognise that, while there may be good original economic grounds for policies pursued, the whole structure of institutions, ideas and purposes built up from these grounds takes on a life of its own and becomes its own justification. Those who claim to be Marxists need to be at least as marxist as Marx in this matter and should not cite Marx's authority for the crudest type of economic determinism.[36] One aspect of the cold war is precisely the defence of capitalist positions against communist encroachment. But communist encroachment and colonial liberation are not the same thing, although both communists and capitalists would sometimes lead us to imagine so. Both tend to exclude the possibility that non-communists may lead colonial liberation movements. Colonel Nasser, whose jails are filled with communists, should have made the point clear.

The cold war is also more than just the defence of capitalist and imperialist positions. In the first place, it is concerned with the overall capitalist position, the whole way of life of what is called 'the free world'. Furthermore, it naturally falls under the leadership of the most powerful and most technically advanced capitalist grouping – that in the United States of America. For both reasons, specific imperial positions may well be abandoned in the general interest. Thus, Indonesia was abandoned in the end; a compromise was reached in Indo-China dividing the country at the Seventeenth Parallel; British and French actions at Suez were not supported by the United States.

Again, the military moves of the cold war have gained a logic and momentum of their own quite unrelated to any economic considerations from which they may derive. There would seem to be no possible advantage, in terms of economic interest to the United States, in the continued support of the Chiang Kai-shek regime on Formosa and in not recognising the government of the mainland, long after the possibility of changing the course of economic development in China had ended. For Britain there have been real economic disadvantages in adhering to the embargoes on trade with China for so long.

The fourth point is probably the most important. United States economic interests are not so much concerned with exercising privileges in protected spheres of influence as with preventing other powers from doing so. The United States has thus not sought to 'pick up' the colonies dropping from the grasp of the older imperial powers, but has insisted on the opening-up of protected markets.* In this respect, the U.S.A. today is in the position of Britain in the mid-nineteenth century and for the same reason: that her technological lead in a very wide range of products and her massed capital resources give her a competitive edge over all other capitalist states. Thus the principles of free trade – the open door, low tariffs, non-discrimination, convertibility of currencies – have entered into United States ideology. They

* Secretary of State Cordell Hull's crusade to include a commitment to multilateralism in the Atlantic Charter, the Lend-Lease Agreement and the Keynes Loan forms a fascinating chapter in Anglo-American Diplomacy.[37]

are the marks of the 'free world', as they once were of the *Pax Britannica*. As Marx insisted, free trade (and not protection or monopoly) is perhaps, after all, the essential characteristic of capitalist development;[38] it is necessarily the ideology of the predominant capitalist power.

The outstanding example of the United States drive for free markets was the treaty signed with Chiang Kai-shek in November 1946. Each party opened its doors freely to each other's trade and investment. The other capitalist powers were left at the start without even the benefit of their old unequal China port treaties. 'It is to the vast unawakened markets of India and the Far East that American exporters are looking,' wrote a well-informed American correspondent, 'and China is the first of these markets.'[39] But it was not to be, and U.S. political and economic diplomacy has still not recovered from the body blow sustained by the communist victory over Chiang Kai-shek in 1949.

We shall return to U.S. foreign economic policy, and especially to U.S. overseas investment, when we consider how an international economy may be built up (Chapter 10). Here we need only to note, first, that, unlike Britain in the nineteenth century, the U.S. has not applied the principles of free trade to its own tariffs and quotas and, second, that U.S. private foreign investment has been on a much smaller scale compared both with her own national income and with the level of world trade than was Britain's in the nineteenth century. Exploitation of oil reserves has been the only major foreign interest of American investors (see Table XXX at end of Chapter 10), although other important interests have been pursued. On the other hand, U.S. governmental aid since the war has been on a really grandiose scale (Table XI below). This aid has done much to sustain the level of U.S. exports as British capital investment did for British exports. Indeed it has often been an explicit reason for the granting of aid.[40]

We need to ask at once whether the effects on the recipient countries of the granting of U.S. aid have been similar to the

effects of British overseas capital investment. The main
limitation, from the receiver's point of view, to this flow of
capital we saw to be not so much that the rate of return on the
loans was high – in many cases loans were defaulted on so that
the capital provided was in effect the same as aid – but that so
little of the capital went to the least developed lands, and so
much to Europe and the developing lands of European
settlement. How far, then, has U.S. aid spread to these less
developed lands?

It is again in the cold-war context that we must see the aid
that has been provided, mainly by the United States, to the ex-
colonial and other underdeveloped lands. In the fifteen
years since the war, the United States has provided aid to the
extent of between five and six billion dollars each year. Table
XI shows what a high proportion of this has been military
aid; even within the total of economic aid, the greater part,
after 1951, consisted of aid allocated in fact under the Mutual
Security Programme for 'defence support' or 'direct forces
support'. It will be noticed that, after the developed lands of
western Europe, the main recipients have been those
countries in the Far East which have been most deeply
involved in the cold war – Korea, Formosa, Indo-China. The
sums received by the underdeveloped lands, such as India,
Iran, Egypt, Yugoslavia, Bolivia, Afghanistan, have come
from the bare 10 per cent of the total aid programme set aside
for development and technical co-operation. India, Brazil,
Yugoslavia, Japan and Indonesia have also, it is true, been
major recipients of surplus agricultural stocks.

The total U.S. aid has involved huge sums by any
standards, and these suggest some idea of the American
commitment to the defence of 'the free world'. The effects of
receipt of this aid we shall consider later. What we have to
note here is not only the military justification for the major
part of the allocations, but the nature of the governments to
which they were made. We have already traced the extraordinary efforts that were made by the imperial powers after

1945 to secure successor governments to their colonial rule which would respect their economic interests. Once they have been established in power American money has been used to keep them there. Any list which included Chiang Kai-shek, Syngman Rhee, Ngo Dinh Diem, Marshal Pibul, Firoz Khan Noon, Nuri es-Said, General Zahedi, Adnan Menderes and General Franco as the main beneficiaries of 'free world aid' would seem pretty offensive to free men. Indeed, several on the list have already lost the toleration of their people and been replaced, not always, perhaps, entirely for the better. All of the countries concerned, except Iraq, remained thereafter within the American defence alliances – NATO, CENTO and SEATO – adherence to which had won them their money.

Internal and External Limitations to Economic Independence

The cold-war dependence of these countries on the United States alliance and on military and economic aid illustrates precisely the limitations inherent in the achievement of independence by people who have once been the colony of a great power. These limitations they share, of course, with other small underdeveloped countries which have never actually had colonial status. National independence in the modern world requires not only formal political sovereignty, but also the possibility of pursuing all-round economic development. The tragedy of so many of the ex-colonial countries is that their governments, by their very nature, have not put such all-round economic development at the forefront of their policies. In this they have been held back by both internal and external factors. The internal factors are now probably the more important. They derive partly from the nature of colonial rule and partly from the cold-war context of liberation.

We may summarise very crudely the points established earlier in this book, taking the example of Pakistan:

The British established the zamindars as landowners in the Punjab at the end of the eighteenth century in order to strengthen their dominion. Later, the British built up an Indian Army manned and even officered from the so-called 'martial races' of the north and committed to the defence of British rule. When nationalism emerged in India, the British were able to take advantage of a split in the movement and to encourage the establishment of a Moslem landlord-based party, the Moslem League. Since the war, Pakistan has been ruled by the Moslem League and the representatives of the few thousand land-owners who own more than a third of all the land – men like Firoz Khan Noon. When these could hold the position no longer, a one-time British Indian Army General, Ayub Khan, took over in a situation that threatened to become a revolutionary one.* What is more natural than that such governments, fearing communist threats of land reform more than the devil, should join the anti-communist alliance – the Baghdad Pact, now called CENTO – and qualify for American aid?

It is precisely the resistance of such governments to land reform that holds back the economic development of their countries and perpetuates their economic and, therefore, to an extent, their political dependence on the great powers. We shall examine in detail in Chapter 11 the restraints which ancient systems of private land-ownership put upon economic development. We may simply note here that it is not only that the high level of the landlords' rent skims off the whole surplus that the peasant creates, but that this leads to a steady decline in the size of the surplus. Yet it is upon that surplus that the whole economic and industrial development of the land depends.[42]

* Lest anyone be deceived by General Ayub's excellent public relations into believing that he is now going to carry through a true measure of land reform,[41] it should be remarked that the new regulations conform entirely to those proposed already in 1951 by none other than his predecessor, now in jail, Firoz Khan Noon (see Chapter 11 for the details of the reform).

Beside the internal restraints connected with land-ownership, there are many other limitations upon economic development which colonialism has left behind, and which we considered in the preceding chapter. These are mostly connected with the fact that the middle class, which has emerged in most colonies as the leadership of the nationalist movements for liberation, had been built up around the colonial system itself. Thus the native traders and merchants were concerned primarily with the collection and sale of crops for export. They were 'comprador' capitalists, who had no interest in or bent for industrialisation. In the early history of capitalism and empire, we saw that merchant capital did not of itself stimulate industrialisation. It is still true today. 'It is wrong to think you can mobilise capital through our traders,' one of Dr Nkrumah's ministers is reported to have said; 'that isn't the way they like to live.' And another added: 'We have spent a lot of money in trying to get our capitalists to go into industry, and what happens? Nasty messes, or nothing at all.'[43]

In ex-colonial countries, where merchant business has been built up around imperial companies, resistance to the development of native manufacturing may be very great. To these limitations on economic development may be added all the hangovers of what Myrdal has called 'the regimentation, red tape, petty bureaucracy, with which the metropolitan powers ruled foreign peoples of inferior status'.[44] These are the points at which the internal and external limitations on economic development meet. We shall take up this matter again in Chapter 11.

What we have still to consider is whether the external limitations on the economic development of the colonies since the war have been strong enough to justify the fear that forms of economic power might continue even after political independence is won. We have already noted that, until an ex-colony can achieve all-round development, it is bound to be economically dependent to a great measure on the larger industrial powers. This may range from dependence on one industrial market for their products to actual direct economic intervention by the ex-colonial power or by imperial companies, over which the government of the one-time colony has little or no control. We must now turn, therefore, to the operation of currency blocs and protected markets by the ex-imperial powers, and to the rule and influence of the imperial companies. For it has not at all been the post-war experience that the dominating position of these companies in colonial economies and the high rate of return on their investments has come to an end on the day of liberation of a colony from imperial rule; rather the opposite has been the case.

TABLE XI

DISTRIBUTION OF U.S. FOREIGN AID, 1945–59
(All figures in $ billions at current prices)

Year	Military Aid	Loans	International Organisations	M.S.P. (non-mil.)	Surplus Food	Other	Total
1946	—	1·7	4·3	—	—	1·3	7·3
1947	0·1	3·9	1·1	—	—	1·6	6·7
1948	0·3	0·1	1·0	—	—	1·7	3·1
1949	0·2	0·1	0·2	6·2	—	1·7	8·4
1950	0·1	0·3	0·1	3·6	—	1·1	5·2
1946–50	0·7	6·1	6·7	9·8	—	7·4	30·7
1951	1·0	0·1	0·1	2·6	—	0·6	4·4
1952	1·5	0·1	0·1	2·0	0·1	0·3	4·1
1953	4·2	0·4	0·1	2·0	—	—	6·8
1954	3·4	—	0·1	2·2	0·1	0·1	5·8
1955	2·4	0·3	0·1	1·9	0·5	—	5·2
1951–55	12·6	0·9	0·5	10·7	0·6	1·0	26·3
1956	2·9	0·2	0·1	1·6	0·9	—	5·6
1957	2·1	0·5	0·1	1·7	1·1	—	5·5
1958	2·3	0·8	0·1	1·3	0·7	—	5·2
1959	2·3	1·2	1·4	1·3	0·8	—	7·0
1956–59	9·6	2·7	1·7	5·9	3·5	—	23·3
Grand Total 1945–59, of which to	22·9	9·7	8·9	26·4	4·1	8·4	70·3
Europe	13·2	5·8	4·9	15·0	0·6	4·6	44·1

Notes: 1. 'Loans' include Development Loan Fund 1958–59.
2. 'International Organisations' include UNRRA and I.M.F. & I.B.R.D. Contributions.
3. M.S.P. = Mutual Security Programme.
4. 'Other' includes Civilian Supplies.

Sources: United States International Co-operation Administration, *Report on U.S. External Assistance, 1945–1959* (Washington, D.C., 1960).

TABLE XI (contd.)

RECEIVING COUNTRIES

1946–50 UNRRA Aid 1946–8		1951–55 Economic Aid (M.S.P.)		1956–59 Economic Aid (M.S.P.)		1946–59 Surplus Food	
Italy	0·7	Europe Total, 5·6		Europe Total, 1·9		India	0·6
China	0·4	of which		of which		Pakistan	0·2
Poland	0·4	France	1·2	Yugoslavia	0·5	Yugoslavia	0·3
Yugoslavia	0·3	U.K.	1·0	Spain	0·6	Brazil	0·15
Greece	0·3	W. Germany	0·6	Turkey	0·5		
Argentina	0·2	Yugoslavia	0·5	Indo-China,		*Military Aid*	
		Korea	3·3	etc.	3·5	France	4·5
Civilian Supplies		Indo-China,		Korea	1·3	Formosa	1·9
1946–50		etc.	1·0	Pakistan	0·6	Italy	1·9
W. Germany	2·4	Formosa	0·5	Formosa	0·5	Turkey	1·8
Japan	2·2	Latin America	1·0	Latin America	2·0	Greece	1·3
				Africa	0·4	Korea	1·2
Loans 1946–7		*Military Aid*				Indo-China,	
U.K.	3·8	Europe	8·5	*Military Aid*		etc.	1·2
France	1·2	Far East	2·2	Europe	4·0	Belgium	1·2
		Near East	1·2	Far East	2·8	Netherlands	1·2
M.S.P. 1949–50				Near East	1·8	U.K.	1·0
Europe Total, 9·0						Germany	0·9
of which						Japan	0·8
U.K.	2·6					Pakistan	0·5
France	2·0						
W. Germany	1·0						
Italy	1·0						
Netherlands	0·9						
Belgium	0·5						
Austria	0·4						
Philippines	0·5						

References

1. W. S. Woytinsky and E. S. Woytinsky, op. cit., Table 19: Area and Population of 115 Countries in 1950.
2. *The Atlantic Charter*, 14 August 1941, H.M.S.O. Cmd. 6321.
3. Official Declaration of H.M. Government, 9 September 1942.
4. Broadcast of President Roosevelt, 22.2.42.
5. L. K. Rosinger, ed. *The State of Asia, passim.*
6. H. Campbell Johnson, *Mission with Mountbatten*, Faber, 1949.
7. L. K. Rosinger, op. cit., especially the section on Malaya by V. Thompson and R. Adloff, p. 332 ff.
8. M. Kennedy, *Short History of Communism in Asia*, Weidenfeld and Nicolson, 1957.
9. See, e.g. Letter from Nehru to Jinnah, January 1937, quoted in R. Palme Dutt, *India Today*, p. 381.
10. D. G. E. Hall, *History of South East Asia*, Macmillan, 1955, Chapter 45; and L. K. Rosinger, op. cit., chapter on Indonesia.
11. D. Woodman, *The Republic of Indonesia*, Cresset Press, 1955, Chapter XI.
12. Keesing's *Contemporary Archives*, 6–13 June 1953, p. 12959.
13. International Co-operation Administration, *U.S. External Assistance, Annual Reports.*
14. UNESCO, *World Illiteracy at Mid-Century*, p. 39.
15. Statement by Sir Winston Churchill, House of Commons, 6.12.61.
16. V. Thompson and R. Adloff, chapter on Malaya, in L. K. Rosinger, op. cit., p. 333.
17. V. Purcell, *Chinese in South East Asia*, Oxford, 1951, Chapter XXIV.
18. H.M. Government, *Declaration* of February 1947.
19. H.M. Government, *The Statute of Westminster*, H.M.S.O., 1931.
20. H. Herring, *History of Latin America*, p. 768 ff.
21. R. P. Dutt, *Crisis of Britain and the British Empire*, pp. 15–16.
22. Whitaker's *Almanack 1961*, 'Dominions, Colonies, etc'.
23. The Labour Party, *Labour's Colonial Policy*, iii, 'The Smaller Territories', June 1957.
24. Article on 'Gambia and Mali', in *West Africa*, London, 25.6.60.
25. Basil Davidson, *Report on Southern Africa,* p. 99.
26. Address delivered by Dr Kwame Nkrumah at the Conference of Heads of States of non-aligned countries, Belgrade, 2 September 1961, reported as a supplement to *Ghana Today* of 13 September 1961.
27. For much of what follows see T. Hodgkin, *Nationalism in Colonial Africa*, Muller, 1956.
28. W. M. Macmillan, 'African Development', an essay in *Europe and West Africa*, Oxford, 1940.

29. J. Woddis, *The Lion Awakes*, Lawrence and Wishart, 1961, Chapter II.
30. T. Hodgkin, op. cit., pp. 98–9.
31. ibid., pp. 142–3.
32. J. Woddis, op. cit., p. 35 ff.
33. T. Hodgkin, op. cit., p. 63 ff.
34. K. Younger, *Public Service in the New States*, Oxford, 1960.
35. J. Woddis, op. cit., p. 252 ff.
36. e.g. I. Cox, *Empire Today*, Lawrence and Wishart, 1960.
37. R. N. Gardner, *Sterling-Dollar Diplomacy*, Oxford, 1956, p. 12 ff.
38. Karl Marx, *Address on Free Trade*.
39. *The Financial Times*, Washington Correspondent, 26.3.46.
40. G. Stein, *The World the Dollar Built*, Dobson, 1952, Chapter VI.
41. e.g. Kingsley Martin, *New Statesman and Nation*, 16.4.60.
42. W. A. Lewis, *Theory of Economic Growth*, Allen and Unwin, 1955, p. 120 ff.
43. Basil Davidson, article on 'Ghana' in the *New Statesman and Nation*, 19.11.60.
44. G. Myrdal, *Economic Theory and Underdeveloped Regions*, p. 61 ff.

CHAPTER 7

What Remains of Empire?

If colonialism is dead or dying, what remains of the old imperial economic ties? The advantage of these ties for the imperial powers consisted first in their unrestricted freedom of trade and, second, in the protected and privileged markets and profitable fields of exploitation of food and raw materials that the colonies provided. It has been the thesis of this book, however, that what has mattered more has been the overall unequal relations which developed between the advanced industrial powers and the lands that were left economically underdeveloped. In the next two chapters we shall have to decide how far these unequal relations may be expected to persist after liberation from colonial status. We have noted already the political hangovers from the colonial régime; we must now examine the economic ties that remain.

In this chapter we shall first examine the continuance of their membership of the Sterling Area by most British colonies even after the day of liberation. Then we shall consider the remaining stake of British investors, and particularly of the giant vertically-integrated combines, in the ex-colonial lands overseas, where so many of the raw materials of British industry are produced. The oil companies will take up the major part of our study. We shall leave to the next chapter the wider consideration of the scale, nature and rationale of the new wave of British overseas investment today.

The Sterling Area – A New Form of Imperialism?

Most of the British colonies have elected to stay within the Sterling Area. The commitment was generally made before independence. What has it involved? Today the Sterling Area is no longer the large Sterling Bloc of pre-war days, which was a loose association of countries with exchange rates tied to sterling because London was their banker, financier and chief trading-partner. Nor is it, on the other hand, the tight wartime organisation of Britain and her empire that gave to London full control of dollar spending and piled up Britain's wartime debts to the other members in the form of sterling balances held, and for the most part blocked, in London.[1] Since the war, Israel, Egypt, and Iraq have left; but the rest of the pre-war empire has stayed in, including Burma, Jordan, Eire and South Africa, which are not now members of the Commonwealth, and always excluding Canada.

The essential feature of the Area today is that all members hold their foreign-exchange reserves in the form of sterling in London and leave to the Bank of England the management of their gold and foreign-currency earnings. Drawing on the dollar pool and running down of reserves (the Sterling Balances) are, however, a matter of gentlemen's agreements based on the assumption of reasonable restraint all round.[2] The fact that most of the banks throughout the Commonwealth are branches of London banks, and that the various Central Banks were launched with 'the active encouragement and co-operation . . . and actually set on their way with the help of personnel . . . from the Bank of England',[3] has made possible this gentlemanly arrangement. So long as members had colonial status, their drawings were, however, regulated by Currency Boards acting on behalf of the Colonial Office.[4]

There can be little doubt that, in the ten years after 1945, the system worked very unfavourably for the colonies. In the first place, Britain, Australia and Southern Rhodesia were able to change some of their soft-currency earnings into hard currency by drawing on the gold and dollar earnings of colonies like Ghana and Malaya and Northern Rhodesia.[5] Secondly, the Sterling Balances of the colonies, arising from the excess of their exports (and particularly dollar exports) over their imports, were allowed to accumulate steadily in London. Colonial holdings of sterling rose in the ten years after 1945 from 12 per cent to 32 per cent of the total holdings. To put it another way, British debts to the colonies rose from £450 million in 1945 to nearly £1,300 million in 1955 (see Table XV, at end of Chapter 8).

Over most of this period the interest received by the colonies on these balances, which were mainly invested in short-term stock, did not rise above 3 per cent. The colonies suffered in several ways. First, they did not have the funds to buy dollar goods as they might have wished. Second, the price of British goods rose, while the value of the Sterling Balances actually fell in the devaluation of 1949. Third, the rate of interest was very much lower than might have been earned elsewhere.

At the same time, and as a direct result, sterling and hard currencies became available for British investors to put into long-term securities overseas carrying much higher rates of return. London was borrowing short and lending long, and doing well on it. No wonder that Professor Arthur Lewis used to complain that it was 'the African and Malayan peasants who are putting capital into Britain'[6] and that Professor Paish should conclude that 'so far from Britain providing finance for the colonial territories, the colonial territories have been providing finance for Britain and the rest of the Sterling Area'.[7] The process of accumulation, however, was terminated after 1955, as short-term interest rates rose prohibitively and as independence day for the colonies drew near.

There are other important results that have followed from

the working of the sterling exchange system in the colonies. The Colonial Currency Boards have insisted on 100 per cent, and even 110 per cent, backing in sterling for all local currency issued.[8] This ultra-conservative financial policy has meant that the normal means of a modern government for expanding the economy by central credit expansion has been ruled out in the British colonies. Not until 1959 was this restrictive policy relaxed in Nigeria and the West Indies, and a fiduciary issue of currency up to 40 per cent of the total permitted for the first five years, and thereafter up to 60 per cent. Currency Boards have, after 1959, moreover, at last begun to make local investments.[9]

Currency Board restrictions were not the only ways in which funds were channelled from the colonies to Britain. Colonial ordinances have generally provided that at least two-thirds of the deposits of savings banks and similar funds should be invested in the Commonwealth and outside the territory of the colony.[10] Moreover, local banks, being branches of London banks, have generally invested some part of the funds deposited with them outside the territory. On the other hand, it must be said that their very large reserves have enabled these banks to tie up a greater proportion of their funds in non-liquid assets than a purely local bank could have afforded to do. One of the worst features of the close relations of colonial and metropolitan banking, however, has been that high rates of interest imposed in Britain for internal economic purposes are almost automatically transferred to the colonies, for which they are quite inappropriate and may, indeed, result in holding back development quite seriously. Even if the colonies could to some extent insulate their internal interest rates from pressures exerted by London rates, they would still be affected as borrowers.

The conclusion must be that the freedom of an ex-colony to control its own credit and fiscal policies is essential for economic development. Membership of the Sterling Area in itself has precluded this for a colony in the past, but need not necessarily any longer preclude this for an independent state in the future. The hangover from colonial days, and particularly the dominant position of the branches of London banks, may, however, last for some time and, in the meantime, have deleterious effects upon economic development.

Should Ex-Colonies leave the Sterling Area?

The other main aspect of the Sterling Area pooling of reserves is the weapon of economic sanctions that this puts into the hands of London. But this problem exists for any country which decides that it is convenient to invest funds in London. Egypt had already left the Sterling Area for some years before 1956, but this did not stop the British Government from freezing the Egyptian holdings of sterling, when Colonel Nasser proposed to nationalise the Suez Canal. What worries many ex-colonies is the question of convertibility. Will they be permitted to convert their sterling, which was often accumulated as the result of dollar earnings, into hard currencies if they choose to leave the Sterling Area?

The case of Iraq is, at first sight, reassuring. When Iraq withdrew from the Sterling Area in 1959, all her previously accumulated balances of sterling were made convertible.[11] The whole problem for the City of London in edging slowly but surely forward towards convertibility since the war, however, has been that nothing but the gentlemen's agreements of the Sterling Area members has stood between them and a mad rush to convert pounds into dollars as in 1947.[12] It may be presumed that the City decided that, since he did not intend to nationalise the Iraq oil-fields, General Kassim could be relied upon to act like a gentleman, even when outside the Sterling Area.

The fact is that today, although Britain's sterling debts are far in excess of her gold and dollar reserves (Table XVI at end of Chapter 8), sterling is a currency which is regarded as worth holding both as a medium for financing trade and as a foreign-exchange reserve. It has been the main objective of Conservative economic policy since 1951 to strengthen sterling, at the expense of much else, as we shall see later. Sterling is not so strong, however, that it could stand many applications to withdraw from the Area, particularly from a country which had less likelihood of earning hard currency from its current exports than Iraq has with its oil. The question must remain whether General Kassim would have been considered a gentleman, and allowed the freedom to convert his sterling, if he had threatened to take over the oil companies. The experience of Dr Moussadeq, which we will consider in the next chapter, is not reassuring.

There are undoubted advantages for a small ex-colony, not only in the large duty-free British market for its exports, but in the large capital flows, the massed reserves and the present high rates of interest to be gained in the Sterling Area. The main problem would arise for Britain, if ex-colonies in launching development programmes drew heavily on their reserves to buy goods from Europe or North America (or even from Russia), and not from Britain, as India in fact has done. Britain's only hope here, as in much else that we shall consider shortly, is to remain competitive as a supplier of capital goods. If she cannot do this, it is doubtful if she can avoid the consequences by using once more the war-time and post-war technique of blocking balances.

In addition to tying their currencies to sterling and holding their reserves in sterling, the members of the Sterling Area also open their doors fairly freely to each other's capital, labour and goods. At the very least, they offer each other's goods a margin of preference over other people's on the old basis of the Ottawa Agreements of 1932. There are no agreements, however, providing for free trade or free movement of capital or labour, such as the United States signed with the Dollar Area countries of Latin America before the war, or with China and the Philippines after the war.[13] Such agreements may rightly be regarded as unequal in so far as they are agreed to under duress and do really fetter the junior partner's freedom of action, for example, to impose tariffs so as to protect infant industries. We saw this in the opening-up of the markets of Asia and South America by Britain in the nineteenth century, and noted, at the same time, the freedom of the lands of European settlement to protect themselves.

Whether an ex-colony decides to stay in or to leave the Sterling Area will depend largely upon its estimate of the balance of advantage in its particular case – that is on the strength of existing ties of capital investment, on possible sources of finance for industrialisation, on the nature and direction of its trade. It will also depend on the future development of the international provision of aid and of an international payments mechanism. In the meantime, sterling is a sound currency to hold, so long as London short-term finance, broking and insurance services remain second to none,[14] so long as the British market remains the largest for most foodstuffs and raw materials and some conventional manufactures like textiles, and so long as Britain remains a source of development capital and, perhaps most important, of high quality machinery and technical know-how.

What is the Importance of Imperial Preference Today?

Independent members of the Sterling Area are now quite free to impose tariffs and quotas, to alter exchange rates, to vary interest rates, to restrict imports or exports of capital or labour. There remain the Ottawa Agreements giving mutual preferences to each other's goods. Even here changes have recently been negotiated. How important is the Ottawa system now for the member states? In the years before the war, the mutual preferences granted were of benefit mainly to the food producers selling in Britain's home market; but the movements of prices after the war led to Britain receiving more advantage for her manufactures in Commonwealth markets than the empire countries received in Britain's market. This is mainly because, whereas preferences on manufactures were reckoned in percentages, preferences on food products were reckoned in shillings and pence per pound. Inflation has naturally eroded the advantage. Nevertheless, Britain's open door to Commonwealth producers is still, in a world of tariffs and import levies, an asset of immense value to them.[15]

Ex-colonial countries like India and Ghana, moreover, give no margin of preference to Britain (except on cars, and chemicals also in the case of India), and in the remaining colonies, such as Kenya, Uganda, Tanganyika, Borneo and Hong Kong, preferences are very small or non-existent. At the same time, subject to quotas the British market remains open to empire manufactures.[16] This is of increasing importance as these countries build up their industries. The main beneficiaries of the Ottawa system have always been the old Dominions. In the first place, Britain takes most of their primary produce – 90 per cent of lamb and butter, for example.[17] At the same time, they are not tied to the British market. New Zealand, in particular, which was anxious to be able to offer some preferential treatment to other customers than Britain, in order to encourage them to increase their purchases of foodstuffs, recently negotiated agreements to this end.[18] The Ottawa system provides genuine mutual advantages to Britain and the Commonwealth.

What will happen to the Ottawa system if Britain enters the Common Market is something that can only be determined by the outcome of the negotiations. Britain's membership of the European Free Trade Association created a new pattern of preferences which were not enjoyed by the Commonwealth partners. In certain products this may have restricted the advantage enjoyed by them in the British home market and provides an argument in favour of bringing together E.F.T.A. and the Commonwealth into closer economic co-operation. But most E.F.T.A. products are not competitive with Commonwealth products. The E.E.C. farm produce quite frankly is. In the event of Britain's joining the 'Six', it seems certain that some *quid pro quo* will have to have been obtained by Britain for her Commonwealth partners – what Mr Heath called 'comparable outlets'[19] – at least for a time, in exchange for the unilateral reduction of their preferential treatment in the British market. What is at issue, however, is not so much preferential treatment but the open market in Britain and this the whole agricultural policy of the 'Six' and their inward-looking protectionism seems bound to deny (see Chapter 10 below).

On the other hand, if any overseas Sterling Area products are given better treatment in the Common Market than those of other outsiders, the 'Six' are bound to ask for something near to parity with Britain in the overseas Sterling Area market. What would be the effect of this? West German, Italian, United States and other competitors are already and increasingly challenging British exporters in Sterling Area markets. Britain's share in the Area's total imports of manufactures fell between 1954 and 1960 from nearly 59 per cent to under 45 per cent, the heaviest fall taking place in 1959 and 1960 (Table XII below). Some part of this fall is due to the return of Germany and Japan to traditional markets; but West Germany had already surpassed her pre-war performance in the old Dominion markets in 1954 and doubled it by 1960, and Japan had overtaken her pre-war share by 1960, except in the Indian market. It is in India that United States exporters have been competing most strongly, having raised their share of the market for manufactures from 10 per cent pre-war to nearly 20 per cent in 1960.[20] Rapid growth has also been exhibited by the other Common Market countries as well as West Germany, that is by France, the Netherlands and Italy. As a result, in 1960 the 'Six' held nearly a quarter of the overseas Sterling Area trade in manufactures (see Table XII).

Britain's losses have been greatest in Australia, Rhodesia, Malaya and Pakistan but heavy also in South Africa and New

Zealand. In India and West Africa losses have been somewhat smaller.[21] How far has all this been the result of the
reduction of discrimination against non-British producers,
and particularly against Japan and the United States, which
have had extra restrictions to overcome in the past in
addition to the Imperial Preferences? The commodity-
distribution figures give us some answers.[22] United Kingdom
exporters' main losses have been, first, in cotton textiles –
these can be directly accounted for by the ending of discrimination against Japan – and, second, in motor vehicles,
but here there has been a continuing very high preference in
favour of British goods. It is true that in New Zealand where
the preference was highest the fall in the British share was
least.

In general, it would seem that British goods were simply
not competitive, even despite the preferences; and this is
confirmed by the very uneven showing of British exports of
different types of machinery where preferences do not vary.
Thus Britain's losses in the market for metal-working and
electrical machinery have been much worse than in power
and other machinery. In two particular fields – in sales of iron
and steel and of tractors – British exporters have actually
expanded their share of the market.

Table XII gives some support to the suggestion that
British exports lost most ground when the market was
expanding most rapidly, that is, possibly beyond the power of
British firms to supply; but the fact is that the overseas
Sterling Area market as a whole has not been expanding very
fast compared with the Common Market and North American markets. Its share in the total of world markets for
manufactured exports, indeed, declined from 18 per cent to
14 per cent between 1954 and 1959. The conclusion must be
that the Sterling Area can no longer be regarded as a safe
market for British exporters; but the margins of preference
in it, varying as they do from 3 per cent right up to 35 per
cent,[23] may well have been of crucial importance in cushion-

ing the challenge of West German, United States and other industrial competitors of British manufacturers. They may also have done much to delay the taking of the measures necessary to face the challenge. For the future, however, the growth of continental European exports in the Sterling Area market overseas will depend on the preparedness of continental countries to import Sterling products, especially from the less developed lands. Trade is a two-way business and this applies to Britain also.

The Sterling Area market has been of far more importance for Britain than for any of the other industrial countries. Even in 1960–61 the Overseas Sterling Area was still taking nearly 40 per cent of Britain's manufactured exports; it took less than 10 per cent of the exports of the U.S.A. or of the Common Market 'Six' and only a quarter of Japan's exports.[24] Behind this lies the even more important fact that by far the greater part of British overseas investment – about two-thirds of the annual flow between 1954 and 1958 – went to the Sterling Area (see Tables XVII and XVIII at end of Chapter 8). Whether this had the effect of increasing British exports, through the finance of capital development, the establishment of assembly plants, etc., or of reducing them by substituting the products of local factories we shall have to consider later. The flow of capital, amounting to an average of over £200 million a year (see Tables XVII and XVIII), was certainly designed to retain the economic ties between British capital and the British Commonwealth. How far was it successful?

The best estimates of the flow of long-term capital – private, governmental and international – into the overseas Sterling Area between 1948 and 1958 suggest a figure of £3,550 million, of which Britain provided some 60 per cent and the United States some 20 per cent.[25] But these figures do not include the Middle East oil investment, where the United States stake is estimated to yield the Big Five Companies nearly $1,000 million a year.[26] Nor do they show the much more rapid growth of United States capital in the Sterling Area during recent years, mainly accounted for by the re-investment of profits in Australia and South Africa, and by the loans to India.[27] (Aid on a grant basis is not shown either or the United States' share would again be much bigger.) Finally these figures do not show the more rapid growth of Soviet and West German loans after 1958, which were estimated to be adding another £50 million a year.[28] The fact is that Britain's pre-eminence in trade and investment in the Sterling Area is being challenged.

The Challenge to British Privilege

The question of the future direction of Britain's trade is one which we must take up later when we consider the possibilities of expanding the general level of world trade. What we have here to decide is, on the one hand, why the Sterling Area has been failing as a protective device for British goods and capital and, on the other hand, why the choice of economic policies for the ex-colonies is still as open as it is even inside the Sterling Area. What may be done to advance the common interests of the British and ex-colonial peoples will be the subject of the last part of this book.

The answers must lie in the balance of economic power in the world today. First of all, United States capitalism, as we noted earlier, has no need to establish its own protected trading and investment areas. Its technological superiority makes this unnecessary; but it has every interest in breaking into the areas protected for the trade and capital of others. Thus, colonial liberation movements have frequently found United States' official favour, so long as they have not provided openings for Russian influence. The antagonism of the United States State Department to both Mr Lumumba and Mr Tshombe in the Congo can be understood to reflect distaste for both Soviet and Belgian protection. United States policy demands open régimes in what, in a very real sense, it regards as the 'free world'. The history of the freeing of the world, and especially of the old British Empire, to United States goods and capital in the last twenty years is an instructive one.

Britain has been steadily driven by official agreements from the Atlantic Charter, through the Lend-Lease Agreement, the Keynes Loan and G.A.T.T. (the General Agreement on Tariffs and Trade), to Marshall Aid and Dollar Liberalisation to give in to United States pressure against imperial trade discrimination. The most that even Churchill could win from Roosevelt, by way of modification of the clause of the Atlantic Charter guaranteeing 'access on equal terms to trade and raw materials', was that this should be *with due respect for existing obligations*.[29]* The Keynes Loan required free convertibility of sterling (actually introduced for a few crazy weeks by the Labour Government in 1947 until the gold reserve had almost run out);[30] G.A.T.T., signed in 1946, ensured that there should be no increase in discrimination;[31] and Marshall Aid required the liberalisation of restrictions on dollar imports, which has been proceeding steadily ever since.[32]†

Britain in the post-war world has not been in a position to refuse United States pressure without forgoing loans and Marshall Aid, and effecting a total reorientation of her foreign economic policy. Here the second factor in the world balance of power enters the picture. In the face of growing Communist strength, the need for unity and solidarity between British and American capitalism has steadily overridden all the differences that might have emerged between the two. In other words, Britain has had, by and large, to yield to American influence. The last great British colonial gesture – that designed to hold the Middle East at Suez – was

* My italics. M.B.B.
† On the day that these lines were written (14.5.61) *The Observer*'s main headline ran 'Kennedy to Europe: Free Africa Trade. Britain and Six urged to abolish shielded markets'.

a flop; but the United States Mediterranean fleet was at hand in full battle array to intervene if necessary.

Thus the liberated colonies have had a certain freedom to manœuvre between their old colonial masters and the new dominant capitalist power of the United States. But we have already seen both the political strings and the economic implications of United States aid and investment. Retention of ex-colonial lands in the Sterling Area, or *mutatis mutandis* in the Franc Area, is much less important for the great powers than their continued incorporation in the capitalist world. It is within this context that we must estimate the continuing role of the Sterling Area. From our earlier studies of capitalist economic development we should expect to draw two general conclusions.

The first conclusion is that, on the Myrdal-Nurkse model, which we noted in Chapter 5, funds tend to go to safe rather than to risky projects, to private rather than to public enterprise, to advanced rather than to poor economies, unless there are very special opportunities to be exploited, very considerable existing investments to be extended, or very important political purposes to be served. The second is that the free-trade tradition, the imperial preference, the banking arrangements, the pooling of reserves all combine, unless conscious counteraction is taken, to preserve capitalist positions in the power of the imperial companies and in old patterns of trade and investment, none of which may be appropriate to the all-round development of a one-time colony.

The conclusion of this section must be the same as that of the last chapter, that the restrictions on the economic development of the ex-colonies are largely internal. They are the hang-over of colonial rule, exacerbated in some cases by the cold-war context of liberation. But, once full political independence is achieved, there is no limit to what a people may, in the long run, do. They are out in the open, without the imperial political power to instruct or to hinder them. (It is the tragedy of the people of Rhodesia and Nyasaland that they are in danger of losing the protection also of the imperial power against their own white settlers.) They are face to face now with the great imperial companies, just as are the workers in the metropolitan lands themselves. The position has two aspects: in the political field, they may build their countries as they wish; in the economic field, at the present moment, it may well be that the bankers and the great combines will, for some time to come, be calling the tune. The role of the great imperial companies is what we shall turn to next.

'Economic Imperialism' in the Plantation and Mining Companies

In the previous chapter we saw the extraordinary importance which the imperial powers had placed upon securing in their colonies successor governments which seemed likely to be good custodians of imperial investments or, as we should now modify this statement, which seemed likely to keep the country within the capitalist fold. If the Sterling Area is no longer an instrument of colonial exploitation, for the reasons we have suggested, what other forms of economic imperialism may be said to be continuing? Apart, that is, from the internal limitations on the economic development of an ex-colony arising from its colonial past and the nature of the successor government, what external limitations of full sovereignty in economic affairs are still operating?

To answer this question we must look at the foreign economic interests of the old imperial powers and particularly of Britain. In the past we have noted four different and even contradictory groups of interests – those of the plantation and mining companies, those of the great vertically-integrated combines processing colonial raw materials, those of the manufacturing firms at home with an interest in export markets, and, finally, the financial and merchanting interests of the City of London. We shall consider them each in turn, but in this chapter we shall limit our study to the overseas oil, plantation and mining companies whose operations have generally been regarded as lying at the very heart of imperialism.[33]

We shall start with the plantation and mining companies. Their original interest in empire was central to its development. In the 1930s, however, these companies suffered severely from the collapse in the prices of primary products, despite their restriction and control schemes and despite the driving-down of the wages of colonial labour. With the recovery of prices during the Second World War, boosted thereafter by the stockpiling that accompanied the outbreak of the Korean War, these companies made enormous profits. Average net profits of over 20 per cent on capital and reserves were being earned in the early 1950s, by companies producing basic materials and operating mainly or wholly overseas, compared with 12 per cent being earned on home industrials. This situation continued until 1954, when primary product prices began to fall; but even in that year there were still only four out of twenty-eight major primary products whose price had risen less than manufacturers' prices compared with 1938. The long-term trend, however, was against the primary producers; prices and profits began to fall. By 1959 and 1960 profits earned by companies operating overseas were only marginally ahead of those earned at home (see Table XIII below). Within this overall figure, there were, of course, wide variations. Earnings on copper and gold in Rhodesia and South Africa remained consistently at around 20 per cent (Table XIII).

While the importance of the investment in oil has grown, the importance of investment in other minerals and raw materials has declined. Indeed, the two are to some extent connected. The whole trend of modern industrial chemistry has been to substitute synthetic for natural materials. Oil is one of the few imported primary products for which demand has steadily risen in line with the rise in industrial output. Oil has not only been replacing coal as a fuel;[34] petro-chemicals have been replacing rubber and cotton, wool and jute, and other natural fibres. The only other increase of a similar order, apart from certain specialised metals and uranium, has been in the use of aluminium, which is now replacing many other metals.[35]

In the early years of this century, increasing supplies of materials and increasing control over material sources were essential for industrial expansion. Before 1913 and from 1913 to 1937, consumption of raw materials in Britain rose side by side with the increase in industrial production. The situation has now altered radically. In the period from 1938 to 1959, Britain's industrial production was increased by 60 per cent without any increase at all in the volume of basic materials imported (see Table XXI at the end of Chapter 9). This is not only the result of the elimination or utilisation of waste and of substitution by synthetics; the fact is that modern engineering and other industrial products demand more and more working-up and less and less raw material. The cost of materials is of decreasing importance in the final cost of production. The most important example is the reduced demand for textile exports and the increased demand for engineering goods.

Just to list the more obvious examples of substitution is to understand the claim of the G.A.T.T. report of 1955 that 'without these domestically produced substitutes the demand of the industrialised countries last year for raw materials would have been some 40 per cent higher'.[36] We may include synthetic for natural rubber; rayon and nylon, etc., for silk, cotton and wool; plastics in place of wood and metals and leather; aluminium in place of copper; synthetic for natural fertilisers; sulphuric acid made from anhydrites; paper bags in place of jute; bulk transport in place of cartons and sacks and tins; substitutes for tin, for bristles, for oils and colours and dyes.

The results of these changes have been devastating for the

primary producing countries, as we shall see in a later chapter. The independent peasant producer, who can least afford to hold on to his crop and check the fall in price, has suffered worst, as always; but the mining and plantation companies have been hit too. There is little to choose today, as we have just noted, between the rate of their earnings on capital employed and those of the industrial companies at home (see Table XIII). The implications for the relations between Britain and the ex-colonies work in two ways. On the one hand, there is less interest in raw-material production and a smaller proportion of British capital would now be involved in it, were it not for the expanding investment in oil; on the other hand, desperate efforts are being made to retain the migrant-labour system in southern Africa and cheap labour elsewhere, in the hope of keeping up profits even as prices fall. Hence the tragedy of *apartheid* in South Africa, whose gold prices have not risen at all since the war, against an average threefold rise in other prices.[37]

With most prices falling heavily in the field of raw-material production, mining and plantation companies have been bound to intensify their exploitation of labour if they were to maintain profits. Should we not associate with this the strong resistance to the growth of trade unions that led in part to the outbreak of the Communist revolt in Malaya and the intransigence of the Dutch planters in Indonesia? This is certainly the common thread that links *apartheid* in South Africa with white supremacy in Rhodesia, and the desperate attempt of the Belgians to maintain control of a puppet government in Katanga and in Ruanda-Urundi, the main source of mining labour. When the Ghana Government prescribed a 30 per cent minimum wage-increase for miners early in 1960, five British-owned mining companies proposed to shut down and the government had to purchase them in order to keep the mines open. The sum offered to the shareholders was particularly generous – £5 million for shares valued on the market at £2.75 million.[38] African governments with larger foreign mining investments than Ghana may not be able to afford compensation on such terms as these, but they may well be driven to expropriate European assets to protect their workers.

Not all overseas mining and plantation companies have been finding themselves in difficulties. The vertically-integrated combines have been doing well. Unilever was able to double its return (after taxation) on capital employed, from 5.3 per cent to 10.3 per cent between 1952 and 1959, and almost double the dividend, as well as raising the capital employed from £349 million to £577 million by ploughing back profits.[39] The efforts of newly independent governments to defend the prices earned by their peasant producers and to raise wages among their plantation and mining workers, taken together with post-war fluctuations within a general decline in demand, have put an increasing premium on ownership of raw-material sources by the great manufacturing combines. Once more the giants have been buying up the small companies. This is particularly true of the rubber plantation companies, whose numbers reported in the *Financial Times* annual survey of the Trend of Industrial Profits dropped from over 250 to just over 100 between 1957 and 1961.[40] During this period, Dunlop doubled its acreage of rubber plantations, mainly in Malaya, to over 90,000.[41] Unilever's United Africa Company had already doubled its rubber plantation acreage in Africa and increased its palm oil plantations to 20,000 acres from the pre-war level of 13,000.[42]

This is what we saw happening in the inter-war years. The one group of companies operating overseas which gained from low raw-material prices between the wars was the group of newly-established vertically-integrated combines, which controlled all the processes of production from the plantations or mines in the colonies right through to the finished product manufactured at home. The oil companies, of course, come in this group together with such giants as Unilever, Dunlop, Imperial Tobacco, the Distillers Co., Tate and Lyle, Harrison and Crosfield, London Tin Corporation, and Brooke Bond. They had not only been able to buy up small companies ruined by the slump, but could benefit from the low prices at which they bought their raw materials for processing (albeit from their own subsidiaries) by using their near monopoly of the market to maintain their selling price. The fact that the content of raw-material imports in their output is high (about a fifth in oil and chemicals and a sixth in food manufacture, compared with only 7 per cent in engineering[43]) means that the price of raw materials is a crucial factor for them. Their dominant position as almost sole buyer, both from their own estates and from peasant production, gives them the power to cut prices.

We may take Unilever as the outstanding example. It is a giant in the British economy; how much more so in the economies of Ghana and Nigeria from which so large a part of its raw materials derive! The turn-over of Unilever was £1,800 million in 1959 and 1960,[44] almost twice the combined national incomes of Ghana and Nigeria.[45] The capital employed by its main African subsidiary, the United Africa Co., is £125 million,[46] a sum equal to the whole gross fixed capital investment of those two countries in any year.[47] For many years after the war, Unilever was buying more than a third of their whole national output and supplying a third of the goods for private consumption.[48] In 1959, Unilever reported significantly that the profits of United Africa rose rapidly as the result of 'the steps taken to combat rising costs and obtain better margins'.[49] This is only what any capitalist firm must do, but the effects on the economies of primary producing countries are bound to be very great. We shall have to consider later how a newly independent government may counteract such pressure of outside influence upon its economy; but first we must examine how the oil companies have fared.

The Oil Protectorates

Oil is still largely a colonial product. The British Protectorates, in certain oil-bearing lands of the Middle East, are
no more than colonies, and with them we may couple the oil-
bearing colonies of British Borneo, Northern Burma,
Sarawak and Brunei. The sheikhdoms of Kuwait, Qatar,
Bahrein, Muscat and Oman, and the Trucial States are all
territories which might be regarded as nibbles taken out of
the Arab peninsula by the prospecting claims of the British
oil companies. The sheikhdoms have what are called 'Special
Treaty Relations with H.M.G'. The ending of these Treaty
Relations with Kuwait early in 1961 was so rapidly followed
by the occupation of the territory by large British military
forces that it was hard to know thereafter what future
relationships were portended. Up till 1961, their foreign and
defence policy was conducted by a Resident Agent of H.M.G.
and they each employed a British economic adviser.[50] In
considering the present role of 'oil imperialism', we shall
have to look also at Iran and Iraq, which were for long under
either British protection or influence.

The Middle East contains more than half the known
reserves of oil in the world, although only about a quarter of
current supplies were derived from this region up to 1960.
By 1970, as much as a third may be expected to come from the
Middle East.[51] Unlike the oil in the U.S. fields, which has to
be pumped to the surface, the oil in the Middle East rises
under its own pressure. Output from each well, therefore,
averages 185,000 tons a year, while the figure for U.S. wells is
little more than 500 tons. In Iran and Iraq, output rises to
half a million tons a year from each well.[52] This means that
the costs of extraction are very much lower in the Middle
East – estimated in 1945 at 10 to 25 cents per barrel – than in
the U.S.A., where they are between $1 and $1.50 per barrel.[53]
Middle East oil has, therefore, from the very beginning, been
fantastically profitable for the mainly American and British

companies exploiting it. For prices have always been fixed on a world basis to allow the American fields to go on operating at a profit.[54] In fact, the United States continued, up to 1950, to provide more than a half of the world's supplies. By 1960, the American share was only a third and it is expected to fall to a quarter by 1970.[55]

The method of fixing the price has been interesting, depending as it does on the unity and dominating position in the oil business of the eight major companies who control nearly 90 per cent of proved oil reserves outside the U.S.A. and the communist lands.[56] At first, and indeed until the outbreak of the Second World War, it was the practice of the companies holding concessions for oil production in the Middle East to sell the crude oil at something near cost price from the country of origin to a marketing concern outside, which was in fact also controlled by the concessionary company. In this way, the profits on the crude-oil extraction side of the business were kept low, and, therefore, yielded a very small revenue to the government of the country from which the oil came.[57]

Persia was then the major producer. Up to 1932, 57 million tons of oil had been produced in Persia. From this oil the Anglo-Persian Oil Company, in which the British Government holds half the shares, had drawn £171 million and the Persian Government £11 million. The profits on the trading, refining and marketing side of the business had enabled the vast world-wide fleets of tankers, the refineries, the petrol stations and the rest to be built up – almost entirely out of Persian oil sales. Even after 1943, when some improvement in the share of profits was conceded to the Persians, British taxes paid by the company amounted to three times the Persian Government's revenue.[58]

During the Second World War, the American companies established themselves in the Middle East, through the oil concession obtained in Saudi Arabia, to meet the demands of the Allied armies. The American companies wielded the full power of the United States Government in breaking into Britain's Middle East reserve and obtaining the monopoly of Saudi Arabian oil. King Ibn Saud, until then a British puppet, came under the protection of the United States.[59] In the years immediately after the war, the international oil cartel was re-formed and world markets (at least capitalist world markets) were divided up amongst the Big Eight companies, one British, one British-Dutch, one French, the rest American.[60] The practice began of dividing the profit on crude-oil extraction fifty-fifty with the government of the oil-bearing land.[61] This was a big advance on what Persia had been receiving from the Anglo-Persian Oil Company and, although Iraq gained its full half-share, Persia still did not.[62]

The Empires of Oil Today

In 1951, with discontent growing inside the country, Dr Moussadeq's government decided to nationalise Persia's resources of oil. Production and exports by the oil company were immediately suspended. The Persian Government continued production at a low level but was stymied by the world oil companies' completely solid boycott of tankers for Persian oil. Behind the company, with half its capital controlled by a British Labour Government, were marshalled the full forces of the other oil companies, the United States Government and the World Bank, to which Dr Moussadeq unsuccessfully appealed.[63] Trade with Russia was considerably stepped up, but Stalin distrusted 'bourgeois nationalists', and this trade was inadequate to provide a solution.[64]

In 1953, a new Persian Government was formed after an army *coup d'état* led by General Zahedi with outside support. A week later, aid and loans were made available by the United States Government and the World Bank. Within a few months a consortium of British, French and American oil companies was formed for handling oil and, by August

1954, agreement with General Zahedi's Government had been reached. Operations and sales of Persian oil were once more in foreign hands, but as a reward for their support of the British the other companies now got their cut. Persia's share of the profits was raised to come into line with the general fifty-fifty division. The Anglo-Persian – now Anglo-Iranian – Oil Company, meanwhile, was compensated to the tune of £240 million, although it still held £150 million of rights and assets from the new consortium.[65]

The story is an instructive one, not only because of the residual strength of imperial support which the oil companies can evidently rely upon, but because of the nature of the government that was re-imposed upon the Persian people. The good looks of the Shahanshah and his Queen should not conceal the fact that the régime is a dictatorship with most of the opposition in jail. The best land is owned by a few thousand great landlords and the peasant is among the poorest in the world – and this is a country on which Anglo-Iranian's £400 million of assets were built. The sharing of the oil profits after 1954 brought in sums rising to £100 million a year – 60 per cent of which was set aside for the National Development Plan.[66]

Roads, bridges, dams, irrigation works began to be constructed. Corruption and extravagance have been widespread, but the main criticism of the régime is that, with the basic social structure of the country unaltered, the peasant has not the initiative or the resources, after paying his rents and his debts, to make use of the public works being built. As a result, dams stand across the valleys of the Karun and Karaz, but the land beneath them that might now be irrigated remains unreclaimed because the peasants lack the knowledge and the wherewithal to do the job, and because social institutions, instead of helping him, hold him back.[67]

This was precisely the situation which created the revolution in Iraq from which General Kassim emerged. During the years of the Protectorate, the British began the process of alienating the land from the tribes and vesting it in sheikhs and landlords. Often as little as a quarter of the crop was retained by the peasant after payment of rent and debts. The government was dominated by the great landlords. The great dams that were built from the oil profits to control the flooding rivers were a magnificent façade for visiting foreigners and brought wealth to the contractors and ministers who made the contracts. Everything was imported, even the cement; few local technicians were trained; and the peasant fled the land for the booming towns, where some of the new wealth was being spent.[68]

General Kassim, like Colonel Nasser, comes from the middle class which the great landlords had to build up, at least to provide the officers for their armies and police force. Their revolt is, in part, a nationalist one against the control of the imperial powers over their countries; it is also a revolt against the corruption, the extravagance and the inefficiency of landlordism at home. From this they draw peasant support but what they do with it, and how far the oil profits, like the canal dues, will be used to make some real progress on the land, depends still on resistance to pressures from outside. Colonel Nasser resisted.[69]

The reaction of the imperial powers to the Kassim revolt was as sharp as that at Suez, and this time the American Government felt equally involved. Troops were landed in Jordan and Lebanon; but Iraq in 1958 was different from Iran in 1954. Suez had taught a lesson; the Russians were that much stronger and more willing to intervene, and the Kassim forces were not so easily to be dislodged by the army and the tribesmen of the oil companies. But then General Kassim made it clear that he was not going to nationalise the oil companies. Was it only that he had learnt from the Persian oil affair? The companies could have boycotted him too. We can only wait and see how far he will use his share of the profits for some real development plans, while at the same time pressing his claim to increase the share.

Arabia stands as the prime example of the argument that receipts from foreign companies do not of themselves enrich poor lands. For years now, hundreds of millions of dollars a year have poured into the royal coffers of King Ibn Saud at Riyadh only to be invested by the royal family in the United States, or spent on the fabulous luxuries of air-conditioned palaces and banquets brought direct by plane from the kitchens of New York's finest hotels to the Arabian desert. The position in Kuwait, now the main source of Britain's oil imports, is better. Free health and education services cover almost the whole of the tiny population. But a good part even of the half-share of the oil profits which Kuwait receives flows out of the area. It has been estimated that the Sheikh of Kuwait invests about £30 million in Britain every year.[70] The difference between the annual oil revenues received by the governments of all the oil-bearing lands of the Middle East and their annual imports rose to something near £100 million in 1955,[71] and, although the gap was thereafter reduced, it was still about £20 million in 1958.[72] This sum was then available for investment outside the region.

It is not at all to the point to explain that Kuwait's population is not much over 200,000 and cannot possibly need all the hundreds of millions of pounds of oil revenues invested in them. It is precisely the fragmentation of the Middle East by the imperial powers that leads to such absurd calculations and that in fact prevents an all-round programme for economic development in the Middle East as a whole, based on the region's mineral wealth. The standard of living of the Arab people from whose lands the oil flows remains as low as any in the world. The total population of the Arab world outside Egypt – in Saudi Arabia, the Yemen, Aden, Jordan, Syria and Iraq – probably does not much exceed 20 million.[73] It must once have been far more. In Babylonian times, it is said, more than 20 million people lived in the land of Iraq alone, which now barely supports its present five million.[74] The Arabs are not impoverished desert nomads and share-cropping fellahin for choice. One day they will demand the whole of their birthright.

Oil Investment and the British Economy

It is the huge sums flowing out of the oil-bearing lands, at least from those within the Sterling Area, which have been available to the City of London for strengthening the value of the pound and expanding British overseas investment since the war. This is the 'Arab economic aid to Britain' which we noted in the last chapter. A 1958 estimate suggested that the Kuwait investment in sterling balances was between £200 and £300 million, and rising at the rate of £30 to £50 million a year.[75] That would put it at more than a tenth of the liquid capital available in London.[76] This is an important contribution to London's total of long-term investible funds, even if high rates of interest have had to be paid to the sheikhs for the loans. Since 1955, partly as a result of high interest rates and partly as a result of increased spending of balances, particularly by Iraq, the accumulation of balances has slowed down.[77] Arab aid to Britain had done its work.

Even more important is the direct contribution of the oil companies' profits to the British Balance of Payments. The oil companies' share of the profits from extracting oil in the Middle East provided them with some £350 million a year in the late 1950s.[78] One can only hazard a guess at the proportion of this accruing to the British companies, but taking into account their overseas refining activities as well, it seems that the Balance of Payments contribution of the oil companies' earnings may have been of the order of £100 million.[79] That means that oil investment may have been providing an important part of the annual British Balance of Payments surplus since the war, which, until 1958, was averaging between £200 million and £300 million a year (Table XV–A at the end of Chapter 8).

The oil investment has become by far the most important

of British overseas investments; it now provides about half of the annual net investment income flowing in to British investors. (See Table XV–B at the end of Chapter 8.) We noted earlier that a third of U.S. foreign investment since the war has also been in oil (see Table XXX at end of Chapter 10). The world-wide prospecting and drilling operations, the huge investment in pipelines, harbours and quays and refineries, the construction of new tanker fleets, the development of petro-chemicals for fertilisers, plastics and textiles – all from accumulated profits – have gone to make oil the world's major industry. In Britain alone, in the three-year period 1958–60, the oil companies were placing orders at the rate of over £100 million a year and were responsible for some £200 million of investment.[80] That would be more than a tenth of the whole of net capital formation in the company sector.[81] It gives to the oil companies a dominating position in the economy; but there are major drawbacks for the British people as a whole in this situation.

First of all, one of the most remarkable features of the system is that Britain has to pay in dollars for oil imported from the Sterling Area, that is for the supplies that are brought in by the American companies, even though they may come from Kuwait.[82] Of course this is offset by Shell's earnings in the Dollar Area from Venezuelan oil, but the net figure on the Balance of Payments may well involve a dollar loss.

A second debit item for the British people, who are not shareholders in the oil companies, is the military cost of the whole operation. This includes not only special items, such as the war over Suez and the landings in Jordan, but the continuing cost of air bases, naval patrols, garrisons and military subventions in the Middle East. Total overseas military expenditure, according to the Balance of Payments accounts and including the colonial service vote, has been of the order of £200 million in recent years.[83] This is a big sum for the poor taxpayer to find and has all to be paid for in exports.

Third, by 1958, the implications of the growing oil companies' contribution to invisible income in the Balance of Payments were beginning to be felt not only in the overseas military expenditure involved, but in the distortion of Britain's fuel economy. Fuel oil had been pushed by the oil lobby into the position of actually replacing Britain's one natural asset – coal – in home, office and factory heating, in steel-making and even in power-generation. Sales of coal declined from 1956 to 1960 while fuel oil sales doubled.[84] Total oil imports over the same period cost another £150 million. The figures were £334 million in 1955 and £482 million in 1960, of which £270 million were directly competitive with coal.[85] What is left of the £100 million contribution to the Balance of Payments?

Fuel imports are now equal to half the cost of all other imported raw materials,[86] nor does the distortion of the British economy end at the Balance of Payments. The attack on the coal industry represents a threat to the preservation of an irreplaceable natural asset. Pits once closed are not easily reopened and miners who leave the industry will not return. It has meant also the dislocation of the British railway system as the introduction of diesels holds back the large-scale electrification programmes that are needed.[87] Belatedly, in 1961, the British Government followed the example of other European coal-producing countries and imposed a fuel tax, but by then the damage had been done.

The fifty-fifty split of extraction profits gives huge sums for investment to the companies and to the oil-bearing lands, but it means that in Britain we pay an inflated price for our oil. This point is little realised because the petrol tax is so high that the price of the oil itself seems unimportant. The system is, however, already under challenge from independent companies outside the Big Companies' cartel – from the Italian nationalised industry (E.N.I.), the Japanese and the Russians.[88] The latter have been offering cut-price oil, which the Big Companies have so far prevented the British and other governments from accepting; but Dr Castro's action may be catching. In 1960, the Indian Government also agreed to take Russian oil despite protests from the western companies.[89]

The Italians and Japanese, meanwhile, have been offering better terms to the oil-bearing lands, for example, a better profits' cut and a form of partnership in refining, marketing and general policy-making. The chief limitation to this challenge to date has been lack of tankers; but the Russians, Italians and Japanese have all been busy building tankers and the Saudis have ordered tankers from Greek yards for transporting their concessionary oil.[90]

In May of 1960, the Arab League went further and proposed that the governments with oil in their lands should agree on a plan for jointly regulating supplies and prices.[91] The days of the old system of the giant companies' cartel are numbered; but swopping old cartels for new would hardly advantage the European consumer or the Arab oil-worker or fellah. A more helpful, but seemingly hopeless, approach is that of the International Co-operative Alliance, which proposed United Nations control of Middle East oil resources in 1947, but was finally rebuffed in the United Nations Economic and Social Council in 1951.[92]

The effects of the challenge to the system both by the oil-producing countries and by the independents can readily be seen in the drop in net profits per unit of capital employed by the oil companies, as shown in Table XIII below. It is not only that profits have been cut back, but taxation has also been taking a third of the gross profits in the late 1950s instead of a quarter as in the early 1950s. The return on capital was in fact halved between 1952 and 1959 and the Stock Exchange values of oil shares, which recovered so remarkably after Suez, were in 1959 and 1960 at nearly half the peak levels of 1957. Should we see the Suez adventure not only as a last British fling to hold the Middle East against the Americans but also as a last bid to hold back the pressure of nationalism throughout the Arab world? The oil companies, perhaps, knew better than the Stock Exchange what the future had in store for them. By 1960, the threat of Russian oil, of Signor Mattei's Italian state oil enterprise (A.G.I.P.) and of JET petrol had become real. JET was particularly worrying for the big oil companies, for it threatened their chief asset, their ownership of the retail petrol outlets. Ninety per cent of British garages are tied;[93] but they need not remain tied for ever.

The most serious aspect of the Middle East oil operation is the ill will that it has engendered among the Arab peoples, especially by the companies' support for the most absolutely reactionary and corrupt governments. It is an immense advance that the oil companies saw reason, at least in the Middle East, after Suez, and were prepared to accept General Kassim. That he has been given full control over his country's sterling balances, even to being granted the right to convert them into dollars, is a really hopeful sign for future relations with the oil-bearing countries. The advantages to the British people of having governments in these lands which are prepared to make radical changes, in order to advance their economic development, are very great indeed. Poor lands make poor markets. Only the oil shareholders and the City of London have gained in the past from the old system and for them, too, it is nearly played out.

TABLE XII

SHARES IN OVERSEAS STERLING AREA MARKETS, 1938–61

Exporting Country	Shares in Area Imports of Manufactures					Shares in Area Total Imports			
	1954	1957	1958	1959	1960	1938	1951	1959	1961
United Kingdom	57	50	50	48	44	35	30	29	27
U.S.A.	12	14	12	13·5	16	10	10·5	11	11
West Germany	16 }	11	12	12 }	23 }	4 }	2·5	7	7 }
Other E.E.C.		10	11	10				6	7
Sweden, Switzerland and Canada	7	5	6	5	4	5·5	5	5	5
Japan	8	10	9	10·5	13	5	4·5	6	8
Total %	100	100	100	100	100	64·5	59·5	64	65
Current $ billion	5·2	6·7	6·5	6·4	7·6	2·9	12·3	13·2	16·2
Sterling Area Imports as % of World Imports	18	16	15	14	15	12	15	11·5	12·5

Sources: Board of Trade, *Journal*, 5.5.61 and 25.5.62, for Imports of Manufactures. United Nations, *Monthly Bulletin of Statistics*, June 1960 and June 1962, for Total Imports.

TABLE XIII

RETURN ON INVESTMENT IN BRITISH HOME AND OVERSEAS COMPANIES 1953–61

A. *Net Profit as % of Capital in different groups of Companies in the years ending:*

Companies	1953	1954	1955	1956	1957	1958	1959	1960	1961
Gold	16	13·5	14·8	14·7	17	19	19·5	19	19·5
Oil	24	22·5	23	17·3	16	16	12	11·5	10·5
Tin/Copper, etc.	29·5	21·3	31	4·9	28	17	16·5	23	27
Rubber	14	6·8	7	12·3	10	11	12	18	17
Tea	7·3	22	29	13·5	14	8	8·5	9	8
Total Overseas Companies	21·5	19	22	20·3	17·3	16·3	13·3	15	13·7
Total Home Industrials	12·5	13·4	15	15	13	12·5	12	12·5	12·4
Total All Companies	14·2	14·5	16·3	16	13·8	13·2	12·2	13	12·6

B. *Share (%) of Total Capital and Total Net Profit of all Companies, accounted for by Overseas Companies in the years ending:*

Companies	1953	1954	1955	1956	1957	1958	1959	1960	1961
All Overseas Companies									
share of Capital	19	19·5	19·5	18·5	18·2	18·4	20·2	20·5	19·8
share of Net Profits	29	26	26	24	23	23	22·5	23	21·2
of which Oil Companies									
share of Capital	8·6	9·1	9	9·8	10·1	10·6	11·7	12·5	13·4
share of Net Profits	14·5	14·1	13·3	10·6	11·9	13	11·5	11	11·3

C.

	1953	1954	1955	1956	1957	1958	1959	1960	1961
All Companies									
(a) Capital Home and Overseas (£m.)	6,056	6,603	7,203	8,187	8,943	9,674	10,666	11,344	11,304
(b) Profits – Gross (£m.)	2,016	2,185	2,463	2,746	2,769	2,843	2,823	3,105	3,038
Net (£m.)	863	959	1,177	1,316	1,176	1,274	1,300	1,492	1,428

Notes: Capital = Ordinary Capital plus Capital and Revenue Reserves.
Net Profits = Gross Profit less Depreciation and Taxation.
Overseas Companies = U.K. Companies operating mainly overseas.
Source: *The Financial Times* 'Survey of Trends in Industrial Profits', published on the first or second Saturday of each year, 1954–62.

References

1. International Co-operation Administration, *The Sterling Area,* Chapter I.
2. P. W. Bell, *The Sterling Area in the Post-War World,* Oxford, 1956, pp. 3–17 and *passim.*
3. The Bank of England, *Banking in the British Commonwealth, 1952,* p. 467.
4. P. W. Bell, op. cit., p. 275 ff.
5. ibid., p. 409.
6. W. A. Lewis, 'The Colonies and Sterling', *The Financial Times,* 16.1.52.
7. F. W. Paish, *Address* to a Conference on Financing the Economic Development of Underdeveloped Countries, United Nations Association, London, 1955.
8. P. W. Bell, op. cit., p. 273 ff.
9. R. H. Barback, 'Nigeria'; F. Shehab, 'Iraq'; 'Analyst', 'West Indies' in *Symposium on the Sterling Area,* Oxford University Institute of Statistics, November 1959.
10. 'Analyst', article on the West Indies, ibid., p. 364 ff.
11. F. Shehab, article on Iraq, ibid.
12. J. Polk, *Sterling, Its meaning in World Finance,* Royal Institute of International Affairs, 1956, Chapter 4.
13. S. Jenkins, 'The Philippines', in L. K. Rosinger, *The State of Asia,* p. 380 ff.
14. J. Polk, op. cit., p. 151.
15. For this whole paragraph see Economist Intelligence Unit, *The Commonwealth and Europe,* 1960, Chapter I.
16. ibid, Chapters I and VI.
17. ibid., p. 103 and 110.
18. ibid., p. 315 ff.
19. Statement made by Mr Edward Heath to Common Market Ministers in Paris on 10 October 1961 printed in *The Times,* 28.11.61.
20. Board of Trade, *Journal,* 5.5.61.
21. R. S. Gilbert and R. L. Major, 'Britain's Falling Share of Sterling Area Imports', *Economic Review,* National Institute of Economic and Social Research, March 1961.
22. ibid.
23. Economist Intelligence Unit, *The Commonwealth and Europe,* Table 5, Chapter I, p. 17.
24. United Nations, *Monthly Bulletin of Statistics,* Special Series, World Exports by Provenance and Destination, December 1961.

25. A. R. Conan, *Capital Exports into Sterling Countries*, Macmillan, 1960.

26. Burnham & Co., *Foreign Oil*, New York, 1956, Table XI, p. 22.

27. United Nations Economic and Social Council, *International Flow of Private Capital, 1956–58*, New York, 1959.

28. Organisation for European Economic Co-operation, *Flow of Financial Resources to Countries in course of Economic Development, 1956–59*, Paris, 1961; and A. Nove, *Communist Economic Strategy*, N.P.A., Oxford, 1960.

29. R. N. Gardner, *Sterling-Dollar Diplomacy*, Chapter III.

30. ibid., p. 230 ff.

31. ibid., Chapter XVII.

32. United States Congress, *Economic Co-operation Act 1948*, Section 115 (b) 3, Washington, 1948.

33. R. P. Dutt, *Crisis of Britain and the British Empire*, p. 55 ff.; and J. Strachey, *The End of Empire*, Chapter XII.

34. G. F. Ray and F. T. Blackaby, 'Energy and Expansion', *Economic Review*, National Institute of Economic and Social Research, September 1960.

35. General Agreement on Tariffs and Trade, *Trends in International Trade*; and United Nations *World Economic Survey, 1955*, New York, 1956, p. 53 ff.; and *World Economic Survey, 1958*, New York, 1959, Chapter I; and J. H. Rowlatt and F. T. Blackaby, 'The Demand for Industrial Materials, 1950–57', *Economic Review*, National Institute of Economic and Social Research, September 1959.

36. General Agreement on Tariffs and Trade, *International Trade 1954–1955*, Geneva, 1956, p. 6.

37. General Agreement on Tariffs and Trade, *Trends in International Trade*, Geneva, 1958, p. 19 ff.

38. *Ghana Today*, 15.2.61.

39. Unilever, *Annual Report and Accounts*, 1960 and 1961.

40. *The Financial Times*, 'Survey of Trends in Industrial Profits', published on the second Saturday in January each year.

41. According to Dunlop advertisements in the current press, April 1961.

42. United Africa Company, *Statistical and Economic Review*, March 1950, p. 38.

43. H.M. Government Blue Book of *National Income and Expenditure, 1958*, 'Input – Output Tables', H.M.S.O., 1958.

44. Unilever, *Annual Report and Accounts*, 1960 and 1961.

45. United Nations, *Economic Survey of Africa since 1950*, Table 111, p. 15.

46. Unilever *Reports*, 1960 and 1961.

47. United Nations, *Economic Survey of Africa since 1950*, Tables 4.4 and 4.5; pp. 192–3.

48. United Africa Company, *Statistical and Economic Review*, 1948–58;

and United Nations, *Economic Survey of Africa since 1950*, Tables 1. LV and 1. LVI, pp. 94–5.

49. Unilever *Annual Report and Accounts*, 1959.
50. Whitaker's *Almanack*, 'Dominions, Colonies and Protectorates'.
51. P. H. Frankel, and W. H. Newton, 'The State of the Oil Industry', *Economic Review*, National Institute of Economic and Social Research, September 1960.
52. ibid.
53. United Nations Economic Commission for Europe, *The Price of Oil in Western Europe*, Geneva, 1955, p. 14.
54. ibid., p. 11 ff.
55. P. H. Frankel and W. L. Newton, 'The State of the Oil Industry', Table 3.
56. ibid., Table 4.
57. L. P. Elwell-Sutton, *Persian Oil*, Lawrence and Wishart, 1955, pp. 24, 134.
58. ibid., for whole paragraph, p. 170 ff.
59. H. O'Connor, *The Empire of Oil*, Calder, 1955, Chapter 27.
60. G. Lenczowski, *Oil and State in the Middle East*, Cornell, 1960, Chapter X.
61. ibid., Chapter IV.
62. L. P. Elwell-Sutton, op. cit., pp. 108, 115, 172.
63. ibid., Chapter 17.
64. Board of Trade, *Journal*, 16.4.55, p. 845.
65. L. P. Elwell-Sutton, op. cit., Chapter 22.
66. Board of Trade, *Journal*, 11.2.56, p. iii.
67. *The Times* Middle East correspondent, 'Iran Today – spoilt by a Surfeit of Aid', 5 and 6 July 1961.
68. H. O'Connor, *New Light on Iraq*, Union of Democratic Control, 1960, quoting Michael Ionides, British member of the Iraq Development Board.
69. C. Issawi, *Egypt at Mid-Century*, Chapter 13.
70. A. C. L. Day, *Observer*, 3.8.58.
71. Figure calculated on assumption of 162 m. tons of Middle East oil sold at $15 per ton = $2,430 m. less costs at $2.5 per ton, i.e. $405 m. = $2,025 m. apparent profit; 50:50 share gives $1,012 m. revenue for governments against $800 m. imports. Prices and costs taken from United Nations Economic Commission for Europe, *Report on the Price of Oil*. Imports and exports from Board of Trade, *Journal*, 11.2.56.
72. H.M. Treasury, *Bulletin for Industry*, February 1961.
73. United Nations, *Statistical Yearbook, 1961*, New York, 1962.
74. T. Jacobsen and R. M. Adams, article in *Science*, Vol. 128, No. 3334.

75. A. C. L. Day, *Observer*, 6.8.58.
76. *Midland Bank Review*, February 1962, 'New Capital Issues 1948–61'.
77. H.M. Colonial Office, *Monthly Digest of Colonial Statistics*, H.M.S.O., Tables on Holdings of Sterling Assets.
78. H.M. Treasury, *Bulletin for Industry*, February 1961.
79. J. Mitchell, 'Britain's Invisible Earnings', *The Banker*, May 1958; and A. Schonfield, *British Economic Policy since the War*, Penguin 1958, p. 113 ff.
80. *The Financial Times*, 7.6.62; and estimate by Ian Campbell in an unpublished paper on 'Oil and Investment' to which I am indebted for help with material in this section.
81. H.M. Government Blue Book on *National Income and Expenditure, 1961*, H.M.S.O., 1961, Table 59.
82. A. Schonfield, op. cit., p. 113 ff.
83. H.M. Government, *United Kingdom Balance of Payments 1959–61*, (White Paper), H.M.S.O., 1961.
84. G. F. Ray and F. T. Blackaby, 'Energy and Expansion'.
85. H. M. Government, *Trade and Navigation Accounts of the United Kingdom*, December 1955 and December 1960; and G. F. Ray and F. T. Blackaby, op. cit.
86. ibid.
87. Association of Scientific Workers, *A National Fuel and Power Policy*, September 1960.
88. P. H. Frankel and W. H. Newton, *The State of the Oil Industry*.
89. Article in *Far East Trade*, October 1960, p. 1304.
90. P. H. Frankel and W. H. Newton, op. cit.
91. ibid.
92. G. Lenczowski, op. cit., Chapter X.
93. Mammon, 'Pump and Pence', *The Observer*, 3.7.60.

CHAPTER 8

The New Empires —
of the Giant Corporations

British capitalism finds itself in a new situation today. The Sterling Area, which was established after the war as a bulwark against the dollar and as a privileged market for British exports of goods and capital, has had its defences slowly but steadily eroded by American and European pressure and is now under open challenge from the Common Market. At the same time, the old British colonial mining and plantation companies are seeing their profits squeezed by the development of synthetic substitutes and of colonial popular resistance. Even the big oil companies' profits are under threat. Yet the gross figure for long-term British capital investment overseas during this period, most of it to the Sterling Area, has been greater in money terms than in any previous period, barring only the last few years before 1913 (Table IV at end of Chapter 3): and the outward flow of capital shows no signs of abating. Why is this happening, just when the ties of empire are being dissolved and the profits of companies operating overseas are under pressure as never before? This is the question we must answer in this chapter. It may be regarded as the central chapter of the book. But, first, what are the facts about this new phase of capital export?

The New Wave of British Overseas Investment

Official estimates[1] put the flow of gross private capital exports from Britain between 1946 and 1959 at well over £4,000 million (Table XVII). This is a very large sum and is almost certainly an underestimate. It is equivalent in value to the whole British overseas investment before the Second World War, although steadily rising prices over the post-war period have meant that each addition to the stock of capital overseas was of less real value. To put it in perspective, we may note that the outflow of long-term capital of £300 million – £400 million a year was equal to between a third and a quarter of the net investment in fixed capital at home in the same period.[2] This is small compared with the great days of overseas investment before the First World War, when exports of capital actually exceeded investment at home. But the 1910–13 period was exceptional and even in real terms this overseas investment in the decade after 1949 probably exceeded that in any of the last decades of the nineteenth century. It comes, moreover, after two decades in which capital exports almost ceased altogether (see Table IV, Chapter 3).

What was the source of all this capital? In theory, an outflow of capital is supposed to reflect fairly directly the annual surplus in the balance of a country's payments. To give a clear picture, we shall have to present the evidence available in a number of tables; but in no field of British capital operation are the actual financial details more carefully concealed. The Tables at the end of the chapter, and especially Table XVII, are made up from a number of fairly well-informed guesses, some of them official guesses; and none will be happier than the author, if the Tables are challenged and more accurate figures made available.

The basic evidence is supplied by the Balance of Payments figures. There are many net items in the Balance, however, which conceal an outward and an inward movement of capital; of these the net oil-investment income is the largest, but there are others. Reinvestment overseas of British companies' income earned overseas is generally regarded as being much under-estimated in the figures. Short-term movements of funds are hard to distinguish from long-term investment. And, finally, there is the so-called 'Balancing Item' to cover errors and omissions – mainly uncontrolled movements of short-term funds – that is frequently of the order of hundreds of millions of pounds and as large as the Balance itself.[3] Nevertheless, it is the surplus on the Balance of Current Account each year that is the basis of the capital flow. It is to the increase of this surplus, and the strengthening of Sterling that goes with it, that Conservative Chancellors since 1951 have been directing almost the whole of their economic policy. The measures they have employed to this end we shall examine in the next chapter. We shall confine ourselves now to the Balance itself.

A surplus is not found, as is sometimes suggested, by achieving a simple surplus of exports of goods over imports of goods, that is on the merchandise account. All the same, remarkable success has been achieved since the war in bringing export earnings and the import bill very nearly in line. In addition to the merchandise trade, however, the Balance of Payments reflects all the movements of 'invisible' earnings. These include income and payments for shipping and air travel, Government grants and expenditure, the tourist accounts, insurance and banking services, brokerage and merchanting provided by Britons to foreigners and by foreigners to Britons and the flow of interest, profits and dividends to foreigners from their property held in Britain and to British owners of capital invested overseas.

Table XIV shows how all these different kinds of earnings have contributed to make up a surplus or a deficit. Each item is shown in the Table as a figure of net earnings calculated as a percentage of the value of imports in that year. This method of presentation provides a useful comparison between years, particularly because the volume figures for imports shown in the Table (Column 1) reveal the close connection between the level of imports and the ultimate payments balance. Every Payments deficit on the Table is associated with a sharp rise in import volumes, except that in 1946 when immediate post-war conditions resulted in very low exports. By the same token, the success in keeping down the import bill – with consequences to the internal economy that we shall examine in the next chapter – may be said to have been the main cause of the high level of post-war surpluses.

If, however, we add up all the surpluses and all the deficits, taking the post-war period as a whole, the net result is only a surplus of under £300 million (£1,831 million minus £1,563 million). Where, then, did the over £4,000 million of capital exports come from? To find out, we have to look beyond the annual current account of goods and services and invisible income to the capital account as well. The two accounts can be seen together in Table XV-A, where they are divided up into two periods: 1946–57 and 1958–60. The Accounts are also broken down according to the main areas with which Britain had to balance her payments. There is also in the Table the record of the Dollar Account of the Rest of the Sterling Area (R.S.A.), because in fact Britain keeps the Account, as we saw earlier, not only of her own citizens' dollar transactions, but of those of all the Sterling Area members.

From a careful study of the figures in this Table (XV-A), we may distinguish four main sources for the over £4,000 million capital export:

First, dollar loans and grants from the U.S.A. and Canada provided over £1,700 million in the period up to 1957. It has been argued that it is improper to say that this aid provided the capital for overseas investment, because it was spent on dollar goods, and dollar goods would not have been imported without this aid.[4] Nevertheless, goods would have to have been imported from somewhere, even if dollar sources had been ruled out; so the dollars must have helped to create a surplus on the account. In addition, the R.S.A. Account was being greatly assisted by the inflow of capital, mainly from the U.S.A., as the Table shows.

Second, Sterling Area gold-production contributed nearly another £1,400 million before 1957 and over £2,300 million in all by 1960. Again, the gold was used partly to buy dollar goods and partly to offset the deficit in Britain's and the Rest of the Sterling Area's account with the European countries in the European Payments Union, which was often very large.

Third, the colonies not only produced a small part of the gold, but also covered the deficit of other Sterling Area countries in their trade with the Dollar Area. In fact, the Table shows that their surplus on dollar trade was almost exactly equal (at £1,120 million) to the other countries' deficit (of £1,140 million) in the period 1946–57. This was a great advantage to the Dominions accruing from their membership of the Sterling Area.

Fourth, the accumulation of colonial balances of sterling in London before 1957, to the extent of nearly £1,000 million as the Table shows, made possible the paying-off of other creditors both inside and outside the Sterling Area, during the period. We have already spoken of this in an earlier chapter. After 1955, colonial sterling balances ceased to be accumulated; the prevailing rates of interest in London made this an expensive way of borrowing short in order to invest long. Nevertheless, the balances of the oil protectorates, of which we spoke, have continued to rise and no doubt provide a useful source of sterling without the fear of criticism from the peoples of the countries from which they derive.

In all these ways, a net movement of long-term capital of over £2,500 million was made possible in the period up to 1960; this net figure covered a gross outward flow of over £4,000 million (£3,200 million according to estimates given to the Radcliffe Committee for the period prior to 1957, and another £900 million over the three succeeding years) and against this a partly balancing inflow of capital to Britain of some £1,600 million. On the Dollar Area account only estimates can be given of the long-term capital movements over this period, but these suggest that the net inflow of £450 million was made up of about £1,300 million flowing from the U.S.A. and Canada into the U.K. and about £900 million flowing out from the U.K. to North America during the period.[5]

Can it Continue?

The separate tabulation of the three years between 1958 and 1960 in Table XV-A shows that the outflow of funds continued at an even faster rate than in the previous twelve years (unless this is the result of more accurate statistical recording). The Treasury figures for separate years show that the peak point both for exports and imports of private capital was 1956, when exports were £430 million and imports £230 million. This brought the 1952–58 annual average for gross capital exports up to nearly £400 million, including about £50 million of Government grants and aid (Table XVIII). The Government contribution has been stepped up since then, but it seems from the Board of Trade figures in Table XVIII that over £300 million of private capital was being invested overseas year by year right up to 1960. How has this rate been maintained?

The combined Balance of Payments account for 1958–60 in Table XV-A reveals important changes in these three years, compared with the previous period. First, on current account there was no U.K. surplus at all, taking the three years together, and the R.S.A. element took a sharp downward turn compared with the period up to 1957 (as is shown in the lower half of the Table). Imports of the Overseas Sterling Area countries from non-Sterling sources rose, between 1950 and 1960, from £1,000 million to £2,800 million, while their exports to non-Sterling markets rose only from £1,400 million to £2,200 million.[6] It is evident that the contribution of the one-time colonies, particularly to the Dollar Account, disappeared as they gained their independence. They widened their sources of imports more freely, especially from Dollar Areas, and at the same time drew down their sterling balances. The performance of the United Kingdom in trade with non-Sterling Area countries has been rather better. Exports were raised from £1,200 million to £2,300 million, while imports grew only from £1,400 million to £2,000 million.

Second, and even more serious, there has been an adverse change in the Invisible Account. Much of this has been the result of the payments necessitated on the post-war wave of United States investment in both the U.K. and the Overseas Sterling Area, amounting to about £1,000 million in the former and £2,000 million in the latter. The payments to United States investors in the Sterling Area rose from $200 million a year to $600 million a year between 1950 and 1960.[7]

As A. R. Conan has pointed out,[8] such capital movements set up a vicious circle. The more capital flows in, the more interest and dividends have to be paid out, and at least a quarter of the current account deficit in 1960 was due to the deficit on invisibles (see Table XV-B). We shall consider the implications of this inward flow for the home economy in the next chapter. Much of the flow consists in the retention of profits in businesses in Britain mainly by U.S. companies. The Board of Trade survey suggests that earnings and investment in the U.K. of overseas companies were both running at about the same level of £130 million a year in the two years 1959 and 1960.[9] There appears to be no sign of the process coming to an end. In 1961, portfolio investment by foreigners in Britain, as distinct, that is, from direct investment by firms, also became important, possibly in anticipation of Britain's entry into the Common Market. One estimate put this as high as £100 million.[10] The fact has to be faced that dividends have to be paid out of the country on this investment, and, in addition, one may expect to see a larger proportion of the profits of direct investment being repatriated. When this happens, the Balance of Payments on current account will be seriously affected. Britain is caught in the same trap as so many of the less developed lands in the Sterling Area and elsewhere.

Already by 1960, the outflow of income to foreigners on their property held in Britain (which includes, of course, the retained portion of the profits) was equal to two-thirds of the inflow of income from British investments overseas. Before 1952, it was less than a half.[11] Even in 1956, when repayment of the interest on the North American loans had begun, it was still a half. The main changes have been, first, in the growth in payments to private foreign investors holding long-term capital in Britain – this has doubled between 1951 and 1960, as we should expect from the rapid growth of the American stake in British industry[12] – and, second, in the growth in interest payments on short-term holdings in the Sterling Balances. These last were especially large during the era of high interest rates, which added as much as £80 million a year to the sums due; but the payments remained, even in 1959, at about twice the 1951 level (according to evidence presented to the Radcliffe Committee).[13] Meanwhile, government loans in the 1950s have been flowing outward rather than inward, as the United Kingdom government has stepped up its own loans, mostly, it must be said, inside the Sterling Area, while making repayments on the earlier United States and Canadian loans.

At the same time, despite the rising level of overseas investment by British investors, the income received from overseas was actually barely rising from 1958 to 1960 and fell in 1961, while the income being paid overseas was rising. (The figures are shown in Table XV-B.) The cause of the disparate movement appears, in part, to be the decline in the oil companies' profits, of which we spoke earlier. But even when oil is excluded, the rise in income from the other direct British investments overseas was barely 20 per cent over the three years, while the rise in payments on foreign investments in Britain was 60 per cent.[14] There appears to be a lower yield to British investors abroad than to foreign investors in Britain. At this rate, income would soon be absorbed completely by payments.

Other invisible items in the current account have fallen also. As a result, in part, of increased purchases from non-sterling sources, earnings from shipping barely rose in the 1950s while payments for shipping services doubled between 1950 and 1955 and continued to rise thereafter. In 1960, for the first time in history, less than half of the imports into the U.K. were carried in British ships and only 60 per cent of our exports.[15] 'Other services', which include the expenditure of U.S. forces in the U.K. as well as the City of London's services, have declined sharply; the Tourist account and the account of migrants' funds and gifts remain slightly negative on balance.

We have to note, finally, the rapid growth in recent years of the Government element in the Account, which our earlier Table (XIV) made clear, but which is emphasised by the presentation of the figures in Table XV-B. Of the over £300 million of Government current expenditure overseas in 1961 (not including capital loans, etc.) two-thirds was military.[16] Is this the price of overseas investment? If so, it is a high one for the tax-payers who do not share in the investment income.

The outlook cannot be regarded as very good. A. R. Conan commented[17] that the optimistic forecasts of the Treasury in evidence to the Radcliffe Committee, looking forward to larger current account surpluses in the 1960s, seem to have been somewhat premature. The year 1960 showed a deficit of £344 million, subsequently corrected to £288 million, and 1961 a deficit of £70 million, which the Treasury again thought might be corrected, this time into a slight surplus.[18]

It must seem astonishing, in view of all that has been said, that British overseas investment has been maintained. How then has it been done? Support from government loans and colonial balances has had to be replaced by dependence on 'hot money' and on the inflow of long-term private investment. Short-term funds flowing 'hot' from New York and the continent have been attracted by the high level of interest rates ruling in London. Long-term investors have been attracted by Common Market prospects. Over £500 million came in between 1958 and 1960, compared with no more than twice that sum in the previous eleven years (Table XV-A). Some further support has been received by the stepping-up of gold production but reserves have regularly had to be drawn down under cover of borrowing from the International Monetary Fund, each time that the 'hot money' has fled once again from London.

By the nature of things, the accumulation of short-term funds in sterling balances is a temporary expedient, which only leads to further embarrassment when the money flows away. Thus, in 1960 alone, some £1,700 million flowed into London, if the balancing item is added to the official figures. When this began to flow out again at the end of the year, recourse was had to the bankers of the continent to the extent of at least £325 million.[19] A part of this difficulty is inevitable for any country whose currency is widely used in international trade transactions. For traders using sterling will naturally time their payments according to the value and expected value of sterling, 'leading' or 'lagging' appropriately.[20] This is the price that is paid for the foreign exchange earnings from the City of London's services. But the whole problem is made far worse by the attempt to maintain long-term foreign investment on the basis of such short-term funds. In large part, it is this which has led to the permanent régime of high interest rates in London, the effects of which we shall examine in the next chapter.

It is hard to see how the surplus for foreign investment can be re-established unless a big increase takes place in exports and other earnings without any comparable rise in imports and other payments. We should not, however, be mesmerised by these figures. As we have emphasised before, overseas investment and an export surplus are two sides of the same coin. Exports can be expanded by gifts and loans just as investment may be achieved by an export surplus. Moreover, according to Conan's estimates,[21] by 1959 Britain once more became a creditor country with a strong balance of overseas assets to set against the assets of foreigners in Britain and even against Britain's short-term liabilities to foreigners. Table XVI shows the picture. The problem remains, from what we have seen, however, that the return on investment in Britain is higher than that on British investment overseas.

What is now of first importance to discover is whether British overseas investment will nourish a rise in British exports, as it did earlier in the twentieth century. To answer these questions we must look at the direction and nature of this post-war wave of overseas investment.

The Nature of British Overseas Investment Today

The British Balance of Payments figures tell us little except that about two-thirds of the post-war capital flow has gone into the Sterling Area (Table XV-A). Details of the form it took and the countries it reached are scanty, although the Board of Trade Surveys for 1958–60 have begun to provide a picture for long-term direct investment excluding oil and insurance companies.[22] In addition, we may draw upon Conan's figures for the Sterling Area[23] and such evidence as is available from the Balance of Payments of other countries to fill in the picture. Table XVII has been built up in this way. A warning should again, perhaps, be given of the tentative nature of the estimates in it, many of which are based on fairly wild guessing. The Table shows not only the flow of capital since the war, but the figures for 1938 and estimates of the sales during the war and immediate post-war years. By deducting sales and adding new investment to the 1938 figures, totals for 1959 have been obtained. This follows Conan's procedure, but it must involve a considerable underestimate of the real totals, as the value of the pre-war investment has not been adjusted at all for the post-war rise in prices. What does the Table show?

A figure rather nearer £5,000 million than Conan's 'over £4,000 million', or the Radcliffe Committee's £3,750 million up to 1957[24] has been taken for the total post-war additions to British overseas investment, to take account of the oil investment, largely omitted by Conan, and of the well-known underestimate of reinvestment of profits by companies operating overseas. This gives a total of foreign assets nearer to £8,000 million than to his £7,000 million. This may seem to be on the high side; Morgan, in his study of the Structure of Property Ownership in Great Britain,[25] gave a figure of £5,000 million for 1955 and it is unlikely that it was increased by more than £2,000 million in the next six years. On the other hand, the starting figure of £4,500 million from 1938 greatly underestimates the market value of these earlier investments that were not sold during the war, particularly since it was mainly the gilt-edged stock, whose price has not risen, that was sold.

The result of these sales and of the post-war reinvestment of profits overseas can be seen in the sharp change in the distribution of capital between company investment and public debt. Instead of a third of the total being in Government stocks, not much more than a tenth remains so today. The largest sales were of the railways in India and the Argentine, but there were large disposals elsewhere in the Commonwealth and some losses also, as in China and eastern Europe.[26] There have been some new issues on the London Market of Commonwealth, Colonial and Foreign Government stocks since the war, but these have not totalled more than about £350 million. Nearly all were for the Sterling Area and mainly for South Africa.[27] Thus the process which we noticed going on during the inter-war period has been accelerated. The days of the rentier investor in foreign and empire government and railway stock are over. Once upon a time, before the First World War, the rentier supplied far and away the greater part of the capital invested overseas; today it is the great corporations who supply the capital.

The direction of the investment is, however, much the same. The post-war flow of capital to the Sterling Area has brought up the Sterling Area share of the total of U.K. capital abroad from about 50 per cent to about 60 per cent (Table XVII). But the outstanding point that emerges from the Table is the concentration of the private business investment in the more developed lands, both inside and outside the Sterling Area, that is, in the U.S.A. and Canada, in Europe and in the older independent members of the Commonwealth. The result is that, instead of about £1,200 million of the £3,000 million total private business investment overseas (that is about 40 per cent) being in the *more*-developed lands as it was before the war, the position today is that over 50 per cent is in these lands. In the Sterling Area alone, even the increased flow of funds to the colonies and the vast oil investment in the Middle East have not prevented the share of capital going to the *less*-developed lands in the Area from falling.

We shall not forget what was said earlier about the role of the colonies and later of the oil protectorates in providing a large part of the short-term funds on which long-term investment could be based. There are, nevertheless, some indications that, of recent years, not only have the colonies been drawing on their sterling balances, but also that they have been receiving some rather larger part of the flow of private capital from the U.K. India has also been receiving much of the government capital that has recently been available from London. The implications of these recent developments will have to be considered later. More needs still to be said here about the nature of the investments we are considering.

The wildest estimate in Table XVII is that of £700 million invested in oil but there are good grounds for accepting it.* The oil investment reveals the essential nature of the flow of post-war British overseas investment. It has consisted largely of profits retained by British companies in their overseas businesses. Table XVIII shows an estimate of the way the outflow of capital was made up in the 1950s. Excluding Government grants (which have not been considered in most of the figures we have been studying so far), nearly two-thirds of the total outward flow of capital has consisted of company retentions. Fresh capital amounted to little more than a fifth of the total. This, perhaps, only emphasises the

* Conan's figures for the Sterling Area include oil company investments in production and storage and in refineries and distribution in the dominions and colonies, but not their investments in the Sterling Area oil protectorates or in Iraq (before she left the Area).[28] Some part of the investment in Venezuela and in Europe must also appear in Conan's figures, which are reproduced in our Table; the whole of the Middle East Oil investment is excluded by Conan, but set in our Table at £700 million. The figure of £700 million is reached by taking into account the annual capital expenditure of B.P. and of Shell. Investment by B.P. has been of the order of £100–£150 million, some £35–£50 million of which was in exploration and production, including pipe-lines and terminals.[29] Even excluding any investment in locally built refineries, that would mean that about £350 million were spent mainly in the Middle East over the post-war years. In addition, the Middle East share – about a fifth – of Shell's huge capital investment of £350 million a year,[30] a half of which is spent on production and exploration, would provide another £350 million over the period.

We may check this in another way. The oil companies have been setting aside about two-thirds of their net profits to reserves for development, as well as paying a quarter of their gross profits into depreciation.[31] The result is that over £200 million have been available for capital development every year. If we take it that at least a third of this sum has been spent outside the home country, we have a figure of £70 million a year. It may be presumed that £50 million have been spent in the Middle East each year, which, averaged over fourteen years, gives once more a conservative estimate of £700 million.

extraordinary importance of the free sterling that was made available and the dollars that were provided from the colonial earnings banked in balances in London. It also provides us with a clear picture of the type of investment that has been going on.

The great oligopolies, whose pricing policies at home have enabled them to build up huge accumulated reserves of capital for their reinvestment programmes, without going to the market for more than their marginal requirements, have been doing the same thing in their overseas operations also. The retention of some £200 million a year earned overseas is equal to about a third of the property income reported in the Balance of Payments as being received from abroad every year after payment of local taxes (Table XV-B). Probably nearer a half of the income from direct private company investments overseas, excluding, that is, all rentier investment in foreign portfolios and public debt, was being reinvested overseas in this period[32] and as much as three-quarters in the years 1958–60 (see Table XIX).

The size of the figures in the Tables of Estimates which we have been examining is so great that the implications for the economy at home must be considered. This will be the subject of the next chapter, but we should note here that, if these estimates are even approximately correct, then British capital invested in businesses overseas each year is equal to rather more than a third of the net capital of about £700 million invested in companies at home.[33] We may check this by relating the company income earned abroad and company income received at home. In 1958–60, just over £1,000 million, net of depreciation, were earned abroad, while company income at home, after deducting depreciation, came to about £3,000 million.[34] We seem to have reached roughly the right order of magnitudes in our calculations; and the order – of £1 invested overseas for every £3 invested at home – must seem to most readers to reveal a remarkable state of affairs.

Who are the Investors?

That the investors behind the new post-war wave of capital exports are not rentiers as of old, we have clearly shown. That they are largely companies reinvesting their profits is equally clear. British companies, however, invest in foreign companies as well as in their own subsidiaries, and sometimes in companies that are registered overseas but in fact are really subsidiaries. The proportion of the total British overseas investment which is in foreign companies of one sort and another is large, probably about 30 to 40 per cent, taking into account portfolio as well as company investment.[35] At least half of this is in the U.S.A. and Canada.[36] It is significant that the item 'Taxes and Remittances Paid Abroad' in the British Company Income Appropriation Account has been rising rapidly of recent years: from £227 million in 1955 to £386 million in 1960.[37]

Which are the companies most involved in this vast overseas operation? We suggested in the last chapter that the capital of the old mining and plantation companies operating mainly overseas had barely increased since the war, so it cannot have been they. The oil companies, however, we have seen to be increasing their capital very rapidly. The total capital of the British oil companies in 1960 was about £1,500 million, including reserves.[38] Not all this would be invested overseas; but it must mean that something between a sixth and a fifth of the total British overseas investment in private business is accounted for by oil. The other raw material companies' capital and reserves amounted to about £875 million in 1960.[39] Nearly all of this must have been overseas, so that we may say that they provided about an eighth of the total. We may set out our findings so far in a very approximate form and add estimates for the rest as best we can:

Distribution of U.K. Foreign Investment in Private
Business, 1960

In Foreign Companies 30%–40%
    U.S.A. and Canada   15%–20%
    Others   15%–20%

In British Companies operating mainly overseas   25%–35%
    Oil   15%–20%
    Mining and Plantation   10%–15%

In U.K.-based Companies' Overseas Interests   25%–40%
    Vertically integrated   10%–15%
    Solely manufacturing   15%–25%

It must be emphasised that these estimates must be very largely guesswork. The group of which least is known is the last, which comprises the overseas interests of companies that operate mainly in the U.K. We have considered earlier the growth of the great vertically-integrated combines, such as Unilever, Imperial Tobacco and Dunlop, both in the inter-war years and since 1945. A large part of the overseas invest-ment of this group must derive from these great combines; and yet there is much evidence that solely manufacturing companies have been showing the most rapid expansion overseas and may now have an even more important stake in foreign investment than the imperial combines of old. This is confirmed by the evidence of the Board of Trade's survey of U.K. Companies' direct investment overseas that manufacturing industry accounted in 1958 and 1959 for more than half of the total (see Table XIX).

One of the most impressive illustrations of the new trend is the development of manufacturing enterprises overseas by the great processing combines themselves. United Africa, for example, is, in its own words, 'acquiring a new look; it is being rapidly converted from a trading and produce buying concern into a merchandising and industrial business'[40] in

Commonwealth West Africa. These businesses include breweries, soap and perfume factories, vehicle and bicycle assembly, cold storage and association with other British firms in cement, plastics, biscuits and so on. Booker Bros., McConnell, the West Indian trading group, under the progressive leadership of Sir Jock Campbell, has been developing in the same direction with breweries and poultry- and animal-feed factories in British Guiana.[41]

There is no way of obtaining an accurate picture of the distribution of overseas investment by companies or even by industries, but Table XIX gives the picture by industry and area and Table XX gives a list – a rather remarkable list – of the branches of British banks overseas and of the overseas subsidiaries of the larger British commercial and industrial concerns. Mere sales organisations are not included. The Table was compiled from a reading of the reports given in 1960 and 1961 by the chairmen of the leading banking and insurance companies and of the top sixty industrial companies. It may, therefore, well exclude many subsidiaries in areas which did not happen to be mentioned; but the extraordinary part about the reports was the frequency with which overseas developments were mentioned. A check with other years' reports suggested that this was definitely a new feature in 1960 which was continued in the reports given in 1961 and 1962.

Table XX also shows that the banks whose role in the Sterling Area was discussed in the previous chapter have achieved a new importance. In many parts of the Commonwealth there are no other banks than branches of London banks. Many of the banks that cover overseas regions have, from their origins, been closely associated with London merchant banking houses – the Hong Kong and Shanghai with Jardine Matheson, the Bank of London and South America with Lazards and Barings, Barclays D.C.O. in South Africa with Rothschilds (and Oppenheimer), Lloyds in India and Australia with Gibbs and Flemings.[42] This arose

naturally from the specialisation of these houses in the floating of loans, financing of production and trade, and general
merchanting activities in their particular regions of the
world.

The merchant banks are still closely associated with the
finance of trade and of the London commodity markets,
where a large part of the production of the ex-colonial lands
is still sold. Their long experience in this field and their
supply of 'risk capital' makes their services much sought
after today, a point that we shall examine in more detail in
the next chapter. Thus it is that these banks, which were once
at the very heart of British imperialism, are again closely
associated with the formation of subsidiaries and consortia
of industrial companies operating abroad.

In these reports, some special indications may be noted in
the case of the manufacturing companies. The Chairman of
Boots referred to the fact that an increasing proportion of
their £2·5 million sales overseas now comes from local
manufacturing resources.[43] Glaxo's Chairman said that the
twenty-five overseas subsidiaries of Glaxo and Allen and
Hanbury now had a turnover considerably higher than that
of the home and export sales of the parent company, and the
same was reported of the British Oxygen Company in 1962.[44]
The Chairman of G.K.N. announced that the overseas share
of the firm's £18 million capital expenditure had been raised
from £3·5 million to £5 million.[45] It was the same with
Dunlop: £6·5 million out of £10 million of Dunlop's capital
expenditure had been overseas in 1959.[46] The Chairman of
Schweppes, in his report on 1960, stated that the profits of
the company's overseas subsidiaries had risen from £67,000
to £655,000 in the years 1953–60.[47]

The list was continued in 1961 with Mr Paul Cadbury's
statement that £6 million of the capital expenditures by
British Cocoa and Chocolate of £22 million over the next four
years were to be in overseas companies.[48] Where no overseas
subsidiaries were mentioned, as in the case of G.E.C. and

English Electric, there was much talk of the consortia which have been formed for nuclear, thermal and hydro-electrical power development overseas.[49] In these consortia the names of Wimpey, Taylor and Woodrow and Richard Costain and their local subsidiaries frequently appear. In their reports for 1961, Wimpey's give a long list of projects completed in Australia, Canada, Peru, Bahrein, Kuwait, Brazil, Trinidad, Malta and Yugoslavia,[50] and Costains announce their aim to undertake 50 per cent or more of their business in overseas territories.[51]

Most of these last are capital projects, but the outstanding feature of the list of companies operating overseas and the reports on which it is based is the preponderance of firms engaged in consumer goods industries over those in capital goods industries. We shall have to consider the implications of this in Chapter 11.

One group of companies that does not appear in the Table but forms an exceedingly important part of British overseas interests is that of the shipping companies. Peninsular & Orient and the closely connected Wm. Cory, Cunard and Furness Withy, Royal Mail and Ellermans lines join with other lines in the 'Shipping Conference', a cartel which controls the whole shipping of the Commonwealth. They have so far largely succeeded in preventing the establishment of shipping lines by the other Commonwealth countries.[52] The Minister for Commerce and Agriculture in a former Australian Labour Government complained in 1959 that, although Australia was a maritime nation and paid more than £160 million in freight charges every year, 'she did not own one solitary ship' and 'was powerless in the grip of this most powerful monopoly',[53] that is, the Shipping Conference. This would seem to be an outstanding example of imperial companies holding back independent development overseas.

Why so much Overseas Investment?

We are left to determine, from this wide-ranging review of British post-war investment overseas, what have been the motives behind it all. Some part of the answer will become clearer when we look at the state of the economy at home in the next chapter. The main reasons accounting for overseas development must be considered here. There are four: vertical integration, tariffs and quotas, transport costs, and the setting-up of the Common Market:

1. Vertical Integration – It should not be necessary to emphasise any more than we already have the importance of the overseas development of the great vertically-integrated combines. We may note, however, the very rapid development of two new groups in addition to Unilever, Imperial Tobacco, Dunlop, and Tate and Lyle, which have already been cited so many times in this book. These are the paper combines – Bowater, A. E. Reed, and Wiggins, Teape – and the asbestos-processing companies, especially Turner and Newall. Surveys of company assets and income in 1948[54] and 1957[55] showed that the paper and printing group had made especially rapid growth, following only after that in steel and vehicle production, and it appears that the advance in assets continued in 1958 and 1959 despite a check to income.[56] Bowater itself was the fastest growing company between 1948 and 1958, having moved up from 22nd to 5th place in the table of company giants in the British economy; its rival, the *Daily Mirror* group's company, A. E. Reed, similarly rose from 91st to 38th place between 1953 and 1958.[57] The reason for these developments is not only the rising demand for paper in packaging as well as in print, and for asbestos in factory-building, but the necessity here as elsewhere for manufacturers to establish the widest possible control over raw-material sources, in face of fluctuating world prices and the pressure of newly independent govern-

ments to raise the prices of their primary products. This might mean only that the great corporations were once more buying up the small, as the latter found their profit margins being squeezed. There was plenty of evidence of this in 1960 and 1961. It almost certainly means also that investment in machinery is now required to raise productivity at the raw-material producing end of processing. Dunlop's purchase of rubber estates[58] and Bowater's planned integration of pulp and paper production are good examples.[59] It must not be forgotten that costs have frequently been high rather than low precisely where labour has been cheap, and therefore often grossly inefficient. Recent developments in mining in Africa suggest a change in policy from reliance solely on cheap labour for profit to heavy mechanisation. Unskilled wages remain low but productivity has been growing fast and the proportion of skilled labour to unskilled rapidly increasing.[60]

2. Tariffs and Quotas – Newly independent governments have fairly universally been exercising their freedom to develop their own industries by means of tariff walls and other protective devices. We may take the statement of the Chairman of Turner & Newall (the giant £70 million asbestos manufacturing company) in his report for 1960 as representative of many similar statements:

'I am pleased to tell you that during the past year our export trade from the United Kingdom increased by one-eighth, as compared with the previous year; this success was achieved in the face of enhanced competition and also of the numerous restrictions on the import of our materials imposed by countries to which we have exported in the past. In some cases the only way to preserve our markets and to take advantage of developing opportunities is to commence manufacture in countries overseas; this we are eager to do, provided that the risks are reasonable and that the Governments in such countries offer terms under which our enterprise can be expected to succeed. We have formed companies in Ghana and in Eastern Nigeria with the intention of manufacturing asbestos-cement products in both localities and we shall not hesitate to act similarly in other countries should circumstances make such action desirable.'[61]

The most obvious examples of this process are the development of Unilever's manufacturing subsidiaries in West Africa and of Booker McConnell in the West Indies, which we have already referred to. Other examples are the setting up of vehicle assembly plants, and subsidiary motor manufacturing plants, in Australia, New Zealand and Singapore.[62] The effects of the process on the economic progress of under-developed lands will be examined in Chapter 11.

3. Transport Costs – As manufacturing costs are reduced by factory automation, and as the goods entering world trade become more complex and more delicate, so the element of transport in final costs becomes more important. Both where new markets open up in previously underdeveloped countries and where old markets become the object of fierce competition, proximity to the market becomes the over-riding factor making for success or failure.[63] In no part of the world is this truer than in the new Common Market in western Europe.[64] But every new step towards the establishment of the necessary infra-structure of basic services in underdeveloped lands demands new thinking about the siting of refining, processing and manufacturing plants.

The most obvious example is in the textile industry; it simply no longer pays to transport cotton half across the world to be fulled and dyed and woven in Lancashire only to be transported back across half the world for the people to buy who grew the cotton in the first place. And this is not only true of textiles. The steel companies in Britain, secure behind their protective walls at home, seem to be the last to realise that carrying ores from Africa to Britain and carrying back the finished product to Africa again may not always be the cheapest way to supply the Africans with steel. The future evolution of the world division of labour will be the subject of the last part of this book.

4. The Common Market – With monotonous regularity the Chairmen of British manufacturing companies were reporting in 1960 and 1961 on measures taken to establish subsidiaries or associates in the Common Market. *Who Owns Whom* for 1960 lists 150 U.K. companies with subsidiaries in the Common Market.[65] Almost all the large manufacturing companies are to be found there, many of them with more than one subsidiary. The drive behind these moves was, of course, the prospect of a common tariff remaining around the six European Economic Community members while tariffs between them were reduced. Associated with this fear was, however, the consideration of transport costs. The main concentration of investment, not only of the U.K. and the U.S.A. but of E.E.C. members themselves, was in the already highly developed industrial centre of the lower reaches and outlet of the Rhine.[66] Proposals for a Channel tunnel, which suddenly sprang into prominence again after years of pigeon-holing, were dictated by real reasons of economic interest.

The development of the Common Market suggests very clearly the nature of the process in which British capitalism is involved in its new wave of overseas investment since the war. Competition is no longer a local or even a national affair; it is increasingly an international battle, as Lenin foresaw, in which only the giant oligopolies in each major capitalist country can survive. New industrial techniques require larger and larger applications of capital. For these to be profitable, markets must be expanded far beyond the confines of nation states. The Common Market is an attempt to form a new market of 160 million people for the leading oligopolies of the six nations that have joined together in it to exploit. This we shall study in Chapter 10.

Britain's experience with the Sterling Area suggests that protected markets can no longer be maintained. The battle between the Six and the Seven, however, like the battle between the dollar and the pound, is but a part of the world-wide struggle of the giant corporations, in which 'Invest or die' has replaced 'Export or die' as the slogan of the times. The new empires belong to the giant corporations, and this means, today, not only the vertically-integrated processors of food and raw materials, or even only the capital goods producers, as of old, but the new consumer goods manu-facturers who are in the lead in modern mass production, and must market and advertise their goods the whole world over. What all this means for the future of world trade, and for Britain's place in it, and for the future of the underdeveloped lands will be the subject of the last part of this book. We must examine first what it means for the home economy of Britain herself.

TABLE XIV
U.K. IMPORTS AND MEANS OF PAYMENT, 1913–61

Year	U.K. Imports Volume 1938 = 100	U.K. Imports Value in £m. Current Prices c.i.f. 1913–38 f.o.b. 1946–61	Exports	Re-exports	Net Shipping	Net Property Income	Net Invisibles Govt.	Other	Total Earnings	Current Surplus or Deficit (£m.)
			Means of Paying for Imports as % of Imports in each year							
1913	88	769	68	14	13	25	—	5	128	+224
1929	101	1,221	60	9	11	20	2	7	109	+103
1933	88	675	54	7	11	24	—	4	100	0
1938	100	920	56	7	11	19	—	−1	93	−70
1946	67	1,082	80	5	3	4	−30	11	73	−295
1947	76	1,560	70	4	2	7	−10	−1	72	−442
1948	78	1,794	87	3	4	10	−4	0	100	+7
1949	85	1,978	90	3	6	8	−7	3	102	+38
1950	85	2,390	90	4	5	14	−6	5	112	+297
1951	96	3,501	74	4	4	6	−4	4	88	−419
1952	88	2,959	91	5	4	4	−2	6	108	+227
1953	95	2,896	88	4	5	7	−2	3	105	+179
1954	96	3,020	91	3	5	8	−4	4	107	+211
1955	107	3,432	87	3	4	5	−4	3	98	−73
1956	106	3,462	94	4	3	6	−5	5	107	+258
1957	110	3,573	95	4	3	6	−4	4	108	+272
1958	110	3,330	98	4	2	7	−7	5	109	+291
1959	118	3,578	94	4	1	6	−7	2	101	+51
1960	133	4,077	89	3	−1	4	−7	2	91	−344
1961	130	3,998	93	4	−1	6	−8	4	98	−70

Notes: 1. Net Property Income after 1946 is taken from U.K. *National Income and Expenditure* Table of Transactions with the Rest of the World by subtracting Property Income Paid Abroad from Property Income Received from Abroad.

2. Surplus or deficit in 1959 and 1960 subsequently corrected to +£115m. and −£288m. respectively.

Sources: Volumes from London and Cambridge Economic Service, *Bulletin*, Table 'External Trade'.
Other figures for 1913 from Imlah, op. cit.
Other figures for 1929 and 1933 from R.I.I.A., op. cit.
Other figures for 1938 from Abrams, op. cit.

TABLE XV-A

U.K. AND STERLING AREA AGGREGATE BALANCE OF PAYMENTS, 1946–60

(all figures in £ millions)

Items of U.K. Account	1946–57				1958–60		
	R.S.A.[1]	$ Area	Other	All Areas	R.S.A.	Others	All Areas
Current Account: Overall	+2907	−2336	−311	+260	+1034	−1036	−2
Invisibles only	+2422	+301	+635	+3407	+785	−414	+371
Government Loans: net	0	+994	+54	+1048	−134	−118	−256
Government Grants: net	+46	+681	−222	+505	−161	−20	−181
Gold	−1363	+1363	—	—	−655	+655	0
Other Convertible Currency	—	—	—	—	—		
Sterling Balances,	+303	−53		−53	−128	−342	−342
of which: Colonies	+963	—	−600	−297	—	+742	+614
Other Sterling	−660	—	—	—			
Long-Term Private Capital:							
Out	−2300	−900	−436	−3200	−474	−440	−914
In	+200	+900		+1100	−42	+583	+541
Other Transactions and Inter-Area Transfers[3]	+241	−1098	+1515	+658	+246	−605	−359

R.S.A. Account with	$ Area	All Non-£ Areas		R.S.A.	Others	All Non-£ Areas
Current Account: Overall	−21	(−706)		—	—	−1493
Invisibles only	n.a.	(−1244)		—	—	−216
of which: Colonies only[2]	+1120	n.a.		—	—	n.a.
Other Sterling	−114	n.a.		—	—	n.a.
Gold	+1456	(+1081)		—	—	+842
of which: Colonies alone[2]	+85	n.a.		—	—	n.a.
Other Sterling	+137	n.a.		—	—	n.a.
Other Transactions[3]	+178	(+269)		—	—	+101
Long-Term Capital (net)	+1613	(+1144)		—	—	+842
Total R.S.A. Surplus (Inter-Area Transfers)	+3226			—	—	(+1788) … +292

Notes: [1] R.S.A. = Rest of Sterling Area, i.e. excluding U.K.
[2] Colonies include Ghana and Malaya.
[3] Other Transactions include contributions to I.M.F., I.B.R.D., etc., and balances with E.P.U. Inter-Area Transfers include R.S.A. Account in second half of table.
n.a. = not available.
figures in brackets = 1950–57 only.
+ = A receipt.
— = A payment or investment.

Sources: H.M. Treasury, *Balance of Payments*, 1947–57 and 1958–60.

TABLE XV-B

U.K. BALANCE OF PAYMENTS CURRENT ACCOUNT, 1958-61

Year	Imports Value £m.f.o.b.	Imports Volume 1938 = 100	Exports Value £m.	Exports Volume 1938 = 100	Visible Trade Net £m.	Govt. Account[1] Net £m.	of which Military[2] gross £m.	Other Invisibles Net £m.	Balance £m.
1958	3,330	110	3,392	197	62	−268	−187	497	291
1959	3,578	118	3,509	205	−104	−233	−169	452	115
1960	4,077	133	3,711	216	−391	−284	−209	387	−288
1961	3,998	130	3,863	222	−135	−337	−227	402	−70

Details of Other Invisibles

Year	Shipping in £m.	Shipping out £m.	Travel and Gifts in £m.	Travel and Gifts out £m.	Other Services[3] in £m.	Other Services[3] out £m.	Property Income[4] in £m.	Property Income[4] out £m.
1958	637	615	233	252	464	277	676	415
1959	621	624	243	267	508	307	698	426
1960	646	702	280	301	553	334	701	456
1961	658	708	303	319	580	369	701	444

Notes: [1] Government Account has been recast to 1959 to separate out all government items following A.R. Conan, *Westminster Bank Review*, May 1961.
[2] Military Account shows gross figures of debits only except in case of cost of forces in Germany, from which Federal German Republic contributions are deducted. Figures do not include imports of military supplies.
[3] Other Services include civil aviation, banking, insurance, merchanting and U.S. forces expenditure. Increase in 1961 mainly due to higher insurance earnings and civil aviation.
[4] For property Income, definition is not as in Note 1 to Table XIV, but is Interest, Profits and Dividends only, as adjusted after 1958 in White Papers.

Sources: Volumes from London and Cambridge Economic Service, *Bulletin*, Table 'External Trade'.
Other figures from H.M. Treasury, *Balance of Payments*, 1958-60, 1959-61, and
R. S. Gilbert, 'Britain's Invisible Earnings', *Economic Review*, November 1960.
A. R. Conan, 'Factors in the Balance of Payments Problem', *Westminster Bank Review*, May 1961.

TABLE XVI

U.K. NET FOREIGN INVESTMENT BALANCE, 1959

Item	U.K. Assets Overseas (£m.)	U.K. Liabilities Overseas (£m.)	Net Balance (£m.)
Long-Term Private Investment	7,650 (a)	2,150 (b)	+5,500
Government Debts	500 (c)	2,000 (d)	−1,500
Short-Term Balances	1,500 (e)	3,000 (f)	−1,500
Total	9,650	7,150	+2,500

Notes: (a) Makes no allowance for increased market value of pre-war assets and does not cover all reinvestment of profits since the war.
   (b) Includes £1,300m. invested or reinvested by U.S. firms in Britain since 1952.
   (c) Includes holdings in the World Bank, Colonial Development Corp., etc.
   (d) Includes liability outstanding to I.M.F.
   (e) Includes subscriptions to I.M.F. and banking, insurance and commercial balances.
   (f) Total Sterling Balances less those that are really banking funds of London banks with branches in the Colonies, etc.

Source: A. R. Conan, 'The U.K. as a Creditor Country', *The Westminster Bank Review*, August 1960.

TABLE XVII

ESTIMATED DISTRIBUTION OF BRITISH
OVERSEAS INVESTMENT, 1938 AND 1959

	1938	1959	Sales 1938–48	Additions 1946–50
Total Investment (Balance Sheet Values in £m.); % = in Sterling Area	4,500 (50%)	7,450 (60%)	1,700 (60%)	4,650 (67%)
Private Business Total	**3,000**	**6,650**	**650**	**4,300**
(a) outside Sterling Area, of which to	1,750	2,850	400	1,500
U.S. and Canada	400	1,300	100	1,000
Europe	250	500	50	300
Proportion to more-developed lands	40%	60%	37%	87%
Latin America	750	750	200	200
Others	350	300	50	—
Proportion to less-developed lands	60%	40%	63%	13%
(b) inside Sterling Area, of which to	1,250	3,800	250	2,800
Australia	200	600 ⎫		450 ⎫
New Zealand	25	100 ⎪		75 ⎪
South Africa	200	800 ⎬ 100		650 ⎬
Rhodesias	50	200 ⎭		150 ⎭
Proportion to more-developed lands in £ Area	38%	45%	40%	47%
India	300	300 ⎫		100 ⎫
Pakistan	30	50 ⎪		50 ⎪
Ceylon	75	75 ⎬ 150		25 ⎬
Colonies	250	850 ⎭		600 ⎭
M.E. Oil Investment	120	800+	—	700
Proportion to less-developed lands in £ Area	62%	55%	60%	53%
Public Debt Total	**1,500**	**800**	**1,050**	**350**
(a) inside Sterling Area	1,000	575	725	300
India, Pakistan and Ceylon	250		250	—
Australia and New Zealand	580	380	250	50
South Africa	100	25	85	10
Rhodesias	10	100	—	90
Colonies	60	70	140	150
(b) outside Sterling Area	500	225	325	50

Notes: (a) Nominal values for investment outside the £ Area have been adjusted for market valuation in 1959 by arbitrarily doubling were appropriate; see E. V. Morgan, *Structure of Property Ownership in Great Britain.* O.U.P. 1960.

(b) Colonies include Ghana and Malaya.

Sources: A. R. Conan, 'Investment in the Sterling Commonwealth', *The Times,* 19. 19.8.59.

A. R. Conan, *Capital Imports into Sterling Countries* (London: Macmillan, 1960).

Royal Institute of International Affairs, op. cit.

Radcliffe Committee, *Report on the Working of the Monetary System* (London: H.M.S.O., 1959).

Bank of England, *Annual Reports.*

United Nations Economic and Social Council, *International Flow of Private Capital, 1956–58* (New York, 1959).

TABLE XVIII

NATURE OF BRITISH OVERSEAS INVESTMENTS
IN THE 1950s

Estimated Average Annual Movements		1952–58 (£m.)	1958–60 (£m.)
Outward Movement	Total	380	475
Inward Movement	Total	190	270
Non-Sterling Area:	Outward Total	120	
of which to U.S. and Canada		90	
	Inward Total×	170	net +45
of which from U.S. and Canada		90	
Sterling Area:	Outward Total	260	net −250
	Inward Total	20	

Outward Movement made up of:				
Government Grants – Welfare	20	Bilateral Grants	60
– Colonial Services	25	Loans	65
– Other ⊕	50	Multilateral Aid	25
Portfolio (net)	15	Portfolio, Oil and Insurance	130
Company Retentions	200	Other Company – Retentions	140
Fresh Capital	70	– Fresh Capital	55
Total Outward	**380**		**475***

Notes: × includes £60m. Defence and other aid.
⊕ includes Colonial Development Corp., Disbursements to World Bank and Export Credit Guarantees as well as New Government loans.
* Excludes I.M.F. subscription of over £250 million in this period.
Sources: Figures for 1952–58 from:
H.M. Treasury, *Bulletin for Industry*, August and October 1959.
J. Wood and T. M. Rybczinski, 'Should Britain Restrict Investments Abroad?' *The Times* 24.4.58.
Figures for 1958–60 from:
Board of Trade, *Journal*, 6.10.61.
H.M. Treasury, *Balance of Payments, 1958–60* (London: H.M.S.O., 1961).

TABLE XIX

U.K. COMPANY DIRECT OVERSEAS INVESTMENTS
AND EARNINGS, 1958–59, 1960
(by Industry and Area in £ millions)

	Industry and Area	Investment	Earnings
(a) 1958–59 by Industry	Agriculture,	26	47
	of which R.S.A.	21	42
	Mining	21	60
	of which R.S.A.	7	48
	Manufacturing	181	201
	of which R.S.A.	74	100
	N. America	66	58
	W. Europe	25	27
	Latin America	15	14
	Construction	8	7
	Distribution	28	41
	Transport and Communications	14	14
	Other, incl. banking	50	49
	of which R.S.A.	43	43
	TOTAL 1958–59	**329**	**420**
(b) 1958, 1959 and 1960 by Area	**TOTAL 1958, 1959, and 1960**	**537**	**648**
	of which		
	Australia	94	80
	S. Africa	48	65
	India	28	45
	Rhodesias	26	28
	R.S.A. Total	**312**	**400**
	U.S.A.	27	37
	Canada	60	42
	N. American Total	**87**	**79**
	W. Germany	18	25
	E.E.C. Total	**48**	**48**
	Other W. Europe	14	23
	Latin America	17	22
	Other Non-Sterling	14	6

Notes: 1. R.S.A. = Rest of Sterling Area.
2. Company investment = U.K. companies investment in branches, subsidiaries and associates overseas, excluding portfolio investment and
excluding oil and insurance companies.
Source: Board of Trade, *Journal*, 6.10.1961.

TABLE XX

OVERSEAS INTERESTS OF BRITISH COMMERCIAL AND INDUSTRIAL COMPANIES
1959-60

Type of Company	Name of Company	Net Assets 1958-59 (in £m.)	Countries where Company has subsidiary, branch or factory (not merely sales organisation)
BANK	Barclays D.C.O. (and United Dominion Trust)		S. Africa, Rhodesias, E. and W. Africa, W. Indies, Mediterranean, N. America, Common Market
	Lloyds		India, Far East, W. Indies, S. Africa, Rhodesia, Common Market
	Hong Kong and Shanghai (including British Bank of M.E. and Mercantile Bank of India)		Hong Kong, Japan, Philippines, Indo-China, Thailand, Malaya, India, Indonesia, Pakistan, Burma, Ceylon, Borneo, Middle East
	Chartered Bank		Middle East, India, Pakistan, Far East, U.S.A., West Germany
	Bank of London and South America		throughout Latin America and the Caribbean
	Standard Bank of South Africa		S. Africa, Rhodesias, E. Africa
	National and Grindlays Bank		India, Pakistan, Burma, Ceylon, Far East, E. Africa, Rhodesias
INSURANCE	Prudential		U.S.A., Canada
	Royal Exchange, Atlas and Sun		U.S.A., Canada, Australia, New Zealand, Rhodesia, E. Africa
	Commercial Union and N. British		U.S.A., Canada
	Royal Group		U.S.A., Canada
OIL	Shell	567	Venezuela, Middle East, Borneo, N. America, Common Market, India, Indonesia, Australia, Japan, W. Indies, Colombia
	B.P.	355	Middle East, Trinidad, Nigeria, Sahara, Australia, Canada, Common Market
RAW MATERIALS	Burmah Oil	72	Burma, India, Pakistan, N. America, Australia
	London Tin Corporation	10	Malaya, Nigeria, Thailand
	Amalgamated Metal	10	N. America, Australia, Malaya, Common Market
	Consolidated Zinc	29	U.S.A., Australia, Common Market
	Rio Tinto (mining)	32	Spain, Australia, S. Africa, Rhodesia, Canada, Common Market
	Tanganyika Concessions (copper, etc.)	10	Rhodesia, Belgian Congo
	British South Africa Co.	50	Rhodesia, Australia, New Zealand, Canada, U.S.A., S. Africa
PROCESSING	Unilever	570	W. Africa, Common Market, Middle East, Australia, Far East, N. and S. America

TABLE XX (contd.)

Type of Company	Name of Company	Net Assets 1958–59 (in £m.)	Countries where Company has subsidiary branch or factory (*not* merely sales organisation)
	Imperial Tobacco	195	Rhodesia, U.S.A., Canada
	Distillers Co.	112	Canada, Australia, New Zealand, S. Africa, Brazil, U.S.A.
	Dunlop Rubber	87	Malaya and 'throughout the Commonwealth and Continent'
	Bowater Paper	85	Canada, U.S.A., Australia, New Zealand, S. Africa, Eire, Common Market, Scandinavia
	A. E. Reed (paper)	36	U.S.A., Australia, New Zealand, Scandinavia
	Turner and Newall (asbestos)	70	S. Africa, Rhodesias, N. America, India, W. Africa
	Wiggins Teape (paper)	25	Australia, New Zealand, India
	Godfrey Philips (tobacco)	15	Rhodesia, Australia, New Zealand, India
	Bells (asbestos)	3	Canada, S. Africa, Australia, Rhodesia, Malaya, Common Market
	Cape (asbestos)	11	U.S.A., S. Africa, Eire, Canada, Common Market
FOOD AND DRINK	British Cocoa and Chocolate	45	Canada, Australia, New Zealand, S. Africa, Eire, India, Germany
	Arthur Guinness	25	Eire, W. Africa, Caribbean
	Tate & Lyle	27	Trinidad, Caribbean, Canada
	Booker Bros., McConnell (sugar)	12	British Guiana, Caribbean, W. Africa, Rhodesia, Canada
	Schweppes	10	U.S.A., Australia, S. Africa, E. Africa, W. Africa, Rhodesia, Canada
	Brooke Bond (tea)	25	India, Ceylon, E. Africa
ELECTRICAL	A.E.I. (+ B.I.I.C. & Henley)	160	Australia, New Zealand, India, Pakistan, Canada, S. Africa, E. Africa, Brazil
	G.E.C.	82	World-wide associates
	English Electric	68	World-wide servicing organisation and factories in Canada, Australia, S. Africa, India
STEEL, etc.	Tube Investments (+ British Aluminium)	114	Canada, India, Argentina, S. Africa, Australia, Eire, Mexico, Common Market
	G.K.N.	155	Common Market
	Vickers	94	Canada, Australia, India
	Stewart & Lloyd	78	S. Africa, Rhodesias, Australia, New Zealand, India, Canada, Eire
	Lancs. Steel	20	Rhodesia, New Zealand
	Firth Cleveland	20	U.S.A., Canada, Germany, India, Australia
ENGINEERING	John Brown	24	Australia, New Zealand, S. Africa, Canada, Rhodesia, India, Brazil
	British Motors Corporation	70	Australia, New Zealand, S. Africa
	Hawker Siddeley (+ Bristol)	42	Canada
	Rolls-Royce	35	U.S.A., Common Market

Type of Company	Name of Company	Net Assets 1958-59 (in £m.)	Countries where Company has subsidiary branch or factory (not merely sales organisation)
	Leyland & A.C.V.	26	U.S.A., S. Africa, Australia, Common Market, Spain
	Metal Box	39	India, Pakistan, Malaya, S. Africa, Rhodesias, E. and W. Africa, Australia, New Zealand, W. Indies, Common Market
	Joseph Lucas	34	Canada, Australia, Spain, Common Market
	De Havilland	20	Canada, U.S.A., Australia, S. Africa, Rhodesia
	Babcock & Wilcox	31	Australia, W. Africa, S. Africa, Iraq, Brazil, Mexico, Common Market, Scandinavia
CHEMICALS	Elliot Automation	9	Switzerland, Australia, Common Market
	I.C.I.	467	S. Africa, Ghana, N. America, India, Caribbean, Malaya, Australia, New Zealand, Argentina, Common Market
	Beecham Group	61	U.S.A., Australia, New Zealand, India, E. Africa, Eire, Common Market
	Boots	38	Australia, India, S. Africa
	British Oxygen	42	Australia, New Zealand, India, E. Africa, Rhodesia, Malaya, Burma, Ceylon, Canada, Pakistan, Hong Kong
	Fisons	28	S. Africa, E. and W. Africa, Malaya, Australia, India, Ceylon, N. America, Common Market
	B.D.H.	5	Malaya, Eire, Australia, Canada, India
	De la Rue	10	Australia, New Zealand, Common Market
	Glaxo (including Allen & Hanbury and Murphy)	26	Australia, New Zealand, India, W. Africa, Malaya, Argentina, Common Market
	Albright & Wilson	20	India, Common Market
	Aspro & Nicholas	5	Australia, India, Common Market
	Courtaulds (including British Celanese and Pinchin & Johnson)	180	U.S.A., Canada, Australia, New Zealand, S. Africa, Common Market, Spain
	Associated Portland Cement	55	Australia, New Zealand, Malaya, Canada, S. Africa, E. and W. Africa, Pakistan, Mexico
OTHERS	Radio Rentals	7	Australia
	British Plaster Board	15	Canada, S. Africa, Rhodesias, Common Market
	W. H. Smith (books)	3	U.S.A., Canada, Common Market
	Low & Bonar (packaging)	5	Canada, S. Africa, Rhodesia, E. and W. Africa

Notes: (a) With a few exceptions only companies in the top 60 by assets were studied.
(b) There may well be subsidiaries, other than those listed above, which were not mentioned in the Reports.
Source: Individual Company Reports for 1959-60 and 1960-61.

References

1. A. R. Conan, 'The United Kingdom as a Creditor Country', *Westminster Bank Review*, August 1960.
2. United Kingdom, Central Statistical Office, Blue Book on *National Income and Expenditure, 1961*, H.M.S.O., 1962, Table 58.
3. R. L. Major, 'Errors and Omissions in the Balance of Payments Estimates', *Economic Review*, National Institute of Economic and Social Research, February 1962.
4. A. R. Conan, *Capital Imports into Sterling Countries*, Macmillan, 1960, pp. 84–5.
5. A. R. Conan, 'The United Kingdom as a Creditor Country'.
6. United Kingdom, Board of Trade, *Commonwealth and Sterling Area Statistical Abstract, 1960*, H.M.S.O., 1961.
7. A. R. Conan, 'Why Sterling Area Payments have Deteriorated', *The Times*, 23.5.61.
8. op. cit., *The Times*, 24.5.61.
9. United Kingdom, Board of Trade, 'Survey of Direct United Kingdom Investment Overseas', 1958–60, Board of Trade *Journal*, 6.10.61.
10. National Institute of Economic and Social Research, *Economic Review*, May 1962, p. 19.
11. A. R. Conan, 'Factors in the Balance of Payments Problem', *Westminster Bank Review*, May 1961.
12. J. H. Dunning, *American Investment in British Manufacturing Industry*, Allen and Unwin, 1958.
13. Committee on the Working of the Monetary System, *Report*, H.M.S.O., 1959, Cmd. 827, Paragraph 438.
14. A. R. Conan, 'Factors in the Balance of Payments Problem'.
15. R. S. Gilbert, 'Britain's Invisible Earnings', *Economic Review*, National Institute of Economic and Social Research, November 1960.
16. See further Miss D. C. Paige, 'Defence Expenditure', National Institute of Economic and Social Research, *Economic Review*, July 1960.
17. A. R. Conan, 'Factors in the Balance of Payments Problem'.
18. R. L. Major, 'Errors and Omissions in the Balance of Payments Estimates'.
19. National Institute of Economic and Social Research, *Economic Review*, November 1961, p. 16.
20. J. Spraos, 'Speculation, Arbitrage and Sterling', *Economic Journal*, March 1959.
21. A. R. Conan, 'The United Kingdom as a Creditor Country'.

22. United Kingdom, Board of Trade, 'Survey of Direct United Kingdom Investment'.

23. A. R. Conan, 'Investment in the Sterling Commonwealth', *The Times*, 19 and 21 August 1959; and A. R. Conan, *Capital Imports into Sterling Countries*.

24. Committee on The Working of the Monetary System, op. cit., Para 736.

25. E. V. Morgan, *The Structure of Property Ownership in Great Britain*, Oxford 1960, Chapter 11.

26. A. R. Conan, 'Investment in the Sterling Commonwealth'.

27. Committee on The Working of the Monetary System, op. cit., Para 226.

28. A. R. Conan, 'Investment in the Sterling Commonwealth'.

29. British Petroleum, *Annual Reports and Accounts, 1960* and *61*.

30. Shell Transport and Trading Company, *Annual Reports and Accounts, 1960* and *61*.

31. *The Financial Times*, 'Trends of Industrial Profits', published on the second Saturday in January every year.

32. A. R. Conan, 'Investment in the Sterling Commonwealth'.

33. United Kingdom Government, Blue Book on *National Income and Expenditure, 1961*, Table 59.

34. ibid., Table 26 and note on 'Depreciation', p. 80.

35. E. V. Morgan, op. cit., Table 64.

36. H.M. Treasury, *Bulletin for Industry*, August 1959.

37. Blue Book, op. cit., Table 27.

38. *The Financial Times*, 'Trends in Industrial Profits', 15.1.62.

39. Board of Trade, 'Survey of Direct United Kingdom Investment'.

40. Unilever, *Annual Report and Accounts, 1960*.

41. Booker Bros. McConnell, *Annual Report and Accounts, 1960*.

42. Paul H. Emden, *Money Powers of Europe*, Sampson Low, 1946.

43. Boots Pure Drug Co., *Report and Accounts for 1960*.

44. Glaxo, *Annual Report and Accounts for 1959*; and *Half-Yearly Report* of the Chairman to the shareholders of British Oxygen Co. Ltd., June 1962.

45. Guest, Keen and Nettlefold, *Annual Report and Accounts for 1960*.

46. Dunlop Rubber Company, *Annual Report and Accounts for 1959*.

47. Schweppes, *Annual Report and Accounts for 1960*.

48. British Cocoa and Chocolate Co., 'Chairman's Statement', *Economist*, 2.6.62.

49. GEC and English Electric, *Annual Reports and Accounts for 1960*.

50. Wimpey (George) & Co., *Annual Report and Accounts for 1961*.

51. Richard Costain, *Annual Report and Accounts for 1961*.

52. *The Times* Shipping Correspondent, 'The Crisis at Sea', *The Times*, 3 and 4 January 1962.

53. Mr Pollard speaking in the Australian Parliament, October 1959, quoted by A. S. Aaronovitch, *The Ruling Class*, Lawrence and Wishart, 1961, p. 97.

54. National Institute of Economic and Social Research, *Classified List of Large Companies engaged in British Industry*, 1955, extended backwards by the author by means of Moody's Services Ltd. *Summaries of Balance Sheets and Profit and Loss Accounts.*

55. United Kingdom, Board of Trade, *Company Assets and Income in 1957*, H.M.S.O., 1960, summarised in Board of Trade *Journal*, 16.12.60, p. 1415.

56. United Kingdom Government, 'Income and Finance in Public Quoted Companies', *Economic Trends*, H.M.S.O., November 1961.

57. Ranking made by the author from Moody's Services Ltd., op. cit.

58. Dunlop Rubber Co., *Annual Report for 1959*.

59. Bowater Paper Corporation Ltd., *Annual Report for 1960*.

60. United Nations, *Economic Survey of Africa since 1950*, p. 115 ff.

61. Turner and Newall, *Annual Report for 1960*.

62. L. A. Dicks-Mireaux *et al.*, 'Prospects for the British Car Industry', National Institute, *Economic Review*, September 1961, pp. 28-9.

63. E. M. Hoover, *Location of Economic Activity*, New York, 1958.

64. United Nations Economic Commission for Europe, *Economic Survey of Europe in 1956*, Geneva, 1957, Chapter IV, p. 17.

65. O. W. Roskill, *Who Owns Whom*, 1960.

66. United Nations Economic Commission for Europe, *Economic Survey of Europe in 1956*, p. 174.

CHAPTER 9

Capitalism Without Empire

We are now faced with questions of central importance for the future of the British economy and of capitalism itself. What are the implications for the economy at home in the metropolitan country of the remarkable development of overseas investment which we examined in the last chapter? Were there strong pressures at home behind this development, associated first with the breaking of the political ties of empire and secondly with the strengthening of overseas economic ties? Or were the pressures generated entirely outside the home country, as we have so far tended to suggest? If so, what is their effect at home? In the light of the very considerable prosperity of the post-war years, we have to determine once more the balance of advantage from Britain's overseas economic relations – from the terms of trade, from past investment overseas, and from the new investment which we have just been examining.

We have to be clear about what is happening to contemporary capitalism and what the new wave of overseas investment augurs for its future. How does British capitalism now compare with Lenin's composite picture of imperialism in his sense of the word? In particular, we must ask what strength the City of London and the great imperial companies now have in the British economy, and how we may expect the new relationships to develop. This involves reconsideration for our own time of Lenin's thesis of the increasing parasitism and decay of an advanced capitalist economy. Does the end of political empire carry with it the threat of the demise of capitalism, or can capitalism survive this crisis as it has survived others before?

This is a part of the wider question which we have been examining all through this book as to whether the relationship of British capitalism with overseas colonies and with overseas industrialisation through overseas investment has been specific to Britain or generic to capitalism as a whole. When Lenin wrote of imperialism as the highest stage of capitalism, he saw these relationships as essential to capitalism (see Chapter 3). We shall have to defer a final answer to this question until the next chapter, when we consider the future development of capitalism in the United States and in Germany as well as in Britain. In this chapter, we shall concentrate on the movement of the British economy at home and the connection with the overseas developments which we have been considering.

The most important question to examine is the relationship between the fairly continuous world boom in output since the war, with only minor recessions, and the high levels of British overseas investment. For the fifteen years that followed the Second World War witnessed a considerable expansion of wealth in the capitalist lands, as well as in the lands that are now under communist rule. In the capitalist world most of the expansion of wealth has taken place inside the more developed lands and it has mainly been concentrated in manufacturing output (see Table I, Chapter 1). By 1960, manufacturing output in the capitalist world had risen to about two and three-quarter times the pre-war level. Much of this was accounted for by the huge increase in United States production during the war and immediate post-war years. Nonetheless, in the years between 1948 and 1960, when North American output only increased by 40 per cent, output by the rest of the capitalist countries was more than doubled. Even in Britain output was raised by more than a half (see Table XXI and also Table XXXI at end of Chapter 10).

This growth was not by any means continuous, and there appears to have been a fairly general break in the rate of growth at some point during the years 1953–55 (see Table XXI). One is bound to compare this check to growth some eight years after the war with the rapid growth of output from 1919 to 1929, and the crisis and stagnation thereafter. Manufacturing production rose by 1929 to a level half as high again as in 1913, but it was only about a third above the 1913 level in 1938 (Table XXI). There is, however, a major difference between the two periods: while the 1930s were marked by a long and deep slump and by a continuing high level of unemployment, especially in Britain, the period since 1955 has seen only minor recessions and some stagnation of activity, but no real slump. Employment, especially in Britain, has been at a continuously high level, although there have been signs of a rising residue of permanently un-employed after each recession in the United States.[1]

We have to find explanations for the growth up to 1955 and the avoidance of deep depression, and at the same time for the check to growth, especially in Britain, after 1953–55. It seemed clear when we examined the earlier period between the wars that the drive of the great corporations towards monopoly and their accumulation of profits, while real wages fell behind the rise in productivity, led to overproduction and the crash of 1929. Yet we have seen an even greater drive of great corporations towards monopoly since 1945, but no slump. What has been happening, and, particularly, what has been the relevance of the ending of colonial empire and the rise of corporate empires?

The Causes of the Post-War Boom

(a) MORE TRIBUTE

One explanation might be to suggest that the post-war

boom was the result of intensified exploitation of empire, and that the dissolving of political ties of empire has had a delayed reaction; thus the check after 1955, especially to growth in Britain, could, since Britain had liberated almost the whole of her colonial empire by that year, be seen as the result of this dissolution of empire. The view that prosperity depended on empire was put forcefully enough in 1946 by Mr Ernest Bevin, in defence of the Labour Government's policy of intervention in Greece, where the possible emergence of a communist government seemed to threaten the Mediterranean lines of communication of the British Empire. 'I am not prepared,' he told the House of Commons, 'to sacrifice the British Empire, because I know that if the British Empire fell . . . it would mean the standard of life of our constituents would fall considerably.'² Is that what has happened?

Intensified exploitation, if it had taken place since the war, might be expected to comprise such factors as we have noted in the accumulation of colonial earnings in the sterling balances, the very high rate of return on investment in raw material production up to 1956, the especially high earnings of the oil companies up to 1955 (see Table XIII at end of Chapter 7), the expansion of overseas investment and thus of overseas investment income, the re-establishment of the commodity markets and the role of the City of London in world trade. And in all these respects there was indeed a boom that collapsed around 1955. Overseas investment reached its peak a little later, in 1956–57, when it was at some £80 million over the average of about £380 million a year for the 1950s as a whole. Income from property overseas went on growing until 1958 and income from the 'other services' of banking and merchanting and the U.S. Forces' expenditure continued thereafter, so that the total of property income in the balance of foreign payments went on rising. (See Table XV-B at end of Chapter 8.)

By 1958, then, if we include the 'other services', income

from overseas had reached 5 per cent of the total British national income and an almost equal figure was maintained during the following two years. Mr R. P. Dutt was led to comment in a review of John Strachey's *The End of Empire*: 'The blood of imperial tribute (in a hundred more forms than simply the overseas investment income) courses through all the veins of the British economy and gives it the feverish glow of a spurious and transient prosperity.'[3]

But was this really the cause of the prosperity at that time and in the earlier post-war years? That there had been a check in the middle 1950s to the growth of the investment income and of some of the other 'hundred ways' – the accumulation of colonial sterling, the profits of overseas companies, and particularly of the oil companies – Mr Dutt would, of course, be the first to agree. The corollary of the rising investment income was certainly a rising bill in over-seas military expenditure and in out-going payments to foreigners for their funds invested in Britain, which we examined earlier (Table XV-B, Chapter 8). These are the contradictions in which capitalism is caught. But aren't they so contradictory that the overseas 'tribute' simply cannot be claimed as an explanation of post-war prosperity?

As far as concerns the income from overseas investment, even in 1958 its contribution to national income barely reached the level attained in the 1930s, when Britain was far from prosperous. And if we take the net contribution after deducting payments to foreign owners of property in Britain, then we have to compare a figure of little more than 1 per cent today with nearly 3 per cent before the war (see Table IV at end of Chapter 3). Can we seriously consider a 1 per cent addition to national income as the basis of post-war prosperity? Mr Dutt asks us to remember the 'hundred other ways'. We have remembered the sterling balances and the increased profits of companies operating overseas, which we saw contributing so much to the re-establishment of British overseas investment. But we have not yet considered the terms of trade, which are generally regarded as outstanding among other ways in which exploitation of colonial and overseas producers may be intensified. Here we find that it was precisely in the years immediately after the war, when Britain's output boomed, that the terms of trade moved favourably for primary producers, and that, when they turned once more against the primary producers, the check took place to Britain's growth (Table III, Chapter 2).

This is only what we should expect from our earlier studies. When we examined the economic condition of Britain in the 1930s we reached two conclusions: first, the additional wealth that income from overseas investment, some part of it in the empire, brought to Britain was small and tended to be offset by adverse effects on the economy at home from policies designed to encourage investment overseas; second, the impoverishment of overseas producers, though it made available cheap food and raw materials, led to stagnation and unemployment in our export industries and thus, in the end, also worked back to check the growth of the whole economy at home. The strongly contrasting period of growth since the Second World War might then be expected to have been associated not only with expanding investment at home but with improved terms of trade for overseas primary producers. And this proves in fact to be exactly the case, at least for the years up to 1955, when the first serious check to growth took place in Britain.

(b) MORE EXPORTS

The buoyancy of foreign demand for British goods was certainly an important factor in the post-war boom. The volume of exports was raised by 1951 right back to the pre-1913 level at a figure nearly double that of 1937 (see Table XXI below). By 1950, the value of exports was equivalent to a fifth of the national income compared with a tenth before the war (Table IV, Chapter 3). Nearly a third of the whole output of the engineering industry was being exported in the

1950s[4] and engineering products were accounting for more than a half of all exports compared with a third before the war (Table VII, Chapter 3). Another eighth was accounted for by the chemicals and petroleum refining industries,[5] which were exporting a fifth of their total output.[6] These new industries had at last finally and completely displaced the textile industries as the mainstay of British exports. Textiles, which still provided nearly a quarter of all exports before the war and almost maintained their share until the textile crisis of 1952, were only providing a twelfth in 1958 (Table VII, Chapter 3).

Up to 1950, Britain's exports grew extremely rapidly (Table XXI). This was partly because shortage of dollars, despite dollar aid, prevented countries outside the Dollar Area from buying American goods, and partly because Britain's chief competitors, Germany and Japan, were knocked out of the race. But these reasons only explain the rise in Britain's share of world exports; they do not explain the very rapid rise of world exports as a whole (Table XXX, Chapter 10). Much of this took place precisely in the less-developed lands, where primary producers were making use of their improved war-time and post-war earnings to develop their economies by measures of industrialisation (Table XXV, Chapter 10). Many of these lands were British dominions, colonial and other lands in the Sterling Area, which gave British manufacturers an easy opening to expand their exports. The details here are of importance.

The total imports of the overseas Sterling Area countries from all sources almost trebled between 1937 and 1951, and during the same period the share of Britain's exports going to the Area rose from just over 40 per cent to just over half.[7] The remaining colonies, that is after India, Pakistan, Ceylon and Burma had won their independence, shared in this expanding trade, but less than they might have done owing to the policy we have already examined of banking their earnings in sterling balances in London. Nonetheless, the

post-war colonies were taking 14 per cent of Britain's exports
by 1952, twice as large a share as these same lands took before
the war.[8] All the colonies and protected areas participated in
this increase. It may be regarded as a major change; but we
shall see that it was not maintained (see Table VI, Chapter 3).

It was a change of crucial importance for our study,
because it suggests once more that improved terms of trade
for primary producers were favourable also for increased
trade and economic growth in Britain. Table XXI shows
what happened. After the rapid post-war growth which we
have seen, British exports simply did not grow from 1951 to
1954, and, after another brief period of growth in 1955 and
1956, there was a further period of stagnation. For the whole
fifteen years after 1945 there was a more than usually clear
correlation between the volume of British exports and the
movements in the terms of trade; the volume rising as the
terms moved against British exports and in favour of the
primary producers, and falling as they moved in favour of
Britain and against the primary producers. During the war,
the terms of trade had moved about 30 per cent in favour of
the primary producers and the improvement continued for
them until 1951 with the rapid rise of raw material prices
during the boom following the outbreak of the Korean War
(Table XXV, Chapter 10).

After 1951, the fall was almost continuous, apart from a
slight recovery in 1954–5, and the terms were little better in
1961 for primary producers than they were in 1939. As
before, it was the more rapid rise and then the more rapid fall
of their export prices than of their import prices that swung
the terms of trade first up and then down for the primary
producers (Table XXV, Chapter 10). We have already
associated the movements of the terms of trade with war-
time and post-war shortages leading to a stimulation of
productive capacity of both food and raw materials overseas,
and to the development of substitutes and home food-
production in the industrial lands. All this increased capacity

could be absorbed so long as industrial production, particularly in Britain, was rising, but the damping-down of
demand in the mid-1950s hit overseas earnings as much as
earnings at home (Table XXI, first and last columns).

Once more it has been argued that this unfavourable
movement in the terms of trade for primary producers after
1951 brought important advantages to the British economy
in the form of cheaper imports of food and raw materials.[9]

On the face of it, it would seem that this must be so,
although it is somewhat surprising that there was practically
no growth after 1951 in the volume of Britain's imports of
food and raw materials (Table XXI). What has grown has
been, in fact, the imports of manufactured goods and
machinery which doubled between 1955 and 1960.[10] Of
course the same quantity of food and raw materials was being
imported and it could be said that the lower prices permitted
the increased imports of manufactures. But what was being
argued was that there was a total gain to the British economy
from the movement in prices. It might be suggested that the
terms of trade embody the new relations of intensified
exploitation of primary producers even after colonial
liberation, and are to be accounted for as an attempt to
maintain the level of overseas tribute.[11] That they injure the
primary producers will not be denied, but once more we have
to ask how far they benefit an industrial economy like
Britain's.

The argument is based on a hypothesis that we may well
doubt, viz. that paying more for imports involves a forgoing of resources that would otherwise be enjoyed at home,
while paying less involves an addition to resources at home.[12]
In a period of stagnation of activity associated with a decline
in exports, this argument has no basis. The extra resources
available were simply not utilised. Industrial activity and
exports were both stagnant between 1955 and 1958. Only in
1959 did they both rise again and, while industrial output
leapt ahead, exports rose only sluggishly. The terms of trade

remained unfavourable to primary producers and Britain's exports collapsed once more at the end of 1960 (Table XXI).

The most serious aspect of the situation is that, quite contrary to previous experience in the nineteenth century and the early years of the twentieth century, British exports have not grown as a result of the wave of overseas investment. In fact, markets in Europe and North America have grown, but in the less-developed lands there has been little growth outside those under communist rule. We saw in the last chapter that the Sterling Area was receiving British investment to the value of some £200 million a year, during the 1950s, so that by 1959 some two-thirds of all British overseas investment was in countries in the Area. Yet, during this very period the Area share of British exports fell from 50 per cent to below 40 per cent. The decline was least, however, in the old dominions, where most of the capital was directed (Table VI, Chapter 3). The real collapse was in the trade of the newly-liberated colonies, whose falling share of the British market, uncompensated by any large capital flow, left them without the earnings to sustain their own purchases from Britain.

We have already seen that Britain was especially hard hit by the failure of her main markets in the primary producing lands to grow in line with those of the industrialised lands. Only the running down of reserves and the provision of aid has enabled the primary producers to stave off heavy cuts in their purchases. As these reserves and aid ran out at the end of 1961, it became clear that the end of the road was approaching both for the primary producing lands and for their British suppliers.

The prospects for Britain's future share in world trade we must look at in detail in the next chapter. Here we need only note the importance of the rising levels of world trade, especially in the five years prior to 1953 (see Table XXV, Chapter 10) as a factor contributing to Britain's post-war prosperity. But it would be remarkable if the export market accounting for even so much as a fifth of national output, as exports were doing in the 1950s (compared with an eighth in the 1930s; Table IV, Chapter 3), should have been accounting for the whole rise in demand in the post-war period. This would then be a case of the tail wagging the dog. There were many other elements in the post-war boom: the pent-up demand for consumer goods and capital re-equipment after war-time restrictions were lifted; the increased share of Government expenditure both on welfare and on arms, compared with the pre-war period; the continuing techno-logical revolution through which industry was passing. All these factors will be examined shortly, but we need first to look at one change to which much importance has been attributed, and that is the apparently large redistribution of incomes in favour of the lower-income groups, over the years between 1938 and at least 1951.

(c) MORE EQUAL INCOMES

This is the change which John Strachey[13] regards as the foundation of post-war prosperity and – what is very important for our study – as the reason for the relaxation of imperial ties. Trade-union and political pressure, he argues, has at last ended the conditions which created the drive for overseas investment and with it the drive to empire. Bearing in mind the great expansion of overseas investment after 1945, which we were considering in the last chapter, the conditions, whatever they were, that gave rise to it do not seem to have ended. Strachey's argument was based upon Hobson's premiss, which we examined earlier, that it was the lack of consuming power of the masses at the end of the nineteenth century and in the early years of this century that led to the drying-up of investment opportunities at home and thus to the outward pressure of capital and the extension of imperial rule to protect the capital exports.

We have already exposed the lack of any direct connection

between overseas investment and imperial rule in Hobson's day, when the two took place mainly in different areas. Now, when the ties of empire are being dissolved and overseas investment is rapidly expanding, the connection would seem once more to be a doubtful one. Strachey's argument could, however, be saved at least in the recent period, by dividing the post-war years at 1953. Then it might be shown that, before 1953, a progressive redistribution of incomes was associated with a high level of investment at home and a low level of investment overseas and, after 1953, that these processes were reversed. There is some evidence to support this argument.

Table XXII below presents the evidence. The share of wages in the total of pre-tax incomes rose sharply during the war and very slightly thereafter. A similar and not much greater change took place in post-tax incomes. By making the calculation in terms of 1938 purchasing power, Dudley Seers was able to suggest a reversal of the trend after 1950.[14] (See Table XXII, second half.) Even before then, the real redistribution of incomes was probably not as great as appears. In the first place, post-tax incomes are of course only post-income-tax incomes, and the great increase in post-war taxation has been in indirect taxes while income-tax rates have been cut. Even though some may regard both drink and tobacco as luxuries, indirect taxes are, in fact, a much more regressive form of taxation than direct taxes. Second, a large part of the higher share of wages was simply the obverse of the lower share of distributed profits. Businesses ploughed back more of their profits and rewarded their shareholders with capital gains (untaxed) rather than with higher dividends. Some attempt was made by H. E. Lydall to show this in his apportioning of additional benefits accruing to the higher income groups over and above their allocated incomes[15] (see Table XXII).

Lydall's figures finish in 1957; up to that time it seems to be clear that there was, during and after the war, an improvement of several percentage points on the pre-war situation, when 80 per cent of the income receivers took only 50 per cent of the income. By 1957 they were taking over 60 per cent. This change, taken into account with the overall ratchet-effect of higher incomes, undoubtedly gave buoyancy to long-term business prospects. Prosperity breeds prosperity as slump bred slump in the 1930s. Security of employment has resulted in a higher propensity to spend and even to dis-save by hire purchases.[16] If we accept the Keynesian analysis that it is consumption and not saving that leads to investment, we can readily see that the result of all this was the capital investment boom, which got under way after 1953.[17] But this was precisely the time at which overseas investment began to expand and there has been little sign of a let-up in the corresponding growth of home investment since then. How are we to explain this expansion of investment at home and overseas simultaneously and at the same time as output was stagnating?

We have clear evidence that there was a progressive redistribution of incomes up to 1954 and a high probability that the decontrol of rents, the reduction in income and surtaxes, while indirect taxes were maintained, the growth of capital gains, the increasing use of business-expense accounts, all combined to reverse the redistribution of incomes after 1954. But this did not cause a swing from home to overseas investment. The explanation may be in part that Keynesian theory, with its assumption that lower-income earners have a higher propensity to consume, no longer has the validity it once had. The very nature of some of the new factors tending to raise the share in the national income of the higher-income earners – that is the capital gains and the use of business-expense accounts – have tended to involve increased consumption. Moreover, there was a markedly high rate of personal saving between 1952 and 1956 when real wages were rising fast (Table XXIII), and a tendency to dis-save through hire purchase when real wages were checked after

1956.[18] The ratchet-effect of higher incomes and greater economic security tends to some extent to even out the swings of saving and consumption.

We shall return to the question of the influence of wage levels at home on investment overseas. But we are bound to look for other causes besides income redistribution for the rise in home demand after 1945, and for the check to growth in output after 1955 despite the continued rise in investment at home and overseas. There are at least two other causes to be considered – the rise in public expenditure and the pace of technological change.

(d) MORE GOVERNMENT SPENDING AND TECHNOLOGICAL CHANGE

Up to 1953, Government expenditure as a proportion of national income was considerably raised compared with the level obtaining before the war – from just over a quarter to just under a third.[19] We must, however, note the direction in which this took place. The change has been in the share of capital and not of current expenditure. Spending on current goods and services by public services, though it rose in the early 1950s to over 16 per cent of national income, declined almost to the 1938 level of 10 per cent thereafter.[20] During the post-war period over half of this expenditure has consisted in payments to persons – pensions and subsidies – at a level more than double pre-war – 7 per cent to 8 per cent compared with less than 3 per cent of the national income. The net effect was only to raise the total public share of current expenditure by two or three percentage points to a little over, instead of a little under, one-third of the national income. Where the big change took place was in the public contribution to capital investment. This was the result of the nationalisation of fuel, power and transport. Investment in the nationalised industries has been taking over 3 per cent of national income; investment in school and house building and capital investment for defence were also for a time in the mid-1950s at a higher level than pre-war; but only for the two years of 1952 and 1953.[21]

The result was that, in the years before 1955, the public sector was generating more than half the total demand for fixed capital formation in Britain. Until 1955, investment in the private sector did not rise in real terms above the 1938 level.[22] On the other hand, the public-sector spending on capital equipment and on consumer goods encouraged an accelerated investment programme in the private sector to meet it. It was only in 1954 and 1955 that the huge sums set aside each year by the great industrial corporations as reserves for future development began to be used on a large scale.[23] When private investment at home did begin, everyone joined in at the same time and on top of the heavy public-sector investment programme. This led to the mad rush for labour and materials in 1955; which caused the Government to cut back the level of public expenditure and introduce deflationary measures into the economy.

This is the penalty paid by an unplanned economy, and the deflationary measures taken to control the 1955 boom were undoubtedly the major cause of the check that followed, as we shall see. We must emphasise again that the check to growth in 1955 was a check to production both for home and export markets. Investment at home and overseas continued to rise year by year (Table IV, Chapter 3). How do we explain this? Part of the answer is that Government investment continued at a high rate, especially in the public corporations. Some further part of the answer lies in the continued Government encouragement of private investment not only by its orders for goods, both civil and military, but by taxation concessions, investment allowances, and the like, which were retained even while other deflationary measures – bank-rate and credit squeeze, for example – were being applied. The last, and perhaps the greatest, part of the answer lies in the nature of oligopolistic competition in a period of technological change.

Certainly the pace of technological change has forced a higher and higher level of investment at home by the great corporations. Stimulated by technical developments in warfare, several industries have begun to approach the transition to automation.[24] There has been some resistance to creating excess capacity, especially in the steel industry, but in electronics, in aircraft, in plastics and other chemicals, research carried out during the war and in the rearmament programme after 1950 opened up possibilities which industrialists were naturally anxious to exploit.[25] We have noticed already that, in the late 1930s, British capital did at length succeed in developing a modern industrial structure, albeit with fearful ruthlessness and inefficiency. By 1945, after six years of war, British industry was still backward in steel production, ship-building, housing and machine-tool manufacture, but had an advanced base in chemicals, electricity, motors and aircraft.[26] It was the products of these last four industries that accounted for a large part of the rapid expansion of exports after 1945, for their share was raised from a sixth of the total of goods exported in 1938 to as much as a third by 1952.[27]

We shall return shortly to the role of the giant oligopolies in the British economy since 1945, but we have first to consider how it could happen that, with such an impressive list of factors tending to sustain growth after 1945, the check in 1955 was nonetheless so sharp as it was and the stagnation that followed so persistent.

The somewhat more equitable distribution of incomes, the increased propensity to consume in all classes, the technological revolution through which we have been living, the huge reserves of the great corporations, the higher level of Government expenditure especially on the capital development of the nationalised industries, the buoyancy of overseas demand must, then, all be included as factors in the boom. And to them should be added another which, though of less importance, should not be overlooked: the improved administrative techniques of private management and of government alike. What then caused the check to growth in 1955?

The Check to Growth in Britain after 1955

The figures in Table XXI show the extent of the check to Britain's economic growth after 1955. As much as £1,000 million of industrial output, or 10 per cent of the 1959 total, may be said to have been lost as a result of the failure of growth to be sustained at an annual rate of 3 per cent to 4 per cent during the three years, 1956, 1957 and 1958. Moreover, the rapid recovery in the second half of 1959 and first half of 1960 was checked again in the second half of 1960. Before we look at the details of the economic stagnation in Britain after 1955, we should remember that this check to growth occurred in other countries besides Britain.

We noted earlier that the rate of industrial growth throughout the capitalist world in the five years prior to 1953 was considerably greater than in the six years that followed (see Table XXXI, Chapter 10). In part, this may be explained by the speed of post-war reconstruction especially in Germany and Japan, but pre-war levels of world output were soon surpassed and, in fact, doubled by 1953. Much of this was the result of the massive growth of the United States manufacturing output in the war and post-war years (Table XXXI, Chapter 10). The year 1954, however, marked the second post-war recession in the United States (the first had been in 1949). Once again, American productivity had outstripped the capacity of American and foreign consumers to buy back the rising tide of industrial production. Thanks to the momentum of the West German reconstruction boom, Europe was less seriously affected than in 1949. World trade continued to climb and Britain's exports recovered from the textile crisis of 1952.[28] By 1955, Britain was in the middle of a boom in exports and in capital equipment at home and drawing in imports far beyond her capacity to pay for them.

We may consider two explanations of the stagnation that followed. First, it was said by Labour Party spokesmen that the check to the boom was simply the result of Government incompetence in using such heavy-handed measures to curb excess demand at home. Was this all, or were there forces at work inside capitalism as such tending to restrict growth and especially affecting Britain? Growth in the United States and in Belgium was also slow after the mid-1950s, but Japan, West Germany and other European industries continued to advance. Britain's problem was the problem of inflation. A mild degree of inflation is probably helpful to capitalist growth; it reduces the money value of accumulated debt, it wipes out some part of the gains to workers from wage increases and it encourages business confidence. At the same time, it not only erodes the value of fixed incomes, but reduces the international standing of a country's currency and the competitiveness of its goods in world markets.

Inflation, as the word implies, is a process that is useful in getting economic activity off the ground, but at a certain point the process gets out of hand, unless some controlling force is used; without cables, in fact, 'the balloon goes up'. Under capitalism, the profit motive is relied upon to determine how much of which goods are produced; the conscious planning of output is anathema. Nevertheless, governments today are expected to exercise some control over economic activity, at least to prevent the extremes of boom and slump. To this end they adjust their own expenditure, which, as we have seen, is now a sizeable proportion of the national income, they influence the supply of credit, and they manipulate interest rates in such a way as to exercise a restraining influence and even 'deflate the balloon'. Reinflation may be more difficult, especially if deflation was accomplished by fairly savage blows at business confidence. Stagnation is likely to result and inflation is not cured, because the cut-back in output raises average unit costs, which are then passed on as higher prices.

In fact, inflation has been worst, not in the years of growth, but in the years of deflation when output was cut back (Table XXIII below). On the one hand wage rates, particularly in non-productive employments, are pushed up to catch up with earnings that have risen in the booming growth industries. On the other hand, oligopoly and price agreements enable prices to be kept up when costs are reduced from working at full capacity in the boom and raised when costs rise as the boom is checked. Indeed, inflation is built into the economy by the practice of replacement-cost pricing in the annual depreciation provisions of the great corporations.

In the crises between the wars, boom-time profits collapsed as real wages failed to keep up with the growth in real output per man. Since the war, real wages have grown in line with productivity, but only because Government restrictions have checked output. Profits have been cut back after short-lived booms as a result of working equipment well below capacity. In trying to check inflation by maintaining a margin between output and capacity, as its advisers recommend, the Government has in fact checked the whole rate of growth. Imports have been held back successfully, but exports have not been expanded. Firms which were supposed to turn to export markets when the home market was restricted have been unable to do so. Their prices were simply not competitive; and this was directly because running their equipment well below capacity raised their unit costs.[29]

For the essence of deflationary measures in a market economy is their indiscriminatory effect. Thus when demand rises in several sectors of the economy at once, as it is bound to do on the multiplier principle, all claimants for scarce resources are cut back by the blunt tools of credit squeeze and monetary control that have to be used. Any form of planning or discriminatory control was eschewed by Conservative Governments until 1961. How far the National Economic

Development Council can be turned from an election gambit into a real planning agency will depend on the extent to which the trade-union members can put forward and win public support for positive steps to control the investment decisions and pricing policies of the great corporations in the public interest. It will not be easy. As Dr Balogh has suggested,[30] the refusal to plan arises from an awareness that any successful planning would lead in the end to popular control over economic decisions. To retain their own power, the leaders of finance and industry must create enough uncertainty in the economy for it to seem that uncontrollable economic forces determine events.

Thus Mr Anthony Tuke, the chairman of Barclays Bank, explaining the cut-back in demand after 1957, speaks of the Trade Cycle's 'pendulum swing governed by the inexorable natural forces of supply and demand'.[31] He blames the decline in primary commodity prices, which began in December 1956 and continued throughout 1957 and 1958. But what caused the declining prices, if it was not the cut-back in demand in the industrial countries after 1955 ? There is much evidence that decisions were taken in 1953 and 1954 quite independently by leading capitalists in Europe and America that inflation had to be checked. Deflationary measures were explicitly proposed in the call of the British Employers Federation in September 1954.[32] It was not so much a conspiracy of wicked capitalists as a necessary decision forced upon them by the contradictions of an unplanned economy.

The point at issue is that raw-material prices are regarded by industrialists in the same light as wages – to be kept down if profits are to be raised. The deflationary policies pursued in the United States and in Britain after 1953 were just as much designed to cut back the rise in raw-material prices as they were to cut back wage demands. What Dr Balogh has described as the 'deliberate creation of uncertainty'[33] in order to reduce the strength of the trade unions, by encouraging a certain measure of unemployment at home, is just as effective in holding back the demands of primary producers overseas. Like the worker with his labour power, the peasant with his produce cânnot afford to withhold from the market the one thing he has to offer. It was the increasingly organised strength of the primary producers overseas, with governments of their own today to support them, as well as the increasing strength of the unions at home, that forced the issue.

Should We Blame the City?

An alternative explanation must now be considered – it was one of Mr Andrew Schonfield's main themes[34] – that the stagnation of the British economy after 1955 could be blamed on an excessive anxiety for the defence of sterling at all costs. This was said to emanate from the City of London, who were still harking back to the palmy days before the First World War when sterling was the world's currency, and there was always a balance of payments surplus for overseas investment. If this, in fact, were the case, it would provide us at once with a link between the overseas developments which we considered in the last chapter and the check to growth at home after 1955. Certainly, successive Tory Chancellors have made it abundantly clear that, in Lord Amory's words, 'The strength of sterling remains the primary objective of our economic policy.'[35] To this end, policies have been pursued of damping-down the whole economy in order to check the rise in imports and of using high interest rates to attract short-term capital into the London market. In both these ways, it may be argued, a surplus has been found for overseas capital exports. But what evidence is there that these measures have been carried beyond the point that was necessary in order to check inflation, given the rejection of comprehensive planning?

There are, in fact, several important pieces of evidence: First, there is the general evidence of the Government's preoccupation with the pull of home demand upon resources as the main source of inflation. Demand pull was certainly the explanation of inflation in the immediate post-war and Korean War crises, but since then, as Keynes used to say, 'the practical men are the slaves of fifteen-year-old ideas, which changed circumstances have rendered defunct'.[36] All the Government's measures of monetary restriction may be said to have derived from this preoccupation and to have led to the stagnation of the economy which we have been examining. But raising bank rate has always had a double motive – not only to check home demand, where its effect on its own may be regarded as doubtful, but also to encourage foreign investors to hold their money in London.

Second, then, we must consider some specific evidence of preoccupation with the defence of the pound. There was the retention of investment allowances against company profits' taxes right up to February 1956, that is over twelve months after the régime of high interest rates and credit squeeze had been introduced;[37] there was the raising of bank-rate to 7 per cent in September 1957, not as the result of pressure of demand at home or even of balance of trade pressure, but of international financial pressure;[38] there was the long delay – a whole year after September 1957, while the economy was in recession – before bank-rate was reduced once more below 5 per cent;[39] there has been the pressure for full convertibility for sterling, which has been the merchant bankers' Holy Grail,[40] and which has certainly made the economy much more open to outside influence than it need have been. This is all evidence to suggest reasons other than inflationary pressures at home for manipulating interest rates and keeping down imports.

Are we then to conclude that the City of London, and the merchant bankers in particular, were distorting the economy at home in the interests of their overseas operations? That the merchant bankers still have the power to do so, through their close connections with the Government, the Bank of

England, the Joint Stock banks and the top industrial corporations, was indicated at the tribunal on the bank-rate leak and documented in subsequent articles.[41] But did they use their power against the interests of British industry?

When we saw the British Government pursuing deflationary policies in the 1920s, in order to build up the strength of sterling, we blamed the City of London and its predilection for overseas investment. Today, we have to recognise that a capital export surplus is as important to the giant oligopolists as to the City financiers. Exports of goods are no longer the test of international success for the giant industrialists; overseas investment in subsidiaries is now their criterion, as we have seen. Retention of earnings in their overseas companies has been making up two-thirds of the total capital exports by Britain in recent years, but this can only go on so long as the country's balance of foreign payments permits it.

In 1960 the dreaded moment came: there was no surplus on the balance of payments for capital export and it did not look as though there would be one in 1961. The check to investment at home and to expanded output had left British goods unable to compete in export markets or even in the home market for many lines of manufactured goods. Imports of manufactures were rising far faster than exports.[42] At the same time, as we saw in the last chapter, income on 'invisibles' was falling. The only solution seemed to be the devaluation of the pound, the very thing the City of London's policies had been designed to prevent. A real conflict of views was developing between the industrialists, anxious to compete overseas, and the City, anxious to maintain sterling as the second world currency.

Industrial groups might be expected to take sides according to their economic position; and this was largely determined by the relative importance of imports in their input and of exports in their output. Thus the great food-processing and tobacco combines, with 15 per cent of their input coming from imports but selling only 4 per cent of their output abroad, should line up with the City. On the other hand, the engineering industries, including the motor industry, with only 7 per cent of their input made up of imports and 29 per cent of their sales consisting of exports, should be ranged on the other side. The textiles industries and chemicals, including oil refining, might be expected to stand in the middle, since the import content of their input and the export content of their output were about the same – 26 per cent in the case of textiles and 18 per cent in the case of chemicals.[43] But, in industries where import content is so large a figure, import prices might well be more important for them than export prices; and they would stand to lose by devaluation, especially where a large element of monopoly in the market or, in the case of the oil companies, cartel agreements take final prices out of the realm of competition.

For some time, it is true, the new industrialists of the Midlands were, like Sir Ivan Stedeford, critical of deflationary policies or, like Mr Lionel Fraser, demanding a national Five Year Plan[44] and in 1962 Mr Selwyn Lloyd established the N.E.D.C. But industrialists are as anxious for an overseas investment surplus as anyone; the problem was how to get it. In this they face a real contradiction, which we have seen before and which is a very simple one: a surplus on payments for one country means a deficit in another; and if the other country is a trading partner a deficit will lead him, if he can, to cut his imports, which will reduce the exports of the country that had the surplus. Winning larger shares of the world's trade may mean checking the growth of the trade as a whole. We may examine this problem by considering the rapid growth of West German and French output and exports compared with Britain's.

The Comparison with West Germany and France

West Germany has succeeded in combining rapid growth

with a much smaller rise in prices than Britain has experienced. Although British export prices only rose 6 or 7 per cent faster than German export prices between 1950 and 1960 (Table XXI), consumer prices at home rose by 50 per cent in Britain compared with only 20 per cent in Germany.[45] Over the same period, British industrial output grew by about 40 per cent, while German output more than doubled. When British growth was stagnant between 1955 and 1958, West Germany continued to expand her output – by nearly 20 per cent over the three years – and with an 8 per cent price increase compared with Britain's 12 per cent (see Table XXI).

What Western Germany did between 1950 and 1960 was to check inflation by holding back wage demands and find a market for her increased production in foreign countries, the home market being restricted by the check to wages. Table XXIV below shows what happened. The share of exports in West Germany's gross national product rose from 12 per cent in 1950 to 25 per cent in 1959, while the share of home private consumption declined from 64 per cent to 58 per cent. The share of public consumption was maintained at 14 per cent, while capital formation was raised from 19 per cent to 23 per cent of the national product. West Germany was able, by keeping her prices down, by keeping her rate of capital investment up, by avoiding a high level of armaments expenditure, and by aggressive sales technique, to capture markets throughout the world from the other capitalist powers. Such a policy is by its very nature not open to more than one or two powers at a time; and exports at the expense of home consumption have left German standards of living still somewhat below Britain's.[46] But if growth can be maintained, the prospects are much brighter in Germany than in Britain.

This is the crucial question. German growth was considerably slowed down in 1960 and 1961.[47] At the same time, prices began to rise. It seems reasonable to see behind these phenomena not only the ending of the flood of new labour from the East, but also some of the same problems that have faced Britain since 1955. As the first waves of post-war reconstruction and the development of modern industries of mass consumption break, there is an inevitable check. Investment continues; indeed, it may become excessive. In Britain, compared with Germany, the low level of capital investment as a share of national income conceals a high level of investment per head of the working population.[48] Some element of excessive investment as well as of demand restriction lies behind the small increase in productivity in Britain since 1955. By May of 1961, it was certainly troubling the Stock Exchange, and a year later investors watched the biggest collapse in share values since 1929.

In some markets, those for radios and television sets for example, it is probable that, in Germany as well as Britain, saturation point was being reached by 1961–2. In others future sales depend on reduced prices; but heavy advertising costs and improved shopping facilities, to win consumers from other forms of spending, taken together with the huge capital cost of equipment for large-scale output, all mean that production must be near to capacity for prices to be kept down. Expanding markets are vital; hence the drive of German industry into the Common Market. This is a competition of giants now to win the existing markets for durable consumer goods. The creation of new markets among the less-developed lands becomes a secondary consideration. They cannot afford cars, TV sets, refrigerators and washing machines. The battle is for the rich consumer.

British exports were the first to suffer from German competition in European as well as in Sterling Area and other overseas markets. The same attempt was made in Britain as in Germany to keep down costs by freezing wages, but with less success. German workers were much less well organised than their British comrades and had the steady flow of refugees from the East to keep the labour market permanently weakened. The very considerations that we have noted as contributing to the British post-war boom and absence of depression, while leading to the expansion of the British home market, tend of course to reduce the competitiveness of British exports in face of such competition as Western Germany has presented. The rise of real wages in line with productivity in Britain since the wage freeze ended in 1950 (Table XXIII below), the high level of Government expenditure and particularly of arms expenditure, and the raising of interest rates since 1955 have all combined to reduce the availability and competitiveness of British goods in export markets.

Economic recovery was almost as impressive after 1953 in France as in West Germany. Industrial output and exports were both doubled by 1961, that is during a period when the British increases were about 33 per cent.[49] France started from extremely low levels having barely recovered by 1953 to the 1929 level of industrial output and exports after the decline of the 1930s and the destruction of the 1940s.[50] French industry then proceeded to carry through in the 1950s what British industry had largely achieved in the 1930s and 1940s. French economic planning – or the setting of targets for industrial output – has been given much of the credit for this success.[51] There can be little doubt, however, that the main reasons were the low starting level and the determination of French planners and governments to proceed with industrial expansion, even at the expense of the French balance of payments.[52]

France is far less dependent on imports than Britain, being largely self-sufficient in foodstuffs. The contrast with the British position is clear and the corollary should be equally evident: if the open economy of Britain cannot, like the largely closed economy of France, risk foreign exchange crisis to avoid stagnation, the major efforts of British policy must be directed to an expansion of world trade within which the British economy also may grow; and this may involve eschewing the cut-throat battle for the consumer durables market and developing capital equipment industries for the markets of the underdeveloped world. In the Common Market French and German industry, and the other countries' industries, too, are committed to battle for the 170 million consumers. What is at stake can be seen from the estimate that, by 1965, in Western Europe demand for motor-cars will be of the order of seven or eight million, while the capacity to supply this demand will be in excess of ten million.[53] What has drawn British industry to favour entry into the Common Market is precisely the similar concentration of British industrial investment on consumer durables. But for Britain entry into the Common Market presents a real choice.

Britain after 1955 probably got the worst of both worlds: neither the advantages of inflationary growth at home nor those of deflationary competitiveness overseas. But Britain was especially hit by the fact that her main markets both in the Sterling Area and elsewhere were among primary producers; and some of the major blows of deflationary policies in Europe and North America, were taken, as Mr Tuke came to realise, by the primary commodity producers. West Germany, by keeping her prices down, could win markets in the industrial producing countries. British deflation undermined markets not only at home but overseas. Britain's trade depended on world growth; world growth in part on Britain's trade. The effect of the cutting-back of Britain's imports was to impoverish British overseas markets. This is where the close interdependence of the British economy and the less-developed and developing lands overseas distinguishes Britain from other capitalist powers. It is not only that Britain is dependent on imports for so much of her food and raw materials; it is that Britain has for long earned a large part of her living by producing goods, and a large part of them capital goods, for overseas buyers in developing lands.

Herein lies the essential difference between the position of Britain and the original six countries of the Common

Market, which has caused most of the difficulty in negotiating Britain's entry. Only 3.5 per cent of Britain's occupied population is engaged in agriculture; the proportion is 25 to 30 per cent among the Six.[54] We import half our food; they import only a few tropical products from outside the Market. Britain's trade has always been based on the assumption of free imports of food and raw materials as the basis for free exports of machines and manufactures. The Six plan to develop their production of synthetic materials and expand their agricultural output, particularly that of France, even using import levies to do so.[55]

Britain remains a major market for the products of the as yet underdeveloped lands. Even the British market is not, however, so open to imports as it was, and an increasing proportion of Britain's imports have been coming from the more developed countries. In Britain too, as a result of subsidies, more food is being produced at home – about a half of total supplies instead of a third as it was before the war.[56] Synthetic substitutes are reducing the demand for imported natural raw materials. Restrictions are imposed on imports of textiles and other manufactured and semi-manufactured goods, even from Commonwealth countries.

It is the result of all these developments that the growth of world agricultural production since the war has been at half the rate achieved in industrial production. There is the further factor of uncertainty about future levels of demand. Ever since the ending of the Labour Government's bulk purchase agreements and the re-establishment of the commodity markets, fluctuations in the prices of primary products have been both wide and unpredictable, and, after 1954 and 1955, the trend was unmistakably downward (see Table XXV, Chapter 10).

Britain was once more, as in the 1930s, caught in the trap of a trade relationship which produced cheap imports at the expense of impoverished export markets; and in the 1960s the cheap imports of food and raw materials are less important, the export markets more important, than they were in the 1930s to the British economy. There are two alternative solutions for Britain today – to complete the present process and intensify agricultural and raw material output as well as industrial production and sales in the more developed lands and particularly in the rich 'West End' of Europe; or to take every possible step to assist the rest of the world to industrialise and expand the whole level of world trade in the process. This is the true challenge of the Common Market which we shall have to consider in the next chapter.

Has Capitalism Changed?

We have now to examine more closely just what sort of system it is that has to be adjusted to these changed circumstances – the system that we call 'capitalism' in Britain today. Its outstanding feature of recent years is the rapid increase by bid and merger in the concentration of ownership. The *Financial Times* record of bids and deals totalled over £600 million in 1960 and nearly £900 million in 1961;[57] but the process has been a continuous one since the end of the war.

Many factors have entered into this concentration of industry: the huge scale of the production technique of modern industry; the giant size of the orders placed by public authorities for modern power stations, modern aircraft, modern defence equipment; the immense cost of promotion and advertising of launching new products for mass consumption; and the difficulties experienced by small firms in raising funds during a period of high interest rates and credit squeeze, when the larger firms could still call upon their internal reserves. The growth in the scale of production may be seen in the fact that considerably more than a third of all manufacturing workers work in factories with over 1,000 workers; there were less than a fifth in such large plants before the war.[58] This, moreover, says nothing of the concentration in ownership of the large plants: I.C.I. employs 110,000; A.E.I. 150,000; B.M.C. 75,000.[59]

The studies of the National Institute have shown the rapid increase in concentration.[60] We can test the size of the giant corporations best by looking at their profits. In 1957, the profits of the top seventy companies accounted for nearly a third of all company trading profits or, more significantly, for nearly a half of the profits of all companies quoted on the Stock Exchange. Two-thirds of the profits earned by the quoted companies were taken by 157 companies. Moreover, the profits of the largest companies have tended to grow much faster than the average for all companies (see Table XXIII). Between 1954 and 1957, the assets of the largest companies (that is, the seventy with over £25 million net assets) grew just twice as fast as those of the quoted companies with under £1 million each in net assets.[61] One must conclude that investment by the largest companies not only plays the major part in total investment, but plays the leading role in the economy.

It is these giant companies which have been pioneering technological advances and moving forward towards automation. The new mode of operation of oligopoly since the war has naturally favoured rapid growth. Monopoly and price agreements between the oligopolies have enabled prices to be charged which permitted high margins of profits.[62] At the same time, dividend restraint has led to the building-up of reserves for investment. Although the very fastest growing firms have in fact gone to the capital market for as much as a half of their investment finance,[63] the average company quoted on the Stock Exchange has drawn more than three-quarters of its finance from reserves and only 5 per cent from bank loans and less than 20 per cent from capital issues.[64] The corporations have become their own investors; shareholders are increasingly coupon-clippers.

This is the point at which it is argued that capitalism is no longer what it was. With such large units of production, relying on their own reserves of capital, and with management divorced from the capital market and share ownership, the modern industrial corporation, it is claimed, need no longer be caught in the anarchic market of capitalism by the necessity for profit maximisation.[65] The managers, and not the owners of capital, control the corporation's investment policies, it is said, and they do so with public and not private gain in mind. But even if it were true that technical managers were now predominant on the boards of directors of the big companies – which it is not,[66] unless we call bankers the managers of money – and that managers had different aims from shareholders – which they do not since they are the same people[67] – the struggle of the market would drive them to maximise profits. And if they do not do this, they will soon be ripe for a take-over bid by someone who will. Such is the ineluctable experience of recent years. It was not the Courtaulds managers that saved them from I.C.I. in 1961 but the insurance companies' already swollen holdings of I.C.I. stock, which made them reluctant to hold any more eggs in one basket.[68]

The truth is that industry and commerce are not only more concentrated in giant 'diversified' corporations than ever before, but that they are more integrated with the centralised finance of the big banks and insurance companies than they have ever been. Interlocking directorates have reduced the number of controllers of the economy to a few hundred who make the main investment decisions of the whole economy.[69] Can it be said, then, that they can, from their positions of power, at least escape from the anarchy of the market and the tendency to over-production? The answer must be a negative one; for they are still bound to compete with their rivals in the international market, even if they have eliminated all rivals at home; and they are, in fact, too big to limit their operations to the home market alone.

There is little doubt that the controllers of finance and industry are today much better informed and better served by national and global statistics; but there is scant evidence that they are driven by any other consideration than the maximising of profit, for this is the basis of the whole system. If they cannot raise profits in line with their world-wide competitors, they will go to the wall. What they can do is to bring wider and wider areas of competition under their control, through merger, amalgamation, price leadership at home and overseas, and ultimately through international cartels. What has changed is not the nature of the controllers, as some suggest, from being owners to being managers of capital, but the scale of the capital they control and so the power they have to move things their way. And their way will mean the destruction of small competitors, the concentration of sales on the products of the giant companies by advertising and other sales techniques, and the establishment of branches and subsidiaries overseas. But while they may raise their share of the market in this way, they cannot so easily expand the market.[70]

When one expands they all expand, as if the consumption of the whole world were their only limit;[71] and the search for maximum profit leads them to use their monopolistic position to resist cutting their own prices or raising primary producers' prices, which alone would absorb their new levels of output. At the same time, they can concede higher earnings by bonus and piece rates in their own expanding sectors, passing on the higher wage costs in higher prices to the consumer. But here they meet a real contradiction. For inflation, while it may expand the market at home, reduces their competitiveness abroad. They must sell abroad, however, because Britain's fifty million are too small a market for modern industry producing durable consumer goods on a vast scale.[72] Hence the drive to expand sales, if necessary by establishing subsidiaries, throughout the richer industrialised lands of the world.

At one time, overseas investment was a rentiers' affair, which kept up the rate of profit, brought great wealth to the City of London and, though it involved some stagnation at home which kept down wages, nevertheless opened up new sources of food and raw materials throughout the world and developed new markets for exports. Today it more than ever follows Lenin's vision of the struggle for the division of the world between the international capitalist combines. Given the necessity for widening markets and given the existence of tariffs and the advantages of geography in the placing of factories, each of the great corporations must invest overseas as well as at home to keep up in the struggle.

The Role of the Giant Corporations

It would be wrong, however, to conclude that there has been no change in capitalism. External and internal pressures to reform are increasingly strong. Indeed, the crucial question for capitalist economies is the extent to which the great oligopolies can be forced by home and overseas pressure to keep down their rates of profits and encourage all-round growth at home and real economic development overseas. There is a growing awareness of the importance of expanding the whole market overseas just as there is of the importance of expanding the whole market at home, but the attraction of the rich consumers at home and of the richer lands abroad remains.[73] Yet there are some capitalists who realise that only if real economic development follows in the lands where investment takes place can growth be maintained in the total level of world trade and reduced costs of production be made without reduced real earnings of the people.[74]

What chance is there, then, of the great corporations embarking upon policies of world-wide industrial expansion? We may first ask how far these giants of the economy at home and overseas are dependent for their profits upon unequal economic relations between Britain and the lands whence their raw materials are derived. How far do they need to use their power to keep labour cheap and capital scarce, in order to maximise their rates of profit? The poverty of workers in oil-fields, in gold- and copper-mines, on sugar and cotton plantations is so evident that one is bound to feel that much of the wealth of the great companies must depend upon this. Some of it undoubtedly does; but we have continually had to notice in this book, first, that only a very small part of investment has been in lands of cheap labour and scarce capital – most of it has gone where labour was scarce and capital growing – and, second, that cheap labour does not necessarily imply cheap production, nor *vice versa*; the cheapness of margarine, for example, is certainly due far more to the high degree of mechanisation in its processing and packing than to the low level of wages of West African growers of oil-seeds.[75] This is not to say that Unilever does not profit from low wages, but only that this profit may be but a small part of the total. It is likely to be smaller than ever today because the share of the raw material in the final value of the products of modern industry has been steadily declining and with the increasing development of synthetic materials seems likely to continue to decline.

Raw material prices, of course, are still kept down wherever possible. Factories are established where labour is cheaper than at home, by American firms in Britain, by British firms in Holland.[76] Labour is certainly one of the determining factors; the wider market remains, however, the most important factor. This gives rise to the hope that capitalist firms and governments will see, as they seem to be seeing in India, albeit under pressure of competition from the Soviet Union, that economic development in the as yet underdeveloped lands is very much in their interest. For this development will certainly benefit their people at home as well as those in the poor lands overseas. It seems hardly to be in the nature of capitalism to undertake such development; but British capitalism did it once for the lands of European settlement and we must consider the possibility of continuing the job in the less developed lands of Asia and Africa.

This will be the subject of the next two chapters. Here we may consider a little further how the great oligopolies, whose position is now so dominating, operate at home and abroad.

We have suggested that the giant oligopolies are driven forward by each other's expansion, knowing full well that the one that does not keep up in the production of new lines and of new cost-saving equipment will lose his share of the market. Even inside the cartels there is a constant struggle for position, for shares of the market and of raw material resources. We have only to note the competitive placing of petrol stations and petrol advertising by the rival oil companies. Nowadays, this oligopolistic competition does not stop at the home market. The giants of contemporary industry are international – General Motors, Ford and B.M.C., the two G.E.C.s and Siemens, I.C.I., Farben and du Pont, Shell-B.P. and Esso.

When we considered the operations of the oil companies in Chapter 7, we saw what a large share their investments amounted to in the total of home as well as overseas investment by British firms. It was not for nothing that the largest British companies were those that were most involved in operations overseas – the oil, tobacco, paper, chemicals, cement, asbestos and sugar companies, the shipping lines and non-ferrous metal mining and refining companies; but, as we saw in the last chapter, the overseas interests of the largest steel, engineering, motor-car, and drug companies are those that have been growing most rapidly of recent years, particularly those manufacturing durable consumer goods. They are driven to invest overseas, simply in order to keep up in the world-wide competition of the giants; and because of the anarchic nature of capitalism they are all attracted at one and the same time into the most profitable lines and the most profitable markets.

Thus, over 10 per cent of all capital formation in British manufacturing in the mid-1950s was taking place simultaneously in the motor and aircraft industry and a similar proportion took place in the paper, printing and publishing industry in the late 1950s.[77] At the same time, whole sectors of the economy are neglected and fall into decay. The concentration of profit leads to over-production and excess capacity and the great corporations look around for new fields for diversification at home and new ventures overseas. And there the same process takes place. The flood of capital first to Canada and then to the Common Market threatens to drown the investors themselves, as excess capacity mounts in the rich lands and the poorer lands are left poorer still. Capitalism tends always to collect rather than to diffuse wealth, and the pikes devour the weaker fish. The quotation from Robert Southey printed at the beginning of this book describes the process that we find at home and that we shall see at work in the underdeveloped lands of the world.[78]

Home versus Foreign Investment

Does it matter, then, that so much investment goes overseas? What are the respective advantages from investment at home and overseas?[79] The resulting gain to the national economy, from £100 million invested at home or from the same sum invested abroad, will depend on a wide range of factors – on the level of employment at home; on the nature of the investment overseas, whether it is in food and raw material for export or in real estate or in local manufacturing; on the rate of return on the capital invested; on the comparative degree of monopoly of the investor in the home and overseas market; on the competitiveness of home exports to take advantage of the stimulus given to overseas development; and, above all, on the level of taxation and manner of distribution both at home and overseas of the earnings resulting from the investment.

It is this last which is probably the crucial point. The relative gains to the economy may be difficult to assess, but the difference in distribution of income resulting from investment at home and overseas may be quite clearly seen. The result of investment at home is a direct return to employment, wages and profits at home. The result of investment overseas is a direct return to profits at home and only an indirect return to wages at home through the investment and spending of profits at home and through higher wages overseas leading to increased exports. In so far as capital is earning a higher return overseas than at home, there will be a redistribution of incomes in favour of profit-earners, unless the whole increase is taken away by taxation, and there may be little increase in wages overseas and so in demand for exports.

This may seem to be a reason why further United States and other foreign investment in Britain should be encouraged. There are, of course, many reasons against such investment, and particularly the influence on political decisions, such as the decision to nationalise an industry, that foreign economic interests may exercise. The rate of return on the capital invested is, however, the crucial economic factor. This is likely to be high where an international corporation can exploit a monopoly or semi-monopoly position and can marshal great resources, not only of finance but of sales and advertising power, behind its investment. The first problem arising from such foreign investment for the country in which the investment takes place is that the country has to earn enough from goods and services sold abroad to pay for the profits on the capital invested. We have already noted the critical position of the U.K. and Sterling Area Balance of Payments as the direct result of the recent outward flow of investment income to foreigners.

The second problem is that powerful international corporations are capable of killing local firms and, in effect, thereby retarding local enterprise. The stimulus to efficiency so enthusiastically sought through Britain's entry into the Common Market may kill as well as cure. The important point for us to recognise in judging the effect of increased U.K. investment overseas is that the gains to investors from higher rates of return on their capital will not necessarily bring gains to the people as a whole in the country from which the capital emanates. This is precisely because such gains will tend to have a regressive effect on income redistribution.

Any steps which increase maldistribution of incomes at home will tend to lessen economic stability and undermine prosperity. And there is a somewhat greater danger of this happening today when investment is being attracted rather more than of old into underdeveloped lands; for here some part of the attraction is, as it was in colonial enclaves, that low wages overseas are brought in to balance high wages at home. In the past, the so-called super-profits drawn from territories where capital was scarce and labour cheap were counterbalanced to some extent, at least, for the home economy by cheap imports of food and raw materials and by the development of export markets. There is no similar counterbalance today.

The third problem is that concentration on mass production of durable consumer goods for more-developed lands may be at the expense of developing the most suitable capital equipment for the less-developed. In fact, as we saw earlier, most of Britain's post-war investment has been in the more-rather than in the less-developed lands, that is in Australia, Canada and South Africa, where economic development has been taking place, and even in the fully-developed lands of the United States and the Common Market. In these cases there is no question of super-profits from overseas, but rather of establishing bases in the world market and particularly for the sale of durable consumer goods. The danger of such investment is that, if it is at the expense of basic investment at home, it will in the long run weaken the industrial base at home, from which a country's competitive strength in the last resort must stem. There is much evidence that this has in fact been happening in Britain, as we shall see in the next chapter.

Provided investment at home is adequate to preserve competitive strength, what matters especially for Britain in the field of overseas investment is that such investment, by expanding the wealth of developed and underdeveloped lands, so raises the whole level of world trade as to create a general demand for British goods.

We have failed to find earlier in any weakened condition of demand at home an explanation for the post-war drive of British industry into overseas investment. We also found no connection between overseas investment and imperial expansion; indeed, the investment has taken place just when the ties of empire were being cut. We did find intense political activity on the part of the capitalist powers to retain the ex-colonial lands within the framework of capitalism; but the proportion of investment directed to them has continued to be small. We are now in a position to reply to Strachey's thesis on the end of empire.[80] Strachey sought to revive Hobson's analysis[81] which made empire a function of overseas investment, which was itself a function of declining investment opportunities at home, caused by lack of consuming power of the masses. The analysis is once again untenable. Overseas investment has not ended with the end of empire nor with the rising share of wages in the national income.

There was always a contradiction in the argument, which Lenin was not free from in his insistence that the impoverishment of the workers at home was one of the pressures forcing oligopolies outwards.[82] Profits which declined because of the impoverishment of the masses at home were supposed to be sustained and even made into 'super-profits' through the still greater impoverishment of the masses overseas. We have to accept that, if the oligopolies are being driven overseas today, it is not by low wages at home, but rather by high wages at home. Real wages rose pretty well in line with productivity after the ending of the wage freeze in 1952; and more recently rates of profit have been falling (see Table XXIII). Yet investment at home has been raised steadily, even while investment overseas has grown.

What then has been happening? We have seen that the pressure to cut raw material costs remains and has been in part the cause both of deflationary measures and of further vertical integration in industrial processing. At the same time, the vertically-integrated processing combines, while still wielding great power in the economy, are less important than they were and are no longer the sole or even the main source of overseas investment. It is the new corporations manufacturing consumer goods, and particularly durables for the mass market, who are now investing abroad to maintain and expand beyond the fifty million of the home market, which is no longer adequate for the scale of modern technology. They are driven by their rivals to do this. For the fact is that high wages and low productivity at home (compared with other industrial powers) have been reducing the competitiveness of British exports; protective barriers are being raised against them in Europe and the newly-independent lands overseas. British industry is being forced to set up shop outside the home country.

The question remains whether this process is inevitable or can be reversed. The answer will largely depend on whether the new wave of overseas investment – largely directed, as it is, to the already developed lands – can create the expansion of world trade upon which Britain's prosperity depends.

In the nineteenth century, the real advantage to Britain from the overseas investment was that it actually did develop the economies of the lands of European settlement, and, therefore, not only cheapened British imports of food and raw materials, but expanded British export markets.

In the first decade of this century, and again in the third, we found that overseas investment and imperial rivalry of many sorts were associated with the world-wide struggle for privileged markets and sources of supply by the vertically-integrated combines of the advanced industrial powers, which Lenin so clearly characterised. But Britain's position as the first industrial power and as the largest foreign investor gave her an interest in free trade rather than protection, which her possession also of the largest empire tended rather to conceal. Lenin accepted Hobson's premise that overseas investment led to direct political rule. But this was never so important as it seemed, because investment in the colonies was so small a part of the total. More important than colonial rule was world-wide economic power, backed up if necessary by force, to restrict the number of lands that were industrialised and thus to maintain the advantage of industrial over primary production. But even more important was the fact that Britain could then still benefit from the industrialisation of the lands of European settlement. Today, the lands that remain to be industrialised are the lands that had been restricted to primary production.

British capitalism now, therefore, faces a real dilemma: to industrialise the primary producers is to reduce the privilege of industrialisation; not to do so is to be driven into the struggle of the giants for the existing industrial markets. In this struggle we can see again the slow growth which Lenin predicted in the lands that are rich in capital and the more rapid growth in lands less engorged by their own capital assets.[82] British capitalism has come at length to be dominated by the great corporations, whose growth we watched in the 1930s, and begins to reveal all the features of concentration, finance domination and 'over-ripe' development at home leading to expansion abroad that Lenin described as the highest or 'imperialist' stage.

These developments have brought the people of Britain to an historic parting of the ways. As the oligopolies become the dominant element in the economy in Britain, as well as in the U.S.A. and Germany, and as the competition of the international giants for the existing world market sharpens,

Britain's traditional trading relations with the less-developed lands of the world are challenged as never before. This is the real issue presented by the Common Market. For economic growth in the less-developed lands has been markedly slow, much slower than in the Common Market. We may repeat our earlier conclusion that the Common Market poses for Britain the alternative of immediate participation in cut-throat competition for the existing rich industrial markets or the development of new, at present poor but potentially much larger, industrial markets over the coming years. In the next chapters we have to examine the growing points of world industrialisation and of world trade in order to find the right choice for Britain today.

TABLE XXI

INDUSTRIAL AND EXPORT PERFORMANCE OF U.K. IN RELATION TO OTHER MANUFACTURING COUNTRIES, 1913–61

Year	U.K. Industrial Production Index	U.K. Materials Import Volumes	Trade in Mfgs. U.K. Export Volumes	World Volumes[4]	Shares in Manufactured Exports (%)				Prices		U.K. Terms of Trade[5]
					U.K.	U.S.A.	Germany	Japan	German Exports	U.K. Exports	
1913	62	88[1]	173[2]	109	27	10	22	1	—	25	69
1919	54	78[1]	95	—	—	—	—	—	—	71	80
1920	62	78[1]	123	84	21	16	17	4	—	92	88
1929	79	97	142	112	21	20	20	7	—	41	83
1937	103	112	113	100	—	—	—	—	31[3]	36	92
1938	100	100	100	—	—	27	—	—	100	37	100
1948	112	83	154	120	22	—	—	—	91[3]	92	85
1949	119	90	171	—	21	—	—	—	92[3]	94	86
1950	126	95	195	148	26	27	7	3	100	100	80
1951	130	100	197	172	22	27	10	4	122	118	72
1952	127	88	180	172	21	26	12	4	132	124	77
1953	134	98	181	185	21	26	13	4	123	119	85
1954	142	98	190	193	20	25	15	5	118	118	83
1955	150	103	206	210	20	24	15	5	121	120	82
1956	150	100	218	230	19	25	16	6	125	125	84
1957	153	104	223	248	18	25	17	6	127	131	87
1958	151	92	214	240	18	23	19	6	127	130	93
1959	160	98	223	260	17·4	21	19	6·7	123	128	93
1960	171	107	235	300	16·8	22	19	6·3	124	131	94
1961	172	99	241	310	15·8	20·5	20·4	6·9	131[6]	132	97

Notes: 1 U.K. Materials Import Volume in 1913, 1919, 1920 = Total Import Volume.
2 U.K. Manufacturing Export Volume in 1913 = Total Export Volume.
3 German Export Prices Prior to 1950 = Continental W. Europe Export Prices.
4 World Manufactured Exports excludes Trade of the Communist bloc.

5 U.K. Terms of Trade = $\dfrac{\text{U.K. Export Prices}}{\text{U.K. Import Prices}}$ on base 1938 = 100.

6 After 5% revaluation of the Mark.

Sources: For World Trade in Manufactures, World Volumes and Shares:
United Nations, *Monthly Bulletin of Statistics*, special series linked to 1938 by E. A. G. Robinson, 'The Problem of Living within our Foreign Earnings. Some Comments', *Three Banks Review*, June 1955, and to 1913 by League of Nations' *World Economic Survey* and National Institute's *Economic Review*.
German Export Prices from O.E.E.C., *General Statistics*.
All other figures from London and Cambridge Economic Service *Bulletin*, Tables on 'External Trade' and Board of Trade, *Journal*,

TABLE XXII

CHANGES IN DISTRIBUTION OF INCOME IN THE U.K., 1938–57

Before and After Tax Shares (%)

	1938		1949		1954		1957	
	Before	After	Before	After	Before	After	Before	After
A. Shares of Income by Percentile Groups								
Top 1%	16·2	11·7	11·2	6·5	9·3	5·4	8·0	4·9
including 'benefits'	19·5	15·2	18·5	10·5	—	9·6	15·0	9·1
2nd–5th %	12·8	12·4	12·3	10·8	11·2	10·0	10·2	9·1
6th–10th %	9·0	9·3	9·5	9·6	9·5	9·7	9·8	9·5
11th–20th %	12·0	12·3	14·5	15·4	16·0	16·8	13·5	14·5
Top 20%	50·0	46·4	47·5	42·3	46·0	41·9	41·5	38·0
Remaining 80%	50·0	53·6	52·5	57·7	54·0	58·1	58·5	62·0
Total	100	100	100	100	100	100	100	100
Income After Tax in £m.		4,156		7,890		11,025		13,635
of which 'Benefits' in £m.		227		771		1,466		1,937
of which received by Top 1% in £m.		177		402		604		742
B. Source of Income								
Wages	37·8	⎱ 40	41·9	⎱ 50	42·6	47	42·9	—
Salaries	17·9	⎰	20·5	⎰	21·6		22·6	—
Other Employee Income	3·8	21	6·0	27	6·6	27	6·5	—
Total Employment	59·5	61	68·4	77	70·8	74	72·0	—
Professions	2·3	—	2·1	—	1·7	—	1·5	—
Farmers	1·4	—	3·2	—	2·7	—	2·4	—
Other Self-Employed	9·1	—	7·8	—	6·6	—	6·1	—
Total Self-Employment	12·8	⎱ 33	13·1	⎱ 15	11·0	⎱ 18	10·0	—
Rent, Dividend and Interest	22·3	⎰	11·4	⎰	11·1	⎰	11·1	—
Government Transfers	5·4	6	7·1	8	7·1	8	6·9	—
TOTAL	100	100	100	100	100	100	100	100

Notes: 'Benefits' = Effect of adding Life Assurance, Capital profits, Social Service, Indirect Taxes.

After Tax Shares in Sources of Income are not on the same basis as pre-tax shares and 1949 figures are in fact for 1950.

They are taken from Dudley Seers O.U. Bulletin of Statistics, February 1956.

Sources: H. F. Lydall, Royal Statistical Society, *Bulletin*, Part 1, 1959.

Dudley Seers, op. cit.

51

TABLE XXIII

ANNUAL MOVEMENTS IN REAL PRODUCT, CONSUMPTION, WAGES, PRICES AND PROFITS, 1948–61

(% changes over previous year)

	National Income					Profits			Manufacturing Industry			
	1	2	3	4	5	6	7	8	9	10	11	12
Year	Real Product	Real Consumption	Real Wage Bill	Money Wage Bill	Consumer Prices	All Companies	Quoted Companies	Top 100 Companies	Output P.M.Y.	Earnings Per Man	Labour Costs Per Unit	Wage Rates
1948	+4·8	−0·2	+5·6	+11·8	+8·0	—	—	—	—	—	—	+5·0
1949	+4·6	+3·1	+2·8	+5·9	+2·6	+2·0	+6·0	—	+5·0	+4·5	−1·0	+3·0
1950	+4·6	+2·7	+1·1	+4·2	+3·1	+15·0	+23·0	+26·0	+5·5	+4·0	−1·0	+1·5
1951	+2·3	−0·8	+1·0	+10·5	+8·0	+17·5	+19·5	+20·5	+2·0	+9·0	+8·0	+8·5
1952	−0·8	−0·3	−1·6	+7·2	+6·0	−12·0	−11·0	−9·0	−4·5	+8·5	+13·0	+9·0
1953	+4·9	+4·4	+2·5	+5·5	+1·7	+6·0	+11·5	+16·0	+4·5	+6·0	+1·0	+4·8
1954	+5·2	+4·5	+5·2	+7·0	+1·7	+11·0	+14·2		+7·0	+6·5	0	+4·0
1955	+3·8	+3·0	+5·1	+9·6	+3·4	+12·0	+8·0		+3·0	+7·5	+5·0	+7·0
1956	+0·3	+0·3	+3·0	+8·1	+4·5	+3·0	+4·6		−1·0	+8·5	+9·0	+7·8
1957	+1·6	+1·7	+1·7	+5·8	+3·1	+9·0	+6·0	average +14·5	+2·0	+6·0	+4·0	+5·0
1958	−0·5	+1·8	+1·0	+1·8	+2·8	−0·5	+2·0		0	+3·0	+3·0	+3·8
1959	+5·0	+4·0	+2·5	+3·0	0	+6·0	+13·5		+6·5	+3·5	−3·0	+3·0
1960	+4·0	+3·6	+6·0	+7·7	+1·5	+8·0	+10·0	—	+3·5	+7·0	+3·0	+2·5
1961	+2·0	+1·6	+2·1	+5·0	+2·8	−2·0	—	—	−1·0	+4·7	+5·5	+4·0

Sources and Notes:

Columns 1, 2, 4, 5, 6 from *National Income and Expenditure Blue Book*, except for 1961, which is taken from *Preliminary Estimates of National Income and Expenditure* plus London and Cambridge Economic Service, *Bulletin*.

Column 3 = Column 4 deflated by Retail Price Index.

Column 7 from 'Income and Finance of Quoted Companies, 1949–60', *Economic Trends*, April 1962.

Column 8 from N.I.E.S.R. *Classified List of Large Companies, 1949–53*, plus Board of Trade, *Company Assets and Income in 1957*.

Column 9 from N.I.E.S.R., *Economic Review*.

Column 10 from London and Cambridge Economic Service, *Bulletin*.

Column 11 = Column 10 ÷ Column 9.

Column 12 from London and Cambridge Economic Service, *Bulletin*.

TABLE XXIV

DISTRIBUTION OF WEST GERMAN NATIONAL PRODUCT, 1950-59

	Shares of National Product at Market Prices		
	1950	1954	1959
Private Consumption	64	59·5	58
Public Consumption	14·5	14	14
of which Defence	(4·5)	(3·8)	(3·2)
Gross Fixed Capital Formation	19	21	23
Changes in Stocks	3·8	2·2	1·1
Exports of Goods and Services	12	20	25
less Imports of Goods and Services	− 13·5	− 17	− 21·5
Total	100	100	100
G.N.P. at Market Prices (D.M. m.)	97,200	156,400	247,000
Subsidies	490	130	1,180
less Indirect Taxes	− 13,100	− 23,250	36,100
G.N.P. at factor cost	84,590	133,280	212,080
Net Income To/From Abroad	− 30	550	500
G N.P. Index (1954 Prices)	100	138	190

Source: O.E.E.C., *General Statistics*, (Paris, January 1961).

References

1. United Nations, *World Economic Survey, 1960*, New York, 1961, p. 135.
2. Ernest Bevin speaking as Foreign Secretary in the House of Commons, 21.2.46.
3. R. P. Dutt, *Daily Worker*, 7.1.60.
4. U.K. Government, Blue Book on *National Income and Expenditure for 1958*, Input-Output Tables.
5. U.K. Government, *Annual Abstract of Statistics for 1960*, H.M.S.O., 1961, Table 264.
6. Blue Book on *National Income and Expenditure for 1958*, Input-Output Tables.
7. United Nations, *Monthly Bulletin of Statistics*, New York, June 1960, Special Table 'A'.
8. U.K. Board of Trade, *Commonwealth and Sterling Area Statistical Abstract 1956*, H.M.S.O., 1957.
9. A. C. L. Day, article in *Lloyd's Bank Review*, July 1958.
10. G. F. Ray, 'British Imports of Manufactures', National Institute, *Economic Review*, May 1961.
11. R. P. Dutt, *Daily Worker* article.
12. A. C. L. Day, *Lloyd's Bank Review* article.
13. J. Strachey, *The End of Empire*, Chapter XVI.
14. Dudley Seers, 'Has the distribution of Income become more unequal?', *Bulletin of the Oxford University Institute of Statistics*, February 1956.
15. H. F. Lydall, 'The Long-Term Trend in Size Distribution of Income', *Journal of the Royal Statistical Society*, Part I, 1959.
16. J. B. Lansing and H. F. Lydall, 'An Anglo-American Comparison of Personal Saving', *Bulletin of the Oxford University Institute of Statistics*, August 1960.
17. Joan Robinson, *Introduction to the Theory of Employment*, Macmillan, 1956.
18. U.K. Government, Blue Book on *National Income and Expenditure, 1961*, H.M.S.O., 1962, Table 6.
19. ibid., Tables 1 and 4.
20. F. W. Paish, 'Saving and Investment in the United Kingdom', *London and Cambridge Economic Bulletin*, December 1957.
21. ibid., and Blue Book, op. cit.
22. F. W. Paish, 'Saving and Investment in the U.K.'
23. ibid.
24. S. Lilley, *Automation and Social Progress*, Lawrence and Wishart, 1957.
25. D. Burn, ed. *The Structure of British Industry*, Cambridge, 1958.

26. H. W. Richardson, 'New Industries between the Wars', *Oxford Economics Papers*, October 1961.
27. U.K. Government, *Annual Abstracts of Statistics, 1935–46* and *1956*, H.M.S.O., 1947 and 1957.
28. United Nations, Economic Commission for Europe, *Economic Survey of Europe since the War*, Geneva, 1953, Chapter X.
29. R. C. Tress and J. M. Fleming, 'Waiting for Exports', *London and Cambridge Economic Bulletin*, June 1962.
30. T. Balogh, 'The Economics of World Tension', *New Statesman and Nation*, 12.12.59.
31. Barclays Bank, *Chairman's Report*, January 1959.
32. British Employers' Federation, *Press Statement*, 15.9.54.
33. T. Balogh, op. cit.
34. A Schonfield, *British Economic Policy Since the War*, Penguin, 1958, especially Chapter 6.
35. Mr (as he then was) Heathcote Amory, as Chancellor of the Exchequer, in the House of Commons, 15.4.58.
36. quoted by *The Economist*, 3.2.62, p. 394.
37. A. Schonfield, op. cit., Chapter 9.
38. J. Spraos, 'Speculation, Arbitrage and Sterling', *Economic Journal*, March 1959.
39. Radcliffe Committee *Report on the Working of the Monetary System*, Para 425.
40. D. J. Robarts, *National Provincial Bank, Chairman's Report*, January 1959.
41. Symposium in the *Manchester School* on 'The Bank Rate Tribunal', January 1959; and M. Barratt Brown, 'The Controllers, I', *University and Left Review*, No. 5, Autumn 1958.
42. G. F. Ray, 'British Imports of Manufactures'.
43. U.K. Government, Blue Book on *National Income and Expenditure, 1958*, Input-Output Tables.
44. Letter to *The Times*, 15.11.57 and letter to *The Times*, 5.1.61, respectively.
45. Organisation for European Economic Co-operation (O.E.E.C.), *General Statistics*, Part I, Paris, January 1962, p. 54.
46. R. G. Opie, 'West Germany's Economic Miracle', *Three Banks Review*, March 1962.
47. O.E.E.C. *General Statistics*, op. cit., p. 2.
48. Political and Economic Planning, *Growth in the British Economy*, 1960, Chapter 9.
49. O.E.E.C., *General Statistics*, op. cit., pp. 2 and 45.
50. I. Svennilson, *Growth and Stagnation in the European Economy*, Table 67, p. 219.

51. P. Bareau, 'Economic Miracle in France', *Three Banks Review*, March 1961.
52. Political and Economic Planning, *Growth in the British Economy*, Chapter 9.
53. L. A. Dicks-Mireaux *et al.*, 'Prospects for the British Car Industry', National Institute *Economic Review*, September 1961.
54. M. Tracy, 'Agriculture and European Union', *Westminster Bank Review*, February 1961.
55. D. Jay, 'Common Market, The Real Choice', *New Statesman and Nation*, 25.5.62.
56. E. A. G. Robinson, 'The Cost of Agricultural Import Saving', *Three Banks Review*, December 1958.
57. *The Financial Times*, 'Record of Bids and Mergers', 25.7.61 and 20.1.62.
58. U.K. Government, *Annual Abstracts of Statistics, 1938–48* and *1961*.
59. 'Directory of Foreign Companies 1959', *Fortune*, August 1960. 1960.
60. R. Evelyn and I. M. D. Little, *Concentration in British Industry*, Cambridge, 1960 and National Institute of Economic and Social Research, *Classified List of Large Companies*, compared with Board of Trade, *Company Assets and Income in 1957*.
61. ibid.
62. J. P. Miller, *Competition, Cartels and their Regulation*, especially T. Wilson, 'Restrictive Practices', North Holland Publishing Company, Amsterdam, 1962.
63. R. F. Henderson, article in *Lloyd's Bank Review*, January 1959.
64. 'Income and Finance of Quoted Companies', *Economic Trends*, December 1960.
65. C. A. R. Crosland, *The Future of Socialism*, Cape, 1956, p. 68 ff.
66. M. Barratt Brown, 'The Controllers, I', Autumn 1958.
67. L. R. Klein, *et al.*, 'Savings and Finance of the Upper Income Classes', *Bulletin of the Oxford University Institute of Statistics*, November 1956.
68. R. Jenkins, 'The Thwarted Giant', *The Observer*, 1.4.62.
69. M. Barratt Brown, 'The Controllers, I', Autumn 1958.
70. ibid., Part III, Summer 1959.
71. Karl Marx, *Capital*, Vol. III, Chapter 13.
72. J. Jewkes, 'The Size of the Factory', *Economic Journal*, Vol. 62, 1952; and D. Schwartzman, 'Methodology of the Theory of Returns to Scale', *Oxford Economic Papers*, February 1958.
73. A. C. L. Day, 'The Economic Case for Joining the Common Market', *The Listener*, 19.10.62.
74. Sir John Campbell, *Report of the Chairman* of Booker, McConnel for the Year 1961.

75. C. Wilson, *The History of Unilever*, Book III.
76. J. H. Dunning, 'United States Overseas Investment and European Economic Integration', *National Provincial Bank Review*, May 1960.
77. U.K. Government, Blue Book on *National Income and Expenditure, 1961*, Table 57.
78. R. Southey, *Sir Thomas More, or Colloquies on the Progress and Prospects of Society*, London, 1831, Colloquy, No. 7, pp. 193–4.
79. see discussion by A. Schonfield, *British Economic Policy since the War*, p. 177 ff.; and comments by A. E. Jasay, 'The Social Choice between Home and Overseas Investment', *Economic Journal*, March 1960.
80. J. Strachey, *The End of Empire*, Chapters 6 and 7.
81. J. A. Hobson, *Imperialism*, Chapter 6.
82. V. I. Lenin, *Imperialism*, 1944 edition, Little Lenin Library, p. 54.

PART THREE

Towards an International Economy

CHAPTER 10

The World Trade Blocs

We have now to consider the future of the world economy and the future of capitalism in particular. In these next three chapters, we shall examine the prospects for development of the new relationships between the chief industrially advanced countries and the underdeveloped lands, and not only between Britain and her one-time empire, with which we have been chiefly concerned so far. At the same time, we shall have to look at developments in the communist third of the world.

The essence of the unplanned relationships of capitalism is ambivalence similar to what the psychologists now call a love-hate relationship. Exploitation, the attempt to win by superior bargaining strength an ever-larger share of the value of what is produced, is in the long run a largely self-defeating process. The worker without capital can only live by offering his labour power to some owner or manager of capital, and must suffer exploitation in the process or drive his employer out of business. The capitalist can only live by exploiting labour, but must keep his workers' earnings up or they will be unable to buy his products. The merchant cannot fleece without limit the producers of one lot of goods, to whom he also hopes to sell another lot. The result is that individuals may hope to benefit from the process of buying cheap to sell dear; but in doing so they impoverish whole communities.

Capitalism has two faces: the accumulation of capital in a few hands encourages growth and technical progress; the accumulation of hands without capital encourages poverty and decay. The story of Mr Walter Reuther, President of the Auto-Workers Union of America, and Mr Henry Ford, jun. touring the automated workshops of Ford's latest factory is instructive. 'Look at those machines,' says Mr Ford, 'they can't go on strike!' 'No!' says Mr Reuther, 'neither can they buy motor-cars.'[1] Modern technology requires not only the planning of processes of production but also of the relations of production and consumption.

The aspect of this problem which concerns us is the relationship involved in capitalist foreign trade. We have seen example after example, over the years since Britain became industrialised, of attempts to hold back development among primary producers. The opening-up of markets to free trade in the first place, the high rates of profit obtained by exploitation of cheap labour, the establishment of one-crop and one-mineral economies with enclaves of development oriented towards the metropolitan market, the retention of refining and processing factories outside the lands of primary production, the vertical-integration of plantations or mines with manufacturing combines – these have all been attempts to exploit the unequal relationship in the terms of trade once established between advanced and underdeveloped lands.

Nevertheless, we have always had to conclude that these attempts, though they brought high profits to a few and though they undoubtedly succeeded in holding back economic development among primary producers, were not the cause of Britain's prosperity – at least since the early years of the nineteenth century. This wealth was the result rather of rising productivity in industry and of an expanding market overseas. But again, after the first important days of the opening-up of India and China and South America, markets were expanded not as the result of holding back the economic development of primary producers but rather of encouraging it. Britain's economic advance, one may almost say, was saved from the worst effects of capitalism by the economic development of the lands of European settlement.

For these lands could not be so easily exploited: they soon won Dominion in place of colonial status; they had no problem of native populations to be ruled and, therefore, no need to retain outmoded social classes in the interests of indirect rule; they could thus expand their agricultural output without fetters; investors from the home country were prepared to lend them money at fixed interest and often to lose it; the European settlers were fortunate enough to find lands and climates suitable for crops that were in world demand; they could impose their own tariffs to protect their infant industries and thus carry through industrialisation out of the earnings from their sales of primary products.

Today this process is nearly completed and Britain's trade which has benefited so much from it is stagnant. The question now is whether capitalist methods can carry through the industrialisation of the other underdeveloped lands, which the whole process so far has neglected. Can the systems of trade established between industrial and primary producers permit such a development? Can capitalism do the job inside the heavily populated lands that remain underdeveloped? Can the tendency of capitalism to grow by jerks, with intermittent checks to growth which have such harmful side-effects on primary producers, be corrected by international action? The last two questions will be the subject of the next and last chapters.

In this chapter, we have to decide how far it is inevitable that capitalism should concentrate wealth rather than diffuse it and that capital should always be attracted to existing wealth and repelled from existing poverty, so that, in the vicious spirals of enrichment in the rich lands and impoverishment in the poor, the two grow ever further apart.[2] For purposes of comparison, we must also examine what is the basis of the rapid expansion of trade inside the communist countries of the world and how far their methods may be applied in the uncommitted, but underdeveloped, lands elsewhere.

Table XXV below illustrates the close interdependence of world production and trade in manufactures and the earnings of primary producers. As a great trading nation, Britain is peculiarly dependent on the growth of world trade as well as on her share in the total. For more than 150 years, Britain's main markets have been in lands in process of development and, in view of the present stagnation of this trade, the problem would seem now to be to decide what may be done to help the still undeveloped lands to develop, as we once helped the lands of European settlement. But, first, we need to consider an alternative conclusion from the facts: viz. that, as the trade of the industrialised lands has been growing faster than that of the underdeveloped lands, it is in the existing industrial lands of North America and western Europe that Britain's exporters should look for new markets. British exports are said to be too heavily concentrated on non-industrialised lands; two-thirds of our exports are directed to such lands, whereas only a half of United States exports and only a third of West German exports go that way.[3] The conclusion for Britain, it is argued, should therefore be to turn even more towards the already industrialised lands rather than to help other lands to industrialise.

The Trade of the Industrialised and Non-Industrialised Lands

Trade with the underdeveloped lands, according to this argument, is a luxury we simply cannot afford and which, in any case, is not required of us. The basis of the argument, which is pressed particularly strongly by supporters of Britain's entry into the Common Market,[4] is that the industrialisation of underdeveloped lands is tending to reduce rather than to increase their trade with the industrialised lands of Europe and North America, and to give more importance to their trade with the new semi-industrialised neighbouring lands. These semi-industrialised lands are said to have replaced their exports of primary products to the industrialised lands by exports of manufactures to their neighbours who are at a lower stage of development. The view is taken that this tendency for trade to grow among the less-industrialised lands will increase. The conclusion follows that the more industrialised lands must concentrate on their exchanges with each other of the specialised products of their more advanced industries.[5] It will be suggested here that this is a specious argument designed in fact to restrict the present non-industrialised lands to primary production.

We must get the facts straight. First, it is true that exports of primary products from the semi-industrialised lands to the industrialised have been dropping sharply as a proportion of world trade (Table XXVII–A below); but it is not true that this has been more than very slightly compensated for by exports of manufactures to their neighbours. The fall in their share of world exports has been an all-round one, as we can see from Table XXVII–A. They may have been using more of their primary products for their own consumption and have failed to expand their output, particularly of agricultural produce, or they may have been losing markets for their primary produce; but they have not yet been able to turn to any great extent from export of primary products to export of manufactures. We have to note which countries are included in the Table, as being semi-industrialised. They are Argentina, Brazil, Mexico, Australia, India, South Africa, Finland, Yugoslavia. They account for some 80 per cent of manufacturing activity outside the more advanced industrial areas; but, apart from Australia and South Africa, and very recently the two smallest countries of Finland and Yugoslavia, they can barely be termed even semi-industrialised yet.

India, Argentina and Brazil have suffered especially severely since the war from the nature of the products they have to offer on the world market, viz. food and agricultural raw materials, which the industrialised lands have increasingly been supplying or substituting from their own resources. One has only to list the countries to realise that they cannot possibly be expected to supply the manufactured requirements of the non-industrialised lands. They may well be able to develop exchanges of manufactures among themselves and take advantage of intra-regional division of labour. There are especially big opportunities for developing intra-regional trade in food and raw materials. Many of the smaller countries, moreover, could not hope to provide on their own a home market large enough for all-round industrial production. Economies of scale may be obtained by co-ordinating plans, which are already in hand for developing production of fertilisers, textiles, pulp and paper, cement, steel and some of the less advanced industrial goods.[6] Such economies are the justification for existing proposals for Common Markets in South America, Africa and South-East Asia.[7] After all this has been said, these regions will remain among the most important markets for industrial products and particularly for capital goods from the fully industrialised lands. The growth of this trade has simply been held back by the difficulties of the underdeveloped lands in earning the wherewithal to buy the goods they need.

Second, it is of crucial importance to note that the falling share of the non-industrialised lands in world exports is not simply due to a decline in the importance of primary products in world trade. Such a decline certainly occurred in the years up to 1954, as a result of increasing home food-production and substitution of synthetic for natural materials inside each of the industrialised lands. Since 1954, however, the volume of world trade in primary products has been growing as fast as the volume of trade in manufactures (see Table XXV). But falling prices for primary products (Table XXV) have reduced the share of primary products in world trade – from 54 per cent to 47 per cent (Table XXVII–B).

At the same time, something else has happened, even more

devastating for the non-industrialised lands, which depend on exports of primary products. Each of the industrialised lands has gone beyond meeting its own needs for food and materials to meeting increasingly the needs of others. As a result, the share of the non-industrialised lands in the world trade in primary products themselves has been declining – from 58 per cent to 51 per cent between 1953 and 1960. This has been due mainly to their losses in trade in food and agricultural materials; they have held on to their position better in metal ores and fuels (Table XXVII-B).

This leads us to consider the third group of facts about the size of the trade of the non-industrialised lands and to consider just how large a market for industrial goods they now provide. While it is true that the non-industrialised lands, as a whole, have been falling behind the industrialised in the volume of exports they have been putting on the world market; it is not true so far that as importers they have also been falling behind (see Table XXVII-A, last two columns). The difference between their declining exports and rising imports has increasingly been made up by loans and aid, to the extent of some $3 billion to $4 billion a year (see Table XXIII), and by drawing on reserves. After 1958, however, their reserves were being rapidly used up.

How big, then, is the market in the non-industrialised lands, and we may include here the semi-industrialised lands in the capitalist world and the whole bloc of lands under communist rule? Some of the latter, and particularly the Soviet Union, are approaching full industrialisation, but their standards of living are still well below those in the main industrial lands under capitalism. It is one of the weaknesses of much writing on this subject that world trade is generally spoken of as if the communist countries simply did not exist. This has been the result of the non-availability of statistics from the U.S.S.R. and China; but, now that this gap is being filled, there is little excuse for continuing to exclude the communist share in international trade and the U.N. statisticians

z

are to be congratulated on their efforts to be all-embracing in their reports.[8]

Table XXVII-A gives us the picture of the main flows of world trade over the years. In the late 1920s, the non-industrialised lands exported 40 per cent and took 36 per cent of the goods entering world trade; during the 1930s, although they increased the volume of their exports, their earnings hardly rose; this was because of the poor prices they received for their primary products, and they ended the period still with only 37 per cent of the world's imports. With better prices received during and after the Second World War, they raised their share of exports by 1954 to 45 per cent and of imports to 43 per cent. There was a sharp decline in their share of exports following the fall in earnings in 1954, but the use of aid and credits and reserves raised their share of imports to 43 per cent again in 1958. Since then it has been falling once more. Now this proportion is a sizeable share of the world market, and it is extremely important to note that the period when it grew most was the period of the most rapid expansion of world trade as a whole.

Table XXIX below distinguishes three periods since the war in the growth of the world's trade. There was the immediate and rapid recovery from very low war-time levels of trade, the pre-war volume being regained in 1948; there followed five years of further rapid growth (with an annual average growth rate of 7.5 per cent) up to 1953; then five years of somewhat less rapid growth (with a growth rate of 5 per cent per annum) up to 1958; and now we are in a new period which may, or may not, show more rapid growth.

We have already, in the previous chapter, noted the check to growth around 1953–55, and we attributed it in large part to the world-wide adoption of deflationary policies by the industrial powers. When industrial growth was checked, the demand for primary products declined. As after the First World War, so after 1945, primary production capacity grew in anticipation of growing industrial demand. Shortages pushed up prices, especially in the stockpiling boom that followed the outbreak of the Korean War. Then the combined effects of increased food production in the advanced industrial lands, of their growing use of substitute materials and of the deflationary measures brought the prices tumbling. Table XXV below shows what happened. Even if we exclude 1951 as an exceptional year, the terms of trade had improved for primary producers during the war and post-war years by between 30 per cent and 40 per cent. At least half of this gain was lost in the five years after 1955.

Some lands suffered more than others, both in the period up to 1954 when trade in primary products was growing more slowly than that in manufactures, and in the period after 1954 when the volume of trade was growing in line with that in manufactures but prices were falling. This varied experience of different lands was the result of varied movements in output and price for different commodities. Table XXVI below shows that, while in the first period output of bauxite, iron-ore, zinc, petroleum and jute, tea and cocoa were all well ahead of manufacturing output, in the second period only petrol of these commodities kept ahead of manufactures, but was joined by rice and coffee while iron-ore and bauxite just managed to keep in line. In the matter of prices the differences were greater. In the first period, only wheat, rice, oil-seeds, butter, zinc, cotton, wood-pulp and jute failed to keep up with manufactured goods' prices, while in the second period only rubber actually kept up although zinc, tin and coal almost kept up. The big price falls in the second period were in the beverages, especially in cocoa and coffee, in wool and, once more, in cotton. This varied experience reflects the wide variations in industrial output. Petrol and chemicals have been the main growth industries since the war; metal products grew rapidly up to 1954 but less rapidly thereafter; while textiles have been falling behind, although clothing and footwear staged something of a recovery after 1954.[9]

Thus, with the exception of the oil-producing lands and certain metal producers, the experience of a slowing-down in the rate of growth of output and of an actual fall in prices has led to a sharp decline in earnings by non-industrialised lands relying on sales of primary products. They have then had to cut back their purchases from the industrialised lands. This, in its turn, has tended to reduce activity in the export trades of the industrial lands, in Britain particularly, and to set off a whole vicious circle of declining demand such as we have seen before. But the decline in primary producers' earnings had further repercussions. Higher earnings in the post-war years had encouraged the beginnings of economic development; industrialisation programmes were embarked upon. The check to earnings brought all these plans into jeopardy.[10] The momentum which had given new pace to the growth of world trade began to run down, and only heavy drawings on reserves and on foreign aid were enabling the flow of capital equipment into the underdeveloped lands to be maintained.

Up to 1960, the underdeveloped lands were raising their industrial output at the same rate as the developed lands, despite the decline in their trade, but the future was more uncertain. Projections of demand for primary products in the 1960s do not suggest a growth rate of imports from underdeveloped into developed lands of much more than 2 per cent per year.[11] That would be quite inadequate for maintaining industrialisation programmes in the under-developed lands on the basis of their primary-product sales. This is evidently of extreme seriousness for them, but we need to consider the implications also for the industrialised lands, who have been expanding their trade among themselves, and particularly the implications for Britain.

The point that we need to notice is that the rapid expansion of trade among the industrialised lands themselves in the years after 1955 was not enough to keep up the rate of growth established in the earlier period when the primary producers were doing well. This is but one more example of the principle we have been establishing throughout this book, that terms of trade that are unfavourable to primary producers are not necessarily, therefore, favourable to their industrial trading-partners. Unless there are now apparent new forces of growth inside the industrialised lands that would lead to a rapid expansion of world trade as a whole, in which Britain could take part, the conclusion must be that Britain should seek ways of developing the non-industrialised lands. This is precisely the question raised by the apparently strong growth of the six countries in the Common Market. We must turn, then, to examine the nature of the recent growth in the trade of the already industrialised lands.

The Rise of Trade Blocs

Rates of growth of exports have varied considerably between one industrial land and another as well as between them and the non-industrialised lands. We noticed earlier how different also has been the trade experience of the various non-industrial lands, the rapid growth of the trade of petroleum and minerals exporters contrasting with the slow growth of those who had only food and agricultural materials to sell. The differences among the industrial lands have partly been differences in the period of growth (see Table XXIX). Before 1948, the most rapid growth was in the trade of the U.S.A. and of Canada, and particularly in trade with each other, which more than doubled in a decade.[12] The next forward jump was that of Britain in the years up to 1950. After that West Germany took up the running and succeeded in trebling her exports over pre-war levels in eight years. Most recently, Japan, in 1959, at length surpassed her pre-war level of exports, after doubling their volume in five years. These separate leaps forward in different countries suggest that in each there were special pressures which, after a time, worked themselves out. In looking for a reason, we shall need to examine also the steady and extremely rapid expansion of the trade of the Soviet Union over the whole period since the war.

The most remarkable feature of these varied surges of growth in the trade of the industrialised lands is that they have taken place in every case inside a trading bloc of countries especially associated with one of the most advanced industrial powers. We can see this in Table XXVIII below. Thus, the main growth of United States trade was inside the Dollar Area, Britain expanded inside the Sterling Area, West Germany inside what is now the Common Market, the Soviet Union inside the communist bloc and, finally, Japan has been doing her best with what is left. As a result, the proportion of the world's trade carried on inside these great trading blocs has risen from little more than a third before the war, taking the countries that are now inside blocs together, to more than a half today, and the trade between the blocs has correspondingly declined. This calculation assumes that the countries which are not in the Dollar, the Sterling or the Rouble Areas, nor members of the European Six or Seven, make up a bloc of their own, a sort of Asian-South American bloc of uncommitted lands, though this, of course, they do not do in any strict sense. But even if we exclude these countries, half the world's trade is carried on today inside the four main groups: Dollar, Sterling and the Seven, Rouble, and the Common Market.

What has happened is not only that trade has become concentrated inside the blocs, but that the countries outside the blocs have simply not kept up with the rate of growth inside. This has applied especially to the larger of these 'uncommitted lands' – to Argentina, Brazil, Indonesia and Egypt, and to Japan herself, whose exporters have been giving much attention precisely to the markets of these lands. Smaller 'uncommitted' lands, and especially, of course, the oil-bearing lands of the Middle East, have done better.

The two biggest concentrations of trade inside blocs have

taken place inside the Dollar and the Rouble Areas. The share of the world's trade carried on inside the Dollar Area doubled between 1938 and 1948 to account for about a third of the world total, and much of this growth has been maintained. Trade between member countries of the Rouble Area barely existed before the war; today it amounts to about 9 per cent of the total of world trade.[13] By contrast, the growth in the share of trade carried on inside western Europe has, in fact, contrary to general opinion, been small compared with before the war. There has actually been a decline from 12 per cent to 8 per cent in the share of world trade carried on inside the Sterling Area; the Sterling countries' trade was already highly concentrated inside the Area before the Second World War (see Table XXVIII).

What conclusions are we to draw from this compartmentalising of world trade into great trading blocs? First, the exclusive nature of the blocs was bound to lead to some reduction in the trade of those countries excluded and, since the blocs have been built up around the major industrial powers, those excluded were bound to be non-industrialised lands. But there is a second point: it would be surprising if the process had not involved some measure of economic dependence for the non-industrialised members of each bloc; and such dependence, we have seen, has never tended to encourage economic development in the dependent countries, but has rather tended to retain their character as primary producers. Thirdly, there is the effect of the dividing-up of the newly liberated colonies into different blocs. This is most obvious in the case of Africa, where many small territories are divided between the Common Market, the Sterling Area and the 'uncommitted remainder'.

Further study of the working of the blocs may suggest that the only way for the small primary producing countries to strengthen their bargaining power in a world of giants may be for them to establish their own common markets, for example for the whole of Africa, for southern America or for

South-East Asia. We must look at the blocs more closely.

The Sterling Area

We have already examined the nature of the relationships between Britain and the rest of the Sterling Area and here need only develop some of the points that were made earlier. The Area consists of one advanced industrial land and several lands of British settlement, which are fairly well advanced in industrialisation, thanks to British investment – Australia, New Zealand, South Africa and Rhodesia – and a large number of primary producing lands, whose economic development has been very slow, viz. India, Pakistan, Burma, Ceylon, Malaya, West and East Africa, the oil states and the many smaller colonies. The pattern of trade has been the supply of primary products by the overseas territories and of manufactures by Great Britain, with a large proportion of capital equipment in the exports to the developing lands of British settlement. Trade among the Sterling Area members, other than the flow between Britain and the rest, has been small and has shown little sign of growing.[14]

The share of Britain's trade concentrated inside the Sterling Area rose in the post-war years from a pre-war figure of about 35 per cent (30 per cent for imports; 40 per cent for exports) to nearly 50 per cent (only slightly more for exports than for imports). A similar concentration had always been maintained by the other member countries.[15] With 1954 came the peak year; after that the importance of the Area for Britain declined (to a figure of about 33 per cent for imports and 39 per cent for exports in 1961, see Table VI, Chapter 3). This was the result of the more rapid expansion of markets in North America and in Europe. The same process affected the overseas countries. The importance of the Sterling Area declined. But the Area as a whole, and Britain in particular, remain the most important but no longer the major market for the other Area members.[16] The causes of the continued concentration of trade are more easily found than the causes of the declining degree of concentration. They consist partly in Imperial Preference, partly in the ties of traditional markets and partly in the ties of Britain's investment in her one-time Empire.

We may take these reasons one by one. First, Imperial Preference continues to be granted by Commonwealth countries to each other's goods, but its primary importance was and remains in the encouragement of trade between Britain and the older dominions, that is, the lands of British settlement, including Canada. After the war, the method of its operation came to give rather more protection to British goods entering overseas markets than to overseas goods entering British markets; but Britain has made a number of concessions of recent years which have done something to correct this unequal development.[17] The main advantage to the Commonwealth countries is, of course, the open door to their foodstuffs and raw materials. Britain has continued to import half her foodstuffs and to rely on natural materials for two-thirds of her raw material requirements. Less than 4 per cent of Britain's occupied population is engaged in agriculture. This is in strong contrast to the increasing self-sufficiency in materials and foodstuffs of the Common Market countries, with 25 per cent to 30 per cent of their population in farming.

At the same time, Imperial Preference has undoubtedly given to British exporters quite definite advantages in the Commonwealth. These advantages are all now challenged by the prospect of Britain's association with the Common Market and we must note the probable effect of this challenge. As long as British goods were competitive elsewhere, there was no reason to suppose that the arrangement harmed either Britain or the ex-colonies; but many British exports are manifestly not competitive in other markets. We saw earlier (Chapter 7) how British exports were already being driven out of Sterling Area markets, as much as out of other markets where German and United States goods suffered from no preferential margins in competition with British. The overseas Commonwealth countries have thus been receiving an inferior or expensive product, while British exporters have been feather-bedded and have thus failed to take the necessary steps to make their goods in fact competitive in other markets.

The protection given by Imperial Preference was very much reinforced by ties of tradition, the most important of which were the traditional arrangements for marketing imperial products through British agents and the London commodity markets, or directly through the great vertically-integrated combines such as the oil companies and Unilever or the tobacco and sugar companies. Many ex-colonies have sought to bring their foreign trade into the hands of their own nationals, but the main effect of legislation to this end has been to force British companies operating overseas to register themselves in the lands where they operate. This at least brings them within the bounds of local taxation; the drawbacks for the ex-colonies of having their sales tied to a single firm or market remain.

The prospect of Britain's joining the Common Market brings out the dilemma of overseas producers specialising in production for the British market. The outstanding example is New Zealand's producers of butter, cheese and lamb. On the one hand, Imperial Preference assures them of a privileged market, which Britain's entry into the Common Market can be expected to terminate; on the other hand, the opening of other European markets to their produce would be of benefit in reducing their dependence on British demand. The main objection of the overseas Commonwealth countries to Britain's entry into the Common Market is, as we shall see, precisely that the market will not be opened to their agricultural products on equal terms with the European producers. While the market for industrial products inside the Economic Community will be free, the agricultural market is to be managed by regulating prices as well as by imposing tariffs and import levies on imports from outside.

The working of free trade inside an area like the Sterling Area is of vital importance. Britain's open market to overseas primary products undoubtedly benefited overseas producers, especially of foodstuffs, as well as benefiting Britain. But, in the case of the colonies, the *quid pro quo* was open markets to Britain's industrial products; and this, as we have emphasised before, inevitably held back economic development in the colonies. The most important result of colonial liberation is that with political freedom has come the right to impose tariffs, quotas and import controls in order to protect infant native industries. Even where this protection may be overcome by the establishment of firms from the metropolitan countries inside the ex-colonies themselves, this very diversification of output nevertheless does much to strengthen the bargaining position of the lands of primary production.

The manner of disposal of their products remains of vital importance for the primary producers' terms of trade. This has been our finding throughout this book; and here, while the farmers of dependent or recently dependent lands are in a weaker bargaining position than those in the older dominions, all may suffer from the workings of the market for their output. We need, therefore, to consider this closely. Where there are many sellers and only one buyer or a ring of buyers, it is possible for prices to be kept artificially low and for other forms of economic pressure to be applied by the buyer. Where buyers compete with each other, but in a single market, there may still be disadvantages for the sellers in being tied to the general price movements of a single market. Quite small movements in relative supply and demand may lead to very large swings in price. Since 1951, it has been really very small margins of excess of supply over demand that have led to the very heavy falls in the price of primary commodities.[18] The ending after 1951 of the Labour

Government's bulk purchase agreements and the re-establishment of the London commodity markets pushed many primary producers back into the uncertainty and low prices which marked the 1930s. And these tendencies were reinforced by the deflationary policies pursued by British Governments after 1954.

These drawbacks suffered by primary producers might not have been so serious for the less-developed lands, had the high level of investment by Britain in the Sterling Area since the war led to a generally high level of economic growth throughout the Area. We have already seen, however, that most of the investment has gone to the more-developed lands. Indeed for many years the Sterling Area financial arrangements were seen to have been drawing capital by way of the Sterling Balances *from* the less-developed lands *to* Britain and the other more-developed lands of the Area. Although this process ended for the most part in 1955, we suggested earlier that the hangover of British banking and of the interests of the great imperial companies in the ex-colonies was continuing to limit economic freedom and economic growth and perpetuate the concentration of wealth in the already richer lands.

The nature of post-war private company investment still leaves the matter in doubt, even in India, as to how far and how fast industrialisation is to spread beyond the lands of Europe and of European settlement to the other primary producing lands of the world. And in so far as industrialisation fails to spread, the trade of the world as a whole will fail to grow. The initial spurts of growth inside each of the protected blocs will work themselves out and decline will set in as it has in the Sterling Area. Further consideration of the effects of the recent increase in British investment in the less-developed lands must be left over to the next chapter. But we should now be clear about the causes of the failure of Sterling Area trade growth.

Nevertheless, the positive aspect of Sterling Area trade must

not be overlooked. Britain does provide a duty-free market
for Commonwealth foodstuffs and raw materials. Moreover, in one new feature of Commonwealth trade, Britain's
role has been progressive and this shows the importance of
the multi-racial and mixed grouping of rich and poor nations
that make up the Commonwealth today. This new feature
is the admission free of duty or on preferential terms of semi-
processed and processed materials – canned food, vegetable
oils, leather products, newsprint, aluminium – and of conventional manufactures, particularly cotton textiles, into the
British home market. Despite the gentlemen's agreements
to limit these last imports by quota, the British market has
enabled many new industries to be built up in the less-
developed as well as the more-developed Commonwealth
countries.

It is, however, just these flows of trade that will be most
hard-hit by Britain's entry into the Common Market. To
take but one example, whereas all Indian exports enter the
U.K. at present free of duty, all but 10 per cent are subject to
tariffs and taxes in the Common Market. The result already
is the serious unbalance of India's present trade with the Six.
The blow to Indian trade, a quarter of which is with the
U.K., and thus to Indian economic development, of Britain's
entering the Common Market cannot be exaggerated. But
the blow will fall upon us too; for if India is prevented from
selling her goods to us, she will by the same token be unable
to buy our goods. An inward-looking Europe will create an
inward-looking India and the whole level of world trade
exchanges will be reduced.

The tendency to concentrate trade and investment among
the richer lands, and retain other lands in the role of primary
producers has been even more a feature of the Common
Market and Dollar Area than it has been of the Sterling
Area. Let us now turn to these other great trading blocs.

The Dollar Area

The immensely rich raw-material resources of the western hemisphere had largely been developed in the nineteenth century by British capital, but, during the Second World War, the United States capital investment rose to some $6,000 million in Canada and to the same figure in Latin America, or about four times the British capital holding in each.[19] The process had begun before the war in Canada and, after 1934, in Latin America with the inauguration of President Roosevelt's 'Good Neighbour' policy.[20] The reciprocal trade agreements then signed became the basis for establishing the Dollar Area. The movement of trade was freed, so that the Latin American republics, including U.S. companies operating there, secured a market for their rich endowment of primary products – sugar, coffee, fruit, copper, tin, petroleum – while United States industrialists secured markets for their manufactures.

The essence of the agreements was reciprocal freedom of the movement of goods and capital. On the face of it, this seems to be a liberal concept, but we have seen enough of the effects of British free trade in the Empire and the Sterling Area in freezing the division of labour between industrial and primary producers, to know that such free trade is only equitable among equals. Where one party to the agreement is a powerful industrial country and the other a poor under-developed land, the result is to encourage the development of the rich and hold back the development of the poor.

The effect of the agreements was, thus, to freeze the Latin American economies as primary producers, mainly of one crop or mineral, for the American market, and to hold back the development of local industry. The outbreak of war concentrated trade more than ever on the United States; but, as shipping difficulties increased, Latin American industry was given the chance to develop to replace U.S. imports. A steel plant in Brazil even began to produce a million tons of steel a year, and industrial output in Latin America rose by nearly a half during the war years.[21]

After the war, the pre-war pattern of trade was re-established by the Clayton Plan, which was presented to the 1945 Conference of American Republics as an Economic Charter for 'free trade', 'free investment', 'free enterprise'. *Fortune* magazine commented, 'The South American market must be closed; it must become an exclusive United States trade area.'[22] Local industry was once more checked. United States investment grew – in fruit, sugar and coffee in Central America, in minerals in South America and especially in Venezuelan oil. Only in Canada was there investment on a large scale in industry as well as in minerals and other primary products.[23]

The currencies of the whole hemisphere, with the exception of the southern lands of Argentina, Brazil, Peru, Chile and the few scattered British possessions in the Caribbean, were tied to the dollar. Between two-thirds and three-quarters of the trade of these Dollar Area countries became directed towards the U.S.A., instead of a third as it had been before the war (see Table XXVIII). When primary product prices began to decline, the Latin American countries were particularly badly hit.[24] Although in some cases, Cuban sugar for example, the U.S. Government offered special prices above world levels for her imports, in order to protect home farmers, in other cases, Philippine pineapples for example, the growers simply found the American market closed to them.[25] Yet the income on United States investments had still to be paid.

The contrast of the wealth of Latin American resources and the poverty, illiteracy and backwardness of the peoples could hardly be greater. What was most serious for the economic development of Latin America, more important even than poor prices or high rates of return on investment or dependence on a single market, was the lack of freedom to raise tariffs, and protect and encourage the development of local industry. South American governments had political freedom; what mattered, however, was the type of government maintained in power by United States influence backed by the United States Marines and United States loans. 'Thirty-one times in this century has the United States sent its troops into one or other of the republics of Central America.' This was the opening sentence of *The Times* New York correspondent's appraisal of the problems raised by the failure of intervention in Cuba some weeks earlier and the assassination of the dictator, Trujillo, in Quisqueya shortly afterwards.[26]

Latin American governments could, and sometimes did, impose tariffs on imports, even on U.S. imports, to protect the growth of local industries, but what happened? No local entrepreneurial class existed to take advantage of the opportunity. The ruling class was a combination of feudal land-owners and merchants engaged in trade with the U.S.A. What would one expect? Luxury industries were established and local building encouraged. Magnificent flats were built for the government ministers and their relations and for the local merchants and 'compradors' associated with the export crop.[27]

Often the manufacturing and building firms established were United States subsidiaries. Development was lopsided. Essential public services actually fell into disrepair and practically no advance was made in building up basic industries. A World Bank mission to Nicaragua commented, 'If 10 per cent of the incomes of the upper 1 per cent of income recipients were to be invested productively, the current productive investment rate would increase by 50 per cent.'[28] Yet Latin American countries which attempted to develop their own industries have been penalised when they nationalised a local industry, as was the case with the oil industry in Mexico, by being starved of United States capital; what was worse, Mexican oil, like Persian oil later, was boycotted from American markets under United States influence.[29] Most serious, the United States support for landowning ruling groups has meant that agricultural output has been held back by the perpetuation of conditions of virtual serfdom on the great estates. Once more this is where the internal and external restraints on economic development meet – at the point where a backward economic class is maintained in power over a backward economy.

We may test the matter at once by reference to the position of Cuba in the summer of 1960. Not for just over fifty years had Cuba been under direct sovereignty of the United States. Seven hundred million dollars of United States capital was, however, invested in the island; most of the plantations and many of the factories, refineries and other industrial and commercial enterprises were owned by United States citizens.[30] Governments of Cuba had for fifty years been freely made and unmade by the will of the United States. The last before the revolution of Dr Castro, that of Fulgencio Batista, had not been more than usually corrupt but had suspended all constitutional guarantees, dissolved all political parties and executed hundreds of workers while arresting thousands more. Cuba's economy was concentrated, as it had been as a Spanish colony, on producing one major crop, sugar, and one minor crop, tobacco. The United States was the main market for both, and supplied three-quarters of Cuba's imports.[31] Capital and goods moved freely between the two countries; the Cuban peso was tied to the U.S. dollar.

Any government, such as Dr Castro's, which wished to raise the standard of living of the people and develop the economy, would have to win enough economic as well as political independence at least to raise the rate of taxation, and control the direction of investment. For the profits made on the sale of Cuba's products mostly flowed out of the country to United States investors, and investment was limited to the export crops. The first step to economic independence would be to find an alternative market for part of the sugar crop and this would mean in exchange increasing Cuba's imports from outside the U.S.A. For the first time, there was, in the late 1950s in the communist countries, an alternative market and an alternative supplier to those of the capitalist countries. The United States Government, in refusing to buy any of Cuba's sugar, and the U.S. oil companies, in refusing to have their refineries refine any oil but their oil, were attempting to exploit to the full the unequal economic relations between themselves and Cuba.[32]

It is not even as if the United States' own home market for imported food and raw materials had been a rapidly expanding one. While U.S. exports had risen three-fold in volume between 1938 and 1957, imports had only risen half as much.[33] As a share of the U.S. national income, imports had remained between 4 per cent and 5 per cent.[34] At one time, in the 1952 'Paley Report', it was estimated that U.S. imports of many raw materials would have to rise rapidly in the next twenty-five years.[35] Halfway through that period, it seemed that, although U.S. output had risen faster than was projected, consumption of materials, with the outstanding exception of aluminium, had risen hardly at all.[36] In some items there had been an actual decline, which is only what our study of British industry would have led us to expect.

On top of this, it must be said that, for an advanced industrial country, the United States has been most reluctant to open its markets to foreign goods. The opening up of the market to foreign motors is well known to all, but the closing of the market to foreign bicycles, textiles, watches and many kinds of foodstuffs is in strong contrast to the free-trade position adopted by Britain when she was the world's dominant economic power.[37] It is not only that tariffs are often high, but all kinds of escape clauses, 'peril points', 'Buy American' Acts and just sheer technical complication in customs formalities surround the United States market.[38] There seems to be no sign at all of the realisation of a

U.S. Commerce Department forecast of 1946 that 'the need to change over from an economy supporting an excess of exports to one supporting an excess of imports will probably come between 1955 and 1960'.[39]

Foreign Investment of United States Capital

Every year since the war there has been a difference of several billion dollars between U.S. exports and imports (Table XXX below). This has been covered by military and economic aid, by overseas expenditure of United States forces and by private investment. Until 1956, it was only inside the Dollar Area that the flow of private capital played any great part in balancing United States foreign payments.[40] Reinvestment of profits and some new investment have been especially important in balancing the surplus of U.S. exports in trade with Canada. As a result, a third of United States foreign investment is now in Canada (Table XXX).

Canada has become the one land to be industrialised with United States capital, but with the result that at least a third of Canada's industry is now owned by United States companies.[41] With many countries in the world, however, the United States established after the war what is sometimes called a 'mature creditor' position; that is to say that income from old investments exceeded both new investment and reinvestment of profits taken together.[42] This was an additional cause of the world's dollar shortage and of the steady flow of gold and other assets to the United States up to 1956.

Since 1956, the situation has radically altered. The dollar-gap has continued to be bridged by aid and military expenditures, but in addition the outward flow of private capital, long-term and short-term, became so great as to cause a steady outward movement from the U.S. of gold and similar assets, amounting to over two billion dollars in 1958 and a billion dollars in 1959.[43] The flow of long-term capital itself rose from two billions in 1955 (including a billion of profits reinvested) to four billions in 1958.[44] This is a huge figure, which is widely regarded as an underestimate. Although it is not much more than 1 per cent of United States national income, it is a tenth of home investment[45] – somewhat smaller than the proportions that we saw in Britain.

The implications of this spread of United States capital, not only in the Dollar Area now but all over the world, are very great. Already it was estimated that, in 1955, the sales of the subsidiary companies of U.S. firms operating outside America are more than twice the annual value of U.S. exports.[46] This is the new pattern of economic relations which we found when we examined British capitalism. And again, as in Britain, this development is most advanced in the case of the giant corporations. The top two hundred corporations in the U.S. are said to derive a quarter of their income from foreign investments.[47]

This recent development begins to make sense of the insistent emphasis of American spokesmen that foreign aid programmes were primarily for this purpose: 'Maintenance of the American way of life is the controlling one' (the State Department on the Marshall Plan, 1947);[48] 'Particular emphasis is . . . given . . . to the stimulation of a greatly expanded flow of private investment' (the State Department on Point Four, 1949);[49] '. . . the encouragement of a hospitable climate for such investment in foreign countries . . .' (President Eisenhower's State of the Union message, 1953).[50] All the little strings attached to the granting of aid seem small by comparison with this. The purchase of American in preference to other supplies of grain,[51] tobacco and steel,[52] the sale of shares in Tanganyika Concessions,[53] the acceptance of the bans on East-West trade,[54] the commitment to military expenditure at high levels[55] and the submission of national forces to American commanders[56] – what are all these but the servile concessions of governments 'that will create the right sort of atmosphere for our investments'

(Randall Commission, 1954)?[57] The pattern of United States expansion in the Dollar Area has been applied to the rest of the world. We noted in an earlier chapter the type of governments to which most of the aid had flowed (Chapter 6).

If the flow of American capital abroad continues, we shall have further confirmation of the competitive pressure for the markets of the world among the giant corporations in every major industrial land. In studying the economy of Britain we emphasised that the growth of the home market, the increase in state expenditures and the rise of industries less dependent than in the past on imports, had all contributed to a more stable economy. We should have reached the same conclusion about the United States before 1954.

From 1954 onward, the national income of the U.S. grew more slowly, unemployment both of men and of industrial capacity remained at a high level even during periods of boom;[58] the arms programme continued to account for not much less than 10 per cent of the national product.[59] All these new developments taken together might suggest a greater outward pressure of American capital towards foreign markets and investment opportunities and a greater American stake in preserving governments that will protect American investments the world over. We must beware of exaggerating. In 1959, gross income from foreign investment at $4 billion only just equalled again 1 per cent of the United States national income as it did before 1929; it was only 5 per cent of all property incomes.[60] Nevertheless, as we noted earlier, it may matter more that it provided a quarter of the profits of the top 200 corporations.[61]

What is crucial for our purpose is that this new flow of capital is not mainly directed to underdeveloped lands, except for the oil-producing countries (see Table XXX). On the contrary, as with the earlier concentration of United States investment on Canada, this new flow is concentrated on the most industrialised lands: Britain, West Germany and other West European lands. This is also, as we saw earlier (Table XI,

Chapter 6) where most of the United States government aid went. Private capital imports from the U.S.A. were indeed in part balancing Europe's dollar payments in place of the defence aid, which after 1955 began to tail off in West Europe. Such overseas investment provided an important alternative to the armament budget as an outlet for American goods and capital, but it was still on a comparatively small scale; 1 per cent of United States national income is small compared with the 10 per cent devoted to arms between 1955 and 1959.

The decision of the United States government in 1960 to provide $500 million in aid to South America is a small gesture,[62] to be compared with an annual investment income flowing from Latin America to the U.S.A. of about twice as much,[63] and a total of grants to other parts of the world of $8 billion (Table XI, Chapter 6). Most important, it is limited to social development and specifically excludes industrial projects.

The figures for United States aid seem big, until they are compared with the needs of the receiving countries and the size of the U.S. economy. Nothing less than a vast expansion of foreign aid or investment at home or abroad would take up the slack that would follow disarmament,[64] but this is a point to which we shall return in the last chapter.

The Common Market

The Common Market differs from the other blocs in not having one outstanding industrialised member. West Germany is only the first among near equals, but the fact that the Common Market grew from the European Coal and Steel Community should give us the clue. The Community was established in 1952, not only to provide tariff-free movement of coal and steel between the Six countries – West Germany, France, Italy, the Netherlands, Belgium and Luxemburg – but also to bring German steel production under international control. The French people, in particular, were frightened at the prospect of the German steel barons being able to prepare once more for war. It was evidently impossible to enforce a low limit to the size of the German steel industry, but the French hoped to set some limit to its growth, to break up the great monopolies and to get cheap German coal for their own French steel industry.[65] In all these aims they failed: German and French output of steel in 1952 was about 10 million tons in each country; in 1960 German output was 36 million tons and French 17 million tons. By 1960 German steel production was once more in the hands of just four giant combines.[66] And, although double pricing of German coal had been ended, West Germany was providing subsidies for German coal-users.[67]

The fact was that there were other forces than the French popular desire to protect themselves from German military strength behind the setting up of the Coal and Steel Community – the same forces which had proposed a Rhineland Palatinate state in 1919 and again in 1945 to protect German and French steel and coal from the threat of nationalisation.[68] Although the threat was removed on both occasions, the desire for unity between the coal and steel combines across the national frontiers continued. For in the coal and steel industries of the six nations, ownership of the largest concerns is and has for long been most closely interlocked.[69] Schneider-Creusot and de Wendel of Paris between them hold the majority of the shares in the giant Luxemburg United Steel Works (ARBED), much of the remaining capital being Belgian. ARBED in turn owns the Felten and Guillaume steel and engineering works and the Eschweiler Mining Union and much else in West Germany. The French Sidechar Consortium has a major interest in the coal, steel and engineering empire of Friedrich Flick as well as in Belgian mining. The Dutch steel group (KNH) is associated with the largest of the German coal and steel combines, the Thyssen Group, in Dortmund Hoerder, the giant Foundry Union. This is itself associated with Hoesch as well as

Thyssen in other foundries and mines in West Germany. Another Dutch group is associated with Kloeckner, the fourth of the giants in German coal and steel production.

It is even reported that, since the establishment of the Community, Italian steel firms have been investing in the West German steel industry. Similar interlocking can be found to a lesser extent in banking, chemicals, rayon, electric lamps, glass and margarine.[70] It is difficult not to see the Common Market, like the Community before it, as the fruit of the union of the highest levels of German, French, Belgian, Dutch and Italian capital.

West German finance and industry must naturally assume the leadership in the Common Market, because of their sheer size. Nearly half the steel and much more than half the coal of the Community are produced in West Germany (see Table XXVIII), and, when overproduction occurred for the first time in 1958, it was not the re-equipped and modernised works in West Germany that were closed down, but the smaller, older and less efficient units elsewhere, and especially in Belgium.[71] West Germany also enjoys the key central geographic position on the lower Rhine and around the Ruhr valley, where low transport costs, ease of communication, skilled labour and availability of raw materials and commercial services have been attracting the new plants of firms throughout the Common Market and from the United States and Britain as well.[72] We saw in Chapter 8 the extent to which British firms were establishing subsidiaries in the lower Rhineland and other parts of the Common Market.

Once more the essence of the bloc is seen to be the free movement of capital and goods which gives to the most advanced economy the greatest opportunities and fixes the less advanced in primary production. As *The Economist* once remarked *à propos* the Common Market: 'the advantage lies with the big battalions'.[73]

Free trade opens up the whole area to the largest and most efficient producers, who can then manage the market through the cartels and their extension in the supra-national in-stitutions of the community. The position of West German finance and industry is that of a dominant partner inside a cartel; indeed they are dominant partners inside a whole range of cartels – in steel and chemicals and artificial textiles, etc.[74] The West Germans are the leaders, but they agree with their fellow members – in uneasy, unstable, competitive agreements that are always subject to revision as conditions change.

It is in the supra-national organisations, beginning with the Community's control of coal and steel output and prices and going on to the creation of the Common Market, that the cartels become the giant 'Cartel' of the European Economic Community. The Coal and Steel Community at all times compromised with the cartels,[75] but its officials complained that they could not control coal and steel policies without control of wider economic policy.[76] The Common Market provides the opportunity. The three Executives – Coal and Steel Community High Authority, Common Market Com-mission and Euratom Commission – consist of non-elected officials, experts drawn mainly from Big Business including even officials from the cartels. The Common Market Com-mission have power of decision on their own (Article 155 of the Rome Treaty) but they work in consultation with a Common Council of Ministers, which retains the final power of decision and must for the first years reach decisions unanimously, thereafter by a qualified majority (Article 148).

There is a whole range of institutions – a Court of Justice for settling disputes and an Assembly appointed from the national Parliaments which can by a two-thirds majority dismiss the Commission (Article 144) – but the essence of the new European Economic Community (the Common Market's proper title) consists in the constitutional provision that the Council of Ministers makes its decisions on the basis of propositions put before it by the Commission (Article 148). The Commission alone has the power of initiative and

the supra-national powers to enforce principles of free competition, which in the world of modern industry means freedom for the largest corporations to control the economy,
unhindered by state intervention (Article 92); and this in
effect means that the cartels have the power.

Writing in *Lloyds Bank Review* in April, 1953, R. Aron
described the Plan for the Coal and Steel Community as 'a
sort of constitutional law setting up a ministry of industrial
production for Europe, a ministry whose authority extends
for the time being only to two markets – those for coal and
steel – but whose authority could easily be widened'.[77] It
remains the best description of the intentions that lay behind
the establishment six years later of the Common Market
under the Rome Treaty. The responsibilities of the Common
Market Commission go far beyond the mere supervision of
tariff cuts, import quotas and control over the origin of
goods flowing into the Union. There is, first, the question of a
common foreign commercial policy, the common tariff
surrounding the 'Six' (Articles 20 ff. and 111 ff.). There are
the questions of the balance of payments of each of the
members with each other and with the outside world
(Articles 105 ff). There is the 'harmonising' of social, welfare
and taxation policies (Articles 93 ff., 100 ff., and 118 ff). There
is the investment policy of the $1,000 million Investment
Bank of Europe, to which the Italian and other less-advanced
members look for help in developing their poorer regions
(Articles 129–30). There is the $600 million Overseas
Development Fund for what is already being called 'Eurafrica', the colonial territories which the Six Powers brought
into the Community with them (Articles 130 ff.).

There is the operation of the European Agricultural
Market, which is to be 'managed' by price regulation, not
opened to free trade (Article 40). There is the work of
Euratom, with $215 million to be spent over the next years in
developing the production of atomic energy.[78] There are also
thermal and hydro-electric power schemes to supply a

Central European grid and finally the improvement of rail, canal, river and road transport connexions. Anyone who has seen the plans for *Europort*, the new port to be built at the mouth of the Rhine, with its docks, shipyards, steel-mills and engineering works, will have gained some picture of the scale on which this new economic community is being developed.[79]

It is not surprising that British firms in 1960 and 1961 were rushing in to establish themselves in the Rhine palatinate and that voices were heard on all sides, before the British Government took the plunge, pressing for us to go in with the Common Market, lest we lose what trade we already have in the Area – in 1961 about a sixth of our exports – and to build a channel tunnel to make sure. As this is written, the outcome of the negotiations is not known, but some points are clear.[80] First, Britain will have to abandon her imperial preference in order to get in. If that were all, few would complain, although British manufacturers will meet even stiffer competition in Commonwealth markets (Table XII, Chapter 7). But it is not all; the second point to note is the ending of the free entry for Commonwealth products in the British market. Our trade with our main Commonwealth partners, Canada, Australia and New Zealand, is bound to suffer. It might be said that they can afford it. The real objections to entry lie elsewhere – in the effect on the underdeveloped lands of the Common Market's protectionist policies and in the supra-national powers of the commission over the economies of the member countries.[81]

As far as the last point is concerned, there can be no doubt that the economic integration of the Community must lead inevitably to political integration – in the United States of Europe (Article 1 of the Rome Treaty says so). Nor can there be any doubt that the central drive behind it is capitalist, the capital of the giant combines, and not in West Germany only. It is German and Belgium steel companies that are jointly exploiting new sources of iron in French North African territories; it is the *Deutsche* Bank that is forming consortia with French and other capital to develop the Sahara.[82] German industry was always more concentrated than British and more permeated by Finance Capital. It formed the basis of Lenin's vision of imperialism. Today, it is more concentrated than ever, despite Allied efforts at decartelisation. Sixty giant companies, most of them controlled by just fourteen industrial groups, own half the public share capital in West Germany.[83]

The establishment of a United States of Europe and Eurafrica is rapidly becoming a copy-book illustration of Lenin's thesis of the continual tendency of capitalism toward monopoly – first local, then national, then continental and finally world-wide. And Lenin was surely right to emphasise, in contradiction of Karl Kautsky,[84] that this development, far from leading to a wider internationalism, divides the world more sharply, as the giants come into conflict with each other on a world scale.

What it does not do is industrialise underdeveloped lands. Indeed, the contrasting arrangements for industrial and for agricultural goods inside the Common Market might seem almost to have been designed to fix the overseas associated territories of the Common Market and the poorer agricultural producers in southern Italy as producers of primary products for export in perpetuity. For, while the industrial market is to be opened to free competition, thus placing a premium on the most advanced industrial units, agricultural markets are to be 'managed' centrally by price regulation with tariffs, import levies and consumer taxes to keep out competition. Prices are likely to be kept high to find markets for increased French agricultural output as well as to protect high costs and inefficient German farmers; but the effect is to prevent overseas producers from diversifying their production and above all to use the overall strength of the great industrial powers inside the Common Market to weaken the bargaining position of primary producers.

What is worse is that, even in primary products, the emphasis inside the Common Market is to be on development within Europe of food supplies, with aid from the import levies to increase efficiency,[85] and of synthetic materials, with aid from external tariffs on natural materials from outside. Moreover, the associated territories in Africa are committed under Article 133 of the Rome Treaty to lowering their tariffs on imports from the Six. This means that they will be unable to protect their infant industries or to develop regional arrangements with other African lands for joint industrial development. A clear indication of the attitude of the Six to the African territories is that in the first few years of its operation the European Development Fund has been spent entirely on developing primary production; not a single unit of account has been devoted to industrialisation.[86] It is particularly significant that the main objection of the Six countries to the admission of the rest of the Sterling Area to the Common Market along with Britain, and their main fears even about admitting Britain, have been concerned with their resistance to cheap manufactures and processed materials from India and Hong Kong entering their market as a result.[87] In fact, they are not free-traders even in industrial goods, if they see the danger of real competition. The overseas territories associated with the Common Market are, as we have seen, to be restricted to primary production, and even the import of their primary products is to be managed.

The African nations are thus caught in a trap. Exclusion from the Common Market means that their neighbours who are inside can snatch European markets from them. But going in to gain new markets for their products is to jeopardise their future chances of industrialisation. Their only way forward is to form their own Common Market large enough to permit of economies of scale in industrial development. The sense of African unity shown in the formation of a single Trade Union Federation suggests that the new African states will not permit this to be prevented either by manœuvre from outside or by their own divisions into the mainly English-speaking 'Casablanca' and mainly French-speaking 'Monrovia' groups, based largely on their colonial inheritance.[88] To this point we shall return, but we must first look at the last great trading bloc – that of the communist lands.

The Rouble Area

We began this chapter in search of forces of growth in world trade and in world economic development. We have so far discovered in the great trading blocs, into which the world is now divided, rather forces of concentration of trade and development upon the more-developed lands, and movements of capital that tend to perpetuate this concentration. This was true of the Sterling Area, with its main movement of trade and capital between Britain and the 'white' Dominions; it was true of the United States and Canada's position in the Dollar Area; and now we have seen the concentration of West European growth upon the lower reaches of the Rhine valley. We have noted a marked tendency in the great blocs to retain external barriers to keep other traders out: Imperial Preferences, 'Buy American' Acts and now the common tariff of the Common Market all reflect the struggle of the giant combines for spheres of influence in a competitive capitalist world. The blocs also imply a less-developed economic status for primary producers. Is this also the basis of trade in what we may call for convenience the Rouble Area of the communist-led third of the world?

Certainly, the concentration of trade within the bloc is higher in the Rouble Area than in any of the other areas. But the total rate of growth is higher too, and this high rate of growth is not limited to the most industrialised member, the Soviet Union (Table XXIX). Moreover, the low level of these countries' trade outside their own Area was not mainly the result of exclusive decisions taken by the Rouble Area countries, rather the reverse. In fact, immediately after 1945 there was a great expansion of 'East-West' trade and, even in the discussions of General Marshall's offer of aid to Europe, Mr Molotov seemed at first genuinely prepared to co-operate, although not to the extent of permitting what he regarded as American interference in the Soviet economy.[89]

From what we now know of the United States' intentions, the break must seem inevitable. Those who served with U.N.R.R.A. will remember that a black list on U.S. rehabilitation supplies to communist countries was being operated as early as 1944 and that the work of U.N.R.R.A., most of whose relief supplies went to the eastern lands of Europe, on the basis of greater devastation, was closed down by an American decision that 'the need for further aid was not established'.[90] Negotiations for loans from the United States and from the World Bank for the Soviet Union and Poland had also broken down before the Marshall offer.[91] At all events, after 1947 capitalist bans on trade with the 'East' became increasingly strict and, after the Chinese communists established their rule over the Chinese mainland in 1949, the bans were applied still more strictly on trade with China, as well as with Russia and eastern Europe.[92]

The communist lands were thus driven to develop what trade they could among themselves. The Soviet Union had never been a major trading nation, the value of her exports of primary products being much depressed in the 1930s;[93] but the eastern European lands had before the war had an aggregate foreign trade turnover four times that of the Soviet Union.[94] They had provided a fairly considerable proportion of West Europe's imports of grain (a third before 1931) and most of West Europe's imports of coke, coal, timber, woodpulp, bauxite, vegetable oils and dairy produce. This was the result partly of the strong eastward orientation of Germany's trade.[95] China's exports had been almost entirely of agricultural products – eggs, tea, soya and other oils, silk, cotton and bristles – exchanged for West European manufactures.[96]

After 1948, a new pattern of trade had to be established. At first, this consisted mainly of eastern European exports of machinery to the Soviet Union, Soviet exports of food and raw materials and of some machinery to East Europe and Soviet exports of machinery to China in exchange for Chinese raw materials.[97] At the same time, Soviet technicians were sent everywhere and joint stock companies were established to develop transport and communications and production of oil, bauxite and other raw materials. The whole Area was potentially self-sufficient, except in rubber, copra, coffee and industrial diamonds, but was largely undeveloped.[98]

It is frequently charged that the Soviet Union established in its trade relations a form of imperialist exploitation of the peoples of the other communist lands. Certainly the complaints of the Poles and the Hungarians in 1956 suggested that there was some truth in this charge.[99] The basis of the charge lay in Stalin's evident determination to wring reparations from the ex-enemy countries – Germany, Poland and Romania. Reparation payments from these countries continued into 1952 and 1953, in which year they amounted for East Germany to a half of her total exports,[100] and the East Germans continued to pay occupation costs thereafter.[101] Poland suffered from being a party to the East German reparation agreement. In addition, there seems to be some evidence of under-pricing of raw material exports; Hungarian uranium was one of the instances given.[102]

The main complaint was against the working of the joint stock companies; even Stalin is reported (by the Yugoslavs) to have admitted that they were only appropriate for ex-enemy countries.[103] In any case, they were broken up in 1954, with the exception of the company which controlled the Romanian oil industry,[104] and the plants handed over to the countries concerned on compensation terms that have never been published, but are not thought to be worse than those offered by Dr Castro to the expropriated United States owners of Cuban industry. Most of the compensation payments were later cancelled by the U.S.S.R.[105]

To emphasise the negative aspects of Soviet trade policy is to make the positive achievement seem all the more remarkable. For what has happened in the Rouble Area is nothing less than the exact reversal of the concentration process, which we have observed elsewhere, and as a result of a deliberate attempt to aid the establishment of industry in the less-developed parts of the Area. The movement of capital has been centrifugal rather than centripetal. Inside the Soviet Union itself, it had long before the war been the practice to devote a higher proportion of the national budget than was called for on a population basis to the development of backward areas.[106] In this way, the standard of living in the Central Asian republics in respect of schools, medical and welfare services had been brought up very much in line with standards in the more advanced parts of the Union.[107] As these republics had been colonies of Tsarist Russia, the contrast with the situation in Britain's colonies, to which Leonard Barnes drew attention in *Soviet Light on the Colonies*, is worth pondering.[108]

The same principle was applied after the war in the development of heavy industry in Poland, Hungary, Bulgaria, Romania and China, which had previously been underdeveloped primary producing countries. It is quite clear that Stalin had in mind the development in this way of a strong military base and that the corollary was a very high level of military expenditure. It is also clear that Stalinist methods and the copying automatically of Soviet experience led, especially in Hungary, to confusion and waste and, in the end, to utter breakdown, as well as to political savagery. But the fact remains that, with all the ruthlessness (and industrialisation is always a ruthless business, as we have seen), these countries have today a strong industrial base in heavy industry, upon which to begin developing their economies and raising their social, cultural and economic standards.[109]

We shall look at this achievement again in the next chapter, because it was, mainly, not the result of Soviet aid but of the mobilisation of internal resources by governments committed to planning their economies with Soviet encouragement. Soviet provision of credits and loans before 1956 was small, with the exception of the credits to Poland in 1948–50 and to China in 1950 and 1954. The total of these did not exceed the equivalent of a billion dollars divided roughly equally between the two countries.[110] After 1956, Soviet loans equal to a further billion dollars were made, mainly to Poland and Hungary. These were to cover periods of several years and cannot be regarded as very large against a total annual trade turnover inside the region equivalent to about $7 billion.[111]

The most important Soviet aid has probably been the provision of expert advisers and the education of very large numbers of foreign technicians at Soviet universities. In addition, the export of complete industrial enterprises has probably been crucial in China's development. One has only to imagine the effect that fifty or so of Britain's top engineering and industrial concerns would make if they were to contract to build 150 heavy industrial enterprises, provide the equipment that could not be made in China, train Chinese personnel to take over, and then get out and leave all the plants in Chinese possession. Yet this is just what the Russians did in China between 1952 and 1956.[112]

Has this aid, then, involved a sacrifice for the Soviet Union and the other more-advanced lands in the Rouble Area? The reverse would seem to be the case. One of the most important features of trade in the Rouble Area has been the increasing degree of specialisation of production among the member countries. This is no longer the old division of labour between primary producers and manufacturers, but a specialisation within manufacture. More than a third of all trade inside the Area consisted by the mid-1950s in the exchange of machinery and equipment.[113] For a long time, despite grandiose proclamations, most trade consisted of exchanges of specific requirements under bilateral agreements; but, after 1956, Five-Year Plans were more closely geared together and agreements were reached on many different kinds of specialisation and on joint plans such as Czechoslovak and East German co-operation in developing Polish brown coal.[114]

C.O.M.E.C.O.N., the Council for Mutual Economic Assistance, was thereafter given much greater responsibilities, and decisions were made jointly on production targets, trade quotas, exchange of information, patents and designs and on joint exploitation of raw materials and joint development of transport and communications, fuel and power sources. While it is possible that Soviet counsels predominate, and while the division of labour has not been pushed very far to overcome the wastage of duplication, yet it is not to be doubted that great economic advances are being made and in the previously least-developed parts of the Area.

It is worth emphasising here the point that, while the essence of the Common Market arrangements is in freeing restrictions on the movement of goods and labour and capital, the essence of C.O.M.E.C.O.N. lies in joint enterprise, and mutual consultation and planned development. The former is suited to countries with equally advanced industrialisation; the latter is more appropriate to countries at different stages of development, who wish to retain control over their foreign trade and ensure a consciously planned advance. Economic co-operation rather than trade liberalisation is likely, therefore, to be of more interest to the less-developed lands, a point to which we shall return in the last chapter.

It is clear that there is no intention to make C.O.M.E.C.O.N. self-sufficient. After 1954, the trade of the communist countries was at the same time considerably developed outside their own Area. The proportion of trade carried on inside the Area was reduced from about 80 per cent to nearer 70 per cent.[115] A great part of this increase in trade outside the Area was the result of expanding trade between East and West Germany, but Soviet trade with Asia and the Middle East was also raised by the provision of Soviet credits to India, Indonesia, Egypt and Afghanistan. Soviet trade with China slumped in 1960.[116] The Chinese had already been expanding their trade in Asia and using also the sterling earned through Hong Kong and from emigrants' remittances to buy machinery from Western Europe, and more recently they used these to buy food grains from Canada and Australia.[117]

This whole development has been a notable breakthrough from the concentration of trade inside the great blocs, which we have been looking at. The effect of Soviet competition in India, in the oil industry, in the Middle East, in Cuba and South America, although so far on an extremely small scale, is beginning to have widespread repercussions. This is partly because the Soviet Union provides an alternative non-capitalist source of supply, for example of oil, partly because Soviet credits are provided on quite generous terms, but, perhaps most important of all to primary producing lands, because the Soviet Union is prepared to be repaid not in scarce currency but in the staple products of the country to whom the loan is given.

For those in capitalist countries who are becoming increasingly disturbed by this development, and it is not only the Soviet Union but other East European countries that are breaking into world markets, the moral is to sell more of the technically advanced products to the Soviet bloc itself.[118] As a result of the Macmillan-Khrushchev talks in London in 1956,[119] some increase in British exports to the Soviet Union was made in 1957, but it was not maintained.[120] Certain bans on exports still remained even at the time of the British Trade Fair in Moscow in May 1961, and often on the most technically advanced items;[121] although no one can any longer believe after the display of Soviet rocketry that such bans make any difference to Soviet technical advancement. Indeed the view is widely held that the bans in the past may positively have stimulated Soviet technological advance, by forcing her to concentrate on developing machinery which she had previously relied on importing. The result of this concentration in any case is that the Soviet bloc is extremely short of just the types of consumer goods and especially durables that the West produces in excess. With such a vast market as that of the Rouble Area expanding at its present rate, it is nothing but wilful blindness that maintains any restraints on the free development of trade.

Apart from the bans, one of the other obstacles to trade is the apparent refusal of the oil companies to allow Soviet oil to be imported into Britain.* There is also evidence of a similar refusal to permit imports of Chinese tobacco, although it is Virginian leaf, the tobacco manufacturing companies being too closely associated with American and Empire growers. In this matter Dr Castro has shown us the way.

The chief moral of this chapter is, however, the possibility which the Rouble Area trade experience suggests, not only of breaking out from the concentration of trade inside the blocs, but of helping the development of the less-developed lands. The evident advantages for the more-developed lands like the Soviet Union, East Germany or Czechoslovakia in the process, as well as for the less-developed lands, is of the greatest relevance for Britain with her high share of trade with underdeveloped lands. The key to the rapid industrialisation of China and the underdeveloped lands of eastern Europe was to be found, we suggested, in the internal measures which they have taken and which they

* Mr Maudling's comment at the highly successful British Trade Fair held in Moscow in May 1961, that 'we have plenty of oil',[122] is particularly disingenuous, since Britain imports almost every gallon of the oil we use and pays in dollars at inflated prices for a large part of it.[123]

have evidently been encouraged by the Soviet Union to take.

We in Britain should not be put off by the fact that the scale of development of the non-industrialised lands, and even of the communist lands, seems small compared with that of the industrialised giants. An extrapolation of growth rates in manufacturing industry over the years 1953–9 (Table XXXI below) suggests in any case that, by 1970, the communist bloc will have within its borders nearly half of the world's output. And this is based on two conservative assumptions: first, that China's rate of growth over the next period will only be at half that supposed to have been achieved over the last period, and, second, that a considerably lower estimate is taken for the shares in world industrial output for 1959 than is claimed by the Soviet leaders themselves. The industrialisation of eastern Europe and China has been proceeding at a remarkable pace by any standards. The growing points of the new are what we should be looking for. It is to the measures necessary for industrialisation in other underdeveloped lands where there is still a chance of forestalling communist ruthlessness and to the aid that these lands may need in the process that we must now turn.

TABLE XXV

CAPITALIST WORLD PRODUCTION, TRADE AND PRICES OF MANUFACTURES AND PRIMARY PRODUCTS, 1876–1961

Year	World Production					World Trade Volume		Prices in World Trade						Terms of Trade	
	Food	Agri-cultural Materials	Mining	Oil	Manu-factures	Primary Products	Manu-factures	Food	Agri-cultural Materials	Mining	Oil	All Primary Products (except oil)	Manu-factures	For U.K.	For Primary Producers
1876–80	48	19		1.5	19	27	35	—	—	—	—	170	91	164	54
1913	80	64		18	75	85	109	—	—	—	—	140	88	143	63
1925	88	80		35	87	84	100	—	—	—	—	218	162	120	74
1929	92	95		70	109	105	112	287	279	156	—	—	223	122	—
1932	104	70		75	69	—	—	—	—	—	—	106	104	98	98
1937–38	100	100		100	100	100	100	100	100	100	100	100	100	100	100
1948	114	133		180	145	94	120	325	284	227	242	311	193	118	64
1951	—	—		—	—	111	172	330	390	239	233	350	191	139	55
1952	125	159		240	187	107	172	345	306	245	236	312	195	129	59
1953	127	163		250	202	113	185 (100)	355	278	229	238	294	187	119	62
1954	132	164		260	202	118 (101)	193 (100)	393	278	230	240	303	184	120	61
1955	132	177		290	224	126 (107)	208 (108)	340	284	234	243	291	185	122	65
1956	137	188		313	234	137 (116)	230 (119)	344	281	250	252	303	193	119	65
1957	140	193		324	242	146 (124)	245 (127)	347	281	264	270	297	200	116	70
1958	139	187		328	236	146 (124)	239 (124)	333	250	250	245	276	200	107	75
1959	146	195		346	260	160 (136)	258 (124)	316	261	236	—	273	198	107	76
1960	154	206		362	275	170 (142)	288 (149)	309	270	232	—	273	204	106	80
1961		214		379	280		296 (153)	301	256	227	—	265	206	103	82

Notes: 1. World Prices, pre-1925 = U.K. Import Prices.
2. Post-1945 figures exclude communist countries.
3. 1937–38 Production figures = 1934–38 Averages.
4. Terms of Trade = Import prices divided by Export prices.
5. Figures in parentheses based on 1954 = 100; all other figures on 1937–38 = 100.

Sources: World Production:
Pre-1945: League of Nations, *World Economic Survey*, Geneva, annually from 1931.
Post-1945: United Nations, *Statistical Yearbook*, 1961 (New York, 1962).
World Prices:
Pre-1938: Schloete, op. cit., Table 26.
Post-1938: United Nations, *Statistical Yearbook*, 1961, linked to 1929 and 1938 by United Nations, *World Economic Survey* (New York, 1956), Table XXIV.
World Trade:
Pre-1945: League of Nations, *World Economic Survey*, Geneva, annually from 1931.
Post-1945: United Nations, *Statistical Year-book*, 1961.

TABLE XXVI

OUTPUT AND PRICES OF SELECTED PRIMARY COMMODITIES

A = 1948–54; B = 1954–60
(First year of period = 100 in every case)

Commodity	Output Growth A	B	Prices Movement A	B	Main Exporters
All Food and Materials	118	116	97	85	
Foodstuffs					
Wheat	118	117	108	81	U.S.A., Canada, Australia
Rice	110	130	70	90	Thailand, Burma, U.S.A.
Sugar	130	150	85	90	Cuba, San Domingo, Philippines
Coffee	135	125	102	95	Brazil, Colombia, Kenya
Cocoa	130	170	280	55	Ghana, Brazil, Fr. Africa
Tea	150	130	150	50	India, Ceylon
Lamb	147	115	117	85	New Zealand
Butter	120	115	170	96	New Zealand, Denmark
Oils, Oilseeds	120	125	88	90	Nigeria, Fr. Africa
Tobacco	103	115	78	97	U.S.A., Turkey, Rhodesia
Agricultural Materials	118	112	93	96	
Wool	120	125	165	75	Australia, New Zealand, S. Africa
Cotton	129	120	89	65	U.S.A., Egypt, U.S.S.R.
Jute	156	110	57	105	Pakistan
Lumber	110	120	104	93	Canada, Sweden
Wood-pulp	—	130	88	95	Canada, Sweden
Rubber	125	112	112	170	Malaya, Indonesia
All Fuels	118	122	99	106	
Coal	104	130	96	110	U.S.A., U.K.
Petroleum	148	152	100	100	Venezuela, Middle East

TABLE XXVI (contd.)

Commodity	Output Growth		Prices Movement		Main Exporters
	A	B	A	B	
All Metals	128	145	101	105	
Iron-Ore	171	140	149	100	Sweden, France
Zinc	142	105	81	110	Canada, Mexico
Tin	117	80	106	110	Malaya
Copper	128	150	143	108	Rhodesia, Canada
Bauxite	192	140	95	—	Guianas, Jamaica
All Manufactures (for comparison)	140	140	95	111	

Sources: GROWTH from United Nations, *Statistical Yearbook, 1960*.
PRICES from United Nations, *Price Indexes for Basic Commodities Entering International Trade*,
New York, 1961.
MAIN EXPORTERS from Economic Intelligence Unit, *Economic Atlas of the World*, Oxford,
1952.

TABLE XXVII-A

TRADE OF INDUSTRIAL AND NON-INDUSTRIAL LANDS, 1928–60

Year	Total Trade ($b.)	'A' Shares in World Exports (%) of different Groups				'B' Shares in World Trade (%) of flows between different Groups			
		Indust.	Semi-Indust.	Non-Indust.	Eastern Bloc	Indust. to Indust.	Non-Indust. to Indust.	Indust. to Non-Indust.	Indust. to Non-Indust.
1928	35·8 100	60	11·5	18·5	9	38	26	22	14
1937–38	25·2 100	60	11·5	21·5	7	35	29	25	12
1953	81·7 100	55	10	25	10	33	24	22	21
1958	106·75 100	60	7·5	21·5	12	37	21	24	19
1960	125·47 100	63	25		12	42	20	21	17

Notes: Industrialised Lands = U.S.A., Canada, U.K., Continental West Europe, Ireland, Japan.
Semi-Industrialised Lands = Australia, South Africa, India, Argentina, Brazil, Mexico, Finland, Jugoslavia.
Non-Industrialised Lands in 'B' *Shares in World Trade* include semi-industrialised lands and Eastern Bloc.
Eastern Bloc. = U.S.S.R., China, Eastern Europe.

Sources: GATT (General Agreement on Tariffs and Trade), *Trends in International Trade*, Geneva, 1958.
GATT, *International Trade*, for 1957–58, 1959, 1960, Geneva.
United Nations, *Monthly Bulletin of Statistics*, New York, June 1960.

TABLE XXVII-B

TRADE OF INDUSTRIAL (I) AND NON-INDUSTRIAL (NI) LANDS, 1953, 1956, 1960

Commodities	1953 I	1953 NI	1956 I	1956 NI	1960 I	1960 NI
All Exports (in $b.)	45·2	24·4	61·8	28·5	79·4	31·0
as shares of World Total (%) made up to 100 by Communist Share (%)	58·3	31·5	61·5	28·4	63·3	24·7
	10·2		10·1		12·0	
Exports of Manufactures (in $b.)	29·4	2·6	41·1	2·6	53·6	3·5
Exports of Primary Products (in $b.)	15·8	21·8	20·7	25·9	25·8	27·5
of those I and.NI shares (%)	42	58	44·5	55·5	48·5	51·5
of which:						
Agric. Materials ($b.)	4·7	6·5	6·3	7·4	7·7	7·6
of these Textiles ($b.)	1·4	3·3	1·7	3·2	2·2	2·9
Metal-Ores ($b.)	2·1	2·2	3·7	2·8	4·4	2·9
Food & Tobacco ($b.)	7·5	8·6	8·7	9·3	10·4	9·4
Fuels ($b.)	1·5	4·5	2·0	6·4	3·3	7·6
Exports of Primary Products as % of Total Exports – for each	35	90	33	91	32·5	89
for both	54		51·5		47·5	

Notes: Agric. Materials = SITC 2 & 4 – 28; Metal Ores = SITC 28 & 68 – 681;
Food & Tobacco = SITC 0 & 1 ; Fuels = SITC 3
Source: GATT, International Trade, Geneva, annual reports since 1954.

TABLE XXVIII

WORLD TRADE BLOCS, 1959

Bloc and Country	Population (millions)	National Income ($b. Current Values)	Crude Steel Prod. (m. tons)	Hard Coal Prod. (m. tons)	Electric Power Prod. (b.k.w.h.)	Petroleum Oil Prod. (m. tons)	Exports (Current $b. Values)	Share of Trade with bloc (%) 1938	1939	Share of World Exports (%) 1938	1959	Growth in Volume of Exports, 1937–59 (1937=100)
STERLING and the Seven	825	200	35	320	265	100	23	43	40	31	26	170
of which U.K.	52	60	22	190	100	—	9	43	50	10	8	170
The 7.	45	50	5	5	100	—	8	32	31	8	7	200
India etc.	570	40	4	50	12	—	2	56	45	4	1	180
DOLLAR	300	475	115	400	850	540	28	36	48	20	26	260
of which U.S.A.	175	400	105	380	720	350	17	27	38	13	17	260
ROUBLE	1,000	300	90	980	390	150	14	10	63	7	13	400
of which U.S.S.R.	200	180	56	370	240	130	5	1	73	1	3	1,000
China	680	60	13	350	40	4	2	0	73	2	1	500
COMMON MARKET	225	150	60	240	230	10	25	10	34	23	23	300
of which W. Germany	52	50	30	141	105	5	10	30	33	9	8	380
France	45	43	15	57	62	2	6	25	27	4	5	250
OTHERS	550	75	15	60	90	180	15	10	30	17	13	100
of which Japan	92	28	12	50	85	—	3	43	20	5	3	75
TOTAL WORLD	2,900	1,200	315	2,000	1,825	980	114	33.5	55	100	100	200

Notes: 1. Some of these figures are inevitably only approximate.
2. National Income = Net National Product at Factor Cost.
3. Common Market includes dependent territories.
4. The Seven here exclude U.K. = Denmark, Norway, Sweden, Switzerland, Austria, Portugal.
5. India, etc. = India, Pakistan, Ceylon, Burma.
6. Germany 1938 = pre-war frontiers.

Sources: United Nations, Statistical Yearbook, 1960.
United Nations, Monthly Bulletin of Statistics, June 1961.
O.E.E.C., General Statistics, Paris, January 1961.
I.M.F., International Financial Statistics, New York, monthly.
U.S.S.R. Central Statistical Administration, Statistical Yearbook, Moscow, 1960.
Chinese Central Statistical Bureau, op. cit.

TABLE XXIX

RATE OF GROWTH AND SHARES OF WORLD TRADE, 1938–59

Group and Country	Shares (%) in Exports (Current Values)				Export Volume Growth Rates p.a. (%)			Volume Index 1938–59 Exports/Imports
	1938	1948	1953	1959	1938–48	1948–53	1953–59	
Capitalist World Total	91	94	90	87.5	–0.2	7.5	5	190/193
U.S.	12	22	19	15	7.1	4.3	1.4	255/250
U.K.	9	11	8.5	8	3.2	4.3	3.2	170/110
W. Germany	8.5	2	6	8.5	–6.1	50.4	14.3	385/350
Other E.E.C.	11	9.5	14	13.5	–1.9	12.5	8.4	250/220
Japan	4	—	2	3	–6.8	37	19	75/100
R.S.A.	12	15	16	12	0.4	4.8	3.9	170/200
Other	34	34	24.5	27.5	—	—	—	—
Industrial Lands	66	58	63	67	0.3	9	5.5	225/185
Non-Industrial Lands	34	42	37	33	–0.5	4.3	4.3	155/195
Communist World Total	9	6.5	10	12.5	2.7	12.5	15	approx. 400
U.S.S.R.	1.5	2	4	5	10	15	15	approx. 1,000
E. Europe	6	3	5	6	–3.5	11	12.5	approx. 200
China etc.	1	1	1.5	2.5	—	12.5	25	approx. 550
Total	100	100	100	100				225
in $b.	25.8	57.3	81.7	114.5				

Notes: Other E.E.C. = Italy, France, Belgium, Netherlands, Luxembourg.
R.S.A. = Rest of Sterling Area, excluding U.K.
China etc. includes Trade of N. Korea, N. Viet Nam and Mongolia.
Industrial and Non-Industrial lands in capitalist world only.

Sources: United Nations Economic Commission for Europe, *Bulletin*, Geneva, September 1960.
United Nations, *Monthly Bulletin of Statistics*, for June 1960 and June 1961.
GATT, *Trends in International Trade*, Geneva, 1958.
GATT, *International Trade*, for 1960, Geneva, 1961.

TABLE XXX

UNITED STATES BALANCE OF PAYMENTS AND LONG-TERM FOREIGN INVESTMENT, 1919–59

(Annual Averages in $b. at current prices)

	1919–21	1922–29	1930–39	1946–49	1950–54	1955–59
A. Balance of Payments						
(1) *Current Account*						
Exports	8·2	5·25	3·1	15·6	15·2	16·7
Imports	−5·2	−4·9	−2·9	−7·9	−12·9	−13·2
Balance on Goods and Services	3·0	0·35	0·2	7·7	2·3	3·5
Investment Income { Gross	0·6	0·9	0·6	1·4	2·6	4·0
Net	0·5	0·7	−0·1	1·2	2·2	3·1
Gross Foreign Investment Income as % of National Income	·75	1	1	·5	·75	1
(2) *Capital Account*						
Outflow – Government	−0·9	nil	nil	−6·8	−4·4	−5·7
Private	−1·1	−1·3	nil	−1·3	−1·55	−3·0
Reinvestment				−0·3	−0·7	−1·0
Inflow – Long Term and Gold	−0·3	0·3	−0·9	−1·2	1·9	2·6
Net Short-Term Movement and Errors	−1·4	−0·3	0·2	0·7	0·1	0·5
Gross Private Foreign Investment as % of Private Home Investment	n.a.	1	nil	5	4·5	6

TABLE XXX (contd.)

	1919–21	1922–23	1930–39	1946–49	1950–54	1955–59
B. *Total Long-Term Foreign Assets* (at end of each period in $b.)						
Government Investment	n.a.	—	—	14	15	12
Portfolio Investment	n.a.	7	4	5	7	10
Private Direct Investment	n.a.	8	7	11	18	30
Distribution of Direct Investment at end of each period (%)						
(a) by Regions – Canada	n.a.	25	n.a.	31	n.a.	33
Latin America	n.a.	33	n.a.	39	n.a.	35
Europe	n.a.	19	n.a.	14·5	n.a.	16
Others	n.a.	23	n.a.	15·5	n.a.	16
(b) by Types – Manufacturing	n.a.	24	n.a.	33	n.a.	32
Mining	n.a.	16	n.a.	10	n.a.	10
Oil	n.a.	15	n.a.	29	n.a.	33
Utilities	n.a.	21	n.a.	11	n.a.	9
Others	n.a.	24	n.a.	17	n.a.	16

Sources: United States Department of Commerce, *Balance of Payments of the United States*, Washington, D.C., annually.
  United States Department of Commerce, *Survey of Current Business*, Washington, D.C. monthly.
  UNESCO, op. cit.
  Royal Institute of International Affairs, op. cit.

TABLE XXXI

GROWTH RATES AND SHARES OF WORLD MANUFACTURING INDUSTRY, 1937–59,
WITH AN ESTIMATE FOR 1970

| | Annual Growth Rates | | | Index | Share of World Mfg. Output | | | Estimated |
	1937–48	1948–53	1953–59	1937–59	1937	1948	1959	1970
Capitalist World	2·5	6·5	4·6	240	82	82	73	53
Excluding U.S.A.	0	10·0	6·8	220	48	38	40	35
U.S.A.	5·0	5·0	2·35	265	34	44	33	18
U.K.	1·2	3·8	3·2	170	10	9	7	4
W. Germany	(−4·5)	22·7	8·5	220	8	3	6	7
Other E.E.C.		5·8	7·0	200	10	8	7	8
Japan	(−4·4)	27·4	13·2	280	3	1	2	4
Others	3·5	4·8	5·8	270	17	17	18	12
Communist World	2·9	8·1	12·6	640	18	18	27	47
U.S.S.R.	4·8	17·3	10·3	685	10	13	17	27
E. Europe	0	19·0	12·0	480	7	5	8	14
China	0	26·1	26·2	1,290	1	1	3	6
World	2·5	9·0	7·0	295	100	100	100	100

Sources: Capitalist World Index and Growth Rates:
    United Nations *Statistical Yearbooks* and *Monthly Bulletins of Statistics*.
  Communist World Index and Growth Rates:
    U.N.E.C.E., op. cit.
    U.S.S.R. Central Statistical Administration, op. cit.
    Chinese Central Statistical Bureau, op. cit.
  The Two Worlds' Shares for 1937 and 1948:
    Woytinsky, op. cit., p. 1000.
  Shares for 1959 found by splitting the difference between Mr Koslov's and Mr Allen Dulles's
  claims in 1959, as reported in U.S. 86th Congress Joint Economic Committee, 'Comparison of
  the United States and Soviet Economies', *Hearings* (Washington, D.C.: U.S.G.P.O., 1960).

References

1. quoted in S. Lilley, *Automation and Social Progress*, Lawrence and Wishart, 1957, p. 133.
2. G. Myrdal, *Economic Theory and Underdeveloped Regions*, Chapter 2.
3. H.M. Treasury, *Bulletin for Industry*, November 1961.
4. Economist Intelligence Unit, *Britain and Europe*, 1957, p. 12.
5. General Agreement on Tariffs and Trade, *International Trade, 1956*, Geneva, 1957, p. 11.
6. United Nations, Economic Commission for Asia and the Far East, *Economic Bulletin* for December 1961 on 'Economic Development and Planning in Asia and the Far East', Bangkok, 1962, p. 68 ff.
7. ibid., p. 52. ff.; and see United Nations, Department of Economic and Social Affairs, *The Latin American Common Market 1959*, New York, 1960, especially statement by Mr Raoul Prebisch, p. 141 ff.
8. United Nations, *Monthly Bulletin of Statistics*, New York, June 1960.
9. United Nations, *Statistical Yearbook, 1960*, New York, 1961.
10. United Nations, *World Economic Survey, 1958*, New York, 1959, p. 53 ff.; and see United Nations, Economic Commission for Latin America, *Economic Survey of Latin America, 1955*, New York, 1956, p. 3 ff.
11. United Nations, Food and Agricultural Organisation, *Commodity Review, 1961*, Rome, 1962, and Special Supplement, *Agricultural Commodities – Projections for 1970*, p. 36, Part I.
12. United Nations Economic Commission for Europe, *Economic Survey of Europe in 1949*, Geneva, 1950, p. 133.
13. General Agreement on Tariffs and Trade, *International Trade, 1960*, Geneva, 1961, Table 3, p. 9.
14. United Kingdom, Board of Trade *Journal*, 25.5.62, 'Sterling Area Trade Summary'.
15. P. W. Bell, *The Sterling Area in the Post War World*, p. 290.
16. Board of Trade *Journal*, 25.5.62.
17. Economist Intelligence Unit, *The Commonwealth and Europe*, 1960, Chapter I.
18. United Nations, *World Economic Survey, 1958*, New York, 1959, p. 41 ff.
19. United States, Department of Commerce, *Balance of Payments Statistical Supplements, 1919–1953*, and United Nations, Economic and Social Council, *The International Flow of Private Capital, 1946–52*, and *1956–58*, New York, 1954 and 1959.
20. R. F. Behrendt, *Inter-American Economic Relations*, New York, 1933.
21. United Nations, Economic Commission for Latin America, *Economic Survey for 1951–52*, New York, 1953.

22. *Fortune*, March 1941.
23. United Nations, *International Flow of Private Capital, 1946–52.*
24. United Nations, *World Economic Survey, 1956*, New York, 1957, p. 20 ff.
25. S. Jenkins, 'The Phillipines', in L. K. Rosinger, *The State of Asia*, p. 380 ff.
26. *The Times*, London, 1.6.1961.
27. R. Nurkse, *Problems of Capital Formation in Underdeveloped Countries*, Oxford, 1960, p. 117.
28. quoted in A. H. Hanson, *Public Enterprise and Economic Development*, Routledge, 1959, p. 191.
29. H. O'Connor, *The Empire of Oil*, John Calder, 1956, Chapter 30.
30. L. Huberman and P. M. Sweezy, *Cuba, the Anatomy of a Revolution*, Monthly Review Press, 1960, p. 22.
31. ibid., p. 141.
32. ibid., p. 169, quoting the *New York Times* petroleum editor.
33. United Nations, *Statistical Yearbook, 1960*, New York, 1961, Table 152.
34. U.S. Government, *Statistical Abstract of the United States, 1956*, Washington, 1957, Tables 350 and 1106.
35. U.S. Government, *Resources for Freedom, A Report to the President* by the President's Materials Policy Commission, Washington, June 1952.
36. General Agreement on Tariffs and Trade, *International Trade 1956*, Geneva, 1957, p. 17 ff.
37. United Nations Economic Commission for Europe, *Economic Survey of Europe since the War*, Geneva, 1953, p. 106 ff.
38. United Nations Economic Commission for Europe, *Economic Bulletin*, Geneva, November 1955.
39. quoted in P. Abrams, *Britain and her Export Trade*, p. 321
40. United States, Department of Commerce, *Balance of Payments, 1919–53.*
41. *New York Herald Tribune*, 27.2.50.
42. United Nations, *World Economic Survey, 1955*, New York, 1956, p. 82.
43. United States Department of Commerce, *Balance of Payments of the United States* and see United Nations, *World Economic Survey 1959*, New York, 1960, p. 166, Table 4–20.
44. United Nations Economic and Social Council, *The International Flow of Private Capital 1956–58*, pp. 21 and 34.
45. *Statistical Abstract of the United States, 1960.*
46. V. Perlo, *The Empire of High Finance*, New York International Publishers, 1957, Table 24, p. 294.
47. ibid., p. 295.

48. U.S. Government, *Outline of European Recovery Programme, Draft Legislation and Background Information* submitted by the State Department for use of the Foreign Relations Committee, Washington, 1947, p. 26.
49. United States, State Department, *Press Release on President Truman's Inaugural Address, Point Four*, Washington, January 1949.
50. President Dwight D. Eisenhower, *State of the Union Message*, Washington, January 1953.
51. Statement of the French delegate to the meeting of the United Nations Economic Commission for Europe, Geneva, June 1953.
52. Averell Harriman, *Report to the President*, Washington, 7.11.47, p. 89.
53. Senator Vandenburgh, *Private Papers*, Gollancz, 1952, p. 360.
54. United States Government, *Economic Co-operation Act*, Washington, 1948, Section 117 d.
55. *The Times*, 3.3.52.
56. North Atlantic Treaty Organisation established in January 1951.
57. Report of the Randall Commission on *United States Foreign Economic Policy* made to President Eisenhower, Washington, February 1954.
58. United Nations, *World Economic Survey, 1960*, New York, 1961, Table 4–3, pp. 132 and 134.
59. United Nations, *Economic and Social Consequences of Disarmament*, New York, 1962, Table 2–1, p. 55.
60. United States Government, *Statistical Abstract of the United States, 1960*, Tables 345 and 1107.
61. V. Perlo, *Empire of High Finance*, p. 295.
62. *Manchester Guardian*, 'Conditions for U.S. Aid to Latin America', 15.3.61.
63. United States Department of Commerce, *Survey of Current Business*, August 1960.
64. United Nations, *Economic and Social Consequences of Disarmament*.
65. E. Strauss, *Commonsense about the Common Market*, Allen and Unwin, 1958, p. 60.
66. Organisation for Economic Co-operation and Development, *General Statistics*, Paris, January 1962, pp. 14 and 22.
67. E. Strauss, op. cit., p. 70.
68. B. Davidson, *Germany What Now?*, Muller, 1960, p. 126; and J. S. Martin, *All Honourable Men*, New York, 1950, p. 241.
69. J. S. Martin, op. cit., *passim*; and G. Baumann, *Eine Handvoll Konzern Herren*, Berlin, 1953; and Deutsches Wirtschaftsinstitut, *Bericht 3*, Berlin, February 1959.
70. Deutsches Wirtschaftsinstitut, *Bericht 3*.

71. European Coal and Steel Community, High Authority, *Ninth General Report on the Activities of the Community*, Luxembourg, 1961, p. 128.

72. United Nations, Economic Commission for Europe, *Economic Survey of Europe in 1956*, Geneva, 1957, Chapter IV, p. 17; and *Economic Survey of Europe in 1957*, Geneva, 1958, Chapter V, p. 12,

73. Economist Intelligence Unit, *Britain in Europe*, p. 20.

74. *The Times Review of Industry*, January 1954.

75. S. Williams, *The Common Market and Its Forerunners*, Fabian International Bureau, 1958; and see *Financial Times*, 'Ruhr Coal Syndicates', 25.10.61.

76. E. Strauss, op. cit., p. 72 ff.

77. R. Aron, 'Problems of Economic Integration', *Lloyds Bank Review*, April 1953.

78. E. Hirsch, 'Euratom Planning', *The Challenge of Europe*, published by *The Financial Times*, 27.11.60.

79. *The Times*, 13.1.60.

80. Statement by Mr Heath in the House of Commons, 13.6.62.

81. W. Pickles, *Not with Europe*, Fabian International Bureau, 1962.

82. Deutsches Wirtschaftsinstitut, op. cit., p. 19.

83. ibid., p. 21 ff., and pp. 4–5.

84. V. I. Lenin, *Imperialism*, Little Lenin Library, 1944 edition, p. 102.

85. *The Financial Times*, 15.1.62; and T. Balogh 'Africa and the Common Market', *Common Market Studies I*, Blackwell, 1962.

86. European Economic Community Commission, *Fourth General Report*, Brussels, May 1961, Tables 5 and 6, pp. 188 ff.

87. Sir Roy Harrod, *The Times*, 2.1.62.

88. President Olympia of Togo at the Lagos Conference of French-speaking African States, reported in *West Africa*, 10.2.62.

89. V. M. Molotov, *Problems of Foreign Policy*, Moscow, 1949, p. 467.

90. United States delegate speaking at the fifth session of the UNRRA Council in August 1956; see J. J. Joseph 'European Recovery and United States Aid', *Science and Society*, New York, Summer 1948.

91. J. J. Joseph, op. cit.

92. United States, *Mutual Defence Assistance Control Act of 1951*, Washington, 1951, introduced by Senator Battle.

93. R. Baykov, *Soviet Foreign Trade*, Oxford, 1946, p. 7 ff.

94. United Nations, *Monthly Bulletin of Statistics*, New York, June 1960.

95. United Nations, Economic Commission for Europe, *Report on Potentialities for Increased Trade and Accelerated Development in Europe*, Geneva, 1948.

96. British Council for the Promotion of International Trade, *China's Foreign Trade*, July 1954.

97. N. B. Scott, *Sino-Soviet Trade*, Soviet Studies, October 1958.

98. Economist Intelligence Unit, *Oxford Regional Economic Atlas of the USSR and East Europe*, Oxford, 1956; and *Oxford Economic Atlas*, Oxford, 1954.

99. Statements respectively by Premier Gomulka, reported in *The Times*, 26.10.56, and by Premier Kadar in *The Times*, 17.11.56.

100. United Nations, Economic Commission for Europe, *Economic Survey of Europe in 1954*, Geneva, 1955, pp. 121-2.

101. Premier Gomulka, op. cit.

102. Premier Kadar, op. cit.

103. V. Dedijer, *Tito Speaks*, Weidenfeld and Nicholson, 1953, pp. 294-6.

104. United Nations, *Economic Survey of Europe in 1954*, pp. 121 ff.

105. United Nations, *Economic Survey of Europe in 1957*, Geneva, 1958, Chapter VI, p. 2.

106. W. P. and Z. K. Coates, *Soviets in Central Asia*, Lawrence and Wishart, 1951, p. 109 ff.

107. ibid., p. 114.

108. L Barnes, *Soviet Light on the Colonies*, Penguin, 1944, Chapter VIII.

109. United Nations, *Economic Survey of Europe in 1959*, Geneva, 1960, Chapter III.

110. United Nations, *Economic Survey of Europe in 1954*, pp. 114-15.

111. United Nations, Economic Commission for Europe, *Economic Bulletin*, Geneva, June 1959, p. 62 and Table I, p. 40.

112. United Nations, *Economic Survey of Asia and the Far East, 1955*, p. 98, and *1957*, p. 103.

113. United Nations, Economic Commission for Europe, *Economic Bulletin*, June 1959, Table 1, p. 40, and Table 3, p. 45.

114. ibid., p. 55 ff.

115. ibid., Table 2, p. 42.

116. United Nations, Economic Commission for Europe, *Economic Bulletin*, Vol. 13, No. 1, Geneva, 1960, pp. 22-3.

117. *Far East Trade*, 'Annual China Review', p. x, October 1961.

118. *The Statist*, 19.11.55.

119. *The Financial Times*, 1.5.56.

120. U.K. Government, *Annual Abstract of Statistics, 1961*, Direction of External Trade.

121. *The Statist*, 20.5.61.

122. *The Financial Times*, 18.5.61.

123. United Nations, Economic Commission for Europe, *The Price of Oil in Western Europe*.

CHAPTER 11

Industrialisation of the World

In this chapter we shall be concerned to discover what are the conditions necessary for the industrialisation of the present underdeveloped lands. We shall bear in mind the experience of the European countries and of the lands of white settlement overseas, which have been industrialised by capitalist methods. We have already noted that these methods have so far not only failed to advance industrialisation elsewhere but seem even to have held it back. We have to ask whether capitalism can in fact do the job now, either by the extension of capitalist enterprises from the more-advanced industrial lands or by the emergence of indigenous capitalist entrepreneurs. We shall finally consider what successes the communist-controlled lands have had in the matter of industrialisation and determine what may be learnt from them by those who wish to get the results of socialist planning without the methods of communism.

We began this book with a study of the contrast between the rich lands and the poor lands of the world and of the widening gap between them. The people in the lands which have been industrialised have been able to double their real wealth in every generation, and they have done this for at least three generations,[1] while the people in the non-industrialised lands have barely advanced (Table I, Introduction). Indeed, there is some evidence that the real wealth of the Indian and Chinese peoples actually declined from the middle of the seventeenth century.[2] When a higher standard of life is so evidently associated with industrialisation, the people of the non-industrialised lands can only be expected to wish to embark upon the process as urgently as possible.

The Necessary Conditions for Industrial Development

It is often argued in criticism of the desire for industrialisation that some predominantly agricultural lands are rich.[3] Australia, New Zealand and Denmark are given as examples; but in fact none of these countries has as much as a quarter of its labour force engaged in agriculture. By the outbreak of the Second World War each had raised the proportion of the labour force engaged in industry to nearly one-third, with at least another quarter in trade, commerce, transport and communication. This is a point of the greatest importance. India, by contrast, has more than two-thirds of her people living and working on the land and there are many under-developed lands where the proportion is three-quarters and even more.[4]

This is the crux of the matter. All rich lands have at least a quarter of their people engaged in manufacture; India had until recently a bare tenth.[5] Many lands have less. Only increased mechanisation, applied not only to industry but to agriculture also, can raise output per man in such a way as to improve the standard of life of the people. Australia and New Zealand have in effect mechanised their agriculture. Machinery has been well described as 'stored-up or accumulated labour',[6] available to be applied to the easing and speeding of labour processes, and as such it is essential to a higher standard of living.

It is sometimes suggested that the underdeveloped lands are so because they lack sources of power and industrial raw materials which could be developed.[7] This is a hangover of thinking from the conception of a supposed natural division

of labour in the world between primary and industrial producers. There never was such a 'natural' division; it was one
that the imperial powers imposed. None of the larger underdeveloped lands lacks sources of power, from coal or from
water, nor do they lack iron or many of the other essential
metals.[8] If one superimposes a raw materials map of the
world upon a population map, the sites of another fifty or
sixty new industrial regions immediately suggest themselves,
in addition to the present twenty or so.[9] Indeed, it is Europe,
not the underdeveloped lands, that lacked many of these
resources in large quantity and had to colonise the world to
make good its deficiencies.

The conditions necessary for carrying through the process
of industrialisation are not so easily come by, as we have had
good reason to notice more than once in this book. From the
simplest point of view, it is necessary to put men to work to
construct and then to operate industrial undertakings. This
means that manpower must be freed from other work (pre-
sumably in agriculture) and nevertheless fed while working
in industry. Surpluses of labour and of food must, therefore,
be created if they do not already exist. In addition, certain
technical skills must be learnt, or otherwise obtained from
outside, and similarly the necessary machines must either be
made or imported.

From another point of view, in a money economy, we may
think of the early stages of this process as the accumulation of
capital, by the extraction of a surplus from current production
for investment in advances to labour, payments for raw
materials, and the like. There is a danger, however, that this
conception may conceal the real needs – for food, for labour,
for materials, for skills – which the holding of mobilisable
financial resources no more than symbolises. As a matter of
history, the emergence of entrepreneurs with capital or access
to capital may strike us as the crucial event; but this event was
itself the product of a more complex process involving
technical changes in agriculture leading to the possibility of a

surplus of food and labour, no less than technical changes in manufacturing leading to machine production of goods. It is a mistake, therefore, to think of industrialisation as a diversion of resources from agriculture or handicrafts, without bearing in mind that it involves in its essence increased productivity, that is an increased total output from the existing labour force, and this requires increased use of mechanical aids.[10]

It is of great significance that some of the biggest differences in productivity between developed industrialised lands and underdeveloped lands are in agricultural production.[11] The whole emphasis of this book has been on the quite artificial nature of the division of labour between industrial lands and lands of primary production. The real difference lies between lands with an accumulation of mechanical aids (rich in capital, we might say) and those without mechanical aids (poor in capital). Improved agricultural productivity is itself dependent on increased industrial production.

It must be emphasised that the process of industrialisation is a total process, technical change, the division of labour and capital accumulation interacting together. It is also a cumulative process, each advance opening up the possibility of new advances, especially if the early advances include the establishment of basic heavy industries which will nourish the growth of the whole industrial sector. It is this cumulative process, or the lack of it, which we have seen to lead to the widening gap between the rich developed lands and the poor underdeveloped lands, and to the vicious circle of rich lands attracting capital and poor lands repelling it.[12] To make the break into the process of industrialisation thus requires some special transformation in the total situation. It is not enough that this should be the discovery of some new resource that can be developed, such as coal or petroleum, or some new technique, such as the application of atomic energy to providing power; for such discoveries, as we have seen so often, lead to no new development without a critical change in the scale and ownership of capital, in the availability of labour from the land, in the raising of agricultural output, in the opening-up of a wider market for manufactures and in the rise to power of a new class of decision-makers.

The Checks to Development

What, then, are the main checks which now hold up the break through to industrialisation in underdeveloped lands? Not labour; there is no shortage of labour. Improved hygiene and medical treatment have created surplus populations throughout Asia and Africa and southern Europe.[13] Unemployed throng the towns; 'disguised unemployed',[14] that is underemployed seasonal farm-workers, fill the countryside. The surplus may amount to as much as one-third of the total labour force in many countries in Asia.[15] Technical skills are short, but there are far better possibilities today than before (though they are still not enough) of making up this deficiency through national and international scholarships, technical aid programmes, etc. Most still depends on fuller utilisation of the existing skills.

Nor are the resources lacking for development. Iron and coal, water-power, petroleum and other necessary minerals abound throughout Asia and Africa and South America, in the last two especially on a scale far in excess of the reserves of Europe.[16] These resources have for long been developed to a limited extent by Europeans and, as European and North American reserves of metals and power sources are run down, the development of Asian, African and South American reserves has been expanded.[17]

We have seen earlier why this has not led to industrialisation of the lands where the raw material resources have been developed. The material has been exported for refining and manufacturing elsewhere. The profits as well as the materials have been taken from the country, in some cases leaving behind nothing more to show for the wealth that once lay in the ground than a large hole.

'When we have finished,' the manager of the new iron-ore mine in Mauretania has boasted, 'there will be no landscape.'[18] There will also be no iron and steel works in Mauretania, although coal is available in neighbouring Nigeria or could be obtained by sea from Europe. The same process is taking place in Guinea, in Liberia, in British Guiana, in Venezuela and elsewhere. As the mountains of iron-ore are removed for use in the steel works of the extracting companies – British, American, French, German – development in the countries of origin is limited to the ports and railways. Yet things are changing; today half the profits of the operation are to go to the governments of Guinea, Liberia and Mauretania in the case of the mines being opened up in these lands.[19] Here is the basis for industrialisation. What else is needed?

Some of the most crucial problems vary from land to land. In India the problem is to assure the food supply for industrial workers, in Africa to develop technical and entrepreneurial skills, in Latin America to control the competition from North American manufactures. Behind all three lies the common need to challenge a social system that holds back development.

In studying the history of the lands that have become industrialised, we saw how the young industrialists had to break through the restraints of both feudal landlords and merchant capitalists in order to start the process of accumulation, free the labour and open up the market. We have suggested in subsequent chapters that the external restraints on development involved in colonial rule have become less important than the internal restraints. These are themselves a hangover from colonial rule, through semi-feudal landownership and the power of merchant and 'comprador' capital, and are often, as we have seen, encouraged by the old imperial powers.

It is time that we spelt out the nature of these restraints, so that we may understand how the non-industrialised lands may free themselves from them. The operation of fully feudal relationships, holding back accumulation, the freeing of labour and the opening of the market are not widely to be found today. Only on the great *latifundios* that remain in South America, and in the villages of some very backward countries such as Tibet, can human labourers properly be regarded as serfs. Yet this is still the case in Brazil, where a great landlord could boast but recently that 'in this house are bought only iron, salt, gunpowder and lead', all else being produced on the estate.[20] The *latifundios* may be very large, running to hundreds of thousands of acres;[21] but there is clearly no market in such an economy for manufacturing industry.

Where there is a much less complete form of feudal land-ownership, and labour is free to move and a national market exists, economic development may still be frustrated. One has to ask, first, what is the effect of the system of land-ownership on the efficiency and scale of agricultural output; second, what happens to any surplus output that is available. Is it available for feeding industrial workers? How much can be sold abroad to pay for imports of machines?

In most of the lands of South-East Asia and South America the landlord collects what might become surplus, in the form of rent, often to the extent of 50 per cent of each crop; he may take even more through his role of money-lender and he may claim the labour of the peasant also for work on his garden and for other levies and dues.[22] What does he do with the rent? This is what matters. He does not invest it in industry. Why should he? He lives only too well off the land. He does not even use it to reinvest in the land; he generally lives in the town and is interested only in the collection of his dues, having no technical knowledge of the processes of production whatever.

This is the main charge of Mr Zahid Hussein, the late

Chairman of the Pakistan Planning Board, writing about his draft Five-Year Plan.[23] How then does the landlord spend his dues? 'He is fond of pomp and show and likes to possess expensive cars and spends lavishly on luxury goods,' says Mr Masud, another senior Pakistan civil servant, writing in a minute of dissent to the Sind Hari Enquiry Committee Report of 1948.[24] The vital surplus of agricultural output goes to feed those who supply luxury goods and services. This is not only wasteful in a land with millions of people living at starvation level; it also leads to the spending of scarce foreign exchange on luxury items, for many of these luxuries, such as cars, have to be imported. This only repeats the picture which we saw when we looked at the expenditures from the oil profits of the Arab sheikhs.

The result of this conspicuous consumption is, however, worse than just wasteful; some part of the landlord's rent might be taxed by the Government for development expenditure, although a government of landlords would hardly do this, and taxation on rents is peculiarly open to evasion. What is worse is the effect of high rents on the peasant. His demand for manufactured goods, for textiles, tools, household equipment and the like, which might stimulate the growth of local industry, is naturally reduced to the minimum. But, more than this, he ceases to be interested in the efficient cultivation of his land, when so much of the fruit of his labours is enjoyed by others and when his own tenure of the land is so insecure. He may, indeed, be incapable of efficient cultivation owing to undernourishment and inability to afford proper equipment, seed and fertilisers. The dung of his animals he must often use to cook the food he eats. This is not an exaggerated picture but one that may be observed throughout South-East Asia and Latin America.[25] It is this that has made land reform the crucial issue for industrialisation.

The Need for Land Reform

Land reform is also desired by the millions of landless labourers. A brief glance at the structure of land-ownership in India will give us the picture we have to understand.[26] In India there are fifteen million households without land, and more than twice as many with under five acres. That accounts for nearly fifty million households. At the other extreme, there are a million and half landowning households who own nearly twice as much land as all the poorest fifty million. Fortunately, there is also a strong middle layer of another fifteen million households, who own perhaps half the land and can provide a small surplus of food for the towns.

Such middle-sized peasant producers in most agricultural countries are the main source of the marketable food surplus available for industrial investment.[27] Their average holding of land is not much more than ten acres per family, and their capacity to increase their output is severely limited, without great intensification of output by the application of machinery, fertilisers and irrigation. It is, however, a large and immediate surplus of food that is required for industrialisation to be speeded up. Productivity in agriculture may rise quickly if the 'disguised' unemployed leave the land. The prospect of work in industry may bring them thronging into the towns, but they do not bring their food with them from the country. One of the first problems of industrial development in India has been to mobilise a food supply for the town populations and absorb the unemployed into work before new thousands join their ranks to push up the demand – and the prices – of food in the towns.[28]

In Britain, the agricultural revolution, as we saw earlier (Chapter 1), partially preceded the industrial revolution, and, at the same time as it increased the food supplies, it provided some of the labour from the land for the factories in the towns. The greater part came from the rising birth-rate and infant survival-rate. In other capitalist lands agriculture was developed by capitalist means side by side with industrialisation. This is an impossible procedure for a land where at least two-thirds of the people form peasant households. The Government would face vastly greater unemployment even than at present exists and uncontrollable peasant discontent. Nevertheless, in India it is clear that increasingly the Government has been relying on the development of capitalist farming.[29] Enterprising farmers have bought land that has come on to the market cheap with the threat of land reform and have proceeded to amalgamate strips and even to use tractors instead of the inefficient, albeit cheap, labour available. The problem of mobilising a really adequate food supply still depends on raising peasant enthusiasm and efficiency to a much higher level, since capitalist methods cannot be applied to the whole job, without increasing the problem of unemployment.

Redistribution of the land will not of itself be successful either, unless state assistance with seeds, tools and fertilisers, and with marketing, accompanies the redistribution. Even then the problem will remain of getting hold of the food surplus for the towns, that is of obtaining a marketable surplus of food, unless crops are to be commandeered directly by the state. If this is not done, all that happens is that the peasant feeds better. Moreover, the raised standards of living of a more efficient peasantry may create a market for manufactured goods from the towns, but, unless industry can supply this, prices rise and the surplus is mopped up without encouraging growth.

Some rise in prices both of foodstuffs and manufactures may be inevitable during a period of rapid growth; but the essential point is that increased agricultural production is of little use, unless it is accompanied by taxation or other means of getting the food surplus on to the market. Taxation of peasants is proverbially difficult to achieve and must obviously not be at such a high rate that it acts as a deterrent to increased production. For the same reason, although investment in heavy industry is necessary for creating the momentum for a rapid rate of growth, some investment in consumer goods' industries must take place at the same time to meet the needs of the agricultural sector, not only for tools and farm equipment, but for the goods that will maintain the incentive to the peasant to go on raising production.[30]

Raw material resources, a surplus of labour and a marketable surplus of food will still not ensure industrialisation without enterprise and technical know-how, and these are especially lacking in a landlord-ridden economy.[31] When we looked at Britain's industrialisation, we saw the crucial importance of the fact that the small English landlord never became wholly separated from the processes of production. Elsewhere, too often the serf or slave had no incentive, and the lord no knowledge of production, to make the small improvements that cumulatively create an agricultural and an industrial revolution. It is the same today, as we noted in considering conditions in Pakistan. Great landlords do not, except in special circumstances, make capitalist entrepreneurs; nor, moreover, do merchants.

Again, our historical study (Chapter 1) showed us, and we have noted since, that merchants and traders are generally themselves quite removed from the processes of production. Merchant capital has rarely become industrial capital; the merchants' enterprise – making big profits on a risky but quick turnover, buying cheap and selling dear – is not what is needed for developing industry. We have also noted earlier (Chapter 5) how much of native capital has been associated with the special enclaves of development, the extraction of minerals and crops for export, that have been the main latter-day interest of the colonial powers. We called this 'comprador' capital. Our main interest before was to note that such 'compradors' continued as loyal custodians of imperial investment, but we must realise now also that they are likely to have little knowledge of, or interest in, industrialisation.

It was the main theme of an earlier chapter (6) that, even after liberation from colonial rule, both internal and external restraints on economic development remain, and that the two forms of restraint came together most clearly in the cold war alliances and the aid given by capitalist governments in the advanced countries to feudal and 'comprador' governments in the underdeveloped lands. It is precisely the successor governments themselves in many ex-colonial territories that are holding back development. Yet it may be doubted whether it is any longer in the direct interests even of foreign capitalists that this should be so, since foreign capital investment in the underdeveloped lands has begun recently to be directed towards industrialisation. Of this we shall see more later.

Industrial Evolution or Revolution

How then with all these restraints upon development are the non-industrialised lands to move forward? The central question we have to answer is whether private capitalist investment by firms from the industrialised lands can do the job; and if not, what then? It has not done the job so far. The earlier history of industrialisation may here be a bad guide, but we should be wise to look at it again. Every country that has industrialised has received some form of foreign aid to carry it 'over the hump' of accumulating enough wealth today to start building for tomorrow. Britain, as the first, took longest and needed most aid, which she obtained as tribute from the wealth of America and India. Once the way had been pioneered, other countries could draw upon British experience, not only her technical and mechanical inventions but the necessary financial organisation of banking and joint-stock companies. Britain gave the world the railway and provided the first machines for industry, in Europe and in North America. She also provided the capital for the in-dustrialising lands to buy the railways and the machines.

Britain gained too, of course, from the corresponding development of new sources of food and raw materials and the opening-up of new markets, until our capitalists began to rest back on the income from past investments (Chapter 4).

The essential elements in this early wave of industrialisation overseas with British capital may easily be missed. First, British capital provided the basic industrial structure and made no attempt to limit in North America, Europe or Australia, the development of local capitalist enterprise. Indeed the most important contribution of Britain to North American and Australian economic development may well have been the immigrants, who brought with them their enterprise and technical knowledge, and often a little capital, and stayed. To some extent this is happening in Central Africa again today.[32]

The second, and perhaps not less important point, was that Britain provided an open market in which the newly developing lands might sell their products and thus repay the money they had borrowed. Thirdly, much of the capital invested overseas by British rentiers was in Government stocks, which gave to the foreign government, rather than to British capital, the power to develop the economy. Indeed, loans were quite often defaulted on, so that they amounted, in effect, to direct grants from Britain. These are all crucial points to which we shall return.

One other aspect of earlier industrialisation, to which attention is now being drawn, is the order of events in the process. First, it is said, came the agricultural revolution, then the building-up of an infra-structure of transport and communications, then textiles and consumer goods industries, which themselves demanded a capital goods industry.[33] This is supposed to be the natural evolutionary process, that creates the appearance of revolution only by the cumulative speed of the changes. It is not, however, a correct description of what took place, even in Britain, where the process of industrialisation lasted longest. In the first place, agricultural changes took place side by side with industrial change – in the early seventeenth century, in the middle of the eighteenth century and at the end of the nineteenth century. Secondly, some development of heavy industry, of power and machines, had of necessity to precede the establishment of light industries, textiles, and so on. The revolutionary point of change came with the making of the machines themselves that gave man a way of storing up labour and increasing power to control his environment.

This argument about a 'natural' and 'evolutionary' order of events is similar to that which we examined earlier about a supposed 'natural' division of labour between primary and industrial producers. It is very evident today that the less-developed lands have only been able to establish light industries; but this is not because it is 'natural' for them with their large reserves of labour power and small accumulation of capital to develop 'labour-intensive' industries rather than those which are 'capital-intensive'.[34] It is because they have not been able to compete with imports from the industrialised lands, and because, by the very nature of their colonial status in the past, they have not been able to protect and develop their native industries. Now that this situation has changed, it is primarily the internal restraints which we have been speaking of that are holding them back.

Yet it is precisely the development of heavy industry that provides the cumulative momentum for accelerating the whole process of development. In the short run, an immediate increase in wealth may be achieved by investment in consumer goods industries. In the long run, a much greater increase in wealth will follow from the establishment of a heavy industrial base.[35] This is very simply because with larger foundations a larger building may be built. It should not, therefore, be supposed that every small underdeveloped land must have its steel combines. This is the way the argument has been ridiculed by advisers from the World Bank.[36] It is certainly true, however, that every small underdeveloped land should join together with other small under-developed lands to form a common market around a new heavy industrial complex. It may be said that this is precisely how they are now oriented around the advanced capitalist powers. But we have seen enough of this relationship to know that, in this way, new heavy industrial bases in those under-developed lands which are suited to such industrialisation will never be established; it is a very important point, how-ever, that the main weight of recent overseas investment by British *heavy* industry has been in the *more*-developed lands (Chapter 8). Investment in the *less*-developed lands has been mainly by firms in *light* industries manufacturing consumer goods. The main industrial base has remained at home in the advanced industrial country.

Can Capitalism do the Job?

The case of the steel mill which British firms are building in India precisely illustrates our point. Discussions had gone on for years without the project getting any nearer to realisation, when the Russians offered to build a mill for the Indians. The whole question began to involve British prestige in the competition between capitalism and socialism. British Government finance was obtained; this persuaded the City of London to come in and the capital for the job was found.[37] Why then have British firms not been interested in develop-ing basic industries in the non-industrialised lands, apart from North America, Australia and Southern Africa?

The answer is twofold. First, there is the hangover from the past. The neglected overseas lands were precisely those where competition was destroyed and markets for British industry were built up. Since the first destruction of com-petitors, there has always been some reluctance to see local industry develop, which might compete for labour with the mines and plantations established in so many colonial lands and thus push up wages and eliminate the very profitable exploitation of cheap labour. But deliberate neglect can only give us a part of the answer.* The second part is given by the internal restraints on development of which we have spoken.

The main reason for the failure of capitalism to invest more in the industrialisation of the less-developed lands has arisen from a real doubt about the possibilities of success, and, therefore, of a profitable return. Investment in heavy industry is a big business, on which a return may only be seen in the very long term. There must be good reasons to believe that the whole overseas economy will develop in such a way as to nourish a market for capital goods. Many problems of power, transport and communications, the housing and training of labour have to be overcome. It is not surprising that capitalist firms and financiers, including those who have the spending of the funds of the World Bank in their hands, should prefer to wait and see how the establishment of light industries and the development of power supplies and a marketable surplus of food goes, before wishing to sink their capital in heavy industry.[39]

There is the risk, moreover, that they may be expropriated by nationalisation, when local capital and labour grow strong enough to resent the hold that foreign capital has upon their existence. The fact is that the 'natural' and 'evolutionary' process of industrialisation has suited very well the capitalist development of empty lands which have been settled by European migrants, but its application to lands with huge and proud populations, whose patterns of life and thought have long been fixed, and often distorted by colonial rule, is a very different matter. It is well not to forget that it needed a revolution to establish capitalism in Britain.

In the emergence of British industrial capitalism, it was

* It is a surprising weakness in Paul Baran's *The Political Economy of Growth* that he gives so much weight to the fear of encouraging higher wages for the failure of capitalism to invest in the industrialisation of the less-developed lands, when he has himself analysed so brilliantly the *internal* 'morphology of backwardness'.[38]

necessary for the young manufacturing class to break completely the power of the feudal landlords and of the merchant monopolies. This was the political revolutionary counterpart to the industrial revolution. Even North American industry was unable to develop fully until the power of the semi-feudal slave-owning South had been broken. Just so we cannot expect capitalism to carry through industrialisation in India, Pakistan or in other underdeveloped lands, without breaking completely the power of the semi-feudal land-owning class.

Yet alien capitalist investors can scarcely do this job; indeed, we have seen that they have tended to preserve feudal ruling groups in power by the cold-war alliances. Moreover, the 'comprador' orientation of merchant capital has stood in the way of the emergence of a native industrial capitalist class. What is more, the competition of the subsidiaries of foreign firms in the underdeveloped lands has actually set back the development of what local enterprise already existed. There have been several examples of British and American firms established recently in consumer industries in Pakistan, actually driving local capitalists out of business.[40] Feudal and 'comprador' elements become only the more entrenched.

This is a point of central importance. The establishment of modern manufacturing based on the latest technology may not only damage local industrial competition, but by its unplanned development may undermine the whole basis in rural and domestic handicrafts of future industrial development. This is precisely what imports of British textiles and manufactures did in India in the early nineteenth century. Myrdal's cumulative processes of enrichment of the rich and impoverishment of the poor are being established today *inside* the underdeveloped countries as well as between the advanced and the underdeveloped.[41]

If it seems already not a little doubtful whether the natural and evolutionary process of capitalist industrialisation will accomplish the job in the as yet undeveloped lands, because of the hangover of distortions from colonial rule, our doubts become all the greater when we consider two new factors which we have not yet mentioned. The first is the rate of growth of population. The one major result of European science in the underdeveloped lands has been the reduction of the death-rate, particularly of the infant mortality rate, by measures of hygiene and inoculation.

Capitalist industrialisation took a long time to accomplish, even in the specially favourable circumstances of the colonial wealth that Europe and North America could draw upon. In many lands besides India, the rate of population growth is such that a slow rate of economic growth will simply be inadequate to start the cumulative process of industrialisation. This means that a rate of economic growth of, let us say, 2 to 3 per cent per year is reduced by population growth everywhere of about 2 per cent per year to practically no advance in income per head. What is even more serious, the growth of population has not been accompanied in the less-developed lands by any comparable application of modern science to the production of food.[42] The problems of mobilising a food surplus and of employing the overcrowded population on the land have thus become the central problems of the countries which are embarking on industrialisation.

In North America and in Australia, population growth always followed after economic growth, and the result was both to encourage capital investment in view of the high cost of labour and to bring immediate yields in higher living standards from the growth that was made.[43] Even more important, food supplies could be raised by applying industrial capitalist methods to the largely virgin lands, without the need to feed a displaced agricultural population. There is an absolutely crucial difference between this situation and the situation in India today.

Capitalist agricultural methods cannot solve India's or Pakistan's food problems without creating rural unemployment on a gigantic scale. The moral is not that Indian and

Pakistan development must be limited to labour-intensive schemes. Industrialisation will never be accomplished if the means are excluded of building up a large mass of 'stored labour' by establishing a heavy industrial base to the Indian economy; the moral must be that other means than those of normal capitalist industrialisation and capitalist farming must be found.

Planned Economic Development

This is the more necessary because the history of capitalist growth has been marked, as is well known, by periodic checks, which appear to be built into the system. These are especially serious in the effect on the underdeveloped lands, as we noted in considering the 1930s and as we have seen again since 1954. The result of these checks in development is, first, to reduce the demand of the industrialised lands for food and raw materials and so cut back the earnings of the non-industrialised lands from their sales of primary products; and this interrupts their imports of industrial equipment.

The secondary effects of a check to capitalist growth may be even more serious, because of the check to profit expectations and thus to the whole cumulative and interacting processes of economic development. To some extent, as we have seen, the European and North American economies could live through these crisis periods by taking advantage of the correspondingly cheaper food and raw materials they could import at such times and by drawing on the fruit of past investments abroad. This living off their fat, as it were, is not open to the underdeveloped lands of today.

The crucial problem for them is not only somehow to maintain their imports of equipment, when their export earnings decline – this may be achieved by various forms of aid and by running down reserves – but they have also to maintain a climate of development, when the general atmosphere of profit expectations, so essential to capitalist growth, has received a check. Herein lies the immense advantage of planned economic development: that the framework of growth is more easily held up and the expectations of individual entrepreneurs of what will happen in other sectors of the economy can be sustained.[44]

Many countries embarking on industrialisation today have drawn up plans, including India, Pakistan, Burma and Ceylon as well as the communist countries.[45] Such plans are essential if a sharp increase is to be made in the rate of investment or a sharp change in the direction of investment, as, for example, into heavy industry. At the same time, some planning is also required to match the output of different sectors of the economy, when such rapid changes are being made, to match wages and prices and to match imports with. exports and other sources of foreign currency including aid.[46] Such matching is essential if grave dislocation and inflation are to be avoided. There still remains the problem of implementing the plans.

In the countries under communist leadership, the main means of production have been brought into social ownership. In such countries the success of the plan will depend on the accuracy of the information from which the plan starts, on a correct understanding of the relationships and interaction of the different sectors of the economy, on sound estimates of how fast each unit and each sector will expand, on training management and workers and, finally, on developing incentives, including the general *élan* of the people, to carry the job through.[47] Where a large part, or the greater part, of the means of production are in private hands, it is the private owners to whom the incentive has to be applied.[48]

The very existence of a plan removes some of the 'unknowability' about the future and about the activities of other complementary producers, which would otherwise be one of the factors holding back private owners from taking the necessary risks. But what is required is new enterprise and

our earlier studies suggested that there may simply not be the
new entrepreneurs. A special problem arises in India from the
fact that 80 per cent of productive assets are still under
management agencies acting for absentee local or foreign
owners.[49]

This is precisely the situation that we have been anticipat-
ing in describing the hangovers of colonial economies. In
these circumstances the state has to step in not only with
incentives for existing entrepreneurs but with its own enterprises and its own training schemes for management and
technical education. This is what has happened in India
where development in steel, coal, electric power, oil,
aluminium and fertilisers is largely, but not wholly, in state
enterprises.[50] With a large state sector and a comprehensive
plan, it is not impossible to secure the necessary interconnection between different sectors of the economy that will
sustain the momentum of growth. There remains the
problem of raising the national product, particularly in
agriculture, and thus of investing a sufficiently high proportion of the national product to create the momentum.
Can this be done with private capital ownership?

What we have said so far suggests that a negative answer
must be returned. Individual private companies will only be
encouraged to invest in a new enterprise where there is an
existing market inside the country or abroad for the product
of the enterprise. Large countries like India have, therefore,
more chance of attracting private capital than have the small
ones. The unification of small, newly liberated colonial
territories in Africa and elsewhere becomes the more
necessary from this point of view, also, as well as for the
purpose of bargaining with the great powers. A large
population, at a low standard of living, however, only means
a large potential market. To make the potential real requires
just those measures of planning to balance development
between different sectors of the economy, which no individual private enterprise can supply. This, as we have seen,

is especially important in relating agricultural and industrial development.

We must now consider what has been done in countries under communist leadership, where planning has been most comprehensive.

Communist Agricultural Policy

To begin with the land, the first task of the communists was to destroy feudalism and redistribute the land of the great landlords through land reform. This did not generally result in any great increase in the marketable surplus produced; the peasant simply ate more himself.[51] Even when better seeds and tools have been provided, the extra return has been inadequate to meet the growing needs of the industrial workers. The old problem of mobilising the surplus from the land appeared in a new form. Individual peasants on tiny strips of land are neither able to produce an adequate surplus nor easily persuaded to part with it when they have it.[52]

Moreover, the tendency for smaller and less efficient producers to become indebted in bad years to the larger and more efficient continued. This is the problem that faced the Russians in the early 1920s.[53] Either the larger peasants were to be given further encouragement, as they were in the N.E.P. period, and a marketable surplus be obtained from them, or completely new measures were required. What happened was that the peasants were collectivised by force on the old lands, and state farms were established to cultivate the new lands. In this way, mechanisation was introduced on a large scale and compulsory deliveries to the state for use in industry were exacted. The low prices paid by the state, however, diverted the collective farmers' efforts into their private plots and kept investment in the agricultural sector at a very low level.

The Chinese communists gave the peasant land, at the same time levying heavy taxes on his crop; then they persuaded him to farm co-operatively and finally brought him into the communes.[54] Various means of pressure have been used in eastern Europe to establish collective or co-operative farming. It should be noted that these measures, however ruthless they may have been, should not, except transitionally and in bad harvests, involve a reduction in the amount of agricultural output consumed per head by workers on the land. Only the proportion of agricultural output remaining in the hands of landworkers of course went down, as the supplies of food were drawn on to feed the workers moving into the towns to work in industry.[55]

It is beside the point to be sentimental about the peasant with his five acres and a cow. There was never anything sentimental about the landlord and the money-lender when New Year came round and the debts had to be paid.[56] An agricultural revolution is a ruthless affair. The trauma of the enclosures and the driving of the peasants off the land in England was as terrible as any great change in the whole of our national history.[57] The test must be the hard-headed one of whether the measures worked. On this test the Russian collectivisation must be seen as the only way open to Stalin to mobilise the necessary food surplus for industrialisation. Russia alone of all the industrial powers carried through her industrialisation without foreign aid. Even a small measure of help from more advanced lands might have made possible the provision of more consumer goods and better agricultural machinery, which would have made the Russian peasant more willing and more efficient. The Chinese and the East European communists have at least been able to some extent to combine the stick of 'persuasion' with the carrot of better tools and household goods. Again, judged by results, the Chinese have been the most successful in raising their food production.

China's grain crop was doubled in ten years to a total of over 250 million tons. That is nearly four times India's output, and the population of China is less than double that of

India. Even if there is still an element of exaggeration in this figure, after the revisions made to the much larger claims of 1958, the increases must be impressive.[58] The remarkable fact is that, despite the worst natural calamities of flood and drought and locusts suffered for decades, Chinese agricultural output was maintained in 1959 and 1960. This was the result of the immense effort that had been put into water-control works in the previous ten years.[59] Even the correspondents of the western press in Hong Kong, who have become worthy successors of the correspondents in Riga in the 1920s, admit that there have been no signs of malnutrition among refugees.[60]

For the first time in Chinese history, a series of natural calamities has not been followed by famine deaths of millions, but only by severe shortages. China's problems remains, however, to feed the rapidly rising population, as well as to mobilise a food surplus for the towns and develop non-food agricultural products for export. Indeed, the major mistake of the Communist authorities, apart from their excessive enthusiasm for deep ploughing, would appear to be that they gambled on good harvests in diverting so much land to industrial crops. It was bad luck rather than bad policies that gave them three successive years of winter flood and spring drought. Hence the import of five million tons of Canadian, Australian and other grains in 1960 and 1961; China had 60 million more mouths to feed in 1961 than in 1957.[61]

Even before the disasters of 1959–61 there were, however, food shortages in the cities, which suggest that it was not easy to collect the grain crop from the peasants, who were only too glad to eat the extra amount they grew. It may indeed be that it is more difficult to collect from the communes than it was from the smaller co-operatives; but it should not be, as the commune is a large enough unit to make the concealing of stocks a difficult business.[62] Success here will depend on the machinery and other manufactures, the tractors and the fertilisers, that the industrial centres have to offer in exchange for food.[63] Collection of non-food crops, particularly of raw materials for export, seems to have gone better. Output of these is said to have been much more than doubled between 1950 and 1960; tobacco output to have increased tenfold.[64]

The importance of this agricultural revolution for Chinese economic development cannot be exaggerated; and it is not surprising that many Indian Congress leaders have been recommending the adoption of co-operative farming in India.[65] The problem is, first, that the great landholdings would have to be broken up in order even to begin to win peasant support. The movement for voluntary land distribution in India has failed;[66] in Pakistan the new land reform does not do more than nibble at the fringe of the great estates, by reducing the maximum holding of land to 1,000 acres, or 500 acres of irrigated land and 250 acres of orchard.[67] This so-called land reform, which Gen. Ayub Khan has so widely publicised, is no more than what his predecessor, Firoz Khan Noon, himself one of Pakistan's greatest landowners, had promised. By the time Ayub Khan carried the measure through, all holdings of over 1,000 acres had been carefully subdivided among individual members of the landowning families.

The second part of the problem is, then, to get the peasant to combine his newly-won land with that of his fellow villagers and farm it jointly. If the job is to be done without the stick of communist labour brigades and communal leadership, the carrot will have to be all the larger. Chinese experience suggests that the sight of tractor ploughing and team work on a few demonstration schemes did more good than the flood of propaganda. With increasing co-operation yield per acre in many districts was doubled between 1949 and 1956.[68]

One cannot help thinking that the equivalent value of farm machinery would do more lasting good than the three million tons of grain that India has been getting every year from

American farm surpluses, especially in reclaiming the 200 million acres suffering from soil erosion.[69] This is a point of great importance when the value of aid is being considered. China's agricultural advance has certainly been dependent on the tools and equipment that the new industrial plants were able to provide for the farmer to reclaim and irrigate lost land; and this may well be the most important aspect of the communes, and of all the little local steel works, that the output of farm tools and of small-scale machinery was really stepped up; and, finally, that communal labour could be applied to the giant tasks of water control.[70] The point has been made before, but it is worth repeating, that industrial and agricultural advance must proceed together, for each is dependent on the other.

This does not mean that India should necessarily attempt to become self-sufficient in all food supplies. International exchanges and in particular intra-regional trade, for example of Indian manufactures for Burmese rice, would help both parties to save foreign exchange earnings in industrial lands solely for imports of capital equipment and use capital at home only for investment in those fields where natural advantages are greatest.[71] One of the main objections to Indian imports of grain from the United States is precisely that it reduces imports of rice from neighbouring underdeveloped lands like Burma.

From what was just said, it might be implied that the way forward for a country with a very large unemployed and underemployed population like India or China, might be by the mobilisation of great armies of labour to carry out construction schemes. In fact, geological conditions, in dam-building, for example, generally demand a combination of labour- and capital-intensive methods. Moreover, the economic dangers of inflationary pressures on available goods have still to be met if more labour is employed without a higher rate of saving or taxation.[72] The propensity to save and the possibility of increasing taxation among labourers absorbed from rural unemployment are not high. Even with starvation wages, it must be clear from what was said earlier, that labour-intensive efforts will not by themselves industrialise a country; there must also be the capital-intensive development of heavy industry, if the foundations for industrialisation are to be laid and consumer goods produced to meet the demand of the new earnings of more fully employed labour.

The balancing of investment in capital goods industries and investment in consumer goods industries is a particularly difficult one. Left to itself, the demand of the agricultural sector for goods may easily swing the whole trend of development away from heavy industry and towards production of consumer goods. Just to raise the price of consumer goods would leave large profits in the hands of the light industries, which would tend to re-invest in further consumer goods production. What the Russians did, and the practice has been copied in other communist-controlled economies, was to institute a variable turnover tax. The variation of rates of such a tax from industry to industry permitted prices of consumer goods to be raised and prices of capital goods to be lowered and an indirect transfer of profits to take place from one to the other.[73]

The Indian and Chinese Plans Compared

How can these important measures adopted by communist governments, where almost the whole of industry and much of agriculture and trade is in social ownership, be applied where a large private industrial and agricultural sector remains, and where the extension of democracy is regarded as important, as, for example, in India? The rate of economic growth under the Chinese Five-Year Plans has been in the past much faster than that under the Indian plans; and a comparison of the two countries' plans may be the best way to discover what is involved in achieving a high rate of economic growth. The rate of China's industrial advance has been very rapid; the fixed assets of industrial enterprises have been increased fourfold in ten years; and industrial output has been multiplied ten times.[74] China has risen during this period from the lowest ranks to the top ten in the world in production of steel, coal and electricity.[75]

It should not be supposed that China is now an industrialised land or anything like it; only the base in heavy industry has been built. Some of the biggest problems remain: developing modern industries on a very large scale with a very small number of scientists, technicians and skilled workers; raising productivity when there are no more unemployed, underemployed and 'disguised' unemployed on the land to call upon. With all the reservations we may have about Chinese figures, about the establishment of the Chinese Party as 'the new class', and about Chinese policies towards intellectuals, towards the cold war or towards Tibet, one cannot, however, doubt the impressiveness of the industrial advance. How does this compare with the Indian experience?

Table XXXII below presents figures to show, that, whereas between 1952 and 1960 the national income of India was expected to increase by 50 per cent, China's income was to be doubled.[76] Taking the annual average rates of growth over this period, that of China was to be twice as fast as India's (just under 10 per cent compared with just under 5 per cent). As a result, despite the more rapid growth of China's population, the income per head was to be raised by £12 in China and by £4 in India, assuming that both started from the same level of £17. (In this calculation the Indian figures are adjusted to include only the same items as Chinese national income statistics include, that is figures for personal, professional and government services, including those of the armed forces, are left out in the totals for both countries.) The reason for this much more rapid expected growth in China may easily be seen when we compare the proportions of the national income set aside for investment in each country. Those for China are double those for India.

The Table shows that not only did China start with a very high rate of investment (15·5 per cent of national income compared with India's 7 per cent), but that China raised the rate to over 23 per cent during the first Five-Year Plan. This meant that, in those five years, four-fifths of the additional income realised each year was being ploughed back into new investment. Yet this very rapid rate of growth was not achieved, as is so often argued, by a cut in living standards. Consumption per head continued to rise, at a higher rate actually than in India, despite the heavy investment by the Chinese in capital equipment. This was made possible, in other words, because the total national output was being raised so considerably each year.

After the first five years, the Chinese expected to be 'over the hump'. The rate of investment was to be dropped slightly; consumption per head was to rise faster than investment. When we translate these figures into real terms, we can see what was being done in those crucial five years in China. Steel output was more than trebled, electric power output was nearly trebled, cement output was trebled, coal output was doubled, metal-cutting machine tools were more than doubled.[77] China had established a secure industrial base; the output of these industries was in all cases raised to three or four times those of India.[78]

Yet it may need to be emphasised once more that, at the same time as these big increases in output of heavy industry were being made, production of consumer goods was also stepped up considerably, albeit at a slower rate. Between 1952 and 1957, output of many foodstuffs like sugar and vegetable oils was more than doubled, cotton-textiles production was raised by 50 per cent, cigarettes, matches, paper and rubber footwear showed 75 per cent increases or thereabouts.[79] In India, over the same period, increases in output of all these items were also made but, with the exception of sugar, output of which was doubled, the increases were all quite small, of the order of 15 per cent to 20 per cent.[80] It should now be clear from all this evidence that a high rate of investment need not mean a cut in consumption.

The 'hump' was not so easily overcome. What followed after 1957 in China was in fact a very rapid stepping-up of plans for investment and output in 'the year of the great leap'. Statistics certainly took a gigantic leap, as the work of the central statistical office was devolved and the 'partisanship principle' in statistics (that is of only recording the favourable ones) was introduced. It would, nonetheless, be a great mistake to reject out of hand the subsequent revisions to the first wild claims which show a very remarkable continuing rate of growth, of the order of 20 per cent per year in industry. There was a real leap forward in 1958 and it is undoubtedly the poor harvests after 1959 that have held back growth since then. Food and consumer goods have been short, but basic industrial investment has continued at a high level.[81]

We suggested earlier that there were at least three steps involved in starting the process of industrialisation, once the initial decision is taken that the thing must be done, and assuming the country concerned has a large enough national market to justify an industrial base of its own. These steps were to mobilise the necessary food surplus for investment, the necessary labour, the necessary enterprise and technical knowledge. We know how the Chinese got the food and we noted at the same time that they got hold of a food surplus for investment by taxing the peasant; the rest they obtained, as we have just seen, by keeping down the rate of growth of consumption and reinvesting from state-owned industries the greater part of the new value created.

Here lies the first big contrast with the Indian situation. In so far as reliance is put on private investment, the incentive to invest must be the expectation of profit. If the greater part of this profit is to be reinvested, private investors, and particularly those who are used to quick merchant and trading

profits, will simply not play, unless they can be persuaded
that there is a very big return in the long run. On the other
hand, if inducement measures are too generous, restrictions
have to be imposed upon resource allocation and the net
result may be to hinder rather than develop the full realisation of private investment.[82]

In fact, it seems to have been somewhat easier than had
been expected to get Indian businessmen to reinvest the
profits, but the operation has so far been on a fairly small
scale.[83] Taxing the surplus from the land, in order to step
up the whole rate of investment in India, has proved to be a
far more intractable problem. Land revenue in 1959 brought
in a mere £75 million a year to a budget of £1,500 million.[84]
India has remained grossly undertaxed and the apparently
high taxation of the rich is simply not effective.[85]

A higher rate of taxation would make possible the larger
plan which India must have to get over the 'hump', as the
Chinese are doing. We are back at the issue of making a
real change in landownership. There can be little doubt that,
unless this change is made, the end of two or three Indian
economic plans will still leave the country without any solid
industrial base. The moral for new countries embarking upon
industrialisation is evident. Indeed it is not too much to say
that, if land reform is not carried through by democratic
socialists, it will be done in the end by communists.

Mobilising the enterprise and technical knowledge for
industrialisation is perhaps, despite all that we have said, still
one of the most difficult hurdles for a backward country to
overcome.[86] One solution is to attract foreign firms to establish subsidiaries in the country and leave them to provide the
enterprise, technical knowledge and the capital. On the face
of it, the solution seems attractive; but we have already
suggested that it has limitations. Foreign companies tend
to be chary of establishing heavy industries, while in light
industries they tend to destroy local enterprises by competition. Moreover, even though they reinvest their profits

in the business over the first few years, they are bound to expect to be able to repatriate a fair part of them thereafter, and thus actually to withdraw some of the investable surplus from the developing country. The problem of repayment, which we shall consider in a moment, then arrives.

An alternative is to import machinery – this has to be done under the previous method also – and import technical advisers with it, so that they may train local managers and technicians. There remains the problem of finding the local entrepreneurs. We have emphasised frequently that merchants and landlords do not make industrialists. Not only are men required with wide technical knowledge, but also men with organising and administrative ability, the self-confidence and energy to take risks and make big decisions.

There is no reason why such men should not be found among merchants and landlords, though their technical knowledge may well be limited; but there is every reason why they should not go into industry, so long as they can do very well out of the land and out of merchanting. Their whole bias is against having to do with the actual processes of production.[87] It should be remembered that it was not until well on in the nineteenth century that the upstart industrialists were admitted into 'polite' English society.[88] Of course, if the avenues to wealth and power via landowning and merchanting are closed it will be easier to attract gifted and educated men into industry.

There is no doubt, however, that the adoption of a planned economy, and even more the revolution from private to social ownership, helps here too. For it not only tends to release large reserves of talent from previously submerged strata of society, but also, by encouraging co-operation reduces the need for the highly individualistic industrial pioneer who is so rare a bird, and creates an environment where lesser mortals with good sense and good technical understanding can take his place. This is a major argument for public enterprise in underdeveloped lands.[89] The weakness here under communist rule is that central planning leads at least temporarily to the dictatorship of the Party, the aggrandisement of the new leaders into a new class and their not inconsiderable alienation from the masses of the people.

As we noted briefly in an earlier chapter (10), the Chinese solved the problem of finding the technical skills they required in a very interesting way. They obtained Russian experts to build them a hundred and fifty major enterprises and imported whatever equipment was necessary for the job.[90] The Russians trained Chinese technicians to take over from them at every level and, when they had got the plants running, went back home. In this way the Chinese had the best of both worlds – the full range of experience of Russian enterprises and the plants in their full ownership at the end. Russia has, at the same time, been training a very large number of technicians from the rest of the communist world in her universities, technical colleges and enterprises; and, as we saw earlier (Chapter 10) in considering the Rouble Area, all the members of the Area have gained greatly from the free exchange of designs and techniques and from agreements on specialisation. Nevertheless, even in the Rouble Area, machines and experts have to be paid for. We come to the last of the problems of an underdeveloped land: how to pay for the extra imports of machines and equipment and for the technical advisers, and also for the profits which have to be repatriated in foreign currency.

The Role of Foreign Aid

A final contrast may be drawn between Chinese and Indian planning. Table XXXII shows the small proportion of the Chinese import bill that has been covered by foreign aid; this would look even smaller if Chinese aid to Korea and Viet Nam had been set against Russian aid to China, instead of being set against the items of 'Other earnings or payments' in the Table.[91] (The latter are especially high in the case of China because of the high level of remittances home of Chinese living abroad.) By contrast, India was not only drawing down her sterling balances at a very rapid rate and drawing on the I.M.F. (to the extent of nearly £500 million in the Second Five-Year Plan), but was receiving large sums of foreign aid and smaller amounts of private capital, to the extent of about £200 million a year. Moreover, the Indian planners do not expect to be able to balance their foreign payments over the period of the Third Plan without more than £400 million a year of foreign aid.[92] The reasons for the sharp increase are, on the one hand, that the sterling balances have run out and, on the other, that funds will from now on have to be found to begin payments on previous foreign loans and investments. China after 1960 was also having to find £150 million a year for the next few years, for amortisation of the Soviet loans.[93]

These figures all emphasise once more the extraordinary importance of the development of agricultural production so as to produce, not only a surplus of food for applying to investment at home, but also a surplus of agricultural raw materials for use in industry and for export. But they emphasise two other points also – the importance of Russian preparedness to receive payment in the products of the debtor country, and the advantages of planned foreign trade to complement planned development at home. On the first point, the fact is that, even if India could greatly step up her output of crops for export, it is by no means certain that she could find a sale for them on the world market. What is causing India's problem of finding the earnings from exports to pay for essential imports for her industrialisation, is not only that India's exports are extremely unresponsive to changes in prices, but that the prices she has been receiving for her exports have been declining consistently over the last few years.[94] This is a fact which we have considered before in relation to all the underdeveloped lands which are primary producers.

It leads to the second point of the need for planned foreign trade. On the one hand, fluctuations in world demand for primary products make planning at home almost impossible.[95] This can only be overcome by bilateral or multilateral trade agreements or commodity control schemes between developed and underdeveloped lands. On the other hand, the search for self-sufficiency at least in food supplies and other agricultural products by each underdeveloped land leads to serious losses of possible advantage from the international division of labour.[96] This can only be overcome by mutual co-operation, not only between developed and underdeveloped lands but among the underdeveloped lands themselves on the lines of the COMECON agreements of the communists and as recommended at the Conference of Asian Economic Planners in December 1961[97] and in the Latin American Common Market discussions in April and May of 1959.[98] We shall have to consider the implications of these two points for advanced industrial lands like Britain in the next chapter, when we shall consider also the amount of aid that is available for world industrialisation.

We noted earlier that nearly all countries that have industrialised have received some form of foreign aid or investment to assist the process. We should now have seen enough of what is involved in the industrialisation of an underdeveloped land to know what forms of aid are likely to be of most use. We may say at once what aid is likely to be of little use. This is aid provided to governments representative of feudal and other backward classes in the community, or aid tied to a high level of military expenditure, or aid limited only to agricultural development without any corresponding industrial development, or aid limited to the establishment of light industries only, or aid that discourages co-operation among underdeveloped lands. Yet, in fact, American economic aid has often been limited in just these ways, as has much private capital investment and much of the capital of the World Bank.[99] Moreover, the advice of the World Bank experts has not only tended to underplay the importance of investment in heavy industry, but has also been strongly opposed to the kind of state enterprise which we have suggested as essential to overcome the rigidities of traditional private enterprise in a backward economy.[100]

The kind of aid that, by contrast, the underdeveloped lands need is the kind that would encourage state enterprise in industry and the development of co-operative farming in agriculture, and would be on a large enough scale to create the momentum necessary for getting over the 'hump' of building up an industrial base and sustaining thereafter a rapid rate of growth in all sectors of the economy. Repayment of loans would need to be phased to come after the 'hump' was surmounted and to be made in commodities that the debtor country could be expected to supply. Multilateral agreements involving mutual exchanges among underdeveloped lands and between them and the developed lands, including long-term agreements on commodity sales and prices, would be of much greater value than the disposal of surplus agricultural stocks by the United States. We only need to remember here that the poor producing areas lost far more by the fall in the price of their exports after 1954 than they received by way of economic aid.

What chances are there of aid of the kind here suggested being provided? It is a question of great moment; for on the scale and kind of aid provided to the underdeveloped lands in the next few years will depend the entire success of the Plans of the poor lands within the non-communist part of the world. And with their success or failure, the British economy is deeply involved. More than this, upon their success may well depend the peace of the world. The tragedy of our world is that in the communist as in the capitalist blocs alike the great wealth of resources available is being increasingly turned towards preparation for war.[101]

TABLE XXXII

THE INDIAN AND CHINESE PLANS COMPARED

Items	INDIA				CHINA		
	1952 Actual	1956 Actual	1960 Estimate	1965 Plan	1952 Actual	1956 Actual	1960 Estimate
National Income £m.	6,000	7,000	9,000	12,000	10,000	14,000	20,000
Population m.	360	385	430	480	600	650	700
Income per head £.	17	18	21	25	16·5	21·5	28·5
Investment – Public in £m.	215	350	550	1,000	1,550	3,250	4,150
– Private in £m.	200	325	550	600			
as % of Nat. Income	7	9·5	12	13·5	15·5	23	21
Resulting Annual Average Growth Rates — National Income %	1952–56 = 3·5	1956–60 = 5·2	1960–65 = 7		1952–56 = 10·5	1956–60 = 8·7	
Population %	1952–56 = 1·5	1956–60 = 1·8	1960–65 = 2		1952–56 = 2·0	1956–60 = 2·0	
Income per head %	1952–56 = 2·0	1956–60 = 3·4	1960–65 = 5		1952–56 = 8·5	1956–60 = 6·7	

TABLE XXXII (contd.)

	INDIA				CHINA		
	1952 Actual	1956 Actual	1960 Estimate	1965 Plan	1952 Actual	1956 Actual	1960 Estimate
Balance of Payments							
Imports £m.	−500	−600	−710	−850	−480	−1,000	−1,350
of which Machinery and Materials £m.	(300)	(370)	(500)	(600)	(400)	(900)	(1,200)
Other Payments or Earnings £m.	−20	−60	−50	−100	+20	+40	+30
Exports £m.	460	460	500	540	360	910	1,300
Sterling Balances £m.	20	100	50	—	—	—	—
Private Foreign Investment £m.	20	20	10	10	—	—	—
Foreign Aid £m.	20	100	240	400	100	60	—

Notes: 1. Indian national income has been scaled down to compare with Chinese statistics, i.e. incomes from private, professional and government services (including armed forces) have been left out.

2. Chinese Foreign Aid is the gross figure; aid given by China has been deducted from item of Other Earnings.

Sources: S. J. Patel, 'Comparison of Indian and Chinese Plans', *Indian Economic Review*, February 1957. Balance of Payments and 1960–65 Plan figures from Indian Government Planning Commission, *The Third Five-Year Plan*, New Delhi, 1961. Chinese Central Statistical Bureau, op. cit.

References

1. Woytinsky and Woytinsky, *World Population and Production*, Tables 180 ff., p. 383 ff.
2. W. H. Moreland, *India at the Death of Akbar*, London, 1920, pp. 286–7; and R. H. Tawney, *Land and Labour in China*, London, 1925.
3. W. A. Lewis, *The Theory of Economic Growth*, Allen and Unwin, 1955, p. 333 ff.
4. Woytinsky and Woytinsky, op. cit., Table 193, p. 424.
5. V. Anstey, *The Economic Development of India*, Table VI, Occupational Census, p. 612.
6. Marx, *Wage-Labour and Capital, Selected Works*, Martin Lawrence, 1933, Vol. I, p. 263.
7. e.g. Ritchie Calder, *The Inheritors*, Heinemann, 1961, pp. 265–6.
8. L. Dudley Stamp, *Our Developing World*, Faber, Table xxvi and *passim*.
9. J. D. Bernal, *World without War*, Routledge, 1958, map, p. 247.
10. M. H. Dobb, *Some Aspects of Economic Development*, Delhi, 1951, first lecture.
11. United Nations, *Economic Survey of Europe in 1948*, Geneva, 1949, pp. 224–5.
12. R. Nurkse, *Problems of Capital Formation in Underdeveloped Countries*, p. 10; and G. Myrdal, *Economic Theory and the Underdeveloped Regions*, p. 11 ff.
13. W. A. Lewis, *Theory of Economic Growth*, p. 304 ff.; and see D. Warriner, *Revolution in Eastern Europe*, Turnstile Press, 1950.
14. J. Robinson, *Essays in the Theory of Employment*, Macmillan, pp. 40–2.
15. United Nations, *Economic Survey of Asia and the Far East, 1949*, p. 84.
16. L. Dudley Stamp, op. cit.; and United Nations, *World Iron Ore Resources*, New York, 1950.
17. Paley Report, op. cit.; and United Nations, *Economic Survey of Africa since 1950*, p. 115 and 125.
18. *The Times*, 12.12.59.
19. J. Woddis, *Africa, The Roots of Revolt*, Lawrence and Wishart, 1960, p. 240.
20. H. Herring, *Good Neighbours*, p. 178; J. A. Crow, *The Epic of Latin America*, p. 701; and J. de Castro, *Geography of Hunger*, p. 8.
21. G. Freyre, *The Masters and the Slaves*.
22. J. de Castro, op. cit., p. 156; and A. Schonfield, *The Attack on World Poverty*, Chatto and Windus, 1960, p. 124.
23. quoted in *Pakistan Today*, 'Land Reform Number', Vol. 2–3, p.8.
24. ibid.

25. J. de Castro, *Geography of Hunger*, p. 155.
26. Government of India, *National Sample Survey, Eighth Round*, New Delhi, June 1958. I am indebted to a lecture by Prof. K. N. Raj of Delhi University given at the London New Left Club in 1959 for much of the material in this and the following paragraphs.
27. W. A. Lewis, *Theory of Economic Growth*, p. 120 ff.
28. M. H. Dobb, *Some Aspects of Economic Development*, second lecture.
29. K. N. Raj, op. cit.
30. M. H. Dobb, *Some Aspects of Economic Development*, second lecture.
31. P. Baran, *Political Economy of Growth*, p. 172.
32. B. Davidson, *Report on Southern Africa*, p. 224.
33. M. H. Dobb, op. cit., p. 54.
34. W. B. Reddaway, *The Development of the Indian Economy*, Allen and Unwin, 1962, p. 68; and M. H. Dobb, *On Economic Theory and Socialism*, Routledge, 1955, p. 138 ff.
35. M. H. Dobb, *Some Aspects of Economic Development*, second lecture.
36. Murray D. Bryce, *Industrial Development*, New York, 1961, pp. 17–19.
37. *The Statist*, 3.3.51, p. 231.
38. P. Baran, *Political Economy of Growth*, p. 197.
39. Murray D. Bryce, op. cit., p. 45.
40. See *Pakistan Today*, Vol. I, No. 1; and M. D. Bryce, op. cit., p. 58.
41. G. Myrdal, op. cit., Chapter II.
42. F. E. Le Gros Clark, 'The Malthusian Heritage', *Four Thousand Million Mouths*, Oxford, 1951.
43. S. Kusnetz, 'Underdeveloped Countries and the pre-Industrial Phase in the Advanced Countries', *The Economics of Underdevelopment*, Oxford, 1958.
44. M. H. Dobb, *Some Aspects of Economic Development*, p. 59; and M. H. Dobb, *Economic Growth and Planning*, Routledge, 1960, Chapter 1.
45. United Nations, 'Economic Development and Planning in Asia and the Far East', *Economic Bulletin for Asia and the Far East*, December 1961, Bangkok, 1962.
46. P. M. Sweezy, 'Economic Planning', *Monthly Review*, May 1960.
47. United Nations, *Economic Survey of Asia and the Far East, 1957*, Chapter 4; and M. H. Dobb, *Soviet Economic Development since 1917*, Routledge, 1948, Chapter 13; and O. Lange, *Essays on Economic Planning*, Asia Publishing House, 1960.
48. Government of India, Planning Commission, *Second Five Year Plan*, New Delhi, 1956, Chapter II.
49. United Nations, *Economic Survey of Asia and the Far East, 1958*, p. 77.

50. *Far East Trade*, 'India – Towards the Third Plan; iii: Public and Private Sector Debate', November 1959, p. 1470.
51. M. H. Dobb, *Some Aspects of Economic Development*, Lecture 3.
52. W. A. Lewis, *Theory of Economic Growth*, p. 133 ff.
53. M. H. Dobb, *Some Aspects of Economic Development*, Lecture 3.
54. S. Adler, *The Chinese Economy*, Routledge, 1957, Chapters VI and VII.
55. ibid.
56. P. Townsend, *China Phoenix*, Cape, 1955, Chapter III.
57. J. L. and B. Hammond, *The Village Labourer*, Methuen, 1921.
58. Choh-Ming Li, *The Statistical System of Communist China*, University of California, 1962, Table 2, p. 90.
59. S. Adler, op. cit.
60. *The Times*, Hong Kong Correspondent, 9.11.60 and 22/23.5.62.
61. *Far East Trade*, 'Annual China Review', October 1961, p. ii.
62. J. D. Bernal, *A Prospect of Peace*, Lawrence and Wishart, 1960, Chapter 6.
63. G. Regis, 'Development in China's Agriculture', *Far East Trade*, January, March and April 1962; and Chao Kuo-Chun, *Agricultural Development and Problems in China Today*, New York, 1958.
64. United Nations, *Economic Survey of Asia and the Far East, 1957*; and G. Regis, op. cit.
65. Mr Dhebar, Congress President, addressing the 63rd session of Congress on the subject of Land Reform, *The Hindustan Times Weekly Edition*, 19.1.58; and *Report of Indian Delegation to China on Agricultural Planning and Techniques*, New Delhi, 1956.
66. René Dumont, 'India's Agricultural Defeat', *New Statesman and Nation*, 19.2.59.
67. *Pakistan Today*, 'Land Reform Number'.
68. Lord Boyd Orr and P. Townsend, *What's Happening in China?* Allen and Unwin, 1958; and M. Shapiro, *Changing China*, Lawrence and Wishart, 1957.
69. United Nations, 'Economic Development and Planning in Asia and the Far East, p. 65 ff.
70. Paul Johnson, 'The Tortoise and the Hare', *New Statesman*, 1.6.62, and compare A. Schonfield, *Attack on World Poverty*, p. 16.
71. United Nations, 'Economic Development and planning in Asia and the Far East', p. 65 ff.
72. I. M. D. Little, 'The Strategy of Indian Development', National Institute *Economic Review*, May 1960, p. 28; and I. M. D. Little, 'A Critical Examination of India's Third Five Year Plan', *Oxford Economic Papers*, February 1962.
73. United Nations, *Economic Survey of Europe in 1955*, Chapter 7.

74. The Chinese State Statistical Bureau, *The Ten Great Years*, Peking, 1959; and see Choh-Ming Li, *The Statistical System of Communist China*, Table 2, and the same author, *Economic Development of Communist China*, Berkeley, 1959.

75. United Nations, *Statistical Yearbook*, 1960, New York.

76. S. J. Patel, 'Growth in Income and Investment in India and China, 1952-60', *Indian Economic Review*, February 1957, pp. 53-67.

77. Chinese State Statistical Bureau, *The Ten Great Years*.

78. United Nations, *Economic Survey of Asia and the Far East, 1957*, Chapter 4.

79. Chinese State Statistical Bureau, *The Ten Great Years*, op. cit.

80. Government of India, Planning Commission, *Appraisal and Prospects of the Second Five Year Plan*, New Delhi, May 1958.

81. *Far East Trade*, 'China Annual Review', 10.10.61.

82. United Nations, 'Economic Development and Planning in Asia and the Far East', p. 24.

83. K. N. Raj, 'The Marginal Rate of Saving in the Indian Economy', *Oxford Economic Papers*, February 1962.

84. Reserve Bank of India, *Report on Currency and Credit, 1959-60*, New Delhi, 1961.

85. I. M. D. Little, 'The Strategy of Indian Development', p. 29.

86. A. H. Hanson, *Public Enterprise and Economic Development*, Chapter XV on Problems of Personnel, quoting Arthur Lewis, Gunnar Myrdal and M. Zinkin, *Development of Free Asia*, London, 1956, pp. 128-9.

87. A. H. Hanson, op. cit., p. 35 ff., 'Obstacles to Economic Development', quoting especially, H. G. Aubrey, *Investment Decisions in Underdeveloped Countries*, Princetown, 1955, pp. 397-440.

88. A. Briggs, *Victorian People*, Longmans, 1955.

89. A. H. Hanson, op. cit., Chapter V and *passim*.

90. S. Adler, *The Chinese Economy*, p. 72.

91. United Nations, *Economic Survey of Asia and the Far East, 1955*, p. 98.

92. I. M. D. Little, 'A Critical Examination of India's Third Five Year Plan', *Oxford Economic Papers*.

93. *Far East Trade*, 'Annual China Review', 10.10.61.

94. G. D. A. MacDougall, 'India's Balance of Payments', *Bulletin of the Oxford University Institute of Statistics*, May 1961.

95. United Nations, *Economic Survey of Asia and the Far East*, 1957, Chapter 6 on 'Export Instability in the Primary Exporting Countries'.

96. United Nations, 'Economic Development and Planning in Asia and the Far East', p. 56 ff.

97. ibid.
98. United Nations, Economic Commission for Latin America, *The Latin American Common Market*.
99. F. Benham, *Economic Aid to Underdeveloped Countries*, Oxford, 1961, especially his criticism of Professor Bauer, p. 100.
100. E. R. Black, *The Diplomacy of Economic Development*, Harvard, 1960, pp. 45 and 67.
101. United Nations, *Economic and Social Consequences of Disarmament*.

CHAPTER 12

Britain in a World of Equals

In this concluding chapter, we have, first, to summarise our answers to the questions raised in the Introduction about the character of the unequal relationships established in the past between the European peoples and the rest of the world, that are widely referred to as 'imperialist'. We shall then have to answer the central question we raised about the consequences of the beginning that has been made in ending these unequal relations. We should, thus, be able to see more clearly what may now be done to maintain and accelerate the advance of the one-time colonial lands to full equality, by means of industrialisation. What is required to be done in the underdeveloped lands themselves has already been treated in the previous chapter. But certain implications must now be faced: first, of the types of government in these underdeveloped lands to which the British people must give their support; second, of the urgent necessity of developing pressure in the advanced lands for international action to assist world industrialisation; and, finally, of the very considerable adjustments that will have to be made inside the British economy to meet this new development.

The Questions Answered: A Summary of Conclusions

Our answers to the questions posed in the Introduction

may now be summarised (a) from the point of view of
Britain and other advanced industrial lands and (b) from the
point of view of the ex-colonies and the other underdeveloped
lands.

1 (a) The wealth of the rich lands such as Britain has not been
a function of the poverty of the poor lands, but has
followed rather from the steadily growing productivity
of industry over nearly two centuries, supported of
recent years by some stabilisation of the economic
system. Indeed, with few exceptions, Britons have
suffered rather than gained from colonial impoverishment. Nevertheless, there have been advantages
accruing to Britain from imperial possessions. In the
eighteenth century, colonial tribute did aid the in-
ception of Britain's industrial revolution. In the nineteenth century, overseas investment did greatly reduce
the costs of imported food and raw materials, but
mainly from non-colonial lands, and did help to expand
overseas markets for Britain's industrial goods mainly
in non-colonial lands of European settlement.

In this century, the main strength of the great
vertically-integrated combines has been drawn from
exclusive control over the sources of their raw materials
in colonial and other lands confined to primary production. Throughout the whole period of colonial rule,
very great wealth has flowed back from the colonies to a
small class of British investors. Finally, some advantage
has been gained, especially in the 1920s and 1930s, by
the British people from the terms of trade with colonial
producers. But this was at the expense of heavy unemployment of men and women between the wars, of
long periods of stagnation of the economy at home and
particularly in the export industries, and of increasingly
costly colonial wars.

(b) On the other hand, the poverty of the poor lands has
certainly been in large part the result of their dependent

colonial relationship with Britain. Their poverty has been brought about not only by the direct tribute drawn from them, but by the destruction of native industries, the concentration on primary production, the distortion of even this production into narrow export channels, the employment of slave and migrant labour and also by the political support given to reactionary tribal, feudal and 'comprador' leaders in the colonies, as part of the policy of indirect rule.

2 (a) Britain was able to establish capitalism and industrialise ahead of the rest of the world for a complex of reasons, which include the long peace after 1066, the premium put upon individual initiative in the forms of agriculture appropriate to Britain's land and climate, and the special geographical position of the British Isles. Almost equally good opportunities existed in other parts of Europe. But similar opportunities were not so easily taken either on the lands of tropical forest, savannah and desert or in the centralised hydraulic societies developed along the great river valleys of the East, threatened always by invasion from the north.

(b) The division, however, between advanced industrial producers and backward primary producers is not a natural division based on human or natural resources, but an artificial division resulting from the original industrial superiority achieved by Britain and other European powers. To break through to industrialisation, underdeveloped lands have always needed, first, to be able to protect their own infant industries from competition with more advanced industries outside and, secondly, to destroy their own surviving backward forms of society in order to raise agricultural productivity and encourage industrial investment – just as Britain had to do in the seventeenth century.

3 (a) Britain's world-wide expansion into empire was the result, first, of the search by a merchant interest for

what may as well be called plunder; secondly, of the need of a rising manufacturing interest to open up wider markets and then to use its military strength to preserve them; and thirdly, of the recourse of growing oligopoly interests to private preserves of raw materials and markets in face of competition from other industrial lands.

In the case of the British Empire, overseas investment was not the cause of the imperial expansion that took place at the end of the nineteenth century. Most of the empire was already there and was, above all, an instrument of free trade; the overseas investment was the result of the special interests of British rentiers and not of British monopolists or oligopolists, and took place largely outside the colonial empire. It was oligopoly interests, however, that gave to the British colonies their importance from the 1920s onward, and it is the drive to monopoly that has lain behind the recent expansion of overseas investment, which has again taken place in the more-developed lands outside the ex-colonies.

(b) Lands of coloured peoples were developed economically less than the lands of white settlement, not because of lack of resources in the former, but because they were ruled as colonies by forms of indirect rule. Such rule, as we have just noted, led to the retention in power of feudal and 'comprador' groups, which have everywhere proved themselves incapable of developing industrialisation or even of expanding agricultural output, when their populations began to increase rapidly in numbers. Moreover, many colonial territories were restricted by the metropolitan power to primary production, in order to guarantee sources of food and raw materials to industrial producers and to weaken the bargaining power of the primary producers in settling the terms of trade.

4 (a) Political rule over colonies is being ended today, partly
      because it is no longer tolerated by the colonial peoples
      or by a growing section of the people at home, partly
      because the value of the colonies is not so great as it was
      when there were no substitutes for their food and raw
      materials and for their military manpower and bases,
      and partly as the result of the growing challenge to
      capitalism in the communist third of the world and
      among the uncommitted emergent nations.

  (b) The economic dependence of the one-time colonies
      remains, however, after political rule is ended, as a
      hangover from colonial status, that is, in their depen-
      dence upon export crops, and upon metropolitan
      markets and capital, in their poor terms of trade and
      general economic weakness and in the continued
      presence in their lands of the giant corporations of the
      advanced capitalist powers. It is still in the economic
      interests of important groups of British and other
      leading capitalists, especially of the oil companies, to
      keep things this way; and to deliberate neglect must
      be added the effect of the support given in the cold
      war to feudal and 'comprador'-based governments in
      ex-colonial lands. The role of United States capitalism
      is here of central importance; on the one hand, like
      Britain at the zenith of her power, the U.S.A., as the
      leading capitalist power today, has no interest in colonial
      possessions, but only in opening them up to her trade
      and capital; on the other hand, the U.S.A. is above all
      anxious to retain as large a part of the world as possible
      within the system of capitalism.

5 (a) Britain in a world of equals need not be poorer; indeed,
      she has every opportunity to become richer by virtue
      of the technical skills of her people. British capitalism is
      now more stable internally than it was, and less depen-
      dent on overseas raw material and overseas invest-
      ment income than it was. Nevertheless, the outward

pressure of capitalism towards monopoly remains. The great wave of post-war overseas investment by private companies is part of the world-wide struggle of the giant oligopolies to hold and to extend their markets. British capitalism would be sorely hit by the expropriation of its overseas subsidiaries. Such expropriation would not, however, necessarily involve the demise of capitalism; but it would be a very different sort of capitalism that survived – more like that found in Scandinavia than that which exists in Britain today. The British working class might still not advance to power, because it is not the corruption of imperial tribute that now holds them back, but rather the failure of Socialists to seize the people with an alternative vision to the present prospects held out by capitalism.

New policies are desperately needed that will unite the interests both of the working people at home in the metropolitan land and of the ex-colonial peoples overseas. The people of Britain have every reason to support the expropriation of the imperial companies' subsidiaries by the ex-colonial peoples, because their own position in relation to these same companies will be strengthened and because of the acceleration in the development programmes in the ex-colonies that may be expected to follow. There is nothing to fear in the industrialisation of the world for a country like Britain and everything to be gained from the development of mutually beneficial trade relations between advanced and underdeveloped lands, without the distorting influence of capitalist combines to come between them. This is the central message of this book for the British working people: their interests and those of their fellows in the ex-colonial and other underdeveloped lands are essentially the same.

(b) The end of political rule in the colonies must, in the long run, mean the ending of economic dependence;

but the run may be very long indeed because of the hangovers from colonial rule, both external, in the role of foreign companies, and internal, in the types of régime left behind. Capitalism, however, either in some indigenous form or in the form of subsidiaries of imperial companies, is unlikely to succeed in carrying through the industrialisation of the remaining underdeveloped lands. Indeed, the great corporations tend actually to hold back industrialisation by pre-empting the most profitable markets themselves and by resisting planned development.

The growing challenge of the communist world in competitive co-existence and the challenge of communist aid can, however, be used by neutralist governments in the emergent lands to force capitalist governments to give real encouragement to their economic development. Planned development and socialised forms of ownership are likely to spread rapidly. How far this will involve communist control with all its ruthlessness will depend on the extent of aid from the richer lands. International aid on a larger scale from the capitalist countries for world industrialisation in fact predicates a greater degree of planning of trade and development than the haphazard bilateral grants and loans and private investment that are made available at present. Aid cannot in fact be used effectively to prevent socialist planning; it can be used to prevent Communism only by encouraging Socialism.

We may add a word on Lenin's analysis of imperialism before going on to examine the way forward for Britain and the lands of the old British Empire today. We have been forced to accept that, by and large, Lenin was right. His insistence on the outward pressure towards monopoly of the great industrial corporations, though inapplicable to Britain before 1913, fitted Germany then and the whole capitalist world in the 1930s and 1950s.

His law of unequal development, under which old mature capitalist states stagnated from the very plethora of their capital assets, while new young capitalist states and those where capital assets had been destroyed at the same time leapt ahead, has been proved anew in each generation. The challenge of the corporate states of Germany, Japan and Italy in the 1930s and the struggle of the great trading blocs today stand as evidence of Lenin's perceptiveness that in the great oligopolies lay the springs of action of modern capitalism.

Some of the elements in the picture which Lenin drew were wrong. The British Empire was not built as a result of the pressure of monopoly capital to invest overseas when profits fell at home. The empire was first established by merchant adventurers, and retained and extended by free traders anxious to open up and keep open to free trade the markets of the world. Overseas investment did not take place primarily in the colonial empire where capital was scarce and labour cheap, but in the self-governing dominions which were thereby assisted to develop economically. Moreover, the tribute from this investment was not the cause of the corruption of the British people, although it was in the interests of those who wished to hold back the strength and unity of the British workers (and their solidarity with colonial workers) to insist that the empire was the source of Britain's high standard of living. It was not colonial exploitation, but higher productivity at home and expanded trade with the developing nations overseas that were the cause of higher living standards; and this point is of profound relevance for our own day.

The Way Forward for Britain

Every attempt in the past to win advantages overseas

which has involved holding back the growth of productivity at home has worsened Britain's position. Thus the flood of capital overseas at the end of the nineteenth century and in the years just before the First World War held back investment at home. The re-establishment of sterling as a world currency linked to gold after 1925 checked the expansion of the economy at home by undermining British exports; the attempt to do so again after 1951 has been once more at the expense of investment at home and of the competitiveness of British exports. It has been the special problem of British capitalism to try to combine the roles of world banker and world trader. The two are fundamentally contradictory, as merchanting and industrial enterprise are contradictory, and no amount of interlocking of bankers and industrialists on the boards of the great companies will reconcile the two.

The union of finance and capital under the leadership of the latter, upon which Lenin insisted as the essential element in imperialism, only glosses over the division of aim between those whose first interest lies in expanding the whole world market and those whose interest is rather to get a higher rate of return or a larger share of the existing market by some monopoly device. You cannot hope to sell goods to customers whom you have previously impoverished. This has been one of the central themes running through this book and is the main lesson to be drawn from our study by those who would hope to preserve what they can of the capitalist system. It is a lesson that British bankers and industrialists seem to be slow to learn, although there were signs of unease among British overseas bankers in 1961 and 1962 at the continuing decline in the earnings of primary producers.[1]

By 1961 the policies of the bankers of the City of London had faced their Nemesis. All the post-war efforts to put the strength of the Pound Sterling before everything else – overseas through accumulating colonial sterling and keeping down the prices of colonial imports, and at home through wage freeze, credit squeeze and high interest rates – had finally resulted in leaving British exporters' goods uncompetitive with their rivals' products and British markets at home and overseas in a condition of stagnation. The Balance of Payments, for which every restriction on demand at home had been designed so that imports would be cut back and a surplus be assured, was in deficit for the second year running. Devaluation of the currency – or the very pound whose strength the bankers' every effort had been strained to defend – faced them as the only way out of the crisis, short of a driving-down of wages which no trade union would have tolerated.

At this point the British Government offered entry into the Common Market of expanding capitalist powers in Western Europe as a solution for stagnation, wages pressure, export markets and political strength to face communist pressure. This is the old economic policy of strengthening the rich at the expense of the poor. But the conclusion of the argument of this book must be that a completely new foreign economic policy is required, that is based on the acceptance that Britain must now find ways of living in a world of equals. The prospect need not frighten us. The unequal relationships of the past, which have held back the economic development of two-thirds of the world, do not bring any advantage to the British people.

Only a very few people may still be said to gain from maintaining gross economic inequalities; perhaps only a very few ever did. Wealth can only be won for a few by exploiting the labour of others. Impoverished primary producers, like underpaid workers, make a poor market for manufacturers. The ordinary folk in an advanced industrial land like Britain are not comfortably off for the most part because two-thirds of the world is poor. We are so today because we have machines to work for us. It is true that our industries were established with the help of wealth taken from other lands and at their expense and that efforts have been made since then to solve our problems at the expense of the poor and unprotected producers of food and raw materials in the world. It has done us no good; their poverty has worked back to make us poorer. We should all be better off, if the rest of the world were richer. This is particularly true for the fifty million of us on our narrow British islands, because we have to live by processing and machining raw materials from the rest of the world into goods to sell to them.

For this reason, we have had in this book to reject the idea that trade and investment can any longer be concentrated upon the already developed lands of Western Europe or the lands developed by white settlers, as has been the case for so long in the past. Yet this concentration is still taking place in North America and in the Common Market. The North-South problem[2] (as it is rather inaccurately termed as a result of the position in America and Italy; in Britain it is a South-North problem!) of the rich and the poor lands, has come to exercise as great an influence on our lives as the East-West problem (also inaccurately termed) between communist and capitalist lands. The polarisation of rich and poor advantages neither.

The most active trade is carried on between the countries, whose industries are most fully developed in all the main branches, but with different specialisations within the branches.[3] This is a most important point. The concentration of markets for manufacturered exports upon the more industrialised lands and of the sources of food and raw materials inside the same lands has already been closely examined (Chapter 10). Britain's entry into the Common Market can only be expected to increase this concentration, but this is precisely to limit the growth of the world market. We may compare once more the position of Australia and Malaya, each today with a population of ten millions, each with rich natural resources. Britain, by providing a market for Australia's products and loans for her industrialisation, finds in Australia her largest trading partner, worth £250 million each way in any year. By contrast the trade with Malaya is worth about £50 million;[4] we have taken Malayan exports, but the Malayans have not been able until recently to use the earnings for economic development. Are we now to rely increasingly on substitutes for Malayan rubber and tin and thus hold back Malayan development still longer?

Or is the moral for a trading nation like Britain to help other countries to develop their industries on the basis of their own resources, as we once helped Australia? For only then can a true division of labour emerge in the world, in place of the artificially imposed division between industrial and primary producers, which is the legacy of imperialism. It is bound to come, this world of equals; but it depends a good deal on what we do how easily and how speedily it comes. The choice lies between *laissez-faire* and planning, between leaving change to the slow and brutal working of economic forces or consciously planning development.

International Aid and Investment

(A) BILATERAL CONTRIBUTIONS:

How much aid are we giving to underdeveloped lands to-day? A glance at Table XXXII below reveals that the largest single element in the movement of funds out of the more advanced industrial lands in recent years has been the investment of private capital. Of course, as we have seen, the greater part of this investment was not directed towards the underdeveloped lands, but within Europe and North America. Nevertheless, it is this movement of funds including private capital to underdeveloped lands which has enabled the United States and Britain to claim that they are already providing more than one per cent of their national incomes to aid programmes.[5] When we considered the contribution of this private foreign investment towards aiding industrialisation, however, we had to conclude that it had serious limitations in its useful effects. It was largely not new capital but the result of the retention of earnings, which would have one day to be repatriated on an even greater scale; it tended not to flow into heavy industry but into consumer goods industries and into luxuries; and it tended to have the result of holding back and even destroying local enterprises.

Of the total of aid, as opposed to private investment, a great part is military aid. This does little to help industrialisation, except possibly by training technicians in military service and by providing roads, railways and, after the armies have finished with them, vehicles, that all add to the country's capital stock. The main objection to this military aid, however, as to so much of United States aid, is that it goes to support governments which are incapable and even undesirous of carrying through the process of industrialisation. Aid provided in loans and grants and food supplies, under the Colombo Plan for economic assistance in South-East Asia, amounted to about $6 billion in the seven years 1953-9,[6] or just over a dollar per head per year for the 600 million people in the area covered compared with just over $3 per head per year obtained over the same period by the 300 million people in Europe.[7] It does not seem very much, and, on examination, we have found the actual amount of technical assistance given to the governments which are genuinely trying to industrialise to be smaller still. The earlier Table (Table XI, Chapter 6) revealed that only a tenth of total American Aid could be said to be used in that way, so much goes for defence support and direct forces support even of the economic aid.

Most of Britain's foreign loans and grants from public sources have gone to the Commonwealth and to the colonies for welfare and development. They amounted in the early 1960s to between £100 million and £150 million a year (Table XVIII, Chapter 8), but we must notice how this was made up. A quarter consisted of the Colonial Service vote, the greater part of which went to the police and military services; another quarter consisted of export credit guarantees and loans of the Colonial Development Corporation.[8]

Useful as these last may be, it should be realised that they go to assist British companies operating overseas and not directly to assist the underdeveloped countries. An even greater proportion of German aid has been of this sort (see Table XXXII).

We have to bear in mind other points about the loans drawn from private sources in the London market (which are in addition to the sums we have just been considering). These loans were carrying a very high rate of interest in the 1950s. When the money was found jointly by the Government and by a consortium of City banks to finance the foreign exchange costs of the Durgapur steel-mill, the total rate amounted to nearly 10 per cent.[9] Moreover, like the private investment, these loans have to be repaid in sterling. This can only be obtained by the borrowing country from exports of commodities, which have first to find a market that earns them sterling.

After taking all these factors into account, one simply cannot say that the aid provided by the industrialised to the underdeveloped lands fulfils the conditions that we saw in the previous chapter were necessary for advancing their industrialisation. Soviet aid comes closest, despite its small scale. Soviet loans can be repaid in commodities and not in currency and, although they are repayable within a rather short period, the rate of interest is very low (not more than 2 per cent). Most important, these Soviet loans are provided for investment in heavy industry and for the kind of programme of technical assistance and training that the underdeveloped lands need. The governments which are really committed to industrialisation, however, would prefer to receive aid through international agencies, so as to avoid any question of strings being attached.[10] This is where we come to the most disappointing figures of all. U.N. technical assistance barely shows up on Table XXXIII in the final item, which includes also the funds for refugees, for children and for Korean relief. Even the loans of the World Bank look rather puny, when it is considered that only $0.8 billion of the $2.5 billion disbursed in the five years from 1955–59 went to underdeveloped lands.[11]

(B) MULTILATERAL CONTRIBUTIONS:

Many hopes were placed upon the work of the World Bank when it was first established at the Bretton Woods Conference in 1944.[12] The Bank was a bold attempt to channel United States overseas lending through international hands. The Bank was designed to deal with long-term disequilibrium between the United States and the rest of the world, while the International Monetary Fund cushioned short-term difficulties. Neither the Fund nor the Bank was allowed to start with the size of funds that the chief British negotiator, Lord Keynes, had hoped to see them control, and neither developed the management by impartial international experts that he had believed possible.[13]

As a State Department bulletin put it in 1946, after their experience with U.N.R.R.A., 'Congress had decided that the U.S.A. should no longer grant large sums under conditions which would leave little or no effective control by the grantor of these funds.'[14] Both the Fund and the Bank have been virtually controlled by the National Advisory Council, a committee of the United States cabinet.[15] The role played by the World Bank has been essentially conservative in financial operations, making loans only where repayment was 100 per cent assured, and essentially in line with State Department policy in political matters.[16] Thus, in its early days, the Bank refused loans to the U.S.S.R. and Poland and later refused both Dr Moussadeq and Col. Nasser, while providing $200 million to Gen. Zahedi.[17]

The World Bank has not only thrown its whole weight against progressive governments, but against 'excessive emphasis on industry for industry's sake, above all heavy industry', as the Bank's report for 1946–53 had it, and against planning. This last is the crux of the matter. But it has favoured private enterprise: 'The Bank had frequently taken steps to encourage a more favourable climate for private business, both domestic and foreign,'[18] says the same report. To confirm this emphasis, the Bank launched the International Finance Corporation in 1957 'to further economic development by encouraging the growth of productive private enterprise in member countries, particularly in the less-developed areas' and 'to stimulate the flow of private capital'.[19]

It is not, perhaps, surprising that the interest of the underdeveloped world turned after that to the possibility that SUNFED (Special United Nations Funds for Economic Development) might at length be established after many years of protracted discussions. These began in 1951 with a United Nations report proposing that the industrially advanced nations of the world should contribute 1 per cent of their national incomes to provide a sum of $10 billion a year to raise living standards in the less-developed lands by 2 per cent per year.[20] That would only be about equal to the total of aid and investment actually provided in the 1950s according to Table XXXIII. The sum would, however, have been in addition to bilateral contributions. In discussion it was, in any case, steadily whittled down to $150 million, as Dr Myrdal has bitterly recorded, until finally the whole scheme was made conditional upon the great powers' reaching agreement on disarmament.[21] The Labour Party in Britain threw in its weight behind the scheme,[22] as did Professor Frederick Benham;[23] but ten years after the first discussions, SUNFED was no nearer realisation.

The association between the release of funds for SUNFED and agreement on disarmament underlines the cold-war context of the whole discussion. United States aid has been used to keep in power virulently anti-communist and anti-socialist governments which have little interest in economic development; at the same time, it has formed part of the total programme of United States military expenditure which has certainly helped to maintain the stability of the United States economy, but is not designed to further overseas economic development. One fifth of U.S. exports has been financed by aid of different sorts – a third of all agricultural exports, two-thirds of grain, dairy produce and cotton.[24] Another fifth has been covered by the outward flow of investment and business retentions (Table XXX, Chapter 10).

Any reduction in the huge military budgets which are shown in Table XXXII would release labour and industrial capacity on a vast scale.[25] Resources would not only become available for aid to underdeveloped lands, but they would, in very truth, have to be turned to world industrialisation, if grave dislocation and instability were to be avoided. It is possible that the British Government, with its greater stake in the civilian side of the economy, in welfare expenditures and the nationalised industries, could effect the conversion with no more than temporary and local pockets of unemployment. Such a transition in the United States, however, where state regulation is still regarded as anathema, might well be expected to be more difficult.

The danger here is important: the cut in military expenditure would make possible a large increase in civilian government expenditure or a heavy cut in taxation. If the latter course were followed, civilian demand for consumer goods would then leap up. At the same time, since much of the burden of taxes is borne by corporations, they would find themselves with huge capital reserves to spend. Investment would be expanded to meet the enlarged consumer and capital goods markets. A bonanza of untaxed profits would follow, until the uncontrolled boom collapsed in an uncontrollable slump, for output from the new unplanned investment would come onto a market that was deprived by high profit-taking of the capacity to buy it back. What the United States military budget does is at least to tax some of the profits and guarantee a market outside the civilian market for the capitalist tendency to overproduce. The alternative of expenditure by the State on health and welfare in place of armaments would do the same job.

The danger which the U.N. Report on the subject[26] glosses over is that taxation for civilian development is less acceptable than armaments to the private corporations, partly because the rate of obsolescence is slower on hospitals than on rockets, and partly because of the implied challenge of a large and prosperous civilian public sector to the established supremacy of the masters of the private sector.

Is there, then, no hope for a plan for world industrialisation? One of the further factors operating against it is that any considerable stepping-up of aid to underdeveloped lands would in fact require more international planning, as well as the establishment of governments in the underdeveloped lands who were prepared to plan. There are, however, certain factors that might lead to the more optimistic view of the U.N. Report being taken. The Report was signed by a Russian and a Pole, and we may well consider the reasons for this apparent revision of Lenin's views on the relation between capitalism and war. First, there is the growth of world opinion in opposition to the arms race and world reaction to the fear of mutual genocide that the H-bomb holds over our heads. Secondly, there is the growing strength of neutralist opinion in the underdeveloped lands, most of which have only just emerged from colonial status and are now demanding in the forum of the United Nations and elsewhere that economic equality should follow political freedom. Third, there is the commitment of all the governments of the world to full or near-full employment for their citizens; and the strength of the trade unions exists to see that the commitment is honoured.

All these factors might have less effect, were it not for a fourth. This is the rapidly increasing strength of the communist third of the world. The struggle for the defence of capitalism has come to demand not only a military response, but the demonstration that capitalism can produce the goods for its own workers and for the less-advanced people more efficiently than communism can. The abandonment of a military posture in favour of entry in the main race of competitive co-existence will only follow from further advances in the communist world, if at the same time there arises still greater pressure from neutralist opinion in both the advanced and the underdeveloped lands. But the prospect is not without hope – if only, in the meantime, a nuclear explosion can be avoided. Indeed, the forces which alone can prevent the two great nuclear power blocs from destroying themselves and the rest of mankind are precisely the neutral and uncommitted lands which stand to gain most from international aid.

The Framework of Positive Neutralism

If capitalism has shown itself incapable of industrialising the non-European two-thirds of the world, as Socialists might in any case have expected, and if Communism can do the job only at the expense of human liberty, as Democrats know, then a third alternative must be found. The whole burden of this book has been that industrialisation of underdeveloped lands today involves the replacement of feudal and merchant power by popular rule, so that land reform and state economic planning become possible. The peoples of these lands cannot afford to go through a capitalist stage to get ultimately to social ownership, in order to secure these ends. At the same time, they do not need to be forced under communist rule and the domination of a 'new class'[27] to get there.

A third way is open to them – the way of democratic Socialism – provided that the peoples of the rich countries, which also aspire to democratic Socialism, can only rally their own strength and confidence to help in time. The demands of the world economy are the same as the demands of world peace. The pressure exerted today to force the whole

world into one or other of the two nuclear-power blocs not
only threatens us all with destruction but renders impossible
the advance to world industrialisation. On both sides the
major industrial effort is channelled into the perfection and
accumulation of instruments of destruction. To the outward
pressures of capitalism, which Lenin saw as the source of
war, we have to add the aggressive posture of a class that
encompasses its own perpetuation in the name of proletarian
dictatorship. Khrushchev's ways may be an improvement on
Stalin's, but the danger from without remains the ultimate
excuse for the monolithic party and the denial of democracy.
In part the danger without is real, as the threat of Communism to capitalist positions is real; but each side has its
own reason for keeping up the tension: the Communists to
hold back criticism from below, the capitalists to maintain
the flow of armament orders.

Thus it will only be possible to force the two blocs to
withdraw from military postures and devote their resources
to industrialising the rest of the world as the result of the
growing strength of neutralist opinion. At the same time,
the only hope for democratic industrialisation in the underdeveloped lands is that their peoples succeed in finding an
alternative to either capitalism or Communism. They need to
combine, on the one hand, the democratic processes won in
bitter struggle by the people of the West without the incubus
of capitalist anarchy, and, on the other hand, the land reform
and social planning of the Soviet Union and China without
the aggrandisement of the 'new class'. But it is not a compromise between capitalism and Communism which they need;
it is a real third way.

The hopes both of world peace and of world industrialisation lie, then, in strengthening the economic and political
ties of the peoples of the rich and poor lands who refuse to
be forced into one or other of the nuclear blocs. The present
weakness of the rich lands where movements towards
neutralism have been growing is their *mésalliance* with

capitalism, i.e. in the Scandinavian countries, Switzerland, Austria, Canada, and above all in Britain. The weakness of the poor lands, among whom there has been a real building up of neutralist opinion, evidenced at the Bandung and Belgrade Conferences,[28] is their economic dependence on aid from one or other of the blocs. It is imperative that aid for the neutralist poor should be made available from the neutralist rich. Only the bringing together of the two into one force, not a bloc but a force to break the blocs and strengthen world-wide association, can overcome the weakness of each. The political and economic viability of both groups requires closer interdependence.

All the proposals that follow require this framework of positive neutralism. What Britain can do is not enough. If the lead, however, can be given by Britain and the other rich lands with neutralist aspirations in providing aid and guaranteed markets to the developing, uncommitted lands and thus underpinning their economic development, then there is hope not only for world industrialisation but for world peace. For peaceful solutions to world problems could more readily be found in such a context. The immediate threat of war can be averted by a neutralist initiative and as world industrialisation proceeds the long-term prospect for peace is improved.

Time is running out, but there may yet be a chance for Britain to rally the democratic socialist governments of EFTA and the neutralist governments of the Commonwealth to reject the narrow aims of the Common Market and embark upon joint policies of world economic development.[29] Here is a formidable group of peoples including not only those of the richest lands after the United States of America, but of the poorest lands – with populations in excess of 700 millions or more than a quarter of the world's total (Table I). It will require, however, a major initiative to replace the blocs by genuine internationalism. It will not be enough for this initiative to be taken in the political forum of the U.N.,

where the neutralist nations of Africa and Asia have already
been establishing their influence, and through the economic
and social agencies of the U.N. and especially through the
U.N. regional commissions, which combine rich and poor,
Communist, Capitalist and Socialist in each of the world's
continents. Such initiatives will be useful but in addition a
fresh start must be made. For this the nucleus of the EFTA
and Commonwealth countries provides the best starting
point.

Higher and More Stable Earnings for Primary Producers

Short of disarmament and much expanded economic aid
for industrialisation, what is there, then, that can be done to
speed and ease the advance of the underdeveloped lands
towards economic equality? The answer is that there are
several steps that might be taken, all of them connected with
the earnings which the underdeveloped countries must rely
on, apart from aid, for buying machines and equipment out of
their sales of primary products. We noted, in an earlier
chapter that the loss sustained by the primary producers in
underdeveloped lands from the drop in their terms of trade
over recent years was far greater than was made up by the aid
received. And we suggested that part of the fall in the terms
of trade was the result of the deliberate deflationary policies
of the industrial countries and particularly of Great Britain;
the other part being the result of the widespread substitution
of synthetic for natural products and of home-grown for
imported foodstuffs.[30]

Because of this last factor, it may seem inevitable that primary producers should suffer in the terms of their trade. First,
however, it is not necessary to exacerbate the suffering by
concentration on European food and raw-materials development. Secondly, it must be clear that, as industrialisation
spreads, the demand for industrial raw materials will go on

rising; large increases in output and a revolution in methods of agricultural production may soon be required. What the primary producers suffer from most, as we have seen, is the instability of their prices; a very large rise and fall in prices follows from quite small changes in supply and demand. The reason for this is partly that peasant producers are unable to hold their product off the market when the price falls, so that the fall is all the heavier, partly that the system of short-term buying and selling in commodity markets, apart from the purchases of the near monopolies like Unilever, greatly exaggerates the movement in prices.

It is a fantastic situation, in which the basic materials of the whole world's industry are subject to violent fluctuations in price; nor does it need to be emphasised again that the far better organised industrialist can protect himself in this situation where the unorganised peasant cannot. Some part of the reason for the deflationary policies recently pursued in the industrial lands has been, as we have seen, to face the better organisation today of the world's peasant primary producers, and not simply of the plantation and mining companies. This problem of the bargaining power of industrial and primary producers has lain at the very heart of this book and recurred in almost every chapter.

We have noted again and again that the vertically-integrated combines and the biggest manufacturers, with a near monopoly of the market, have been able to keep their prices up, and even to raise them during a recession, in which the primary producers' prices have slumped. The only primary producers who have been able to contract out of these terms of trade have been the farmers in the advanced industrial land, for they have been receiving price support in the form of state subsidies, tariffs and levies. But this only creates artificially high prices for their products at the expense of the taxpayer, distorts the balance of agricultural output in favour of the subsidised products, holds back the development of more efficient farming methods and makes the situation of the primary producers in the underdeveloped lands still worse.[31]

To meet this problem, schemes for international control of output and for the building up of buffer stocks have been developed by producers of such varied products as coffee, wheat, sugar, olive oil and tin, but this is the complete list.[32] The weakness of even these schemes is that they deal with particular commodities in isolation, they are not all-embracing, they still depend on the relative bargaining power of producers and consumers and that in many cases the attempt has been made to protect high-cost producers – often in fact those in the more advanced countries.[33] The result has been continued encouragement of overproduction, continued weakness of the small producer and continued instability.

Schemes for bulk purchase over long periods, such as the Labour Government introduced before 1951,[34] have certain advantages both for producers and consumers. Their main drawback was that prices were fixed for too long a period and that they were essentially bilateral agreements. As such they still depended on bargaining and we know already where the strength in such bargaining lies. A jointly negotiated package of many-sided international commodity agreements would have the merit of equalising bargaining power on either side. What some believe to be required is simply an automatic system somewhat similar to the old gold system, which combines stock-piling and price adjustment according to the movement of stocks. Mr St Clare Grondona has devised just such a system, which has been given quite inadequate notice in the economic press.[35]

The object of any system must be to prevent prices from falling precipitately below prescribed and pre-notified levels and to keep prices within relatively narrow fluctuations. An alternative to the Grondona scheme for Price Stabilisation Corporations, automatically adjusting prices according to the volume of stocks held, is the proposal for a 'development insurance fund' whereby richer countries would give temporary assistance to poorer countries suffering from setbacks in earnings.[36] Long-term changes in demand caused by increased output in the more developed lands would remain; so would the tendency of each country to press exports at the expense of imports. What is needed is that a way should be found of uniting the interest of the primary producers, who are trying to develop their industries, and of the industrial producers who have the skills and can provide the equipment for the job, so that the attempt to balance payments by each country does not lead to a reduction in world trade. The best solution would be to develop a scheme for long-term guaranteed purchases of industrial and primary products as part of a multilateral trade clearing system.

In the present state of the world economy it is only too easy for vicious downward spirals to keep developing. These have already occurred in the trade of advanced and under-developed lands as a result of deflationary policies and would be worsened by Britain's entry into the Common Market. If Britain reduces her demand for food and raw materials, the raw material producers have to reduce their demand for our manufactures and so it can go on, holding up the general advance of all. Britain as a major importer of so many commodities, and as an exporter so dependent on rising markets among the primary producers, would have every-thing to gain from finding a common solution to this problem.

Professor Ragnar Frisch has proposed that all countries entering into a Trade Clearing System should state their economic targets, including demand for imports and avail-ability of exports over a period of years and should commit themselves to settling their trade balances at the highest poss-ible level in the long run.[37] This proposal could form part of the fresh start in advancing world development that EFTA and the Commonwealth might initiate as an alternative to entry into the Common Market. It would provide the best solution for the vicious circle of declining trade balances and also for the perennial problem of international liquidity, precisely because it would be based on planned commitments in advance and not on unplanned compensation after the event.

Growing Points of an International Economy

One of the most urgent matters is to find the way to a new multilateral payments system in place of the present division of the world into trading blocs. Settlement between the blocs is at present effected by movements of gold or dollars; one of the advantages of the Grondona scheme is that settlement might then be made by means of other commodities than gold. Even better would be the Frisch proposal for a matrix of guaranteed purchases.

Gold can no longer supply the necessary credit base – that is, in generally acceptable international currencies – to ensure the expanded levels of world trade today. In the last fifty years, gold production has provided less than half of the increase in international reserves and less than a third in the last ten years.[38] The gap has been filled by Balance of Payments deficits financed by short-term dollar and sterling and mark credits. When conservative financiers like M. Jacques Rueff,[39] fearing the dangerously inflated pyramid of credit built upon the narrow gold exchange standard, begin to recommend a scaling-back to the gold basis, we need to be really frightened. A return to gold today would be as disastrous as it was in the 1920s. Nor would it be entirely helpful simply to raise the price of gold, as Sir Roy Harrod has suggested,[40] for this would immensely strengthen the position of the rich United States with two-thirds of the world's gold (and incidentally of Russia and South Africa) at the expense of the poor lands in the rest of the world, although the advantage of thereby encouraging more expansionary internal policies in the U.S.A. should not be underestimated.

The weakness of the present credit arrangements supplied largely by dollars and sterling and, to some extent, by marks is that they are inadequate and that they depend on the U.S.A. and Britain running deficits in their balance of payments for others to be able to get hold of their currencies. And neither the U.S.A. nor Britain has any desire to run permanent deficits; they are both busy doing all they can to alter them into surpluses. Some see the only hope as lying in a strengthening of the International Monetary Fund. The general flurry of world bankers in the spring of 1961 to increase the lending powers of I.M.F., however, seems to have been instigated more by fear of even greater United States import restrictions to meet the outward flow of gold and dollars from the U.S. and by fear of United Kingdom devaluation of sterling to solve the non-competitiveness of British exports than by any belief in the possibility of strengthening the currency basis of world trade.

The dangers inherent in the present arrangements are that the I.M.F. is in the hands of the bankers and that the bankers are essentially conservative people and Mr Per Jacobsson, the secretary-general of the I.M.F., is one of the most conservative.[41] The fears of the bankers, in countries which have surplus funds to lend, that the countries which want to borrow will pursue excessively inflationary policies has greatly reduced the flow of funds and has so far prevented the I.M.F. from playing an expansionist role. Nevertheless it was agreed in 1961 to expand the Fund's lending-power by some $6,000 million: the U.S.A. putting up $2,000 million, the U.K. and Germany $1,000 million, France $550 million and the six other advanced industrial powers providing the balance.[42] The condition was imposed, however, that no loans should be made by the Fund without the lender being consulted and having the opportunity to give or withhold, according to his view of the borrower's economic policies and general financial 'soundness'. Some new world-wide credit base remains a desperate necessity for the poorer and less 'sound' countries whose needs are the greatest.

Two other proposals have been made here: one by the Hon. Maxwell Stamp for the issue of gold certificates by I.M.F. unbacked by actual metal to the tune of some $3,000 million in the first year and more thereafter.[43] These certificates could be put into circulation through United Nations aid funds. The second was made by Professor Triffin,[44] and was for the establishment of a world central bank or at least the founding of regional banks with powers to settle payments and create credit. A beginning could undoubtedly be made with an expansion of regional credit mechanisms through the Regional Commissions of the United Nations in association with the Common Markets that are already emerging in South-East Asia, Africa and South America as well as in Europe. These commissions are the only organisations in which all parts of our divided world – East and West, North and South – come together (with the outstanding exception of the Chinese who are still excluded in favour of the rump government on Formosa). They have been especially valuable in providing a forum for trade exchanges and economic co-operation, albeit on a very small scale, between the capitalist and non-capitalist lands, especially in Europe. But they could do much more, especially if the bans on East-West trade were removed, to facilitate multilateral trade movements in place of the present clumsy bilateral agreements.

Regional Common Markets, however, make all the more necessary the uniting of the rich and the poor lands in a wider Payments or Trade Clearing Union.[45] For nothing else will overcome the present contradiction between the national need to control currencies for balanced internal growth and the international need for expanded trade exchanges. The question is whether the national bankers are prepared to accept the resulting reduction in their own powers. The I.M.F. seems to be the last place to hope for such a progressive initiative. Just as some new source of funds (such as SUNFED) is needed to overcome the narrow capitalist principles of the World Bank, so some new agency is needed to overcome the even narrower precepts of the I.M.F. It is nothing short of ridiculous that governments committed to full employment policies at home and to aid overseas should have to choose between these policies and the defence of their currencies, simply in order to provide room for financial speculators to operate in, and for central bankers to retain their centralised control of world liquidity. Britain, with the greatest need for world-trade expansion, is still held back by the opposing interests of the City bankers.

Once again the way lies open for Britain with EFTA and the Commonwealth to take the initiative. What is required is a Clearing Union, together with a Bank and Development Fund. These should be open for all to join, not closed like the EEC, and should be organised on the basis of the planning of production and trade targets, and not of the *laissez-faire* capitalist finance that we have seen dominates the World Bank and Monetary Fund.

Towards a True Division of Labour in the World

The implications of these proposals for the rich industrial lands like Britain must now be spelled out. Everything depends on the preparedness of the advanced countries to open their markets to free trade not only for primary products but also for the more conventional manufactures, not only of the developed lands, but of the underdeveloped lands, so that they can sell the goods they have to offer, even if this means ending the protection of high cost producers at home. The most important feature of the period when Britain was the workshop of the world, and providing the capital for other lands to industrialise, was that her markets were wide open to the sale of their natural products, and the world-wide expansion of trade that resulted we saw to be precisely the basis of Britain's growing wealth. One of the most serious factors which we have seen to be holding back the earnings, and unbalancing the payments, of underdeveloped lands since the war, has been the evident inability of the United States to do today what Britain did then. No amount of aid can make up for this; and, indeed, aid in the form of surplus United States agricultural stocks actually worsens the situation by reducing the market for the sale of other countries' agricultural produce.

The main dangers of the moves towards a Common Market in Europe, which we noted, are the proposals for tariffs, import levies and taxes to control the trade in foodstuffs, including many of the food products of the associated African territories, for developing synthetic raw materials at the expense of natural products, and for excluding processed and manufactured goods from outside. One of the major contributions which Britain as the world's largest food importer, and the other rich countries in EFTA and the Commonwealth, could make to world industrialisation would be the negotiation of long-term guaranteed purchases of primary products, and of the more conventional manufactures; but the whole burden of this book is that this is as much in our long-term interest as it is in the interest of the developing lands.

Attempts to establish a World Trade Organisation, which was to have been the third of the International Organisations arising from the Bretton Woods Conference, all failed during the years after the war.[46] But a number of countries did sign the General Agreement on Tariffs and Trade, by which they agreed not to raise any new or higher tariffs or to give new or higher preferences. G.A.T.T. has since negotiated a number of concessions and reductions among the member nations, and its new council established in 1960 may provide the opening for building a World Trade Organisation at last.[47] G.A.T.T. has provided a defence against the raising of new barriers to trade among industrial lands, but has done little to help the underdeveloped lands which are bound to protect their infant industries against foreign competition. Moreover, G.A.T.T. has not been able to prevent the raising of a common tariff around the Common Market, which is the corollary of the lowering of trade barriers between the members inside the Market. Here again, as we have already suggested, the way lies open for a positive initiative by Britain and the EFTA-Sterling group to bargain the lowering of their tariffs for a cut in the tariff wall that surrounds the Common Market;[48] at the same time to take advantage without entering the Common Market of the concessions which the U.S.A. is bound to make in order to reduce the effect on U.S. exports of the common tariff wall.

What has been most serious, however, has been the past refusal of the United States and the inability even of President Kennedy to carry reduction of tariffs and import controls very far, while other countries have been steadily 'liberalising' their controls on imports from the U.S.A.[49] The increase of American consumer goods entering Britain and all West European countries in the 1950s was very great, almost making up for the cuts in imports of food and raw materials from the U.S.A. in the same period.[50] Yet on the American side, although United States imports of manufactures, mainly cars, quadrupled in the 1950s, the market remained difficult to penetrate and sales of primary products actually fell.[51] United States economic growth was not very rapid, and imports did not keep up with growth. In the first years of the 1960s, the cost of overseas military operations together with the outflow of United States private capital have driven President Kennedy to step up United States exports.[52] The impression has grown that 'international collaboration' in G.A.T.T. has been, in the words of the Brazilian delegate to the 10th Session, 'only a one-way street'.

It should not be supposed that Britain has been entirely

above blame in this respect, although herself suffering from one-way trade with the United States. We have to accept the fact that the corollary of aid to the underdeveloped lands is that we must open our markets even further also to their products, even to Indian cloth and Japanese textiles.[53] Just to mention such a proposal in Lancashire will raise a storm of protest, and yet we cannot have it both ways – criticise the Americans and do the same thing ourselves. Lancashire needs help in making the adjustment to new types of industry, but this help should not be the protection of old industries. If we want to help the underdeveloped lands to industrialise, so that their purchases of our goods may rise, we must in our turn give them the opportunity to earn the wherewithal to buy from us. This means opening our markets, and those of the other rich lands we can persuade to come with us, not only to raw materials and food, as in the past, but to whatever the underdeveloped lands can produce cheaper than we can; and this may include not only textiles but many other manufactures, including semi-processed materials such as vegetable oils, leather products, crude steel, refined oil, aluminium. In exchange, we shall be able to offer them the more technically advanced products that our more technically advanced position enables us to produce and, as the world division of labour develops, we shall offer in the end only the goods in which we can develop the highest degree of specialisation – in drugs, plastics, electronics, nuclear engineering and the other most advanced industries.

It is argued in some quarters[54] that we cannot help the less-developed lands unless we first become richer ourselves, and this demands our industrial development in a large protected market like the European Common Market. The truth is almost precisely the opposite: we cannot get rich unless we first help the less-developed lands. To develop West Europe's food and raw material as well as all-round industrial output would be precisely to attempt to get rich at the expense of the poor primary producers. A rich man who said, 'Nothing just now; wait till I get a little richer – at your expense,' would get short shrift. But, in fact, it is the burden of this book that it is highly improbable, at least for Britain, that any attempt to get richer at the expense of the poorer nations will in fact succeed. The Six may gain for a time yet, but even their day of reckoning will come, when their own 'home' market is over-supplied and the rest of the world too impoverished to buy. This has already happened with agricultural production in the United States. Must Europe go the same way?

The moral is not to re-establish on a higher level the division of the lands of the world into primary and industrial producers; it is to encourage a true division of labour in every major country or region. At the end of this book, we must repeat again that the division of labour between the industrial countries and the primary producers has been an artificial one that we have imposed. A truer division of labour exists between those equally industrialised lands who exchange products in which they have each variously specialised. We do not need to be frightened of this; the most active trade is already being carried out, as we noted earlier, in just such exchanges. A return to free trade is essential for expansion among the advanced industrial lands, but must not be imposed upon the less advanced.

'Equality of treatment is equitable only among equals,' as Dr Myrdal reports the emphatic declaration of an Indian delegate at a session of G.A.T.T.[55] The underdeveloped countries must be permitted to develop their industries behind protective walls until they are truly equals. If we demand free entry for all our goods and for the subsidiaries of our great companies, their plans for industrialisation will be held back and the attainment of equality delayed.

The crucial point to recognise is that holding back their development only does us harm in the long run, because it impoverishes the markets for our products.[56] It is better to allow some discrimination against our manufactures, while they develop their industries. This does not mean that they

HH

will exclude all our goods; on the contrary, as their in-dustrialisation advances, they will need more and more. It is only necessary, in order to see the point, once more to remember the comparison between British exports to Australia, one of the older dominions, with British exports to Malaya, which only in 1960 freed herself from colonial status. Australia can raise tariffs against us; Malaya until recently could not. But Australia is manifestly the better market.

The implications of the policies here proposed are not inconsiderable. To adjust our economy to producing more not only of the most technically advanced goods, in place of our traditional exports, but also modern capital equipment in place of consumer durables which have come to dominate the economy, will demand planning at home. Otherwise the adjustment will be by the crude forces of competition – of the same slow, ruthless and wasteful kind which we experienced between the wars, and which are enshrined once more in the Rome Treaty framing the Common Market.[57] Workers in Lancashire, to take the example already mentioned, should not be expected to move to the Thames or the Rhine Valley, but will need to be assisted and trained to change over from textile manufacture to electronics and the other branches of modern industry. State aid will be required, aid on a scale far exceeding any so far given to depressed areas and far beyond what the Rome Treaty (Article 92) permits. Indeed, the job may well be better done by establishing government enter-prises rather than by bribing private enterprise, as we are doing now.[58]

To take examples, it is the 'Hover-craft' (developed in fact by state enterprise)[59] and the Land-Rover[60] and a cheap all-purpose flying bus, needing only short and rough landing strips, that we should be developing for use in opening up the underdeveloped lands of Asia, Africa and South America, and not the sleek limousines and high-speed jet air-liners for the rich West Ends of Europe and North America. Let there be no mistake, if we do not do the job consciously now in a planned way, it will in the end be forced upon us. For it follows from the logic of world history. If we leave it to 'blind economic forces', we can only have forced upon us the situation which was spelled out for us in a Conservative Party pamphlet on the Common Market: 'It therefore seems that any disequilibrium (in balance of payments among member states) would always have to be corrected by reducing incomes and by unemployment in the country concerned, just as South Wales solved its balance of payments difficulties with the British "common market" in the inter-war years.'[61] It is precisely this which must be one of our main objections to Britain's joining the Common Market.

It is this abrogation of responsibility to 'blind forces' that in effect leaves power in the hands of those who control the great aggregations of productive capacity in the modern in-dustrial corporations. The result of such a concentration of power is, on the one hand, to withdraw the making of economic decisions from popular democratic control, and, on the other hand, to stunt and dwarf the smaller enterprises, including those in the underdeveloped lands. Just as a considerable measure of national planning, with national control over key sectors of the economy in place of private control, is needed to ensure the full development of the resources of the whole nation, so a measure of international planning is needed to ensure the full development of the resources of the whole world.[62] In the same way that the great industrial corporations have today to be directed by government action into the 'development' areas of Britain, so we shall have to find international means of 'directing' industry into the 'development' areas of the world. Every-thing that we have seen in this book suggests that capitalism leads to concentration of wealth in the richer areas and im-poverishment outside. It would be idle to pretend that the beginnings of international planning, as of national planning, will not demand a major challenge to capitalism.

National planning has been developed by public pressure through the growing stake of national governments in their countries' economies. We have now to increase the stake of international organisations in the world economy. For this is the logical corollary of national planning. It is no step towards this to establish a United States of Europe, with supranational powers, but rather the opposite. If establishing a United States of neighbouring peoples in Europe led to world government, the United States of America would be the leading protagonist of world co-operation. But her policies do not suggest this and it is therefore the growing points of world order that we need to encourage. There is no halfway step across this chasm. But the United Nations, its regional commissions and technical agencies, such as the World Health and Food and Agricultural Organisation, already exist, and new agencies, such as SUNFED or a World Trade Organisation, formed from G.A.T.T., could immediately develop their roles, if they had more money and some greater measure of co-ordination and could be won from their *laissez-faire* policies.

It is precisely a measure of international planning that is now required. This is the logic of our whole argument, and, if this cannot be achieved yet on a world-wide basis, a start can be made among the like-minded peoples of EFTA and the Commonwealth. The aim must be to create the conditions for expansion of the whole world economy and not of one rich corner of it, and in so doing to take the necessary measures, that were not taken in the 1930s, to avert world recession. It will be necessary to create some new institutions, starting with the EFTA and Commonwealth countries. A Clearing Union, a Bank and a Development Fund have been proposed here, but existing world organisations should be used wherever they can be turned to the general aim of planned development.

One example must suffice to point up the choice for Britain. In the field of engineering standards and specifications Britain pioneered the British Standards Institution. The Americans then established their standards; the communists have theirs; now the Common Market is to have their own. British standards are no longer accepted the world over. What should we do? Go in with one of the others, or use the International Standards Conference to obtain international agreement on world-wide standards to replace all the existing ones? For a trading nation like Britain, the latter is the only sane course, but it needs a strong initiative from Britain and her chief trading-partners in EFTA and the Commonwealth.

It is necessary to repeat once more that the aim is not to try to form another bloc like E.E.C., but rather to form in the EFTA and Commonwealth countries a nucleus of a genuine world organisation which would be open to adherents from East and West, from capitalist, communist and uncommitted lands on the basis of planning world trade and development. It is not only that this multi-racial association of rich and poor lands could do much to channel aid to underdeveloped lands in a more effective manner than at present, but they could begin to integrate our divided world of narrow trading blocs into one world of expanding commerce. As inequalities were reduced, they could encourage the conscious development of international specialisation, which we saw beginning in the Rouble Area. It is only on such a basis, as Dr Oscar Lange, the Polish economist, has emphasised, 'that the principle of comparative costs and the international division of labour come into their own and are transformed from ideological phrases, masking the exploitation of the weak countries by the strong ones, into operating principles of economic activity.'[63]

A programme that will advance world industrialisation and a world-wide expansion of trade and commerce must be one that unites the interests of both the peoples of the rich industrialised lands and the peoples of the poor undeveloped lands. A beginning, we have suggested, can be made among the rich and poor lands of EFTA and the Commonwealth.[64] If the central argument of this book is correct, then this is not going to be so difficult as it is always made to seem, for the wealth of the rich lands has not, for many years now, been dependent upon the poverty of the poor lands. A few, a very few, in the rich lands have gained from that poverty; the vast majority have suffered from it, by the reduced rate of growth of the whole world market. As a nation, we in Britain can only gain from a world that is growing richer. Any advantages that were once derived from inequality have long since been surpassed by the advantages of co-operation. International aid and credits, schemes for stabilising prices and earnings, and for balancing payments on a high level, long-term agreement on specialisation – all these are but the means for the giant task that awaits us of applying man's growing knowledge to controlling the whole environment and condition of our lives.

We have to keep our eyes on the long-term prospects for all mankind, poor and hungry though most of them now are, and avoid the short-term attractions of associating only with the few who are already rich. We need not be dismayed that the present examples of genuine world-wide international co-operation seem to be small and feeble compared with the rich corporations and the great world blocs; poor examples they may yet be, but they are the growing points of the new international economy that will follow after imperialism.

TABLE XXXIII

WORLD AID AND INVESTMENT FOR UNDERDEVELOPED LANDS, 1955–59
(in $b.)

Source	Total over 5 years	(As % of National Income)	Short-Term Credit	Loans	Grants	Food	Military	Private Investment	Total Military Budgets (for comparison)	Total Exports (for comparison)
U.S.A.	31	(1·5)	0·3	1·7	7	1·7	13·5	7	230	160
Canada	0·6	(0·25)	0·1	0·1	0·1	—	—	0·3	10	28
U.K.	4·1	(1)	0·4	0·2	0·5	—	—	3	22	48
Japan	1·0	(0·5)	0·2	0·3	0·5	—	—	0·1	3	15
France	5·6	(2)	0·2	1·2	2·4	—	—	1·8	20	25
Germany	2·5	(0·5)	1·0	0·7	0·4	—	—	0·4	17	44
Other Advanced Capitalist	3	(—)	0·6	0·4	0·5	—	—	1·5	15	30
U.S.S.R.	2·5	(0·5)	—	0·4	2·5	—	?·?	—	150	30
China	1·5	(1)	—	—	1·5	—	—	—	15	10
World Bank	0·8	(—)	—	0·8	—	—	—	—	—	—
Other	0·5	(—)	—	—	0·5	—	—	—	—	—
International	—	—	—	—	—	—	—	—	—	—
TOTALS	56		2·8	23		2	13·5	15	500	350

Note: These figures are in many cases no more than inspired guesses, but they probably give the correct order of magnitudes.

Sources: International Economic Aid:
  United Nations, *Statistical Yearbook 1960.*
  O.E.E.C., op. cit.
National Income, Military Budgets and Exports:
  United Nations, *Statistical Yearbook 1960.*
  United States Government, *Statistical Abstracts, 1960,* Washington, D.C., 1961.
  O.E.E.C., op. cit.
  U.S.S.R. Central Statistical Administration, op. cit.
  Chinese Central Statistical Bureau, op. cit.

References

1. Sylvester Gates, *Report of the Chairman*, the Bank of West Africa, 2.6.62.
2. G. Myrdal, *Economic Theory and the Underdeveloped Regions*, Chapter II.
3. United Nations, *Economic Survey of Europe in 1954*, footnote, p. 126.
4. U.K. Government, *Annual Abstract of Statistics, 1961*, External Trade Tables.
5. Organisation of European Economic Co-operation, *The Flow of Financial Resources to Countries in course of Economic Development*, pp. 97 ff. and 109 ff.
6. Colombo Plan, *Annual Reports*, H.M.S.O.
7. calculated from United States *Balance of Payments Statistics*, 1953–59, and International Monetary Fund, *International Financial Statistics*, 'International Bank loans, classified by borrowing country'.
8. U.K. Treasury, *Bulletin for Industry*, May 1961 and April 1962; and U.K. White Paper on *Assistance from the U.K. for Overseas Development*, March 1960.
9. *The Statist*, 3.3.56.
10. Mr David Owen, Assistant Secretary-General for Economic Affairs, The United Nations, reported in *Far East Trade*, September, 1958.
11. *International Financial Statistics*, loc. cit.
12. United Nations Monetary and Financial Conference, *Proceedings and Documents*, Bretton Woods, New Hampshire, 1–22 July 1944.
13. R. N. Gardner, *Sterling-Dollar Diplomacy*, Oxford, 1956, especially pp. 134 and 296 ff.
14. United States, Department of State, *Bulletin*, 1. iii, 1946, quoted by R. N. Gardner, p. 296.
15. R. N. Gardner, op. cit., p. 134.
16. ibid, p. 296 ff.
17. L. P. Elwell-Sutton, *Persian Oil*, pp. 279–80, 313–17.
18. International Bank for Reconstruction and Development, *Report, 1946–53*, Washington, 1954; and see Appendix to the lecture by Mr Eugene Black, the President of the Bank, on the *Diplomacy of Economic Development*.
19. Statement by Mr R. Garner, President of the International Finance Corporation, published in *The Times*, 25.7.56.
20. United Nations, *Measures for the Economic Development of Underdeveloped Countries*, New York, 1951.
21. G. Myrdal, *An International Economy*, Routledge, 1956, p. 123 ff.
22. The Labour Party, *Labour's Colonial Policy*, II *Economic Aid*, 1958.
23. F. Benham, *Economic Aid to Underdeveloped Countries*, p. 106.
24. Food and Agriculture Organisation, *The State of Food and Agriculture, 1960*, Rome, 1961, p. 48.

25. United Nations, *Economic and Social Consequences of Disarmament*.
26. ibid.
27. M. Djilas, *The New Class*, Thames and Hudson, 1957.
28. J. Hughes and M. Barratt Brown, *Britain's Crisis and the Common Market*, New Left pamphlet, 1961.
29. *Britain – E.F.T.A. – Commonwealth Conference*, 16–19 July 1962, Forward Britain Movement.
30. J. A. Rowlatt and F. T. Blackaby, 'The Demand for Industrial Materials', *National Institute Economic Review*, September 1959.
31. General Agreement on Tariffs and Trade, *Trends in International Trade*, p. 66 ff.
32. ibid., p. 72 ff.
33. ibid., p. 95 ff.; and see United Nations Economic Commission for Europe, *Economic Survey of Europe in 1960*, Geneva, 1961, Chapter V, *passim*.
34. Political and Economic Planning, *Britain and World Trade*, 1947, Chapter VI.
35. L. St. Clare Grondona, *Utilising World Abundance*, Allen and Unwin, 1958.
36. United Nations, *International Compensation for Fluctuations in Commodity Trade*, New York, May 1961.
37. Professor Ragnar Frisch, *Britain – E.F.T.A. – Commonwealth Conference*.
38. A. C. L. Day, 'New Money for Old', *The Listener*, August 1961.
39. Jacques Rueff, three articles in *The Times*, 27, 28, 29 June 1961.
40. Sir R. Harrod, *Policy against Inflation*, Macmillan, 1958, Chapter I, and 'Wall Street and Gold', *The Financial Times*, 22.6.62.
41. A. Schonfield, *The Attack on World Poverty*, p. 38.
42. *The Times* 'Report from the Vienna I.M.F. Meeting', 19.9.61.
43. The Hon. J. Maxwell Stamp, 'The Fund and the Future', *Lloyds Bank Review*, October 1958.
44. R. Triffin, 'The Death of a System', *The Listener*, 27.7.61.
45. J. E. Meade, 'The Future of International Trade and Payments', *Three Banks Review*, June 1961, and Ragnar Frisch, op. cit.
46. P. Abrams, *Britain and Her Export Trade*, p. 99.
47. General Agreement on Tariffs and Trade, *The Activities of GATT*, Geneva, May 1960.
48. J. Hughes and M. Barratt Brown, *Britain's Crisis and the Common Market*.
49. *The Financial Times*, 8.6.56, and *The Economist*, 9.12.61.
50. United Nations, 'Economic Commission for Europe', *Economic Bulletin*, Geneva, September 1960, Table 3.
51. United Nations, *World Economic Survey*, 1959, p. 167 ff.

52. President Kennedy, *Message to Congress on Balance of Payments and Gold*, Washington, 6.2.61.

53. Sir R. Harrod, *The Observer*, 6.5.62.

54. Lord Home reported in *The Observer*, 3.6.62, and Mr Harold Macmillan in a *Party Political Broadcast*, 20 June 1962.

55. G. Myrdal, *An International Economy*, Routledge, 1956, p. 291.

56. United Nations Economic Commission for Europe, *Economic Survey of Europe in 1955*, p. 31; and *Economic Survey of Europe in 1960*, Geneva, 1961, Chapter V.

57. Treaty establishing the European Economic Community, 25 March 1957.

58. *The Times* 'Possible Government Aid to Industry over £200m', 7.4.60.

59. *The New Scientist*, 5.9.60.

60. Lord Montagu, 'The Challenge of the Motor Show', *New Statesman* 20.10.61.

61. Conservative Political Centre, *Our Trade with Europe*, 1957.

62. G. Myrdal, *Beyond the Welfare State*, Duckworth, 1960, especially Chapter 14.

63. quoted in P. Baran, *The Political Economy of Growth*, p. 292.

64. *Britain – E.F.T.A. – Commonwealth Conference.*

A NOTE ON THE
SUPPLEMENTARY TABLES OF STATISTICS

Some of the Statistical Tables in the book were the result of what were really voyages of discovery in ill charted realms. In the last ten years the charting of many of these realms has proceeded at an unprecedented rate and publication of recent research work in the field of historical statistics has been widespread. In particular for British historical statistics we have Mitchell & Dean's *British Historical Statistics* and by the time this Note is printed we shall have Charles Feinstein's magisterial extension of the *National Income and Expenditure* Blue Book back to the 1860s. For international historical series A. Maizel's great work on *Industrial Growth and World Trade* was published at almost the same time as *After Imperialism* and is invaluable.

Current statistics are also steadily improving as governments attempt to make decisions on increasingly up to date information. For current British finance the Bank of England *Bulletin* and the Board of Trade *Journal* between them have at length begun to reveal the facts of British overseas investment, although the oil companies' investment is still mysteriously excluded from the count. The United Nations studies of the World economy in the Statistical Yearbooks have become much more precise and now include comparable figures of trade and industrial output for the Soviet as well as the Capitalist worlds. No aggregate statistics can be better than the parts from which they are built up and our knowledge of the national income of many underdeveloped countries must remain hazy until their economic development reaches the stage of requiring a sound statistical service. Interesting new estimates for a number of countries with projections of growth rates in the future appeared recently in Kahn and Wiener's *The Year 2000*.

Up to date figures are therefore more easily available for readers than they were when the book first appeared. There are nevertheless, a number of Tables in the book which are based on scources that are still not so readily available. To bring these up to date I have added supplementary figures in the form of the following Tables. In the case of certain of these Tables the new figures involve revisions of the old, but in most cases what is presented is simply an up dating of the series. These supplementary Tables are referred to in the Preface to the second edition and provide evidence for many of the statements made in this new Preface.

Supplementary Table I

RICH AND POOR 1958 AND 1968

| | National Income | | | | Population | | | | Per Capita Income | | Growth in Per Capita Income |
	$b 1958	%	$b 1968	%	Million 1958	%	Million 1968	%	1958	1968	1958–68
U.S. & Canada	395	35	670	33	192	7	220	7	2050	2950	144
Other Developed	225	20	390	19	270	10	300	9	850	1300	153
Communist	260	24	530	26	325	12	370	11	800	1425	178
Middle Group (Non Communist)	110	9	200	10	365	14	455	14	300	440	146
China	55	5	100	5	680	25	750	23	80	135	170
Other Poor	80	7	150	7	850	32	1155	36	90	130	145
TOTAL	1125	100	2040	100	2680	100	3250	100	420	630	150

Notes: (a) Totals exclude about 200m people in 1958, 250m in 1968 for whom income data unavailable.

(b) Developed Countries in this Table include Western Europe and Oceania but exclude Japan and South Africa which are placed in Middle Group (Non Communist). For details of this group see *After Imperialism* Table IB.

(c) National Income excludes private and government services as figures for these are not available for Communist countries.

(d) The figure for China in 1968 is a wild guess.

Source: United Nations *Statistical Yearbooks* and *Monthly Bulletins of Statistics.*

Supplementary Table XIII

RETURN ON INVESTMENT IN BRITISH HOME AND OVERSEAS COMPANIES 1952–68

Companies	A.		B.			C.	
	Average 1952–60	Year 1961	Year 1961	Average 1961–5	Year 1965	Year 1965	Average 1965–8
1. Share of Capital Investment							
All Home and Overseas Companies	100	100	100	100	100	100	100
Oil Companies	10	13.5	11	10	9.5	11.5	12
Other Overseas	9.5	6.5	3.2	2.4	1.8	1.9	2.1
2. Share of Net Profits							
All Home and Overseas Companies	100	100	100	100	100	100	100
Oil Companies	12	11	10	10	10	13	12.5
Other Overseas	12	10	6	4.5	3.2	2.7	2.8
3. Rate of Return on Capital							
All Home Industrial Companies	13.2	12.4	8.8	7.8	7.9	7.0	6.7
Manufacturing Companies	13.4	12.7	8.9	7.9	8.1	7.1	6.8
Oil Companies	16	10.7	7.8	7.7	7.7	7.1	6.8
Other Overseas	19.2	20	14.5	12.7	10.5	9.0	8.5

Notes: 1. The method of calculation was changed in 1961 and 1965 so these years are presented in two ways,

A = Net Profits = Profits less Depreciation and Tax
= Capital = Issued Ordinary Capital plus Capital and Revenue Reserves .

B = Net Profits = Profits less Depreciation and Tax
= Capital = Net Assets

C = Net Profits = Profits less Charges, Depreciation and Tax
= Capital = Net Assets

2. Other Overseas Companies include companies producing gold, coffee, lead, zinc, tin, rubber, tea and other primary products.

Source: *Financial Times*, "Annual Trend of Industrial Profits"

SUPPLEMENTARY TABLE XVIII
NATURE OF BRITISH OVERSEAS INVESTMENT IN THE 1960s

Annual Movements		Average 1961–5 £m	Average 1966–7 £m
Outward Movement	Total	575	615
Inward Movement	Total	215	410
Non Sterling Areas[1]	—Outward Total	345	330
	—Inward Total	225	430
Sterling Area[1]	—Outward Total	230	285
	—Inward Total[2]	−10	−20
Outward Movement made up of			
Government—Economic Grants		81	88
—Military Grants		19	19
—International Institutions etc.		45	75
—Loans (excl. repayments)		70	90
Portfolio		−25	−25
Direct Company Investment (incl. Oil)		350	385
—retentions etc.		280	345
—new capital (excl. oil)		70	40
Inward Movement made up of			
Government—Grants		—	—
—Loans (incl. repayments)		−5	70
Portfolio[2]		−25	−20
Direct Company Investment (incl. Oil)		245	360
—retentions etc.		165	290
—new capital (excl. Oil)		80	70

Notes: [1] Oil investment is assumed to be equally divided between Sterling and Non Sterling Areas.
[2] A negative inward movement means sales of earlier portfolio investments.
Source: U.K. Balance of Payments.

Supplementary Table XIX
U.K. COMPANY DIRECT OVERSEAS INVESTMENT 1960–67

Industry and Area	Investment Stake (£ millions)		Investment Flows Annual Averages (£m)	
	1960	1965	1961–5	1966–7
By Industry				
Mining	197	271	17	16[1]
Agriculture	294	365	14	8[1]
Manufacturing	1450	2113	132	158[1]
Distribution	431	671	48	39[1]
Other	588	796	39	55[1] [2]
TOTAL (excl. oil and finance)	2950	4215	250	272
Oil	1200	1650	90	) 113
Insurance (excl. other finance)	350	400	10	) —
TOTAL	4500	6265	350	385

By Area for all investment except oil and finance and for manufacturing investment only.

	Percentage		Percentage	
TOTAL	100	100	100	100
U.S.A.	9	9	9.5	15[1]
Canada	15.5	12.5	6	5.0[1]
North America: Mfg only	32	26	12.5	—
E.E.C.	7.5	9	14	18.5[1]
Other W. Europe	2.5	4	6	5.0[1]
W. Europe: Mfg only	11	13.5	18.5	—
Sterling: developed	28.5	31.5	39	32
underdeveloped	28	25	19	11
Sterling: Mfg only	49	53	60	—
Other developed	0.5	1	1.5	2 .5
underdeveloped	9	8	5	11
Other: Mfg only	8	7.5	9	—
All underdeveloped	37	33	24	22[1]

Notes: [1] 1966 only
[2] includes insurance companies investment.
Source: Board of Trade *Journal* 29.1.68 and 19.7.68
    W. B. Reddaway *Effects of U.K. Direct Investment Overseas*

Supplementary Table XXV

CAPITALIST WORLD PRODUCTION TRADE AND PRICES OF MANUFACTURERS AND PRIMARY PRODUCTS 1958-67

	Indices based on 1958=100								
	1959	1960	1961	1962	1963	1964	1965	1966	1967
World Production									
Agriculture—TOTAL	102	106	108	110	113	116	117	119	123
—Food[1]	103	106	107	111	111	116	117	120	124
—Non Food[1]	103	105	106	109	113	115	116	117	118
Minerals—excl. fuels	105	118	120	122	124	132	137	143	147
Oil	108	117	124	134	144	155	167	179	193
Manufactures	110	116	120	129	136	147	157	167	172
World Trade Volumes									
TOTAL	107	118	124	131	141	155	167	180	190
Primary Products	108	118	122	125	133	140	145	150	158
Manufactures	108	122	126	134	145	163	178	195	210
Prices in World Trade									
Food	93	91	90	90	103	106	99	101	100
Agriculture—non food	105	107	103	99	103	105	104	105	97
Minerals	94	93	92	92	92	94	96	96	95
All Primary Products	97	97	95	94	100	103	100	101	98
Manufactures	99	101	102	102	103	104	106	108	108
Terms of Trade[2]									
For U.K.	100	101	104	106	105	103	106	107	110
For Primary Products/Manufactures	98	95	93	93	95	95	95	95	92
For Underdeveloped Lands	98	97	95	93	95	96	94	94	93

Note: 1—includes U.S.S.R. and Eastern Europe
2—Terms of Trade—Export Prices divided by Import Prices
Source: United Nations *Statistical Yearbook:* and *Monthly Bulletins of Statistics.*

Supplementary Table XXVII
TRADE OF INDUSTRIAL AND NON-INDUSTRIAL LANDS 1953–1967

A. *By Area*

There is a misprint in the heading of the last column of this Table in the book which should read Non-Indust. to Non-Indust. The Table is arranged below to bring it up to 1967, and to include Australia, South Africa and New Zealand in the Industrialised Lands.

World Trade Groups	1953	1960	1967
TOTAL TRADE ($b)	81.7	127.8	214.1
Shares of Flows of World Trade (%)	100	100	100
Indust. Lands Exports	64.5	67	70
to Indust. Lands	41	46.7	52.4
to Communists	1.1	2.3	2.9
to Non-Indust.	17.5	16.7	14.2
U.S. Special Category	5.0	1.3	0.5
Communist Lands Exports	9.7	11.8	11.5
to Communist	7.5	8.5	7.0
to Indust.	1.4	2.2	1.7
to Non-Indust.	0.8	1.0	2.8
Non-Indust. Lands Exports	25.8	21.4	18.6
to Indust.	18.8	15.5	13.7
to Non-Indust.	6.3	4.8	3.8
to Communist	0.7	1.0	1.0

Note: Figures do not exactly add up to 100 because of rounding.
Source: United Nations *Statistical Yearbooks*

Supplementary Table XXVII (cont.)

TRADE OF INDUSTRIAL AND NON-INDUSTRIAL LANDS 1928–1967

B. *By Commodity* (current values)

The Table is rearranged to make the intended point clearer, to bring the figures up to 1965, and to include Australia, South Africa and New Zealand in the industrialised lands.

Years	1928	1937	1950	1955	1960	1965	1967
World Trade Total	100	100	100	100	100	100	100
of which Primary Products Share (%)	61	63	55.5	50	45	40.5	38
Industrial Lands Share of Primary Product Exports (%)	50	48	47	50	53.5	54.5	53
Industrial Lands Trade Total	100	100	100	100	100	100	100
of which Primary Products Share (%)	45	44	39.5	34.5	31.5	28	25.5
Non Industrial Lands Trade Total	100	100	100	100	100	100	100
of which Primary Products Share (%)	82	85	88	87	85	83	79

Note: This Table excludes the trade of the Communist countries after 1937.
Source: 1928 and 1937 P. Lamartine Yates 50 *Years of Foreign Trade*
1930–1965 United Nations *Statistica Yearbook*
1967 United Nations Monthly *Bulletin of Statistics*

Supplementary Table XXIX

RATE OF GROWTH AND SHARES IN WORLD TRADE 1950-70

Group and Country	Shares (%) in Exports (current $ values)				Export Volume Growth Rates p.a. (%)			
	1955	1960	1965	Est. 1970	1950-1955	1955-1960	1960-1965	1966-1967
Capitalist World Total	90	88.5	88.4	88.3	5.7	6.0	7.3	6.5
Developed	65	67	69	72	7.0	6.5	7.5	7.0
Underdeveloped	25	21.5	19.5	16	3.0	4.5	5.0	5.0
U.S.A.	16.5	16	14.5	13.2	2.0	4.5	5.5	6.3
E.E.C.	20	23.5	25.5	28	11.5	10	9.0	8.0
U.K.	9	8	7	6	4.0	2.1	3.8	2.0
Japan	2	3.2	45	6.5	20	14.3	15	11
Communist World Total	10	11.5	11.6	11.7	12.2	11	7.5	6.7
USSR & E.Europe	8.5	10	10.5	11.25	12.5	12	8.7	7.7
China	1.5	1.6	1.0	0.75	10	7.3	0	0

Note: 1970 estimated share is on assumption of 1960-67 growth rates continuing.
Source: United Nations *Statistical Yearbooks*

Supplementary Table XXX

UNITED STATES BALANCE OF PAYMENTS AND LONG TERM FOREIGN INVESTMENT 1960–68

A. *Balance of Payments*

	Average 1960–65 ($b)	Year 1965 ($b)	Year 1968 ($b)
(1) Current Account	4.3	5.2	— 0.2
Exports	23.2	27.1	33.8
Imports	—17.0	—20.9	—32.9
Freight & Insurance	—1.2	—1.8	—0.8
Other Services & Property Income (net)	1.6	3.1	2.5
Government Grants	—2.3	—2.3	—2.8
(2) Capital Account	—5.3	—6.7	—1.5
Outflow—Government Loans	—1.1	—1.5	—1.5
—Private Investment—direct	—3.2	—4.5)	0
other	—1.0	—0.7)	
(3) Capital & Current Account Deficit	—1.0	—1.5	1.7

Note: in 1968 the deficit was offset by over $3 billion of short term private capital.

B. *Long Term Foreign Investment*

	Investment Stake			Investment Flow 1961–65 Annual Average ($b)
	1955 $b	1960 $b	1965 $b	
Government Loans	15	18	23	1.1
Private Portfolio	7	13	18	1.0
Private Direct Company	19	32	48	3.2
Distribution of Direct Company Investment				
(a) by Regions (%) Canada	—	34	—	25
Latin America	—	28	—	12
Europe	—	17	—	43
Oceania	—	3	—	10
Other	—	18	—	10
(b) by Type (%) Manufacturing	—	35	—	50
Mining	—	9	—	8
Oil	—	33	—	27
Utilities	—	8	—	7
Other	—	15	—	10

Source: U.S. Department of Commerce *Survey of Current Business*

Supplementary Table XXXI

GROWTH RATE AND SHARES OF WORLD INDUSTRIAL ACTIVITY 1950–1970

Economic Group	Population Growth rate p.a. 1960–65 %	Industrial Growth Rate p.a. 1950–5 %	Industrial Growth Rate p.a. 1955–60 %	Industrial Growth Rate p.a. 1960–5 %	Shares in Industrial Output 1958 %	Shares in Industrial Output 1966 %	Shares in Industrial Output Est.A 1970 %	Shares in Industrial Output Est.B 1970 %
World Total[1]	1.9	7.0	5.4	6.7	100	100	100	100
Capitalist World—TOTAL	2.3	5.9	3.8	6.2	73	70	57	67
Capitalist—Developed	1.3	5.7	3.3	6.0	65.5	62	49	60
—U.S.A.	1.5	5.0	1.0	5.8	37	33	23.5	32.5
—U.K.	0.8	3.5	2.3	3.2	7	5	4	4.5
—E.E.C.	1.3	8.2	6.5	5.5	14	14.5	15	10.5
—Japan	1.0	18.0	13.5	11.6	2	3.5	5.5	4.5
Capitalist—Underdeveloped	2.5	7.0	7.0	6.5	7.5	8	8	7.5
Communist—Soviet Bloc	1.2	12.5	11.0	8.7	27	30	43	33
—China[1]	1.4	(?25)	(?25)	(?)	(?3)	(?)	(?15)	(?)

Notes: [1] Total excludes China except in case of population
Figures in brackets for China would be additional to the total
[2] Output in 1970 Estimate A extrapolated from 1950–60 growth rates.
Estimate B extrapolated from 1960–65 growth rates.

Source: United Nations *Statistical Yearbooks*

Supplementary Table XXXIII

WORLD AID AND INVESTMENT FOR
UNDERDEVELOPED LANDS 1955–66

A. *Aid and Investment* by Types of Capital Flow	1955–60 Annual Average		1961–66 Annual Average	
	$m	$ per head of recipients	$m	$ per head of recipients
1. Capitalist Countries				
Government—Grants	2,300	1.4	3,700	2.1
Loans & Credit	1,250	0.75	1,400	0.8
—Military Aid	1,800	1.1	(1,500)	0.85
International Agencies—				
Official)	400	0.25	} 560	0.3
Private)			160	0.1
Private Investment—Direct)	2,800	1.7	} 1,700	1.0
—Other)			400	0.25
2. Communist Countries				
TOTAL	350	0.25	250	0.15
GRAND TOTAL	8,800	5.45	9,670	5.55

B. *Official Aid (excl, military) by source and Destination*				
1. Capitalist Countries Total	4,250	2.6	5,800	3.2
from U.S.A.	2,300	1.4	3,400	1.9
France	800	0.5	850	0.5
U.K.	350	0.2	430	0.4
W. Germany	300	0.2	400	0.2
Others	500	0.3	720	0.4
to International Agencies	500	0.5	600	0.35
India	300	0.7	900	2.2
Algeria	350	35	400	40
French Franc Zone	250	12.5	400	20
Pakistan	200	2.5	500	5.5
S. Korea	350	16	250	12
Viet Nam	50	4	225	17
Brazil	60	1	225	3.5
Egypt	50	2	200	8
Colombia	70	5.5	140	10
Indonesia	40	0.5	100	1.1
Chile	50	7	100	12.5
Morocco	—	—	100	10
Israel	50	25	100	50
Congo	—	—	100	7.5
Cambodia, Thailand & Laos	50	1.5	90	2
Taiwan	100	10	80	8
Jordan	30	20	80	55
Tunisia	—	—	80	20
Mexico	40	1.5	60	2
Kenya	—	—	55	9
Argentina	25	1.2	50	2.5
Iran	90	4.5	50	2.5

Supplementary Table XXXIII—(*cont.*)

		1955–60		1961–66	
		$m	$ *per head of recipients*	$m	$ *per head of recipients*
2. Capitalist Countries Total		350	0.25	250	0.15
from	USSR	200	0.1	150	0.1
	Others (incl. China)	150	0.1	100	
to	Algeria	—	—	60	6
	India	90	0.3	100	0.35
	Egypt	65	3.0	60	2.5
	Indonesia	70	0.8	40	0.2

C. *Major Donors and Beneficiaries of Official International Aid*
    (excl. Military Aid, private investment and International Agencies)

Donor	Beneficiary	1955–60 (*Annual Average*) $m	1961–66 (*Annual Average*) $m
U.S.A.	TOTAL	2,300	3,400
	S. Korea and S.E. Asia	650	850
	Latin America	450	900
U.K.	TOTAL	350	430
	Sterling—Independent	100	100
	—Dependent	150	225
France	TOTAL	800	850
	Algeria & Franc Zone	600	800

Note: Figures give only rough orders of magnitude but include loans, grants and
    credits but exclude military aid except where indicated.
Source: O.E.C.D. *Flow of Financial Resources to Countries in Course of Development*,
    United Nations *Statistical Yearbooks*

SELECT BIBLIOGRAPHY

The best available bibliography is A. Hazlewood's, *The Economics of Underdeveloped Areas*, Oxford, 1959, which is comprehensive in its own field.

I *General Works on Imperialism*

The two main works in the Socialist tradition which are discussed in this book are V. I. Lenin's *Imperialism* (1916) Little Lenin Library, 1944 and 1948, and J. A. Hobson's *Imperialism* (1902) Allen and Unwin, 1938. N. Bukharin's *Imperialism and the World Economy* (1917) Martin Lawrence, 1930, gives a similar analysis to that of Lenin. Lenin's facts and figures were brought up to date in 1937 by E. Varga and L. Mendelsohn in *New Data on Lenin's Imperialism*, New York, International Publishers, 1940.

Critiques of Lenin's and Hobson's analysis include J. A. Schumpeter's essay on *Imperialism* (1919) New York, Meridian Books, 1955, and more recently, John Strachey's *The End of Empire*, Gollancz, 1959. Both are extremely valuable, which cannot be said of W. W. Rostow's *Stages of Economic Growth – a Non-Communist Manifesto*, Cambridge, 1960.

Victorian thought on Imperialism is exemplified in J. R. Seeley's *Expansion of England*, Macmillan, 1883, and discussed in B. Semmell, *Imperialism and Social Reform* and rather better in C. A. Bodelsen, *Studies in Mid-Victorian Imperialism* (1923) Heinemann, 1960.

D. K. Fieldhouse's article ' "Imperialism" : an Historiographical Revision' in the *Economic History Review*, December 1961, provides a valuable review of the literature, as does

H. B. Davis's article 'Imperialism and Labour: an Analysis of Marxian Views' in *Science and Society*, New York, Winter, 1962.

II *Works on Colonial History*

British colonial history is exhaustively and exhaustingly covered by the *Cambridge History of the British Empire*, 1958, and by A. B. Keith's *Responsible Government in the Dominions* (1912) and *Selected Speeches and Documents in British Colonial Policy 1763–1917* (1918). Economic history is widely surveyed in L. C. A. Knowles' *Economic Development of the British Overseas Empire*, Routledge, 1928, especially Volume I.

The age of mercantilism is fully dealt with in E. Lipson's *Economic History of England*, Black, 1934. Henry Hamilton in the *History of the Homeland*, Allen and Unwin, 1947, admirably summarises the 'Spread of Commerce and the Flag'. J. H. Lawson gives a brilliant and provocative study of American colonial history in the *Hidden Heritage*, New York, Citadel, 1950. Portuguese colonisation may best be studied in G. Freyre's *The Masters and the Slaves*, 1946.

Marx's and Engel's views on colonial history have been brought together in *Marx and Engels on Colonialism*, Lawrence and Wishart, 1960. E. J. Hobsbawm's essays on 'The Crisis of the Seventeenth Century' in *Past and Present*, numbers 5 and 6, shed much fresh light on the old and new colonial systems.

III *Works on Nineteenth-Century British Economic History*

The standard work is Sir J. Clapham's three-volume *Economic History of Modern Britain*, Cambridge, 1934–6, which may be replaced only by reading W. H. B. Court's shorter and duller *Concise Economic History of Britain – 1750 to Recent Times*, Cambridge, 1954, and by the economic and social sections of the Oxford histories and especially of R. C. K. Ensor's outstanding *England 1870 – 1914*, Oxford, 1936.

Marx's *Capital* (1887) Allen and Unwin, 1918, and C. H.

Kerr, Chicago, 1909, is a treasure chest of English economic history and M. A. Dobb's *Studies in the Development of Capitalism*, Routledge, 1946, provides the most valuable Marxist analysis.

W. W. Rostow's *British Economy of the Nineteenth Century*, Oxford, 1948, must be corrected in the light of A. K. Cairncross, *Home and Foreign Investment, 1870–1913*, Cambridge, 1953; J. Saville's 'Comment on Professor Rostow's "British Economy of the 19th Century" ' in *Past and Present*, Number 6; C. H. Feinstein's thesis on *Aspects of British and Foreign Investment – 1870–1913*, Department of Applied Economics, Cambridge, 1960; and D. Coppock's 'The Cause of the Great Depression 1873–1896' in *The Manchester School of Economic and Social Studies*, September 1961.

Technological history may be studied in S. Lilley, *Men, Machines and History*, Cobbett Press, 1948; J. D. Bernal, *Science and Industry in the Nineteenth Century*, Routledge, 1953; H. J. Habbakuk, *American and British Technology in the Nineteenth Century*, Cambridge, 1962; and D. Burn, *Economic History of Steelmaking 1867–1939*, Cambridge, 1940. Statistical material is available in Cairncross and Feinstein, cited above, and in W. G. Hoffman, *British Industry 1750–1950*, Blackwell, 1955; A. H. Imlah, *Economic Elements in the Pax Britanica*, Harvard 1958; J. B. Jeffreys and D. Walters' article 'National Income and Expenditure of the U.K. 1870–1952' in *Income and Wealth – Series V*, Bowes and Bowes, 1955; D. C. Paige's article 'Economic Growth – the Hundred Years' in *National Institute Economic Review*, July 1901; and E. H. Phelps Brown and S. V. Hopkins, 'Seven Centuries of Wages and Prices', *Economica*, February 1961.

IV *Works on Twentieth-Century British Economic History up to 1945*

The best short book on the Edwardian period is W. S. Adams, *Edwardian Heritage*, Muller, 1949. W. A. Lewis's *Economic Survey 1919–39*, Allen and Unwin, 1949; G. D. H. Cole's

Intelligent Man's Guide through World Chaos, Gollancz, 1932; and H. W. Arndt's *The Economic Lessons of the 1930's*, Oxford, 1944, all provide just what their titles indicate.

J. M. Keynes' *Essays in Persuasion*, Macmillan, 1931, and E. A. G. Robinson's articles 'The Changing Structure of the British Economy' in *The Economic Journal*, September, 1954, and 'The U.K's Economic Problems' in *United Kingdom Policy*, Royal Institute of International Affairs, 1950, raise questions of structure within the long historical setting.

V *Works on the British Economy since* 1945

A. Schonfield's *British Economic Policy since the War*, Penguin, 1958, provides an admirable summary. This may be supplemented by M. Shank's *The Stagnant Society*, Penguin, 1961, which devotes five chapters to the faults of the trade unions and one to those of the employers.

An orthodox economic analysis will be found in F. W. Paish, *Studies in an Inflationary Economy*, Macmillan, 1962. Political and Economic Planning's *Growth in the British Economy*, P.E.P., 1961, provides an admirably objective statement of the facts.

Socialist analysis will be found in J. Strachey, *Contemporary Capitalism*, Gollancz, 1956; C. A. R. Crosland, *The Future of Socialism*, Cape, 1956; and D. Jay, *Socialism in the New Society*, Longmans, 1962 – all good Gaitskell men.

Studies in the control of Inflation have been made by Sir R. Harrod in *Policy against Inflation,* Macmillan, 1958, and by J. C. R. Dow in the *Westminster Bank Review*, May and November, 1960, articles on 'Fiscal and Monetary Policy as Instruments of Economic Control'.

More radical proposals will be found in T. Balogh's *New Statesman* article, 12.12.59, on 'The Economics of World Tension', and in two pamphlets by J. Hughes and K. Alexander: *A Socialist Wages Plan*, New Left Booklets, 1958, and *Trade Unions in Opposition*, Fabian Society, 1961.

VI *Works on International Trade*

J. Viner's *Studies in the Theory of International Trade*, Allen & Unwin, 1955, and his editing of *Readings in International Trade Theory*, Allen & Unwin, 1950, provide a complete theoretical framework.

On World Trade P. Lamartine Yates, *Forty Years of Foreign Trade*, Allen and Unwin, 1960, provides a reliable summary and for further detail it is necessary to consult The League of Nations *World Economic Surveys*, annually from 1930, the United Nations *World Economic Surveys*, annually from 1948 and the General Agreement on Tariffs and Trade, *International Trade*, annually from 1952.

For the trade of different regions The United Nations Regional Commissions respectively for Africa, Asia, and the Far East, Latin America and Europe publish Annual *Economic Surveys* and Quarterly *Bulletins*. In addition, for Europe there is the invaluable report of I. Svennilson on *Growth and Stagnation in the European Economy*, Geneva, 1954, covering the period between the wars and the annual reports and statistics of the Organisation for European Economic Co-operation for the years after 1949.

For Britain's overseas trade the basic work is W. Schloete's *British Overseas Trade from 1700 to the 1930's*, Blackwell, 1952, supplemented by A. H. Imlah, op. cit., and R. B. Saul, *Studies in British Overseas Trade 1870–1914*, Liverpool, 1962. The two reports of Political and Economic Planning, *Report on International Trade* (1937), and *Britain and World Trade* (1947), contain useful material. M. Abrams (ed.), *Britain and Her Export Trade*, Pilot Press, 1947, contains some excellent essays, and on Britain's Colonial Trade, K. M. Stahl *The Metropolitan Organisation of Britain's Colonial Trade*, Faber, 1937, is essential.

Britain's trade with Europe and with the Commonwealth respectively have been exhaustively treated in F. V. Meyer, *United Kingdom Trade with Europe*, Bowes and Bowes, 1957, and the two major publications of the Economist Intelligence

Unit, *Britain and Europe* (1957) and *The Commonwealth and Europe* (1960).

VII *Works on Economic Growth and Development*

W. A. Lewis, *Theory of Economic Growth*, Allen and Unwin, 1955, covers a very wide field while D. Baran's *Political Economy of Growth*, New York, Monthly Review, 1957, has a specifically Marxist approach. The first part of H. Hanson's *Public Enterprise and Economic Development* provides an excellent summary of the 'Obstacles to Economic Dvelopment'.

More difficult questions in the analysis of growth are dealt with in A. K. Cairncross, *Factors in Economic Development*, Allen and Unwin, 1962; C. P. Kindleberger, *Economic Development*, New York, McGraw Hill, 1958; S. Kusnetz, *Economic Growth*, Illinois, Free Press of Glencoe, 1959; and N. Kaldor, *Essays on Economic Stability and Growth*, Duckworth, 1960.

Development of underdeveloped lands is treated specifically in G. Myrdal's brilliant *Economic Theory and Underdeveloped Regions*, Duckworth, 1957 and R. Nurkse's *Problems of Capital Formation in Underdeveloped Countries*, Blackwell, 1960. Books on development in specific countries are described below. For more difficult questions of analysis M. Dobb's *Economic Growth and Planning*, Routledge, 1960, is excellent.

On the poverty of underdeveloped lands, J. de Castro's *Geography of Hunger*, Gollancz, 1952, is unrivalled, but Dudley Stamp's *Our Developing World*, Faber, 1960, contains much valuable material.

Economic Aid to underdeveloped lands is described from the point of view of the World Bank by the Bank's Governor, E. R. Black, *The Diplomacy of Economic Development*, Harvard, 1960, and by M. D. Bryce, *Industrial Development*, McGraw Hill, 1960. For a corrective of these official views the reader should examine A. Shonfield's *Attack on World Poverty*, Chatto and Windus, 1960; F. Benham's brilliant *Economic Aid to Underdeveloped Countries*, Oxford, 1961; and J. D. Bernal's comprehensive *World Without War*, Routledge, 1958.

VIII *Works on the Post-War Sterling Area and Commonwealth*

The most comprehensive work is P. H. Bell's *The Sterling Area in the Post-War World*, Oxford, 1956, although the immense work of the Economic Co-operation Administration, *The Sterling Area – an American Analysis*, London, 1951, may also be consulted. A more popular American critique will be found in J. Polk's *Sterling*, New York, Harper Bros., 1956, and for early post-war negotiations with the United States R. N. Gardner's *Sterling–Dollar Diplomacy*, Oxford, 1956, is essential.

Commonwealth Trade is most fully examined in the Economist Intelligence Units *The Commonwealth and Europe,* while Commonwealth investment is described in A. R. Conan's *Capital Imports into Sterling Countries*, Macmillan, 1960.

IX *Works on International Business Interests and Cartels*

The two basic books on the inter-war and last war periods are J. W. Stocking and M. W. Watkins, *Cartels in Action*, Twentieth Century Fund, New York, 1947, and *Cartels or Competition?*, Twentieth Century Fund, New York, 1948. A very valuable recent book is J. P. Miller (ed.), *Competition, Cartels and their Regulation*, Amsterdam, North Holland Publishing Co., 1962, which has a particularly useful survey of 'Restrictive Practices in Britain' by T. Wilson.

The standard work on British cartels prior to 1914 is H. Levy's *Monopolies, Cartels and Trusts in British Industry*, Macmillan, 1927. J. W. F. Rowe's *Markets and Men*, Cambridge, 1936, provides an admirably simple account of inter-war commodity control schemes.

V. Perlo's *Empire of High Finance*, New York, International, 1957, gives a Marxist view of U.S. big business since the war, expanding Anna Rochester's pre-war *Rulers of America*, Lawrence and Wishart, 1936.

H. O'Connor's *The Empire of Oil*, Calder, 1955, is a racy description of the oil companies. More sober analysis will be found in L. P. Elwell Sutton's *Persian Oil*, Lawrence and Wishart, 1955, and in G. Lenczowski's *Oil and State in the Middle East*, Cornell, 1960. The United Nations, Economic Commission for Europe, prepared a monograph on *The Price of Oil in Western Europe*, Geneva, 1955, which was subsequently withdrawn.

On the overseas interests of British firms S. Aaronovitch's two books, *Monopoly*, Lawrence and Wishart, 1955, and *The Ruling Class*, Lawrence and Wishart, 1961, give many essential facts. Others may be found in M. Barratt Brown's articles, 'The Controllers', *Universities and Left Review*, Autumn 1958 – Spring 1959. C. Wilson's two-volume *History of Unilever*, Cassell, 1954–5, provides an impeccably fair case-study.

X *Works on the Economics of Western Europe*

On Western Europe generally Sir J. Clapham's *Economic Development of France and Germany, 1815–1914*, Cambridge, 1938, is essential for the period before 1914. I. Svennilson's *Growth and Stagnation in the European Economy*, Geneva, 1954, is equally essential for the inter-war years.

Works on the Common Market now abound but E. Strauss's *Common Sense about the Common Market*, Allen and Unwin, 1958, remains the best background book and J. F. Deniau's *The Common Market*, Barrie and Rockcliff, 1960, the best brief description. U. W. Kitzinger, *The Challenge of the Common Market*, Blackwell, 1961, states the case for Britain's entry and for the opposite view see M. Barratt Brown and J. Hughes, *Britain's Crisis and the Common Market*, New Left Pamphlets, 1961, and W. Pickles, *Not With Europe*, Fabian Society, 1962.

On Western Germany A. J. P. Taylor's *The Course of*

German History, Hamilton, 1945, is an excellent background book. B. Davidson, *Germany, What Now?*, Muller, 1950, describes the immediate post-war issues. The concentration of economic and financial power before, during and after Hitler is described in J. S. Martin's *All Honourable Men*, New York, Little Brown, 1950; R. Sasuly's *I. G. Farben,* New York, Boni and Gaer, 1947; J. E. Dubois, *Generals in Grey Suits*, Bodley Head, 1953; and G. Baumann, *Eine Handvoll Konzern Herren*, Berlin, 1953. Ludwig Erhard describes his economic miracle in *Germany's Come-Back to the World Market*, Allen and Unwin, 1954, and in *Prosperity through Competition*, Thames and Hudson, 1958.

A valuable comparison of French, German and British economic growth since the war is to be found in Political and Economic Planning, *Growth of the British Economy*, P.E.P. 1961.

XI *Works on the United States Economy and Latin America*

H. F. Williamson (ed.), *The Growth of American Economy*, 1944, supplies the best background study. J. K. Galbraith's three books are essential reading: *The Great Crash – 1929*, Hamilton, 1955, *American Capitalism*, Hamilton, 1957, and *The Affluent Society*, Hamilton, 1958.

G. Stein's *The World the Dollar Built*, Dobson, 1952, provides a brilliant left-wing analysis as a corrective to the President's annual 'State of the Nation' reports which give an invaluable commentary on developments.

On Latin America H. Herring, *A History of Latin America*, Cape, 1954, is comprehensive. J. F. Rippy, *British Investments in Latin America*, Minnesota, 1958, contains valuable material, as does the article by H. S. Ferns, 'Britain's Informal Empire in Argentina 1830–1914', in *Past and Present*, no. 4.

L. Huberman and P. N. Sweezey's study, '*Cuba – Anatomy of a Revolution*', Monthly Review, New York, 1960, should be read by all.

The United Nations Economic Commission for Latin

America annual *Economic Surveys* are of great value especially those for 1954 and 1957.

XII *Works on Africa*

Lord Hailey's *African Survey*, Oxford, 1938, provides weighty background. On early African History B. Davidson's two books, *Old Africa Rediscovered*, Gollancz, 1958, and *Black Mother*, Gollancz, 1961, are essential. R. Robinson and J. Gallagher, *Africa and the Victorians*, Macmillan, 1961, covers nineteenth-century British-African relations admirably.

On Africa since the war B. Davidson's work is essential: *Report on Southern Africa*, Cape, 1952, and *The African Awakening*, Cape, 1955. To these must be added T. Hodgkin's *Nationalism in Colonial Africa*, Muller, 1956. J. Woddis' two books *Roots of Revolt*, Lawrence and Wishart, 1960, and *The Lion Awakes,* Lawrence and Wishart, 1962, provide essential information from a communist angle. For an opposite view see M. Perham's very defensive Reith lectures, *The Colonial Reckoning*, Collins, 1962.

On Egypt there is Lord Cromer's classic, *Modern Egypt*, Macmillan, 1908, and a good recent work is C. Issawi's, *Egypt at Mid Century*, Oxford, 1954.

The United Nations Annual Economic Surveys both of Africa and the Middle East contain valuable statistical material and especially valuable is the United Nations *Economic Survey of Africa since 1950*, New York, 1959.

A. Hazlewood's and P. D. Henderson's 'Nyasaland – the Economics of Federation' in the *Bulletin* of the Oxford University Institute of Statistics is an excellent case study, as is W. T. Newlyn, ' "Take-Off" considered in an African setting', *Yorkshire Bulletin of Economic and Social Research*, May 1961.

XIII *Works on Asia and the Far East*

A first-class background book on all the countries in the region is L. K. Rosinger (ed.), *The State of Asia*, New York,

Knopf, 1951. K. S. Latourette's *Short History of the Far East*, Macmillan, 1947, is a useful historical textbook.

On Indian Economic history V. Anstey's *Economic Development of India*, Longmans, 1952, is essential, supplemented by D. H. Buchanan's *Development of Capitalist Enterprise in India*, New York, 1934. More recent years are covered by W. B. Reddaway, *Development of the Indian Economy*, Allen and Unwin, 1962.

A Marxist study of early Indian history, which includes much of Marx's own *Notes on Indian History*, Lawrence and Wishart, 1960, is R. Mukherjee, *Rise and Fall of the East India Company*, Berlin, 1955. Despite inaccuracies R. P. Dutt's *India Today*, Bombay, 1947, remains an essential reference work.

On Indian planning M. H. Dobb's three lectures on *Some Aspects of Economic Development*, Delhi, 1951, are masterpieces of compression. *Keynesian Economics*, Delhi, 1956, includes a number of useful essays on Indian planning. I. M. D. Little's two essays on the Indian Plans in the National Institute *Economic Review* of May 1960 and in the *Oxford Economic Papers* of February 1962 are very stimulating.

On Japan E. H. Norman's *Japan's Emergence as a Modern State*, Institute of Pacific Relations, 1940, is the basic work. On Burma and Indonesia Dorothy Woodman's two books, *The Republic of Indonesia*, Cressett, 1955, and *The Making of Burma*, Cressett, 1962, are comprehensive.

The United Nations Far East Economic Commission's annual *Economic Surveys of Asia and the Far East* provide very complete detailed material and the *Bulletin* for December 1961 gives a full report of the 1961 conference on Economic Development and Planning. The journal *Far East Trade* maintains a splendid coverage of trade and economic developments.

XIV *Works on Communist Countries*

M. H. Dobb's *Soviet Economic Development since* 1917, Routledge, 1948, remains the standard work. D. Warriner's *Revolution in Eastern Europe*, Turnstile, 1950, covers the post-war changes in Eastern Europe. On more recent developments the sections of the United Nations Economic Commission for Europe annual *Economic Surveys* covering the communist lands cannot be bettered. More detailed studies have appeared in *Soviet Studies*, quarterly from Glasgow University, published by Blackwell.

The statistics of *The U.S.S.R. Economy*, published by Lawrence and Wishart, 1957, have been commented on by N. Jasay, *The Soviet 1956 Statistical Handbook*, Michigan, 1957, and by A. Bergson, *The Real National Income of Soviet Russia*, Harvard, 1961.

On China P. Townsend, *China Phoenix*, Cape, 1955, is an excellent background book, brought up to date by P. Townsend and Lord Boyd-Orr, *What's happening in China?*, 1961. S. Adler's *The Chinese Economy*, Routledge, 1957, is comprehensive. Chinese statistics are available in the Chinese Central Statistical Bureau's *Ten Great Years*, Pekin, 1960, which has been commented on very fairly by Choh Ming Li, *The Statistical System of Communist China*, Berkeley, 1962.

The British Council for the Promotion of International Trade publishes excellent surveys of Chinese and East European trade and economic developments.

XV *Statistical References*

The main source of international Statistics is now the United Nations. *The Statistical Yearbook* is supplemented by *Monthly Bulletins of Statistics* in which the main series are kept up to date. The annual *World Economic Survey* and the regional *Economic Surveys* and quarterly *Bulletins*, already referred to, also contain much statistical material. There are further a *Yearbook of International Trade Statistics*, a *Demographic Yearbook* and a *Yearbook of National Account Statistics*. The Economic and Social Council of the United Nations also makes special studies of the *Flow of Private Investment, Dollar Valuations of National Incomes,* etc.

The International Monetary Fund publishes *International Financial Statistics* monthly, which covers most trade, financial and economic movements for all member countries. The General Agreement on Tariffs and Trade publishes an annual review, *International Trade,* and occasional special studies, e.g. on *Trends in International Trade,* Geneva, 1958. The Food and Agriculture Organisation publishes annually *The State of Food and Agriculture* and in addition regular annual *Commodity Reviews.*

The International Labour Office publishes a *Yearbook of Labour Statistics* and many special studies of particular industries.

The Organisation for European Economic Co-operation (now Organisation for European Co-operation and Development) has a full range of statistical publications including a monthly *General Statistics* and half-yearly *Foreign Trade Statistics* and in addition publishes a vast range of reports on particular industries and commodities.

The European Economic Community and Coal and Steel Community publish their own annual reports and statistics.

Index

Abrams, Mark, Table VI
Africa, 60, 61
  Cold War, 203–4
  Common Market, 378–9
  early history, 26, 168
  nationalism, *see* Nationalism
  see also individual countries,
    Rhodes, etc.
Agriculture
  communist policy, 425ff.
  English 18th-century, 39, 44
    19th-century, 68
  irrigated, 29, 57–8
  labourers leaving, 55
  productivity, differences in, 407
  world production, trade and
    prices, Table XXV
America
  Bullion, 32
  Colonisation, 36ff.
  Revolution, 46, 163
  see also individual countries,
    South America
Anglo-Iranian Oil Company, 237,
  239
Anti-Corn Law League, 61
Apartheid, 233
  land policy, 167
  mineowners' support of, 167
Arab League Oil Proposals, 245

Argentina, 52, 86, 94, 135, 136,
  349, 356
Aron, R., 376
Asia, land ownership, 28, 57
  see also individual countries,
    South-East Asia
Atlantic Charter, 191, 205n, 228
Australia, 55
  agricultural products, 67, 71
  economy compared with
    Malaya, 457
  immigration, 55
  industrialisation, 56, 99, 160
  mutton exports, 67
  non-ownership of ships, 272
  U.K. investment in, 93, 99, 124,
    163–4
Ayub Khan, General, 209

Balance of Payments
  see individual countries
Balance of Trade
  see individual countries
Balfour, A. J. (afterwards Earl of
  Balfour), 103
Balogh, T., 310
Bank of England, 136, 217
Bank Rate, 312
Bank, World, 417, 419, 474, 475
  discussion of, 461

loans to underdeveloped countries, Table XXXIII
Banks
country, 44
role in colonies, 219, 271
U.K. industry in 1930s, 144
Merchant
convertibility of sterling, 312
domination of Government, 106
historic role of, 99
overseas companies, 271
see also Baring Brothers
Baran, Paul, 13n, 419n
Baring Brothers, 52, 86
Baring, Evelyn (Earl Cromer), 87–8, 106
Barnes, Leonard, 383, Table VIII
Beers, de, 89
Benham, Professor F., 462
Bentinck, Lord William Cavendish, see India
Besant, Mrs A., 90
Bevin, Ernest, 294
Bilateral Trade Agreements 1933, 135
enforced on colonies, 161
Birth Control, 90
Bismarck, Prince, 102, 121
Boer War, see War, Boer
Booker Brothers, 270, 275
Booth, Charles, 104
Bradlaugh, Charles, 90
Brazil, 349, 356
steel industry, 365
British
Commonwealth, see Commonwealth
East Africa Company, 88
Guiana, 203, 270
South Africa Company, 88, 89
Bryce, James, 101
Bukharin, N. I., 95
Burma

exports, 172
independence, 197

Campbell-Bannerman, Sir Henry, 93
Canada, 55, 327
agriculture, 68
aid and investment to underdeveloped countries, Table XXXIII
immigration, 55
industrialisation, 56, 99, 160, 163
U.K. investment in, 93–4, 99
U.S.A. investment in, 364, 365, 369
Canning, George, 52
Capital, export of, see Overseas Investment
Capitalism
contemporary, 291, 320ff.
definition, 10n
development of underdeveloped lands, 347ff.
failure to industrialise underdeveloped countries, 417ff.
moribund, 11, 100
Second World War and, 147ff.
structural fault in, 99
two faces of, 346
Cartels
Common Market, 375
definition, 126–7
Germany, 120, 149
World, 125ff., 142, 323, 326
world depression, 135
see also Monopolies, Integration, Trade Associations, mergers
Cassel, Sir Ernest, 106
Castro, Dr F., 367, 382, 387
Central African Federation
aim of, 165
Ceylon
copra, 172

exports, 58, 172
rubber, 60, 171
tea, 171
Chamberlain, Joseph, 80, 90, 91
discussion of, 101ff.
Chartered Companies, 33-4, 37, 39
East India company, 33, 39, 40, 42, 43, 45, 46, 47
Virginia company, 37
Chartists, 61
Cheap labour, 324-5
colonial, 96, 160, 166ff., 419
Chemicals, 83, 126, 143
Chiang Kai Shek, 205, 206
China, 57, 58, 60
agriculture, 29
communist policy, 425ff.
aid and investment to under-developed countries, Table XXXIII
bureaucracy, 29-31, 57
communist successes, 194
early history, 27ff.
foreign trade, 30, 47-8, 382, 386, 387, Table XXVIII
rate of growth and share of world, Table XXIX
industrial production, Table XXVIII
rate of growth and share of world, 429ff., Table XXXI
land ownership, 29, 57
market, 47-8
national income, 431, Tables XXVIII, XXXII
planning, 430ff., Table XXXII
opium trade, 47
population, Tables XXVIII, XXXII
Soviet aid, 384, 426, 436-7, Table XXXII
Chinese labour, 104, 169
Churchill, Sir Winston

return to gold 1925, 132
Atlantic Charter, 191, 228
Clapham, Sir John, 105
Clayton Plan, 365
Clive, Lord Robert, see India
Cold War
Africa and, 203
discussion of, 204ff.
Colombo Plan, 459
Colonial
Constitutions, 195ff.
liberation movements, 190ff.
system, new, 38
old, 36, 40, 43
Colonies
limitations on economic in-dependence, 208ff., Chapter 7
oil bearing, 236
opposing views on in 19th century, 54
small, island, 198
mainland, 199
surplus on dollar account post-1945, 257
Commodity markets
metropolitan countries, 161
Common Market, 275, 316, 348, 357, 363, 456, 476
agriculture, 224, 319, 360, 379
alternatives for U.K., 334-5, 467, 478ff.
Conservative Party pamphlet on, 481
discussion of, 372ff.
foreign investment in U.K. in anticipation of, 259
Imperial preference and, 223, 360, 377
India and, 363
industrial production, Table XXVIII
rate of growth and share of world, Table XXXI

motive for U.K. overseas investment, 276ff.
national income, Table XXVIII
population, Table XXVIII
restrictions on trade, 471
trade, share of world, Tables XXVIII, XXIX
rate of growth, Table XXIX
under-developed countries, 378
Common Markets, Regional, 350, 357, 379, 468
Commonwealth, 197, 471
defence, 197
neutralism, 467
Prime Ministers' Conference, 197
Communism
China, 194
colonial, 191ff.
denial of democracy, 465
rebellion against Japanese, 192ff.
Communist Countries, 4, 17, 351, Table I
agricultural policy, 425ff.
industrial development, 388·
manufacturing industry, rate of growth and share in world, Table XXXI
planned economy, 423
Rouble area, 380ff.
share in world trade, Table XXVII
trade, share in world, Tables XXVII, XXIX
rate of growth, Table XXIX
Comparative costs, 67–8, 480–1
Comprador, 179, 210, 414, 415, 420
Conan, A. R., 259, 261, 263, 264, 266n, Tables XV, XVI, XVII, XVIII
Conference of American republics
Clayton plan, 365

Congo, Belgian, 89, 169, 227, 233
Conservative Party
Common Market pamphlet, 481
Convertibility, 220–1
Corn Laws, repeal of, 53, 61, 63, 67
Cornwallis, Charles, 1st Marquis and 2nd Earl, see India
Cromer, 1st Earl, see Baring, Evelyn
Cuba, 366–8
Cyprus, 89

Dalhousie, 1st Marquis of, 64
Davidson, Basil, 168
Defoe, Daniel, 40–1
Devaluation
U.K. 1931, 136
1932, 137
possibility of after 1960, 313–14
Devonshire, 8th Duke of, 102
Diamonds, 88, 89, 164
Dilke, Sir Charles W., 54
Disraeli, B. (Earl of Beaconsfield), 54, 85, 87, 88, 92
Division of labour
between industrialised lands, 475, 479
manufactures and primary products, 58, 67ff., 71
Dock strike 1889, 92
Dollar area, 139, 297, 356, 357
capital movements post-1945, 257
discussion of, 364ff.
Free Trade, 221
industrial production, Table XXVIII
national income, Table XXVIII
population, Table XXVIII
share of world trade, Table XXVIII
Dominions
economic development of, 99

main beneficiaries of Imperial preference, 223
U.K. investment in, Table V
see also individual countries
Dufferin, 1st Marquis of, see India
Dutt, R. Palme, 13n, 295

East India Company, see under Chartered Companies
East-West Trade, 381, 386–9
Economic resources
development of world, 17
Egypt, 356
British occupation, 87–8
cotton, 60
sterling sanctions against, 220
Elphinstone, the Hon. Mountstuart, see India
Emigration, 55, 90–1, 92
Empire Prime Ministers
first conference of, 101
Empires, slave and peasant, 25ff.
Engels, F., 28, 100, 144
Euratom, 375, 376
Europe
colonisation, 25ff.
U.K. investment in, 98, Table V
U.K. trade with, 63, 81–2
European
Coal and Steel Community, 373ff., 376
development fund, 376, 379
Economic Community, see Common Market
Free Trade Association
clearing union, 471
Imperial preference and, 223
neutralism, 467
Exchange Equalisation Account, 136
Expectation of life, comparative, 7
Export Credit Guarantees Department, 138

Family firms, 84, 142
Fascism, 148–9
Federation of British Industries
agreement with Reichsgruppe Industrie, 129
Feinstein, Charles, 83, Tables IV, V, VI
Feudalism, 6–7, 32, 178–9, 409–10, 420
Finance capital
German, interconnection with monopoly, 97
overseas investment, 12, 97
Firoz Khan Noon, 209n
Ford, Henry, 60
Henry, Junior, 346
Formosa, 205
Forster, W. E., 101
Franc Area, 139, 229
France, 56, 80, 87
aid and investment to underdeveloped countries, Table XXXIII
Coal and Steel Community, 373
Community Overseas, 198
economic growth post-1945 compared with U.K., 317
exports, sterling area, 224
1959, Table XXVIII
national income, Table XXVIII
war with Indo-China, 193
Free trade, 87, 97, Chapter 2
adherents to c.1900, 104–5
aid to industrial development, 416
campaign against, 104ff.
Canning, G., 52
detrimental effect on poor lands, 159
need for at present, 475
opponents of c.1900, 104
U.K. abandonment of, 137
U.K. industrial development and, 52, 67

U.S.A. and, 205–6, 227, 364
see also Manchester
Frisch, Professor Ragnar, 471, 472
Froude, J. A., 101

Galbraith, J. K., 134
Gambia, 199
Gaulle, General Charles de, 198
General Agreement on Tariffs and Trade, 228, 232, 476
German Federal Republic
  aid and investment in under-developed countries, Table XXXIII
  Coal and Steel Community, 374
  exports, 348, 355, Table XXVIII
  manufacturing output, rate of growth and share of world, Table XXXI
  national product 1950–59, Tables XXIV, XXVIII
  post-1945 economic growth compared with U.K., 314ff.
  sterling area exports, 224
    loans, 227
  trade, rate of growth and share of world, Table XXIX
Germany
  1930s, 129–30
  exclusion from colonies, 129–30
  expansionary pressure, 97, 105–6, 118ff., 148
  exports, 119, Table XXI
  gold standard, 81
  industrial development, 36, 56, 80, 81–2, 94, 119ff.
  tariffs, 120
  trusts and cartels, 120, 126, 127, 149
  unemployment between the wars, Table IX

Ghana, 88, 210, 223
  mining wage increase, 233–4
  sterling balances, 218
Gilbert, R. S., Table XV
Gladstone, W. E., 87, 88, 103
Gold
  certificates, 474
  inadequate credit base, 472
  mining, 88, 93, 103, 164ff.
    profits of, 166
  output, world 1850–85, 62
    sterling area post-1945, 257, 262
Gold Coast, see Ghana
Gold Standard
  Germany, 81
  U.K. return to 1925, 132–3
    abandonment 1931, 136
Goschen, G. J. (afterwards Viscount), 106
Great Crash, 1929, 134ff.
Grondona, St Clare, 470, 472

Harrod, Sir Roy, 472
Heath, Rt Hon. Edward, 224
Hertzog, General, 166
Hewins, W. A. S., 104
Hilferding, R., 95
Hitler, Adolf, 129–30, 148, 149
Hobsbawm, Eric, 100
Hobson, J. A., 80, 86, 95, 330
  discussion of views on Imperialism, 91ff.
Hoffmann, W., Table III
Holland, see Netherlands
Hughes, John, 97n
Hull, Cordell, 205n
Hussein, Zahid, 410

Imlah, A. H., 65, 74, Tables II, III, XIV
Imperial Companies, 146, 162, 171, 200, 202, Table XX
  Ghana nationalisation, 233

history and discussion of,
230ff.
manufacturing, 271
overseas economic development, 324ff.
profits in 1950s, 231, 233, 234,
235
re-investment overseas, 264,
268ff, Table XIX
returns on investment, 172
see also Integrated companies,
Unilever
Imperial Federation League, 101
Imperial preference, 53, 104,
135ff., 177, 197, 221, 377
discussion of, 222ff., 359ff.
Imperial tribute
who gained in U.K.?, 142ff.
Imperialism
collapse of, 12
defence of, 8ff.
definitions, 9–11
economic consequences for
colonies, Chapter 5
'Economic Imperialism', 230ff.
Hobson on, 91ff.
Lenin on, 95ff.
military, 42, 53
Socialist criticism of, 7–8
sterling area, 217ff.
summary of conclusions, 447ff.
U.S.S.R. in Rouble area, 382–3
war and, 117ff.
Indo-China
communist-led government,
192
Indonesia, 356
communist-led government,
192
exports, 172
relationship with Netherlands,
173, 233
Industrial
class, 27, 62

development, plunder and, 43–4
U.K. in 17th century, 39
Revolution, 3, 44–5, 416–17
under-developed countries,
415ff.
Industrialisation
contrast between lands of European settlement and other
colonies, Chapter 5
necessary conditions for, 405ff.
Industrialised countries, 4, 5,
Table I
trade, with non-industrialised,
348ff.
with industrialised, 355ff.
Inflation
Germany, 315
U.K., 308ff.
Integrated companies
investment in Colonies, 269
links with Colonies, 148, 161–2,
171–2, 234–5
Integration of Industry, 142,
320ff.
motive behind U.K. overseas
investment, 273–4
International
Co-operative Alliance, oil proposal, 245
Monetary Fund, 262, 461, 473ff.
Inventions, 26, 35, 43, 44, 82
Investment, see individual coun-
tries
India, 57, 59, 84–5, 223
agriculture, 30, 59, 60, 174
need for new policy, 428ff.
Bentinck, 178
Clive, 41, 42, 43, 178
Common Market, 363
conquest of, 41ff., 53
Cornwallis, 178
cotton growing, 64
mills, 176
Dufferin, 180

early history, 27ff.
educational results of British rule, 181
Elphinstone, 180
expectation of life, 7
exports, 58, 59, 84, 174ff., 349, 437
famines, 43, 59, 174
imports, 85
see also India, market
independence, 191
indirect rule by Imperialists, 178
industrial development, 59–60, 64, 176–7, 180, 432
foreign aid, 437, Table XXXII
land ownership, 28–9, 57
land reform, 412ff.
Lytton, 178
market, 45, 48, 64, 85
competition from E.E.C. & U.S.A., 225
Moslem League, 181
National Congress, 180
national income, 431, Table XXXII
native middle class, 180ff.
planning, 439ff., Table XXXII
population, 59, 421, Tables XXVIII, XXXII
railways, 64–5
steel, 177
tariffs, 177
trade with U.K., 100
see also India, imports and exports
tribute from, 40, 42, 44, 175
U.K. destruction of competition from, 45, 47, 48, 59
U.K. income from, 100, 175
U.K. investment, Table V
return on, 172
wealth and poverty of, 174ff.
see also Pakistan

Iran
development after 1954, 239
nationalisation, 238
oil industry and profits, 236ff.
Iraq
oil industry, 13, 45, 48, 221, 236–8
revolution, 239–40
withdrawal from sterling area, 220
Ireland
England's first colony, 54
population, 55
Ismay, Lord, 191
Italy
Coal and Steel Community, 376
expansion in 1930s, 149
exports, sterling area, 224
industrialisation, 36, 121

Jacobsson, Per, 473
Japan
aid and investment to underdeveloped countries, Table XXXIII
expansion in 1930s, 149
exports, 355–6, Table XXVIII
growth and share of world trade, Table XXIX
sterling area, 224
imports, 84, Table XXIX
industrial production, Table XXVIII
rate of growth and share of world, Table XXXI
industrialisation, 57–8, 94, 121
national income, Table XXVIII
population, Table XXVIII
Japanese occupation S.E. Asia
communist rebellion, 192ff.
Jefferys, J. B., Table IV
Johannesburg, 103
Chamber of Mines, 104

Kassim, General, 220, 221, 239, 240, 246
Kautsky, K., 378
Kennedy, President J., 477
Kenya and Uganda, 88
Keynes, J. M. (Lord), 107, 303, 312, 461
Keynes Loan, 205*n*, 228
Kipling, Rudyard, 92
Korean War, *see* War
Krupps, 120
Khrushchev, N., 466
Kuwait, 236, 241
    sterling balances, 242

Labour Party Colonial Policy, 199*n*, 462
Land
    ownership
        Asia, 28
        China, 29
        India, 29
        landlord and share of crop, 6, 178–9, 410ff.
        Pakistan, 411
    reform, 411ff.
        communist 425ff.
Lange, Oscar, 483
Latin America, *see* South America
Lend Lease Agreement, 205*n*, 228
Lenin, V. I., 80, 86, 90, 121, 127, 141, 378
    assessment of, 453–4
    definition of Imperialism, 9–10, 11ff.
    discussion of views on Imperialism, 95ff., 147ff.
    finance capital and overseas investment, 12–13
    Imperialism, collapse of, 12
    international cartels, 125, 127, 128, 324, 330
    law of unequal development of capitalism, 11, 149

stagnation, metropolitan economies, 12, 13, 98
    war, main cause of, 11, 122, 149
    workers, bribery of, 12, 13, 97, 100, 144
Leopold II, King (Belgium), 88
Lewis, Arthur, 133, 218
Limited liability, 83
Livingstone, David, 87
Lloyd, Selwyn, 314
London School of Economics, 104
Lucas, George, 137
Lumumba, Patrice, 227
Lydall, H. F., 302, Table XXII
Lytton, 1st Earl of, *see* India

Macmillan Report, 131
Malaya, 59, 60, 87
    commodity production, 171, 172
    economy compared with Australia, 457
    exports, 172
    sterling balances, 218
    war with British, *see* War
Manchester
    Chamber of Commerce, 52
    free traders, 52, 55
    anti-colonial, 53
Manufacturing output
    Capitalist World, 292–3, Table XXV
    U.K., 292
    U.S.A., 292
Marshall Aid, 228, 369
Marshall, Alfred, 105
Martin, K., 72
Marx, Karl, 11, 57, 64, 98, 105, 127, 204, 206
    falling rate of profit, 98–9
    overproduction theory, 96, 134
    super profit and immiseration, 100, 141
Maudling, Rt Hon. R., 387

McKenna, Reginald, 106
Merchant
  adventurers, 31ff.
  class, 21, 31, 38, 414
  outsiders, 33
  Bankers, *see* Banks, Merchant
Mergers, 83, 144
  see also Monopolies, Trade Associations, Integration, Cartels
Military
  Aid, *see* U.S.A. Foreign Aid
  expenditure, effects of reduction in, 463
Mill, J. S., 105
Mining
  concessions in Africa, 89
  copper, 164ff.
    profits, 231
  development in colonies, 60
  distribution of revenue from Africa, Table VIII
  gold, 88, 93, 103, 164ff., 231
  Ghana wage increase, 233–4
  Rhodesia, 164–5
  South Africa, 165
  tin and lead, U.K., 67
  world production, trade and prices, Table XXV
Mittel-Europa, 120
Molotov, V. M., 381
Moneylenders, 6, 57, 178, 410
Monopolies, 97
  see also Cartels, Mergers, Trade Associations, Integration
Morgan, E. V., 264
Moslem League, 181, 209
Moussadeq, Dr, 221, 238, 461
Multilateral Payments System, need for, 471ff.
Multilateralism, U.S.A. and, 205n
Multiplier theory, 309
Mutual security programme, 207, Table XI

Myrdal, Gunnar, 159, 161, 210, 229, 420, 462, 479

Nasser, Colonel, 204, 220, 240, 461
National Economic Development Council, 309–10, 314
National Income
  comparative, 4, 4n, Table I
  Germany 1950–59, Table XXIV
  relationship to trade and investment U.K., Table IV
  U.K. 1930s, 145
    1948–61 details, Table XXIII
  U.K. and Germany between the wars, Table IX
  U.S.A. post-1954, 372
    1959, Table XXVIII
  world trade blocs, Table XXVIII
  see also Standard of Living
Nationalism
  African, 171, 196, 200
    basis of, 200ff.
Naval strength, 89
Navigation Acts, repeal of, 53
Netherlands, 39, 40
  Coal and Steel Community, 374
  exports, sterling area, 224
  war with Indonesia, 193, 233
  wealth from Indonesia, 173
Neutralism 465ff.
New Zealand, 55, 223
  industrialisation, 56, 160, 163
  mutton exports, 67
Nigeria, 88
  Currency Board, 219
  mines, distribution of revenue from, Table VIII
  poverty, 170
Nkrumah, Dr, 200
Northern Rhodesia, *see* Rhodesia
Nuffield, Lord, 137
Nurkse, R., 159, 229

Nyasaland, 230
mines, 169

Oil
discussion of, 236ff.
growing importance of, 231
Iran, 236ff.
Iraq, 221, 236, 238
price fixing, 237
production, capitalist world, Table XXV
Italian, 244–6
Japanese, 244–6
U.S.S.R., 244–6
Roumania, 382
Saudi Arabia, 237–8
Soviet, 387
U.K. investment in, 266
U.S.A. industry, 236
investment in, 226
Organisation of American States, 198
Overproduction Theory, see Marx
Overseas Investment
role of European in colonies, discussion of, 162ff.
U.K., see U.K.
U.S.A., see U.S.A.

Paish, F. W., 218
Pakistan, 195, 420
discussion of, 209
landlords, 411
Palmerston, Viscount, 54
Patel, S. J., Table XXXII
Peasants, expropriation of, 39
Perham, Margery, Table VIII
Persia, see Iran
Persian Gulf, 89
Planning, 309–10, 480ff.
China and India compared, 430ff., Table XXXII
under-developed countries, 423

Plunder, 33, 40, 42, 44
Population
Arab world, 241
Colonies, 1945, 189–90
1962, 190
European expansion of, 3
India, 59, 421, Table XXVIII
Ireland, 55
U.K. density, 2
growth, 90
urbanisation in colonies, 173, 202
world, 1, Table I
rapid growth, 421
world trade blocs, Table XXVIII
Portuguese Empire, 32
Pigou, A. C., 105
Primary production
advantage to Colony, 171
development of, 58ff.
output and prices, Table XXVI
trade and prices, Table XXV
Primary products
Common Market, 378–9
instability of prices, 161, 468ff.
proposals for stabilisation, 470ff.
substitution by synthetic materials, 231–2
Productivity, 83
Profit
British overseas and home industrial companies, Table XIII
falling rate of, 83, 96, 98, 99
overseas companies, 59, 60, 123

Radcliffe Committee, 257, 260, 261, 264
Raffles, Sir Stanford, 53
Railway building, 55–6, 66
Railways, India, 64–5

Reichsgruppe Industrie
  agreement with F.B.I., 129
Reuther, Walter, 346
Revolution
  English 1688, 38
  American, 45–6, 163
  1848, 61
  Russian 1917, 128
  Cuba, 366ff.
Rhodes, Cecil, 87, 88, 89, 90, 91,
  103, 164
Rhodesia, 230
  health of miners, 169
  see also Central African Federa-
  tion
Rhodesia, Northern, 88, 89
  industrialisation, 164–5
  mines, distribution of income
  from, Table VIII
  sterling balances, 218
Rhodesia, Southern, 88, 89
  industrialisation, 164–5
  mines, distribution of revenue
  from, Table VIII
  local ownership, 170
Ricardo, D., 67–8
Rippy, J. F., 172
Robinson, E. A. G., 67–8, Tables
  VII, XXI
Roon, General A. Von, 102
Roosevelt, F. D., 228, 364
Roosevelt, Theodore, 107
Rosebery, 5th Earl of, 101, 106
Rostow, W. W., 159
Rothschild, House of, 106
Rouble Area, 356, 357
  discussion of, 380ff.
  industrial production, Table
  XXVIII
  national income, Table XXVIII
  population, Table XXVIII
  share of world trade, Table
  XXVIII
Royal Niger Company, 88, 103

Rubber, 60, 130, 161, 172
Russia
  industrialisation, 94
  revolution, 1917, capitalist fear
  of, 128
  see also U.S.S.R.

Sandys, Sir Edwin, 36
Salisbury, 3rd Marquess of, 89,
  103
Saud, King Ibn, 238, 241
Saudi Arabia, American oil in-
  terests in, 237–8
Schacht, Dr, 149
Schloete, W., 74, Tables IV, V,
  VI, VII, XXV
Schonfield, Andrew, 311
Schumpeter, J., 84, 105, 137
  views on cartels, 127–8
Seeley, J. R., 101
Seers, Dudley, 302, Table XXII
Shannon, H., 85
Shipbuilding, 82
Singapore, population, 173
Slave trade, 37, 40, 44
Slavery, 26, 31, 37, 149, 163
Smith, W. H., 102
Smythe, Sir Thomas, 37
Socialism, Democratic, 465
Somaliland, 199
South Africa, Union of, 88, 103,
  203
  Chamber of Commerce, 169
  Chamber of Mines, 167
  industrialisation, 160, 163ff.
  mines, distribution of revenue
  from Table VIII
  gold, 103, 231
  local ownership, 170
  native Africans' living stan-
  dards, 168
  tariffs, 166
  U.K. investment in, 94, 124, 170
  see also Apartheid

South America, 52, 56, 60, 68, 71, 94
  American Aid, 372
  dollar domination, 364ff.
  economic development, 366
  U.K. investment in, Table V
  sale of to U.S.A., 125
  U.S.A. investment in, 365
South-East Asia, 6–7, 60
  Colombo Plan, 459
  Japanese occupation, 192–3
  trade, 172
  see also individual countries
Southern Rhodesia, see Rhodesia
Spanish Empire, 32–3, 107
Stagnation of metropolitan economies
  Lenin on, 12, 13, 80
  U.K. after 1955, 306ff.
Stalin, J. V., 238, 382, 383, 426, 466
Stamp, Hon. Maxwell, 474
Standard of Living, 4–7, 83
  African worker, Table VIII
  Arab peoples, 241
  Kuwait, 241
  South Africa, 168–9
Stanley, H. M., 89
Stanley, Oliver, 129
Statute of Westminster 1931, 197
Stead, W. S., 90
Stedeford, Sir Ivan, 314
Sterling
  convertibility, 220, 312
  defence of and recession, 311ff.
  international currency, 221
Sterling Area, 139, 357, 358
  advantages to ex-colony, 221–2
  Currency Boards, 219
  declining share in world market, 225–6
  definition, 217
  discussion of, 358ff.
  failure as protective device for

British trade, 227ff.
  formation, 136
  Imperialism and, discussion of, 217ff.
  industrial production, Table XXVIII
  investment in, U.K., 226, 362
    U.S.A., 226
    U.S.S.R., 227
    Germany, 227
  management, 217
  membership, 217
  national income, Table XXVIII
  population, Table XXVIII
  restriction on economic independence of colony, 219–20
  sanctions against Egypt, 220
  trade, competition to U.K. from E.E.C. and U.S.A., 224ff.
    proportion of U.K. exports taken, 226
    share of world, Table XXVIII
    shares in overseas Sterling Area markets, Table XII
    with all sources post-1945, 297–8
    with non-sterling sources post-1950, 258–9
  withdrawal of Iraq, 220
Sterling Balances, 218, 221, 260, Table XV
  Arab contributions to, 242
  recent colonial withdrawals, 265
  U.K. overseas investment, 257
Strachey, Sir John, 180
Strachey, Rt Hon. John, 10n, 13n, 42n, 88, 95n, 158, 301–2
Strategic bases
  U.K., 53–4, 87, 88, 107, 199
  Middle East, 243
  U.S.A., 199
Suez
  Canal, 87, 220
  adventure, 205, 228, 245

Svennilson, I., Tables VII, IX
Synthetic raw materials
  substitution for natural, 231–2

Tariffs, Chapter 3
  Canadian, 55
  colonial liberation and, 361
  Dominion, 124
  German, 81, 120
  Indian, 176–7
  McKinley, 82
  motive behind U.K. overseas
    investment, 274–5
  South African, 166
  U.K., 475
  U.S.A., 476
  world depression and, 135,
    137–8
Tariff Reform, 104ff.
  League, 104
Terms of Trade, see Trade, Terms
  of
Thackeray, F. G., 72
Trade
  colonial, development of, 37,
    58–9, 297–8
  Free, see Free Trade
  industrialisation and, 44–5,
    63–4
  industrialised and non-indus-
    trialised lands, 346ff.
  industrialised lands, 355ff.
  regional blocs, 355ff.
  under-developed countries
    and, 357–8
  three-cornered, 40
  World, 62, 348, Table XXI
    after 1945, 297, 300
    before 1800, 159
  see also individual countries and
    List of Tables
Trade Associations, 83, see also
  Monopolies, Mergers, Integration, Cartels

Trade, Board of
  Survey of foreign investment
    in U.K., 259
Trade Cycle, 72–3, 292–3, Table
  III
  effects on under-developed
    countries, 422–3
  post-1945 boom, causes of,
    293ff.
  more equal incomes, 301ff.
  more exports, 296ff.
  more government spending
    and technological change,
    304ff.
  more tribute, 293ff.
  post-1955 recession, 294, 298–9,
    305, 307ff.
  defence of sterling, 311ff.
  government restrictions, 309
Trade, Terms of
  between manufactured and pri-
    mary products, 68, 70ff., 231,
    296, 298ff., 319–20, 353, 361,
    468ff.
  U.K., 72–4, Tables III, XXI
  1930s, 140ff., 150–2
Trade Union Congress
  proposed investment in Africa
    Corporation, 91
  supporting Free Trade c.1900,
    105
Trade Unions
  African, 201–2
  European in Africa, 165
  Malayan, 233
  U.K. membership 1911–14, 101
Transvaal, 104
Triffin, R., 474
Trowell, H. C., 168
Tshombe, M., 227
Tuke, A., 310, 318

Under-consumption theory, see
  Hobson

Under-developed countries, 3, 6–7, Table I
Common Market, 379
development of, 16ff., 347, 354
 capitalism's failure, 417ff.
 checks to, 408ff.
 effect of trade cycle on, 422–3
 necessary conditions, 405ff.
 need for foreign aid, 436ff.
 need for heavy industry, 417, 429–30
 planning, 423ff., 430ff.
foreign aid, 458ff.
 American, see U.S.A. foreign aid
 Soviet, 460
 international aid and investment to, Table XXXIII
origins of, 56–7
restricted purchasing power, 69–71
trade blocs, 357
trade with industrialised lands, 348ff., Table XXVII
Unemployment
Germany between the wars, Table IX
U.K. between the wars, 132ff., 143ff., Table IX
Unilever, 88, 170, 179, 234, 269, 275
 discussion of, 235
Union of Soviet Socialist Republics
 Bi-lateral trade agreements with U.K., 135
 Foreign Aid, 384ff., Table XXXIII
 'Imperialism' in Rouble Area, 382
 manufacturing output, rate of growth and share in world, Table XXXI

national income, Table XXVIII
oil, trade with Cuba, 245
 India, 245
 Iran, 238
Sterling Area, loans to, 227
trade, 357
 competition in world, 386–7
 rate of growth, Table XXIX
 share of world, Tables XXVIII, XXIX
 see also Russia, Rouble Area
United Africa Company, see Unilever
United Kingdom
 advantages of Free Trade, 61ff., 71
 agriculture, 18th-century, 39–40, 44
 19th-century, 67
 contemporary, 318–20
 artificial textiles, 126
 balance of payments, 65, 84, 85, Tables II, XV
 1920s, 131, 133
 dependence on inflow of investment, 262–3
 foreign investment effect on, 259–60
 India, 84
 oil companies profits, 242
 oil debit items, 243–4
 position 1960–61, 261, 313
 post-1945 overseas investment, 254–5, 258
 balance of trade, 65, 100, Table II
 1920s, 131
 post-1945, 255
 bankruptcies, 85
 chemicals, 83, 125, 143
 coal, 82, 126
 competition from oil, 244
 Common Market, see Common Market

devaluation 1931, 126
  1932, 137
distribution of income post-
  1945, 301ff., Table XXII
early industrialisation, reasons
  for, 35ff.
economic   policy   proposals,
  454ff.
economic relations with underdeveloped lands, 17
expansion of Empire after 1880,
  86
expectation of life, 7
exports, 52, 62, 69ff., 72-4, 81,
  94-5, 100, 143, 296ff., 313,
  Tables IV, V, XXI
  capital goods, 63
  chemicals and petroleum pro-
    ducts, 297, 306, 314
  coal, 86, 106, Table VII
  decline in 1920s, 133ff.
  falling prices, 69
  iron and steel, 86, 94, 100,
    106, 143, 225, Table VII
  means of payment for im-
    ports, Table XIV
  metal and engineering goods,
    82, 85, 86, 133, 225, 296,
    314, Table VII
  motors, 225, 306, 314
  post-1945, 297-8, 306
  rails, 56, 64-5
  ships, 82
  Sterling Area, see Sterling
    Area
  textiles, 35, 47, 55, 62, 85, 86,
    94, 100, 104, 133, 143, 225,
    296, 314, Table VII
family firms, 84
future prospects, 451
gains and losses from world
  division of labour, 66ff.
gold and dollar reserves, 220
gold standard 1925, 132

Great Depression, 81ff.
Great Exhibition, 61
Imperial tribute, who gained
  from, 142ff.
  cause of post-1945 boom?,
    293ff.
imports, 72-4, 142, Tables IV,
  XXI
  cotton, 37, 45
  food, 58, 63, 66, 138, 143,
    299, 313-14
  manufactured goods, 299,
    314
  means of payment, Table
    XIV
  oil, 138, 314
  raw materials, 58, 67, 232,
    234-5, 299, 310-11
  textiles, 46
  tobacco, 37, 313-14
industrial development and free
  trade, 52, 62
industrialisation in 17th century, 39
investment
  Europe, 98, Table V
  geographical distribution of,
    Table V
  home, 82, 83, 85, 93, Table IV
    1920s, 131
    oil companies, 243
    post-1945, 304ff.
  home versus foreign, 327ff.
  overseas, 55-6, 64-5, 66, 71,
    84ff., 97, 98, 162ff., Tables
    IV, V, XIX, XX
    1920s, 122ff., 131, 133-4
    aid to industrial develop-
      ment, 415-16
    balance, Table XVI
    character of 1913, 1930 and
      1934, Table VIII
    concentration   on   de-
      veloped lands, 265

disposal of to U.S.A., 124
distribution of, Table XVII
Hobson's views on, 91ff.
income from, 99, 172ff., 175ff., Table IV
new wave after 1945, Chapter 8
exports and, 300
motives behind, 273ff.
nature of, 263ff., 327ff., Table XVIII
peak in 1956–57, 294
sources of, 256–8
oil, 242–3, 266ff.
sale of 1939–45, 264
sources of, 65–6
Sterling Area, 226
under-developed countries, Table XXXIII
see also Sterling Balances
U.S.A. in U.K., see U.S.A.
U.S.A., see U.S.A.
iron, 82
manufacturing output, since 1945, 292–3
growth rate and share of world, Table XXXI
Malayan War, 194–5, 233
military defence of Free Trade, 87ff.
monopoly, growth of, 125ff., 320ff.
monopoly position challenged, Chapter 3
motors, 126, 143
national income, see National Income
naval strength, 89
planning, need for, 480ff.
population, density, 2
growth, 90
post-1945 boom and 1955 recession, see Trade Cycle

post-1945 economic growth compared with, Germany, 315
France, 317
productivity, 83
profits overseas and home industrial companies, Table XIII
protection of overseas investments, 87ff.
17th-century revolution, 38–9
shipbuilding, 82, 105
shipping, 82, 131, 261
means of payment for imports, Table XIV
steel industry rationalisation, 137
tariffs, 476
tariff policy 1930s, 136ff.
terms of trade, see Trade, Terms of
textiles, 35, 45, 62, 82, 143, 275, 478
see also U.K. exports
trade, empire, 63, 94, 100, 346ff., Tables VI, VII
Europe, 64, 81–2, Table VII
geographical distribution, Table V
rate of growth and share of world, Table XXIX
Trade Cycle, see Trade Cycle
Trusts, see Monopolies
unemployment between the wars, 132ff., 143, Table IX
wages, prices and profits 1948–61, Table XXIII
see also Sterling
United Nations, 191, 464, 474, 482
Economic and Social Council, 245
Relief and Rehabilitation Association (UNRRA), 381, 461
aid 1946–48, Table XI

Sunfed, 462, 474, 482
United States of America, 80
balance of payments 1919–59, Table XXX
Civil War, 81
Cold War and colonial liberation, 204ff.
colonial liberation movements, 227
see also Cuba
domination in Latin and South America, 364ff.
dominance in capitalist world, 227ff., 369ff.
exports, 348, 369ff., Table XXI
rate of growth and share in world, Table XXIX
Sterling area, 224
Foreign Aid, 206ff., 370–2, 459, 462, Tables XI, XXXIII
South America, 372
U.K. overseas investment and, 256
founding of, 46, 163
Free Trade, 205–6, 227–8
imports, 369, Table XXIX
industrial development, 82, 94, 163–4
intervention in S.-E. Asia, 194
manufacturing output, since 1945, 292
growth rate and share of world, Table XXXI
national income, post-1954, 371
1959, Table XXVIII
oil industry, 236
interest in Saudi Arabia, 237
pressure on Cuba, 368
overseas investment, 206, 364
1919–59, Table XXX
oil, 226
post-1945, discussion of, 369ff.
prior to Great Crash, 134

Sterling area, 226, 259ff.
under-developed countries, Table XXXIII
U.K. post-1945, 259
assessment of for U.K., 328–9
Paley Report, 368
tariffs, 476
McKinley, 82
trade with U.K., 46, 63, 67, 68, 81–2
U.K. investment in, 56, 63–4, 94, 98, Table V
disposal of, 123–4

Varga, E., 146
Vespucci, Amerigo di, 18
Victoria, Queen, 85

Wakefield, Gibbon, 164
Walters, D., Table IV
War
Ashanti, 88
Boer, 92, 103–4
Cold, see Cold War
First World, 122
Franco-Russian, 81
Greece, 1946, 294
Imperialism and, 117ff., 148ff.
Indo-China, 193–4
Indonesia, 193, 233
Korean, stockpiling, 231
Lenin on cause of, 11, 149
Malayan, 194–5, 233
Matabele, 102
Napoleonic, 53
Second World, 147ff., 190ff.
Suez, 205
U.S.A. Civil, 81
Zulu, 88
Warren Hastings, 46
Welensky, Sir Roy, 165
Welfare state, 13

West Indies, 171, 275
   Currency Board, 219
Witwatersrand, 88
Working class
   chauvinism, 101
   Imperialist sentiment, 91

Lenin on bribery of, 12, 13, 97,
   100, 144
World Bank, *see* Bank, World

Zahedi, General, 238, 461
Zollverein, 120, 127